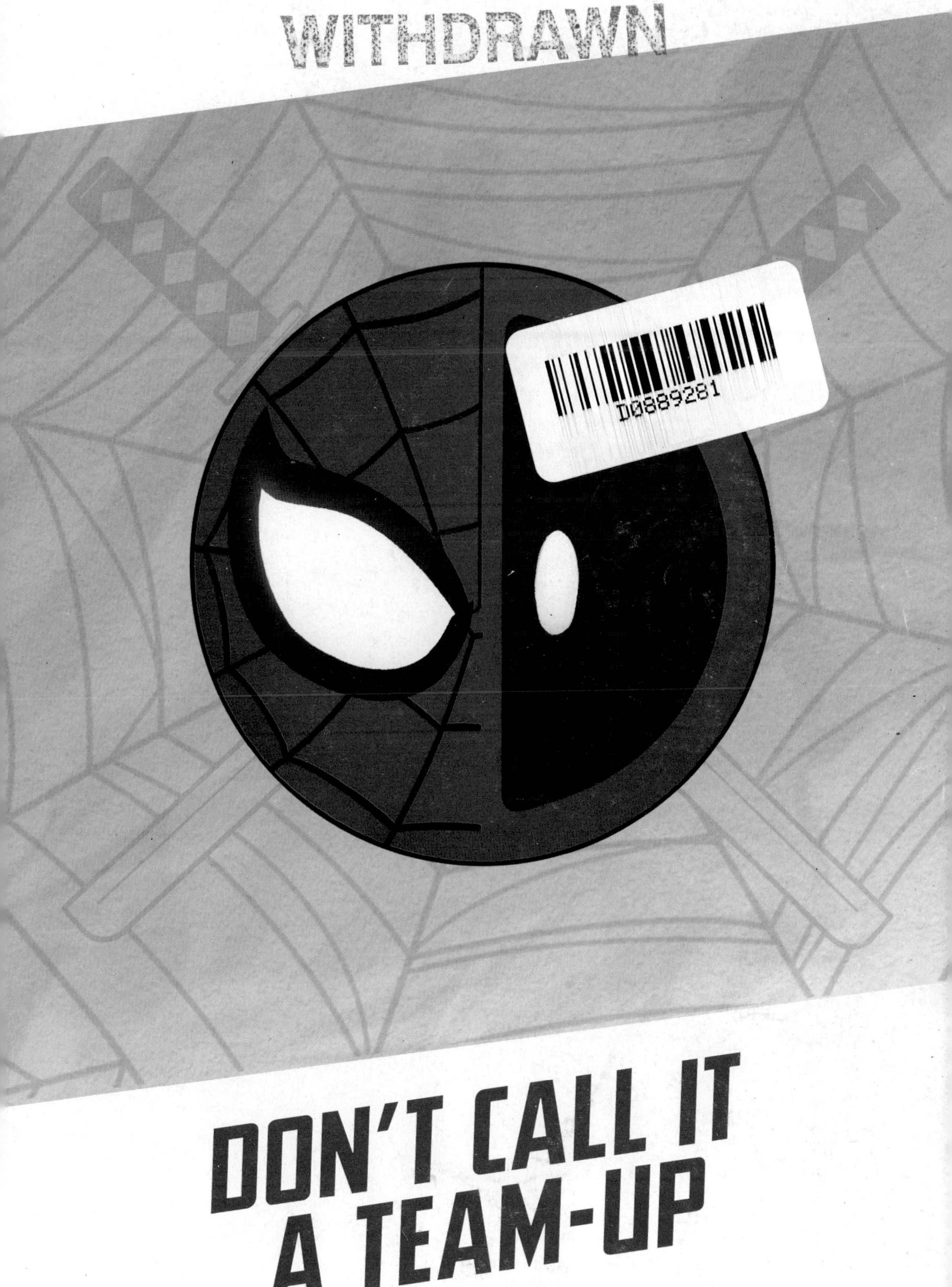

DON'T CALL IT A TEAM-UP

MARVEL COMICS
BEGRUDGINGLY PRESENTS...

PETER PARKER WAS BITTEN BY AN IRRADIATED SPIDER, GRANTING HIM AMAZING ABILITIES, INCLUDING THE PROPORTIONAL SPEED, STRENGTH AND AGILITY OF A SPIDER, AS WELL AS ADHESIVE FINGERTIPS AND TOES. AFTER LEARNING THAT WITH GREAT POWER, THERE MUST ALSO COME GREAT RESPONSIBILITY, HE BECAME THE WORLD'S GREATEST SUPER HERO! HE'S...

THE WORLD'S GREATEST SUPER HERO!

The AMAZING SPIDER-MAN

AVENGER...ASSASSIN...SUPERSTAR! WADE WILSON WAS CHOSEN FOR A TOP-SECRET GOVERNMENT PROGRAM THAT GAVE HIM A HEALING FACTOR THAT ALLOWS HIM TO HEAL FROM ANY WOUND. DESPITE EARNING A SMALL FORTUNE AS A GUN FOR HIRE, WADE HAS BECOME THE WORLD'S MOST BELOVED HERO. AND IS THE STAR OF THE WORLD'S GREATEST COMICS MAGAZINE (NO MATTER WHAT THAT JERK IN THE WEBS MAY THINK). CALL HIM THE MERC WITH THE MOUTH...CALL HIM THE REGENERATIN' DEGENERATE...CALL HIM...

DEADPOOL

DEADPOOL (1997) #11
Writer JOE KELLY
Penciler PETE WOODS
Inkers NATHAN MASSENGILL, AL MILGROM &
JOE SINNOTT
Based In Part On AMAZING SPIDER-MAN #47
by STAN LEE & JOHN ROMITA SR.
Colorist CHRIS SOTOMAYOR
Letterer RICHARD STARKINGS &
COMICRAFT'S EMERSON MIRANDA
Cover Art PETE WOODS & NATHAN MASSENGILL
Assistant Editor PAUL TUTRONE
Editor MATT IDELSON

DEADPOOL (2008) #19-21
Writer DANIEL WAY
Penciler CARLO BARBERI
Inkers SANDU FLOREA WITH JUAN VLASCO (#19)
Colorist MARTE GRACIA
Letterer VC's JOE SABINO
Cover Art JASON PEARSON
Assistant Editor JODY LEHEUP
Editor AXEL ALONSO

DEADPOOL ANNUAL #2
Writer CHRISTOPHER HASTINGS
Artist JACOPO CAMAGNI
Colorist MATT MILLA
Letterer VC's JOE SABINO
Cover Art DAVID NAKAYAMA
Assistant Editor FRANKIE JOHNSON
Editor JORDAN D. WHITE
X-Men Group Editor MIKE MARTS

CABLE & DEADPOOL #24
Writer FABIAN NICIEZA
Penciler PATRICK ZIRCHER
Inkers UDON'S M3TH
Colorist GOTHAM
Letterer VC's CORY PETIT
Cover Art PATRICK ZIRCHER, UDON'S M3TH
& ROB SCHWAGER
Consulting Editors JOHN BARBER &
RALPH MACCHIO
Editor NICOLE WILEY

AVENGING SPIDER-MAN #12-13
Writer KEVIN SHINICK
Artist AARON KUDER
Colorist MATT HOLLINGSWORTH
Letterer VC's CORY PETIT
Cover Art SHANE DAVIS, MARK MORALES &
MATT HOLLINGSWORTH
Assistant Editor ELLIE PYLE
Associate Editor SANA AMANAT
Editor STEPHEN WACKER
Executive Editor TOM BREVOORT

SPIDER-MAN CREATED BY
STAN LEE & STEVE DITKO

DEADPOOL CREATED BY
ROB LIEFELD & FABIAN NICIEZA

AMAZING SPIDER-MAN #611
Writer JOE KELLY
Artist ERIC CANETE
Colorist ANDRES MOSSA
Letterer VC's JOE CARAMAGNA
Cover Art SKOTTIE YOUNG
Assistant Editor TOM BRENNAN
Editor STEPHEN WACKER
Executive Editor TOM BREVOORT

DEADPOOL (2012) #10
Writers BRIAN POSEHN & GERRY DUGGAN
Artist MIKE HAWTHORNE
Colorist VAL STAPLES
Letterer VC's JOE SABINO
Cover Art TRADD MOORE & EDGAR DELGADO
Editor JORDAN D. WHITE

Collection Editor MARK D. BEAZLEY
Associate Editor SARAH BRUNSTAD
Associate Manager, Digital Assets JOE HOCHSTEIN
Associate Managing Editor ALEX STARBUCK
Editor, Special Projects JENNIFER GRÜNWALD
VP, Production & Special Projects JEFF YOUNGQUIST
Research & Layout JEPH YORK
Book Designer ADAM DEL RE
SVP Print, Sales & Marketing DAVID GABRIEL

Editor In Chief AXEL ALONSO
Chief Creative Officer JOE QUESADA
Publisher DAN BUCKLEY
Executive Producer ALAN FINE

Special Thanks To JORDAN D. WHITE

SPIDER-MAN/DEADPOOL VOL. 0: DON'T CALL IT A TEAM-UP. Contains material originally published in magazine form as DEADPOOL (1997) #11, CABLE & DEADPOOL #24, AMAZING SPIDER-MAN #611, DEADPOOL (2008) #19-21, AVENGING SPIDER-MAN #12-13, and DEADPOOL (2012) #10 and ANNUAL #2. First printing 2016. ISBN# 978-1-302-90084-7. Published by MARVEL WORLDWIDE, INC., a subsidiary of MARVEL ENTERTAINMENT, LLC. OFFICE OF PUBLICATION: 135 West 50th Street, New York, NY 10020. Copyright © 2016 MARVEL. No similarity between any of the names, characters, persons, and/or institutions in this magazine with those of any living or dead person or institution is intended, and any such similarity which may exist is purely coincidental. Printed in the U.S.A. ALAN FINE, President, Marvel Entertainment; DAN BUCKLEY, President, TV, Publishing & Brand Management; JOE QUESADA, Chief Creative Officer; TOM BREVOORT, SVP of Publishing; DAVID BOGART, SVP of Business Affairs & Operations, Publishing & Partnership; C.B. CEBULSKI, VP of Brand Management & Development, Asia; DAVID GABRIEL, SVP of Sales & Marketing, Publishing; JEFF YOUNGQUIST, VP of Production & Special Projects; DAN CARR, Executive Director of Publishing Technology; ALEX MORALES, Director of Publishing Operations; SUSAN CRESPI, Production Manager; STAN LEE, Chairman Emeritus. For information regarding advertising in Marvel Comics or on Marvel.com, please contact Vit DeBellis, Integrated Sales Manager, at vdebellis@marvel.com. For Marvel subscription inquiries, please call 888-511-5480. Manufactured between 3/18/2016 and 4/25/2016 by R.R. DONNELLEY, INC., SALEM, VA, USA.

10 9 8 7 6 5 4 3 2 1

Previously, Deadpool's teleporter interacted badly with the space-bending powers of the Great Lakes Avengers' Doorman, hurling Deadpool and his elderly roommate-slash-prisoner Blind Al back in time...and straight into the pages of 1967's AMAZING SPIDER-MAN #47!

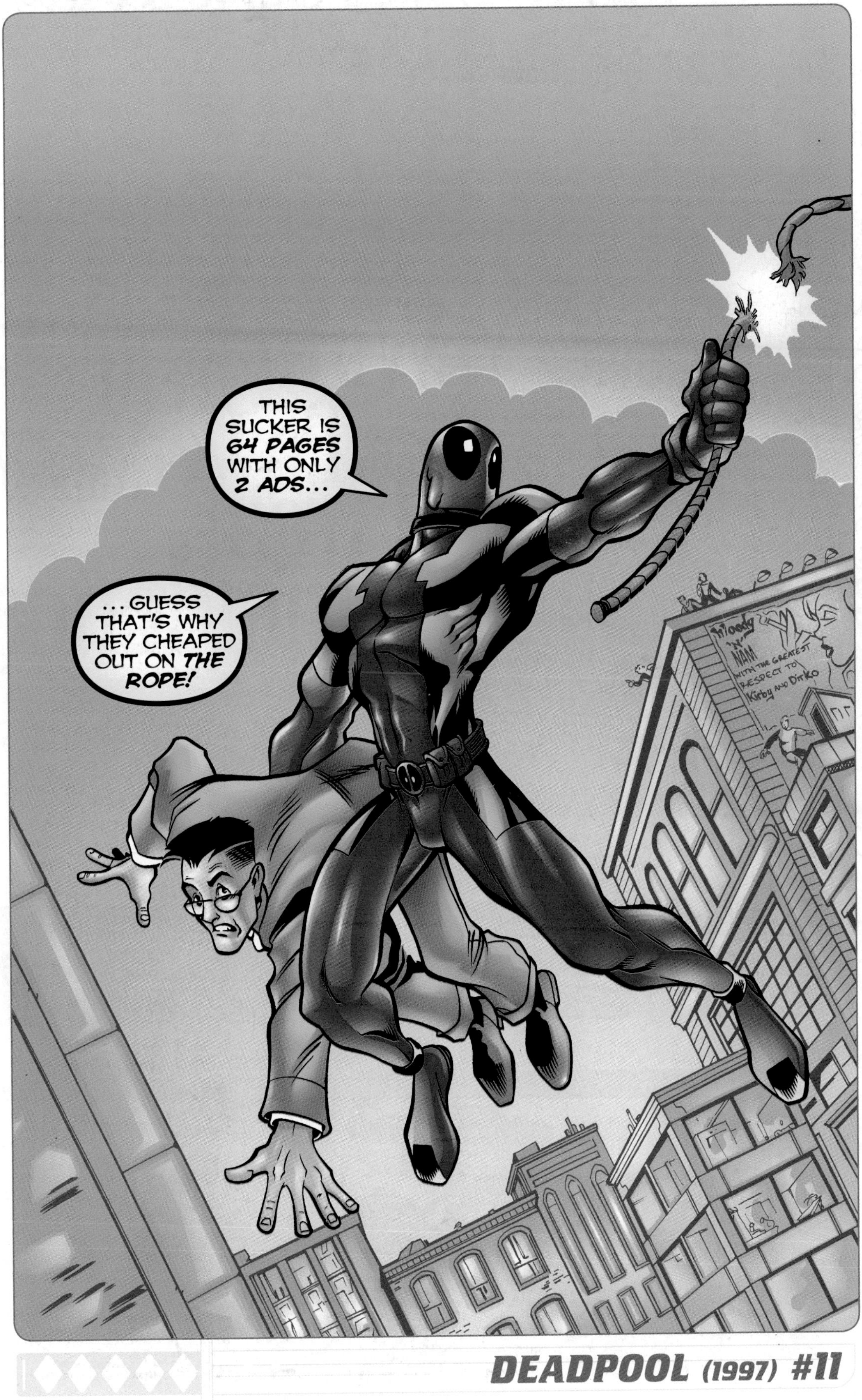

THIS SUCKER IS *64 PAGES* WITH ONLY *2 ADS*...
...GUESS THAT'S WHY THEY CHEAPED OUT ON *THE ROPE!*
Woody
"N"
NAM
WITH THE GREATEST RESPECT TO
Kirby AND Ditko

STAN LEE PRESENTS A VERY SPECIAL DEADPOOL BROUGHT TO YOU ACROSS THE VAST EXPANSE OF SPACE AND TIME BY:

JOE "MARTY MCFLY" KELLY WRITER PETE "H.G. WELLS" WOODS PENCILER NATHAN "TIME TRAVELLER'IN" MASSENGILL INKER ('90s)

AL "TIME BY SEIKO" MILGROM AND JOE "SPACE WARP" SINNOTT INKERS ('60s) CHRIS "SAGAN" SOTOMAYOR COLORIST

R "TIMECOP" S AND COMICRAFT/EMERSON MIRANDA LETTERING PAUL "TIME WARP AGAIN" TUTRONE ASSISTANT EDITOR

MATT "TIME TO MAKE THE DONUTS" IDELSON EDITOR BOB HARRAS TIME LOOP BOB HARRAS TIME LOOP BOB HARRAS TIME LOOP BOB HARRAS TIME LOOP BOB HARRAS TIME LOOP

BASED IN PART on AMAZING SPIDER-MAN #47 by STAN LEE and JOHN ROMITA, Sr.

SPECIAL THANKS TO DARREN AUCK, THE BULLPEN (AND ALL THAT NAME ENCOMPASSES) PATTI DAZZO, RALPH MACCHIO, KAREEM MONTES, WILSON RAMOS, REPRO, POND SCUM AND OF COURSE STAN AND JOHN FOR ALLOWING THIS TRAVESTY TO OCCUR!

With Great Power comes Great Coincidence

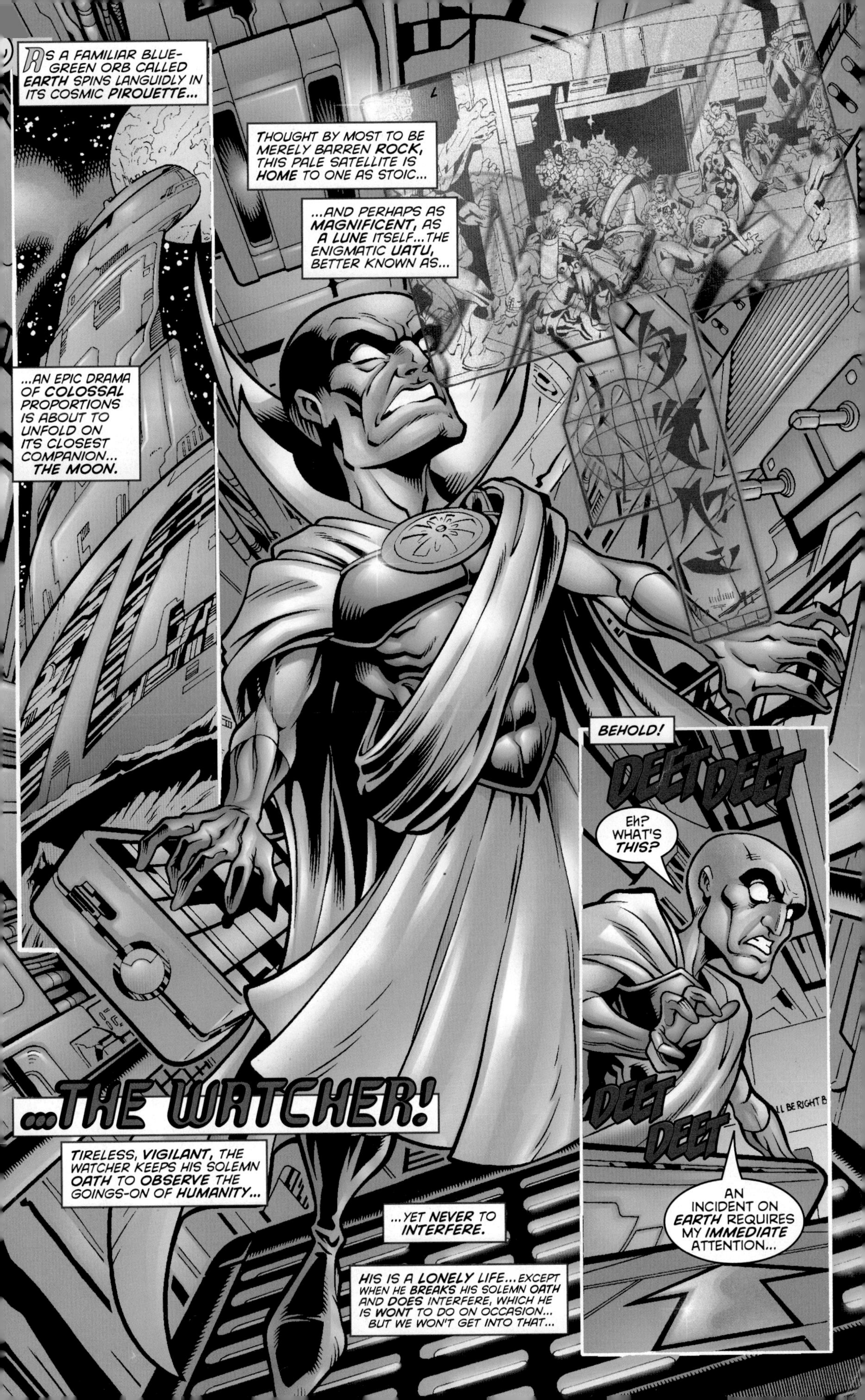

AS A FAMILIAR BLUE-GREEN ORB CALLED EARTH SPINS LANGUIDLY IN ITS COSMIC PIROUETTE...
...AN EPIC DRAMA OF COLOSSAL PROPORTIONS IS ABOUT TO UNFOLD ON ITS CLOSEST COMPANION... THE MOON.
THOUGHT BY MOST TO BE MERELY BARREN ROCK, THIS PALE SATELLITE IS HOME TO ONE AS STOIC...
...AND PERHAPS AS MAGNIFICENT, AS A LUNE ITSELF...THE ENIGMATIC UATU, BETTER KNOWN AS...
...THE WATCHER!
TIRELESS, VIGILANT, THE WATCHER KEEPS HIS SOLEMN OATH TO OBSERVE THE GOINGS-ON OF HUMANITY...
...YET NEVER TO INTERFERE.
HIS IS A LONELY LIFE...EXCEPT WHEN HE BREAKS HIS SOLEMN OATH AND DOES INTERFERE, WHICH HE IS WONT TO DO ON OCCASION... BUT WE WON'T GET INTO THAT...
BEHOLD!
DEET DEET
EH? WHAT'S THIS?
DEET DEET
AN INCIDENT ON EARTH REQUIRES MY IMMEDIATE ATTENTION...

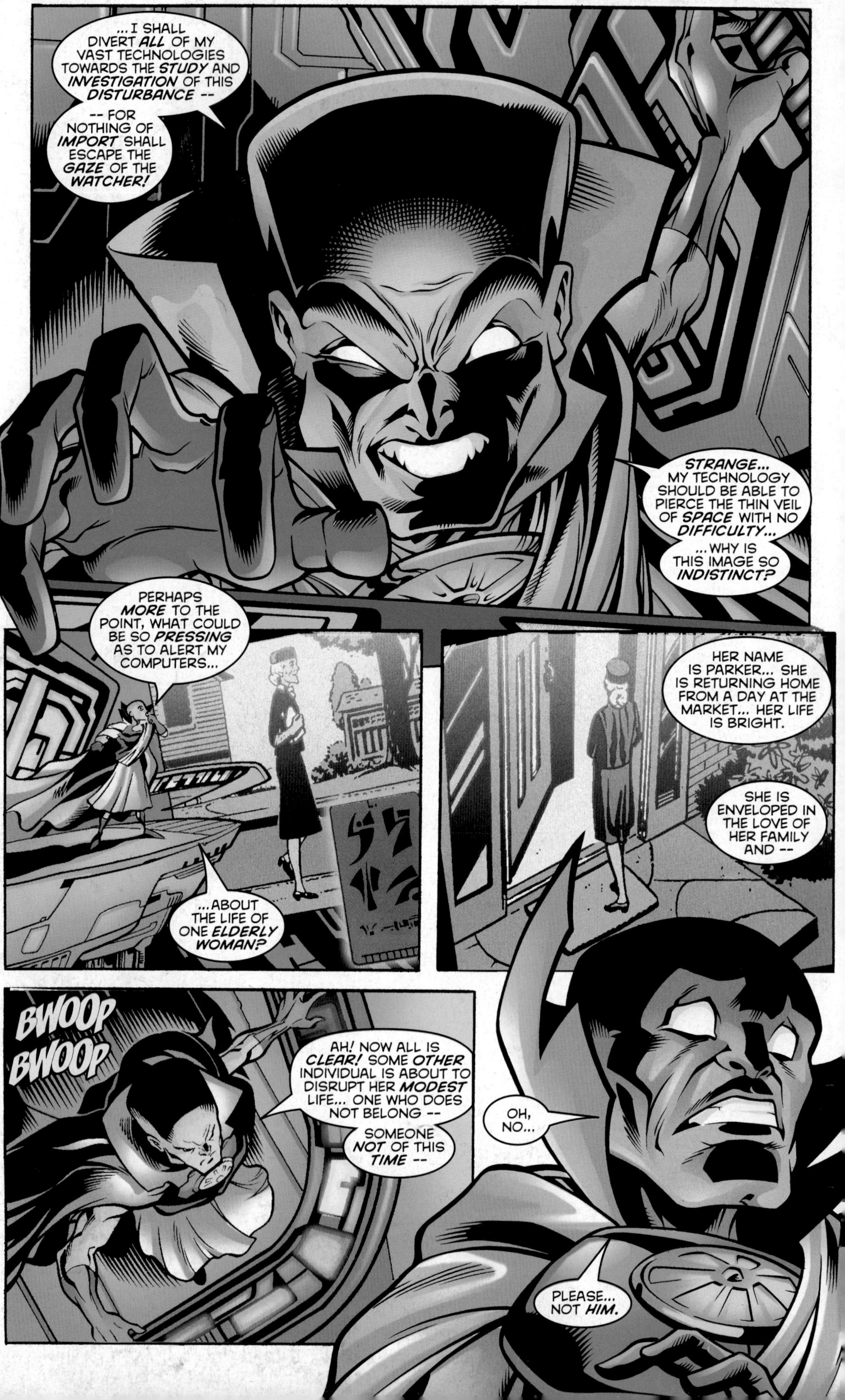
...I SHALL DIVERT ALL OF MY VAST TECHNOLOGIES TOWARDS THE STUDY AND INVESTIGATION OF THIS DISTURBANCE --
-- FOR NOTHING OF IMPORT SHALL ESCAPE THE GAZE OF THE WATCHER!
STRANGE... MY TECHNOLOGY SHOULD BE ABLE TO PIERCE THE THIN VEIL OF SPACE WITH NO DIFFICULTY...
...WHY IS THIS IMAGE SO INDISTINCT?
PERHAPS MORE TO THE POINT, WHAT COULD BE SO PRESSING AS TO ALERT MY COMPUTERS...
...ABOUT THE LIFE OF ONE ELDERLY WOMAN?
HER NAME IS PARKER... SHE IS RETURNING HOME FROM A DAY AT THE MARKET... HER LIFE IS BRIGHT.
SHE IS ENVELOPED IN THE LOVE OF HER FAMILY AND --
BWOOP BWOOP
AH! NOW ALL IS CLEAR! SOME OTHER INDIVIDUAL IS ABOUT TO DISRUPT HER MODEST LIFE... ONE WHO DOES NOT BELONG --
SOMEONE NOT OF THIS TIME --
OH, NO...
PLEASE... NOT HIM.

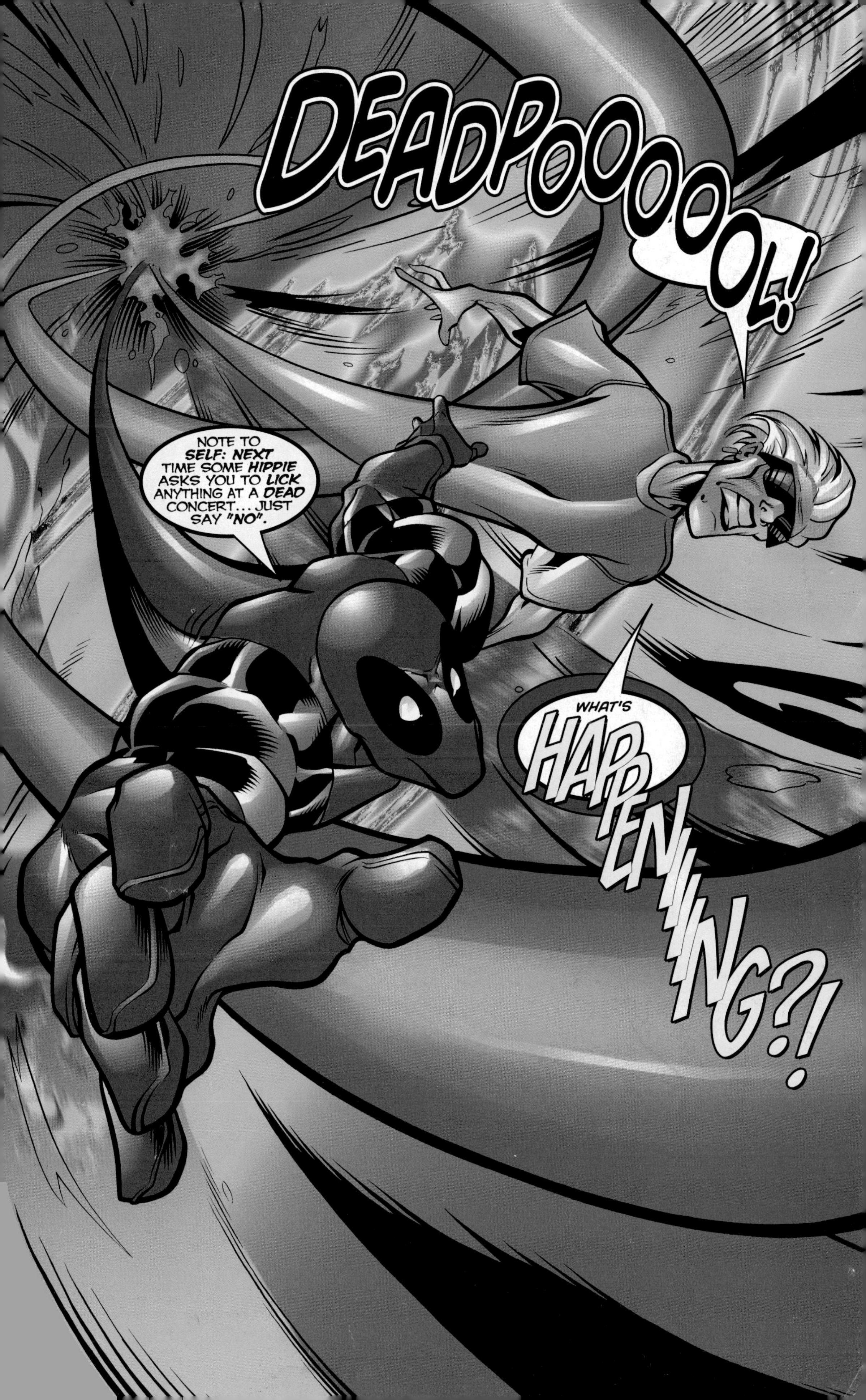

DEADPOOOOOL!
NOTE TO SELF: NEXT TIME SOME HIPPIE ASKS YOU TO LICK ANYTHING AT A DEAD CONCERT... JUST SAY "NO".
WHAT'S HAPPENING?!

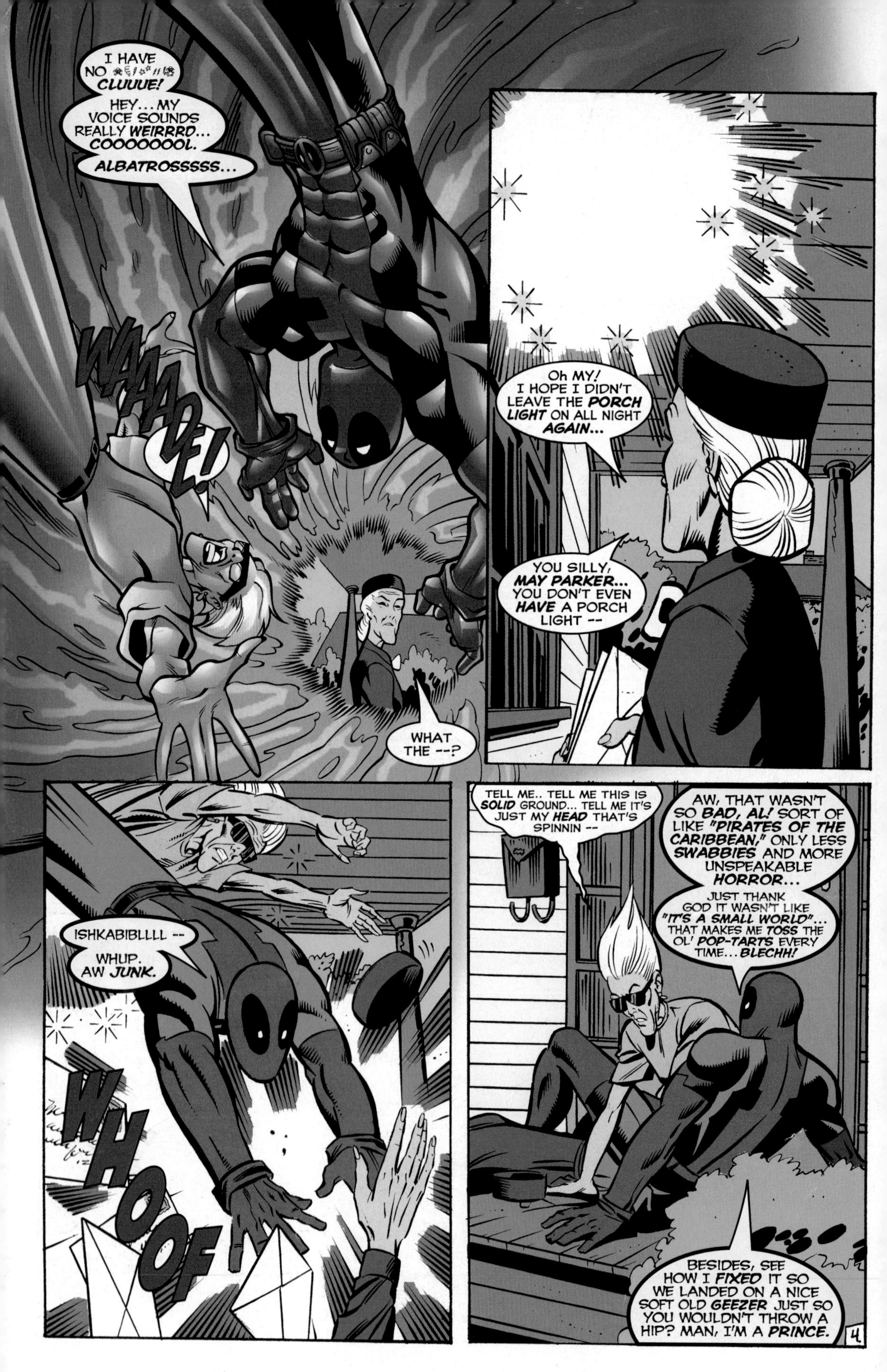
I HAVE NO @$!#%#@ CLUUUE!
HEY... MY VOICE SOUNDS REALLY WEIRRRD... COOOOOOOL.
ALBATROSSSSS...
WAAAAOE!
WHAT THE --?
Oh MY! I HOPE I DIDN'T LEAVE THE PORCH LIGHT ON ALL NIGHT AGAIN...
YOU SILLY, MAY PARKER... YOU DON'T EVEN HAVE A PORCH LIGHT --
ISHKABIBLLLL --
WHUP. AW JUNK.
WHOOOF
TELL ME.. TELL ME THIS IS SOLID GROUND... TELL ME IT'S JUST MY HEAD THAT'S SPINNIN --
AW, THAT WASN'T SO BAD, AL! SORT OF LIKE "PIRATES OF THE CARIBBEAN," ONLY LESS SWABBIES AND MORE UNSPEAKABLE HORROR...
JUST THANK GOD IT WASN'T LIKE "IT'S A SMALL WORLD"... THAT MAKES ME TOSS THE OL' POP-TARTS EVERY TIME... BLECHH!
BESIDES, SEE HOW I FIXED IT SO WE LANDED ON A NICE SOFT OLD GEEZER JUST SO YOU WOULDN'T THROW A HIP? MAN, I'M A PRINCE.
4

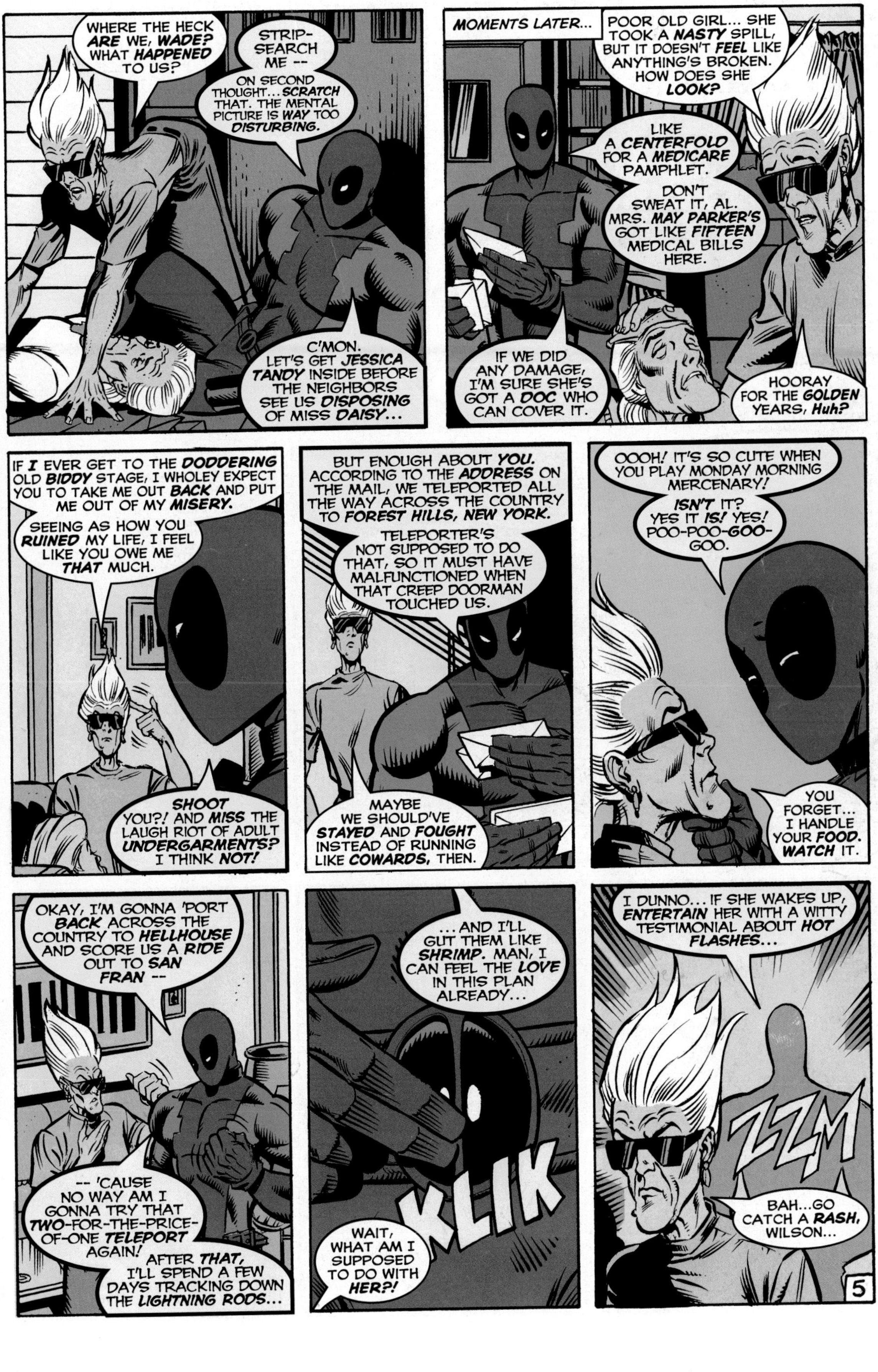
WHERE THE HECK ARE WE, WADE? WHAT HAPPENED TO US?
STRIP-SEARCH ME --
ON SECOND THOUGHT... SCRATCH THAT. THE MENTAL PICTURE IS WAY TOO DISTURBING.
C'MON. LET'S GET JESSICA TANDY INSIDE BEFORE THE NEIGHBORS SEE US DISPOSING OF MISS DAISY...
MOMENTS LATER...
POOR OLD GIRL... SHE TOOK A NASTY SPILL, BUT IT DOESN'T FEEL LIKE ANYTHING'S BROKEN. HOW DOES SHE LOOK?
LIKE A CENTERFOLD FOR A MEDICARE PAMPHLET.
DON'T SWEAT IT, AL. MRS. MAY PARKER'S GOT LIKE FIFTEEN MEDICAL BILLS HERE.
IF WE DID ANY DAMAGE, I'M SURE SHE'S GOT A DOC WHO CAN COVER IT.
HOORAY FOR THE GOLDEN YEARS, Huh?
IF I EVER GET TO THE DODDERING OLD BIDDY STAGE, I WHOLEY EXPECT YOU TO TAKE ME OUT BACK AND PUT ME OUT OF MY MISERY.
SEEING AS HOW YOU RUINED MY LIFE, I FEEL LIKE YOU OWE ME THAT MUCH.
SHOOT YOU?! AND MISS THE LAUGH RIOT OF ADULT UNDERGARMENTS? I THINK NOT!
BUT ENOUGH ABOUT YOU. ACCORDING TO THE ADDRESS ON THE MAIL, WE TELEPORTED ALL THE WAY ACROSS THE COUNTRY TO FOREST HILLS, NEW YORK.
TELEPORTER'S NOT SUPPOSED TO DO THAT, SO IT MUST HAVE MALFUNCTIONED WHEN THAT CREEP DOORMAN TOUCHED US.
MAYBE WE SHOULD'VE STAYED AND FOUGHT INSTEAD OF RUNNING LIKE COWARDS, THEN.
OOOH! IT'S SO CUTE WHEN YOU PLAY MONDAY MORNING MERCENARY!
ISN'T IT? YES IT IS! YES! POO-POO-GOO-GOO.
YOU FORGET... I HANDLE YOUR FOOD. WATCH IT.
OKAY, I'M GONNA 'PORT BACK ACROSS THE COUNTRY TO HELLHOUSE AND SCORE US A RIDE OUT TO SAN FRAN --
-- 'CAUSE NO WAY AM I GONNA TRY THAT TWO-FOR-THE-PRICE-OF-ONE TELEPORT AGAIN!
AFTER THAT, I'LL SPEND A FEW DAYS TRACKING DOWN THE LIGHTNING RODS...
...AND I'LL GUT THEM LIKE SHRIMP. MAN, I CAN FEEL THE LOVE IN THIS PLAN ALREADY...
KLIK
WAIT, WHAT AM I SUPPOSED TO DO WITH HER?!
I DUNNO... IF SHE WAKES UP, ENTERTAIN HER WITH A WITTY TESTIMONIAL ABOUT HOT FLASHES...
ZZM
BAH...GO CATCH A RASH, WILSON...
5

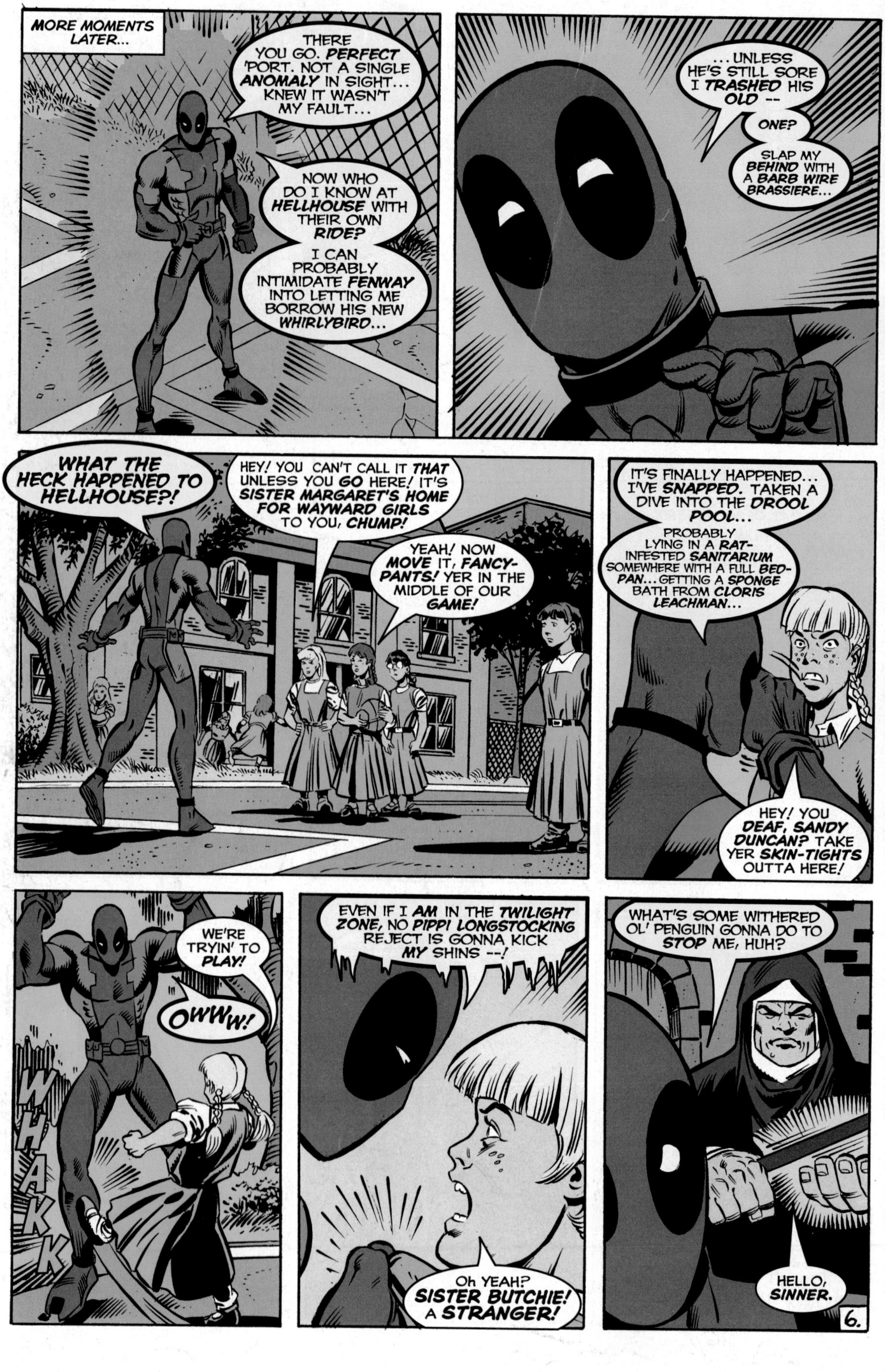
MORE MOMENTS LATER...
THERE YOU GO. PERFECT 'PORT. NOT A SINGLE ANOMALY IN SIGHT... KNEW IT WASN'T MY FAULT...
NOW WHO DO I KNOW AT HELLHOUSE WITH THEIR OWN RIDE?
I CAN PROBABLY INTIMIDATE FENWAY INTO LETTING ME BORROW HIS NEW WHIRLYBIRD...
...UNLESS HE'S STILL SORE I TRASHED HIS OLD --
ONE?
SLAP MY BEHIND WITH A BARB WIRE BRASSIERE...
WHAT THE HECK HAPPENED TO HELLHOUSE?!
HEY! YOU CAN'T CALL IT THAT UNLESS YOU GO HERE! IT'S SISTER MARGARET'S HOME FOR WAYWARD GIRLS TO YOU, CHUMP!
YEAH! NOW MOVE IT, FANCY-PANTS! YER IN THE MIDDLE OF OUR GAME!
IT'S FINALLY HAPPENED... I'VE SNAPPED. TAKEN A DIVE INTO THE DROOL POOL...
PROBABLY LYING IN A RAT-INFESTED SANITARIUM SOMEWHERE WITH A FULL BED-PAN...GETTING A SPONGE BATH FROM CLORIS LEACHMAN...
HEY! YOU DEAF, SANDY DUNCAN? TAKE YER SKIN-TIGHTS OUTTA HERE!
WE'RE TRYIN' TO PLAY!
OWWW!
WHAKK
EVEN IF I AM IN THE TWILIGHT ZONE, NO PIPPI LONGSTOCKING REJECT IS GONNA KICK MY SHINS --!
Oh YEAH? SISTER BUTCHIE! A STRANGER!
WHAT'S SOME WITHERED OL' PENGUIN GONNA DO TO STOP ME, HUH?
HELLO, SINNER.
6.

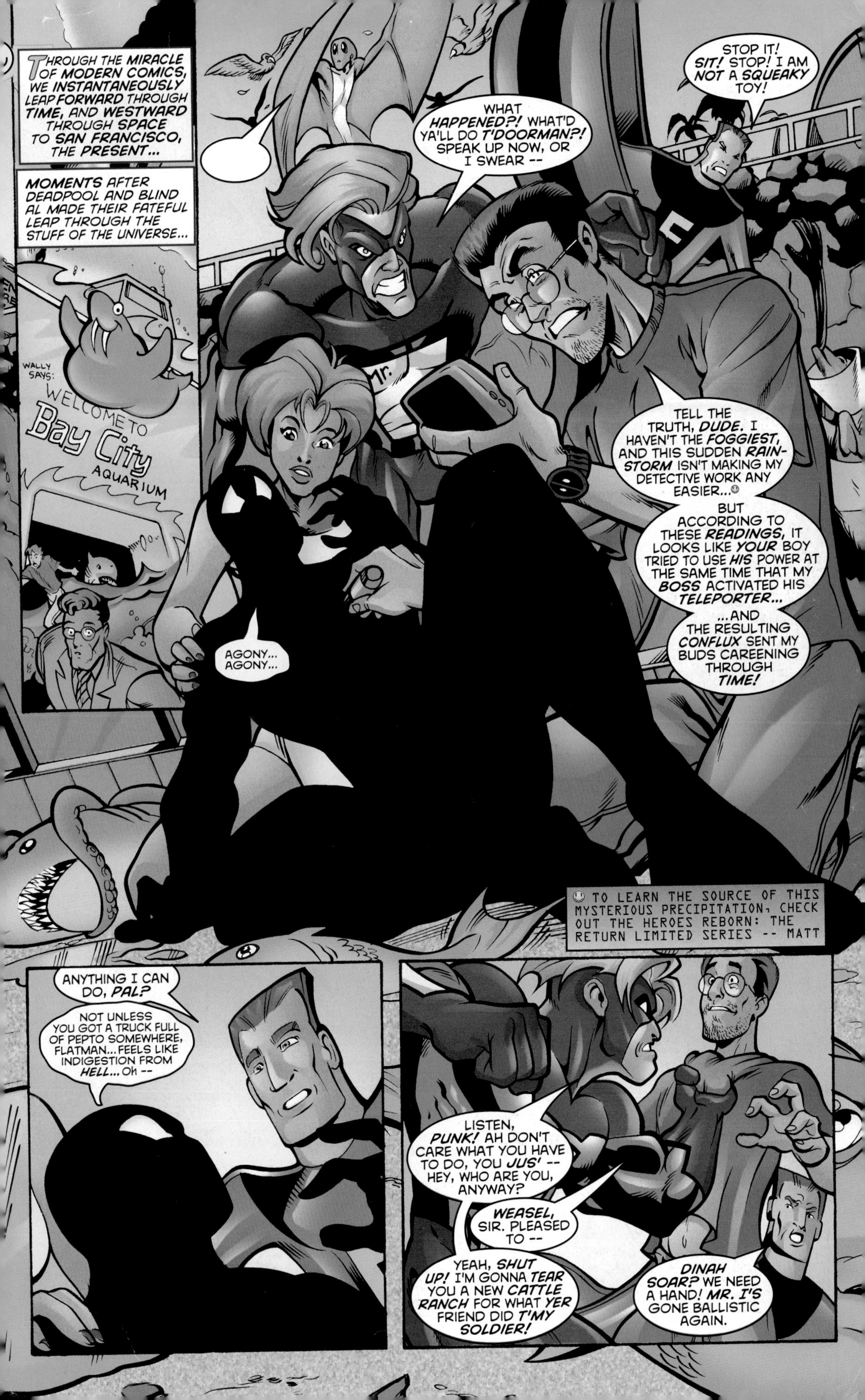
THROUGH THE MIRACLE OF MODERN COMICS, WE INSTANTANEOUSLY LEAP FORWARD THROUGH TIME, AND WESTWARD THROUGH SPACE TO SAN FRANCISCO, THE PRESENT...
MOMENTS AFTER DEADPOOL AND BLIND AL MADE THEIR FATEFUL LEAP THROUGH THE STUFF OF THE UNIVERSE...
WALLY SAYS:
WELCOME TO
Bay City
AQUARIUM
WHAT HAPPENED?! WHAT'D YA'LL DO T'DOORMAN?! SPEAK UP NOW, OR I SWEAR --
STOP IT! SIT! STOP! I AM NOT A SQUEAKY TOY!
TELL THE TRUTH, DUDE. I HAVEN'T THE FOGGIEST, AND THIS SUDDEN RAIN-STORM ISN'T MAKING MY DETECTIVE WORK ANY EASIER...
BUT ACCORDING TO THESE READINGS, IT LOOKS LIKE YOUR BOY TRIED TO USE HIS POWER AT THE SAME TIME THAT MY BOSS ACTIVATED HIS TELEPORTER...
...AND THE RESULTING CONFLUX SENT MY BUDS CAREENING THROUGH TIME!
AGONY... AGONY...
TO LEARN THE SOURCE OF THIS MYSTERIOUS PRECIPITATION, CHECK OUT THE HEROES REBORN: THE RETURN LIMITED SERIES -- MATT
ANYTHING I CAN DO, PAL?
NOT UNLESS YOU GOT A TRUCK FULL OF PEPTO SOMEWHERE, FLATMAN... FEELS LIKE INDIGESTION FROM HELL... Oh --
LISTEN, PUNK! AH DON'T CARE WHAT YOU HAVE TO DO, YOU JUS' -- HEY, WHO ARE YOU, ANYWAY?
WEASEL, SIR. PLEASED TO --
YEAH, SHUT UP! I'M GONNA TEAR YOU A NEW CATTLE RANCH FOR WHAT YER FRIEND DID T'MY SOLDIER!
DINAH SOAR? WE NEED A HAND! MR. I'S GONE BALLISTIC AGAIN.

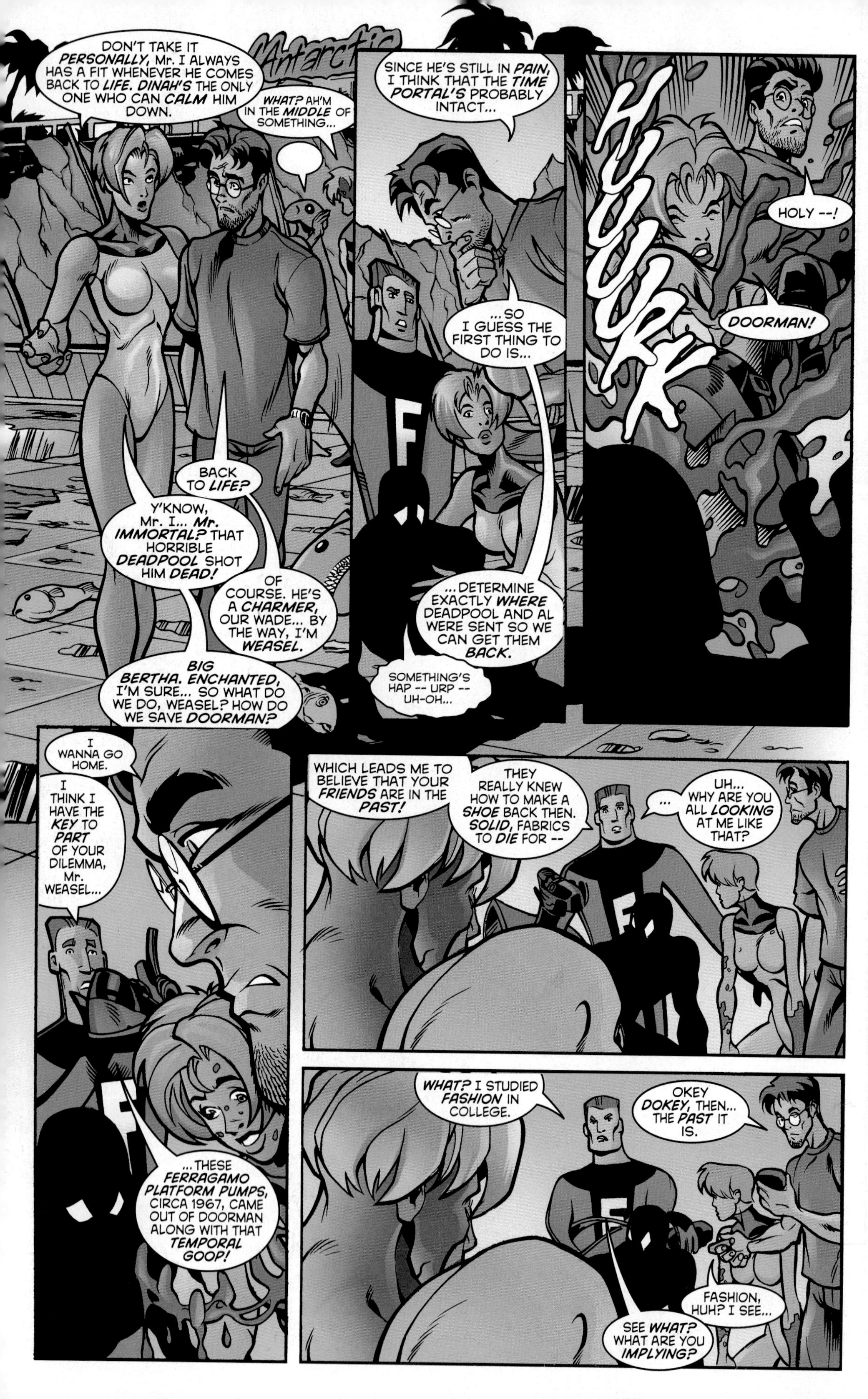

DON'T TAKE IT PERSONALLY, Mr. I ALWAYS HAS A FIT WHENEVER HE COMES BACK TO LIFE. DINAH'S THE ONLY ONE WHO CAN CALM HIM DOWN.
WHAT? AH'M IN THE MIDDLE OF SOMETHING...
BACK TO LIFE?
Y'KNOW, Mr. I... Mr. IMMORTAL? THAT HORRIBLE DEADPOOL SHOT HIM DEAD!
OF COURSE. HE'S A CHARMER, OUR WADE... BY THE WAY, I'M WEASEL.
BIG BERTHA. ENCHANTED, I'M SURE... SO WHAT DO WE DO, WEASEL? HOW DO WE SAVE DOORMAN?
SINCE HE'S STILL IN PAIN, I THINK THAT THE TIME PORTAL'S PROBABLY INTACT...
...SO I GUESS THE FIRST THING TO DO IS...
...DETERMINE EXACTLY WHERE DEADPOOL AND AL WERE SENT SO WE CAN GET THEM BACK.
SOMETHING'S HAP -- URP -- UH-OH...
HUUUURK
HOLY --!
DOORMAN!
I WANNA GO HOME.
I THINK I HAVE THE KEY TO PART OF YOUR DILEMMA, Mr. WEASEL...
...THESE FERRAGAMO PLATFORM PUMPS, CIRCA 1967, CAME OUT OF DOORMAN ALONG WITH THAT TEMPORAL GOOP!
WHICH LEADS ME TO BELIEVE THAT YOUR FRIENDS ARE IN THE PAST!
THEY REALLY KNEW HOW TO MAKE A SHOE BACK THEN. SOLID, FABRICS TO DIE FOR --
...
UH... WHY ARE YOU ALL LOOKING AT ME LIKE THAT?
WHAT? I STUDIED FASHION IN COLLEGE.
OKEY DOKEY, THEN... THE PAST IT IS.
FASHION, HUH? I SEE...
SEE WHAT? WHAT ARE YOU IMPLYING?

MEANWHILE, BACK IN TIME...

DEADPOOL MAY BE FRUITY AS A *LOON*, BUT I KNOW *I'M* NOT SENILE...

SO EITHER *EVERY* CHANNEL ON THIS STUPID TV IS SET TO *NICK AT NITE*... OR...

...I'M LISTENING TO *SHOWS* FROM THE BLOODY *PAST!*

FZASH

NO! NO *MORE* WITH THE RULER! *STOP!* I DON'T *CARE* ANYMORE WHAT YOU'VE GOT ON UNDER THAT *HABIT* --

OH. TELEPORTED... HEH HEH... *HI, AL...*

MAN... I'LL NEVER LOOK AT A NUN WITH ANYTHING BUT FEAR IN MY HEART FROM NOW ON... I *PROMISE.*

SHE MUST'VE NAILED THE TELEPORTING *BELT...* HOPE IT'S *OKAY* --

WADE! WE'RE IN THE *PAST!*

GEE, HOW'D YOU FIGURE THAT ONE OUT, *SHERLOCK?* BLIND GUESS?

OHH. EVEN IN THE *PAST* I STILL GOT IT.

IT'S BAD ENOUGH THAT I'M TRAPPED FOR ETERNITY WITH *YOU,* WADE, BUT IN THE *PAST?!*

I CAN'T *BELIEVE* THIS IS HAPPENING TO US...

IS THAT SUPPOSED TO BE AN *ALLIGATOR* ON TV? AW GEEZ... THIS *BITES...* WHAT ELSE COULD GO WRONG?

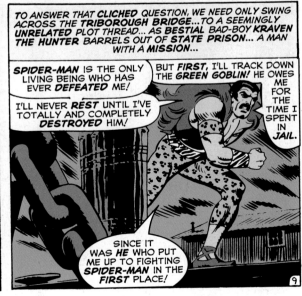

TO ANSWER THAT *CLICHED* QUESTION, WE NEED ONLY SWING ACROSS THE *TRIBOROUGH BRIDGE*...TO A SEEMINGLY *UNRELATED* PLOT THREAD... AS BESTIAL BAD-BOY *KRAVEN THE HUNTER* BARRELS OUT OF *STATE PRISON...* A MAN WITH A *MISSION...*

SPIDER-MAN IS THE ONLY LIVING BEING WHO HAS EVER *DEFEATED* ME!

I'LL NEVER *REST* UNTIL I'VE TOTALLY AND COMPLETELY *DESTROYED* HIM!

BUT *FIRST,* I'LL TRACK DOWN THE *GREEN GOBLIN!* HE OWES ME FOR THE TIME I SPENT IN JAIL.

SINCE IT WAS *HE* WHO PUT ME UP TO FIGHTING *SPIDER-MAN* IN THE *FIRST* PLACE!

9

KRAVEN EFFORTLESSLY BREAKS INTO THE MORGUE ROOM OF THE *DAILY BUGLE* UNTIL HE FINDS...

I'M TOO *LATE!* HE'S *DEAD*, AND *SPIDER-MAN* HAD A HAND IN IT!

LY BUGLE

EN GOBLIN ES IN FIRE!

SPIDER-MAN T SCENE!

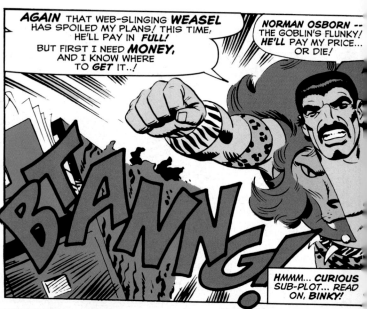

AGAIN THAT WEB-SLINGING *WEASEL* HAS SPOILED MY PLANS! THIS TIME, HE'LL PAY IN *FULL!* BUT FIRST I NEED *MONEY*, AND I KNOW WHERE TO *GET* IT..!

NORMAN OSBORN -- THE GOBLIN'S FLUNKY! *HE'LL* PAY MY PRICE... OR DIE!

BLANNG!

HMMM... *CURIOUS* SUB-PLOT... READ ON, *BINKY!*

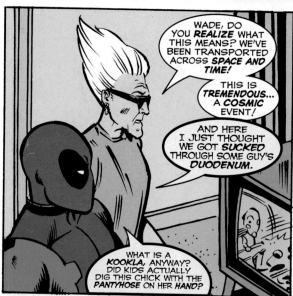

WADE, DO YOU *REALIZE* WHAT THIS MEANS? WE'VE BEEN TRANSPORTED ACROSS *SPACE AND TIME!*

THIS IS *TREMENDOUS*... A *COSMIC* EVENT!

AND HERE I JUST THOUGHT WE GOT *SUCKED* THROUGH SOME GUY'S *DUODENUM.*

WHAT IS A *KOOKLA*, ANYWAY? DID KIDS ACTUALLY DIG THIS CHICK WITH THE *PANTYHOSE* ON HER *HAND?*

WADE!

DON'T YOU *GRASP* WHAT WE COULD DO HERE? STUCK IN THE *PAST*, BUT WITH *KNOWLEDGE* OF THE *FUTURE?*

I *THINK* I SEE WHAT YOU'RE *GETTING* AT...

I COULD FIX *SPORTING EVENTS*...TAKE *CINDY CRAWFORD* TO THE *PROM*... HANG OUT ON THE *GRASSY KNOLL* AND TAKE *POLAROIDS* --

ANYTHING WE DO COULD *MESS* UP THE *TIMESTREAM!* DON'T YOU EVER WATCH *STAR TREK?!*

FOR *EXAMPLE*, IF *YOU* KEPT SOMEONE FROM GETTING ON A *BUS* WHO *SHOULD* HAVE GOTTEN ON, MAYBE THEY'D NEVER MEET THEIR FUTURE *WIFE* --

-- AND THE NEXT *PRESIDENT* MIGHT NOT BE BORN, LEADING TO *WORLD WAR THREE!* ALL BECAUSE *YOU* WANT A *WINDOW* SEAT!

HOLEE *STEPHEN HAWKING*... YOU'RE *RIGHT*...

10

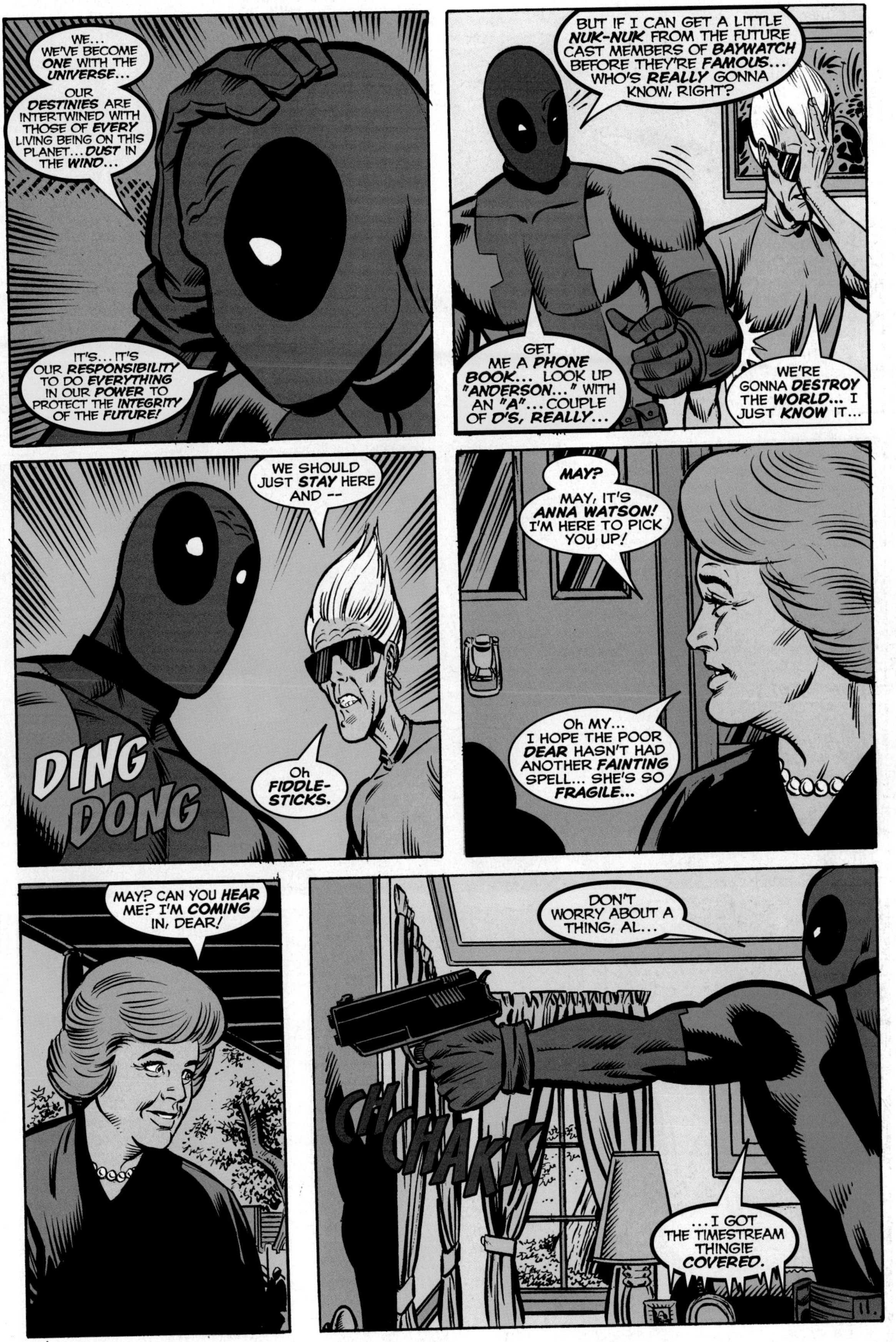
WE... WE'VE BECOME ONE WITH THE UNIVERSE...
OUR DESTINIES ARE INTERTWINED WITH THOSE OF EVERY LIVING BEING ON THIS PLANET... DUST IN THE WIND...
IT'S... IT'S OUR RESPONSIBILITY TO DO EVERYTHING IN OUR POWER TO PROTECT THE INTEGRITY OF THE FUTURE!
BUT IF I CAN GET A LITTLE NUK-NUK FROM THE FUTURE CAST MEMBERS OF BAYWATCH BEFORE THEY'RE FAMOUS... WHO'S REALLY GONNA KNOW, RIGHT?
GET ME A PHONE BOOK... LOOK UP "ANDERSON..." WITH AN "A"... COUPLE OF D'S, REALLY...
WE'RE GONNA DESTROY THE WORLD... I JUST KNOW IT...
WE SHOULD JUST STAY HERE AND --
DING DONG
Oh FIDDLE-STICKS.
MAY?
MAY, IT'S ANNA WATSON! I'M HERE TO PICK YOU UP!
Oh MY... I HOPE THE POOR DEAR HASN'T HAD ANOTHER FAINTING SPELL... SHE'S SO FRAGILE...
MAY? CAN YOU HEAR ME? I'M COMING IN, DEAR!
DON'T WORRY ABOUT A THING, AL...
CHCHAKK
...I GOT THE TIMESTREAM THINGIE COVERED.
11.

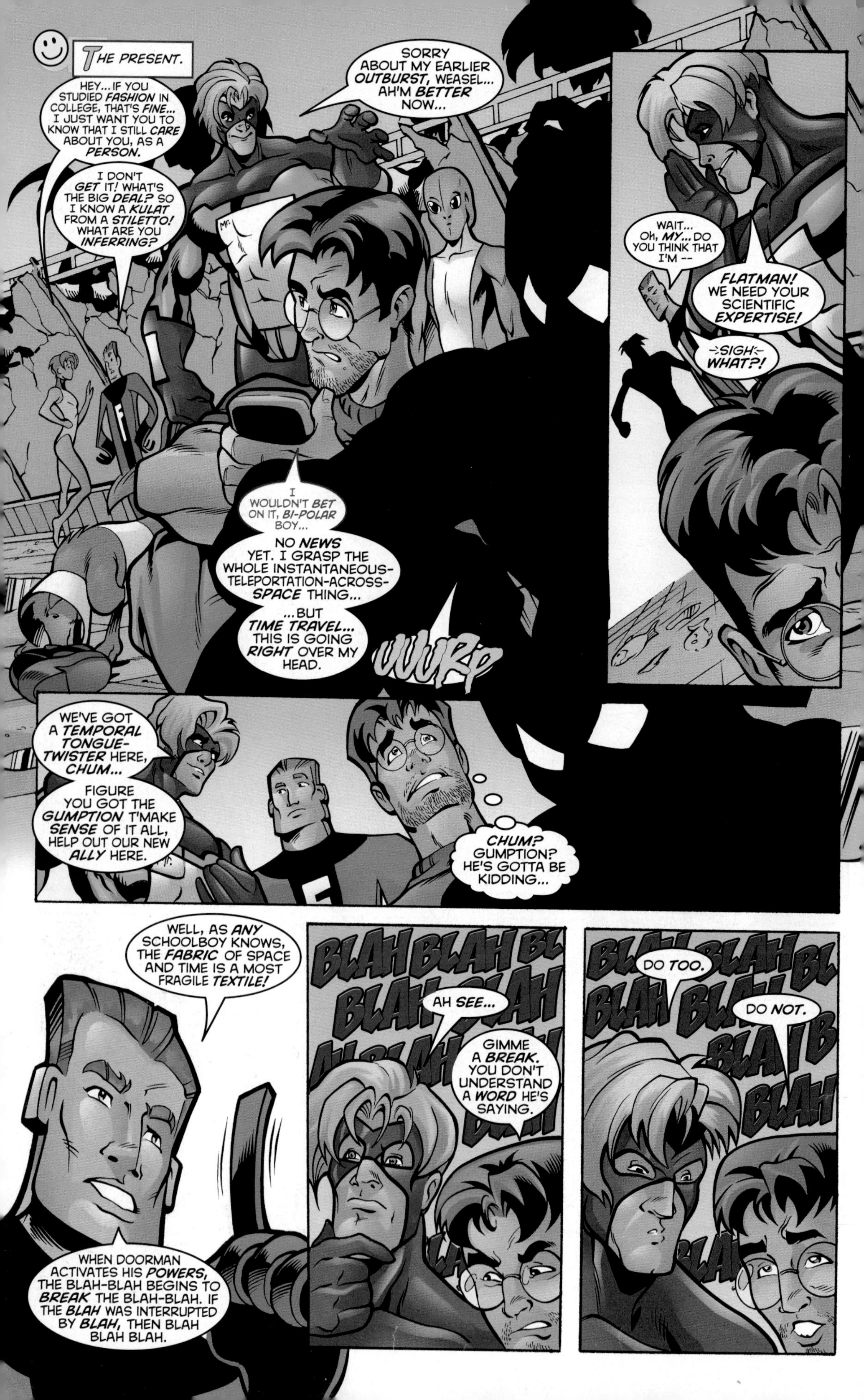
THE PRESENT.
HEY... IF YOU STUDIED FASHION IN COLLEGE, THAT'S FINE... I JUST WANT YOU TO KNOW THAT I STILL CARE ABOUT YOU, AS A PERSON.
I DON'T GET IT! WHAT'S THE BIG DEAL? SO I KNOW A KULAT FROM A STILETTO! WHAT ARE YOU INFERRING?
SORRY ABOUT MY EARLIER OUTBURST, WEASEL... AH'M BETTER NOW...
I WOULDN'T BET ON IT, BI-POLAR BOY...
NO NEWS YET. I GRASP THE WHOLE INSTANTANEOUS-TELEPORTATION-ACROSS-SPACE THING...
...BUT TIME TRAVEL... THIS IS GOING RIGHT OVER MY HEAD.
UUURP
WAIT... OH, MY... DO YOU THINK THAT I'M --
FLATMAN! WE NEED YOUR SCIENTIFIC EXPERTISE!
-SIGH- WHAT?!
WE'VE GOT A TEMPORAL TONGUE-TWISTER HERE, CHUM...
FIGURE YOU GOT THE GUMPTION T'MAKE SENSE OF IT ALL, HELP OUT OUR NEW ALLY HERE.
CHUM? GUMPTION? HE'S GOTTA BE KIDDING...
WELL, AS ANY SCHOOLBOY KNOWS, THE FABRIC OF SPACE AND TIME IS A MOST FRAGILE TEXTILE!
WHEN DOORMAN ACTIVATES HIS POWERS, THE BLAH-BLAH BEGINS TO BREAK THE BLAH-BLAH. IF THE BLAH WAS INTERRUPTED BY BLAH, THEN BLAH BLAH BLAH.
AH SEE...
GIMME A BREAK. YOU DON'T UNDERSTAND A WORD HE'S SAYING.
DO TOO.
DO NOT.

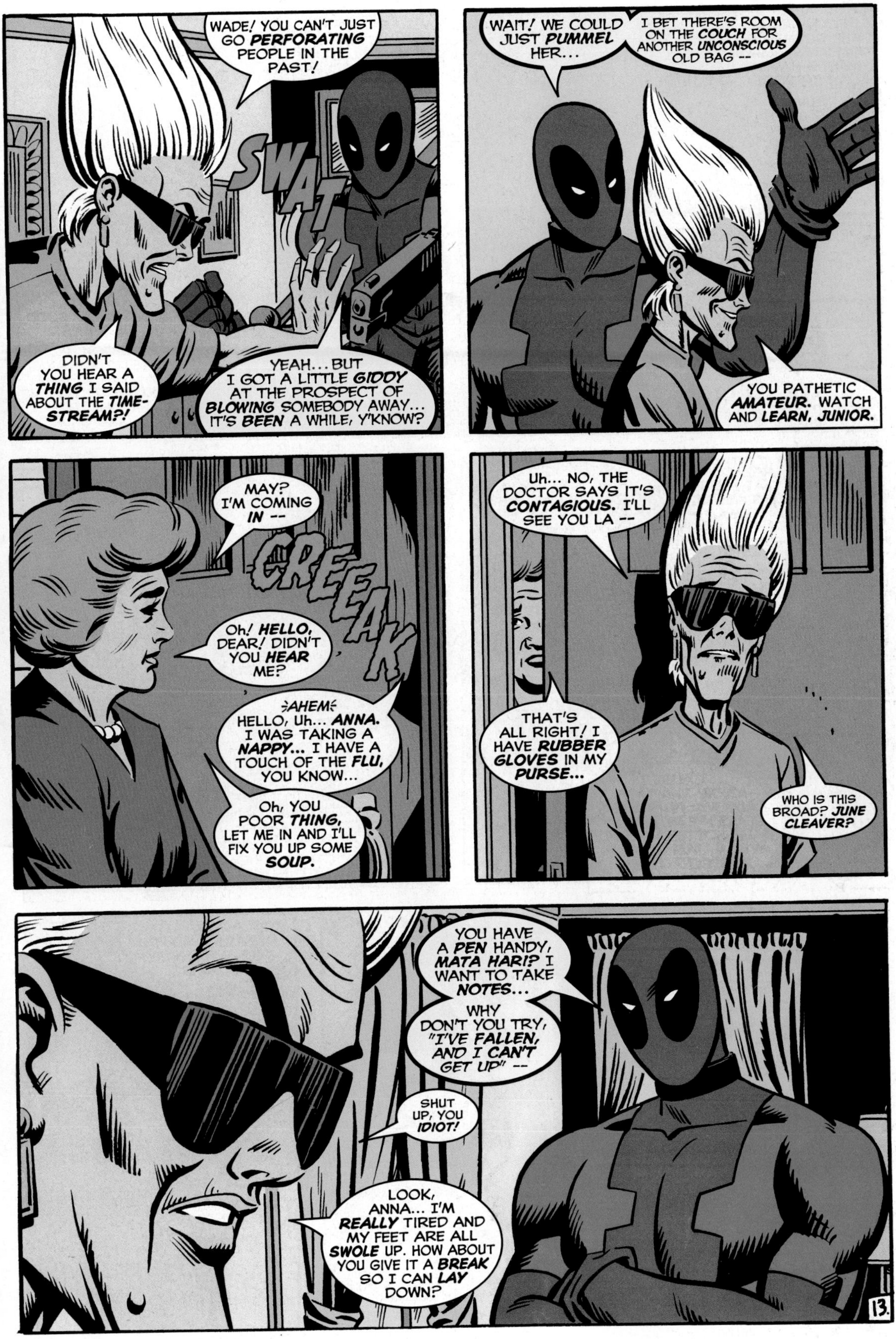
WADE! YOU CAN'T JUST GO PERFORATING PEOPLE IN THE PAST!
SWAT
DIDN'T YOU HEAR A THING I SAID ABOUT THE TIME-STREAM?!
YEAH... BUT I GOT A LITTLE GIDDY AT THE PROSPECT OF BLOWING SOMEBODY AWAY... IT'S BEEN A WHILE, Y'KNOW?
WAIT! WE COULD JUST PUMMEL HER...
I BET THERE'S ROOM ON THE COUCH FOR ANOTHER UNCONSCIOUS OLD BAG --
YOU PATHETIC AMATEUR. WATCH AND LEARN, JUNIOR.
MAY? I'M COMING IN --
CREEEAK
Oh! HELLO, DEAR! DIDN'T YOU HEAR ME?
AHEM
HELLO, Uh... ANNA. I WAS TAKING A NAPPY... I HAVE A TOUCH OF THE FLU, YOU KNOW...
Oh, YOU POOR THING, LET ME IN AND I'LL FIX YOU UP SOME SOUP.
Uh... NO, THE DOCTOR SAYS IT'S CONTAGIOUS. I'LL SEE YOU LA --
THAT'S ALL RIGHT! I HAVE RUBBER GLOVES IN MY PURSE...
WHO IS THIS BROAD? JUNE CLEAVER?
YOU HAVE A PEN HANDY, MATA HARI!? I WANT TO TAKE NOTES...
WHY DON'T YOU TRY, "I'VE FALLEN, AND I CAN'T GET UP" --
SHUT UP, YOU IDIOT!
LOOK, ANNA... I'M REALLY TIRED AND MY FEET ARE ALL SWOLE UP. HOW ABOUT YOU GIVE IT A BREAK SO I CAN LAY DOWN?
13.

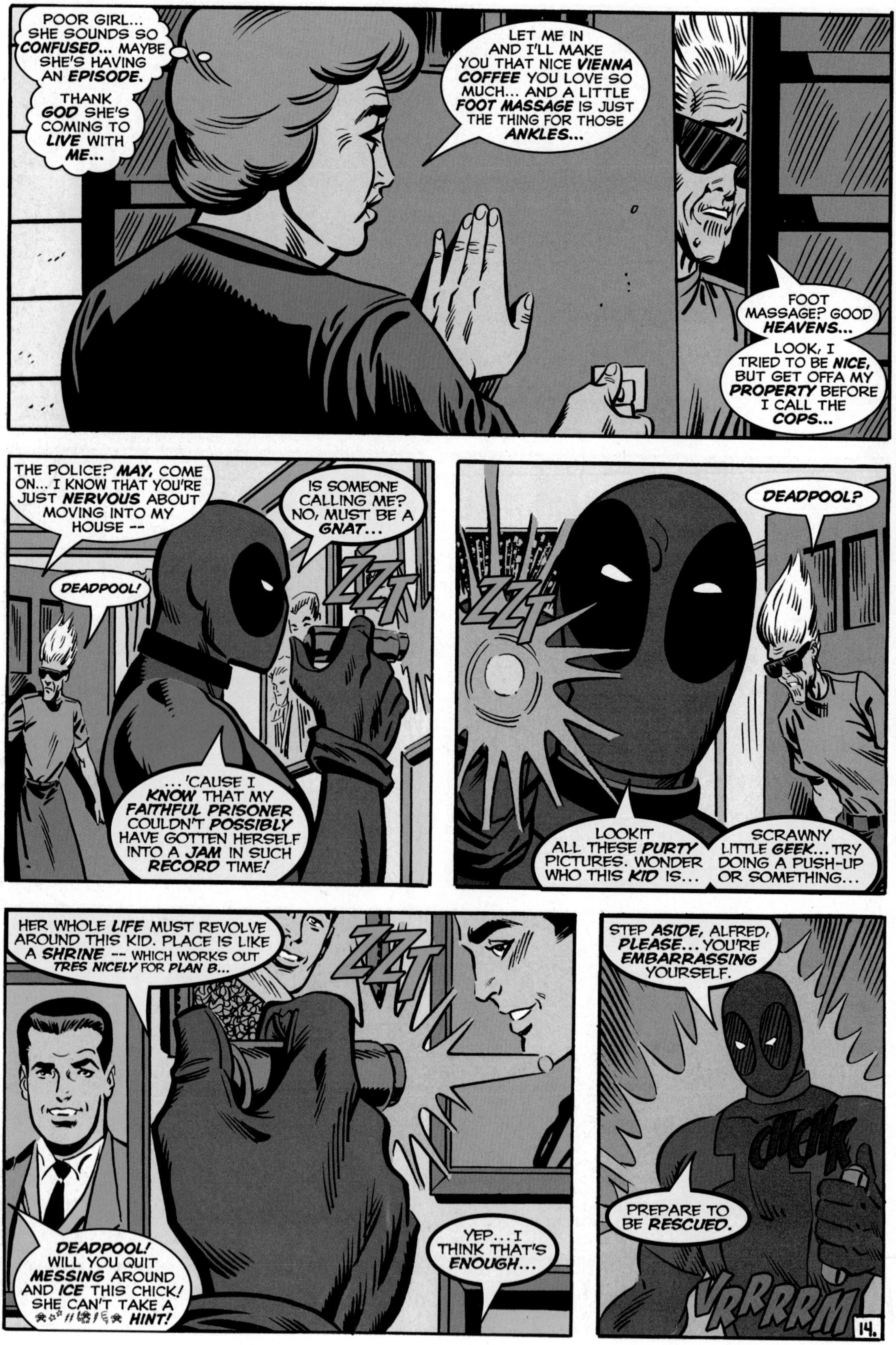
POOR GIRL... SHE SOUNDS SO CONFUSED... MAYBE SHE'S HAVING AN EPISODE.
THANK GOD SHE'S COMING TO LIVE WITH ME...
LET ME IN AND I'LL MAKE YOU THAT NICE VIENNA COFFEE YOU LOVE SO MUCH... AND A LITTLE FOOT MASSAGE IS JUST THE THING FOR THOSE ANKLES...
FOOT MASSAGE? GOOD HEAVENS...
LOOK, I TRIED TO BE NICE, BUT GET OFFA MY PROPERTY BEFORE I CALL THE COPS...
THE POLICE? MAY, COME ON... I KNOW THAT YOU'RE JUST NERVOUS ABOUT MOVING INTO MY HOUSE --
IS SOMEONE CALLING ME? NO, MUST BE A GNAT...
DEADPOOL!
ZZT
...'CAUSE I KNOW THAT MY FAITHFUL PRISONER COULDN'T POSSIBLY HAVE GOTTEN HERSELF INTO A JAM IN SUCH RECORD TIME!
DEADPOOL?
ZZT
LOOKIT ALL THESE PURTY PICTURES. WONDER WHO THIS KID IS...
SCRAWNY LITTLE GEEK... TRY DOING A PUSH-UP OR SOMETHING...
HER WHOLE LIFE MUST REVOLVE AROUND THIS KID. PLACE IS LIKE A SHRINE -- WHICH WORKS OUT TRES NICELY FOR PLAN B...
ZZT
DEADPOOL! WILL YOU QUIT MESSING AROUND AND ICE THIS CHICK! SHE CAN'T TAKE A HINT!
YEP... I THINK THAT'S ENOUGH...
STEP ASIDE, ALFRED, PLEASE... YOU'RE EMBARRASSING YOURSELF.
CHCHK
PREPARE TO BE RESCUED.
VRRRRM
14.

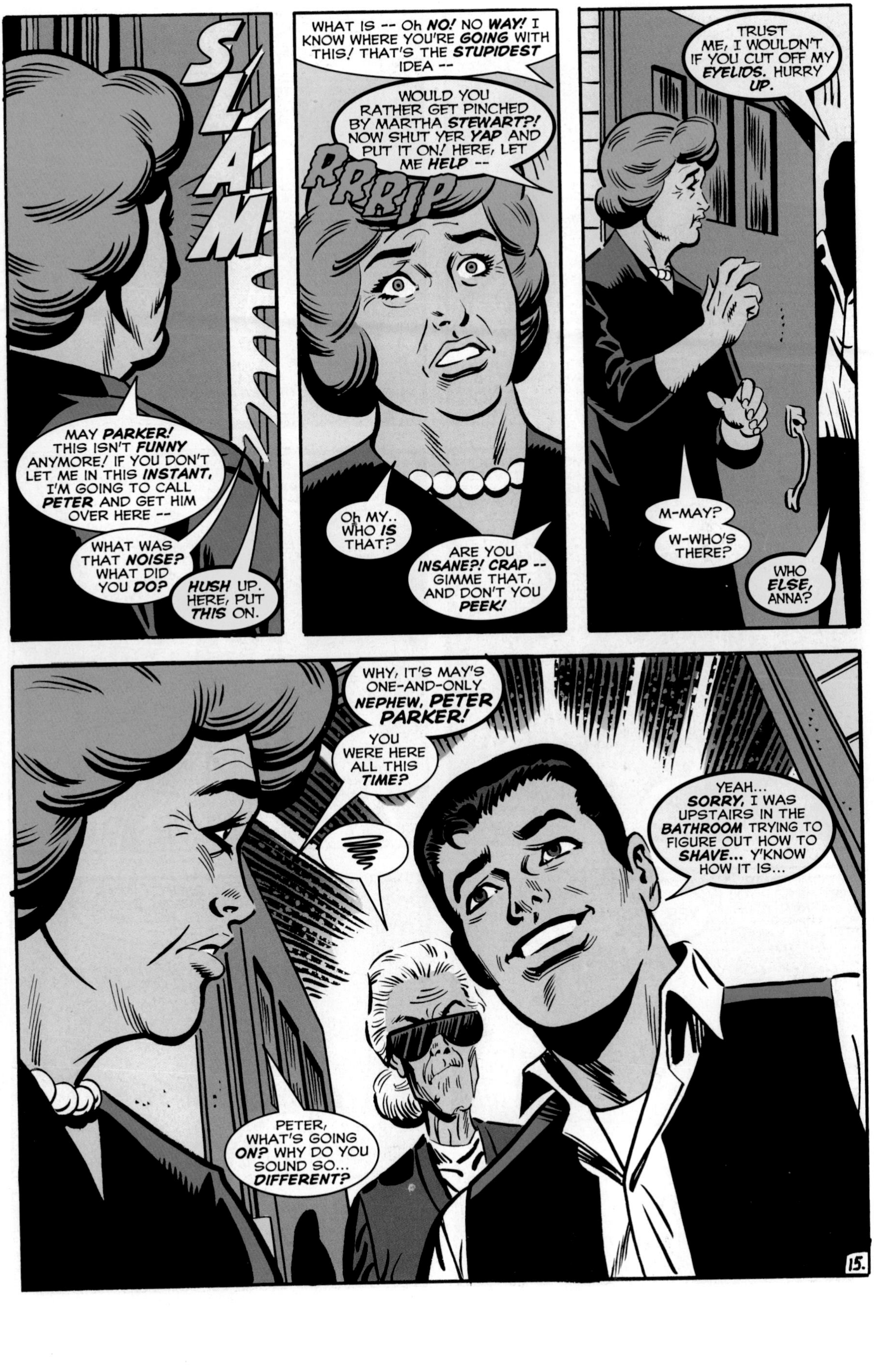
SLAM
MAY PARKER! THIS ISN'T FUNNY ANYMORE! IF YOU DON'T LET ME IN THIS INSTANT, I'M GOING TO CALL PETER AND GET HIM OVER HERE --
WHAT WAS THAT NOISE? WHAT DID YOU DO?
HUSH UP. HERE, PUT THIS ON.
WHAT IS -- Oh NO! NO WAY! I KNOW WHERE YOU'RE GOING WITH THIS! THAT'S THE STUPIDEST IDEA --
WOULD YOU RATHER GET PINCHED BY MARTHA STEWART?! NOW SHUT YER YAP AND PUT IT ON! HERE, LET ME HELP --
RRRIP
Oh MY.. WHO IS THAT?
ARE YOU INSANE?! CRAP -- GIMME THAT, AND DON'T YOU PEEK!
TRUST ME, I WOULDN'T IF YOU CUT OFF MY EYELIDS. HURRY UP.
M-MAY? W-WHO'S THERE?
WHO ELSE, ANNA?
WHY, IT'S MAY'S ONE-AND-ONLY NEPHEW, PETER PARKER!
YOU WERE HERE ALL THIS TIME?
YEAH... SORRY, I WAS UPSTAIRS IN THE BATHROOM TRYING TO FIGURE OUT HOW TO SHAVE... Y'KNOW HOW IT IS...
PETER, WHAT'S GOING ON? WHY DO YOU SOUND SO... DIFFERENT?

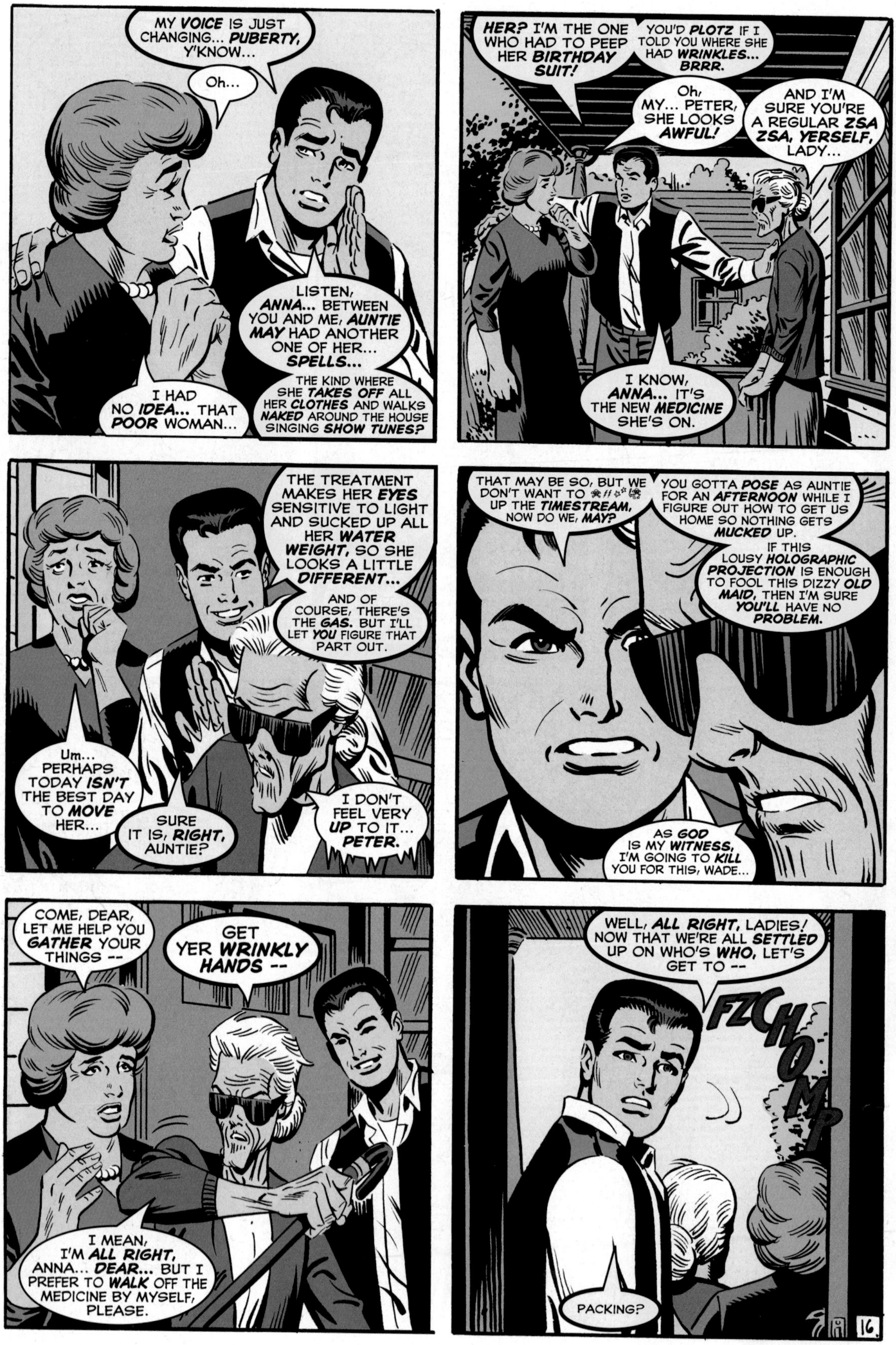
MY VOICE IS JUST CHANGING... PUBERTY, Y'KNOW...
Oh...
LISTEN, ANNA... BETWEEN YOU AND ME, AUNTIE MAY HAD ANOTHER ONE OF HER... SPELLS...
THE KIND WHERE SHE TAKES OFF ALL HER CLOTHES AND WALKS NAKED AROUND THE HOUSE SINGING SHOW TUNES?
I HAD NO IDEA... THAT POOR WOMAN...
HER? I'M THE ONE WHO HAD TO PEEP HER BIRTHDAY SUIT!
YOU'D PLOTZ IF I TOLD YOU WHERE SHE HAD WRINKLES... BRRR.
Oh, MY... PETER, SHE LOOKS AWFUL!
AND I'M SURE YOU'RE A REGULAR ZSA ZSA, YERSELF, LADY...
I KNOW, ANNA... IT'S THE NEW MEDICINE SHE'S ON.
...
THE TREATMENT MAKES HER EYES SENSITIVE TO LIGHT AND SUCKED UP ALL HER WATER WEIGHT, SO SHE LOOKS A LITTLE DIFFERENT...
AND OF COURSE, THERE'S THE GAS. BUT I'LL LET YOU FIGURE THAT PART OUT.
Um... PERHAPS TODAY ISN'T THE BEST DAY TO MOVE HER...
SURE IT IS, RIGHT, AUNTIE?
I DON'T FEEL VERY UP TO IT... PETER.
THAT MAY BE SO, BUT WE DON'T WANT TO # UP THE TIMESTREAM, NOW DO WE, MAY?
YOU GOTTA POSE AS AUNTIE FOR AN AFTERNOON WHILE I FIGURE OUT HOW TO GET US HOME SO NOTHING GETS MUCKED UP.
IF THIS LOUSY HOLOGRAPHIC PROJECTION IS ENOUGH TO FOOL THIS DIZZY OLD MAID, THEN I'M SURE YOU'LL HAVE NO PROBLEM.
AS GOD IS MY WITNESS, I'M GOING TO KILL YOU FOR THIS, WADE...
COME, DEAR, LET ME HELP YOU GATHER YOUR THINGS --
GET YER WRINKLY HANDS --
I MEAN, I'M ALL RIGHT, ANNA... DEAR... BUT I PREFER TO WALK OFF THE MEDICINE BY MYSELF, PLEASE.
WELL, ALL RIGHT, LADIES! NOW THAT WE'RE ALL SETTLED UP ON WHO'S WHO, LET'S GET TO --
FZCHOMP
PACKING?

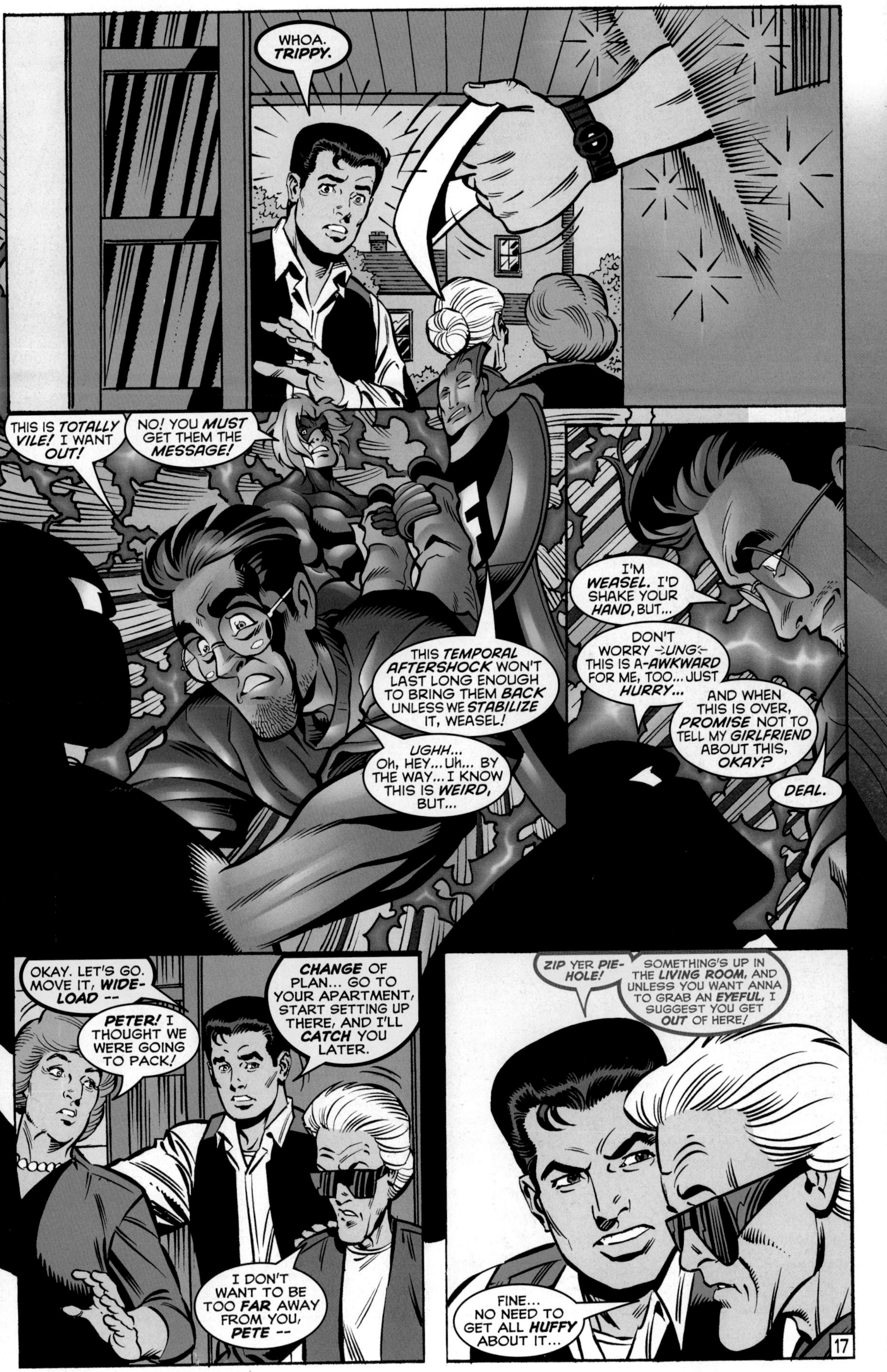
WHOA. TRIPPY.
THIS IS TOTALLY VILE! I WANT OUT!
NO! YOU MUST GET THEM THE MESSAGE!
THIS TEMPORAL AFTERSHOCK WON'T LAST LONG ENOUGH TO BRING THEM BACK UNLESS WE STABILIZE IT, WEASEL!
UGHH... Oh, HEY... Uh... BY THE WAY... I KNOW THIS IS WEIRD, BUT...
I'M WEASEL. I'D SHAKE YOUR HAND, BUT...
DON'T WORRY -UNG- THIS IS A-AWKWARD FOR ME, TOO... JUST HURRY...
AND WHEN THIS IS OVER, PROMISE NOT TO TELL MY GIRLFRIEND ABOUT THIS, OKAY?
DEAL.
OKAY. LET'S GO. MOVE IT, WIDE-LOAD --
PETER! I THOUGHT WE WERE GOING TO PACK!
CHANGE OF PLAN... GO TO YOUR APARTMENT, START SETTING UP THERE, AND I'LL CATCH YOU LATER.
I DON'T WANT TO BE TOO FAR AWAY FROM YOU, PETE --
ZIP YER PIE-HOLE!
SOMETHING'S UP IN THE LIVING ROOM, AND UNLESS YOU WANT ANNA TO GRAB AN EYEFUL, I SUGGEST YOU GET OUT OF HERE!
FINE... NO NEED TO GET ALL HUFFY ABOUT IT...

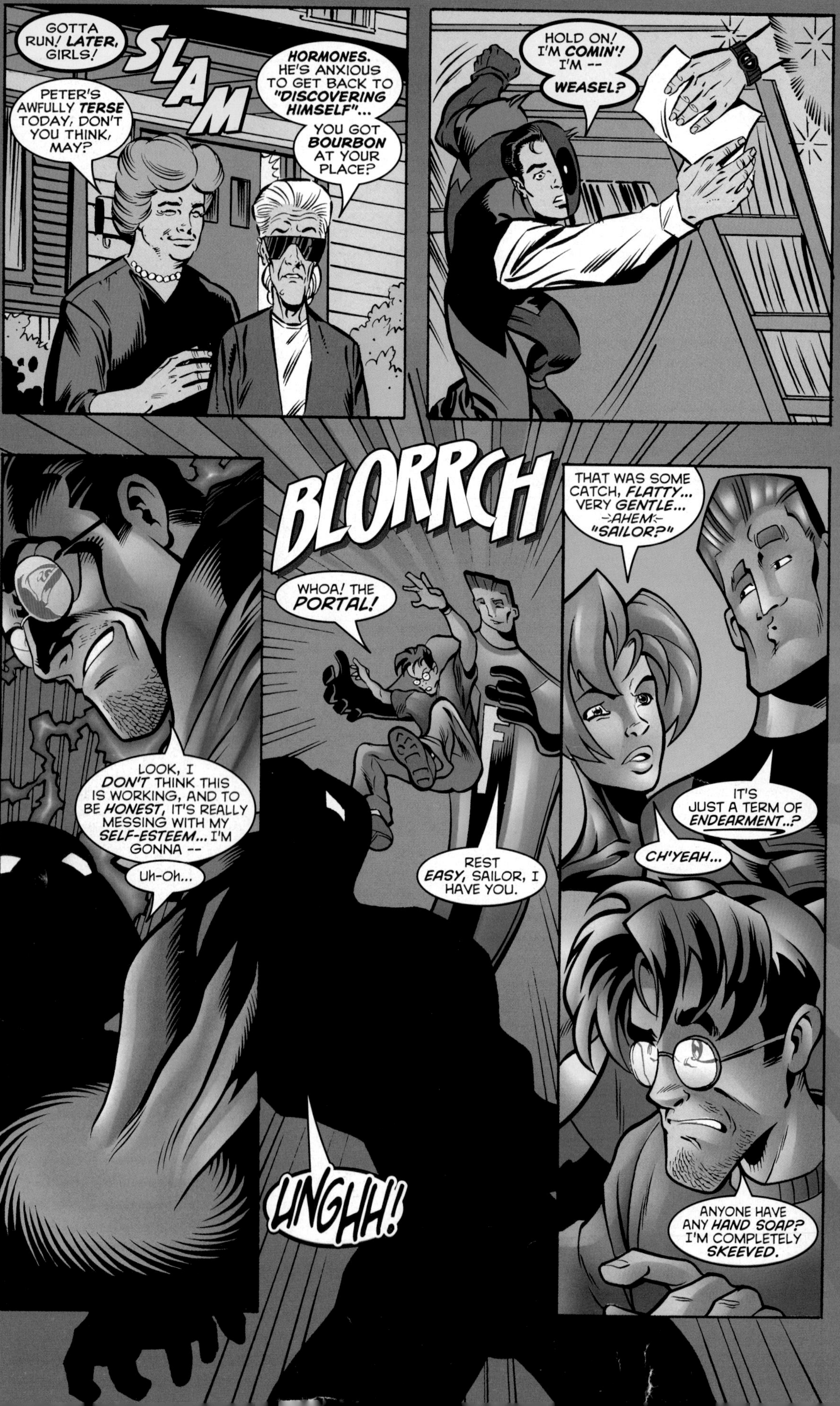

GOTTA RUN! LATER, GIRLS!
SLAM
PETER'S AWFULLY TERSE TODAY, DON'T YOU THINK, MAY?
HORMONES. HE'S ANXIOUS TO GET BACK TO "DISCOVERING HIMSELF"...
YOU GOT BOURBON AT YOUR PLACE?
HOLD ON! I'M COMIN'! I'M -- WEASEL?
LOOK, I DON'T THINK THIS IS WORKING, AND TO BE HONEST, IT'S REALLY MESSING WITH MY SELF-ESTEEM... I'M GONNA --
Uh-Oh...
BLORRCH
WHOA! THE PORTAL!
REST EASY, SAILOR, I HAVE YOU.
UNGHH!
THAT WAS SOME CATCH, FLATTY... VERY GENTLE... -AHEM- "SAILOR?"
IT'S JUST A TERM OF ENDEARMENT..?
CH'YEAH...
ANYONE HAVE ANY HAND SOAP? I'M COMPLETELY SKEEVED.

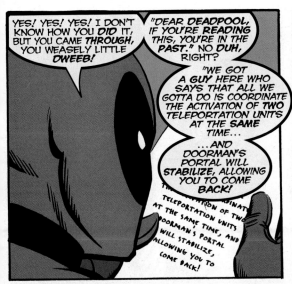

YES! YES! YES! I DON'T KNOW HOW YOU *DID* IT, BUT YOU CAME *THROUGH*, YOU *WEASELY* LITTLE *DWEEB!*

"DEAR *DEADPOOL*, IF YOU'RE READING THIS, YOU'RE IN THE *PAST*." NO *DUH*, RIGHT?

"WE GOT A *GUY* HERE WHO SAYS THAT ALL WE GOTTA DO IS COORDINATE THE ACTIVATION OF *TWO* TELEPORTATION UNITS AT THE *SAME* TIME...

...AND *DOORMAN'S* PORTAL WILL *STABILIZE*, ALLOWING YOU TO COME *BACK!*

THE COORDINATE THE ACTIVATION OF TWO TELEPORTATION UNITS AT THE SAME TIME, AND DOORMAN'S PORTAL WILL STABILIZE, ALLOWING YOU TO COME BACK!

"SO *ACTIVATE* YOUR BELT AT MIDNIGHT, TONIGHT, AND WE'LL COORDINATE THE *REST* FROM HERE."

HEH HEH... *BROKEN.*

"THIS IS SO *COOL*, ISN'T IT? SEE YOU SOON, WEASEL."

BSHHT

STUCK IN THE *PAST.*

BUSTED TELEPORTER.

WHAT WOULD *ALEX P. KEATON* DO?

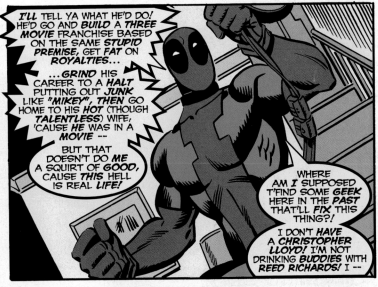

I'LL TELL YA WHAT HE'D DO! HE'D GO AND *BUILD* A *THREE MOVIE* FRANCHISE BASED ON THE SAME *STUPID* PREMISE, GET FAT ON *ROYALTIES...*

...*GRIND* HIS CAREER TO A *HALT* PUTTING OUT *JUNK* LIKE "*MIKEY*", THEN GO HOME TO HIS *HOT* (THOUGH *TALENTLESS*) WIFE, 'CAUSE *HE* WAS IN A MOVIE --

BUT THAT DOESN'T DO *ME* A SQUIRT OF *GOOD*, CAUSE *THIS* HELL IS REAL *LIFE!*

WHERE AM *I* SUPPOSED T'FIND SOME *GEEK* HERE IN THE *PAST* THAT'LL *FIX* THIS THING?!

I DON'T *HAVE* A *CHRISTOPHER LLOYD!* I'M NOT DRINKING *BUDDIES* WITH *REED RICHARDS!* I --

WHAT ARE *YOU* SMILING ABOUT, *PARKER?!*

I'LL KNOCK YOUR WHITE-BOY *TEETH* DOWN YOUR *SCRAWNY THROAT*, YOU --

⌐GASP⌐

SILENCE THE *VIOLENCE...*

19.

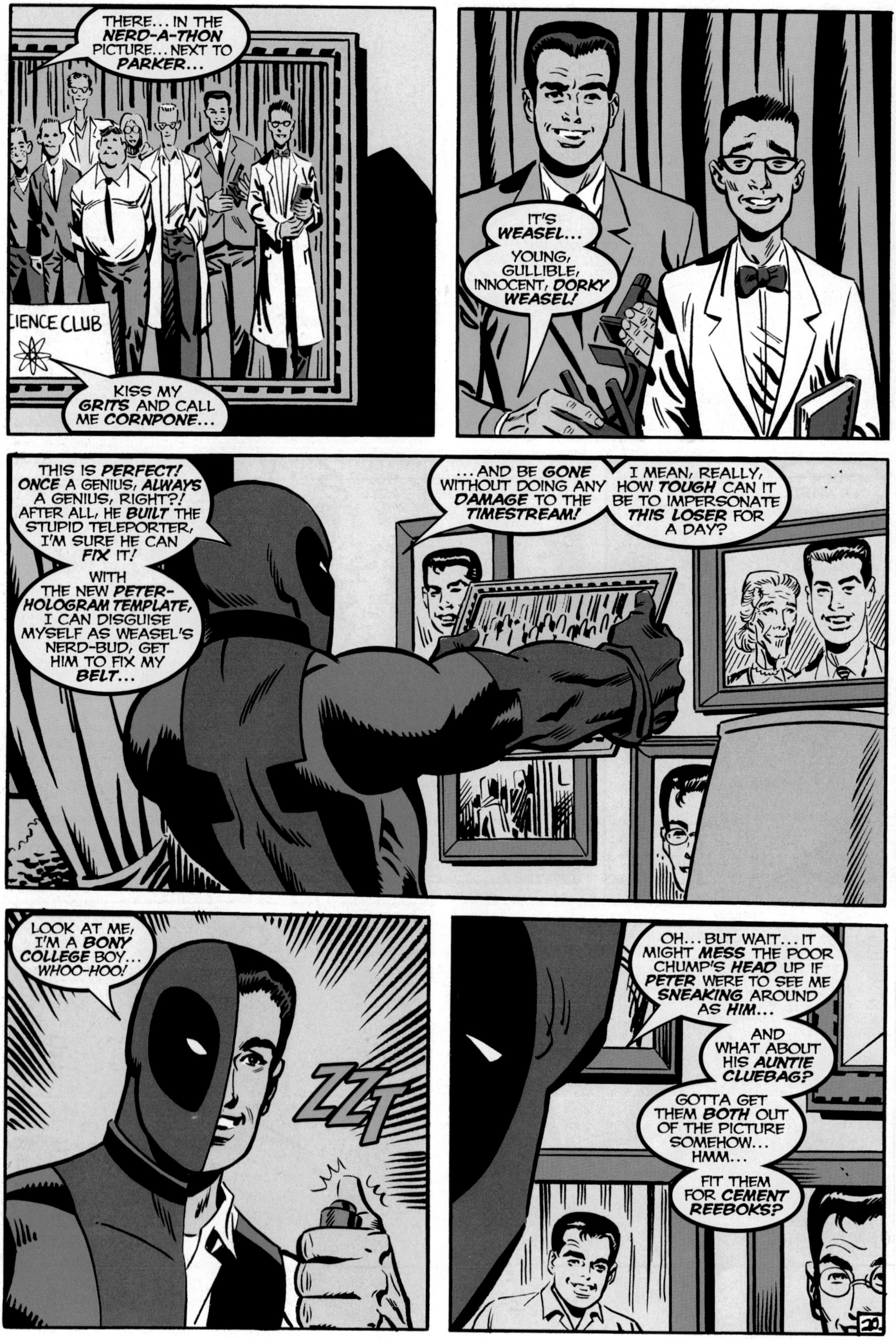
THERE... IN THE NERD-A-THON PICTURE... NEXT TO PARKER...
CIENCE CLUB
KISS MY GRITS AND CALL ME CORNPONE...
IT'S WEASEL...
YOUNG, GULLIBLE, INNOCENT, DORKY WEASEL!
THIS IS PERFECT! ONCE A GENIUS, ALWAYS A GENIUS, RIGHT?! AFTER ALL, HE BUILT THE STUPID TELEPORTER, I'M SURE HE CAN FIX IT!
WITH THE NEW PETER-HOLOGRAM TEMPLATE, I CAN DISGUISE MYSELF AS WEASEL'S NERD-BUD, GET HIM TO FIX MY BELT...
...AND BE GONE WITHOUT DOING ANY DAMAGE TO THE TIMESTREAM!
I MEAN, REALLY, HOW TOUGH CAN IT BE TO IMPERSONATE THIS LOSER FOR A DAY?
LOOK AT ME, I'M A BONY COLLEGE BOY... WHOO-HOO!
ZZZT
OH... BUT WAIT... IT MIGHT MESS THE POOR CHUMP'S HEAD UP IF PETER WERE TO SEE ME SNEAKING AROUND AS HIM...
AND WHAT ABOUT HIS AUNTIE CLUEBAG?
GOTTA GET THEM BOTH OUT OF THE PICTURE SOMEHOW... HMM...
FIT THEM FOR CEMENT REEBOKS?
20

NAH... I GOT A FEELIN' THAT JUST WOULDN'T BE KOSHER... KARMICALLY SPEAKING... THERE'S GOTTA BE A LESS NC-17 WAY TO GO ABOUT THIS LITTLE ENDEAVOR...
DAILY
NEW YORK'S FIN
PHOTO BY PETER PARKER
Hmmm, LI'L PETEY'S A SHUTTERBUG FOR THE BUGLE... ALRIGHT... AN IDEA IS A'BREWIN, BUT FIRST...
LET'S TAKE CARE OF AUNTIE...
LATER, AFTER "TAKING CARE" OF DEAR AUNT MAY, THE FAUX PETER PARKER MAKES HIS WAY TO NEW YORK CITY...
PHASE ONE COMPLETE, ON TO PART B. ALL I HAVE TO DO IS GET TO E.S.U. AND PLAY MY LITTLE GAG ON PETEY-BOY...
SHOULDN'T BE TOO HARD. PEOPLE IN THIS TIME SEEM PRETTY DENSE. "MAKE LOVE NOT WAR?" HOW NAIVE CAN YOU GET?
AND THE CLOTHES! LOOK AT THIS WALKING ACCIDENT...
NICE DUDS, KA-ZAR.
OSBORN HAS AN OFFICE HERE IN THE CITY SOME-WHERE...
KEEP YOUR CITY CLEA
AND IT WON'T TAKE KRAVEN THE HUNTER LONG TO FIND IT!
WEIRDO.
THE WORLD'S GREATEST HUNTER TURNS TO THE PHONE BOOK, AND AFTER A QUICK STOP AT THE COAT SHOP...
I WANT TO SEE NORMAN OSBORN!
I'M SORRY, SIR! I'M AFRAID THAT'S IMPOSSIBLE!
HE'LL BE OUT OF TOWN FOR THE REST OF THE WEEK!
OUT OF TOWN?!
YES, SIR! MAY I ASK WHO'S CALLING?
SIR! IS ANY-THING WRONG?
WHY... ARE YOU... LOOKING AT ME LIKE THAT?
OUT OF TOWN, Eh? HE MUST HAVE HEARD I HAD RETURNED!
WELL, YOU CAN TELL HIM THAT IT WON'T WORK --HE CAN'T HIDE FROM ME FOREVER!
SLAM!
RUNNING INTO THE NEXT ROOM WON'T DO YOU ANY GOOD! TELL HIM THAT KRAVEN WILL BE BACK... DO YOU HEAR?
KRAVEN WILL BE BACK!
MINUTES LATER... BACK AT THE HUNTER'S HIDDEN LAIR...
NO MATTER HOW MANY OBSTACLES ARE THROWN IN MY WAY, THIS TIME, KRAVEN WILL NOT FAIL!
SPIDER-MAN'S MASK WILL YET ADORN MY TROPHY ROOM!
KRAVEN NEVER MAKES THE SAME MISTAKE TWICE!
I WAS DEFEATED LAST TIME BECAUSE OF SPIDER-MAN'S GREATER SPEED!
BUT I'VE HAD MONTHS TO DEVELOP THIS NEW WEAPON... A DOUBLE-BARRELED RAY WHICH CAN MAGNETIZE HIS MUSCULAR ELECTROLYTES!
A COBRA-QUICK ATTACK LIKE THIS, AND HIS ACCURSED SPIDER-SPEED WILL BE GONE!
ZZTAK!
THEN, WITHOUT HIS SPEED, HE'LL BE HELP-LESS BEFORE Y FAR GREATER STRENGTH... AND MY MATCH-LESS ANIMAL POWERS!
MAN! WHAT'S THE DEAL WITH THIS CAT? TO FIND OUT, READ ON, FEARLESS FRONT-FACER...
21

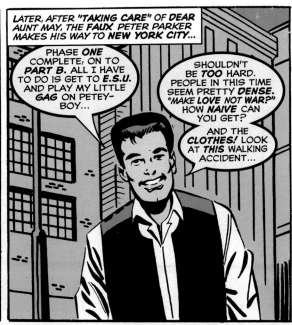

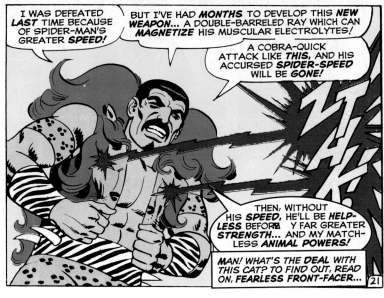

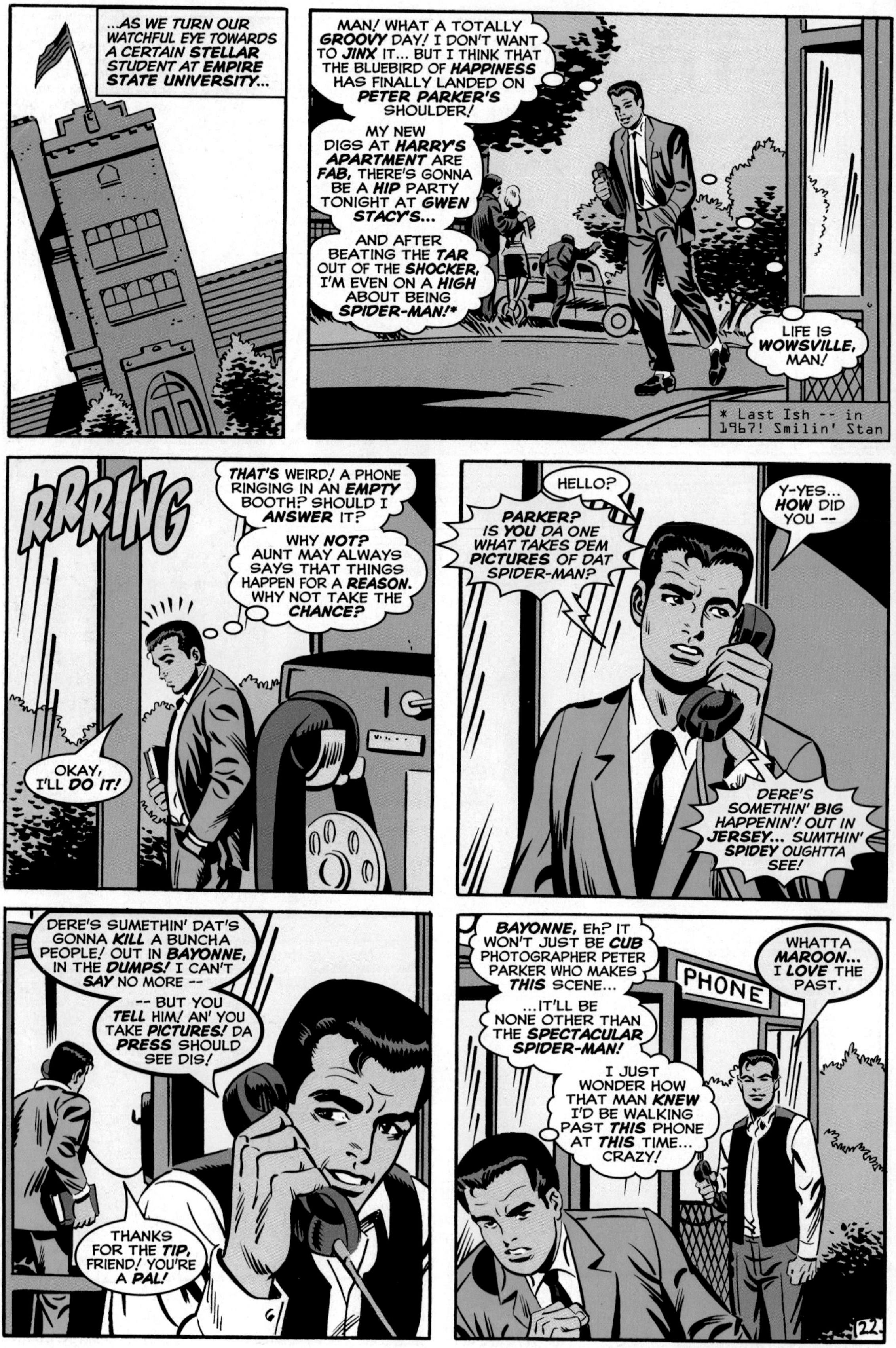
...AS WE TURN OUR WATCHFUL EYE TOWARDS A CERTAIN STELLAR STUDENT AT EMPIRE STATE UNIVERSITY...
MAN! WHAT A TOTALLY GROOVY DAY! I DON'T WANT TO JINX IT... BUT I THINK THAT THE BLUEBIRD OF HAPPINESS HAS FINALLY LANDED ON PETER PARKER'S SHOULDER!
MY NEW DIGS AT HARRY'S APARTMENT ARE FAB, THERE'S GONNA BE A HIP PARTY TONIGHT AT GWEN STACY'S...
AND AFTER BEATING THE TAR OUT OF THE SHOCKER, I'M EVEN ON A HIGH ABOUT BEING SPIDER-MAN!*
LIFE IS WOWSVILLE, MAN!
* Last Ish -- in 1967! Smilin' Stan
RRRING
THAT'S WEIRD! A PHONE RINGING IN AN EMPTY BOOTH? SHOULD I ANSWER IT?
WHY NOT? AUNT MAY ALWAYS SAYS THAT THINGS HAPPEN FOR A REASON. WHY NOT TAKE THE CHANCE?
OKAY, I'LL DO IT!
HELLO?
PARKER? IS YOU DA ONE WHAT TAKES DEM PICTURES OF DAT SPIDER-MAN?
Y-YES... HOW DID YOU --
DERE'S SOMETHIN' BIG HAPPENIN'! OUT IN JERSEY... SUMTHIN' SPIDEY OUGHTTA SEE!
DERE'S SUMETHIN' DAT'S GONNA KILL A BUNCHA PEOPLE! OUT IN BAYONNE, IN THE DUMPS! I CAN'T SAY NO MORE --
-- BUT YOU TELL HIM! AN' YOU TAKE PICTURES! DA PRESS SHOULD SEE DIS!
THANKS FOR THE TIP, FRIEND! YOU'RE A PAL!
BAYONNE, Eh? IT WON'T JUST BE CUB PHOTOGRAPHER PETER PARKER WHO MAKES THIS SCENE...
...IT'LL BE NONE OTHER THAN THE SPECTACULAR SPIDER-MAN!
PHONE
WHATTA MAROON... I LOVE THE PAST.
I JUST WONDER HOW THAT MAN KNEW I'D BE WALKING PAST THIS PHONE AT THIS TIME... CRAZY!
22

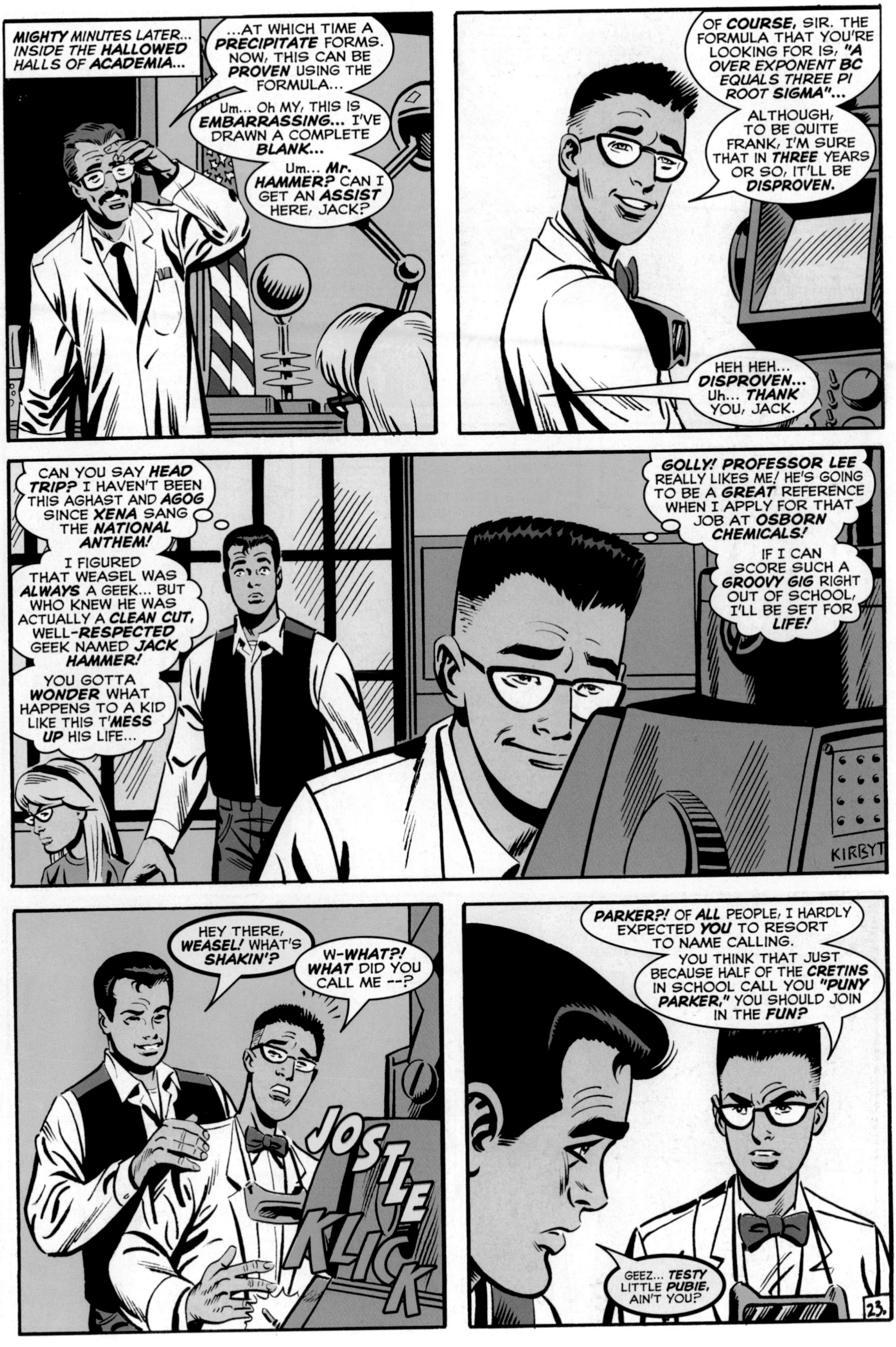
MIGHTY MINUTES LATER... INSIDE THE HALLOWED HALLS OF ACADEMIA...
...AT WHICH TIME A PRECIPITATE FORMS. NOW, THIS CAN BE PROVEN USING THE FORMULA...
Um... Oh MY, THIS IS EMBARRASSING... I'VE DRAWN A COMPLETE BLANK...
Um... Mr. HAMMER? CAN I GET AN ASSIST HERE, JACK?
OF COURSE, SIR. THE FORMULA THAT YOU'RE LOOKING FOR IS, "A OVER EXPONENT BC EQUALS THREE PI ROOT SIGMA"...
ALTHOUGH, TO BE QUITE FRANK, I'M SURE THAT IN THREE YEARS OR SO, IT'LL BE DISPROVEN.
HEH HEH... DISPROVEN... Uh... THANK YOU, JACK.
CAN YOU SAY HEAD TRIP? I HAVEN'T BEEN THIS AGHAST AND AGOG SINCE XENA SANG THE NATIONAL ANTHEM!
I FIGURED THAT WEASEL WAS ALWAYS A GEEK... BUT WHO KNEW HE WAS ACTUALLY A CLEAN CUT, WELL-RESPECTED GEEK NAMED JACK HAMMER!
YOU GOTTA WONDER WHAT HAPPENS TO A KID LIKE THIS T'MESS UP HIS LIFE...
GOLLY! PROFESSOR LEE REALLY LIKES ME! HE'S GOING TO BE A GREAT REFERENCE WHEN I APPLY FOR THAT JOB AT OSBORN CHEMICALS!
IF I CAN SCORE SUCH A GROOVY GIG RIGHT OUT OF SCHOOL, I'LL BE SET FOR LIFE!
KIRBYT
HEY THERE, WEASEL! WHAT'S SHAKIN'?
W-WHAT?! WHAT DID YOU CALL ME --?
JOSTLE
KLICK
PARKER?! OF ALL PEOPLE, I HARDLY EXPECTED YOU TO RESORT TO NAME CALLING.
YOU THINK THAT JUST BECAUSE HALF OF THE CRETINS IN SCHOOL CALL YOU "PUNY PARKER," YOU SHOULD JOIN IN THE FUN?
GEEZ... TESTY LITTLE PUBIE, AIN'T YOU?
23.

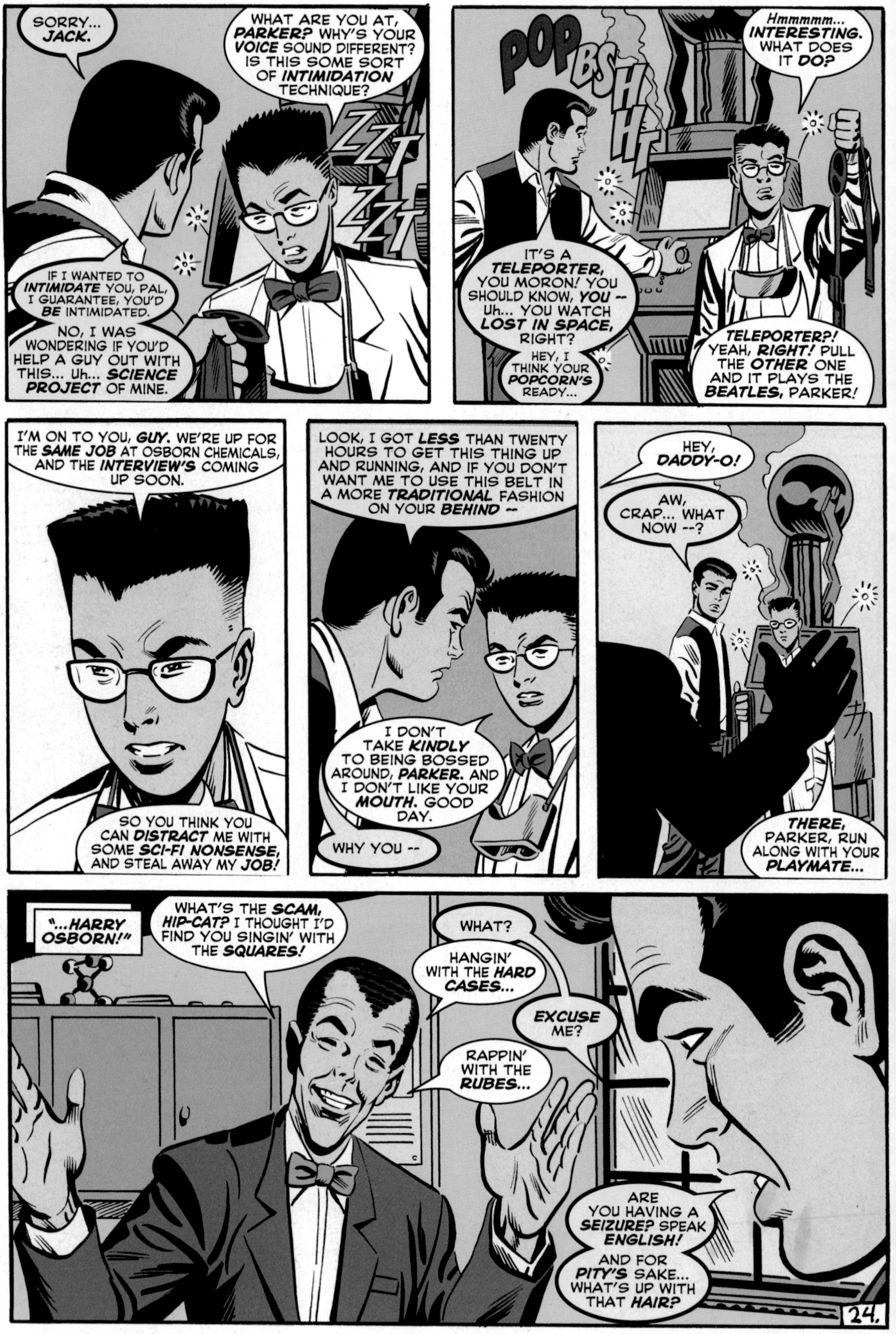
SORRY... JACK.
WHAT ARE YOU AT, PARKER? WHY'S YOUR VOICE SOUND DIFFERENT? IS THIS SOME SORT OF INTIMIDATION TECHNIQUE?
ZZZT ZZZT
IF I WANTED TO INTIMIDATE YOU, PAL, I GUARANTEE, YOU'D BE INTIMIDATED.
NO, I WAS WONDERING IF YOU'D HELP A GUY OUT WITH THIS... Uh... SCIENCE PROJECT OF MINE.
POP BSHHT
Hmmmmm... INTERESTING. WHAT DOES IT DO?
IT'S A TELEPORTER, YOU MORON! YOU SHOULD KNOW, YOU -- Uh... YOU WATCH LOST IN SPACE, RIGHT?
HEY, I THINK YOUR POPCORN'S READY...
TELEPORTER?! YEAH, RIGHT! PULL THE OTHER ONE AND IT PLAYS THE BEATLES, PARKER!
I'M ON TO YOU, GUY. WE'RE UP FOR THE SAME JOB AT OSBORN CHEMICALS, AND THE INTERVIEW'S COMING UP SOON.
SO YOU THINK YOU CAN DISTRACT ME WITH SOME SCI-FI NONSENSE, AND STEAL AWAY MY JOB!
LOOK, I GOT LESS THAN TWENTY HOURS TO GET THIS THING UP AND RUNNING, AND IF YOU DON'T WANT ME TO USE THIS BELT IN A MORE TRADITIONAL FASHION ON YOUR BEHIND --
I DON'T TAKE KINDLY TO BEING BOSSED AROUND, PARKER. AND I DON'T LIKE YOUR MOUTH. GOOD DAY.
WHY YOU --
HEY, DADDY-O!
AW, CRAP... WHAT NOW --?
THERE, PARKER, RUN ALONG WITH YOUR PLAYMATE...
"...HARRY OSBORN!"
WHAT'S THE SCAM, HIP-CAT? I THOUGHT I'D FIND YOU SINGIN' WITH THE SQUARES!
WHAT?
HANGIN' WITH THE HARD CASES...
EXCUSE ME?
RAPPIN' WITH THE RUBES...
ARE YOU HAVING A SEIZURE? SPEAK ENGLISH!
AND FOR PITY'S SAKE... WHAT'S UP WITH THAT HAIR?
24.

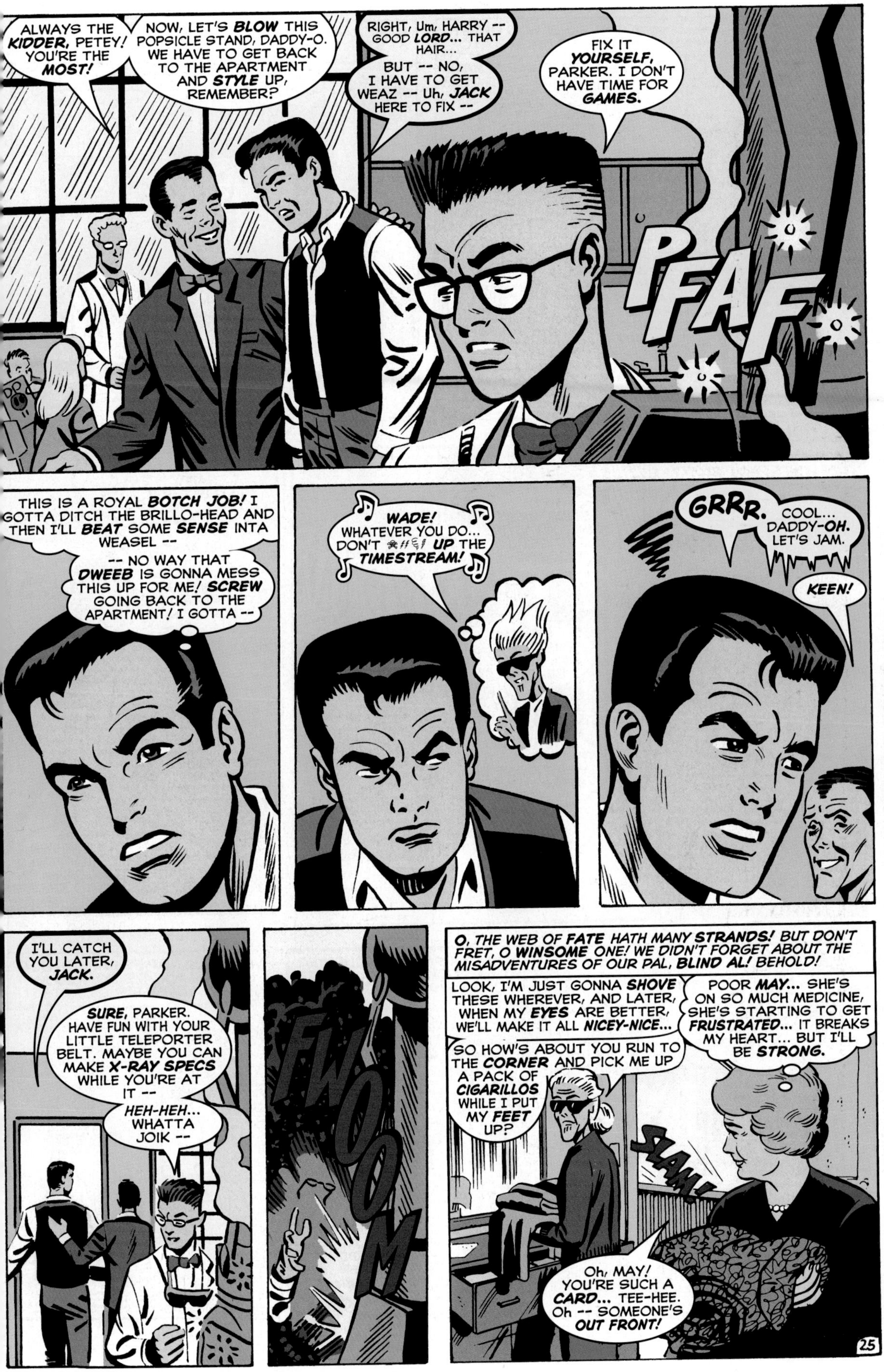
ALWAYS THE KIDDER, PETEY! YOU'RE THE MOST!
NOW, LET'S BLOW THIS POPSICLE STAND, DADDY-O. WE HAVE TO GET BACK TO THE APARTMENT AND STYLE UP, REMEMBER?
RIGHT, Um, HARRY -- GOOD LORD... THAT HAIR...
BUT -- NO, I HAVE TO GET WEAZ -- Uh, JACK HERE TO FIX --
FIX IT YOURSELF, PARKER. I DON'T HAVE TIME FOR GAMES.
PFAF
THIS IS A ROYAL BOTCH JOB! I GOTTA DITCH THE BRILLO-HEAD AND THEN I'LL BEAT SOME SENSE INTA WEASEL --
-- NO WAY THAT DWEEB IS GONNA MESS THIS UP FOR ME! SCREW GOING BACK TO THE APARTMENT! I GOTTA --
WADE! WHATEVER YOU DO... DON'T ☠#$ UP THE TIMESTREAM!
GRRR.
COOL... DADDY-OH. LET'S JAM.
KEEN!
I'LL CATCH YOU LATER, JACK.
SURE, PARKER. HAVE FUN WITH YOUR LITTLE TELEPORTER BELT. MAYBE YOU CAN MAKE X-RAY SPECS WHILE YOU'RE AT IT --
HEH-HEH... WHATTA JOIK --
FWOOOM
O, THE WEB OF FATE HATH MANY STRANDS! BUT DON'T FRET, O WINSOME ONE! WE DIDN'T FORGET ABOUT THE MISADVENTURES OF OUR PAL, BLIND AL! BEHOLD!
LOOK, I'M JUST GONNA SHOVE THESE WHEREVER, AND LATER, WHEN MY EYES ARE BETTER, WE'LL MAKE IT ALL NICEY-NICE...
SO HOW'S ABOUT YOU RUN TO THE CORNER AND PICK ME UP A PACK OF CIGARILLOS WHILE I PUT MY FEET UP?
POOR MAY... SHE'S ON SO MUCH MEDICINE, SHE'S STARTING TO GET FRUSTRATED... IT BREAKS MY HEART... BUT I'LL BE STRONG.
SLAM!
Oh, MAY! YOU'RE SUCH A CARD... TEE-HEE. Oh -- SOMEONE'S OUT FRONT!

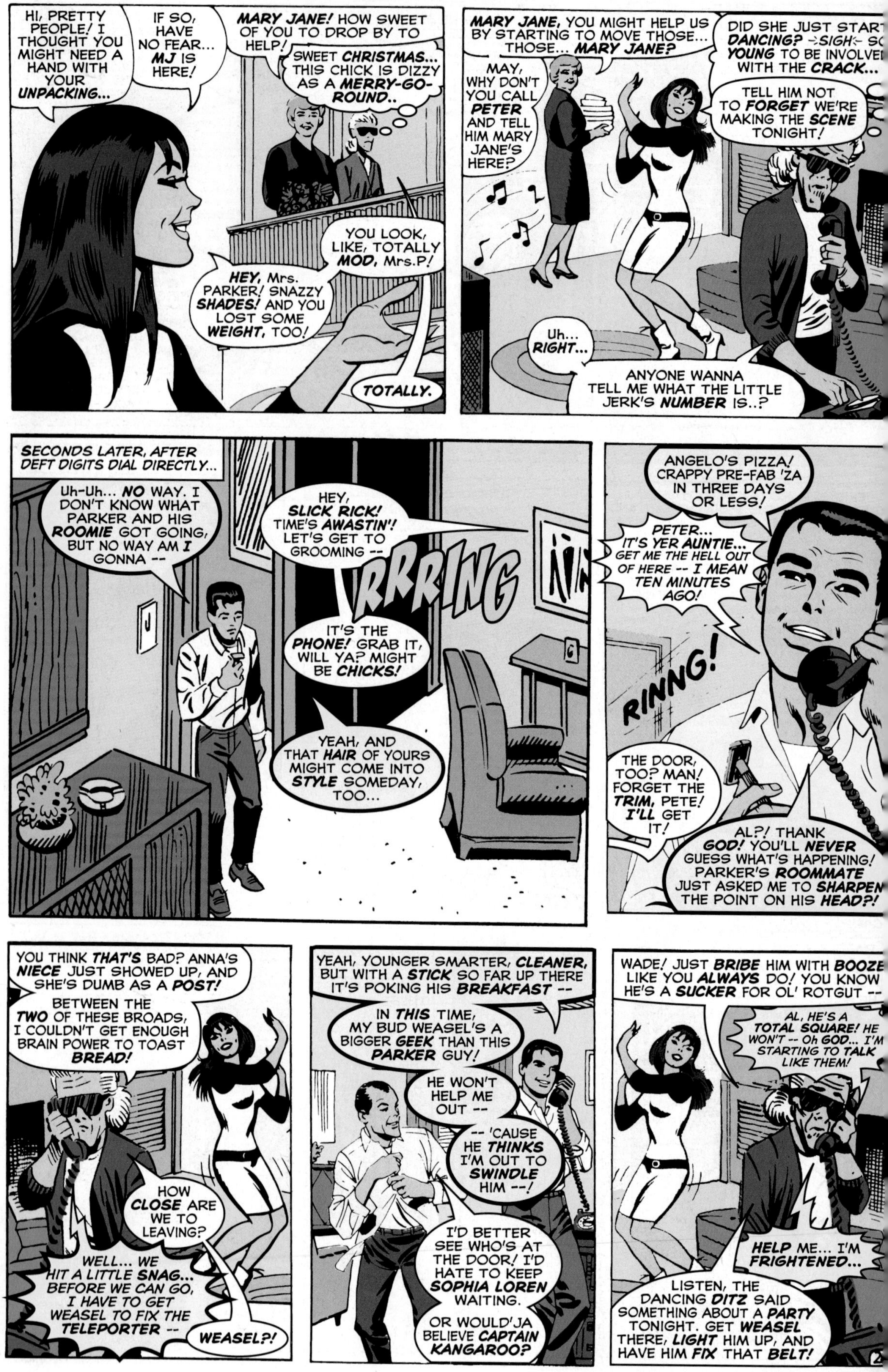
HI, PRETTY PEOPLE! I THOUGHT YOU MIGHT NEED A HAND WITH YOUR UNPACKING...
IF SO, HAVE NO FEAR... MJ IS HERE!
MARY JANE! HOW SWEET OF YOU TO DROP BY TO HELP!
SWEET CHRISTMAS... THIS CHICK IS DIZZY AS A MERRY-GO-ROUND..
YOU LOOK, LIKE, TOTALLY MOD, Mrs.P!
HEY, Mrs. PARKER! SNAZZY SHADES! AND YOU LOST SOME WEIGHT, TOO!
TOTALLY.
MARY JANE, YOU MIGHT HELP US BY STARTING TO MOVE THOSE... THOSE... MARY JANE?
MAY, WHY DON'T YOU CALL PETER AND TELL HIM MARY JANE'S HERE?
DID SHE JUST STAR DANCING? →SIGH← SC YOUNG TO BE INVOLVE WITH THE CRACK...
TELL HIM NOT TO FORGET WE'RE MAKING THE SCENE TONIGHT!
Uh... RIGHT...
ANYONE WANNA TELL ME WHAT THE LITTLE JERK'S NUMBER IS..?
SECONDS LATER, AFTER DEFT DIGITS DIAL DIRECTLY...
Uh-Uh... NO WAY. I DON'T KNOW WHAT PARKER AND HIS ROOMIE GOT GOING, BUT NO WAY AM I GONNA --
HEY, SLICK RICK! TIME'S AWASTIN'! LET'S GET TO GROOMING --
RRRING
IT'S THE PHONE! GRAB IT, WILL YA? MIGHT BE CHICKS!
YEAH, AND THAT HAIR OF YOURS MIGHT COME INTO STYLE SOMEDAY, TOO...
ANGELO'S PIZZA! CRAPPY PRE-FAB 'ZA IN THREE DAYS OR LESS!
PETER... IT'S YER AUNTIE... GET ME THE HELL OUT OF HERE -- I MEAN TEN MINUTES AGO!
RINNG!
THE DOOR, TOO? MAN! FORGET THE TRIM, PETE! I'LL GET IT!
AL?! THANK GOD! YOU'LL NEVER GUESS WHAT'S HAPPENING! PARKER'S ROOMMATE JUST ASKED ME TO SHARPEN THE POINT ON HIS HEAD?!
YOU THINK THAT'S BAD? ANNA'S NIECE JUST SHOWED UP, AND SHE'S DUMB AS A POST!
BETWEEN THE TWO OF THESE BROADS, I COULDN'T GET ENOUGH BRAIN POWER TO TOAST BREAD!
HOW CLOSE ARE WE TO LEAVING?
WELL... WE HIT A LITTLE SNAG... BEFORE WE CAN GO, I HAVE TO GET WEASEL TO FIX THE TELEPORTER --
WEASEL?!
YEAH, YOUNGER SMARTER, CLEANER, BUT WITH A STICK SO FAR UP THERE IT'S POKING HIS BREAKFAST --
IN THIS TIME, MY BUD WEASEL'S A BIGGER GEEK THAN THIS PARKER GUY!
HE WON'T HELP ME OUT --
-- 'CAUSE HE THINKS I'M OUT TO SWINDLE HIM --!
I'D BETTER SEE WHO'S AT THE DOOR! I'D HATE TO KEEP SOPHIA LOREN WAITING.
OR WOULD'JA BELIEVE CAPTAIN KANGAROO?
WADE! JUST BRIBE HIM WITH BOOZE LIKE YOU ALWAYS DO! YOU KNOW HE'S A SUCKER FOR OL' ROTGUT --
AL, HE'S A TOTAL SQUARE! HE WON'T -- Oh GOD... I'M STARTING TO TALK LIKE THEM!
HELP ME... I'M FRIGHTENED...
LISTEN, THE DANCING DITZ SAID SOMETHING ABOUT A PARTY TONIGHT. GET WEASEL THERE, LIGHT HIM UP, AND HAVE HIM FIX THAT BELT!

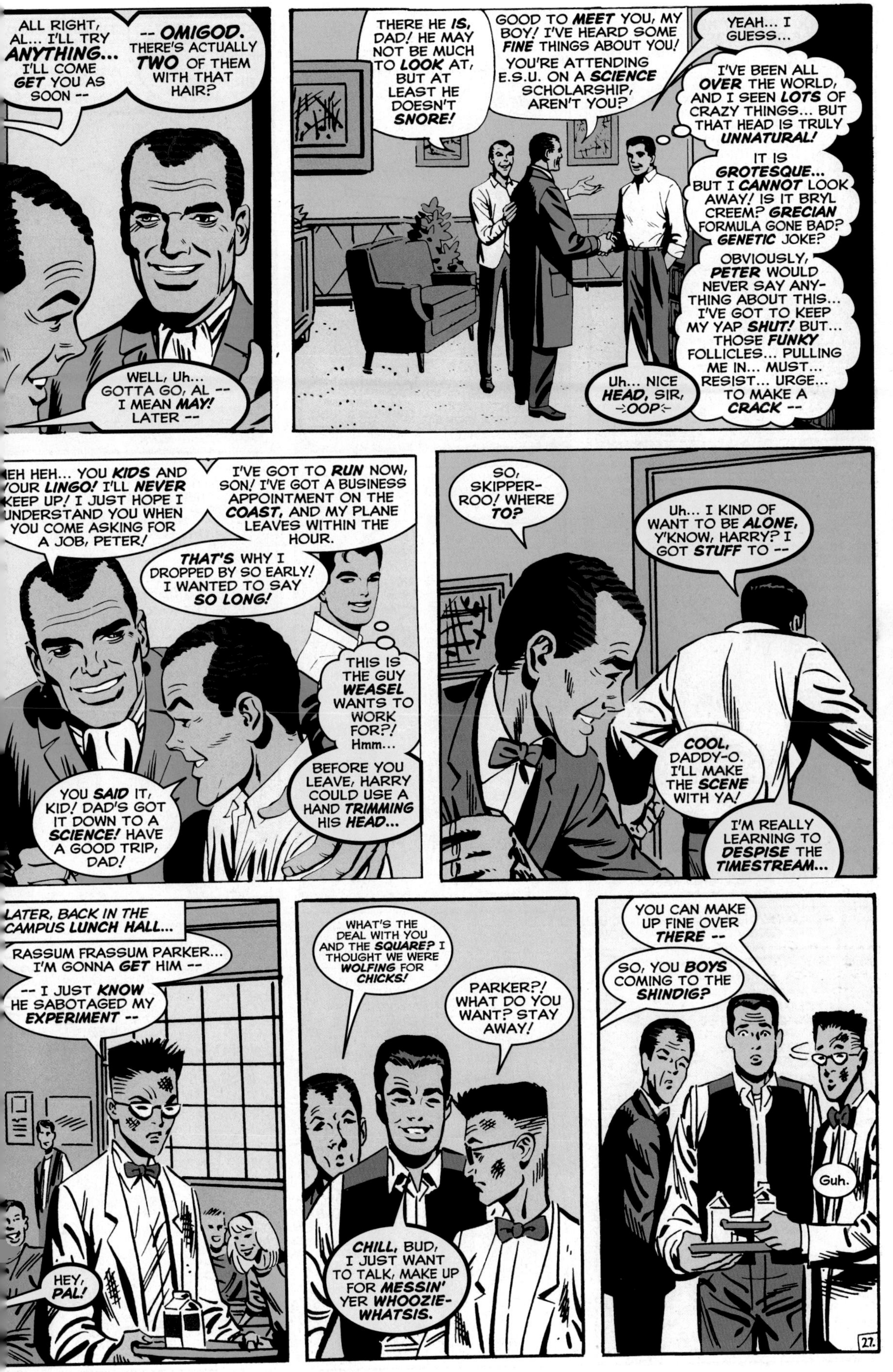
ALL RIGHT, AL... I'LL TRY ANYTHING... I'LL COME GET YOU AS SOON --
-- OMIGOD. THERE'S ACTUALLY TWO OF THEM WITH THAT HAIR?
WELL, Uh... GOTTA GO, AL -- I MEAN MAY! LATER --
THERE HE IS, DAD! HE MAY NOT BE MUCH TO LOOK AT, BUT AT LEAST HE DOESN'T SNORE!
GOOD TO MEET YOU, MY BOY! I'VE HEARD SOME FINE THINGS ABOUT YOU!
YOU'RE ATTENDING E.S.U. ON A SCIENCE SCHOLARSHIP, AREN'T YOU?
YEAH... I GUESS...
I'VE BEEN ALL OVER THE WORLD, AND I SEEN LOTS OF CRAZY THINGS... BUT THAT HEAD IS TRULY UNNATURAL!
IT IS GROTESQUE... BUT I CANNOT LOOK AWAY! IS IT BRYL CREEM? GRECIAN FORMULA GONE BAD? GENETIC JOKE?
OBVIOUSLY, PETER WOULD NEVER SAY ANYTHING ABOUT THIS... I'VE GOT TO KEEP MY YAP SHUT! BUT... THOSE FUNKY FOLLICLES... PULLING ME IN... MUST... RESIST... URGE... TO MAKE A CRACK --
Uh... NICE HEAD, SIR, -OOP-
HEH HEH... YOU KIDS AND YOUR LINGO! I'LL NEVER KEEP UP! I JUST HOPE I UNDERSTAND YOU WHEN YOU COME ASKING FOR A JOB, PETER!
I'VE GOT TO RUN NOW, SON! I'VE GOT A BUSINESS APPOINTMENT ON THE COAST, AND MY PLANE LEAVES WITHIN THE HOUR.
THAT'S WHY I DROPPED BY SO EARLY! I WANTED TO SAY SO LONG!
THIS IS THE GUY WEASEL WANTS TO WORK FOR?! Hmm...
BEFORE YOU LEAVE, HARRY COULD USE A HAND TRIMMING HIS HEAD...
YOU SAID IT, KID! DAD'S GOT IT DOWN TO A SCIENCE! HAVE A GOOD TRIP, DAD!
SO, SKIPPER-ROO! WHERE TO?
Uh... I KIND OF WANT TO BE ALONE, Y'KNOW, HARRY? I GOT STUFF TO --
COOL, DADDY-O. I'LL MAKE THE SCENE WITH YA!
I'M REALLY LEARNING TO DESPISE THE TIMESTREAM...
LATER, BACK IN THE CAMPUS LUNCH HALL...
RASSUM FRASSUM PARKER... I'M GONNA GET HIM --
-- I JUST KNOW HE SABOTAGED MY EXPERIMENT --
HEY, PAL!
WHAT'S THE DEAL WITH YOU AND THE SQUARE? I THOUGHT WE WERE WOLFING FOR CHICKS!
PARKER?! WHAT DO YOU WANT? STAY AWAY!
CHILL, BUD, I JUST WANT TO TALK, MAKE UP FOR MESSIN' YER WHOOZIE-WHATSIS.
YOU CAN MAKE UP FINE OVER THERE --
SO, YOU BOYS COMING TO THE SHINDIG?
Guh.
27.

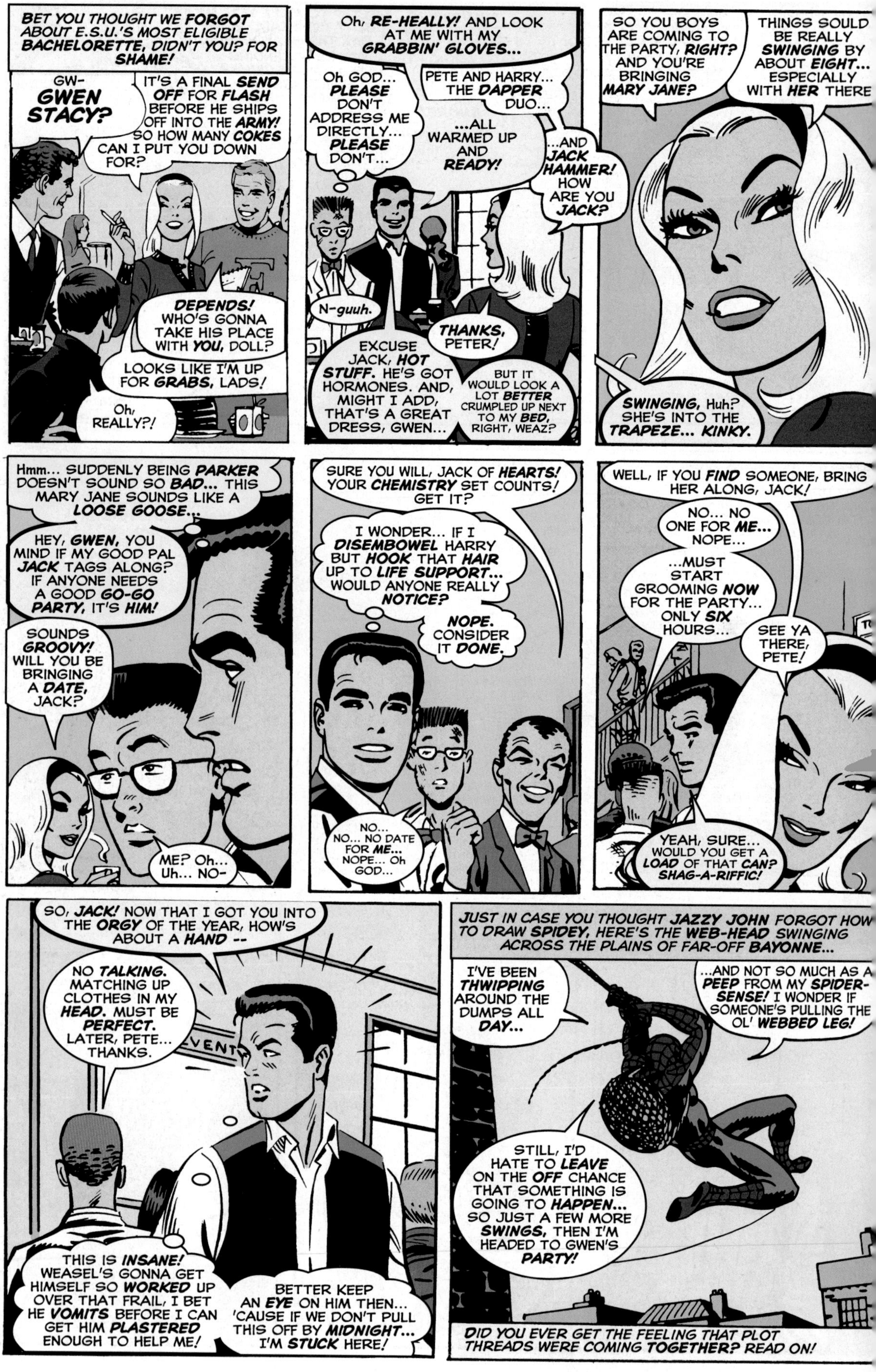
BET YOU THOUGHT WE FORGOT ABOUT E.S.U.'S MOST ELIGIBLE BACHELORETTE, DIDN'T YOU? FOR SHAME!
GW- GWEN STACY?
IT'S A FINAL SEND OFF FOR FLASH BEFORE HE SHIPS OFF INTO THE ARMY! SO HOW MANY COKES CAN I PUT YOU DOWN FOR?
DEPENDS! WHO'S GONNA TAKE HIS PLACE WITH YOU, DOLL?
LOOKS LIKE I'M UP FOR GRABS, LADS!
Oh, REALLY?!
Oh, RE-HEALLY! AND LOOK AT ME WITH MY GRABBIN' GLOVES...
Oh GOD... PLEASE DON'T ADDRESS ME DIRECTLY... PLEASE DON'T...
PETE AND HARRY... THE DAPPER DUO...
...ALL WARMED UP AND READY!
...AND JACK HAMMER! HOW ARE YOU JACK?
N-guuh.
THANKS, PETER!
EXCUSE JACK, HOT STUFF. HE'S GOT HORMONES. AND, MIGHT I ADD, THAT'S A GREAT DRESS, GWEN...
BUT IT WOULD LOOK A LOT BETTER CRUMPLED UP NEXT TO MY BED, RIGHT, WEAZ?
SO YOU BOYS ARE COMING TO THE PARTY, RIGHT? AND YOU'RE BRINGING MARY JANE?
THINGS SOULD BE REALLY SWINGING BY ABOUT EIGHT... ESPECIALLY WITH HER THERE
SWINGING, Huh? SHE'S INTO THE TRAPEZE... KINKY.
Hmm... SUDDENLY BEING PARKER DOESN'T SOUND SO BAD... THIS MARY JANE SOUNDS LIKE A LOOSE GOOSE...
HEY, GWEN, YOU MIND IF MY GOOD PAL JACK TAGS ALONG? IF ANYONE NEEDS A GOOD GO-GO PARTY, IT'S HIM!
SOUNDS GROOVY! WILL YOU BE BRINGING A DATE, JACK?
ME? Oh... Uh... NO-
SURE YOU WILL, JACK OF HEARTS! YOUR CHEMISTRY SET COUNTS! GET IT?
I WONDER... IF I DISEMBOWEL HARRY BUT HOOK THAT HAIR UP TO LIFE SUPPORT... WOULD ANYONE REALLY NOTICE?
NOPE. CONSIDER IT DONE.
NO... NO... NO DATE FOR ME... NOPE... Oh GOD...
WELL, IF YOU FIND SOMEONE, BRING HER ALONG, JACK!
NO... NO ONE FOR ME... NOPE...
...MUST START GROOMING NOW FOR THE PARTY... ONLY SIX HOURS...
SEE YA THERE, PETE!
YEAH, SURE... WOULD YOU GET A LOAD OF THAT CAN? SHAG-A-RIFFIC!
SO, JACK! NOW THAT I GOT YOU INTO THE ORGY OF THE YEAR, HOW'S ABOUT A HAND --
NO TALKING. MATCHING UP CLOTHES IN MY HEAD. MUST BE PERFECT. LATER, PETE... THANKS.
THIS IS INSANE! WEASEL'S GONNA GET HIMSELF SO WORKED UP OVER THAT FRAIL, I BET HE VOMITS BEFORE I CAN GET HIM PLASTERED ENOUGH TO HELP ME!
BETTER KEEP AN EYE ON HIM THEN... 'CAUSE IF WE DON'T PULL THIS OFF BY MIDNIGHT... I'M STUCK HERE!
JUST IN CASE YOU THOUGHT JAZZY JOHN FORGOT HOW TO DRAW SPIDEY, HERE'S THE WEB-HEAD SWINGING ACROSS THE PLAINS OF FAR-OFF BAYONNE...
I'VE BEEN THWIPPING AROUND THE DUMPS ALL DAY...
...AND NOT SO MUCH AS A PEEP FROM MY SPIDER-SENSE! I WONDER IF SOMEONE'S PULLING THE OL' WEBBED LEG!
STILL, I'D HATE TO LEAVE ON THE OFF CHANCE THAT SOMETHING IS GOING TO HAPPEN... SO JUST A FEW MORE SWINGS, THEN I'M HEADED TO GWEN'S PARTY!
DID YOU EVER GET THE FEELING THAT PLOT THREADS WERE COMING TOGETHER? READ ON!

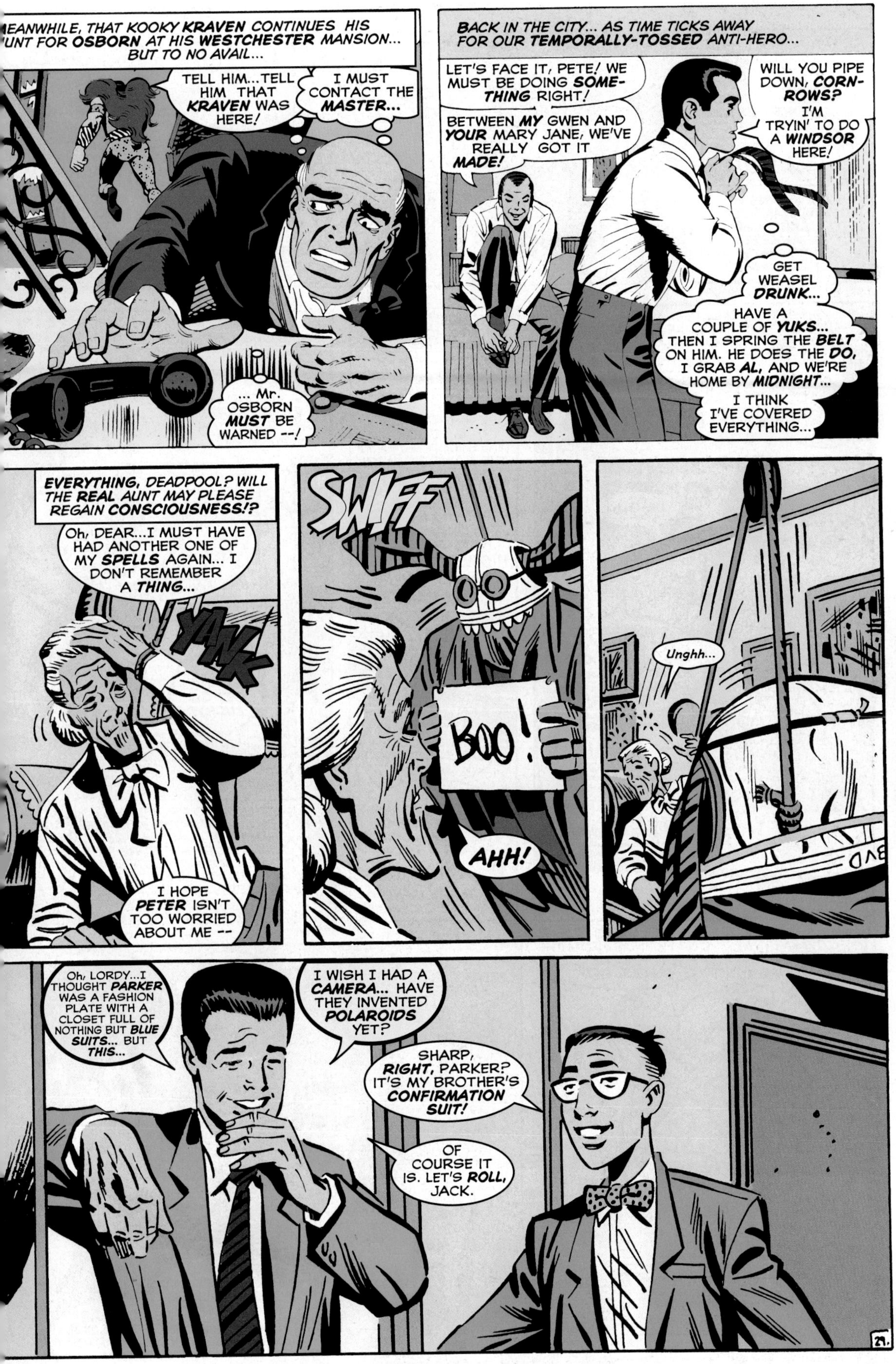
MEANWHILE, THAT KOOKY KRAVEN CONTINUES HIS HUNT FOR OSBORN AT HIS WESTCHESTER MANSION... BUT TO NO AVAIL...
TELL HIM...TELL HIM THAT KRAVEN WAS HERE!
I MUST CONTACT THE MASTER...
... Mr. OSBORN MUST BE WARNED --!
BACK IN THE CITY... AS TIME TICKS AWAY FOR OUR TEMPORALLY-TOSSED ANTI-HERO...
LET'S FACE IT, PETE! WE MUST BE DOING SOMETHING RIGHT!
BETWEEN MY GWEN AND YOUR MARY JANE, WE'VE REALLY GOT IT MADE!
WILL YOU PIPE DOWN, CORNROWS? I'M TRYIN' TO DO A WINDSOR HERE!
GET WEASEL DRUNK... HAVE A COUPLE OF YUKS... THEN I SPRING THE BELT ON HIM. HE DOES THE DO, I GRAB AL, AND WE'RE HOME BY MIDNIGHT... I THINK I'VE COVERED EVERYTHING...
EVERYTHING, DEADPOOL? WILL THE REAL AUNT MAY PLEASE REGAIN CONSCIOUSNESS!?
Oh, DEAR...I MUST HAVE HAD ANOTHER ONE OF MY SPELLS AGAIN... I DON'T REMEMBER A THING...
YANK
I HOPE PETER ISN'T TOO WORRIED ABOUT ME --
SWIFF
BOO!
AHH!
Unghh...
Oh, LORDY...I THOUGHT PARKER WAS A FASHION PLATE WITH A CLOSET FULL OF NOTHING BUT BLUE SUITS... BUT THIS...
I WISH I HAD A CAMERA... HAVE THEY INVENTED POLAROIDS YET?
SHARP, RIGHT, PARKER? IT'S MY BROTHER'S CONFIRMATION SUIT!
OF COURSE IT IS. LET'S ROLL, JACK.

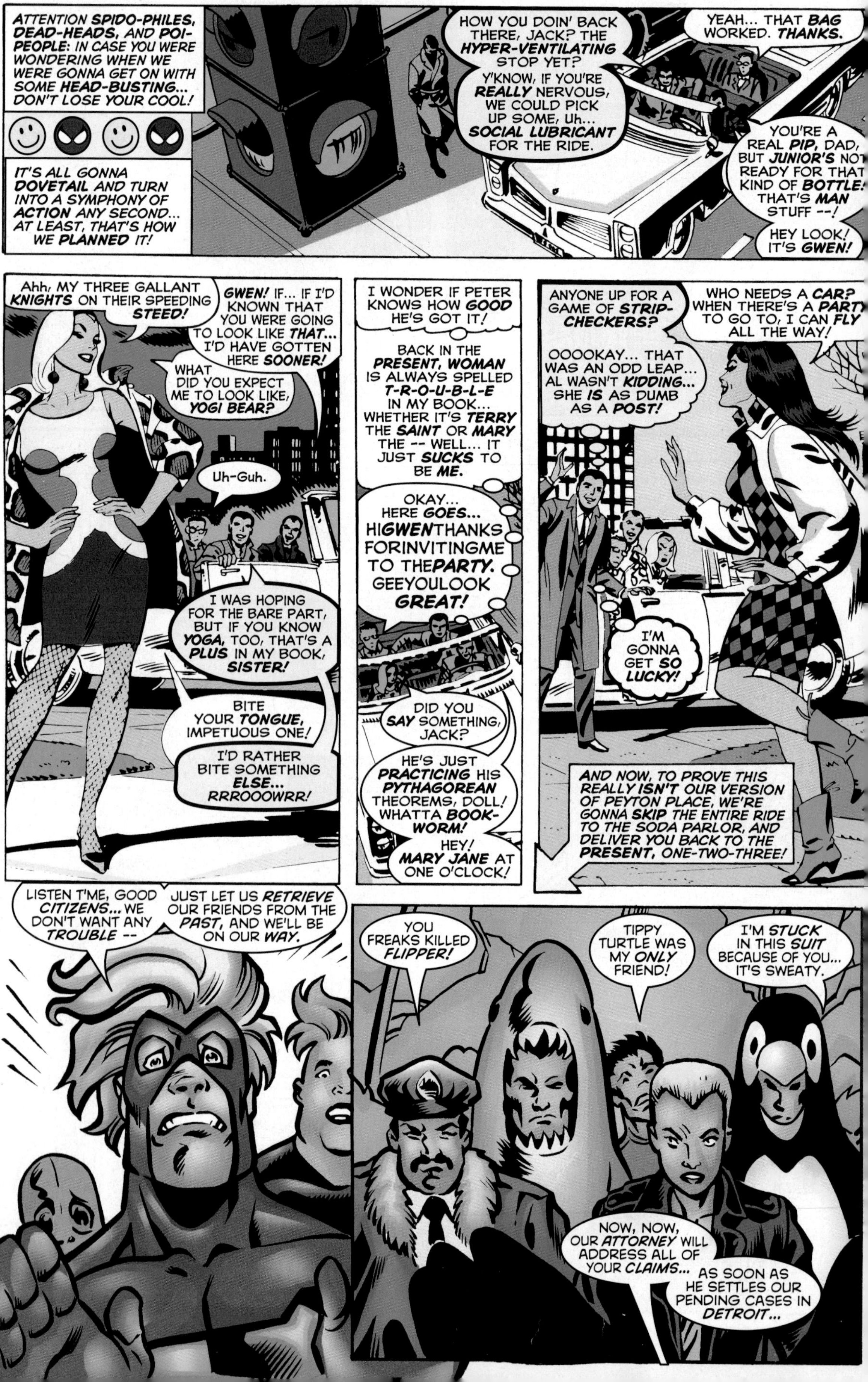

ATTENTION SPIDO-PHILES, DEAD-HEADS, AND POI-PEOPLE: IN CASE YOU WERE WONDERING WHEN WE WERE GONNA GET ON WITH SOME HEAD-BUSTING... DON'T LOSE YOUR COOL!
IT'S ALL GONNA DOVETAIL AND TURN INTO A SYMPHONY OF ACTION ANY SECOND... AT LEAST, THAT'S HOW WE PLANNED IT!
HOW YOU DOIN' BACK THERE, JACK? THE HYPER-VENTILATING STOP YET?
Y'KNOW, IF YOU'RE REALLY NERVOUS, WE COULD PICK UP SOME, Uh... SOCIAL LUBRICANT FOR THE RIDE.
YEAH... THAT BAG WORKED. THANKS.
YOU'RE A REAL PIP, DAD, BUT JUNIOR'S NOT READY FOR THAT KIND OF BOTTLE! THAT'S MAN STUFF --!
HEY LOOK! IT'S GWEN!
Ahh, MY THREE GALLANT KNIGHTS ON THEIR SPEEDING STEED!
GWEN! IF... IF I'D KNOWN THAT YOU WERE GOING TO LOOK LIKE THAT... I'D HAVE GOTTEN HERE SOONER!
WHAT DID YOU EXPECT ME TO LOOK LIKE, YOGI BEAR?
Uh-Guh.
I WAS HOPING FOR THE BARE PART, BUT IF YOU KNOW YOGA, TOO, THAT'S A PLUS IN MY BOOK, SISTER!
BITE YOUR TONGUE, IMPETUOUS ONE!
I'D RATHER BITE SOMETHING ELSE... RRROOOWRR!
I WONDER IF PETER KNOWS HOW GOOD HE'S GOT IT!
BACK IN THE PRESENT, WOMAN IS ALWAYS SPELLED T-R-O-U-B-L-E IN MY BOOK... WHETHER IT'S TERRY THE SAINT OR MARY THE -- WELL... IT JUST SUCKS TO BE ME.
OKAY... HERE GOES... HIGWENTHANKS FORINVITINGME TO THEPARTY. GEEYOULOOK GREAT!
DID YOU SAY SOMETHING, JACK?
HE'S JUST PRACTICING HIS PYTHAGOREAN THEOREMS, DOLL! WHATTA BOOK-WORM!
HEY! MARY JANE AT ONE O'CLOCK!
ANYONE UP FOR A GAME OF STRIP-CHECKERS?
WHO NEEDS A CAR? WHEN THERE'S A PARTY TO GO TO, I CAN FLY ALL THE WAY!
OOOOKAY... THAT WAS AN ODD LEAP... AL WASN'T KIDDING... SHE IS AS DUMB AS A POST!
I'M GONNA GET SO LUCKY!
AND NOW, TO PROVE THIS REALLY ISN'T OUR VERSION OF PEYTON PLACE, WE'RE GONNA SKIP THE ENTIRE RIDE TO THE SODA PARLOR, AND DELIVER YOU BACK TO THE PRESENT, ONE-TWO-THREE!
LISTEN T'ME, GOOD CITIZENS... WE DON'T WANT ANY TROUBLE --
JUST LET US RETRIEVE OUR FRIENDS FROM THE PAST, AND WE'LL BE ON OUR WAY.
YOU FREAKS KILLED FLIPPER!
TIPPY TURTLE WAS MY ONLY FRIEND!
I'M STUCK IN THIS SUIT BECAUSE OF YOU... IT'S SWEATY.
NOW, NOW, OUR ATTORNEY WILL ADDRESS ALL OF YOUR CLAIMS...
AS SOON AS HE SETTLES OUR PENDING CASES IN DETROIT...

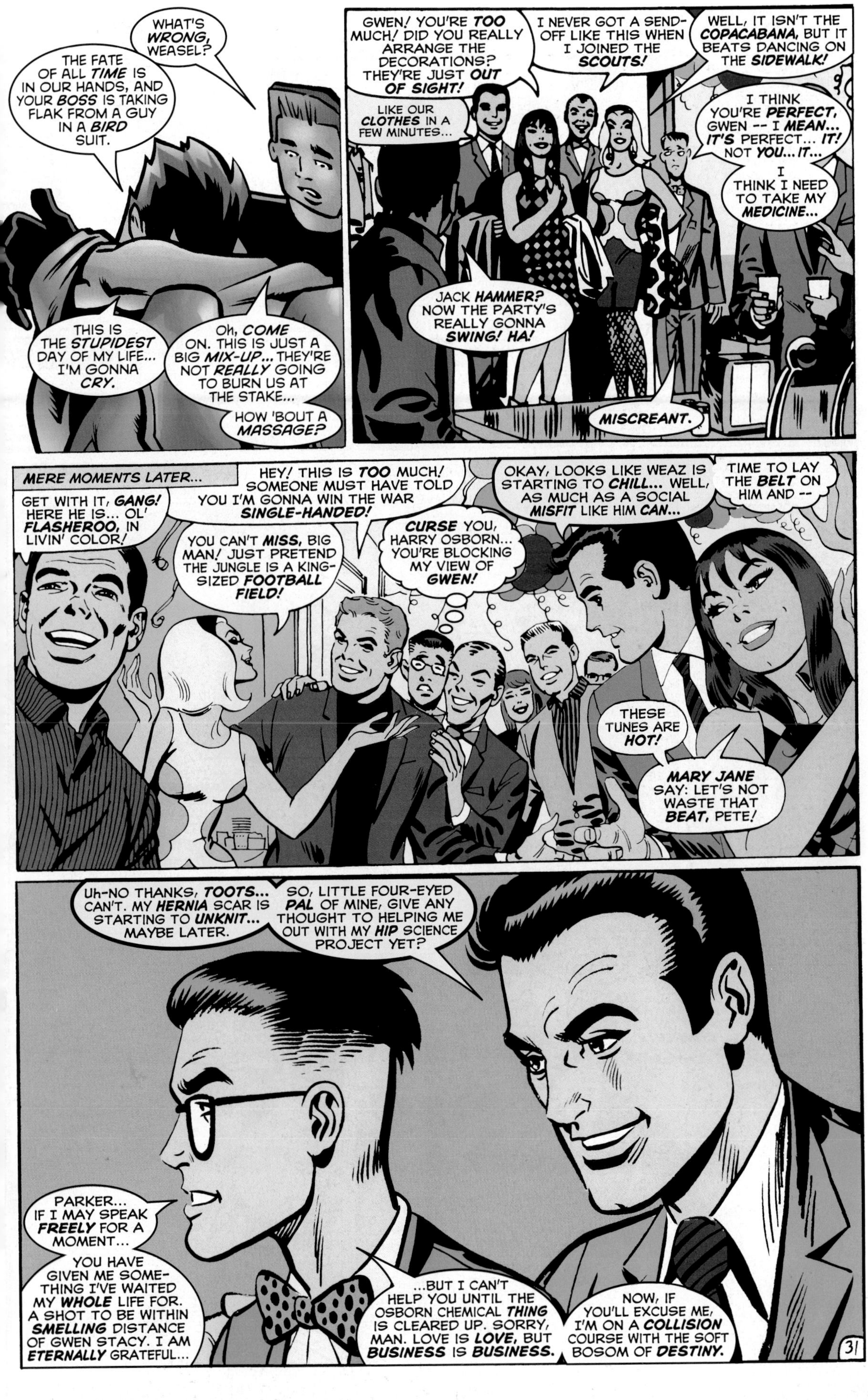
WHAT'S WRONG, WEASEL?
THE FATE OF ALL TIME IS IN OUR HANDS, AND YOUR BOSS IS TAKING FLAK FROM A GUY IN A BIRD SUIT.
THIS IS THE STUPIDEST DAY OF MY LIFE... I'M GONNA CRY.
Oh, COME ON. THIS IS JUST A BIG MIX-UP... THEY'RE NOT REALLY GOING TO BURN US AT THE STAKE...
HOW 'BOUT A MASSAGE?
GWEN! YOU'RE TOO MUCH! DID YOU REALLY ARRANGE THE DECORATIONS? THEY'RE JUST OUT OF SIGHT!
LIKE OUR CLOTHES IN A FEW MINUTES...
I NEVER GOT A SEND-OFF LIKE THIS WHEN I JOINED THE SCOUTS!
WELL, IT ISN'T THE COPACABANA, BUT IT BEATS DANCING ON THE SIDEWALK!
I THINK YOU'RE PERFECT, GWEN -- I MEAN... IT'S PERFECT... IT! NOT YOU... IT...
I THINK I NEED TO TAKE MY MEDICINE...
JACK HAMMER? NOW THE PARTY'S REALLY GONNA SWING! HA!
MISCREANT.
MERE MOMENTS LATER...
GET WITH IT, GANG! HERE HE IS... OL' FLASHEROO, IN LIVIN' COLOR!
HEY! THIS IS TOO MUCH! SOMEONE MUST HAVE TOLD YOU I'M GONNA WIN THE WAR SINGLE-HANDED!
YOU CAN'T MISS, BIG MAN! JUST PRETEND THE JUNGLE IS A KING-SIZED FOOTBALL FIELD!
CURSE YOU, HARRY OSBORN... YOU'RE BLOCKING MY VIEW OF GWEN!
OKAY, LOOKS LIKE WEAZ IS STARTING TO CHILL... WELL, AS MUCH AS A SOCIAL MISFIT LIKE HIM CAN...
TIME TO LAY THE BELT ON HIM AND --
THESE TUNES ARE HOT!
MARY JANE SAY: LET'S NOT WASTE THAT BEAT, PETE!
Uh-NO THANKS, TOOTS... CAN'T. MY HERNIA SCAR IS STARTING TO UNKNIT... MAYBE LATER.
SO, LITTLE FOUR-EYED PAL OF MINE, GIVE ANY THOUGHT TO HELPING ME OUT WITH MY HIP SCIENCE PROJECT YET?
PARKER... IF I MAY SPEAK FREELY FOR A MOMENT...
YOU HAVE GIVEN ME SOMETHING I'VE WAITED MY WHOLE LIFE FOR. A SHOT TO BE WITHIN SMELLING DISTANCE OF GWEN STACY. I AM ETERNALLY GRATEFUL...
...BUT I CAN'T HELP YOU UNTIL THE OSBORN CHEMICAL THING IS CLEARED UP. SORRY, MAN. LOVE IS LOVE, BUT BUSINESS IS BUSINESS.
NOW, IF YOU'LL EXCUSE ME, I'M ON A COLLISION COURSE WITH THE SOFT BOSOM OF DESTINY.

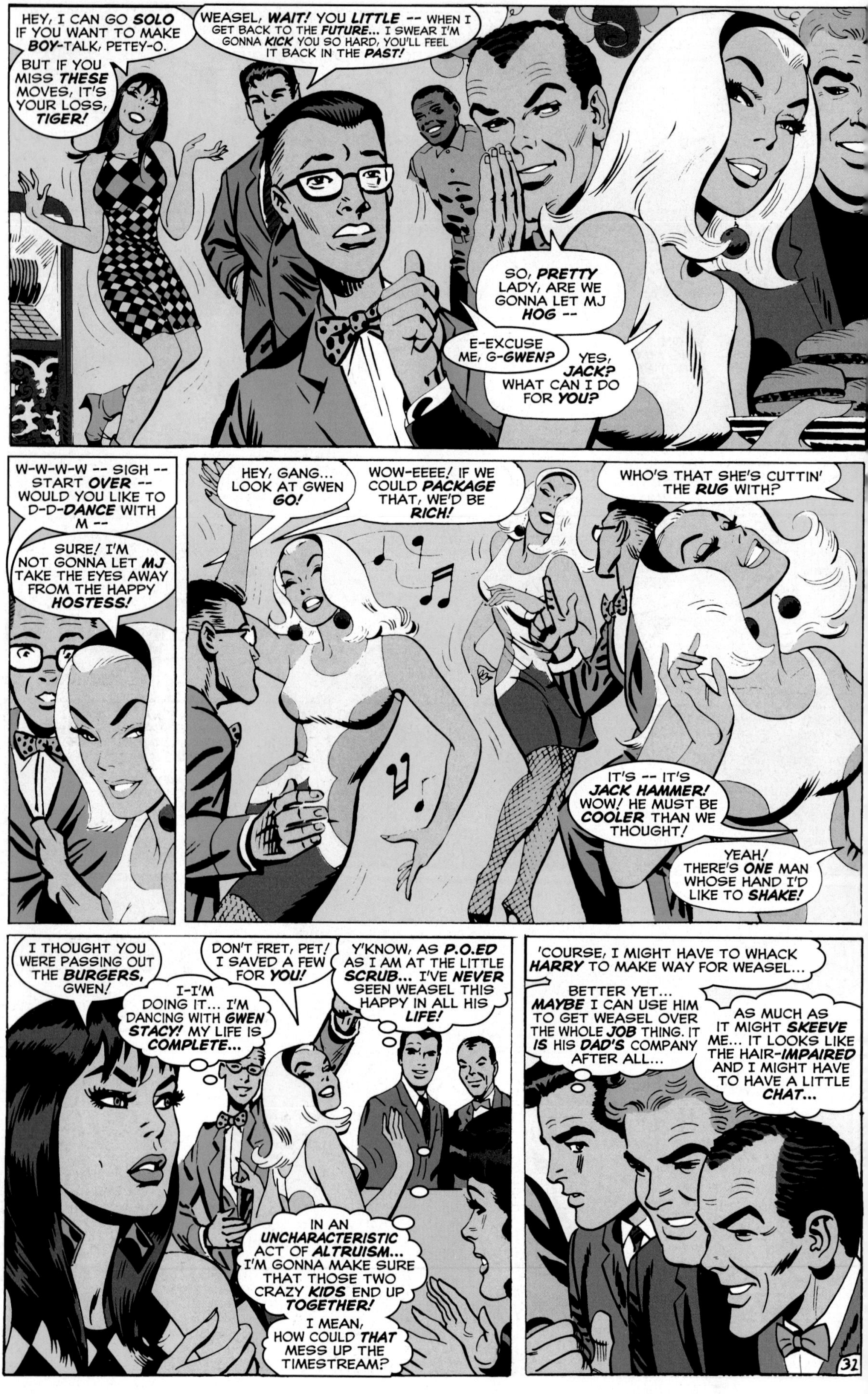
HEY, I CAN GO SOLO IF YOU WANT TO MAKE BOY-TALK, PETEY-O.
BUT IF YOU MISS THESE MOVES, IT'S YOUR LOSS, TIGER!
WEASEL, WAIT! YOU LITTLE -- WHEN I GET BACK TO THE FUTURE... I SWEAR I'M GONNA KICK YOU SO HARD, YOU'LL FEEL IT BACK IN THE PAST!
SO, PRETTY LADY, ARE WE GONNA LET MJ HOG --
E-EXCUSE ME, G-GWEN?
YES, JACK? WHAT CAN I DO FOR YOU?
W-W-W-W -- SIGH -- START OVER -- WOULD YOU LIKE TO D-D-DANCE WITH M --
SURE! I'M NOT GONNA LET MJ TAKE THE EYES AWAY FROM THE HAPPY HOSTESS!
HEY, GANG... LOOK AT GWEN GO!
WOW-EEEE! IF WE COULD PACKAGE THAT, WE'D BE RICH!
WHO'S THAT SHE'S CUTTIN' THE RUG WITH?
IT'S -- IT'S JACK HAMMER! WOW! HE MUST BE COOLER THAN WE THOUGHT!
YEAH! THERE'S ONE MAN WHOSE HAND I'D LIKE TO SHAKE!
I THOUGHT YOU WERE PASSING OUT THE BURGERS, GWEN!
I-I'M DOING IT... I'M DANCING WITH GWEN STACY! MY LIFE IS COMPLETE...
DON'T FRET, PET! I SAVED A FEW FOR YOU!
Y'KNOW, AS P.O.ED AS I AM AT THE LITTLE SCRUB... I'VE NEVER SEEN WEASEL THIS HAPPY IN ALL HIS LIFE!
IN AN UNCHARACTERISTIC ACT OF ALTRUISM... I'M GONNA MAKE SURE THAT THOSE TWO CRAZY KIDS END UP TOGETHER!
I MEAN, HOW COULD THAT MESS UP THE TIMESTREAM?
'COURSE, I MIGHT HAVE TO WHACK HARRY TO MAKE WAY FOR WEASEL...
BETTER YET... MAYBE I CAN USE HIM TO GET WEASEL OVER THE WHOLE JOB THING. IT IS HIS DAD'S COMPANY AFTER ALL...
AS MUCH AS IT MIGHT SKEEVE ME... IT LOOKS LIKE THE HAIR-IMPAIRED AND I MIGHT HAVE TO HAVE A LITTLE CHAT...
31

KRASH

IF YOU VALUE YOUR **LIVES**... **DON'T** ANYONE **MOVE**!

THE **SON** OF NORMAN OSBORN IS HERE... AND I **WANT** HIM!

NO! NOT **NOW**! WE WERE JUST ABOUT TO **RUMBA**!

A **MAN**! HE... HE PUNCHED HIS WAY RIGHT THROUGH THE **WALL**!

WHOA! IT'S THAT **GOON** IN THE **LOINCLOTH** FROM **BEFORE**!

IF **NATURE BOY** NABS OSBORN, I MAY **NEVER** GET HIM TO CONVINCE **WEASEL** TO **HELP** ME!

YOU'RE THE ONE I WANT! I'D RECOGNIZE YOU **ANYWHERE**!

I **KNEW** OSBORN HAD A **SON**, AND IT WASN'T HARD FOR THE WORLD'S GREATEST **HUNTER** TO TRACK YOU **HERE**!

I DON'T **KNOW** YOU! I... I NEVER SAW YOU! WHAT DO YOU WANT WITH **ME**?

BACK OFF, MISTER! **NOBODY** BREAKS UP MY PARTY THAT WAY!

HARRY!

NO... IT'S **JACK**... STAY FOCUSED HERE... **GWEN**?

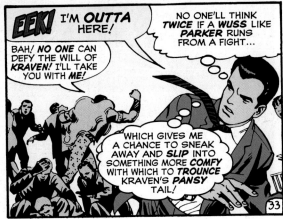

EEK! I'M **OUTTA** HERE!

BAH! **NO ONE** CAN DEFY THE WILL OF **KRAVEN**! I'LL TAKE YOU WITH **ME**!

NO ONE'LL THINK **TWICE** IF A **WUSS** LIKE **PARKER** RUNS FROM A FIGHT...

WHICH GIVES ME A CHANCE TO SNEAK AWAY AND **SLIP** INTO SOMETHING MORE **COMFY** WITH WHICH TO **TROUNCE** KRAVEN'S **PANSY** TAIL!

33

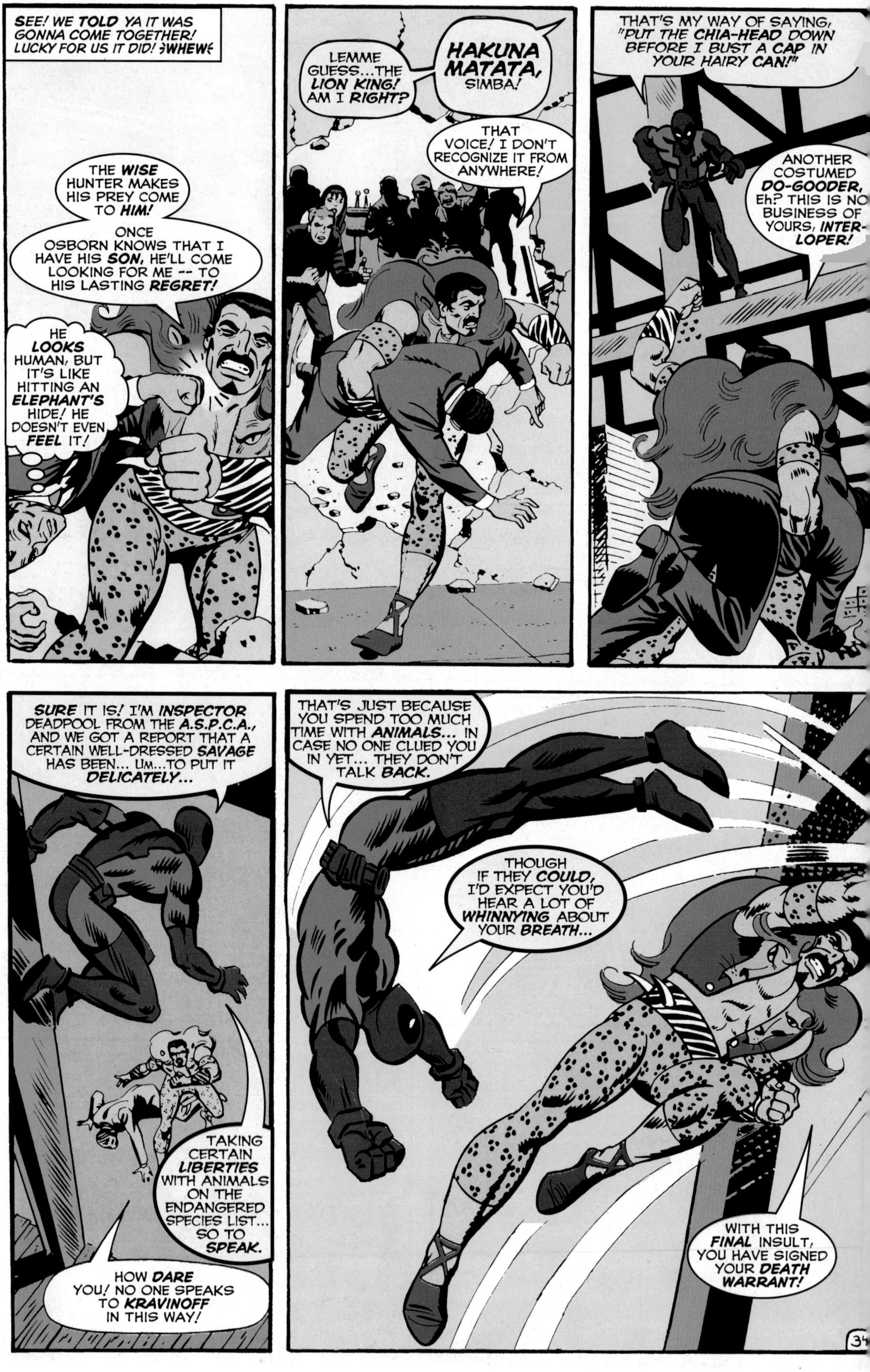

SEE! WE TOLD YA IT WAS GONNA COME TOGETHER! LUCKY FOR US IT DID! WHEW
THE WISE HUNTER MAKES HIS PREY COME TO HIM!
ONCE OSBORN KNOWS THAT I HAVE HIS SON, HE'LL COME LOOKING FOR ME -- TO HIS LASTING REGRET!
HE LOOKS HUMAN, BUT IT'S LIKE HITTING AN ELEPHANT'S HIDE! HE DOESN'T EVEN FEEL IT!
LEMME GUESS... THE LION KING! AM I RIGHT?
HAKUNA MATATA, SIMBA!
THAT VOICE! I DON'T RECOGNIZE IT FROM ANYWHERE!
THAT'S MY WAY OF SAYING, "PUT THE CHIA-HEAD DOWN BEFORE I BUST A CAP IN YOUR HAIRY CAN!"
ANOTHER COSTUMED DO-GOODER, Eh? THIS IS NO BUSINESS OF YOURS, INTERLOPER!
SURE IT IS! I'M INSPECTOR DEADPOOL FROM THE A.S.P.C.A., AND WE GOT A REPORT THAT A CERTAIN WELL-DRESSED SAVAGE HAS BEEN... UM... TO PUT IT DELICATELY...
TAKING CERTAIN LIBERTIES WITH ANIMALS ON THE ENDANGERED SPECIES LIST... SO TO SPEAK.
HOW DARE YOU! NO ONE SPEAKS TO KRAVINOFF IN THIS WAY!
THAT'S JUST BECAUSE YOU SPEND TOO MUCH TIME WITH ANIMALS... IN CASE NO ONE CLUED YOU IN YET... THEY DON'T TALK BACK.
THOUGH IF THEY COULD, I'D EXPECT YOU'D HEAR A LOT OF WHINNYING ABOUT YOUR BREATH...
WITH THIS FINAL INSULT, YOU HAVE SIGNED YOUR DEATH WARRANT!

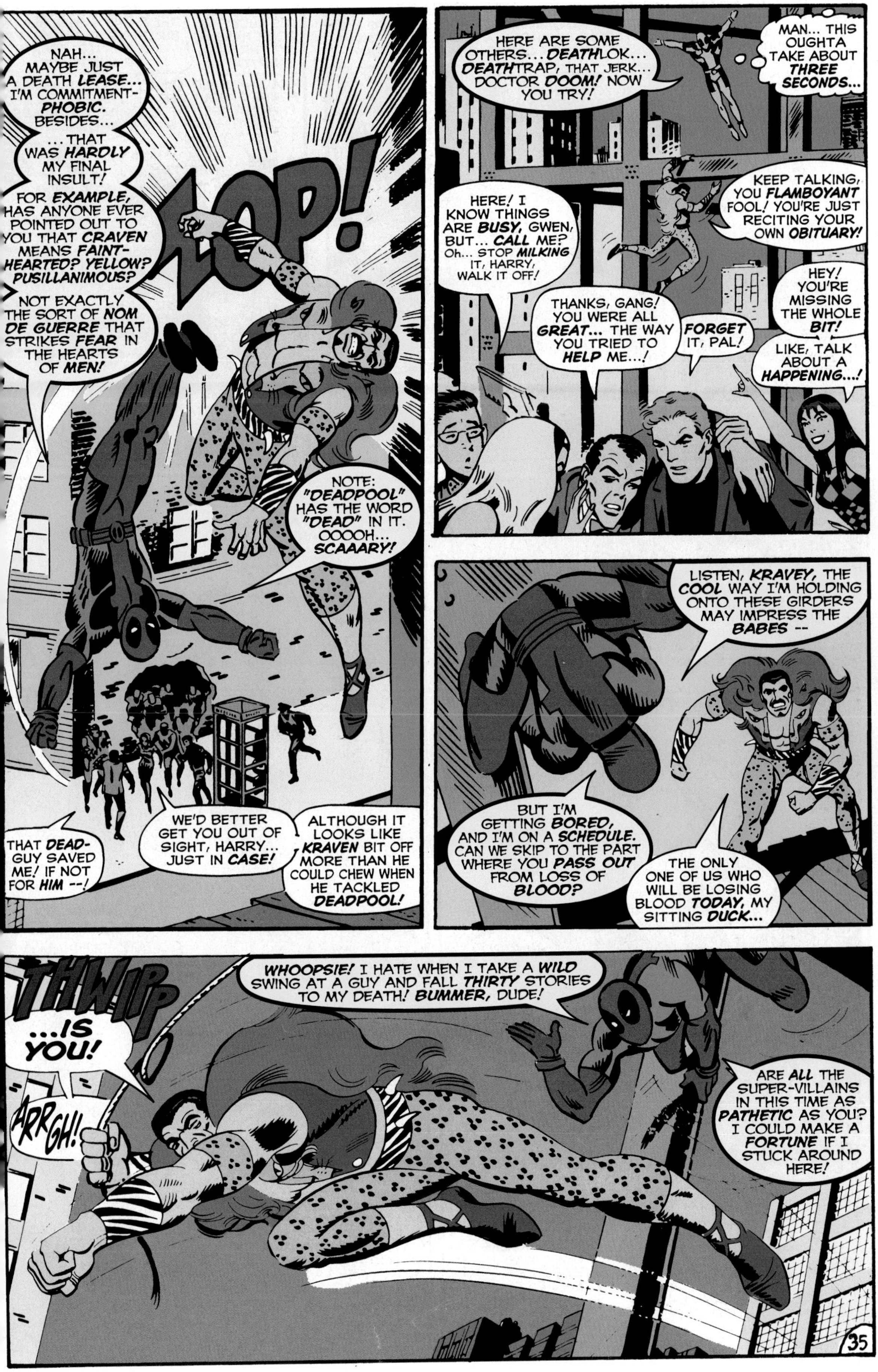
NAH... MAYBE JUST A DEATH LEASE... I'M COMMITMENT-PHOBIC. BESIDES...
... THAT WAS HARDLY MY FINAL INSULT!
FOR EXAMPLE, HAS ANYONE EVER POINTED OUT TO YOU THAT CRAVEN MEANS FAINT-HEARTED? YELLOW? PUSILLANIMOUS?
NOT EXACTLY THE SORT OF NOM DE GUERRE THAT STRIKES FEAR IN THE HEARTS OF MEN!
ZOP!
NOTE: "DEADPOOL" HAS THE WORD "DEAD" IN IT. OOOOH... SCAAARY!
THAT DEAD-GUY SAVED ME! IF NOT FOR HIM --!
WE'D BETTER GET YOU OUT OF SIGHT, HARRY... JUST IN CASE!
ALTHOUGH IT LOOKS LIKE KRAVEN BIT OFF MORE THAN HE COULD CHEW WHEN HE TACKLED DEADPOOL!
HERE ARE SOME OTHERS... DEATHLOK... DEATHTRAP, THAT JERK... DOCTOR DOOM! NOW YOU TRY!
MAN... THIS OUGHTA TAKE ABOUT THREE SECONDS...
KEEP TALKING, YOU FLAMBOYANT FOOL! YOU'RE JUST RECITING YOUR OWN OBITUARY!
HERE! I KNOW THINGS ARE BUSY, GWEN, BUT... CALL ME? Oh... STOP MILKING IT, HARRY, WALK IT OFF!
THANKS, GANG! YOU WERE ALL GREAT... THE WAY YOU TRIED TO HELP ME...!
FORGET IT, PAL!
HEY! YOU'RE MISSING THE WHOLE BIT!
LIKE, TALK ABOUT A HAPPENING...!
LISTEN, KRAVEY, THE COOL WAY I'M HOLDING ONTO THESE GIRDERS MAY IMPRESS THE BABES --
BUT I'M GETTING BORED, AND I'M ON A SCHEDULE. CAN WE SKIP TO THE PART WHERE YOU PASS OUT FROM LOSS OF BLOOD?
THE ONLY ONE OF US WHO WILL BE LOSING BLOOD TODAY, MY SITTING DUCK...
THWIPP
...IS YOU!
WHOOPSIE! I HATE WHEN I TAKE A WILD SWING AT A GUY AND FALL THIRTY STORIES TO MY DEATH! BUMMER, DUDE!
ARRGH!
ARE ALL THE SUPER-VILLAINS IN THIS TIME AS PATHETIC AS YOU? I COULD MAKE A FORTUNE IF I STUCK AROUND HERE!

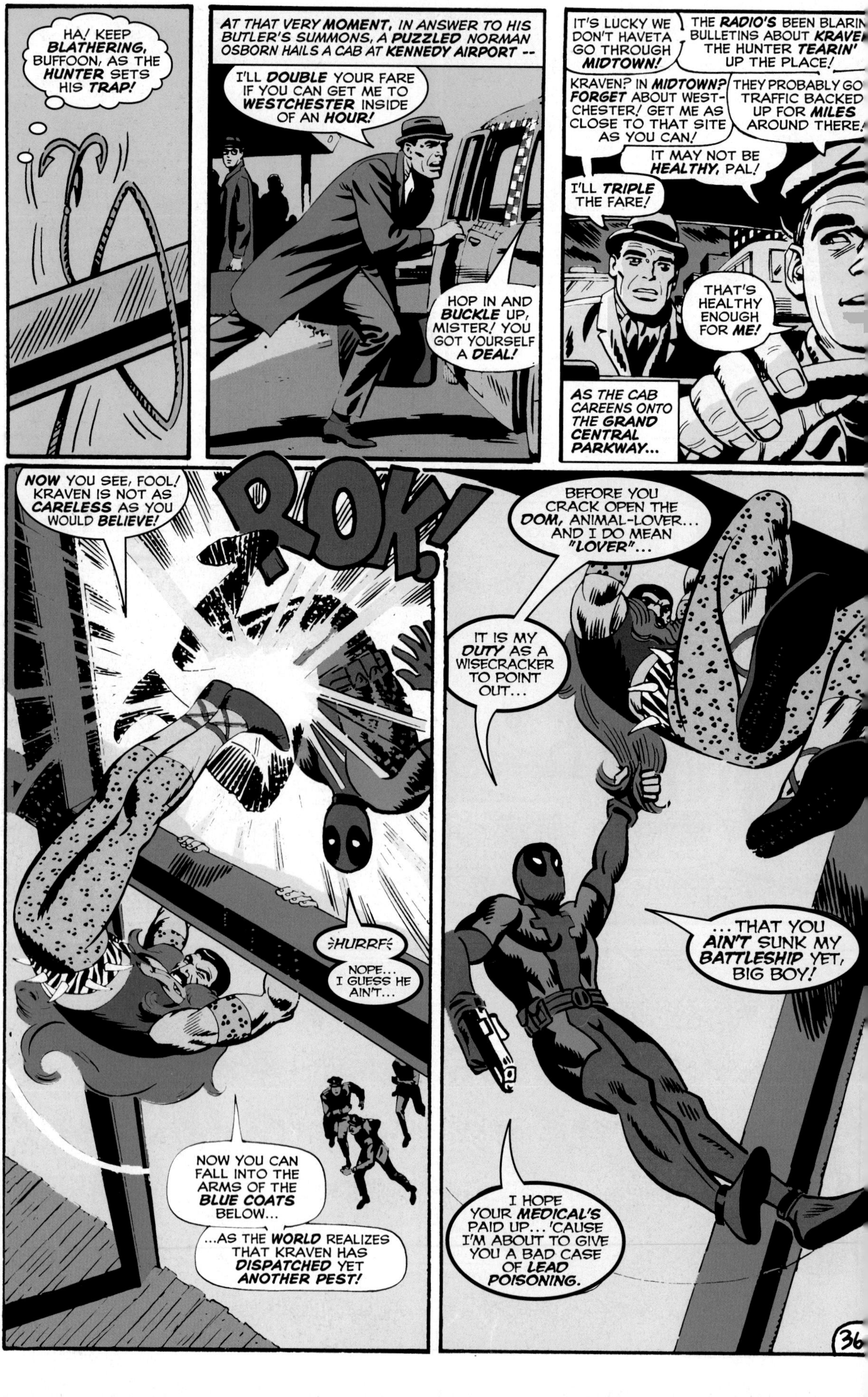
HA! KEEP BLATHERING, BUFFOON, AS THE HUNTER SETS HIS TRAP!
AT THAT VERY MOMENT, IN ANSWER TO HIS BUTLER'S SUMMONS, A PUZZLED NORMAN OSBORN HAILS A CAB AT KENNEDY AIRPORT --
I'LL DOUBLE YOUR FARE IF YOU CAN GET ME TO WESTCHESTER INSIDE OF AN HOUR!
HOP IN AND BUCKLE UP, MISTER! YOU GOT YOURSELF A DEAL!
IT'S LUCKY WE DON'T HAVETA GO THROUGH MIDTOWN!
THE RADIO'S BEEN BLARIN BULLETINS ABOUT KRAVE THE HUNTER TEARIN' UP THE PLACE!
KRAVEN? IN MIDTOWN? FORGET ABOUT WEST-CHESTER! GET ME AS CLOSE TO THAT SITE AS YOU CAN!
THEY PROBABLY GO TRAFFIC BACKED UP FOR MILES AROUND THERE.
IT MAY NOT BE HEALTHY, PAL!
I'LL TRIPLE THE FARE!
THAT'S HEALTHY ENOUGH FOR ME!
AS THE CAB CAREENS ONTO THE GRAND CENTRAL PARKWAY...
NOW YOU SEE, FOOL! KRAVEN IS NOT AS CARELESS AS YOU WOULD BELIEVE!
ROK!
HURRF
NOPE... I GUESS HE AIN'T...
NOW YOU CAN FALL INTO THE ARMS OF THE BLUE COATS BELOW...
...AS THE WORLD REALIZES THAT KRAVEN HAS DISPATCHED YET ANOTHER PEST!
BEFORE YOU CRACK OPEN THE DOM, ANIMAL-LOVER... AND I DO MEAN "LOVER"...
IT IS MY DUTY AS A WISECRACKER TO POINT OUT...
...THAT YOU AIN'T SUNK MY BATTLESHIP YET, BIG BOY!
I HOPE YOUR MEDICAL'S PAID UP... 'CAUSE I'M ABOUT TO GIVE YOU A BAD CASE OF LEAD POISONING.
36

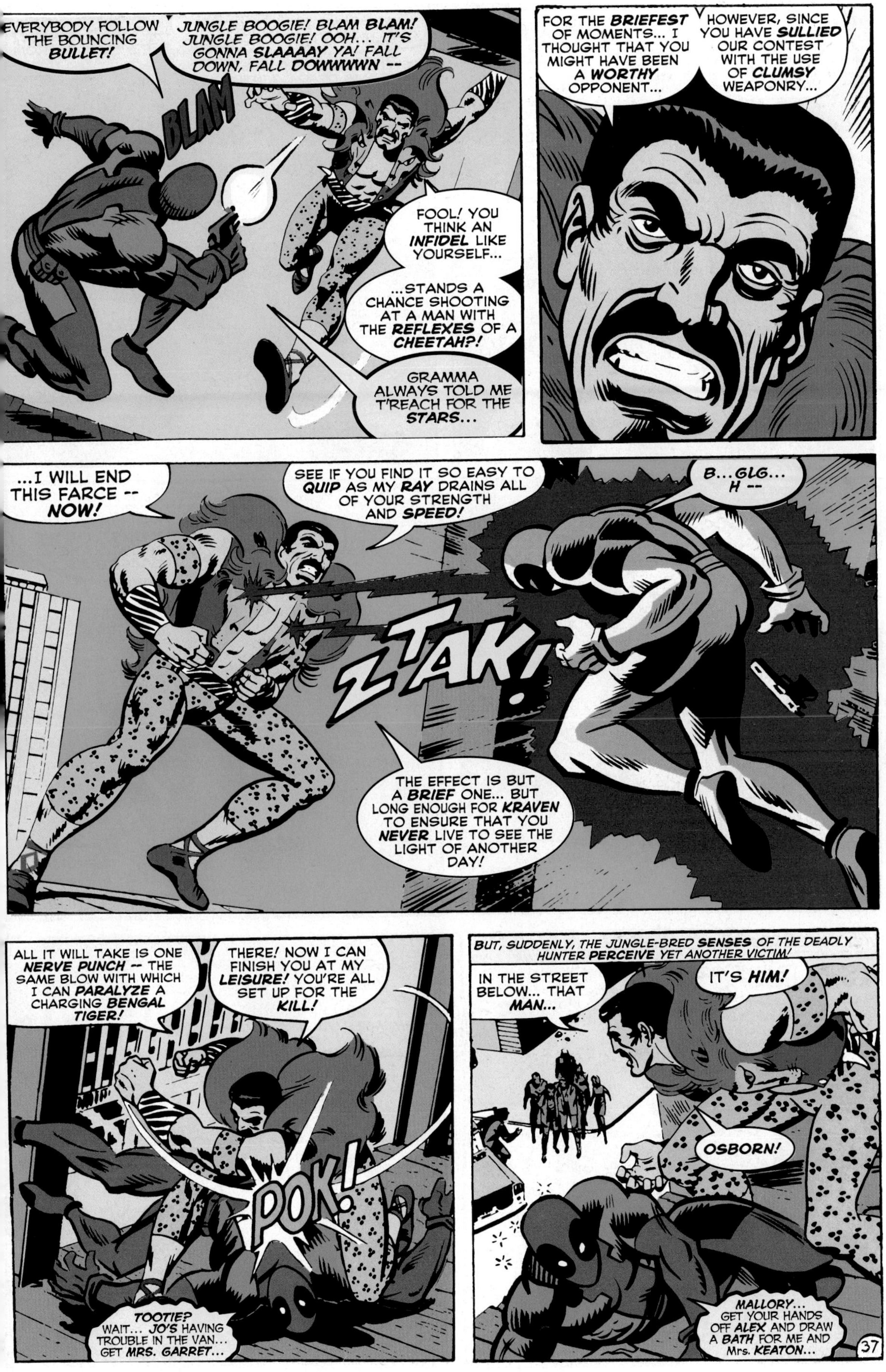
EVERYBODY FOLLOW THE BOUNCING BULLET!
JUNGLE BOOGIE! BLAM BLAM! JUNGLE BOOGIE! OOH... IT'S GONNA SLAAAAY YA! FALL DOWN, FALL DOWWWWN --
BLAM
FOOL! YOU THINK AN INFIDEL LIKE YOURSELF...
...STANDS A CHANCE SHOOTING AT A MAN WITH THE REFLEXES OF A CHEETAH?!
GRAMMA ALWAYS TOLD ME T'REACH FOR THE STARS...
FOR THE BRIEFEST OF MOMENTS... I THOUGHT THAT YOU MIGHT HAVE BEEN A WORTHY OPPONENT...
HOWEVER, SINCE YOU HAVE SULLIED OUR CONTEST WITH THE USE OF CLUMSY WEAPONRY...
...I WILL END THIS FARCE -- NOW!
SEE IF YOU FIND IT SO EASY TO QUIP AS MY RAY DRAINS ALL OF YOUR STRENGTH AND SPEED!
B...GLG... H --
ZTAK!
THE EFFECT IS BUT A BRIEF ONE... BUT LONG ENOUGH FOR KRAVEN TO ENSURE THAT YOU NEVER LIVE TO SEE THE LIGHT OF ANOTHER DAY!
ALL IT WILL TAKE IS ONE NERVE PUNCH -- THE SAME BLOW WITH WHICH I CAN PARALYZE A CHARGING BENGAL TIGER!
THERE! NOW I CAN FINISH YOU AT MY LEISURE! YOU'RE ALL SET UP FOR THE KILL!
POK!
TOOTIE? WAIT... JO'S HAVING TROUBLE IN THE VAN... GET MRS. GARRET...
BUT, SUDDENLY, THE JUNGLE-BRED SENSES OF THE DEADLY HUNTER PERCEIVE YET ANOTHER VICTIM!
IN THE STREET BELOW... THAT MAN...
IT'S HIM!
OSBORN!
MALLORY... GET YOUR HANDS OFF ALEX AND DRAW A BATH FOR ME AND Mrs. KEATON...
37

HARRY! SON, ARE YOU *ALL RIGHT* --

WHAT --?!

DAD!

THWUP!

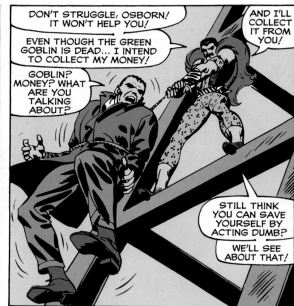

DON'T STRUGGLE, OSBORN! IT WON'T HELP YOU!

EVEN THOUGH THE GREEN GOBLIN IS DEAD... I INTEND TO COLLECT MY MONEY!

AND I'LL COLLECT IT FROM YOU!

GOBLIN? MONEY? WHAT ARE YOU TALKING ABOUT?

STILL THINK YOU CAN SAVE YOURSELF BY ACTING DUMB?

WE'LL SEE ABOUT THAT!

ROW ROW ROW YER BOAT... GENTLY DOWN THE *TIME-STREAM*...

WHOA... *MAJOR* ICE-CREAM HEADACHE... BUT I THINK I'M BACK IN *BUSINESS*...

HEALING FACTOR'S OVER-RIDING THE EFFECTS OF THE *BEAM.*

GROOVY...

DON'T KNOW *MUCH* ABOUT *HISTORY*... BUT I DO KNOW *THIS* -- IT'S WRITTEN BY THE *SURVIVORS*... OR THE GUYS WITH THE *BIGGEST GUNS.*

TIMESTREAM OR *NOT*... THIS IS KRAVEN'S *LAST* FREAKIN' HUNT.

THE GOBLIN MUST BE BIGGER THAN I *THOUGHT* TO HAVE *YOU* AS A FLUNKY!

NO ONE BREAKS A PROMISE TO *KRAVEN* THE HUNTER!

TAKE ME TO YOUR *BANK*, AND *WITHDRAW* WHAT YOU OWE ME!

I DON'T KNOW WHAT YOU'RE *TALKING* ABOUT -- I'VE NEVER EVEN SEEN YOU BEFORE!

IT'S *IMPOSSIBLE* TO LIE TO ME! MY JUNGLE *INSTINCT* --

WAIT...

YOU *DON'T* REMEMBER! YOU DON'T KNOW *ANY-THING!* YOU'RE TELLING THE *TRUTH* --

♪ WADE! WADE! WADE OF THE JUNGLE! STRONG AS HE CAN BE --! ♪

38

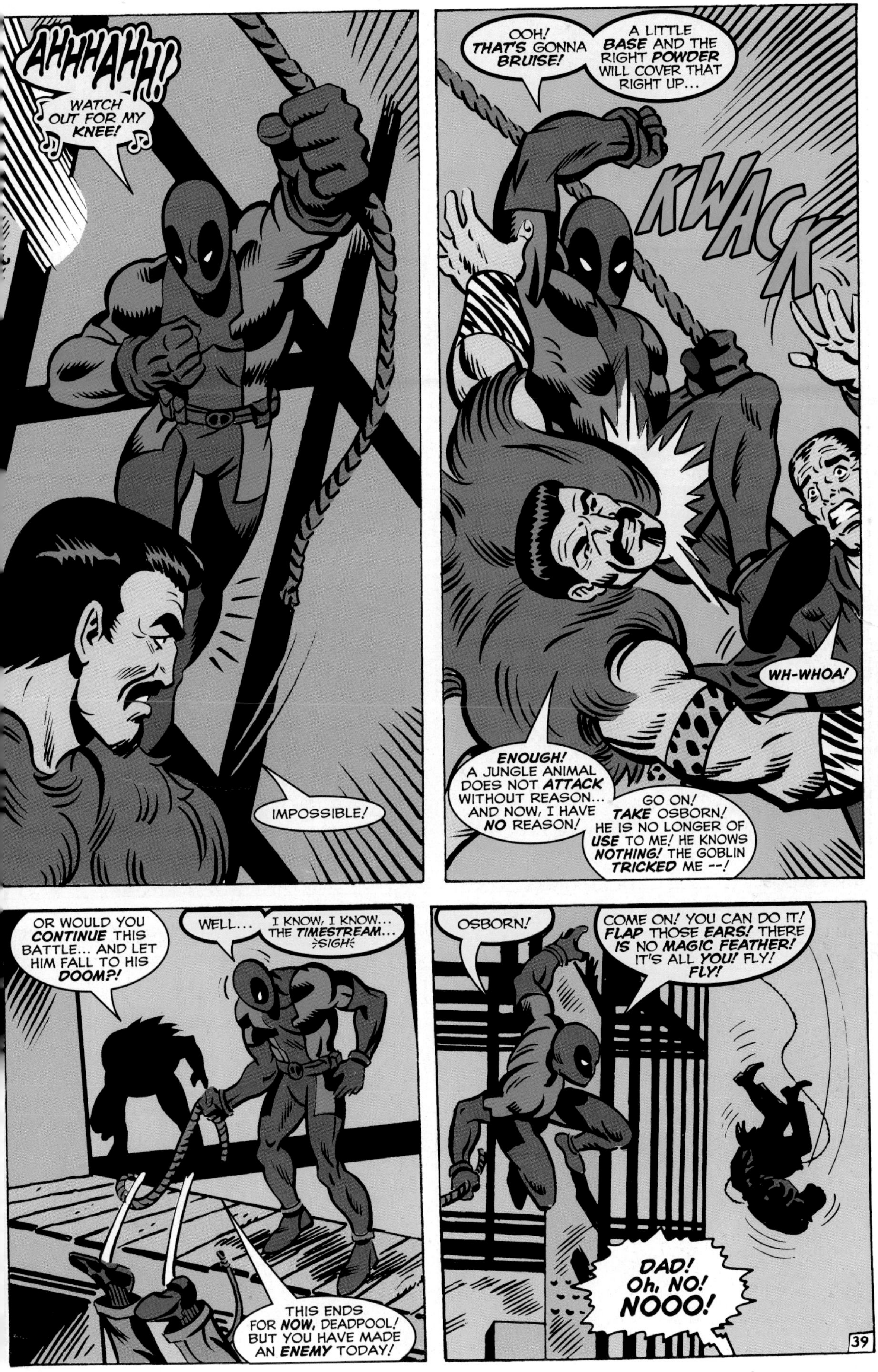
AHHHAHH!
WATCH OUT FOR MY KNEE!
IMPOSSIBLE!
OOH! THAT'S GONNA BRUISE!
A LITTLE BASE AND THE RIGHT POWDER WILL COVER THAT RIGHT UP...
KWACK
WH-WHOA!
ENOUGH! A JUNGLE ANIMAL DOES NOT ATTACK WITHOUT REASON... AND NOW, I HAVE NO REASON!
GO ON! TAKE OSBORN! HE IS NO LONGER OF USE TO ME! HE KNOWS NOTHING! THE GOBLIN TRICKED ME --!
OR WOULD YOU CONTINUE THIS BATTLE... AND LET HIM FALL TO HIS DOOM?!
WELL...
I KNOW, I KNOW... THE TIMESTREAM... *SIGH*
THIS ENDS FOR NOW, DEADPOOL! BUT YOU HAVE MADE AN ENEMY TODAY!
OSBORN!
COME ON! YOU CAN DO IT! FLAP THOSE EARS! THERE IS NO MAGIC FEATHER! IT'S ALL YOU! FLY! FLY!
DAD! Oh, NO! NOOO!

GUESS YOU DIDN'T *CATCH* THAT CARTOON, HUH? FINE... WE'LL DO IT THE *BORING* WAY!

UPSIE-DAISY!

DEADPOOL!

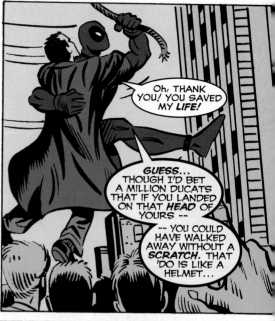

Oh, THANK YOU! YOU SAVED MY *LIFE!*

GUESS... THOUGH I'D BET A MILLION DUCATS THAT IF YOU LANDED ON THAT *HEAD* OF YOURS --

-- YOU COULD HAVE WALKED AWAY WITHOUT A *SCRATCH.* THAT 'DO IS LIKE A HELMET...

HOW CAN I EVER *REPAY* YOU?

GET ME A GUEST SPOT ON THE *JOKER'S WILD*... MY OWN *DUNE BUGGY*... TELL ME THE MEANING OF *LIFE*...

PROMISE TO START WEARING *HATS*...?

SNAP

I GOT IT. LISTEN UP, AND LISTEN *GOOD!* THERE'S A CERTAIN *COLLEGE STUDENT* APPLYING FOR A JOB AT *YOUR* COMPANY...

JACK HAMMER. KNOW HIM?

OF COURSE, HE'S ONE OF THE TOP TWO CANDIDATES, ALONG WITH PETER PARKER.

WELL, THERE'S SOMETHING YOU MIGHT WANNA KNOW ABOUT HIM... AND HIS... *HABITS*...

MEANWHILE, IN A NEARBY ALLEY, THE *REAL* PETER PARKER QUICKLY CHANGES INTO HIS *CIVILIAN SKIVVIES*...

I JUST *BARELY* MADE IT IN TIME FOR THE PARTY! HOPE THERE'S STILL SOME *PUNCH* LEFT!

HEY, ARE THOSE *SIRENS?*

40

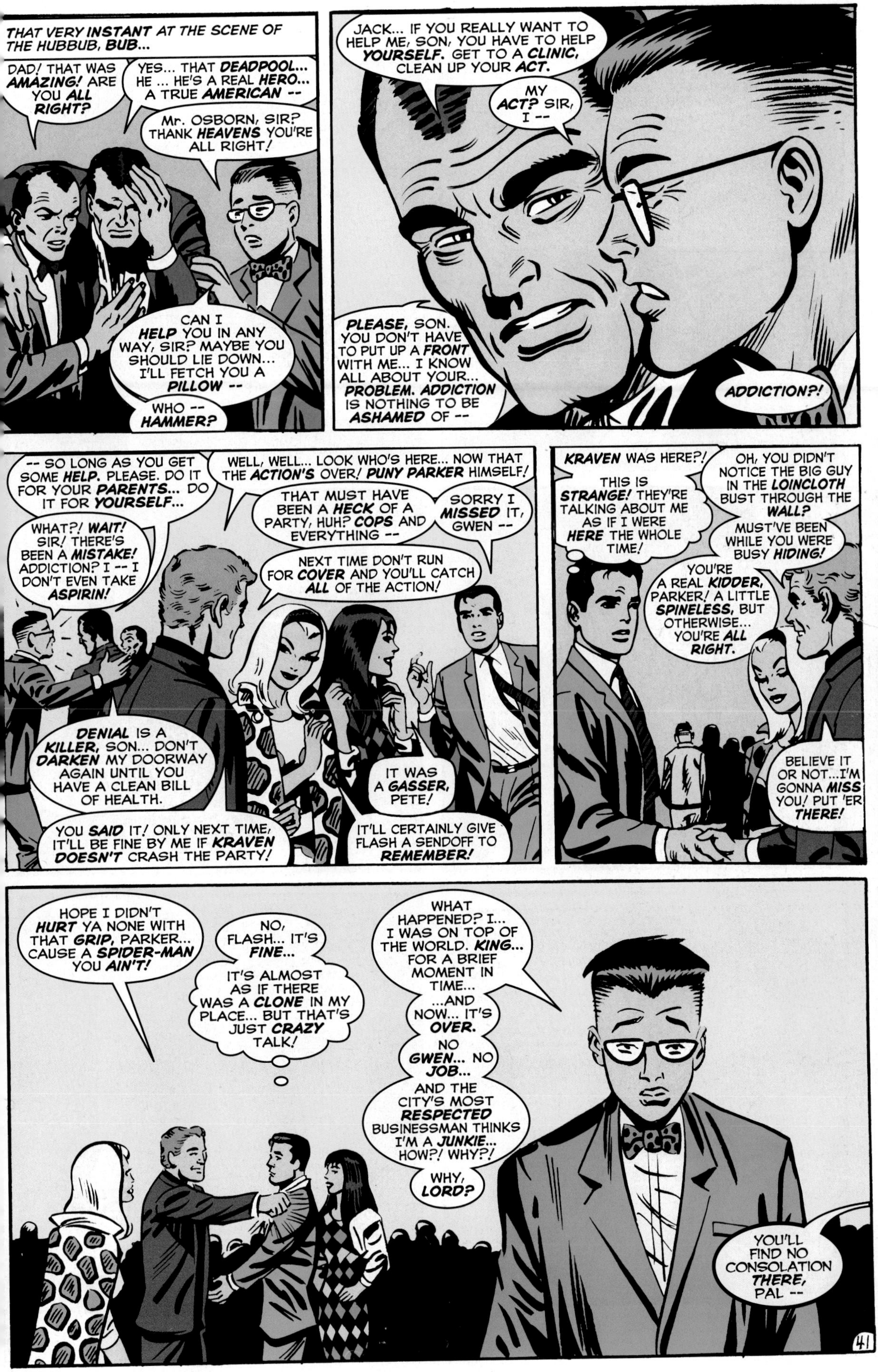
THAT VERY INSTANT AT THE SCENE OF THE HUBBUB, BUB...
DAD! THAT WAS AMAZING! ARE YOU ALL RIGHT?
YES... THAT DEADPOOL... HE ... HE'S A REAL HERO... A TRUE AMERICAN --
Mr. OSBORN, SIR? THANK HEAVENS YOU'RE ALL RIGHT!
CAN I HELP YOU IN ANY WAY, SIR? MAYBE YOU SHOULD LIE DOWN... I'LL FETCH YOU A PILLOW --
WHO -- HAMMER?
JACK... IF YOU REALLY WANT TO HELP ME, SON, YOU HAVE TO HELP YOURSELF. GET TO A CLINIC, CLEAN UP YOUR ACT.
MY ACT? SIR, I --
PLEASE, SON. YOU DON'T HAVE TO PUT UP A FRONT WITH ME... I KNOW ALL ABOUT YOUR... PROBLEM. ADDICTION IS NOTHING TO BE ASHAMED OF --
ADDICTION?!
-- SO LONG AS YOU GET SOME HELP. PLEASE. DO IT FOR YOUR PARENTS... DO IT FOR YOURSELF...
WHAT?! WAIT! SIR! THERE'S BEEN A MISTAKE! ADDICTION? I -- I DON'T EVEN TAKE ASPIRIN!
DENIAL IS A KILLER, SON... DON'T DARKEN MY DOORWAY AGAIN UNTIL YOU HAVE A CLEAN BILL OF HEALTH.
WELL, WELL... LOOK WHO'S HERE... NOW THAT THE ACTION'S OVER! PUNY PARKER HIMSELF!
THAT MUST HAVE BEEN A HECK OF A PARTY, HUH? COPS AND EVERYTHING --
SORRY I MISSED IT, GWEN --
NEXT TIME DON'T RUN FOR COVER AND YOU'LL CATCH ALL OF THE ACTION!
IT WAS A GASSER, PETE!
YOU SAID IT! ONLY NEXT TIME, IT'LL BE FINE BY ME IF KRAVEN DOESN'T CRASH THE PARTY!
IT'LL CERTAINLY GIVE FLASH A SENDOFF TO REMEMBER!
KRAVEN WAS HERE?!
THIS IS STRANGE! THEY'RE TALKING ABOUT ME AS IF I WERE HERE THE WHOLE TIME!
OH, YOU DIDN'T NOTICE THE BIG GUY IN THE LOINCLOTH BUST THROUGH THE WALL?
MUST'VE BEEN WHILE YOU WERE BUSY HIDING!
YOU'RE A REAL KIDDER, PARKER! A LITTLE SPINELESS, BUT OTHERWISE... YOU'RE ALL RIGHT.
BELIEVE IT OR NOT...I'M GONNA MISS YOU! PUT 'ER THERE!
HOPE I DIDN'T HURT YA NONE WITH THAT GRIP, PARKER... CAUSE A SPIDER-MAN YOU AIN'T!
NO, FLASH... IT'S FINE...
IT'S ALMOST AS IF THERE WAS A CLONE IN MY PLACE... BUT THAT'S JUST CRAZY TALK!
WHAT HAPPENED? I... I WAS ON TOP OF THE WORLD. KING... FOR A BRIEF MOMENT IN TIME... ...AND NOW... IT'S OVER.
NO GWEN... NO JOB...
AND THE CITY'S MOST RESPECTED BUSINESSMAN THINKS I'M A JUNKIE... HOW?! WHY?!
WHY, LORD?
YOU'LL FIND NO CONSOLATION THERE, PAL --
41

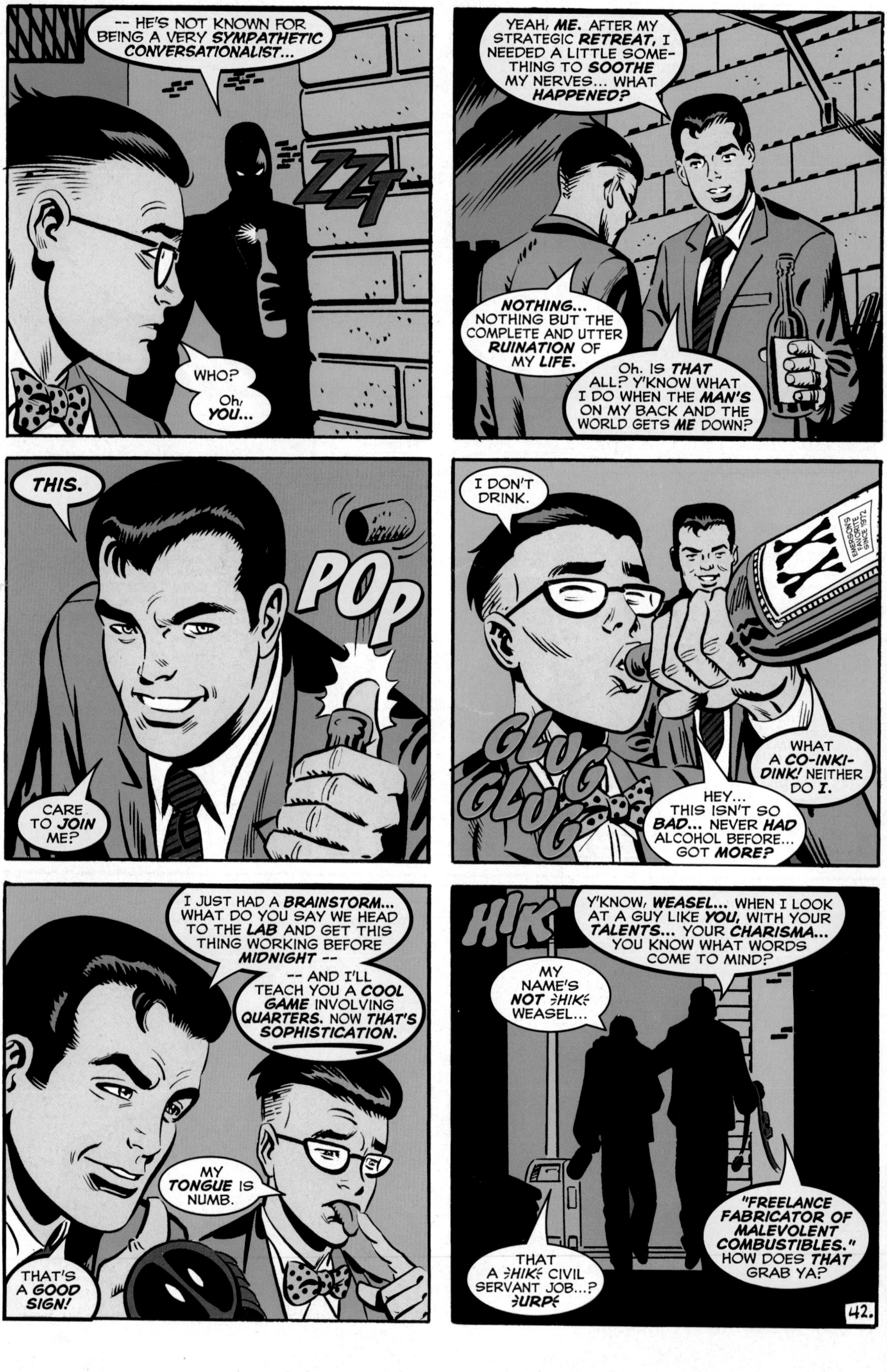
-- HE'S NOT KNOWN FOR BEING A VERY SYMPATHETIC CONVERSATIONALIST...
ZZT
WHO?
Oh, YOU...
YEAH, ME. AFTER MY STRATEGIC RETREAT, I NEEDED A LITTLE SOME-THING TO SOOTHE MY NERVES... WHAT HAPPENED?
NOTHING... NOTHING BUT THE COMPLETE AND UTTER RUINATION OF MY LIFE.
Oh. IS THAT ALL? Y'KNOW WHAT I DO WHEN THE MAN'S ON MY BACK AND THE WORLD GETS ME DOWN?
THIS.
POP
CARE TO JOIN ME?
I DON'T DRINK.
EMERSON'S FAVORITE SINCE 1972
GLUG GLUG
HEY... THIS ISN'T SO BAD... NEVER HAD ALCOHOL BEFORE... GOT MORE?
WHAT A CO-INKI-DINK! NEITHER DO I.
I JUST HAD A BRAINSTORM... WHAT DO YOU SAY WE HEAD TO THE LAB AND GET THIS THING WORKING BEFORE MIDNIGHT --
-- AND I'LL TEACH YOU A COOL GAME INVOLVING QUARTERS. NOW THAT'S SOPHISTICATION.
MY TONGUE IS NUMB.
THAT'S A GOOD SIGN!
HIK
Y'KNOW, WEASEL... WHEN I LOOK AT A GUY LIKE YOU, WITH YOUR TALENTS... YOUR CHARISMA... YOU KNOW WHAT WORDS COME TO MIND?
MY NAME'S NOT ›HIK‹ WEASEL...
"FREELANCE FABRICATOR OF MALEVOLENT COMBUSTIBLES." HOW DOES THAT GRAB YA?
THAT A ›HIK‹ CIVIL SERVANT JOB...? ›URP‹

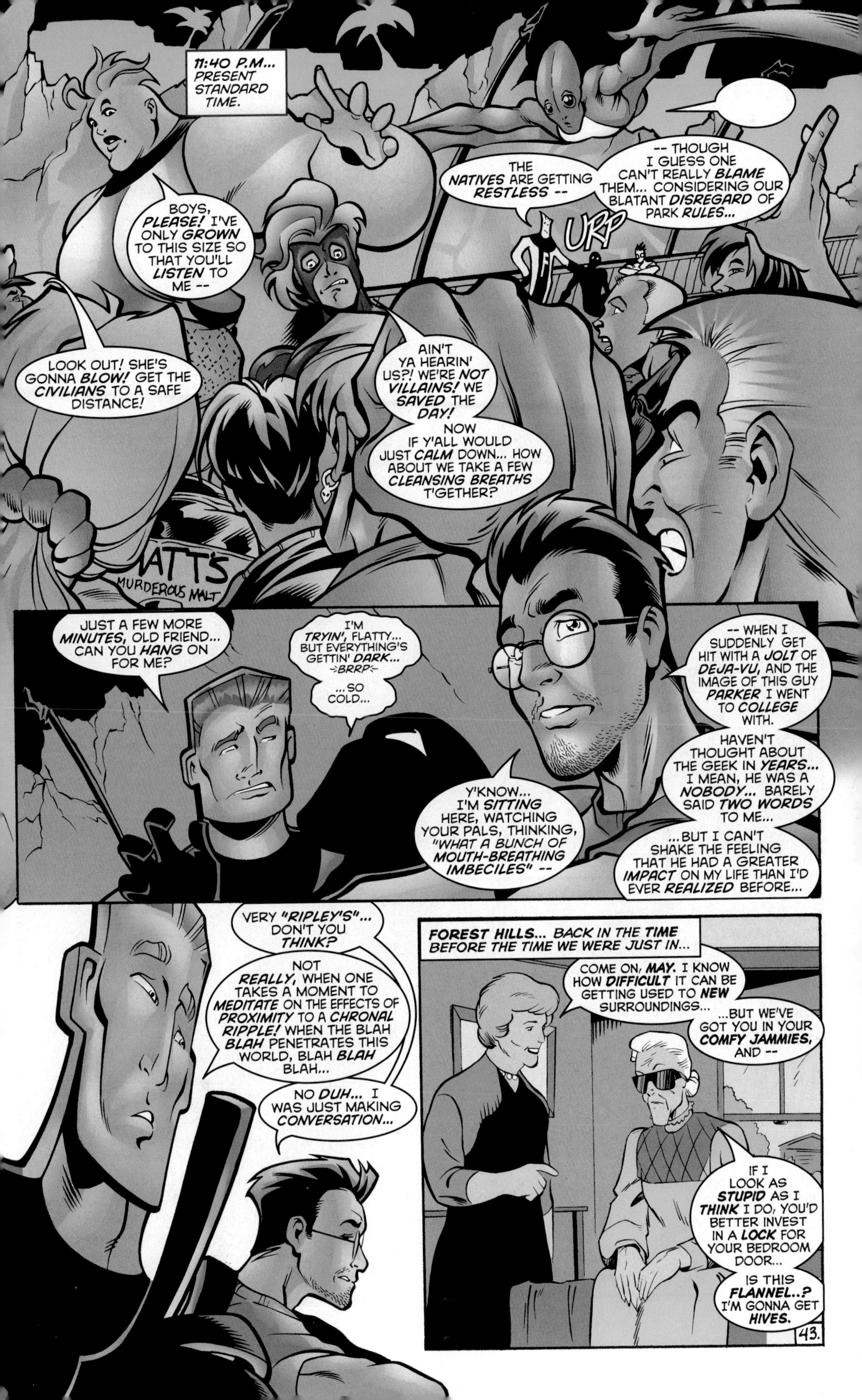
11:40 P.M... PRESENT STANDARD TIME.
BOYS, PLEASE! I'VE ONLY GROWN TO THIS SIZE SO THAT YOU'LL LISTEN TO ME --
THE NATIVES ARE GETTING RESTLESS --
-- THOUGH I GUESS ONE CAN'T REALLY BLAME THEM... CONSIDERING OUR BLATANT DISREGARD OF PARK RULES...
URP
LOOK OUT! SHE'S GONNA BLOW! GET THE CIVILIANS TO A SAFE DISTANCE!
AIN'T YA HEARIN' US?! WE'RE NOT VILLAINS! WE SAVED THE DAY!
NOW IF Y'ALL WOULD JUST CALM DOWN... HOW ABOUT WE TAKE A FEW CLEANSING BREATHS T'GETHER?
MATT'S
MURDEROUS MALT
JUST A FEW MORE MINUTES, OLD FRIEND... CAN YOU HANG ON FOR ME?
I'M TRYIN', FLATTY... BUT EVERYTHING'S GETTIN' DARK... BRRP
...SO COLD...
Y'KNOW... I'M SITTING HERE, WATCHING YOUR PALS, THINKING, "WHAT A BUNCH OF MOUTH-BREATHING IMBECILES" --
-- WHEN I SUDDENLY GET HIT WITH A JOLT OF DEJA-VU, AND THE IMAGE OF THIS GUY PARKER I WENT TO COLLEGE WITH.
HAVEN'T THOUGHT ABOUT THE GEEK IN YEARS... I MEAN, HE WAS A NOBODY... BARELY SAID TWO WORDS TO ME...
...BUT I CAN'T SHAKE THE FEELING THAT HE HAD A GREATER IMPACT ON MY LIFE THAN I'D EVER REALIZED BEFORE...
VERY "RIPLEY'S"... DON'T YOU THINK?
NOT REALLY, WHEN ONE TAKES A MOMENT TO MEDITATE ON THE EFFECTS OF PROXIMITY TO A CHRONAL RIPPLE! WHEN THE BLAH BLAH PENETRATES THIS WORLD, BLAH BLAH BLAH...
NO DUH... I WAS JUST MAKING CONVERSATION...
FOREST HILLS... BACK IN THE TIME BEFORE THE TIME WE WERE JUST IN...
COME ON, MAY. I KNOW HOW DIFFICULT IT CAN BE GETTING USED TO NEW SURROUNDINGS...
...BUT WE'VE GOT YOU IN YOUR COMFY JAMMIES, AND --
IF I LOOK AS STUPID AS I THINK I DO, YOU'D BETTER INVEST IN A LOCK FOR YOUR BEDROOM DOOR...
IS THIS FLANNEL..? I'M GONNA GET HIVES.
43.

SWEET *DREAMS*, MAY... AFTER A GOOD NIGHT'S REST, MAYBE YOU'LL FEEL BACK TO YOUR *OLD SELF*.

SLEEP AS *LONG* AS YOU LIKE... AS LONG AS IT *TAKES*. I'LL BE THERE FOR --

JUST SHUT THE *DOOR*, ALREADY!

≥SIGH≤ SO THIS IS IT... THIS IS WHAT *HELL* FEELS LIKE... FLANNEL *BLOOMERS, PINEAPPLE* BOATS, AND LAME TELEVISION.

IT'S MORE *HORRIFIC* THAN I'D EVER IMAGINED.

ALL I CAN HOPE FOR IS THAT MY BODY BEGINS TO *BREAK DOWN* AHEAD OF SCHEDULE... AND I DIE *QUICKLY*.

S'FUNNY... I'VE BEEN A *PRISONER* OF WADE'S FOR *YEARS*... SUFFERED *ALL* FORMS OF *INDIGNITY*... BUT I *NEVER* CONSIDERED *DEATH* A *POSITIVE* ALTERNATIVE TO MY SITUATION.

BUT TOMORROW... I CHEW *CARBON MONOXIDE*, BIG TIME.

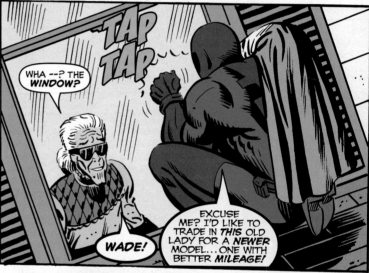

TAP TAP

WHA --? THE *WINDOW*?

WADE!

EXCUSE ME? I'D LIKE TO TRADE IN *THIS* OLD LADY FOR A *NEWER* MODEL... ONE WITH BETTER *MILEAGE!*

GOODBYE, *PAST!* GOODBYE *ANNA!* GOODBYE *FLANNEL!*

OH... PLEASE, AL, A LITTLE *WARNING* NEXT TIME...

SOME OF US AREN'T *BLIND*, Y'KNOW?

44.

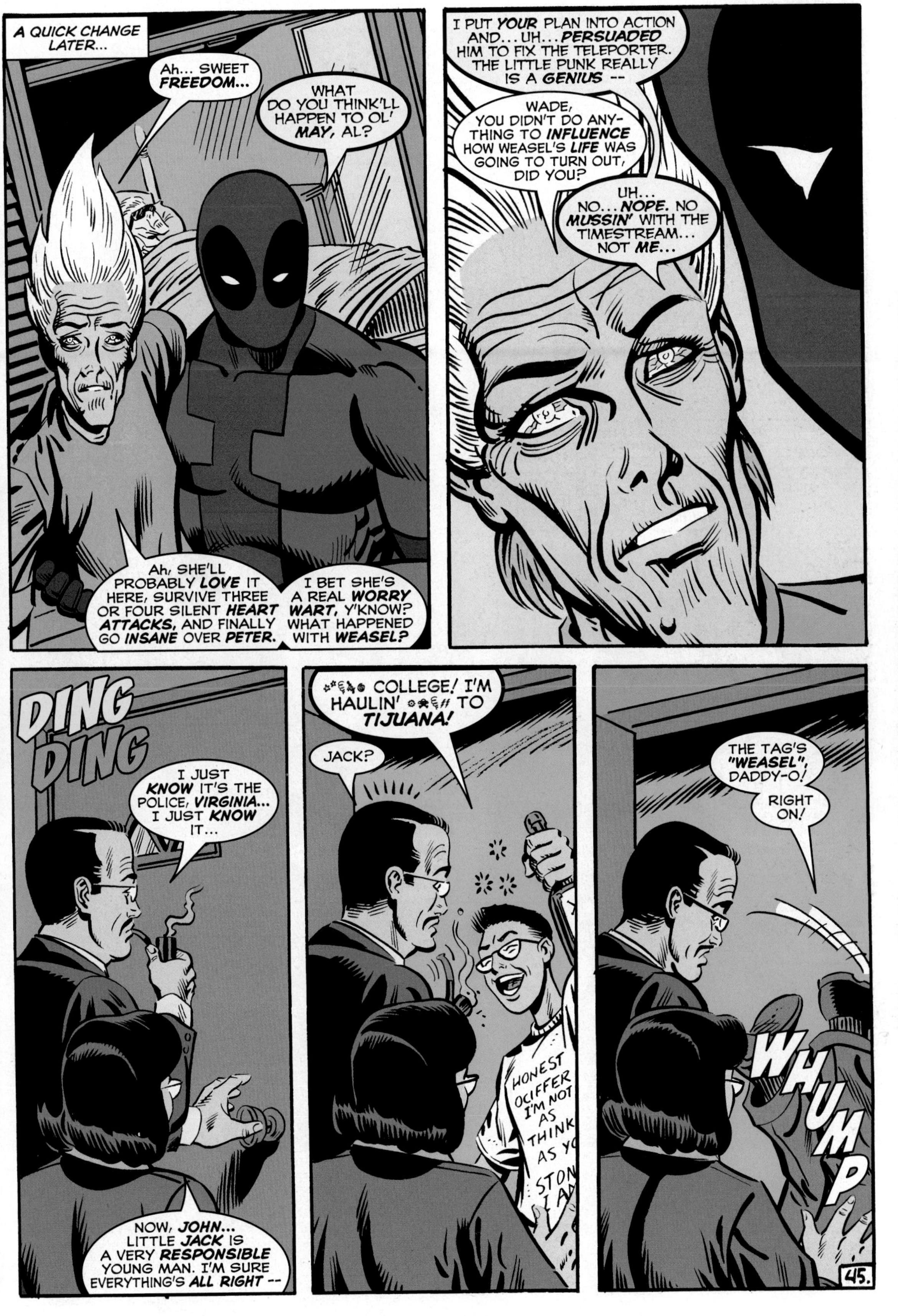
A QUICK CHANGE LATER...
Ah... SWEET FREEDOM...
WHAT DO YOU THINK'LL HAPPEN TO OL' MAY, AL?
Ah, SHE'LL PROBABLY LOVE IT HERE, SURVIVE THREE OR FOUR SILENT HEART ATTACKS, AND FINALLY GO INSANE OVER PETER.
I BET SHE'S A REAL WORRY WART, Y'KNOW? WHAT HAPPENED WITH WEASEL?
I PUT YOUR PLAN INTO ACTION AND...UH...PERSUADED HIM TO FIX THE TELEPORTER. THE LITTLE PUNK REALLY IS A GENIUS --
WADE, YOU DIDN'T DO ANYTHING TO INFLUENCE HOW WEASEL'S LIFE WAS GOING TO TURN OUT, DID YOU?
UH... NO...NOPE. NO MUSSIN' WITH THE TIMESTREAM... NOT ME...
DING DING
I JUST KNOW IT'S THE POLICE, VIRGINIA... I JUST KNOW IT...
NOW, JOHN... LITTLE JACK IS A VERY RESPONSIBLE YOUNG MAN. I'M SURE EVERYTHING'S ALL RIGHT --
COLLEGE! I'M HAULIN' TO TIJUANA!
JACK?
HONEST OCIFFER I'M NOT AS THINK AS
THE TAG'S "WEASEL", DADDY-O!
RIGHT ON!
WHUMP

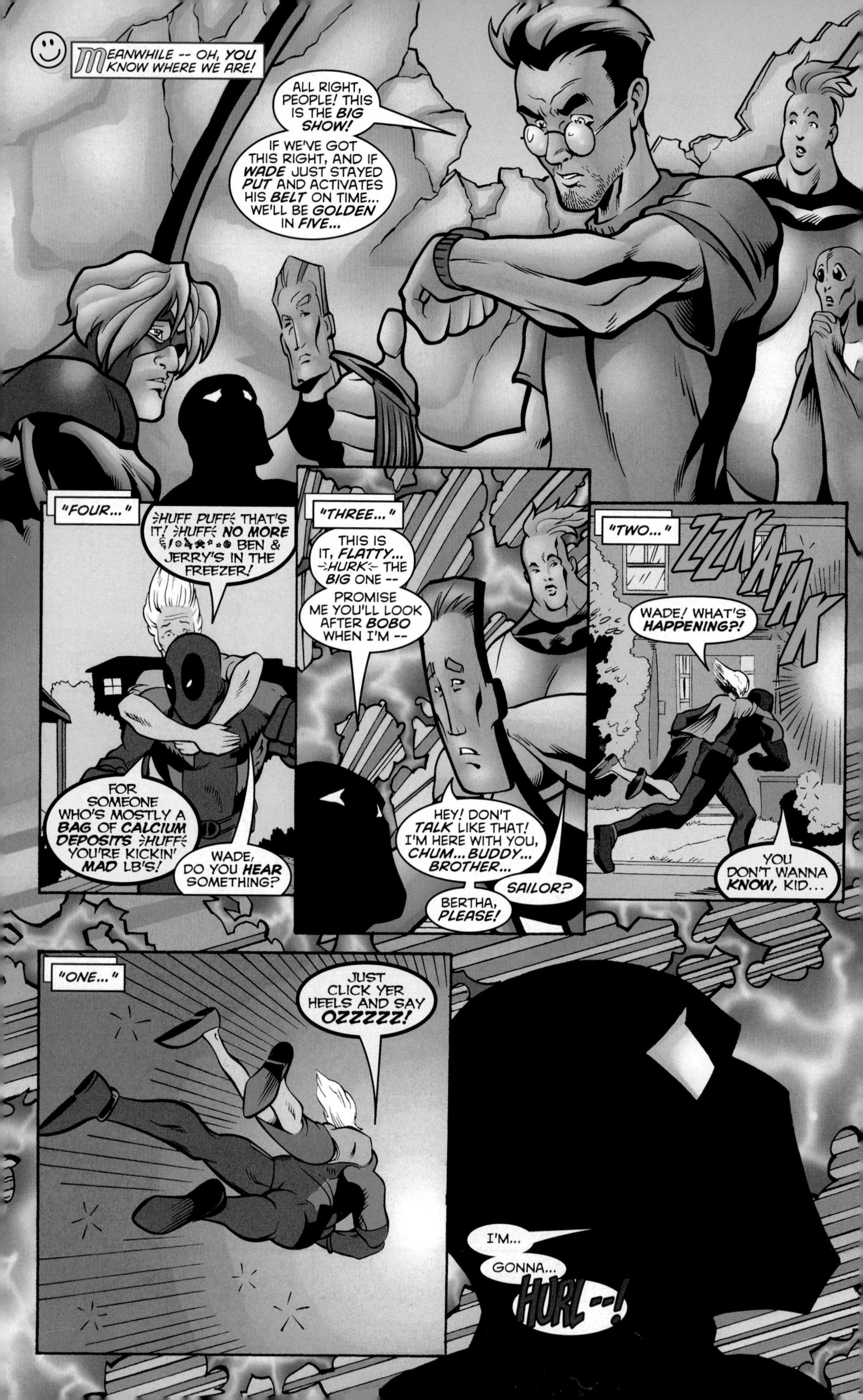

MEANWHILE -- OH, YOU KNOW WHERE WE ARE!
ALL RIGHT, PEOPLE! THIS IS THE BIG SHOW!
IF WE'VE GOT THIS RIGHT, AND IF WADE JUST STAYED PUT AND ACTIVATES HIS BELT ON TIME... WE'LL BE GOLDEN IN FIVE...
"FOUR..."
HUFF PUFF THAT'S IT! HUFF NO MORE BEN & JERRY'S IN THE FREEZER!
FOR SOMEONE WHO'S MOSTLY A BAG OF CALCIUM DEPOSITS HUFF YOU'RE KICKIN' MAD LB'S!
WADE, DO YOU HEAR SOMETHING?
"THREE..."
THIS IS IT, FLATTY... HURK THE BIG ONE --
PROMISE ME YOU'LL LOOK AFTER BOBO WHEN I'M --
HEY! DON'T TALK LIKE THAT! I'M HERE WITH YOU, CHUM... BUDDY... BROTHER...
SAILOR?
BERTHA, PLEASE!
"TWO..."
ZZKATAK
WADE! WHAT'S HAPPENING?!
YOU DON'T WANNA KNOW, KID...
"ONE..."
JUST CLICK YER HEELS AND SAY OZZZZZ!
I'M...
GONNA...
HURL --!

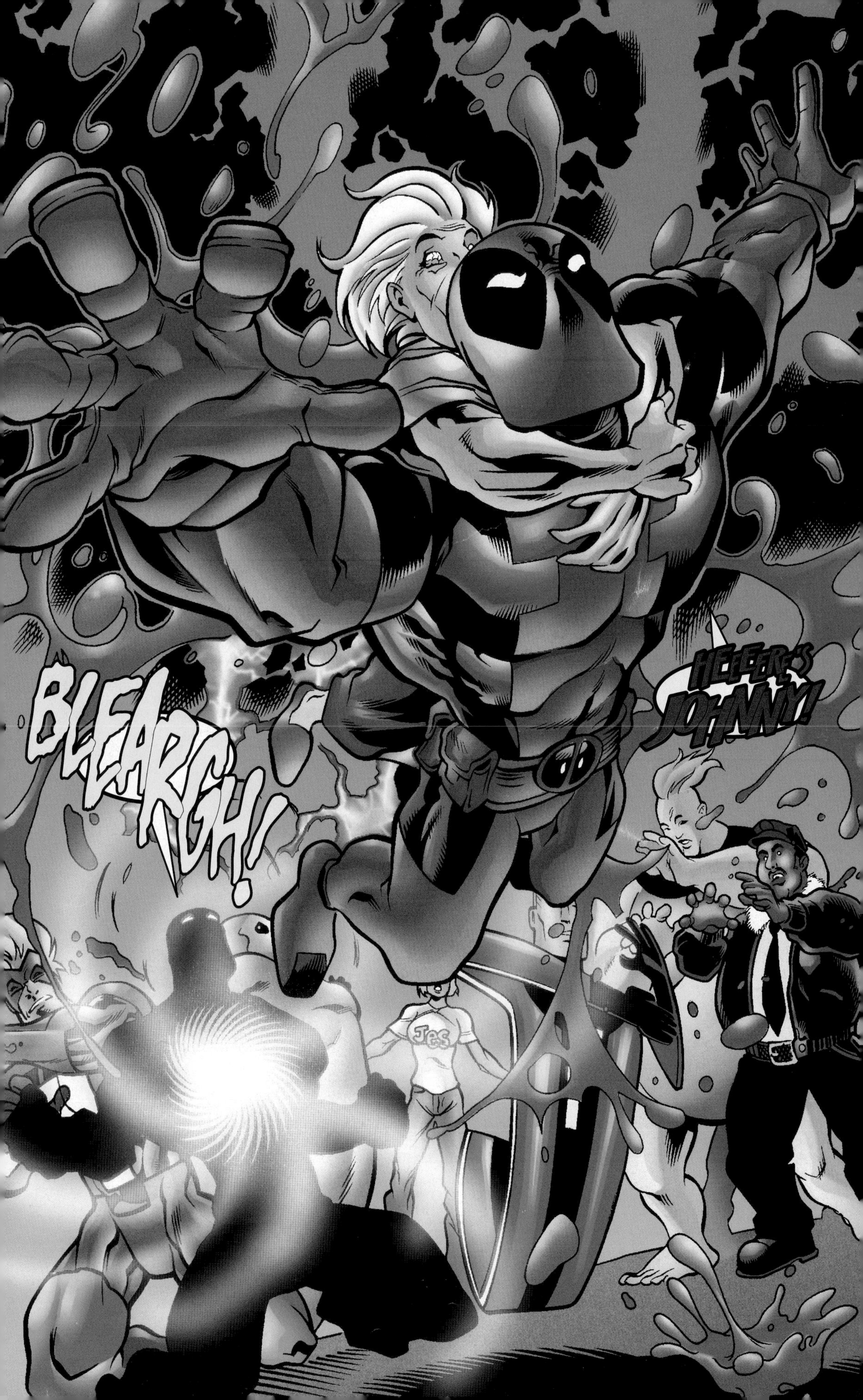
BLEARGH!
HEEERE'S JOHNNY!

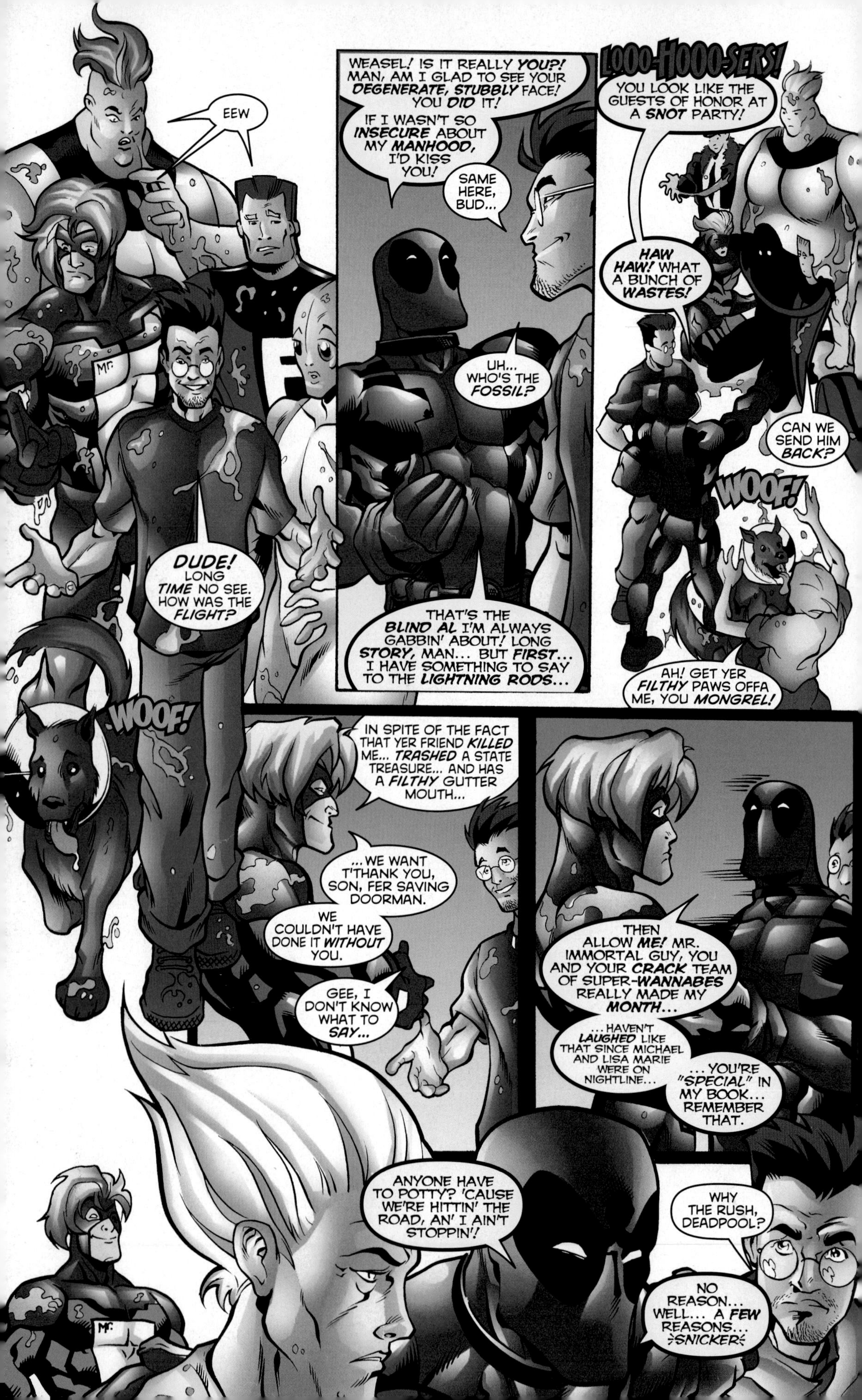
EEW
DUDE! LONG TIME NO SEE. HOW WAS THE FLIGHT?
WOOF!
WEASEL! IS IT REALLY YOU?! MAN, AM I GLAD TO SEE YOUR DEGENERATE, STUBBLY FACE! YOU DID IT!
IF I WASN'T SO INSECURE ABOUT MY MANHOOD, I'D KISS YOU!
SAME HERE, BUD...
UH... WHO'S THE FOSSIL?
THAT'S THE BLIND AL I'M ALWAYS GABBIN' ABOUT! LONG STORY, MAN... BUT FIRST... I HAVE SOMETHING TO SAY TO THE LIGHTNING RODS...
LOOO-HOOO-SERS!
YOU LOOK LIKE THE GUESTS OF HONOR AT A SNOT PARTY!
HAW HAW! WHAT A BUNCH OF WASTES!
CAN WE SEND HIM BACK?
WOOF!
AH! GET YER FILTHY PAWS OFFA ME, YOU MONGREL!
IN SPITE OF THE FACT THAT YER FRIEND KILLED ME... TRASHED A STATE TREASURE... AND HAS A FILTHY GUTTER MOUTH...
...WE WANT T'THANK YOU, SON, FER SAVING DOORMAN.
WE COULDN'T HAVE DONE IT WITHOUT YOU.
GEE, I DON'T KNOW WHAT TO SAY...
THEN ALLOW ME! MR. IMMORTAL GUY, YOU AND YOUR CRACK TEAM OF SUPER-WANNABES REALLY MADE MY MONTH...
...HAVEN'T LAUGHED LIKE THAT SINCE MICHAEL AND LISA MARIE WERE ON NIGHTLINE...
...YOU'RE "SPECIAL" IN MY BOOK... REMEMBER THAT.
ANYONE HAVE TO POTTY? 'CAUSE WE'RE HITTIN' THE ROAD, AN' I AIN'T STOPPIN'!
WHY THE RUSH, DEADPOOL?
NO REASON... WELL... A FEW REASONS... ›SNICKER‹

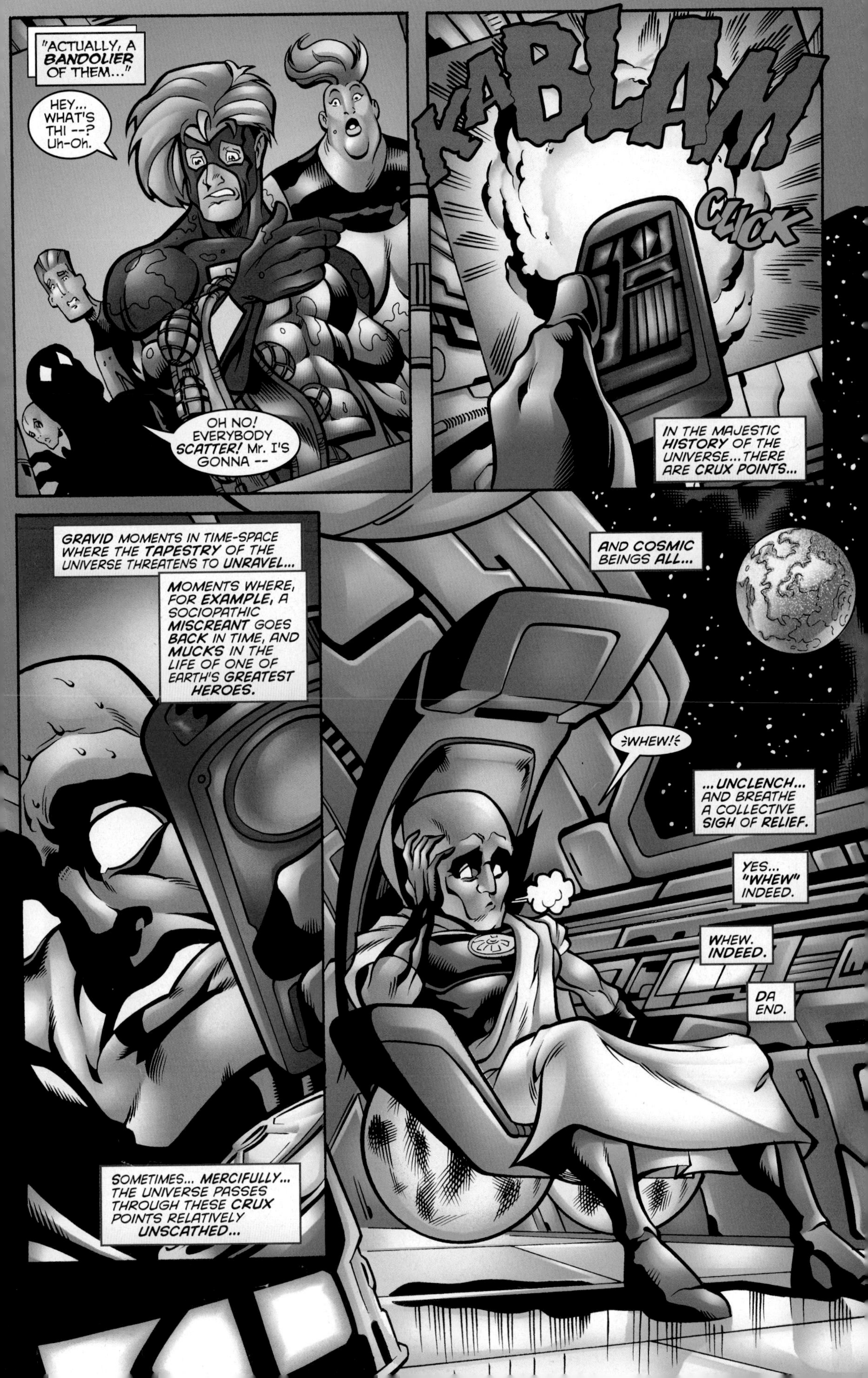
"ACTUALLY, A BANDOLIER OF THEM..."
HEY... WHAT'S THI --? Uh-Oh.
OH NO! EVERYBODY SCATTER! Mr. I'S GONNA --
KABLAM
CLICK
IN THE MAJESTIC HISTORY OF THE UNIVERSE...THERE ARE CRUX POINTS...
GRAVID MOMENTS IN TIME-SPACE WHERE THE TAPESTRY OF THE UNIVERSE THREATENS TO UNRAVEL...
MOMENTS WHERE, FOR EXAMPLE, A SOCIOPATHIC MISCREANT GOES BACK IN TIME, AND MUCKS IN THE LIFE OF ONE OF EARTH'S GREATEST HEROES.
SOMETIMES... MERCIFULLY... THE UNIVERSE PASSES THROUGH THESE CRUX POINTS RELATIVELY UNSCATHED...
AND COSMIC BEINGS ALL...
WHEW!
...UNCLENCH... AND BREATHE A COLLECTIVE SIGH OF RELIEF.
YES... "WHEW" INDEED.
WHEW. INDEED.
DA END.

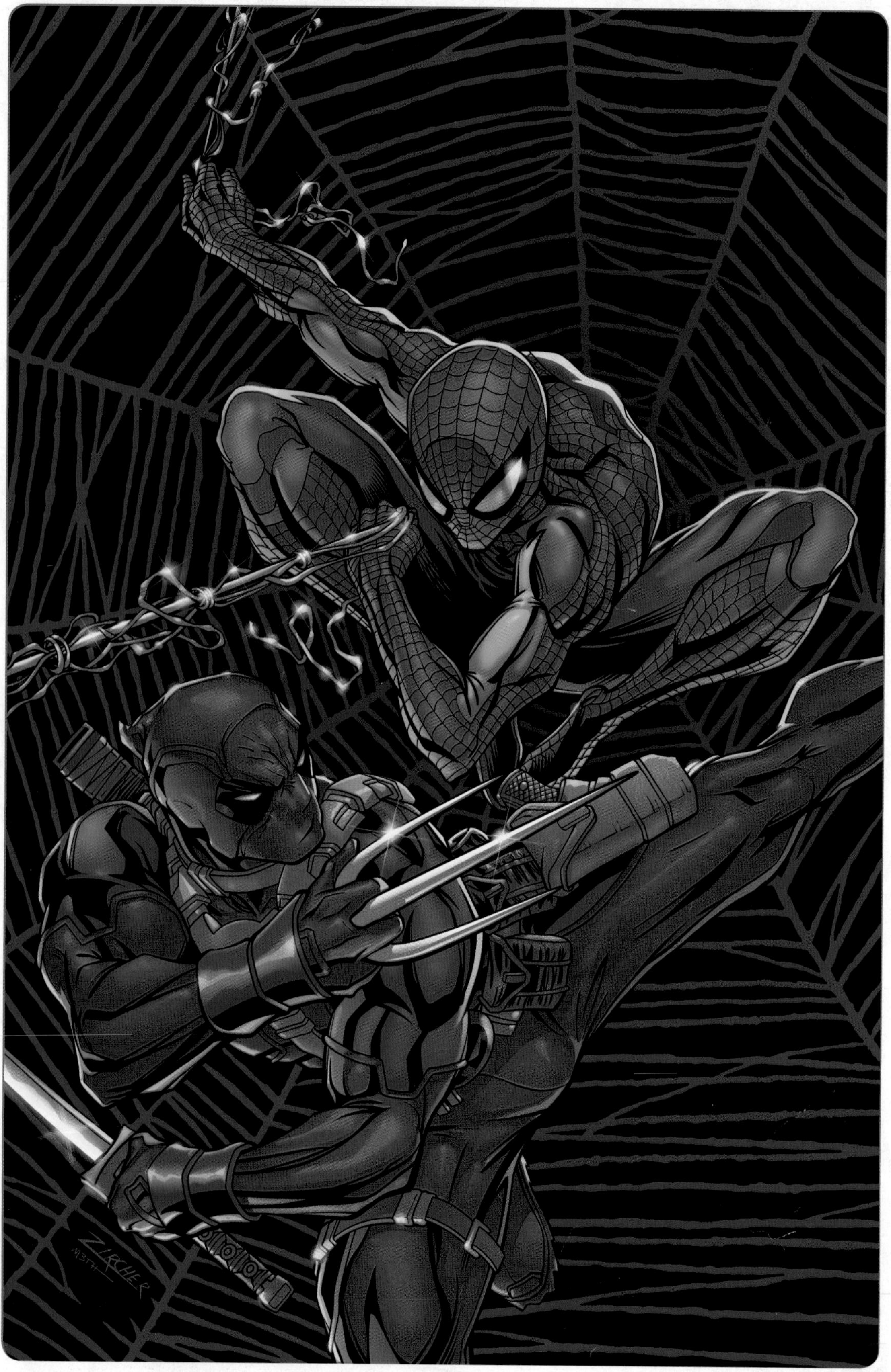
ZIRCHER

CABLE & DEADPOOL #24

"STICKY SITUATIONS"

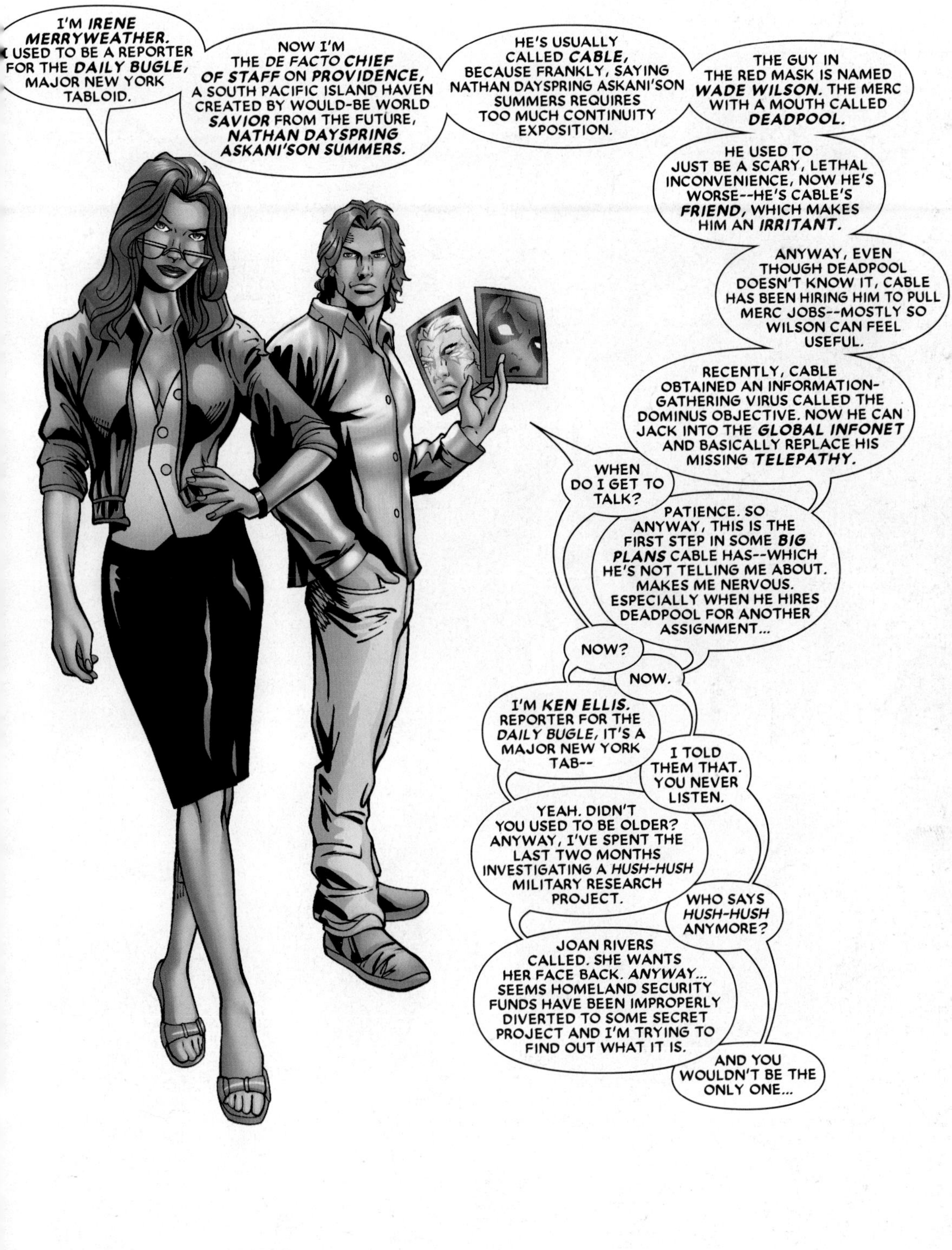

I'M IRENE MERRYWEATHER. I USED TO BE A REPORTER FOR THE DAILY BUGLE, MAJOR NEW YORK TABLOID.
NOW I'M THE DE FACTO CHIEF OF STAFF ON PROVIDENCE, A SOUTH PACIFIC ISLAND HAVEN CREATED BY WOULD-BE WORLD SAVIOR FROM THE FUTURE, NATHAN DAYSPRING ASKANI'SON SUMMERS.
HE'S USUALLY CALLED CABLE, BECAUSE FRANKLY, SAYING NATHAN DAYSPRING ASKANI'SON SUMMERS REQUIRES TOO MUCH CONTINUITY EXPOSITION.
THE GUY IN THE RED MASK IS NAMED WADE WILSON. THE MERC WITH A MOUTH CALLED DEADPOOL.
HE USED TO JUST BE A SCARY, LETHAL INCONVENIENCE, NOW HE'S WORSE--HE'S CABLE'S FRIEND, WHICH MAKES HIM AN IRRITANT.
ANYWAY, EVEN THOUGH DEADPOOL DOESN'T KNOW IT, CABLE HAS BEEN HIRING HIM TO PULL MERC JOBS--MOSTLY SO WILSON CAN FEEL USEFUL.
RECENTLY, CABLE OBTAINED AN INFORMATION-GATHERING VIRUS CALLED THE DOMINUS OBJECTIVE. NOW HE CAN JACK INTO THE GLOBAL INFONET AND BASICALLY REPLACE HIS MISSING TELEPATHY.
WHEN DO I GET TO TALK?
PATIENCE. SO ANYWAY, THIS IS THE FIRST STEP IN SOME BIG PLANS CABLE HAS--WHICH HE'S NOT TELLING ME ABOUT. MAKES ME NERVOUS. ESPECIALLY WHEN HE HIRES DEADPOOL FOR ANOTHER ASSIGNMENT...
NOW?
NOW.
I'M KEN ELLIS. REPORTER FOR THE DAILY BUGLE, IT'S A MAJOR NEW YORK TAB--
I TOLD THEM THAT. YOU NEVER LISTEN.
YEAH. DIDN'T YOU USED TO BE OLDER? ANYWAY, I'VE SPENT THE LAST TWO MONTHS INVESTIGATING A HUSH-HUSH MILITARY RESEARCH PROJECT.
WHO SAYS HUSH-HUSH ANYMORE?
JOAN RIVERS CALLED. SHE WANTS HER FACE BACK. ANYWAY... SEEMS HOMELAND SECURITY FUNDS HAVE BEEN IMPROPERLY DIVERTED TO SOME SECRET PROJECT AND I'M TRYING TO FIND OUT WHAT IT IS.
AND YOU WOULDN'T BE THE ONLY ONE...

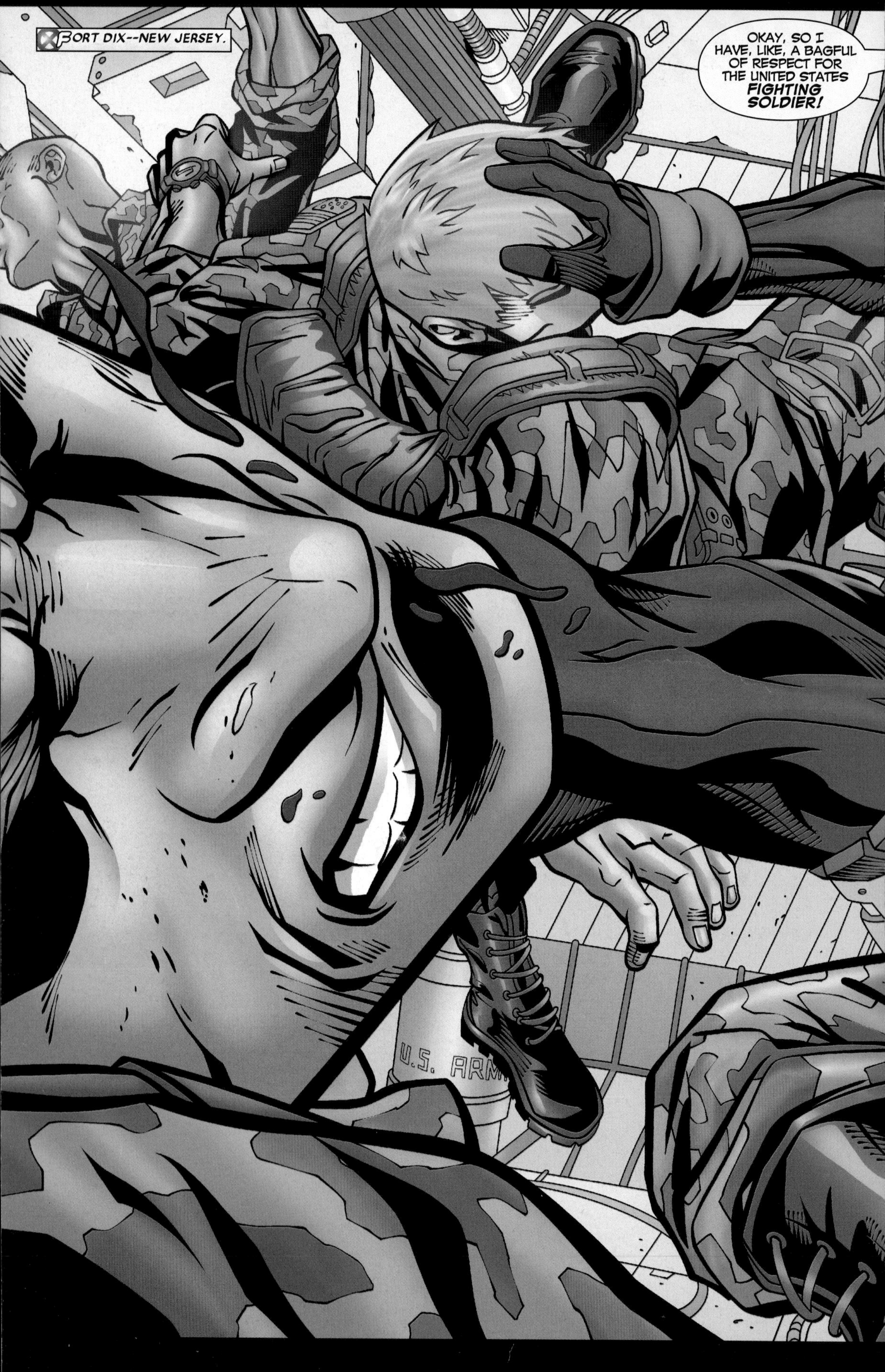
FORT DIX--NEW JERSEY.
OKAY, SO I HAVE, LIKE, A BAGFUL OF RESPECT FOR THE UNITED STATES FIGHTING SOLDIER!
U.S. ARM

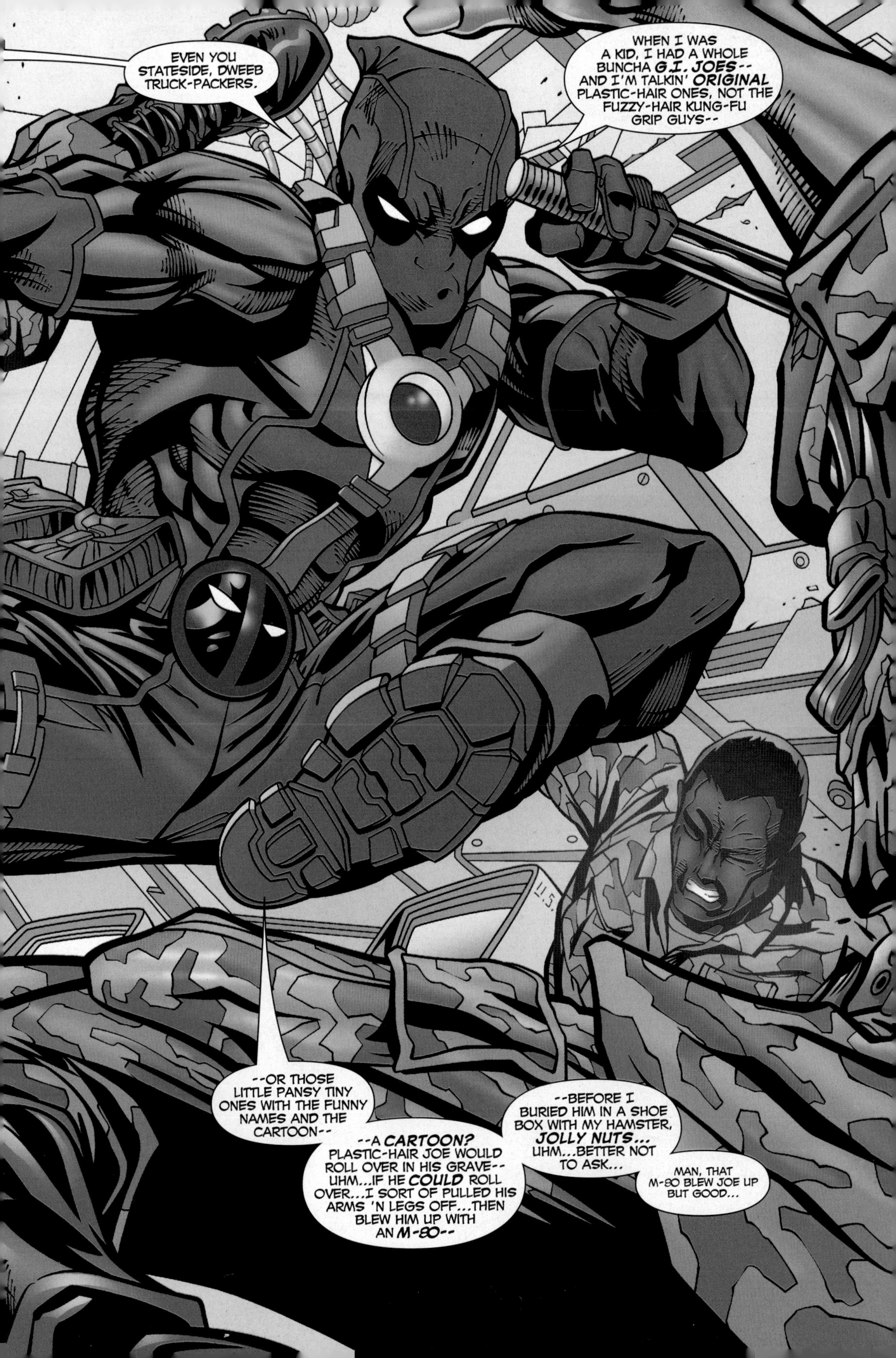
EVEN YOU STATESIDE, DWEEB TRUCK-PACKERS.
WHEN I WAS A KID, I HAD A WHOLE BUNCHA G.I. JOES-- AND I'M TALKIN' ORIGINAL PLASTIC-HAIR ONES, NOT THE FUZZY-HAIR KUNG-FU GRIP GUYS--
--OR THOSE LITTLE PANSY TINY ONES WITH THE FUNNY NAMES AND THE CARTOON--
--A CARTOON? PLASTIC-HAIR JOE WOULD ROLL OVER IN HIS GRAVE-- UHM...IF HE COULD ROLL OVER...I SORT OF PULLED HIS ARMS 'N LEGS OFF...THEN BLEW HIM UP WITH AN M-80--
--BEFORE I BURIED HIM IN A SHOE BOX WITH MY HAMSTER, JOLLY NUTS... UHM...BETTER NOT TO ASK...
MAN, THAT M-80 BLEW JOE UP BUT GOOD...

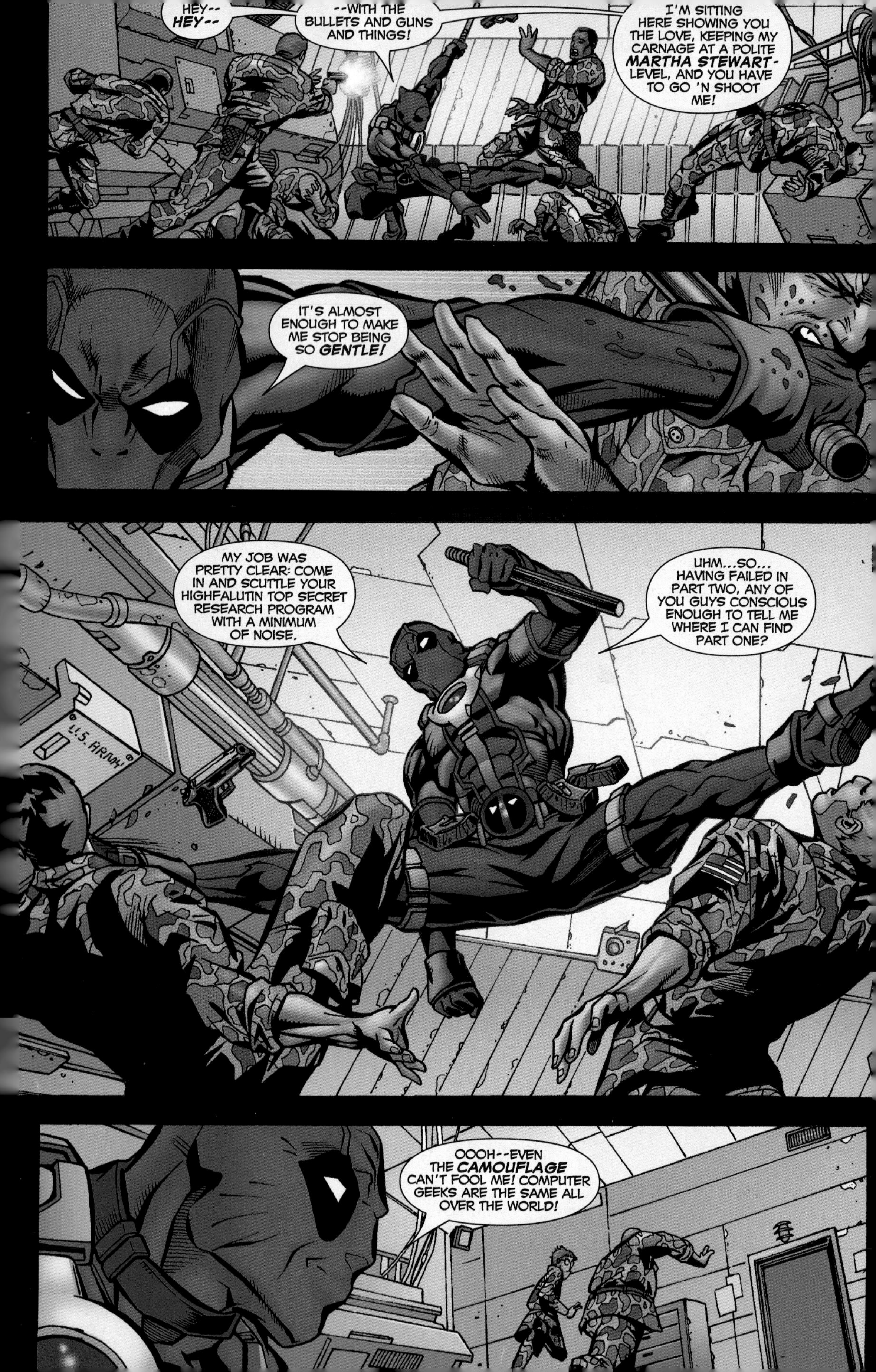
HEY-- HEY--
--WITH THE BULLETS AND GUNS AND THINGS!
I'M SITTING HERE SHOWING YOU THE LOVE, KEEPING MY CARNAGE AT A POLITE MARTHA STEWART-LEVEL, AND YOU HAVE TO GO 'N SHOOT ME!
IT'S ALMOST ENOUGH TO MAKE ME STOP BEING SO GENTLE!
MY JOB WAS PRETTY CLEAR: COME IN AND SCUTTLE YOUR HIGHFALUTIN TOP SECRET RESEARCH PROGRAM WITH A MINIMUM OF NOISE.
UHM...SO... HAVING FAILED IN PART TWO, ANY OF YOU GUYS CONSCIOUS ENOUGH TO TELL ME WHERE I CAN FIND PART ONE?
U.S. ARMY
OOOH--EVEN THE CAMOUFLAGE CAN'T FOOL ME! COMPUTER GEEKS ARE THE SAME ALL OVER THE WORLD!

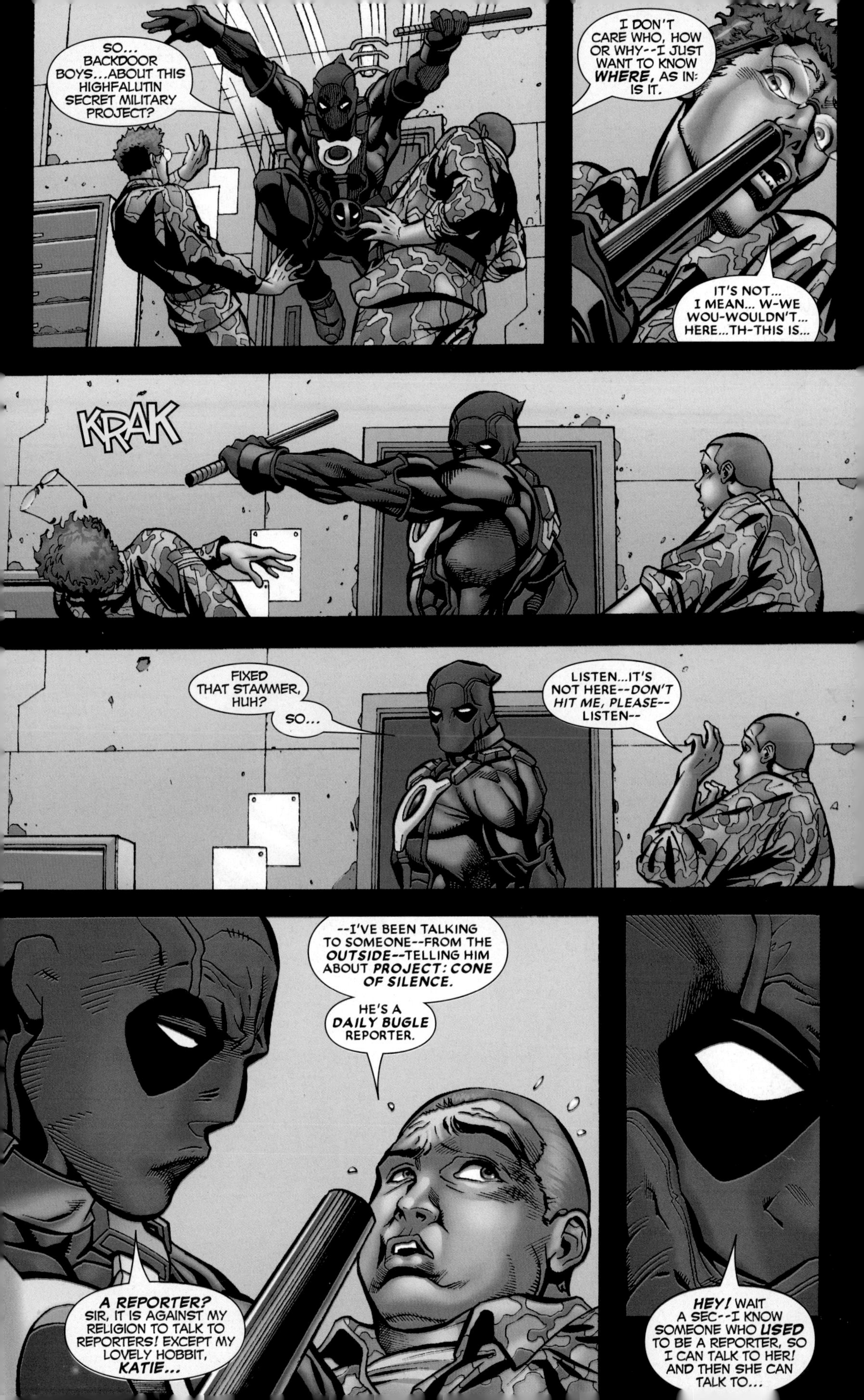
SO... BACKDOOR BOYS...ABOUT THIS HIGHFALUTIN SECRET MILITARY PROJECT?
I DON'T CARE WHO, HOW OR WHY--I JUST WANT TO KNOW WHERE, AS IN: IS IT.
IT'S NOT... I MEAN... W-WE WOU-WOULDN'T... HERE...TH-THIS IS...
KRAK
FIXED THAT STAMMER, HUH?
SO...
LISTEN...IT'S NOT HERE--DON'T HIT ME, PLEASE-- LISTEN--
--I'VE BEEN TALKING TO SOMEONE--FROM THE OUTSIDE--TELLING HIM ABOUT PROJECT: CONE OF SILENCE.
HE'S A DAILY BUGLE REPORTER.
A REPORTER? SIR, IT IS AGAINST MY RELIGION TO TALK TO REPORTERS! EXCEPT MY LOVELY HOBBIT, KATIE...
HEY! WAIT A SEC--I KNOW SOMEONE WHO USED TO BE A REPORTER, SO I CAN TALK TO HER! AND THEN SHE CAN TALK TO...

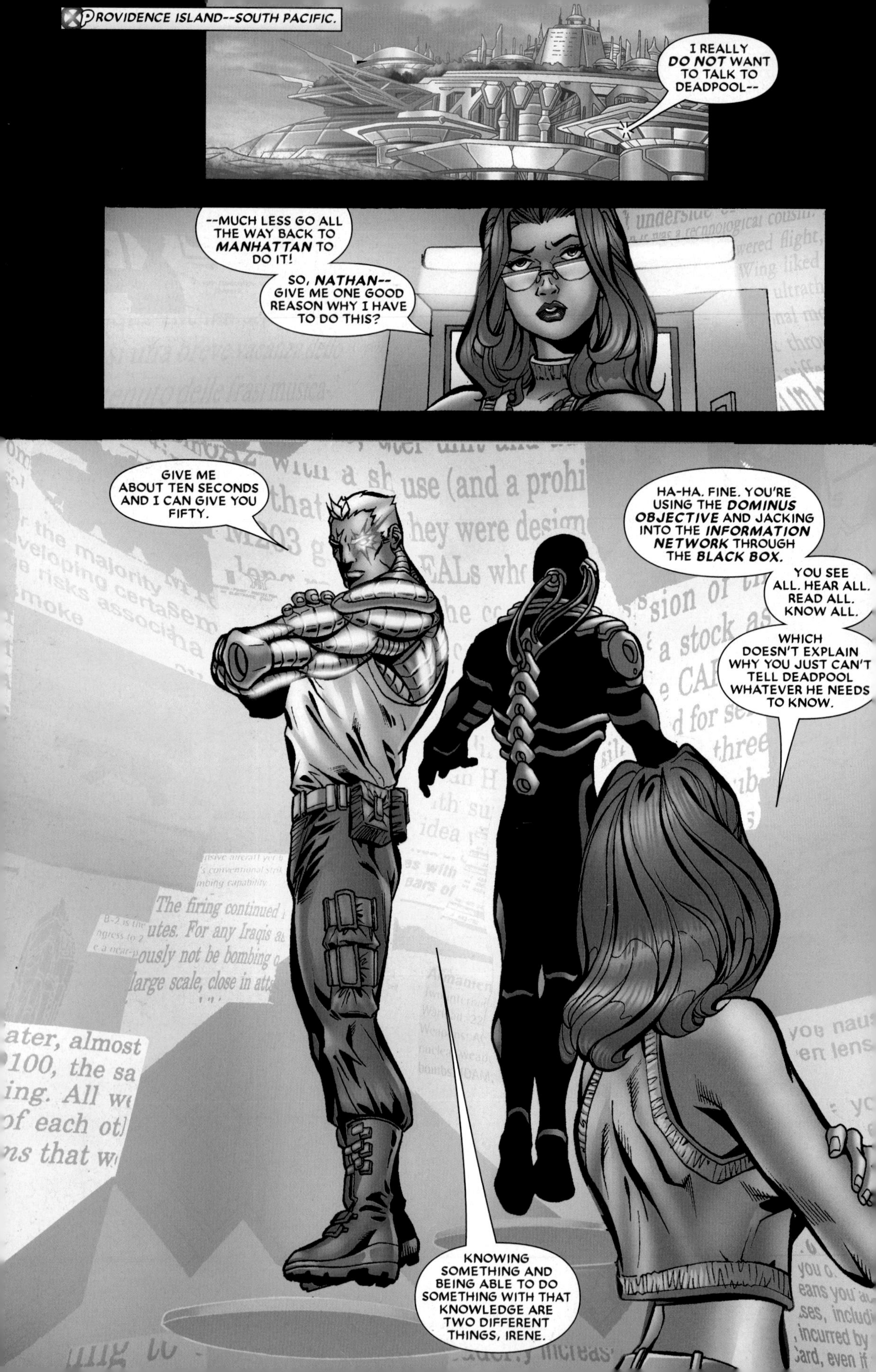
PROVIDENCE ISLAND--SOUTH PACIFIC.
I REALLY *DO NOT* WANT TO TALK TO DEADPOOL--
--MUCH LESS GO ALL THE WAY BACK TO *MANHATTAN* TO DO IT!
SO, *NATHAN*-- GIVE ME ONE GOOD REASON WHY I HAVE TO DO THIS?
GIVE ME ABOUT TEN SECONDS AND I CAN GIVE YOU FIFTY.
HA-HA. FINE. YOU'RE USING THE *DOMINUS OBJECTIVE* AND JACKING INTO THE *INFORMATION NETWORK* THROUGH THE *BLACK BOX.*
YOU SEE ALL. HEAR ALL. READ ALL. KNOW ALL.
WHICH DOESN'T EXPLAIN WHY YOU JUST CAN'T TELL DEADPOOL WHATEVER HE NEEDS TO KNOW.
KNOWING SOMETHING AND BEING ABLE TO DO SOMETHING WITH THAT KNOWLEDGE ARE TWO DIFFERENT THINGS, IRENE.

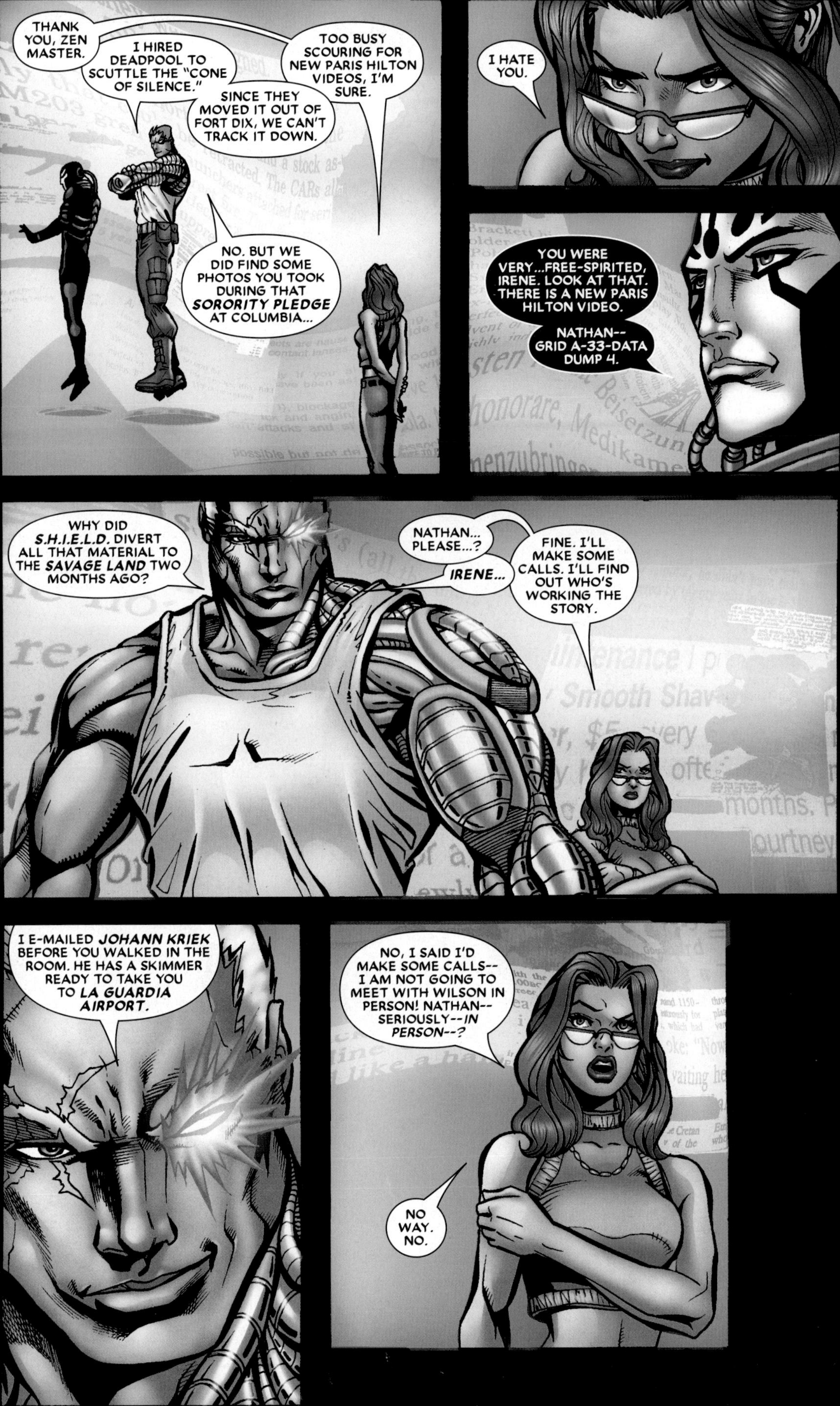
THANK YOU, ZEN MASTER.
I HIRED DEADPOOL TO SCUTTLE THE "CONE OF SILENCE."
TOO BUSY SCOURING FOR NEW PARIS HILTON VIDEOS, I'M SURE.
SINCE THEY MOVED IT OUT OF FORT DIX, WE CAN'T TRACK IT DOWN.
NO. BUT WE DID FIND SOME PHOTOS YOU TOOK DURING THAT SORORITY PLEDGE AT COLUMBIA...
I HATE YOU.
YOU WERE VERY...FREE-SPIRITED, IRENE. LOOK AT THAT. THERE IS A NEW PARIS HILTON VIDEO.
NATHAN-- GRID A-33-DATA DUMP 4.
WHY DID S.H.I.E.L.D. DIVERT ALL THAT MATERIAL TO THE SAVAGE LAND TWO MONTHS AGO?
NATHAN... PLEASE...?
IRENE...
FINE. I'LL MAKE SOME CALLS. I'LL FIND OUT WHO'S WORKING THE STORY.
I E-MAILED JOHANN KRIEK BEFORE YOU WALKED IN THE ROOM. HE HAS A SKIMMER READY TO TAKE YOU TO LA GUARDIA AIRPORT.
NO, I SAID I'D MAKE SOME CALLS-- I AM NOT GOING TO MEET WITH WILSON IN PERSON! NATHAN-- SERIOUSLY--IN PERSON--?
NO WAY. NO.

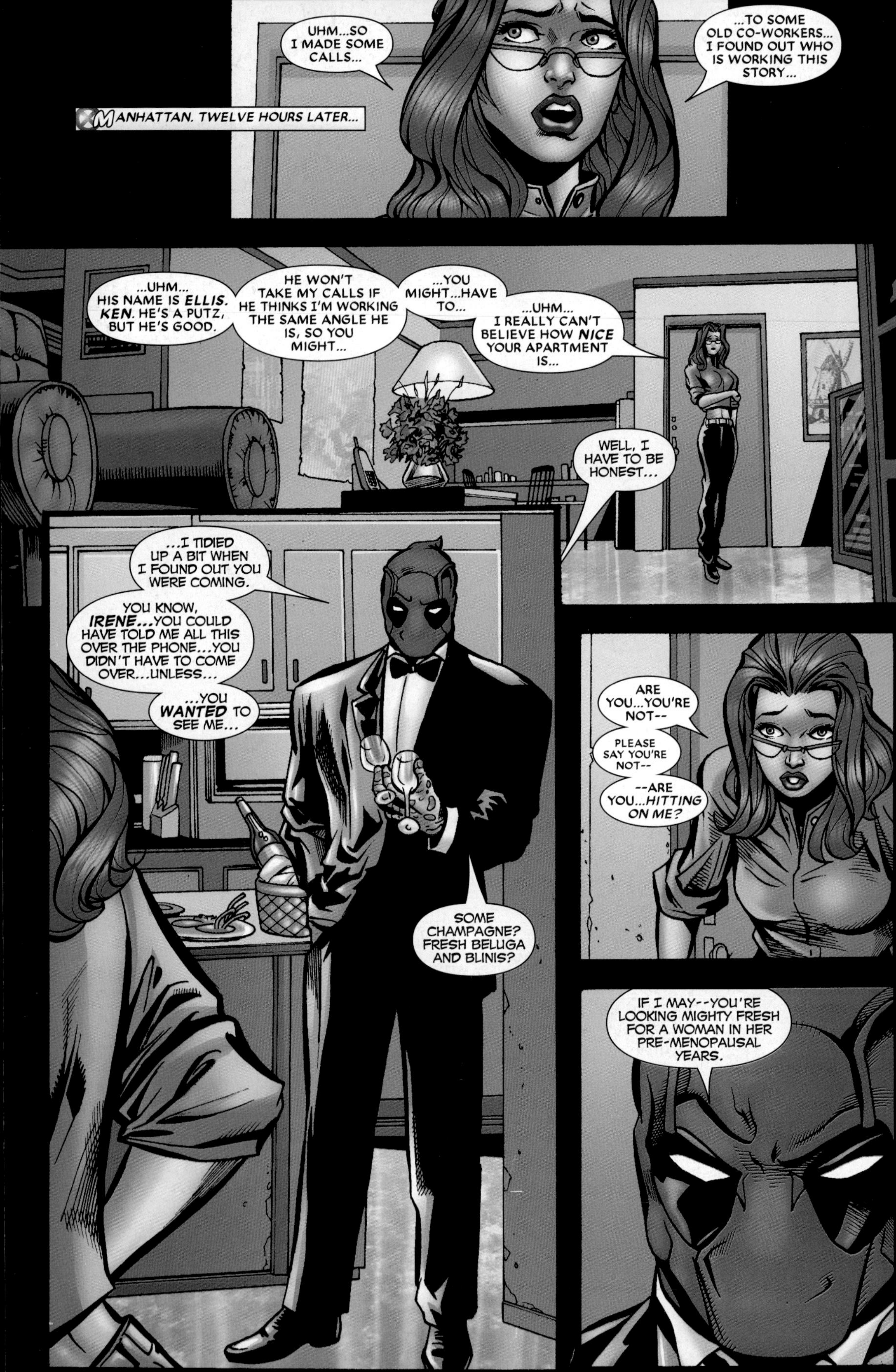
MANHATTAN. TWELVE HOURS LATER...
UHM...SO I MADE SOME CALLS...
...TO SOME OLD CO-WORKERS... I FOUND OUT WHO IS WORKING THIS STORY...
...UHM... HIS NAME IS ELLIS. KEN. HE'S A PUTZ, BUT HE'S GOOD.
HE WON'T TAKE MY CALLS IF HE THINKS I'M WORKING THE SAME ANGLE HE IS, SO YOU MIGHT...
...YOU MIGHT...HAVE TO...
...UHM... I REALLY CAN'T BELIEVE HOW NICE YOUR APARTMENT IS...
WELL, I HAVE TO BE HONEST...
...I TIDIED UP A BIT WHEN I FOUND OUT YOU WERE COMING.
YOU KNOW, IRENE...YOU COULD HAVE TOLD ME ALL THIS OVER THE PHONE...YOU DIDN'T HAVE TO COME OVER...UNLESS...
...YOU WANTED TO SEE ME...
SOME CHAMPAGNE? FRESH BELUGA AND BLINIS?
ARE YOU...YOU'RE NOT--
PLEASE SAY YOU'RE NOT--
--ARE YOU...HITTING ON ME?
IF I MAY--YOU'RE LOOKING MIGHTY FRESH FOR A WOMAN IN HER PRE-MENOPAUSAL YEARS.

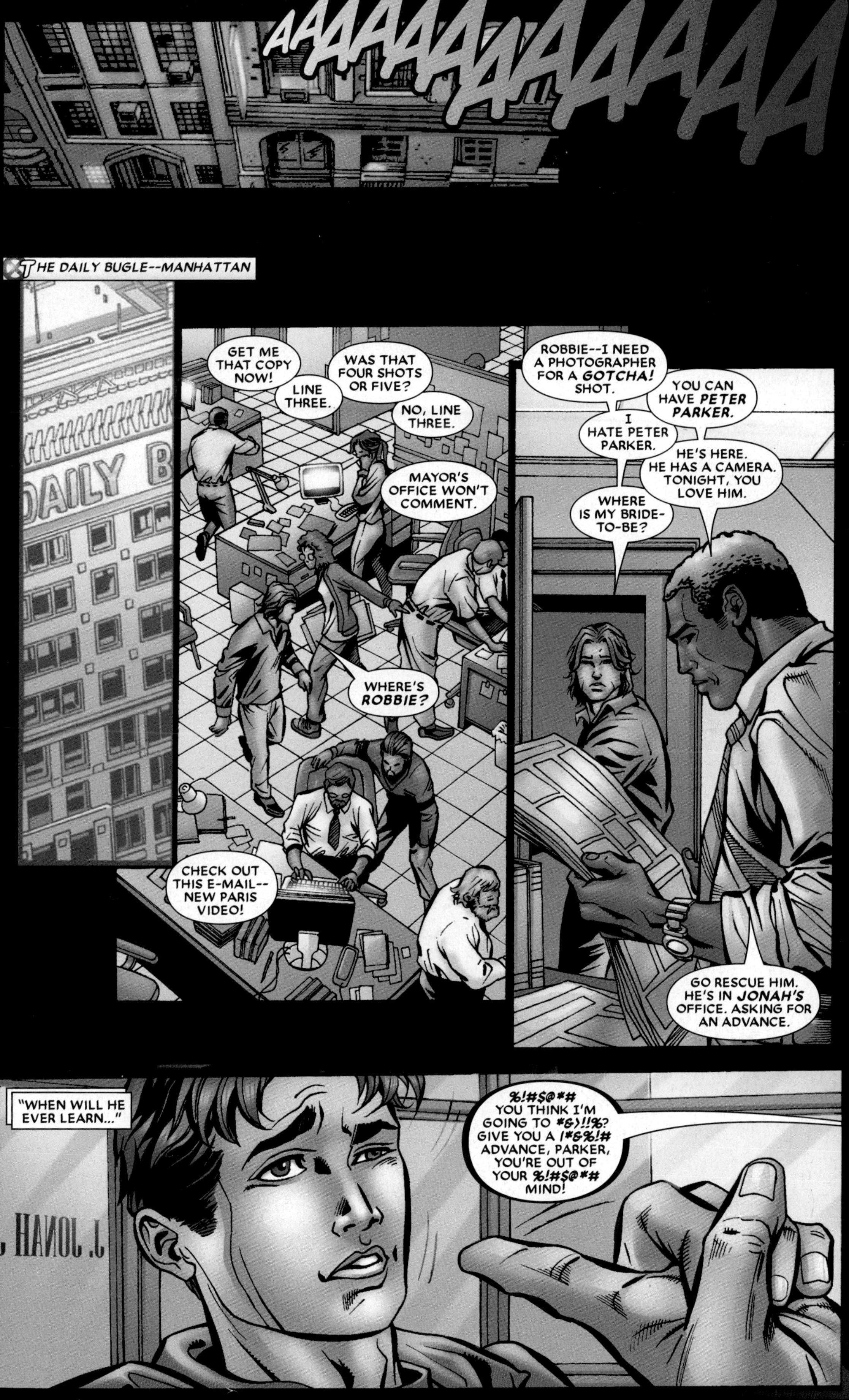
AAAAAAAAAAAAAA
THE DAILY BUGLE--MANHATTAN
GET ME THAT COPY NOW!
LINE THREE.
WAS THAT FOUR SHOTS OR FIVE?
NO, LINE THREE.
MAYOR'S OFFICE WON'T COMMENT.
WHERE'S ROBBIE?
CHECK OUT THIS E-MAIL-- NEW PARIS VIDEO!
ROBBIE--I NEED A PHOTOGRAPHER FOR A GOTCHA! SHOT.
YOU CAN HAVE PETER PARKER.
I HATE PETER PARKER.
HE'S HERE. HE HAS A CAMERA. TONIGHT, YOU LOVE HIM.
WHERE IS MY BRIDE-TO-BE?
GO RESCUE HIM. HE'S IN JONAH'S OFFICE. ASKING FOR AN ADVANCE.
"WHEN WILL HE EVER LEARN..."
%!#$@*# YOU THINK I'M GOING TO *&)!!%? GIVE YOU A !*&%!# ADVANCE, PARKER, YOU'RE OUT OF YOUR %!#$@*# MIND!
J. JONAH

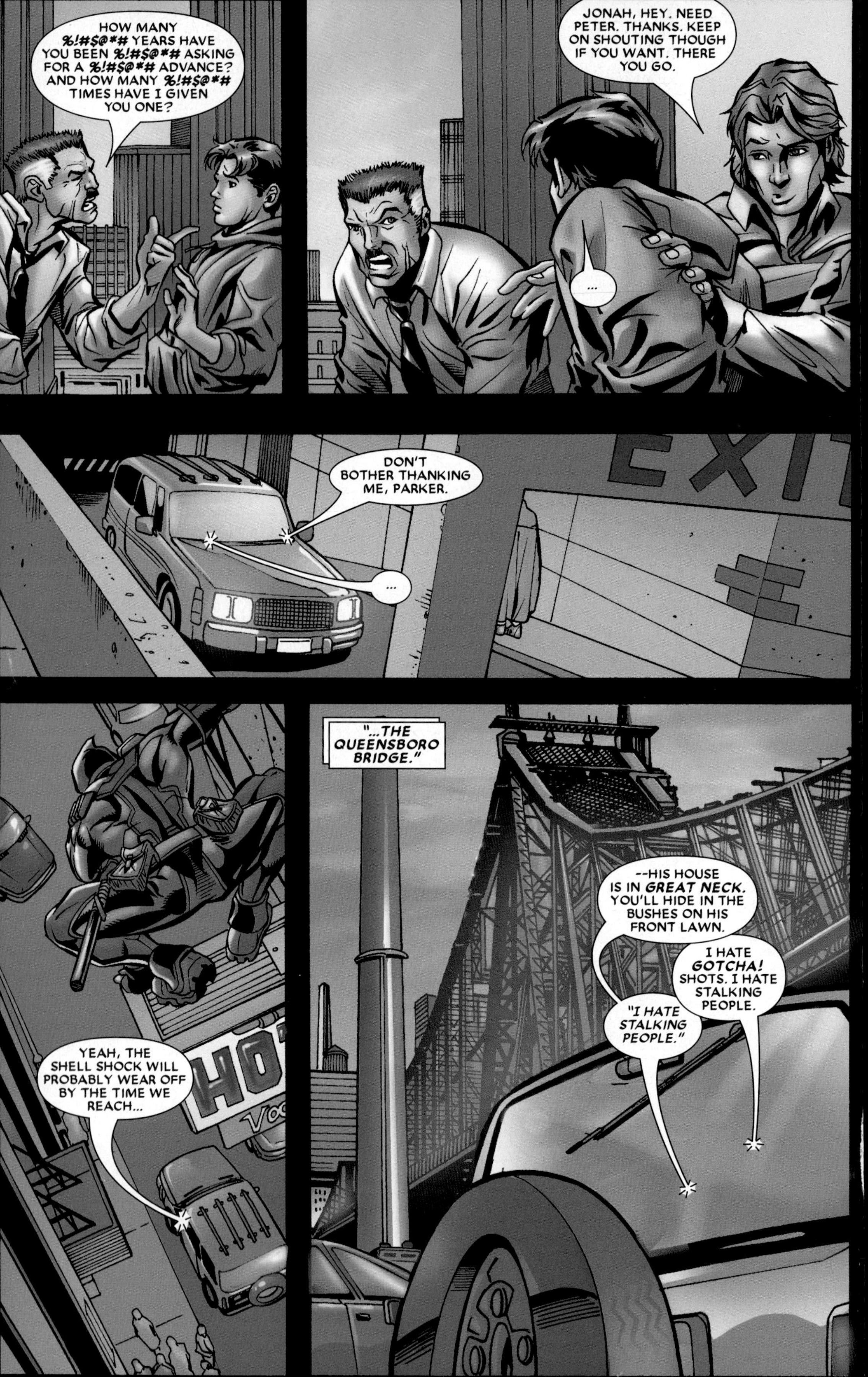
HOW MANY %!#$@*# YEARS HAVE YOU BEEN %!#$@*# ASKING FOR A %!#$@*# ADVANCE? AND HOW MANY %!#$@*# TIMES HAVE I GIVEN YOU ONE?
JONAH, HEY. NEED PETER. THANKS. KEEP ON SHOUTING THOUGH IF YOU WANT. THERE YOU GO.
...
DON'T BOTHER THANKING ME, PARKER.
...
EXIT
YEAH, THE SHELL SHOCK WILL PROBABLY WEAR OFF BY THE TIME WE REACH...
"...THE QUEENSBORO BRIDGE."
--HIS HOUSE IS IN GREAT NECK. YOU'LL HIDE IN THE BUSHES ON HIS FRONT LAWN.
I HATE GOTCHA! SHOTS. I HATE STALKING PEOPLE.
"I HATE STALKING PEOPLE."

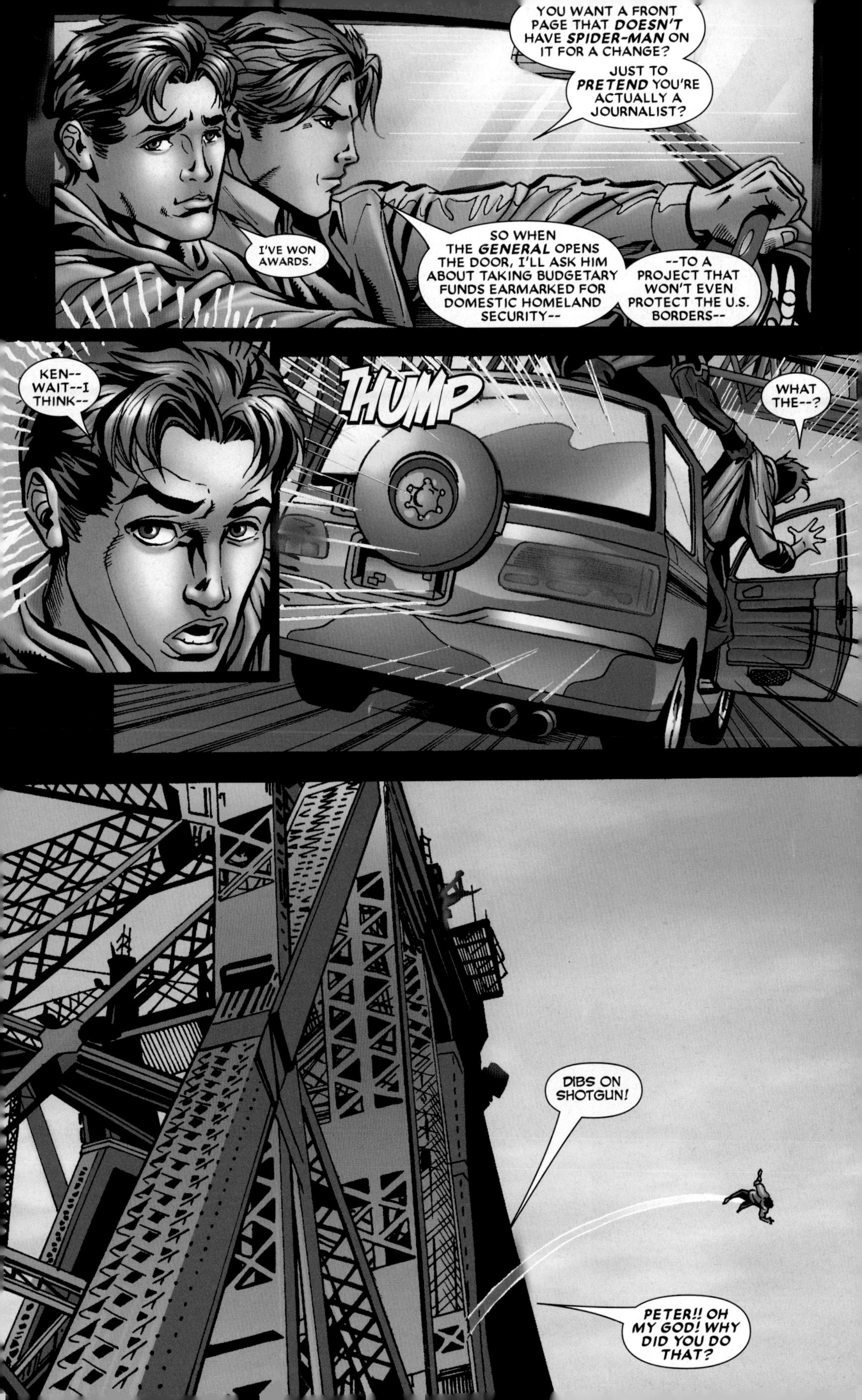
YOU WANT A FRONT PAGE THAT DOESN'T HAVE SPIDER-MAN ON IT FOR A CHANGE?
JUST TO PRETEND YOU'RE ACTUALLY A JOURNALIST?
I'VE WON AWARDS.
SO WHEN THE GENERAL OPENS THE DOOR, I'LL ASK HIM ABOUT TAKING BUDGETARY FUNDS EARMARKED FOR DOMESTIC HOMELAND SECURITY--
--TO A PROJECT THAT WON'T EVEN PROTECT THE U.S. BORDERS--
KEN--WAIT--I THINK--
THUMP
WHAT THE--?
DIBS ON SHOTGUN!
PETER!! OH MY GOD! WHY DID YOU DO THAT?

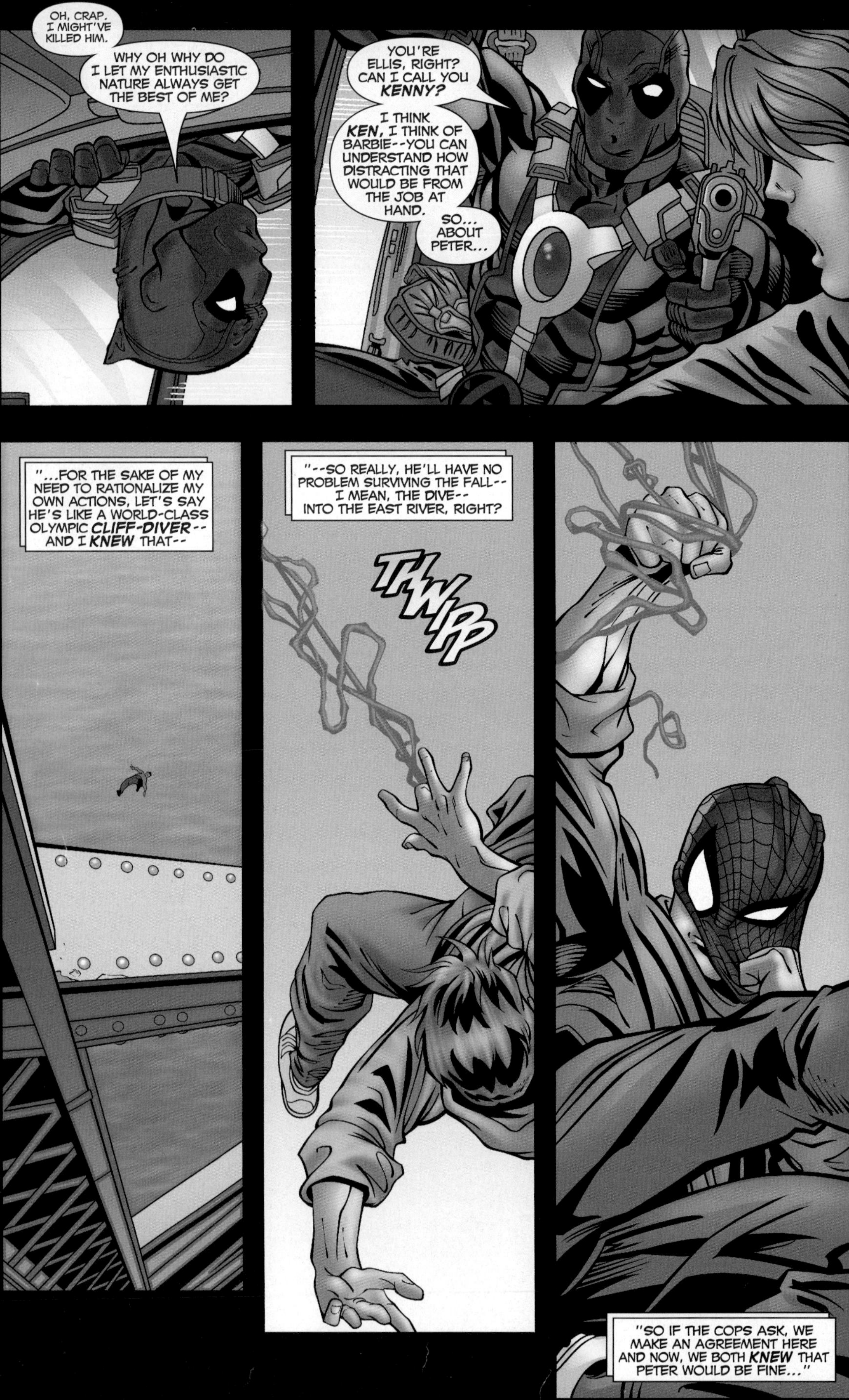
OH, CRAP. I MIGHT'VE KILLED HIM.
WHY OH WHY DO I LET MY ENTHUSIASTIC NATURE ALWAYS GET THE BEST OF ME?
YOU'RE ELLIS, RIGHT? CAN I CALL YOU KENNY?
I THINK KEN, I THINK OF BARBIE--YOU CAN UNDERSTAND HOW DISTRACTING THAT WOULD BE FROM THE JOB AT HAND.
SO... ABOUT PETER...
"...FOR THE SAKE OF MY NEED TO RATIONALIZE MY OWN ACTIONS, LET'S SAY HE'S LIKE A WORLD-CLASS OLYMPIC CLIFF-DIVER--AND I KNEW THAT--
"--SO REALLY, HE'LL HAVE NO PROBLEM SURVIVING THE FALL--I MEAN, THE DIVE--INTO THE EAST RIVER, RIGHT?
THWIPP
"SO IF THE COPS ASK, WE MAKE AN AGREEMENT HERE AND NOW, WE BOTH KNEW THAT PETER WOULD BE FINE..."

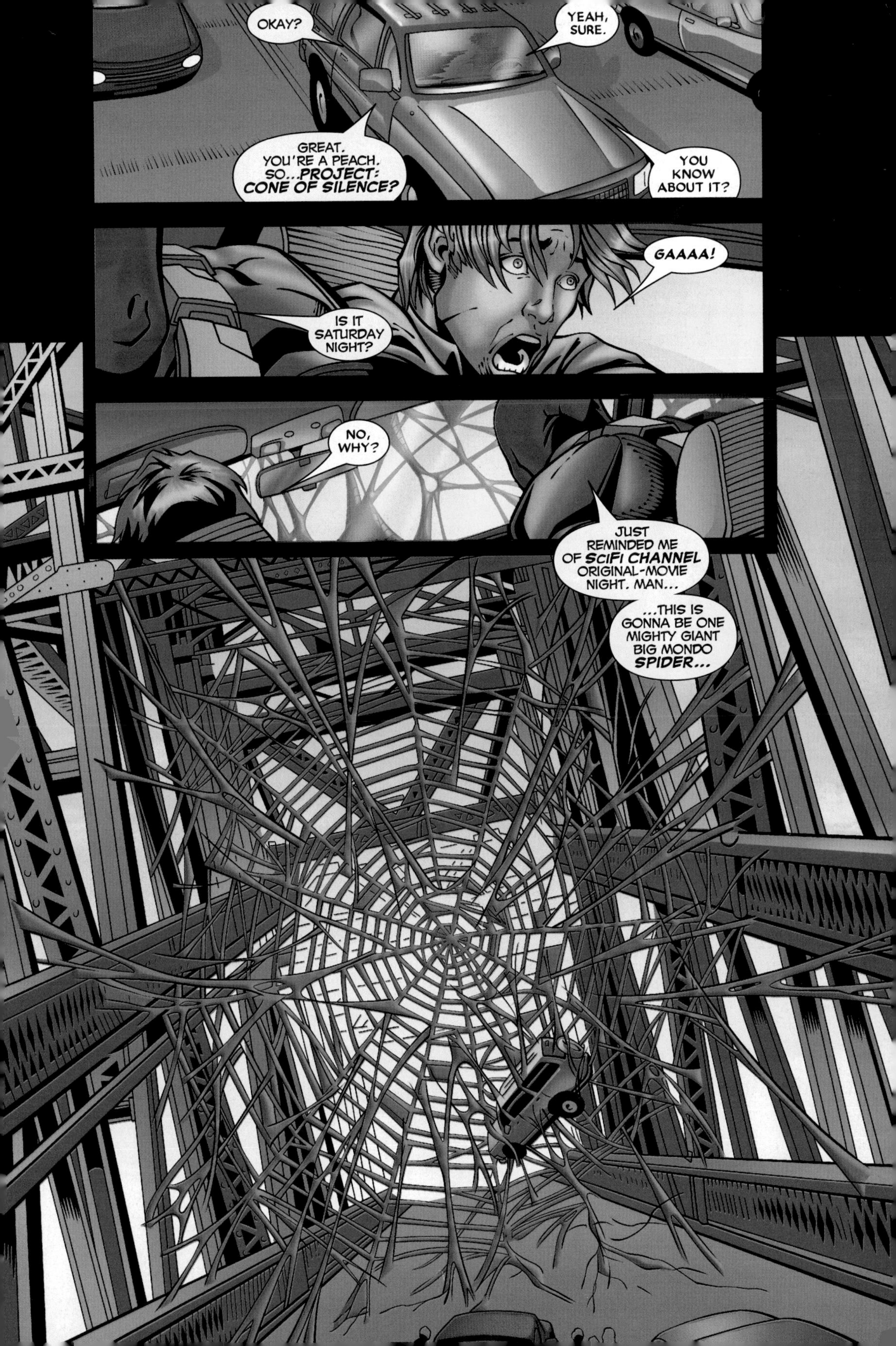
OKAY?
YEAH, SURE.
GREAT. YOU'RE A PEACH. SO...PROJECT: CONE OF SILENCE?
YOU KNOW ABOUT IT?
GAAAA!
IS IT SATURDAY NIGHT?
NO, WHY?
JUST REMINDED ME OF SciFi CHANNEL ORIGINAL-MOVIE NIGHT. MAN...
...THIS IS GONNA BE ONE MIGHTY GIANT BIG MONDO SPIDER...

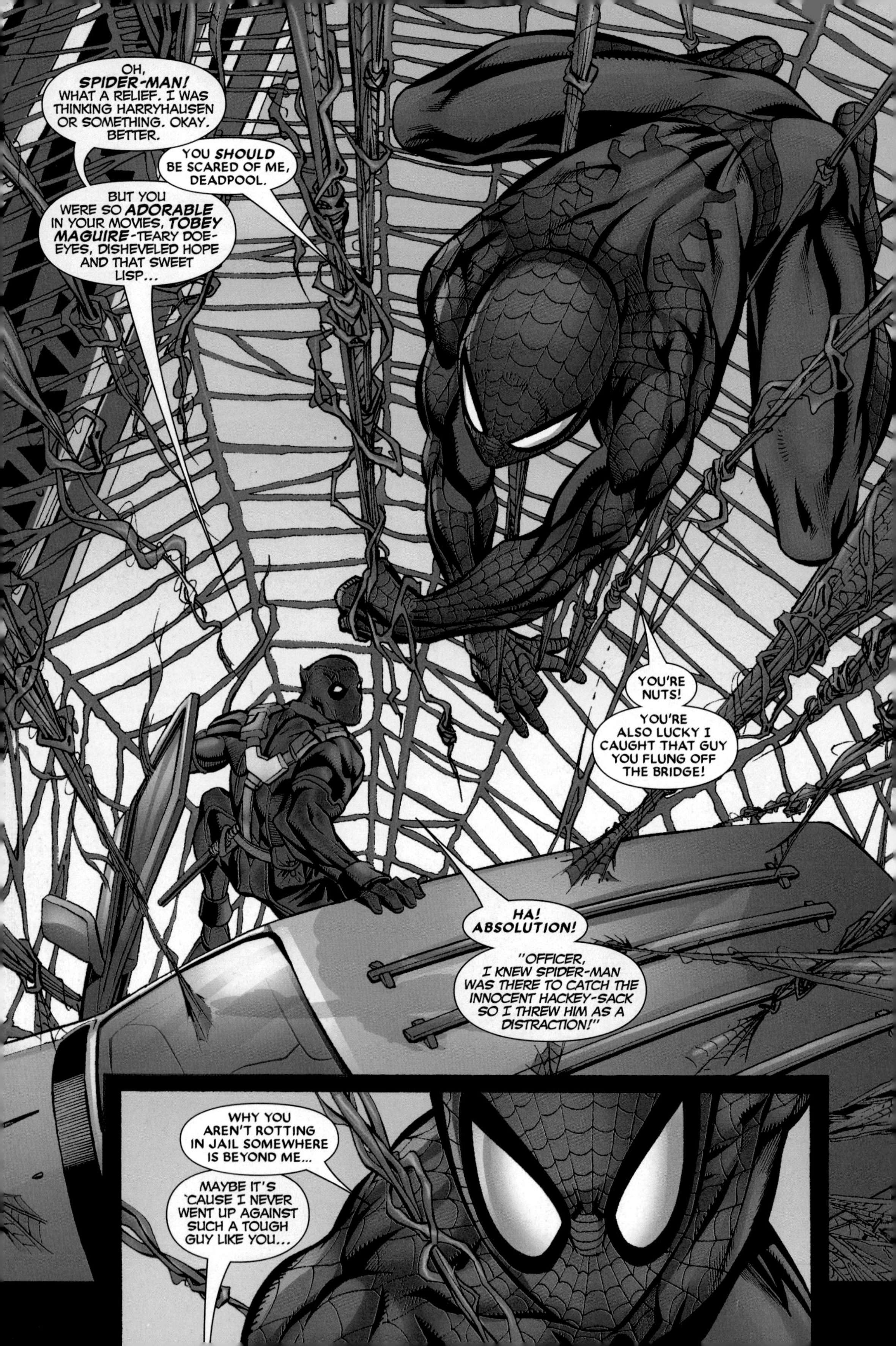
OH, SPIDER-MAN! WHAT A RELIEF. I WAS THINKING HARRYHAUSEN OR SOMETHING. OKAY. BETTER.
YOU SHOULD BE SCARED OF ME, DEADPOOL.
BUT YOU WERE SO ADORABLE IN YOUR MOVIES, TOBEY MAGUIRE-TEARY DOE-EYES, DISHEVELED HOPE AND THAT SWEET LISP...
YOU'RE NUTS!
YOU'RE ALSO LUCKY I CAUGHT THAT GUY YOU FLUNG OFF THE BRIDGE!
HA! ABSOLUTION!
"OFFICER, I KNEW SPIDER-MAN WAS THERE TO CATCH THE INNOCENT HACKEY-SACK SO I THREW HIM AS A DISTRACTION!"
WHY YOU AREN'T ROTTING IN JAIL SOMEWHERE IS BEYOND ME...
MAYBE IT'S 'CAUSE I NEVER WENT UP AGAINST SUCH A TOUGH GUY LIKE YOU...

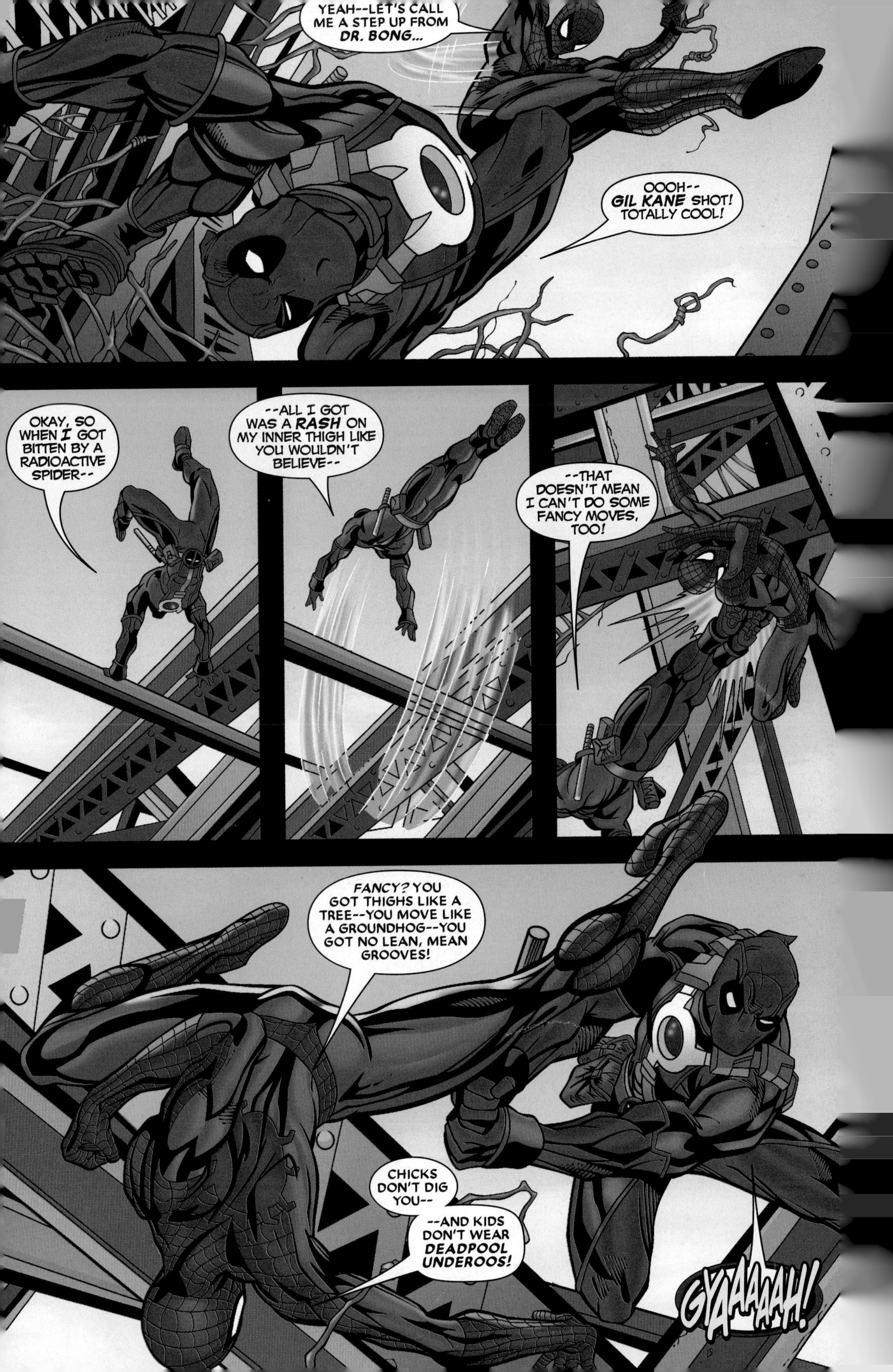
YEAH--LET'S CALL ME A STEP UP FROM DR. BONG...
OOOH-- GIL KANE SHOT! TOTALLY COOL!
OKAY, SO WHEN I GOT BITTEN BY A RADIOACTIVE SPIDER--
--ALL I GOT WAS A RASH ON MY INNER THIGH LIKE YOU WOULDN'T BELIEVE--
--THAT DOESN'T MEAN I CAN'T DO SOME FANCY MOVES, TOO!
FANCY? YOU GOT THIGHS LIKE A TREE--YOU MOVE LIKE A GROUNDHOG--YOU GOT NO LEAN, MEAN GROOVES!
CHICKS DON'T DIG YOU--
--AND KIDS DON'T WEAR DEADPOOL UNDEROOS!
GYAAAAAH!

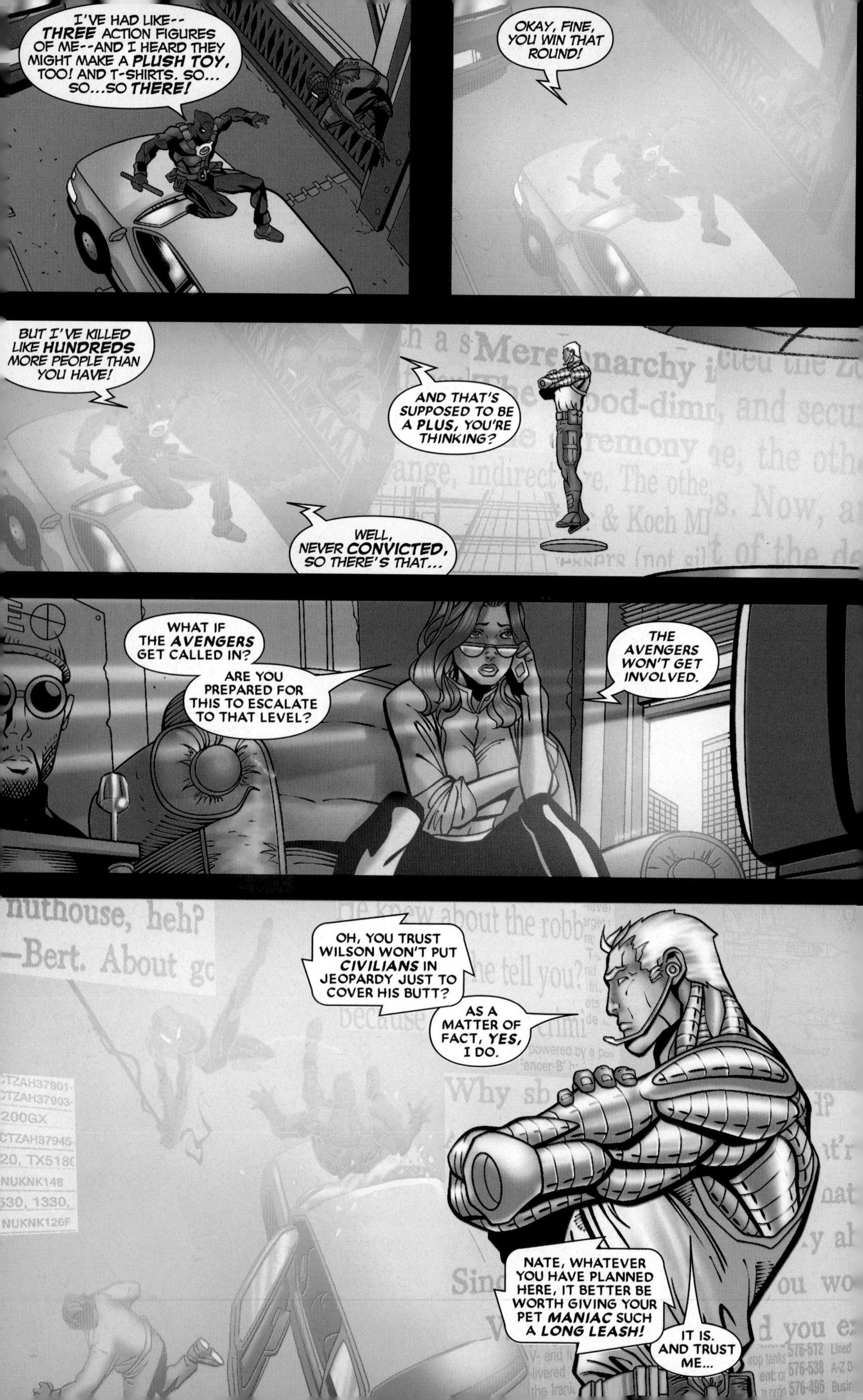
I'VE HAD LIKE-- THREE ACTION FIGURES OF ME--AND I HEARD THEY MIGHT MAKE A PLUSH TOY, TOO! AND T-SHIRTS. SO... SO...SO THERE!
OKAY, FINE, YOU WIN THAT ROUND!
BUT I'VE KILLED LIKE HUNDREDS MORE PEOPLE THAN YOU HAVE!
AND THAT'S SUPPOSED TO BE A PLUS, YOU'RE THINKING?
WELL, NEVER CONVICTED, SO THERE'S THAT...
WHAT IF THE AVENGERS GET CALLED IN?
ARE YOU PREPARED FOR THIS TO ESCALATE TO THAT LEVEL?
THE AVENGERS WON'T GET INVOLVED.
OH, YOU TRUST WILSON WON'T PUT CIVILIANS IN JEOPARDY JUST TO COVER HIS BUTT?
AS A MATTER OF FACT, YES, I DO.
NATE, WHATEVER YOU HAVE PLANNED HERE, IT BETTER BE WORTH GIVING YOUR PET MANIAC SUCH A LONG LEASH!
IT IS. AND TRUST ME...

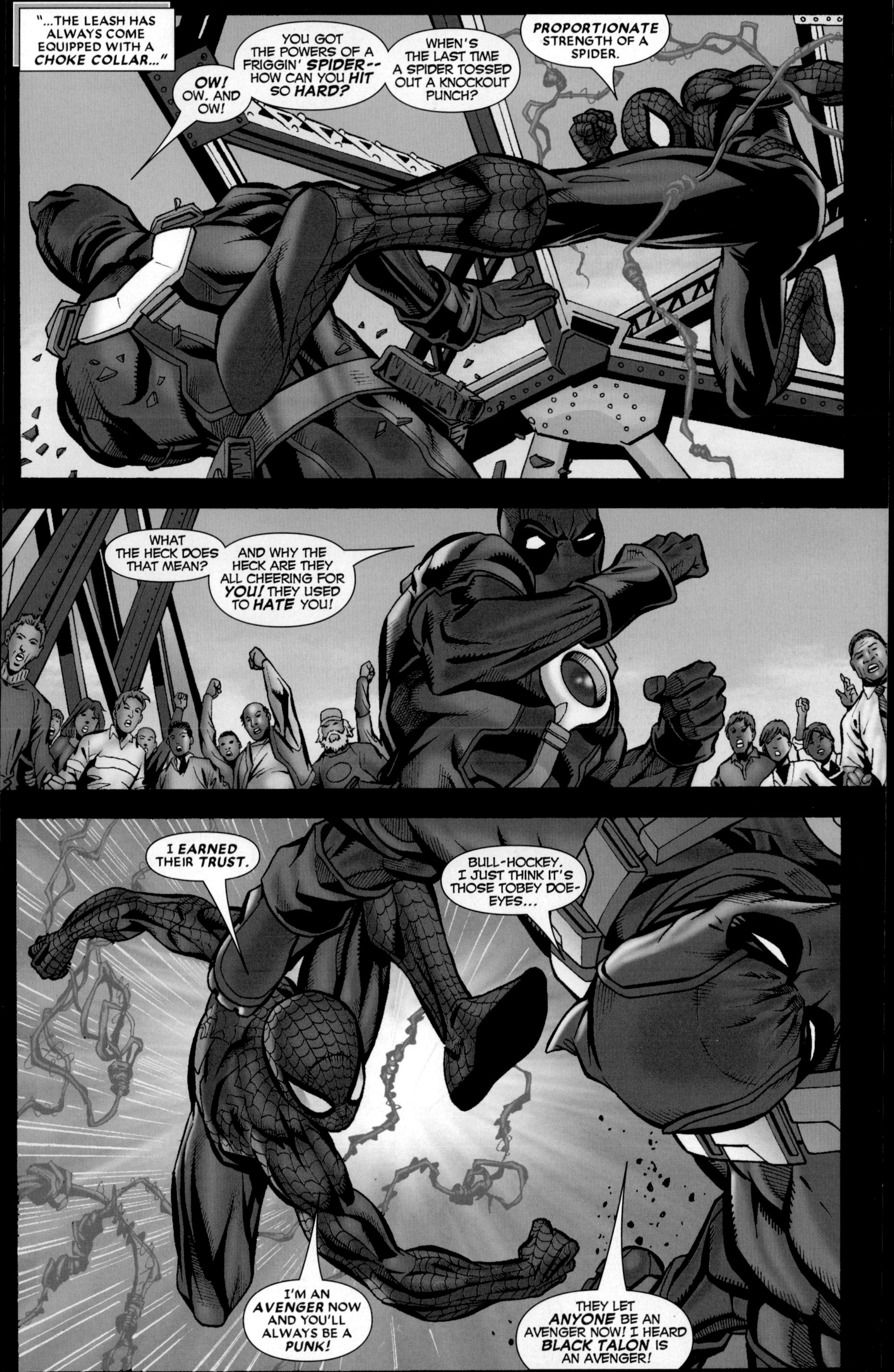
"...THE LEASH HAS ALWAYS COME EQUIPPED WITH A CHOKE COLLAR..."
OW! OW. AND OW!
YOU GOT THE POWERS OF A FRIGGIN' SPIDER-- HOW CAN YOU HIT SO HARD?
WHEN'S THE LAST TIME A SPIDER TOSSED OUT A KNOCKOUT PUNCH?
PROPORTIONATE STRENGTH OF A SPIDER.
WHAT THE HECK DOES THAT MEAN?
AND WHY THE HECK ARE THEY ALL CHEERING FOR YOU! THEY USED TO HATE YOU!
I EARNED THEIR TRUST.
BULL-HOCKEY. I JUST THINK IT'S THOSE TOBEY DOE-EYES...
I'M AN AVENGER NOW AND YOU'LL ALWAYS BE A PUNK!
THEY LET ANYONE BE AN AVENGER NOW! I HEARD BLACK TALON IS AN AVENGER!

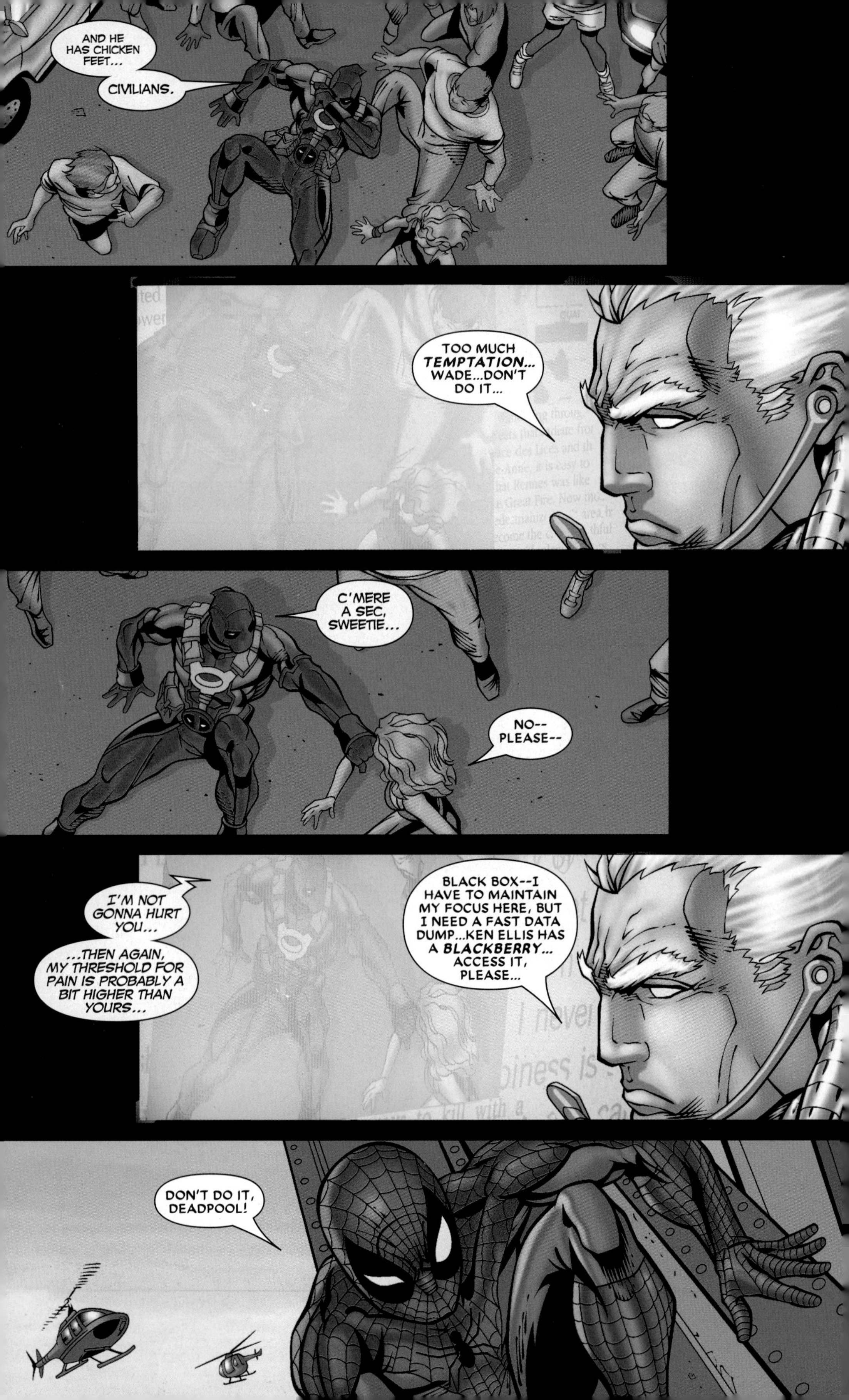
AND HE HAS CHICKEN FEET...
CIVILIANS.
TOO MUCH TEMPTATION... WADE...DON'T DO IT...
C'MERE A SEC, SWEETIE...
NO-- PLEASE--
I'M NOT GONNA HURT YOU...
...THEN AGAIN, MY THRESHOLD FOR PAIN IS PROBABLY A BIT HIGHER THAN YOURS...
BLACK BOX--I HAVE TO MAINTAIN MY FOCUS HERE, BUT I NEED A FAST DATA DUMP...KEN ELLIS HAS A BLACKBERRY... ACCESS IT, PLEASE...
DON'T DO IT, DEADPOOL!

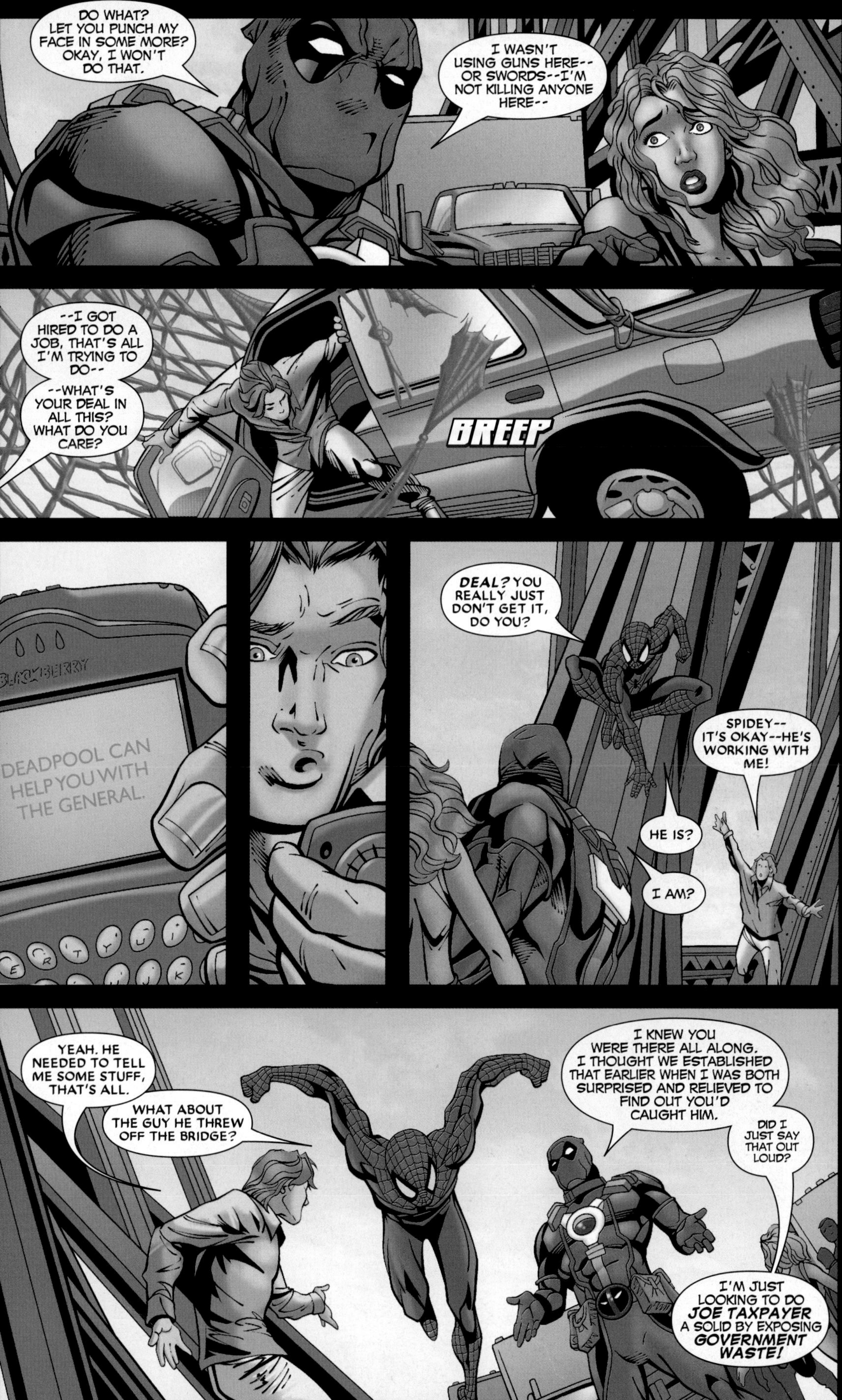

DO WHAT? LET YOU PUNCH MY FACE IN SOME MORE? OKAY, I WON'T DO THAT.
I WASN'T USING GUNS HERE-- OR SWORDS--I'M NOT KILLING ANYONE HERE--
--I GOT HIRED TO DO A JOB, THAT'S ALL I'M TRYING TO DO--
--WHAT'S YOUR DEAL IN ALL THIS? WHAT DO YOU CARE?
BREEP
BLACKBERRY
DEADPOOL CAN HELP YOU WITH THE GENERAL.
DEAL? YOU REALLY JUST DON'T GET IT, DO YOU?
SPIDEY-- IT'S OKAY--HE'S WORKING WITH ME!
HE IS?
I AM?
YEAH. HE NEEDED TO TELL ME SOME STUFF, THAT'S ALL.
WHAT ABOUT THE GUY HE THREW OFF THE BRIDGE?
I KNEW YOU WERE THERE ALL ALONG. I THOUGHT WE ESTABLISHED THAT EARLIER WHEN I WAS BOTH SURPRISED AND RELIEVED TO FIND OUT YOU'D CAUGHT HIM.
DID I JUST SAY THAT OUT LOUD?
I'M JUST LOOKING TO DO JOE TAXPAYER A SOLID BY EXPOSING GOVERNMENT WASTE!

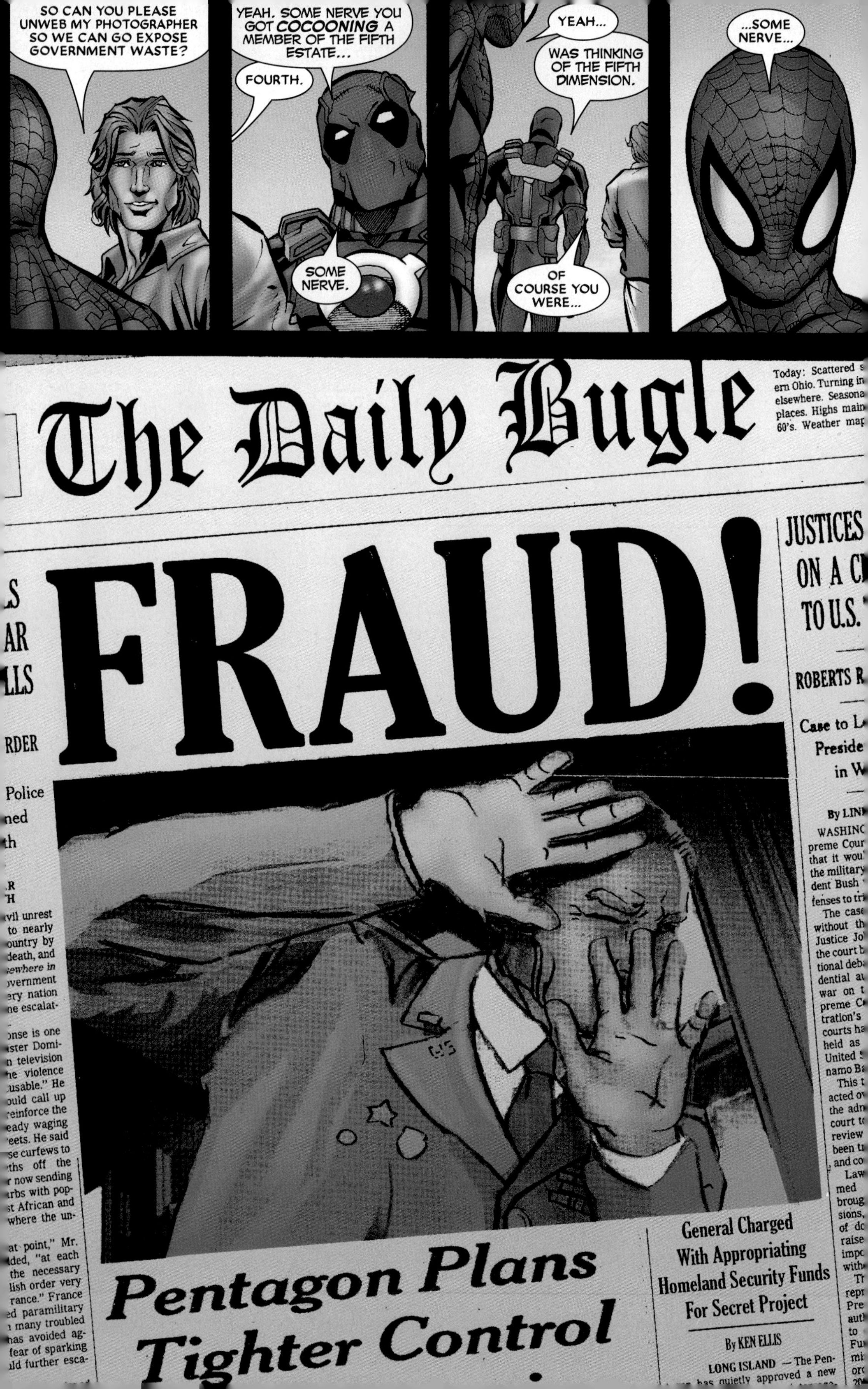

SO CAN YOU PLEASE UNWEB MY PHOTOGRAPHER SO WE CAN GO EXPOSE GOVERNMENT WASTE?
YEAH. SOME NERVE YOU GOT *COCOONING* A MEMBER OF THE FIFTH ESTATE...
FOURTH.
SOME NERVE.
YEAH...
WAS THINKING OF THE FIFTH DIMENSION.
OF COURSE YOU WERE...
...SOME NERVE...
The Daily Bugle
Today: Scattered
FRAUD!
JUSTICES
Pentagon Plans Tighter Control
General Charged With Appropriating Homeland Security Funds For Secret Project
By KEN ELLIS
LONG ISLAND —The Pen-

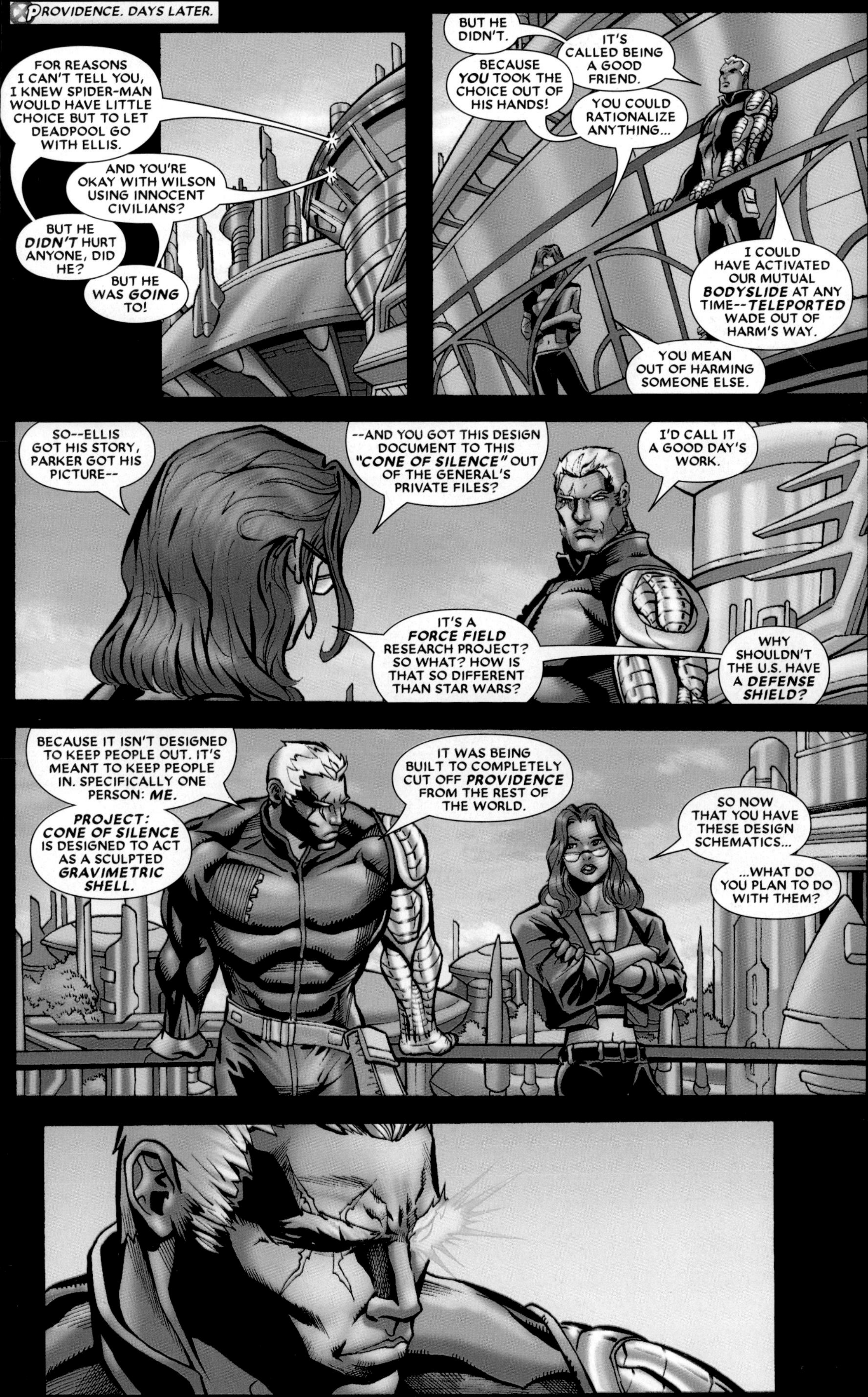
PROVIDENCE. DAYS LATER.
FOR REASONS I CAN'T TELL YOU, I KNEW SPIDER-MAN WOULD HAVE LITTLE CHOICE BUT TO LET DEADPOOL GO WITH ELLIS.
AND YOU'RE OKAY WITH WILSON USING INNOCENT CIVILIANS?
BUT HE DIDN'T HURT ANYONE, DID HE?
BUT HE WAS GOING TO!
BUT HE DIDN'T.
BECAUSE YOU TOOK THE CHOICE OUT OF HIS HANDS!
IT'S CALLED BEING A GOOD FRIEND.
YOU COULD RATIONALIZE ANYTHING...
I COULD HAVE ACTIVATED OUR MUTUAL BODYSLIDE AT ANY TIME--TELEPORTED WADE OUT OF HARM'S WAY.
YOU MEAN OUT OF HARMING SOMEONE ELSE.
SO--ELLIS GOT HIS STORY, PARKER GOT HIS PICTURE--
--AND YOU GOT THIS DESIGN DOCUMENT TO THIS "CONE OF SILENCE" OUT OF THE GENERAL'S PRIVATE FILES?
I'D CALL IT A GOOD DAY'S WORK.
IT'S A FORCE FIELD RESEARCH PROJECT? SO WHAT? HOW IS THAT SO DIFFERENT THAN STAR WARS?
WHY SHOULDN'T THE U.S. HAVE A DEFENSE SHIELD?
BECAUSE IT ISN'T DESIGNED TO KEEP PEOPLE OUT. IT'S MEANT TO KEEP PEOPLE IN. SPECIFICALLY ONE PERSON: ME.
PROJECT: CONE OF SILENCE IS DESIGNED TO ACT AS A SCULPTED GRAVIMETRIC SHELL.
IT WAS BEING BUILT TO COMPLETELY CUT OFF PROVIDENCE FROM THE REST OF THE WORLD.
SO NOW THAT YOU HAVE THESE DESIGN SCHEMATICS...
...WHAT DO YOU PLAN TO DO WITH THEM?

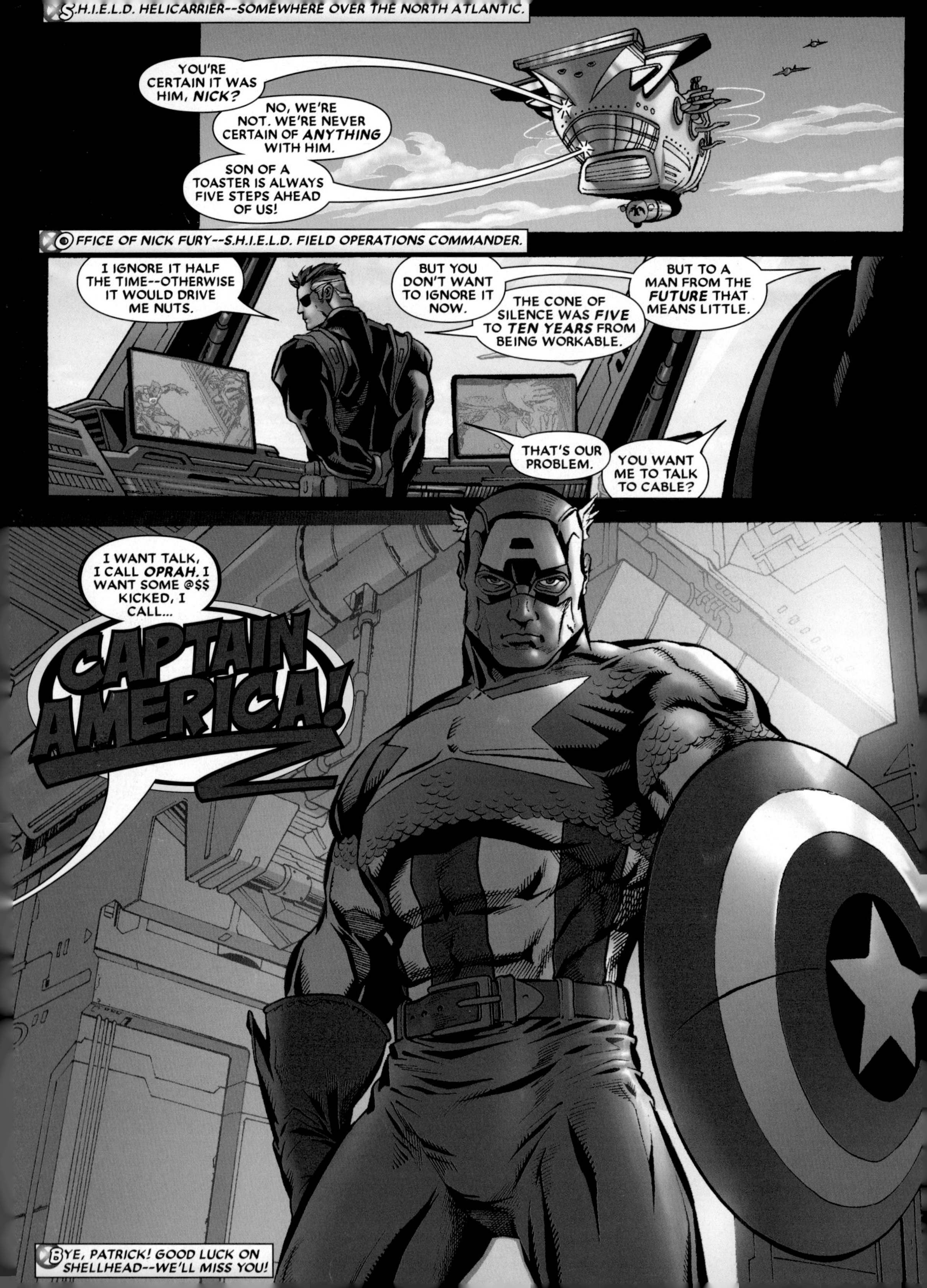
S.H.I.E.L.D. HELICARRIER--SOMEWHERE OVER THE NORTH ATLANTIC.
YOU'RE CERTAIN IT WAS HIM, NICK?
NO, WE'RE NOT. WE'RE NEVER CERTAIN OF ANYTHING WITH HIM.
SON OF A TOASTER IS ALWAYS FIVE STEPS AHEAD OF US!
OFFICE OF NICK FURY--S.H.I.E.L.D. FIELD OPERATIONS COMMANDER.
I IGNORE IT HALF THE TIME--OTHERWISE IT WOULD DRIVE ME NUTS.
BUT YOU DON'T WANT TO IGNORE IT NOW.
THE CONE OF SILENCE WAS FIVE TO TEN YEARS FROM BEING WORKABLE.
BUT TO A MAN FROM THE FUTURE THAT MEANS LITTLE.
THAT'S OUR PROBLEM.
YOU WANT ME TO TALK TO CABLE?
I WANT TALK, I CALL OPRAH. I WANT SOME @$$ KICKED, I CALL...
CAPTAIN AMERICA!
BYE, PATRICK! GOOD LUCK ON SHELLHEAD--WE'LL MISS YOU!

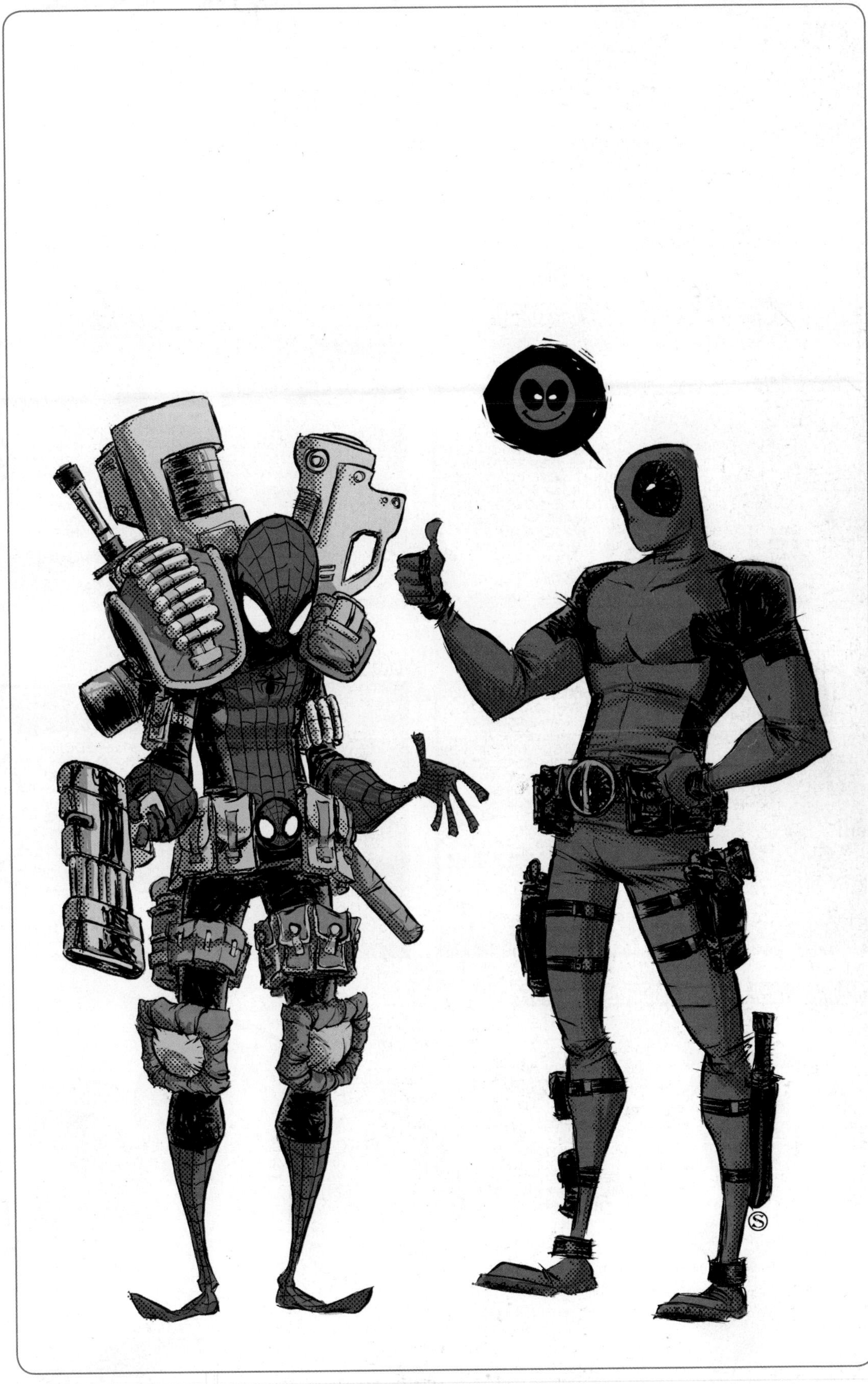

AMAZING SPIDER-MAN #611

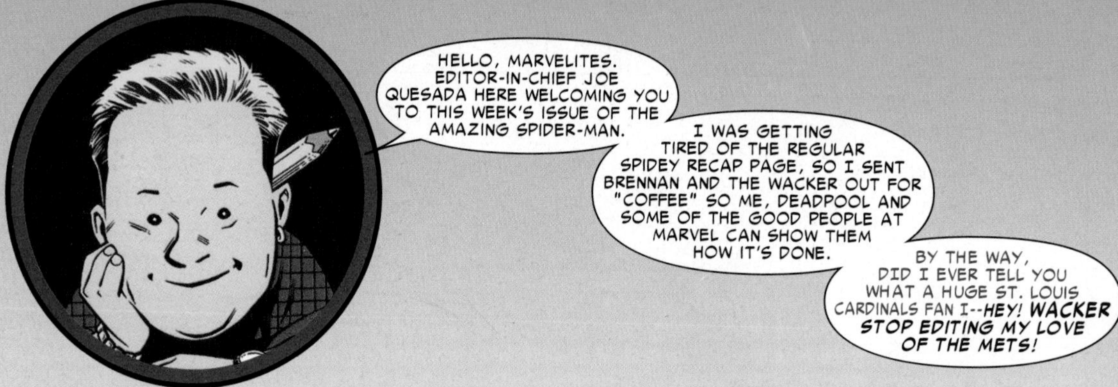
HELLO, MARVELITES. EDITOR-IN-CHIEF JOE QUESADA HERE WELCOMING YOU TO THIS WEEK'S ISSUE OF THE AMAZING SPIDER-MAN.
I WAS GETTING TIRED OF THE REGULAR SPIDEY RECAP PAGE, SO I SENT BRENNAN AND THE WACKER OUT FOR "COFFEE" SO ME, DEADPOOL AND SOME OF THE GOOD PEOPLE AT MARVEL CAN SHOW THEM HOW IT'S DONE.
BY THE WAY, DID I EVER TELL YOU WHAT A HUGE ST. LOUIS CARDINALS FAN I--*HEY! WACKER STOP EDITING MY LOVE OF THE METS!*

EXECUTIVE EDITOR/RAGE-A-HOLIC TOM BREVOORT!

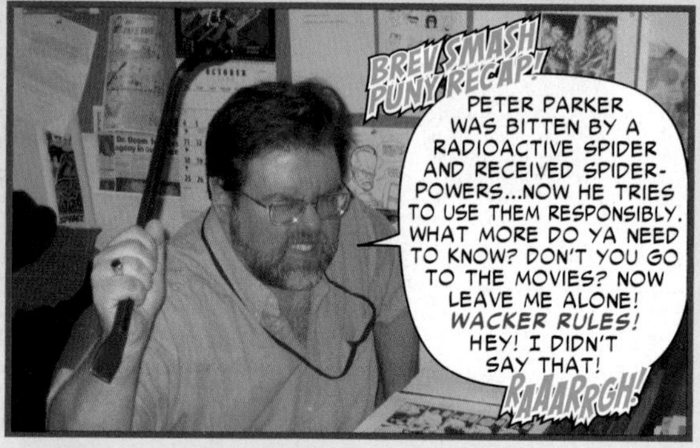
BREV SMASH PUNY RECAP!
PETER PARKER WAS BITTEN BY A RADIOACTIVE SPIDER AND RECEIVED SPIDER-POWERS...NOW HE TRIES TO USE THEM RESPONSIBLY. WHAT MORE DO YA NEED TO KNOW? DON'T YOU GO TO THE MOVIES? NOW LEAVE ME ALONE! *WACKER RULES!* HEY! I DIDN'T SAY THAT!
RAAARRGH!

BULLPEN SCAN-A-HOLIC RANDALL MILLER!

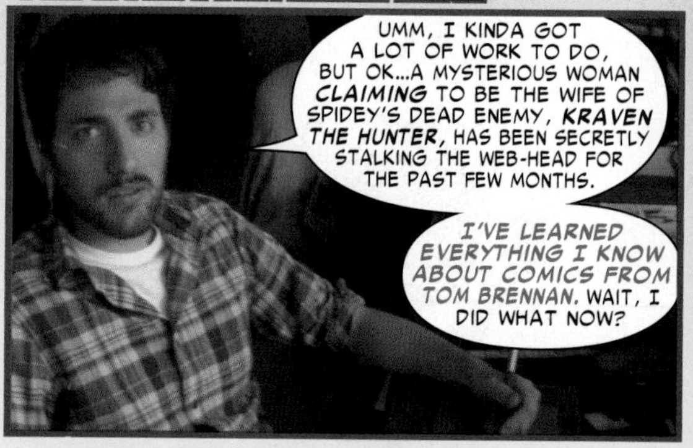
UMM, I KINDA GOT A LOT OF WORK TO DO, BUT OK...A MYSTERIOUS WOMAN *CLAIMING* TO BE THE WIFE OF SPIDEY'S DEAD ENEMY, *KRAVEN THE HUNTER,* HAS BEEN SECRETLY STALKING THE WEB-HEAD FOR THE PAST FEW MONTHS.
I'VE LEARNED EVERYTHING I KNOW ABOUT COMICS FROM TOM BRENNAN. WAIT, I DID WHAT NOW?

X-EDITOR/SNARK-A-HOLIC JEANINE SCHAEFER

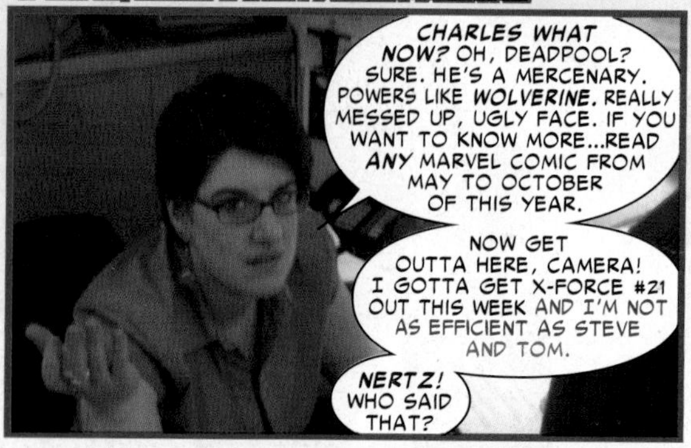
CHARLES WHAT NOW? OH, DEADPOOL? SURE. HE'S A MERCENARY. POWERS LIKE *WOLVERINE.* REALLY MESSED UP, UGLY FACE. IF YOU WANT TO KNOW MORE...READ *ANY* MARVEL COMIC FROM MAY TO OCTOBER OF THIS YEAR.
NOW GET OUTTA HERE, CAMERA! I GOTTA GET X-FORCE #21 OUT THIS WEEK AND I'M NOT AS EFFICIENT AS STEVE AND TOM.
NERTZ! WHO SAID THAT?

PRODUCTION MANAGER SUE CRESPI

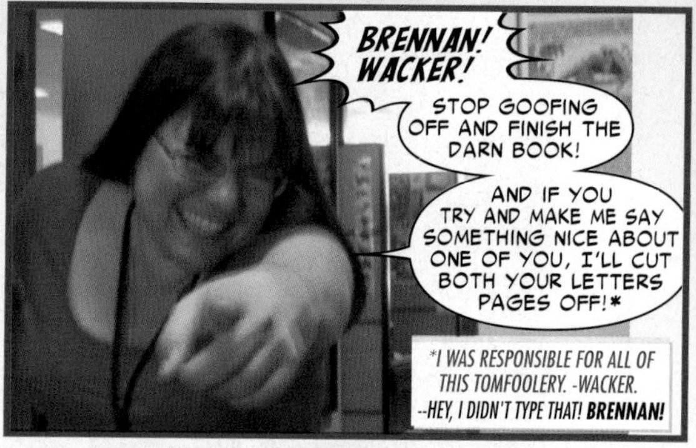
BRENNAN! WACKER!
STOP GOOFING OFF AND FINISH THE DARN BOOK!
AND IF YOU TRY AND MAKE ME SAY SOMETHING NICE ABOUT ONE OF YOU, I'LL CUT BOTH YOUR LETTERS PAGES OFF!*
*I WAS RESPONSIBLE FOR ALL OF THIS TOMFOOLERY. -WACKER. --HEY, I DIDN'T TYPE THAT! **BRENNAN!***

ALL RIGHT THEN...LET'S GET MOVING, BUT FIRST...

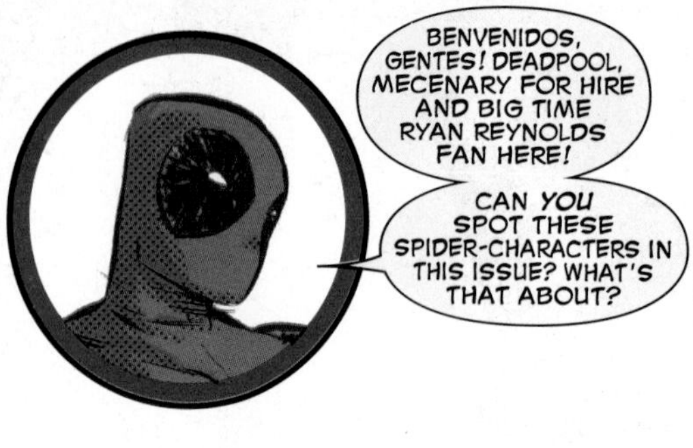
BENVENIDOS, GENTES! DEADPOOL, MECENARY FOR HIRE AND BIG TIME RYAN REYNOLDS FAN HERE!
CAN *YOU* SPOT THESE SPIDER-CHARACTERS IN THIS ISSUE? WHAT'S THAT ABOUT?

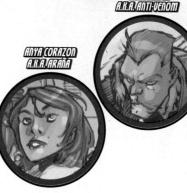

EDDIE BROCK
A.K.A. ANTI-VENOM

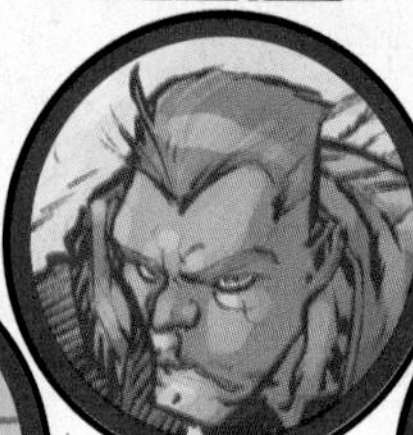

ANYA CORAZON
A.K.A. ARAÑA

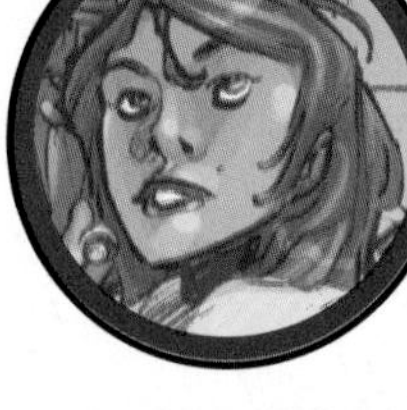

MATTIE FRANKLIN
A.K.A. SPIDER-WOMAN

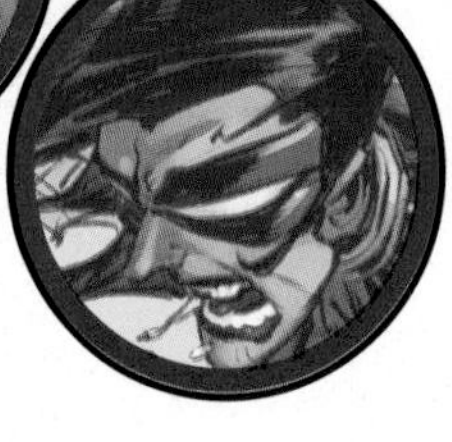

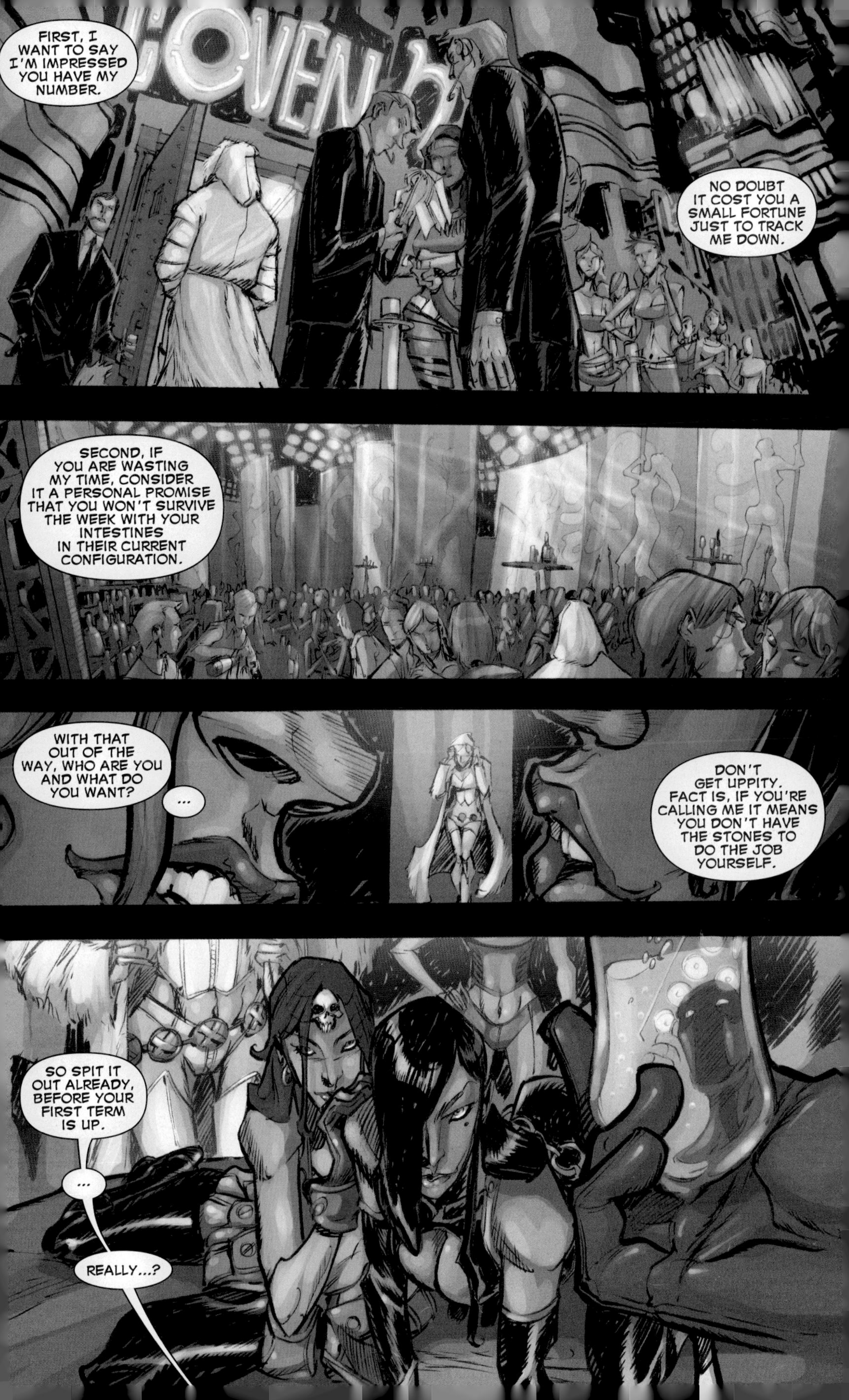
COVEN
FIRST, I WANT TO SAY I'M IMPRESSED YOU HAVE MY NUMBER.
NO DOUBT IT COST YOU A SMALL FORTUNE JUST TO TRACK ME DOWN.
SECOND, IF YOU ARE WASTING MY TIME, CONSIDER IT A PERSONAL PROMISE THAT YOU WON'T SURVIVE THE WEEK WITH YOUR INTESTINES IN THEIR CURRENT CONFIGURATION.
WITH THAT OUT OF THE WAY, WHO ARE YOU AND WHAT DO YOU WANT?
...
DON'T GET UPPITY. FACT IS, IF YOU'RE CALLING ME IT MEANS YOU DON'T HAVE THE STONES TO DO THE JOB YOURSELF.
SO SPIT IT OUT ALREADY, BEFORE YOUR FIRST TERM IS UP.
...
REALLY...?

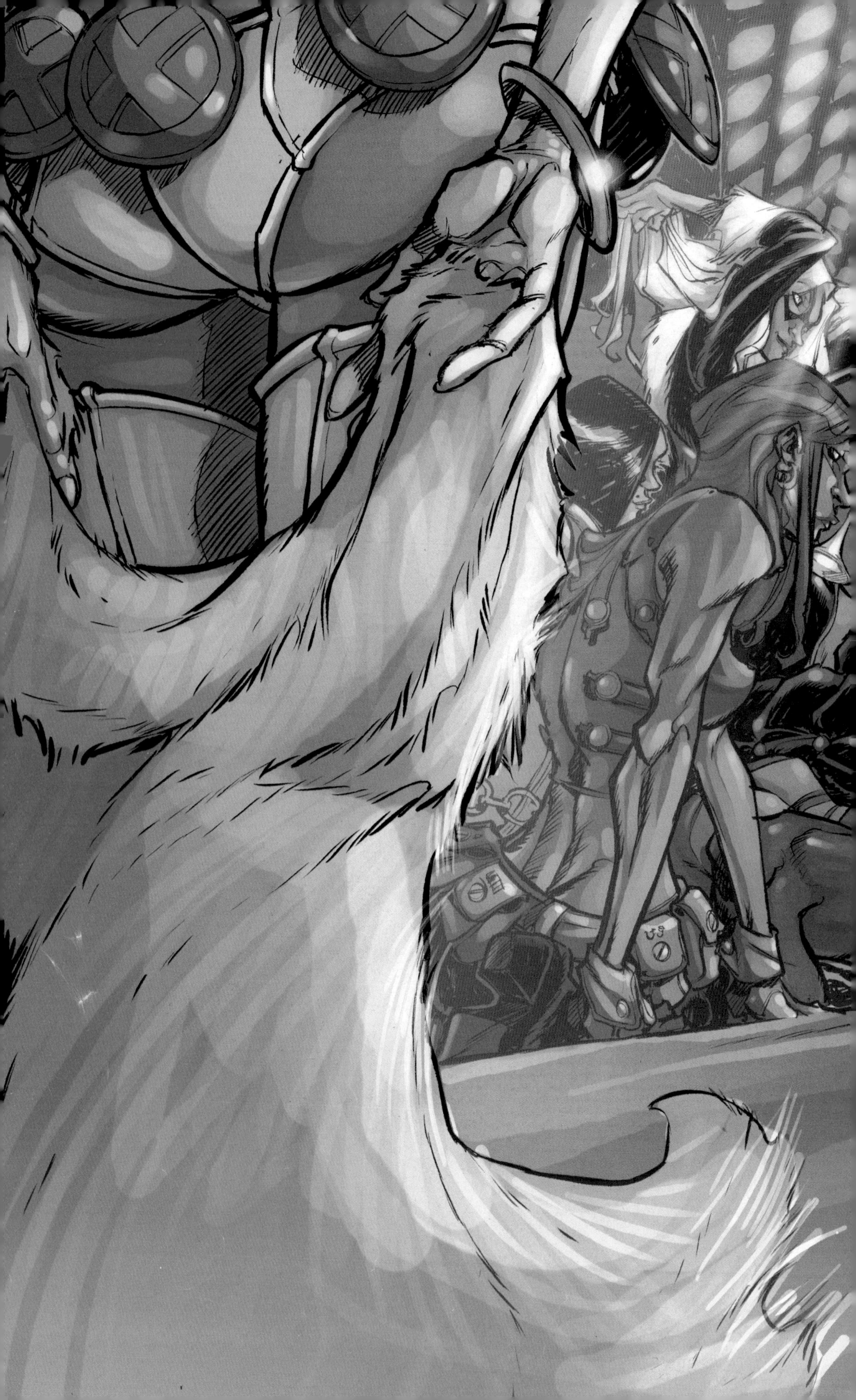

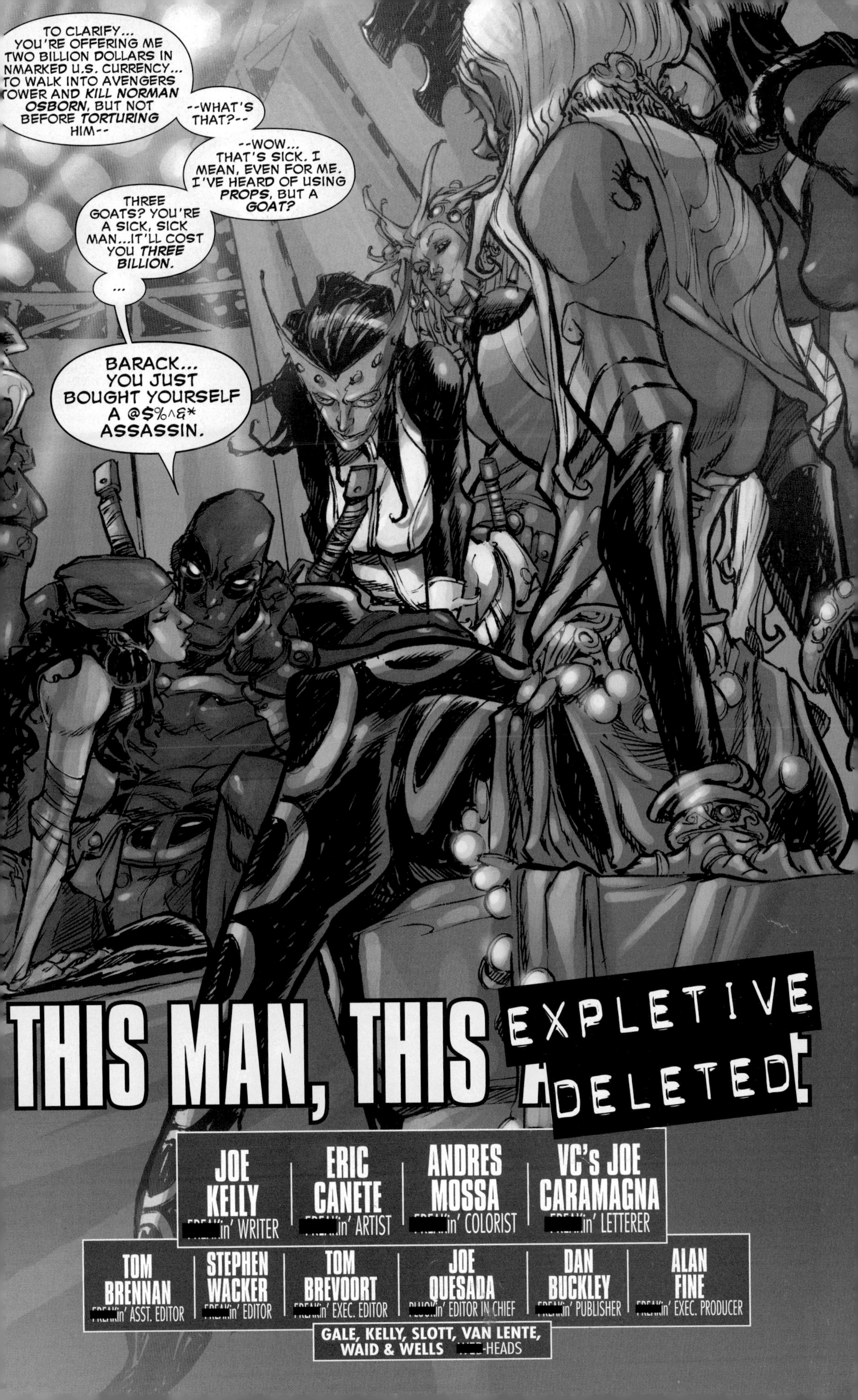

TO CLARIFY... YOU'RE OFFERING ME TWO BILLION DOLLARS IN NMARKED U.S. CURRENCY... TO WALK INTO AVENGERS TOWER AND KILL NORMAN OSBORN, BUT NOT BEFORE TORTURING HIM--
--WHAT'S THAT?--
--WOW... THAT'S SICK. I MEAN, EVEN FOR ME. I'VE HEARD OF USING PROPS, BUT A GOAT?
THREE GOATS? YOU'RE A SICK, SICK MAN...IT'LL COST YOU THREE BILLION.
...
BARACK... YOU JUST BOUGHT YOURSELF A @$%^&* ASSASSIN.
THIS MAN, THIS EXPLETIVE DELETED
JOE KELLY [redacted]in' WRITER
ERIC CANETE [redacted]in' ARTIST
ANDRES MOSSA [redacted]in' COLORIST
VC's JOE CARAMAGNA [redacted]in' LETTERER
TOM BRENNAN [redacted]in' ASST. EDITOR
STEPHEN WACKER [redacted]in' EDITOR
TOM BREVOORT [redacted]in' EXEC. EDITOR
JOE QUESADA [redacted]in' EDITOR IN CHIEF
DAN BUCKLEY [redacted]in' PUBLISHER
ALAN FINE [redacted]in' EXEC. PRODUCER
GALE, KELLY, SLOTT, VAN LENTE, WAID & WELLS [redacted]-HEADS

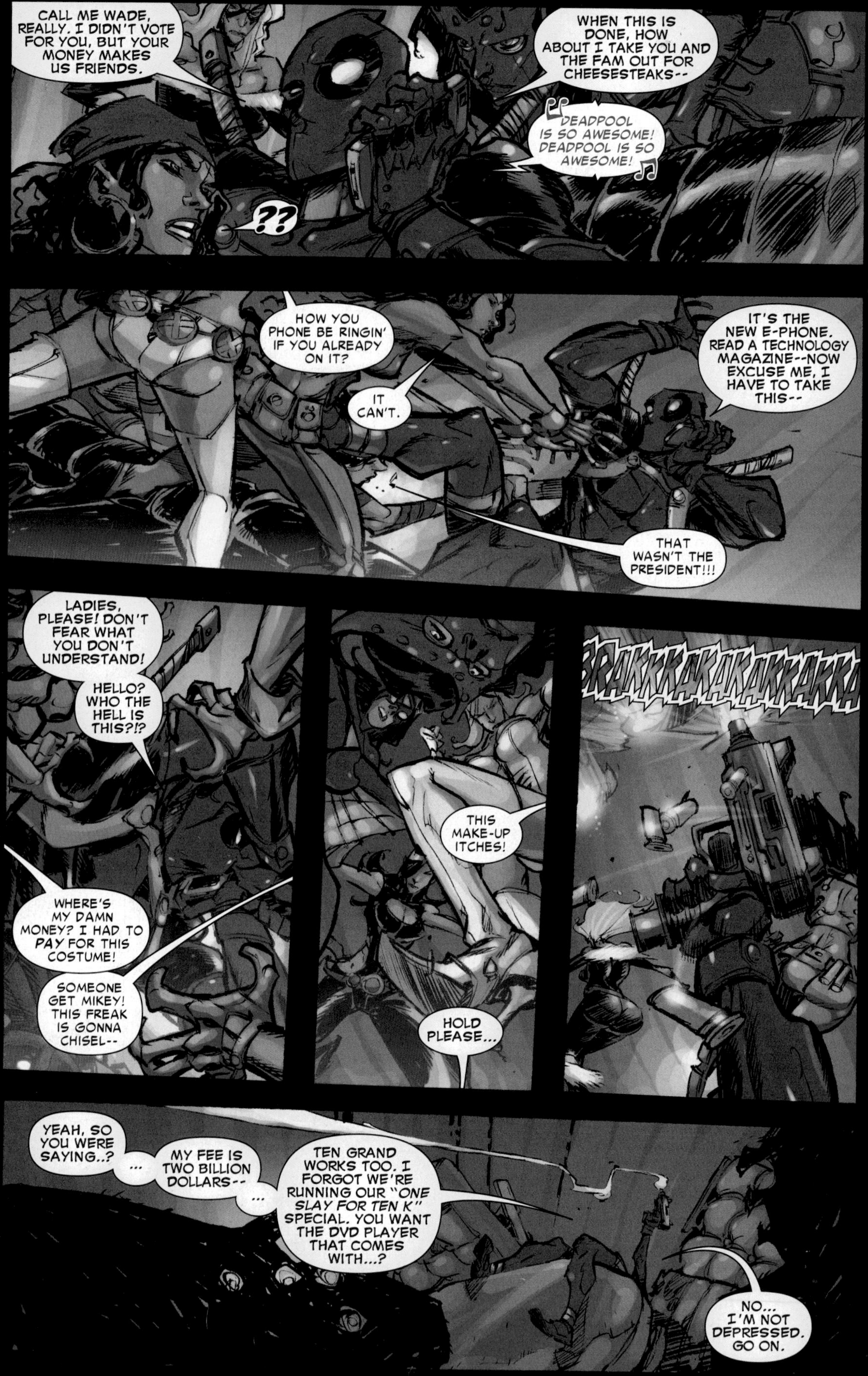
CALL ME WADE, REALLY. I DIDN'T VOTE FOR YOU, BUT YOUR MONEY MAKES US FRIENDS.
WHEN THIS IS DONE, HOW ABOUT I TAKE YOU AND THE FAM OUT FOR CHEESESTEAKS--
DEADPOOL IS SO AWESOME! DEADPOOL IS SO AWESOME!
??
HOW YOU PHONE BE RINGIN' IF YOU ALREADY ON IT?
IT CAN'T.
IT'S THE NEW E-PHONE. READ A TECHNOLOGY MAGAZINE--NOW EXCUSE ME, I HAVE TO TAKE THIS--
THAT WASN'T THE PRESIDENT!!!
LADIES, PLEASE! DON'T FEAR WHAT YOU DON'T UNDERSTAND!
HELLO? WHO THE HELL IS THIS?!?
WHERE'S MY DAMN MONEY? I HAD TO PAY FOR THIS COSTUME!
SOMEONE GET MIKEY! THIS FREAK IS GONNA CHISEL--
THIS MAKE-UP ITCHES!
HOLD PLEASE...
BRAKKKAKAKAKKAKKA
YEAH, SO YOU WERE SAYING..?
...
MY FEE IS TWO BILLION DOLLARS--
...
TEN GRAND WORKS TOO. I FORGOT WE'RE RUNNING OUR "ONE SLAY FOR TEN K" SPECIAL. YOU WANT THE DVD PLAYER THAT COMES WITH...?
NO... I'M NOT DEPRESSED. GO ON.

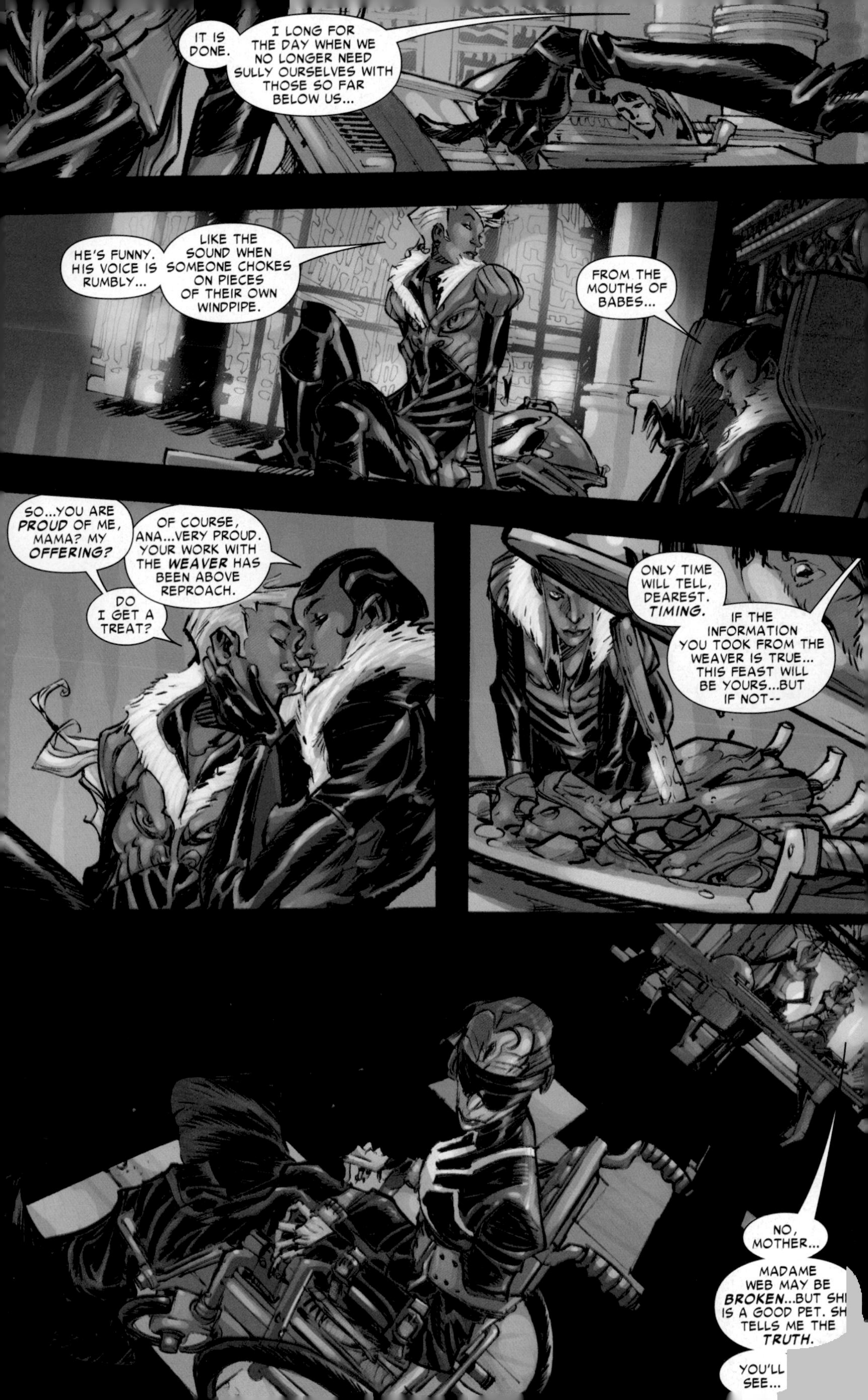

IT IS DONE.
I LONG FOR THE DAY WHEN WE NO LONGER NEED SULLY OURSELVES WITH THOSE SO FAR BELOW US...
HE'S FUNNY. HIS VOICE IS RUMBLY...
LIKE THE SOUND WHEN SOMEONE CHOKES ON PIECES OF THEIR OWN WINDPIPE.
FROM THE MOUTHS OF BABES...
SO...YOU ARE *PROUD* OF ME, MAMA? MY *OFFERING?*
DO I GET A TREAT?
OF COURSE, ANA...VERY PROUD. YOUR WORK WITH THE *WEAVER* HAS BEEN ABOVE REPROACH.
ONLY TIME WILL TELL, DEAREST. *TIMING.*
IF THE INFORMATION YOU TOOK FROM THE WEAVER IS TRUE... THIS FEAST WILL BE YOURS...BUT IF NOT--
NO, MOTHER...
MADAME WEB MAY BE *BROKEN*...BUT SH IS A GOOD PET. SH TELLS ME THE *TRUTH.*
YOU'LL SEE...

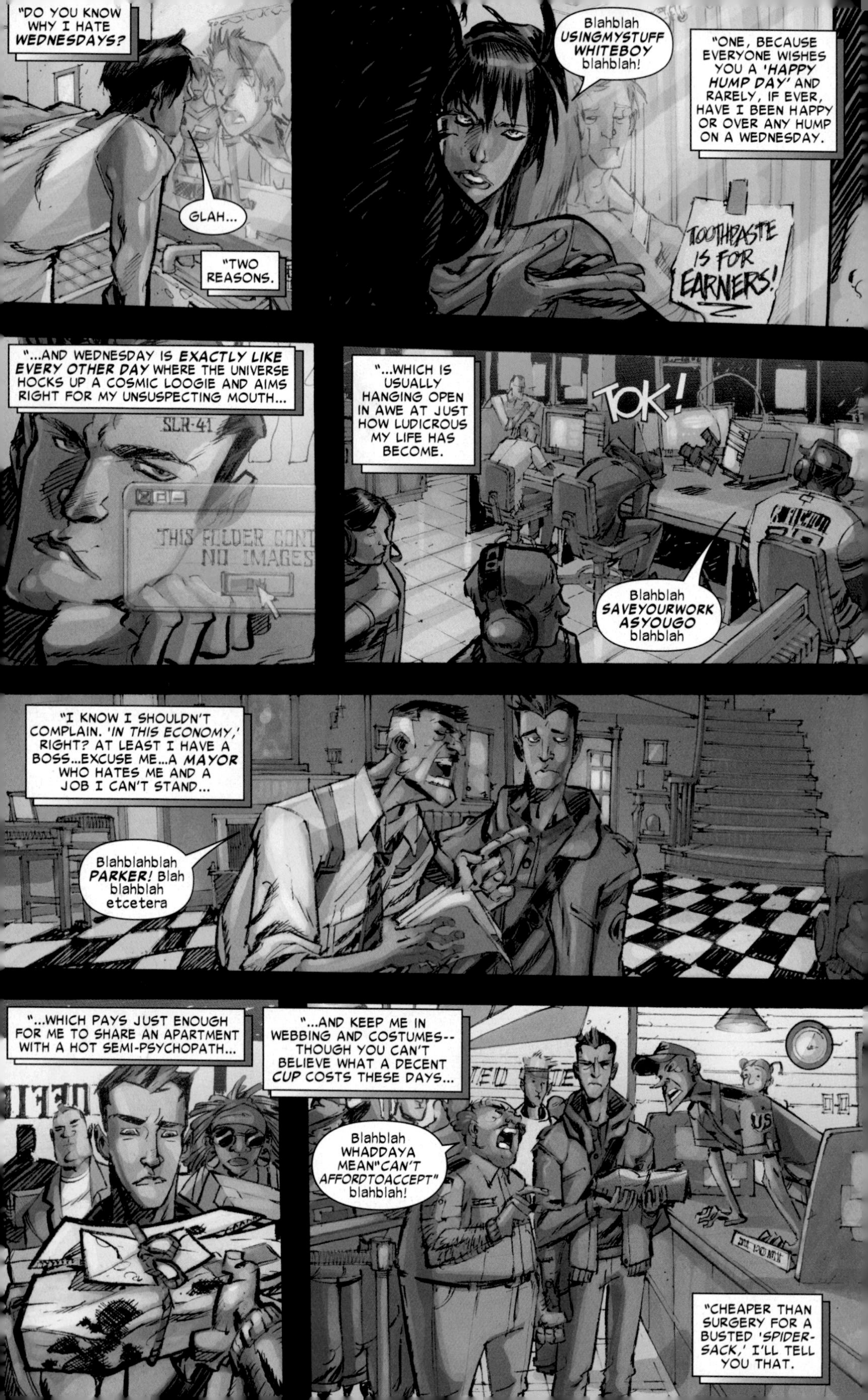

"DO YOU KNOW WHY I HATE *WEDNESDAYS?*
GLAH...
"TWO REASONS.
Blahblah *USINGMYSTUFF WHITEBOY* blahblah!
"ONE, BECAUSE EVERYONE WISHES YOU A *'HAPPY HUMP DAY'* AND RARELY, IF EVER, HAVE I BEEN HAPPY OR OVER ANY HUMP ON A WEDNESDAY.
TOOTHPASTE IS FOR EARNERS!
"...AND WEDNESDAY IS *EXACTLY LIKE EVERY OTHER DAY* WHERE THE UNIVERSE HOCKS UP A COSMIC LOOGIE AND AIMS RIGHT FOR MY UNSUSPECTING MOUTH...
SLR-41
"...WHICH IS USUALLY HANGING OPEN IN AWE AT JUST HOW LUDICROUS MY LIFE HAS BECOME.
TOK!
Blahblah *SAVEYOURWORK ASYOUGO* blahblah
"I KNOW I SHOULDN'T COMPLAIN. *'IN THIS ECONOMY,'* RIGHT? AT LEAST I HAVE A BOSS...EXCUSE ME...A *MAYOR* WHO HATES ME AND A JOB I CAN'T STAND...
Blahblahblah *PARKER!* Blah blahblah etcetera
"...WHICH PAYS JUST ENOUGH FOR ME TO SHARE AN APARTMENT WITH A HOT SEMI-PSYCHOPATH...
"...AND KEEP ME IN WEBBING AND COSTUMES--THOUGH YOU CAN'T BELIEVE WHAT A DECENT *CUP* COSTS THESE DAYS...
Blahblah WHADDAYA MEAN"*CAN'T AFFORDTOACCEPT*" blahblah!
"CHEAPER THAN SURGERY FOR A BUSTED *'SPIDER-SACK,'* I'LL TELL YOU THAT.

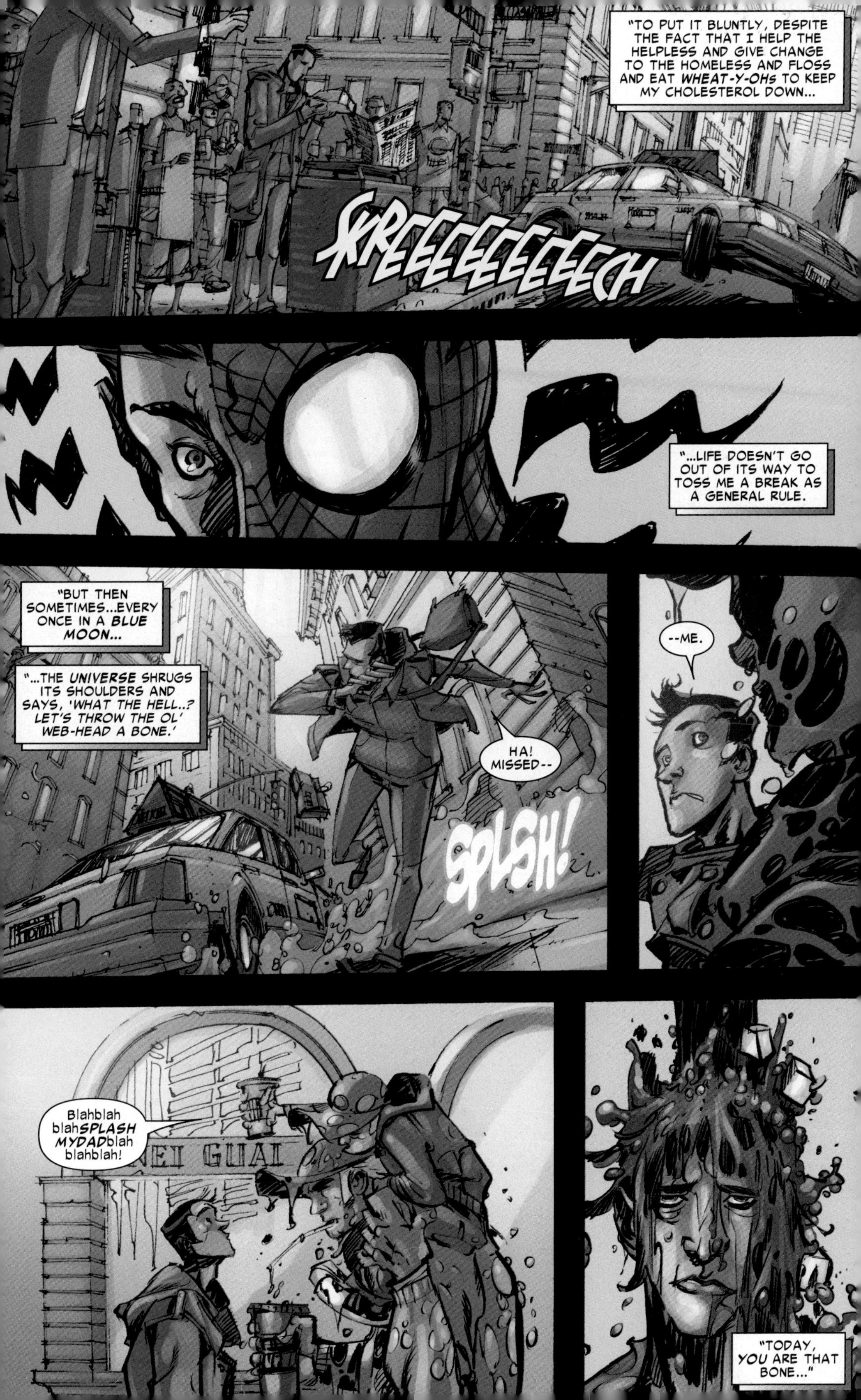

"TO PUT IT BLUNTLY, DESPITE THE FACT THAT I HELP THE HELPLESS AND GIVE CHANGE TO THE HOMELESS AND FLOSS AND EAT *WHEAT-Y-OHs* TO KEEP MY CHOLESTEROL DOWN...
SKREEEEEEEEEECH
"...LIFE DOESN'T GO OUT OF ITS WAY TO TOSS ME A BREAK AS A GENERAL RULE.
"BUT THEN SOMETIMES...EVERY ONCE IN A *BLUE MOON*...
"...THE *UNIVERSE* SHRUGS ITS SHOULDERS AND SAYS, '*WHAT THE HELL..? LET'S THROW THE OL' WEB-HEAD A BONE.*'
HA! MISSED--
SPLSH!
--ME.
Blahblah blah**SPLASH MYDAD**blah blahblah!
NEI GUAI
"TODAY, *YOU* ARE THAT BONE..."

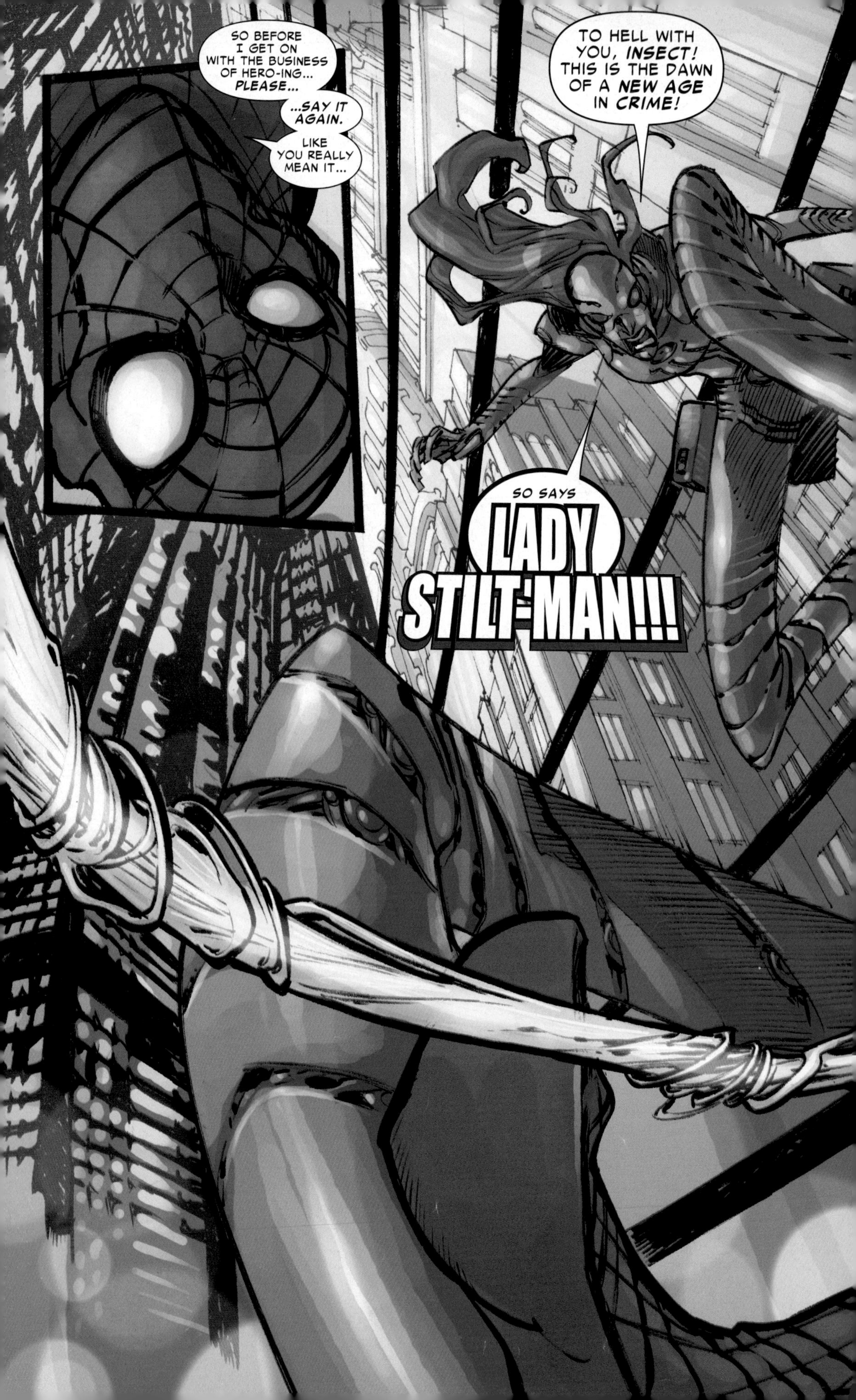
SO BEFORE I GET ON WITH THE BUSINESS OF HERO-ING... PLEASE...
...SAY IT AGAIN.
LIKE YOU REALLY MEAN IT...
TO HELL WITH YOU, INSECT! THIS IS THE DAWN OF A NEW AGE IN CRIME!
SO SAYS
LADY STILT-MAN!!!

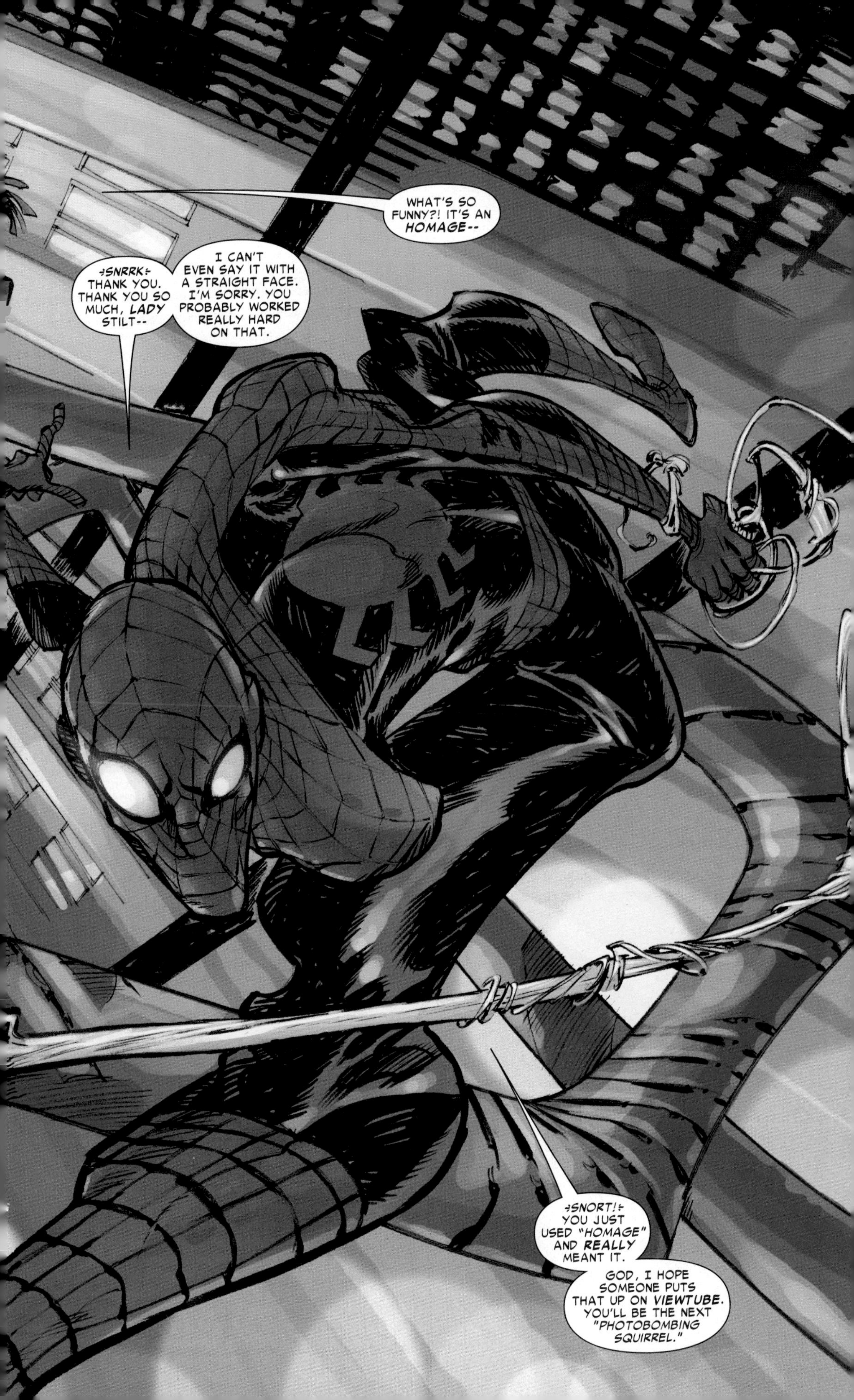
WHAT'S SO FUNNY?! IT'S AN HOMAGE--
I CAN'T EVEN SAY IT WITH A STRAIGHT FACE. I'M SORRY. YOU PROBABLY WORKED REALLY HARD ON THAT.
⇒SNRRK⇐ THANK YOU. THANK YOU SO MUCH, LADY STILT--
⇒SNORT!⇐ YOU JUST USED "HOMAGE" AND REALLY MEANT IT.
GOD, I HOPE SOMEONE PUTS THAT UP ON VIEWTUBE. YOU'LL BE THE NEXT "PHOTOBOMBING SQUIRREL."

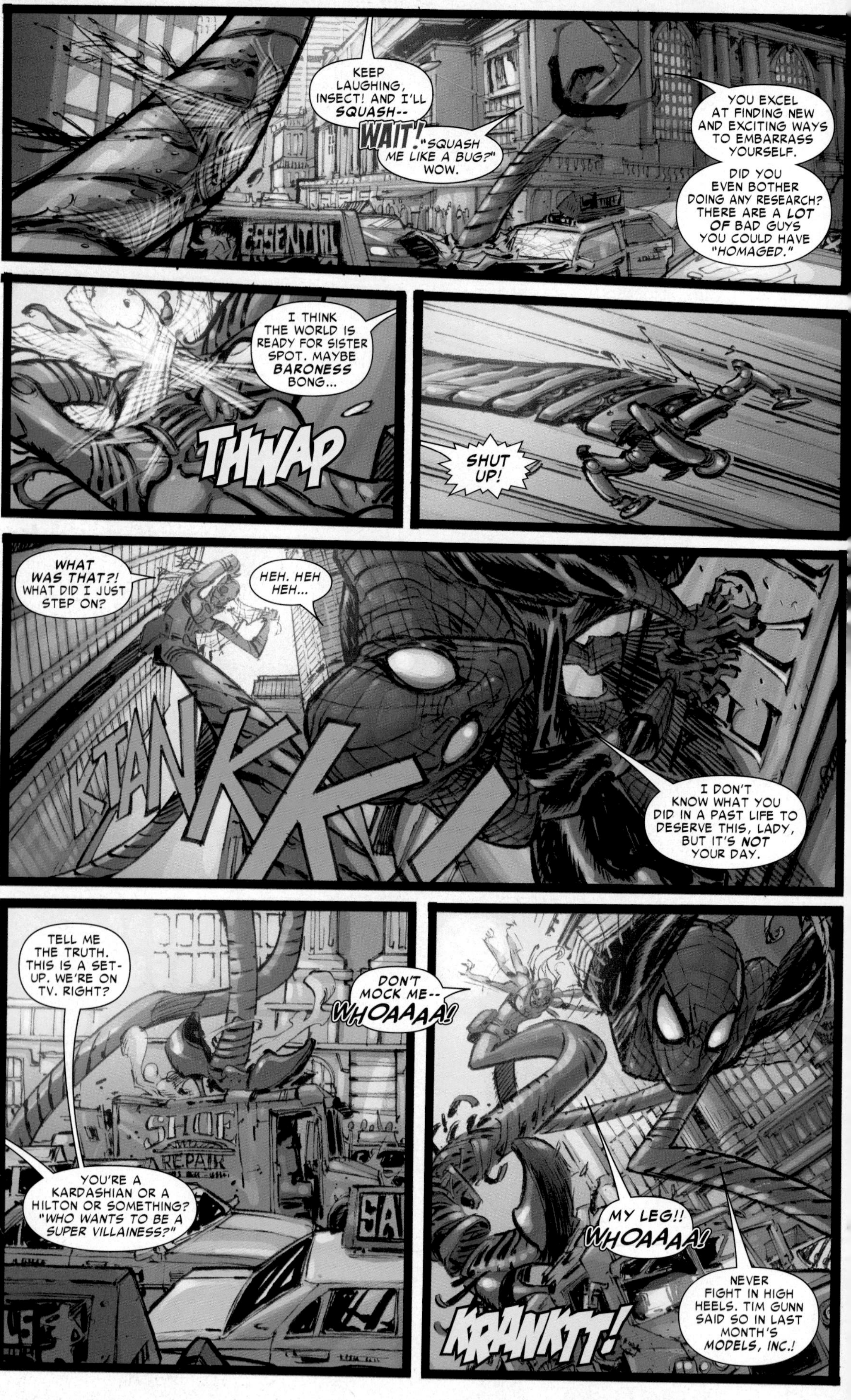
KEEP LAUGHING, INSECT! AND I'LL SQUASH--
WAIT! "SQUASH ME LIKE A BUG?" WOW.
YOU EXCEL AT FINDING NEW AND EXCITING WAYS TO EMBARRASS YOURSELF.
DID YOU EVEN BOTHER DOING ANY RESEARCH? THERE ARE A LOT OF BAD GUYS YOU COULD HAVE "HOMAGED."
ESSENTIAL
I THINK THE WORLD IS READY FOR SISTER SPOT. MAYBE BARONESS BONG...
THWAP
SHUT UP!
WHAT WAS THAT?! WHAT DID I JUST STEP ON?
HEH. HEH HEH...
KTANKK
I DON'T KNOW WHAT YOU DID IN A PAST LIFE TO DESERVE THIS, LADY, BUT IT'S NOT YOUR DAY.
TELL ME THE TRUTH. THIS IS A SET-UP. WE'RE ON TV. RIGHT?
DON'T MOCK ME-- WHOAAAA!
SHOE REPAIR
YOU'RE A KARDASHIAN OR A HILTON OR SOMETHING? "WHO WANTS TO BE A SUPER VILLAINESS?"
MY LEG!! WHOAAAA!
NEVER FIGHT IN HIGH HEELS. TIM GUNN SAID SO IN LAST MONTH'S MODELS, INC.!
KRANKTT!

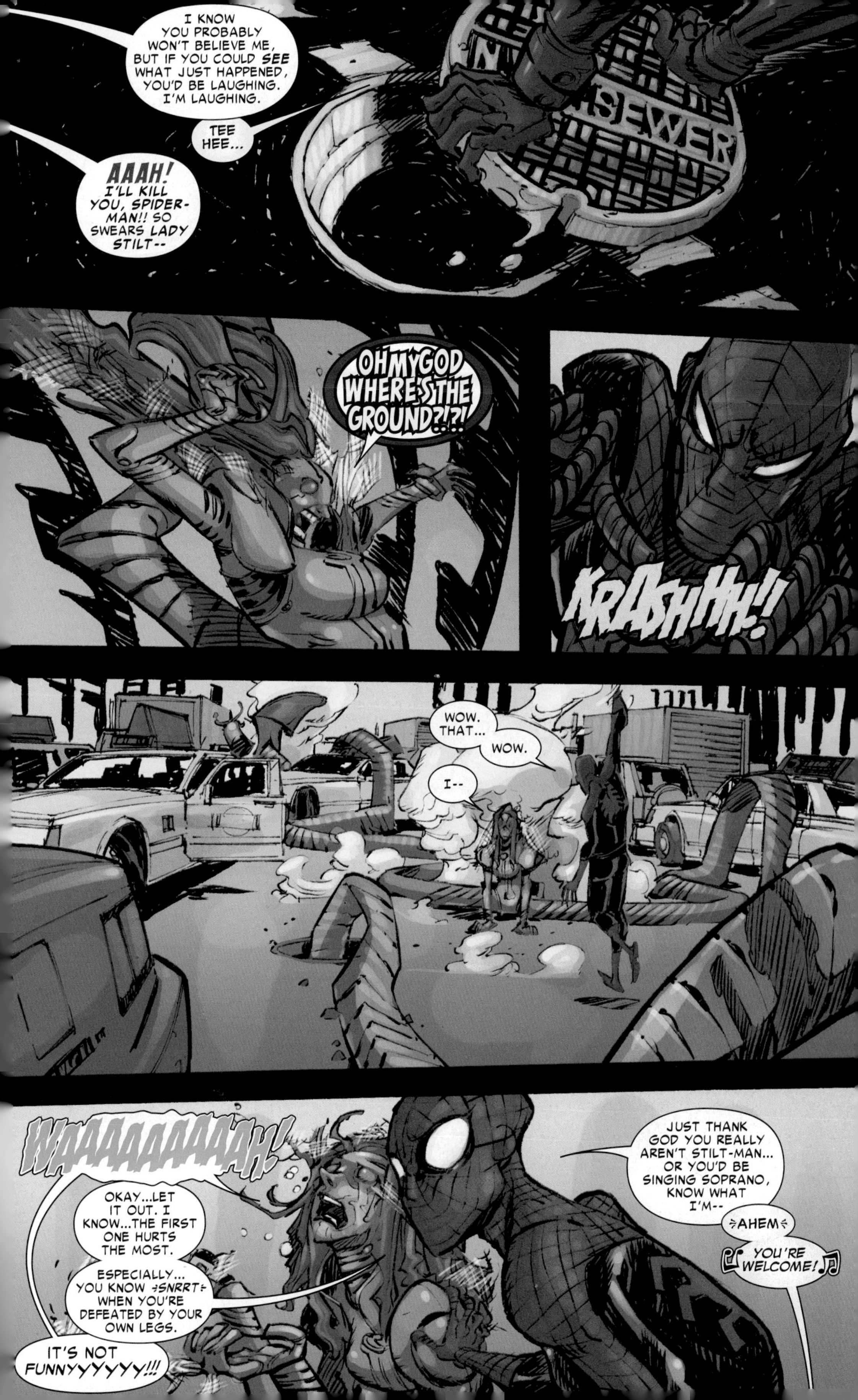
I KNOW YOU PROBABLY WON'T BELIEVE ME, BUT IF YOU COULD SEE WHAT JUST HAPPENED, YOU'D BE LAUGHING. I'M LAUGHING.
TEE HEE...
AAAH! I'LL KILL YOU, SPIDER-MAN!! SO SWEARS LADY STILT--
SEWER
OHMYGOD WHERE'S THE GROUND?!?!
KRASHHH!!
WOW. THAT...
WOW.
I--
WAAAAAAAAAH!
OKAY...LET IT OUT. I KNOW...THE FIRST ONE HURTS THE MOST.
ESPECIALLY... YOU KNOW SNRRT WHEN YOU'RE DEFEATED BY YOUR OWN LEGS.
IT'S NOT FUNNYYYYYY!!!
JUST THANK GOD YOU REALLY AREN'T STILT-MAN... OR YOU'D BE SINGING SOPRANO, KNOW WHAT I'M--
AHEM
YOU'RE WELCOME!

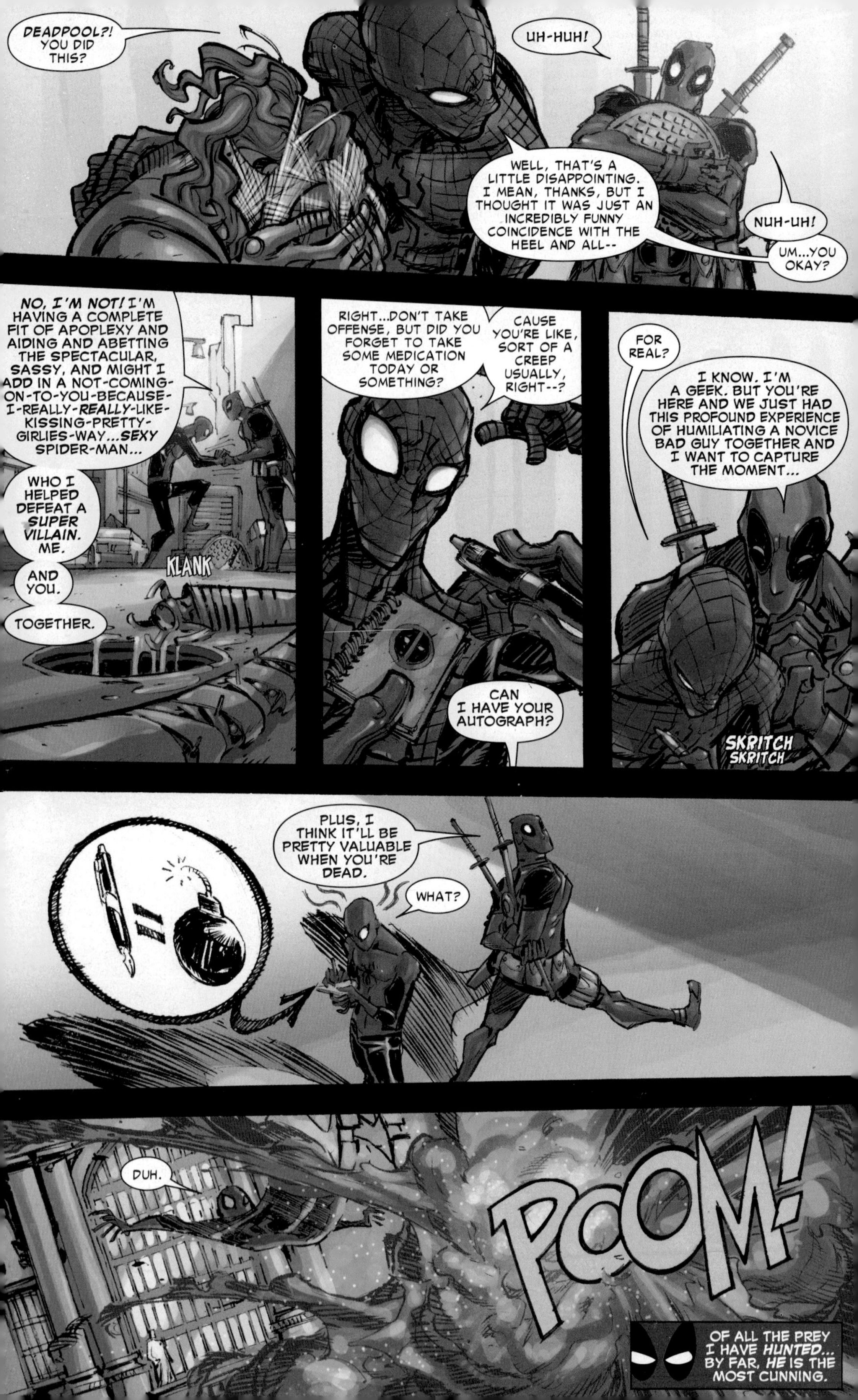
DEADPOOL?! YOU DID THIS?
UH-HUH!
WELL, THAT'S A LITTLE DISAPPOINTING. I MEAN, THANKS, BUT I THOUGHT IT WAS JUST AN INCREDIBLY FUNNY COINCIDENCE WITH THE HEEL AND ALL--
NUH-UH!
UM...YOU OKAY?
NO, I'M NOT! I'M HAVING A COMPLETE FIT OF APOPLEXY AND AIDING AND ABETTING THE SPECTACULAR, SASSY, AND MIGHT I ADD IN A NOT-COMING-ON-TO-YOU-BECAUSE-I-REALLY-REALLY-LIKE-KISSING-PRETTY-GIRLIES-WAY...SEXY SPIDER-MAN...
WHO I HELPED DEFEAT A SUPER VILLAIN. ME.
AND YOU.
TOGETHER.
KLANK
RIGHT...DON'T TAKE OFFENSE, BUT DID YOU FORGET TO TAKE SOME MEDICATION TODAY OR SOMETHING?
CAUSE YOU'RE LIKE, SORT OF A CREEP USUALLY, RIGHT--?
CAN I HAVE YOUR AUTOGRAPH?
FOR REAL?
I KNOW. I'M A GEEK. BUT YOU'RE HERE AND WE JUST HAD THIS PROFOUND EXPERIENCE OF HUMILIATING A NOVICE BAD GUY TOGETHER AND I WANT TO CAPTURE THE MOMENT...
SKRITCH SKRITCH
PLUS, I THINK IT'LL BE PRETTY VALUABLE WHEN YOU'RE DEAD.
WHAT?
DUH.
POOM!
OF ALL THE PREY I HAVE HUNTED... BY FAR, HE IS THE MOST CUNNING.

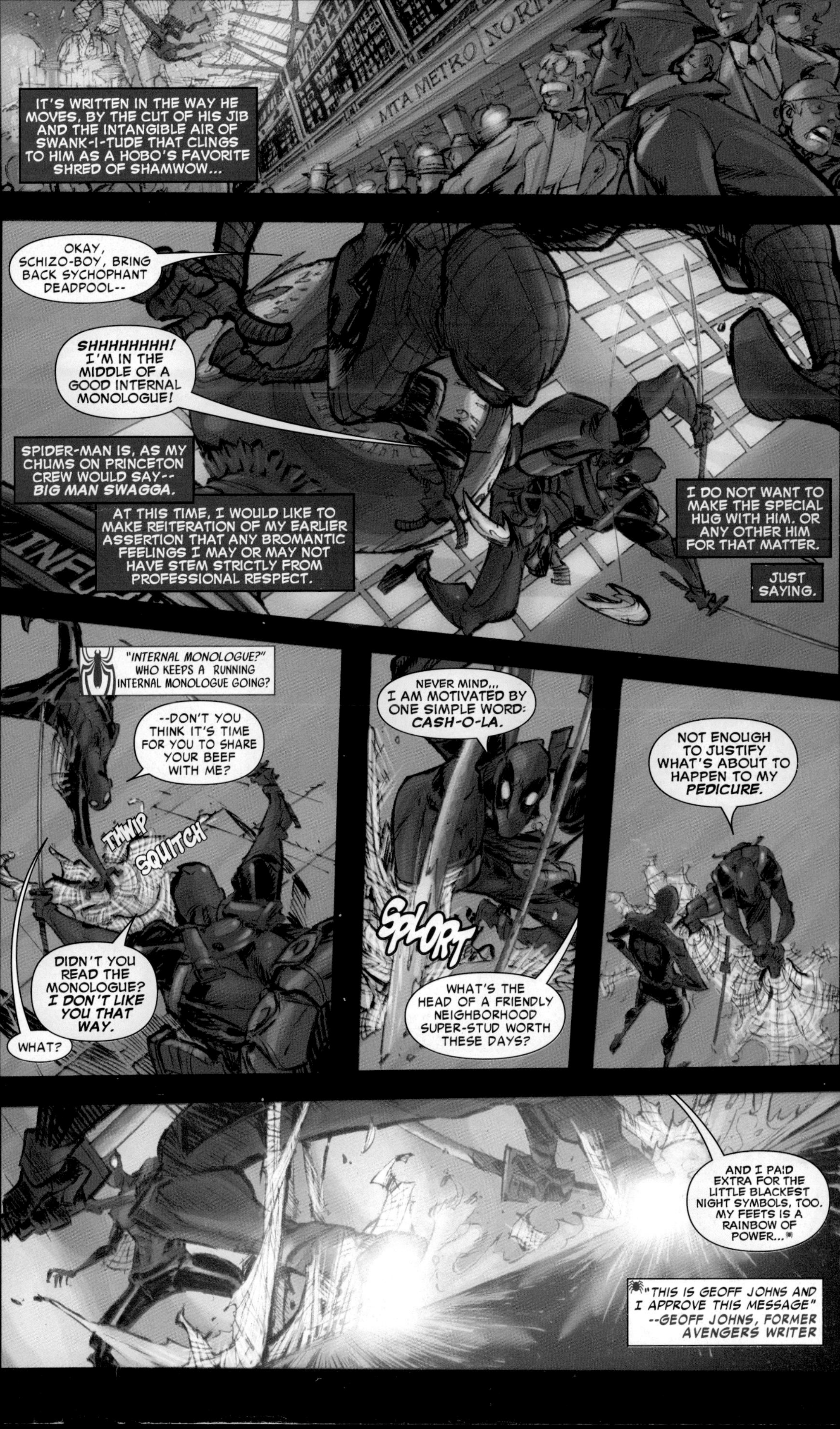
IT'S WRITTEN IN THE WAY HE MOVES, BY THE CUT OF HIS JIB AND THE INTANGIBLE AIR OF SWANK-I-TUDE THAT CLINGS TO HIM AS A HOBO'S FAVORITE SHRED OF SHAMWOW...
MTA METRO NORTH
OKAY, SCHIZO-BOY, BRING BACK SYCHOPHANT DEADPOOL--
SHHHHHHHH! I'M IN THE MIDDLE OF A GOOD INTERNAL MONOLOGUE!
SPIDER-MAN IS, AS MY CHUMS ON PRINCETON CREW WOULD SAY-- BIG MAN SWAGGA.
AT THIS TIME, I WOULD LIKE TO MAKE REITERATION OF MY EARLIER ASSERTION THAT ANY BROMANTIC FEELINGS I MAY OR MAY NOT HAVE STEM STRICTLY FROM PROFESSIONAL RESPECT.
I DO NOT WANT TO MAKE THE SPECIAL HUG WITH HIM. OR ANY OTHER HIM FOR THAT MATTER.
JUST SAYING.
"INTERNAL MONOLOGUE?" WHO KEEPS A RUNNING INTERNAL MONOLOGUE GOING?
--DON'T YOU THINK IT'S TIME FOR YOU TO SHARE YOUR BEEF WITH ME?
THWIP
SQUITCH
DIDN'T YOU READ THE MONOLOGUE? I DON'T LIKE YOU THAT WAY.
WHAT?
NEVER MIND... I AM MOTIVATED BY ONE SIMPLE WORD: CASH-O-LA.
SPLORT
WHAT'S THE HEAD OF A FRIENDLY NEIGHBORHOOD SUPER-STUD WORTH THESE DAYS?
NOT ENOUGH TO JUSTIFY WHAT'S ABOUT TO HAPPEN TO MY PEDICURE.
AND I PAID EXTRA FOR THE LITTLE BLACKEST NIGHT SYMBOLS, TOO. MY FEETS IS A RAINBOW OF POWER...*
*"THIS IS GEOFF JOHNS AND I APPROVE THIS MESSAGE" --GEOFF JOHNS, FORMER AVENGERS WRITER

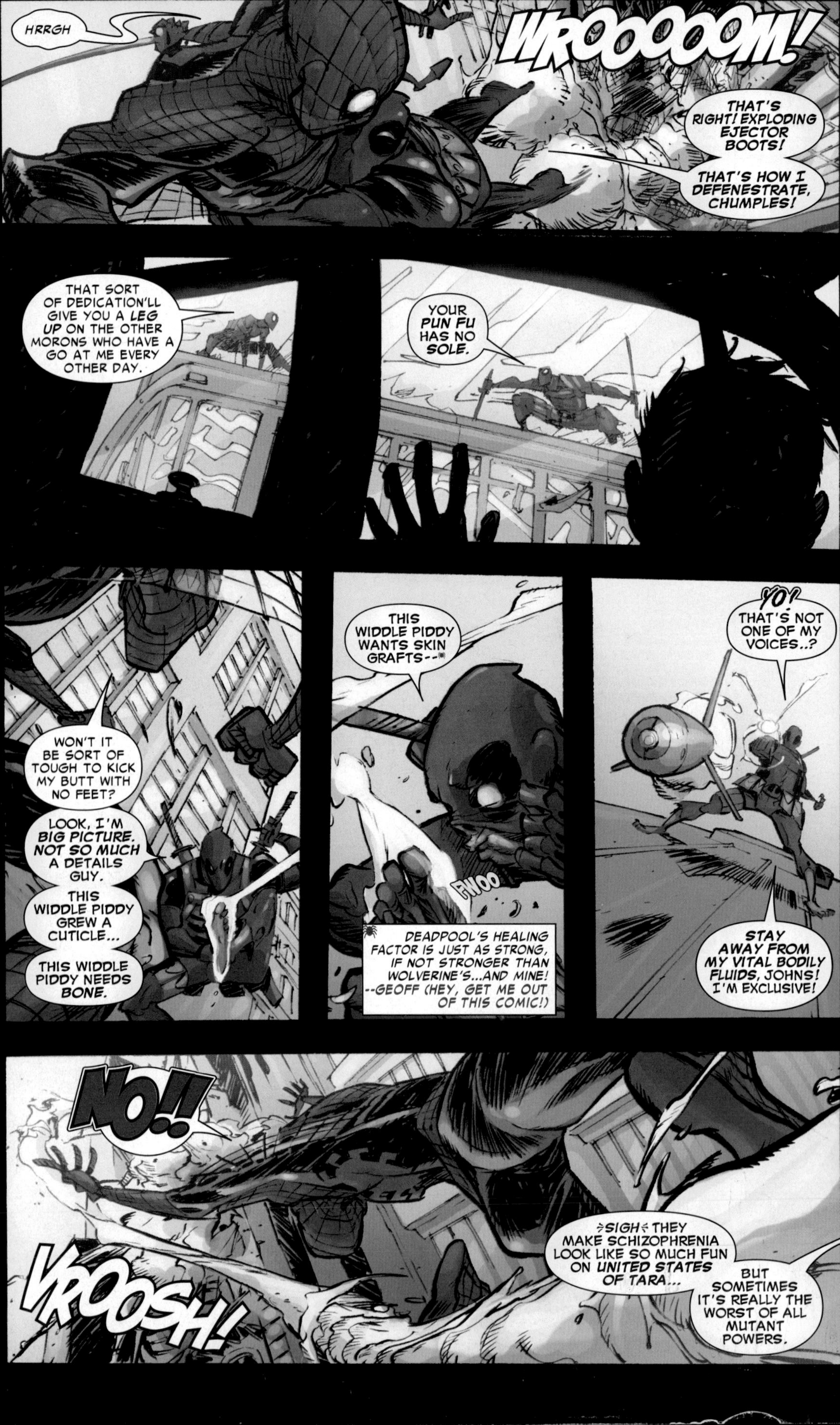
HRRGH
WROOOOOM!
THAT'S RIGHT! EXPLODING EJECTOR BOOTS!
THAT'S HOW I DEFENESTRATE, CHUMPLES!
THAT SORT OF DEDICATION'LL GIVE YOU A LEG UP ON THE OTHER MORONS WHO HAVE A GO AT ME EVERY OTHER DAY.
YOUR PUN FU HAS NO SOLE.
WON'T IT BE SORT OF TOUGH TO KICK MY BUTT WITH NO FEET?
LOOK, I'M BIG PICTURE. NOT SO MUCH A DETAILS GUY.
THIS WIDDLE PIDDY GREW A CUTICLE...
THIS WIDDLE PIDDY NEEDS BONE.
THIS WIDDLE PIDDY WANTS SKIN GRAFTS--
FWOO
DEADPOOL'S HEALING FACTOR IS JUST AS STRONG, IF NOT STRONGER THAN WOLVERINE'S...AND MINE! --GEOFF (HEY, GET ME OUT OF THIS COMIC!)
YO? THAT'S NOT ONE OF MY VOICES..?
STAY AWAY FROM MY VITAL BODILY FLUIDS, JOHNS! I'M EXCLUSIVE!
NO!!
VROOSH!
SIGH THEY MAKE SCHIZOPHRENIA LOOK LIKE SO MUCH FUN ON UNITED STATES OF TARA...
BUT SOMETIMES IT'S REALLY THE WORST OF ALL MUTANT POWERS.

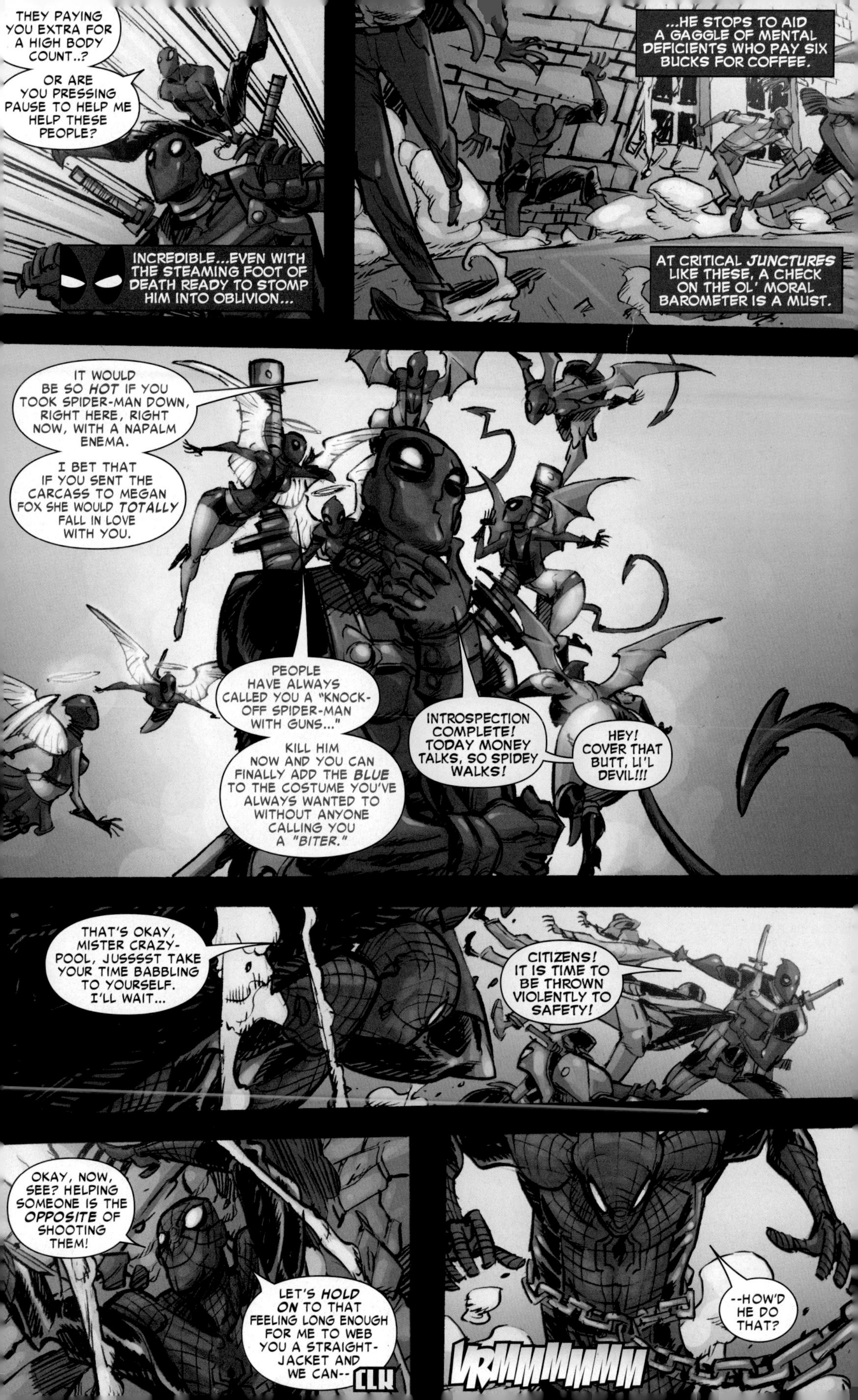
THEY PAYING YOU EXTRA FOR A HIGH BODY COUNT..?
OR ARE YOU PRESSING PAUSE TO HELP ME HELP THESE PEOPLE?
INCREDIBLE...EVEN WITH THE STEAMING FOOT OF DEATH READY TO STOMP HIM INTO OBLIVION...
...HE STOPS TO AID A GAGGLE OF MENTAL DEFICIENTS WHO PAY SIX BUCKS FOR COFFEE.
AT CRITICAL JUNCTURES LIKE THESE, A CHECK ON THE OL' MORAL BAROMETER IS A MUST.
IT WOULD BE SO HOT IF YOU TOOK SPIDER-MAN DOWN, RIGHT HERE, RIGHT NOW, WITH A NAPALM ENEMA.
I BET THAT IF YOU SENT THE CARCASS TO MEGAN FOX SHE WOULD TOTALLY FALL IN LOVE WITH YOU.
PEOPLE HAVE ALWAYS CALLED YOU A "KNOCK-OFF SPIDER-MAN WITH GUNS..."
KILL HIM NOW AND YOU CAN FINALLY ADD THE BLUE TO THE COSTUME YOU'VE ALWAYS WANTED TO WITHOUT ANYONE CALLING YOU A "BITER."
INTROSPECTION COMPLETE! TODAY MONEY TALKS, SO SPIDEY WALKS!
HEY! COVER THAT BUTT, LI'L DEVIL!!!
THAT'S OKAY, MISTER CRAZY-POOL, JUSSSST TAKE YOUR TIME BABBLING TO YOURSELF. I'LL WAIT...
CITIZENS! IT IS TIME TO BE THROWN VIOLENTLY TO SAFETY!
OKAY, NOW, SEE? HELPING SOMEONE IS THE OPPOSITE OF SHOOTING THEM!
LET'S HOLD ON TO THAT FEELING LONG ENOUGH FOR ME TO WEB YOU A STRAIGHT-JACKET AND WE CAN--
CLK
VRMMMMMMM
--HOW'D HE DO THAT?

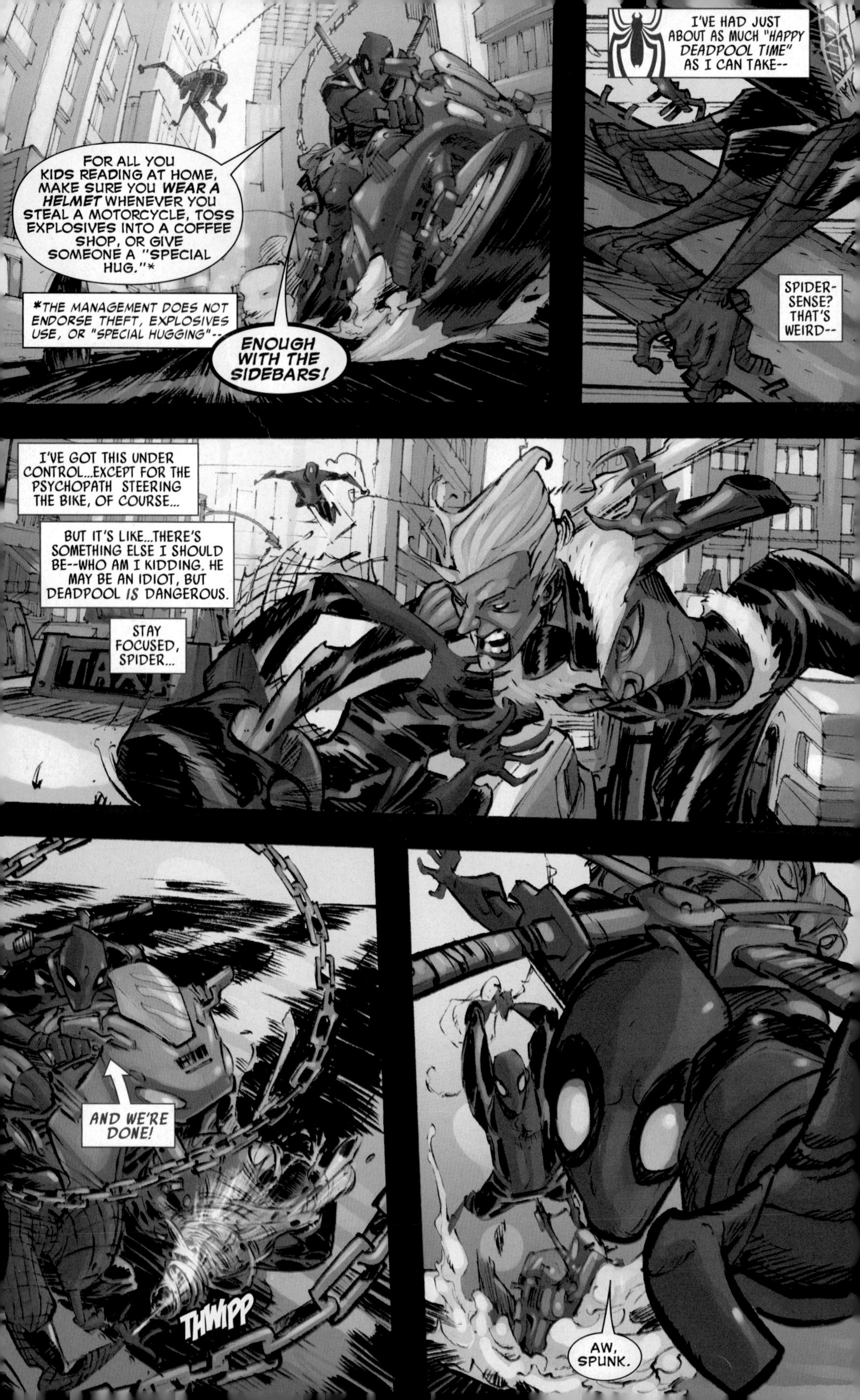

FOR ALL YOU KIDS READING AT HOME, MAKE SURE YOU WEAR A HELMET WHENEVER YOU STEAL A MOTORCYCLE, TOSS EXPLOSIVES INTO A COFFEE SHOP, OR GIVE SOMEONE A "SPECIAL HUG."*
*THE MANAGEMENT DOES NOT ENDORSE THEFT, EXPLOSIVES USE, OR "SPECIAL HUGGING"--
ENOUGH WITH THE SIDEBARS!
I'VE HAD JUST ABOUT AS MUCH "HAPPY DEADPOOL TIME" AS I CAN TAKE--
SPIDER-SENSE? THAT'S WEIRD--
I'VE GOT THIS UNDER CONTROL...EXCEPT FOR THE PSYCHOPATH STEERING THE BIKE, OF COURSE...
BUT IT'S LIKE...THERE'S SOMETHING ELSE I SHOULD BE--WHO AM I KIDDING. HE MAY BE AN IDIOT, BUT DEADPOOL IS DANGEROUS.
STAY FOCUSED, SPIDER...
AND WE'RE DONE!
THWIPP
AW, SPUNK.

🕷 FOR THOSE OF YOU LACKING IN IMAGINATION, CREATE YOUR OWN SOUND EFFECT FOR THIS PANEL BY DRAGGING A SLAB OF BOLOGNA ALONG SOME SANDPAPER. TRY IT IN YOUR PARENTS BED, THEY WON'T MIND! --JOE "I KNOW WHAT A FOLEY ARTIST IS" CARAMAGNA.

OKAY, THAT SIDEBAR WAS ACTUALLY PERTINENT...

Y'KNOW...I NEVER TAKE THE TIME TO NOTICE HOW *PRETTY* MY BLOOD LOOKS ON THE OUTSIDE...

...LIFE IS SO *HECTIC* WITH THE ANARCHY AND MERCENARYING AND COMMEMORATIVE SPOON COLLECTING--

THEN HOW ABOUT A NICE *LONG SINUS-SHATTERING* NAP TO HELP YOU RELAX?

WAIT! I JUST REMEMBERED! A SECRET ABOUT YOUR MYSTERIOUS PAST!

YOUR MOTHER IS SO OLD, ~~SHE EATEN SANDWICH A REIGN ARGUING~~

THAT'S DISGUSTING.

OH, SNAP!

SPIDEY, YOU GONNA JUS' LET THAT PUNK DISS YOU LIKE THAT?!

HE'S TALKIN' ABOUT *YO MAMA!*

IF YOU'LL BACK IT UP A FEW, JUNIOR, YOU'LL SEE I'M ABOUT TO *"DISRESPECT"* HIM MY OWN SELF... AND BESIDES, MY MOTHER'S DEAD--

DEAD OF *EMBARRASSMENT* BECAUSE HER SON WENT TO THE BARBER TO GET HIS *PALMS SHAVED* AFTER HE SHOT WEBBING

OOOOH!

OH, YEAH..? YOUR MOTHER IS SO *UGLY* THAT A *SKRULL* TRIED TO COPY HER DURING THE INVASION AND *DIED*... OF UGLY.

OOOOOOH!

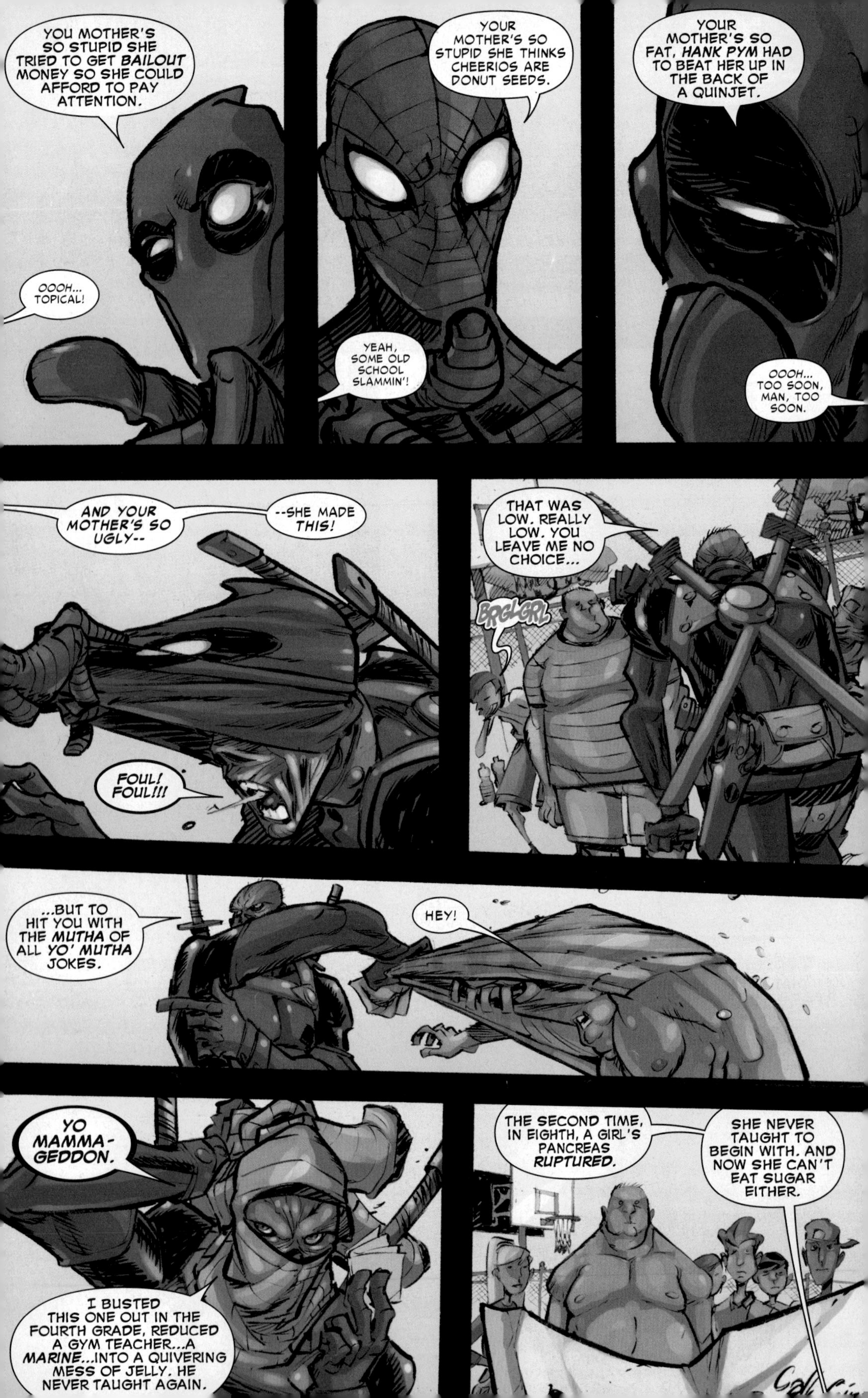
YOU MOTHER'S SO STUPID SHE TRIED TO GET BAILOUT MONEY SO SHE COULD AFFORD TO PAY ATTENTION.
OOOH... TOPICAL!
YOUR MOTHER'S SO STUPID SHE THINKS CHEERIOS ARE DONUT SEEDS.
YEAH, SOME OLD SCHOOL SLAMMIN'!
YOUR MOTHER'S SO FAT, HANK PYM HAD TO BEAT HER UP IN THE BACK OF A QUINJET.
OOOH... TOO SOON, MAN, TOO SOON.
AND YOUR MOTHER'S SO UGLY--
--SHE MADE THIS!
FOUL! FOUL!!!
THAT WAS LOW. REALLY LOW. YOU LEAVE ME NO CHOICE...
BRGLGRL
...BUT TO HIT YOU WITH THE MUTHA OF ALL YO' MUTHA JOKES.
HEY!
YO MAMMA-GEDDON.
I BUSTED THIS ONE OUT IN THE FOURTH GRADE, REDUCED A GYM TEACHER...A MARINE...INTO A QUIVERING MESS OF JELLY. HE NEVER TAUGHT AGAIN.
THE SECOND TIME, IN EIGHTH, A GIRL'S PANCREAS RUPTURED.
SHE NEVER TAUGHT TO BEGIN WITH. AND NOW SHE CAN'T EAT SUGAR EITHER.

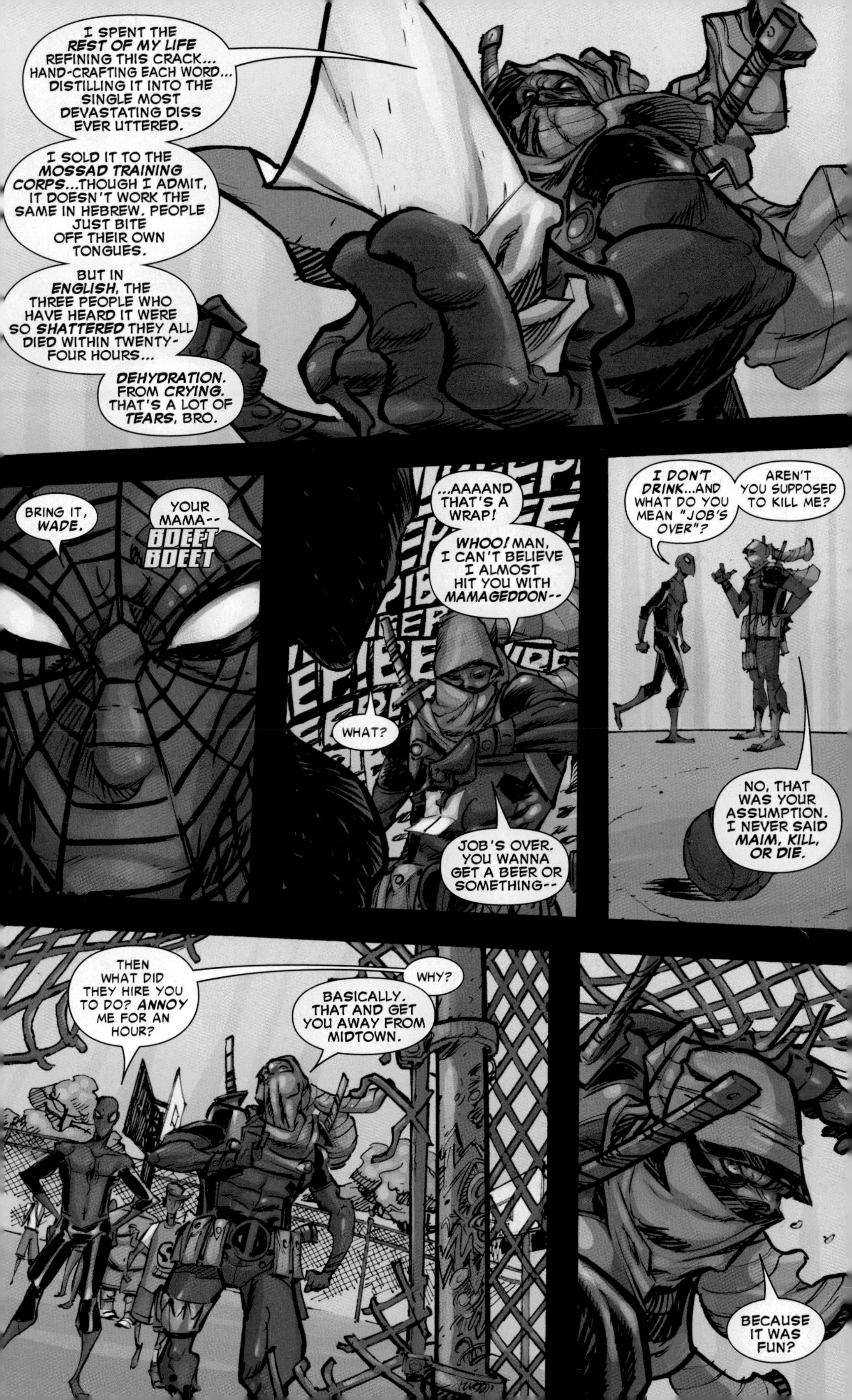
I SPENT THE REST OF MY LIFE REFINING THIS CRACK... HAND-CRAFTING EACH WORD... DISTILLING IT INTO THE SINGLE MOST DEVASTATING DISS EVER UTTERED.
I SOLD IT TO THE MOSSAD TRAINING CORPS...THOUGH I ADMIT, IT DOESN'T WORK THE SAME IN HEBREW. PEOPLE JUST BITE OFF THEIR OWN TONGUES.
BUT IN ENGLISH, THE THREE PEOPLE WHO HAVE HEARD IT WERE SO SHATTERED THEY ALL DIED WITHIN TWENTY-FOUR HOURS...
DEHYDRATION. FROM CRYING. THAT'S A LOT OF TEARS, BRO.
BRING IT, WADE.
YOUR MAMA--
BDEET BDEET
...AAAAND THAT'S A WRAP!
WHOO! MAN, I CAN'T BELIEVE I ALMOST HIT YOU WITH MAMAGEDDON--
WHAT?
JOB'S OVER. YOU WANNA GET A BEER OR SOMETHING--
I DON'T DRINK...AND WHAT DO YOU MEAN "JOB'S OVER"?
AREN'T YOU SUPPOSED TO KILL ME?
NO, THAT WAS YOUR ASSUMPTION. I NEVER SAID MAIM, KILL, OR DIE.
THEN WHAT DID THEY HIRE YOU TO DO? ANNOY ME FOR AN HOUR?
BASICALLY. THAT AND GET YOU AWAY FROM MIDTOWN.
WHY?
BECAUSE IT WAS FUN?

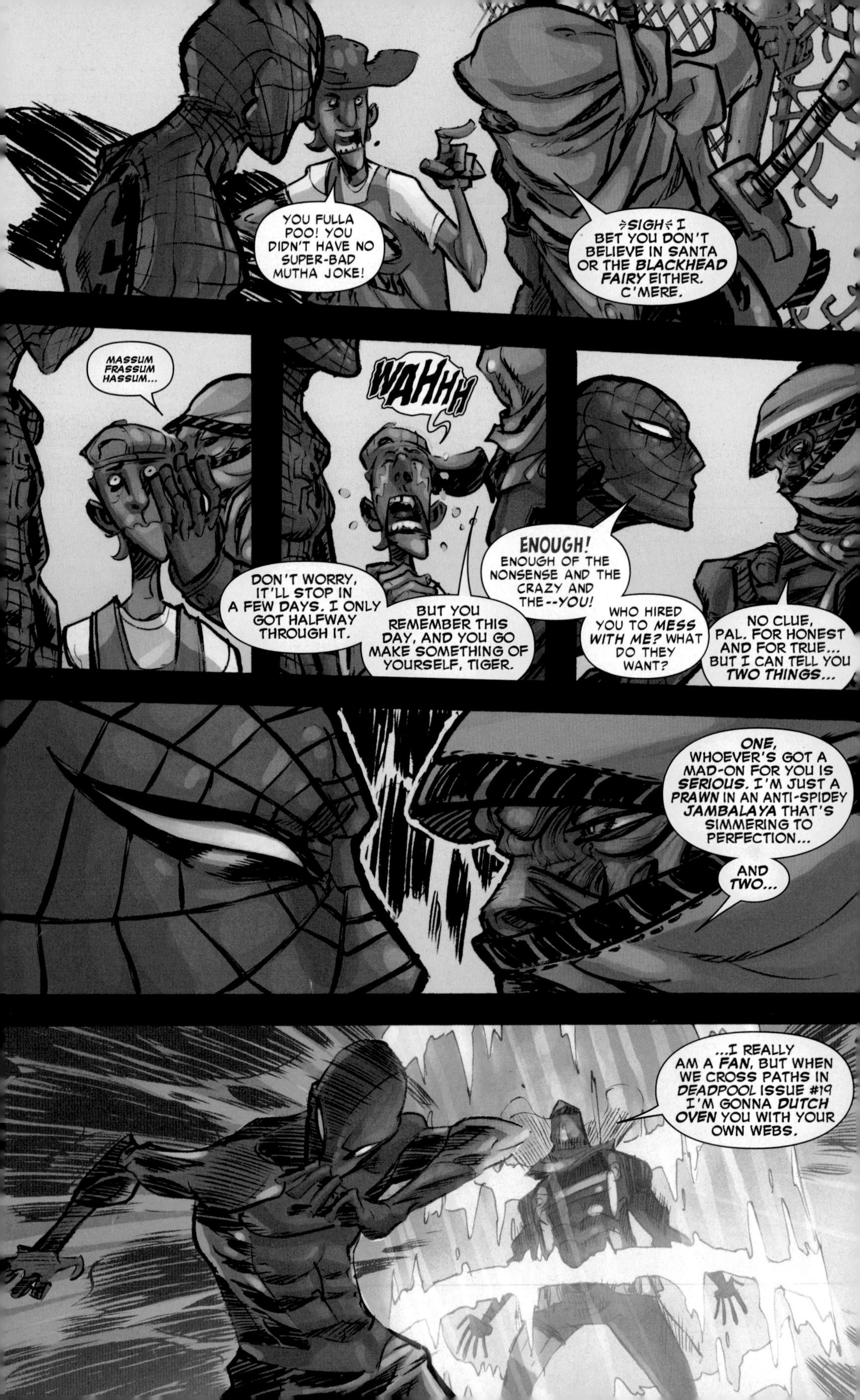

YOU FULLA POO! YOU DIDN'T HAVE NO SUPER-BAD MUTHA JOKE!
SIGH I BET YOU DON'T BELIEVE IN SANTA OR THE BLACKHEAD FAIRY EITHER. C'MERE.
MASSUM FRASSUM HASSUM...
DON'T WORRY, IT'LL STOP IN A FEW DAYS. I ONLY GOT HALFWAY THROUGH IT.
WAHHH
BUT YOU REMEMBER THIS DAY, AND YOU GO MAKE SOMETHING OF YOURSELF, TIGER.
ENOUGH! ENOUGH OF THE NONSENSE AND THE CRAZY AND THE--YOU!
WHO HIRED YOU TO MESS WITH ME? WHAT DO THEY WANT?
NO CLUE, PAL. FOR HONEST AND FOR TRUE... BUT I CAN TELL YOU TWO THINGS...
ONE, WHOEVER'S GOT A MAD-ON FOR YOU IS SERIOUS. I'M JUST A PRAWN IN AN ANTI-SPIDEY JAMBALAYA THAT'S SIMMERING TO PERFECTION...
AND TWO...
...I REALLY AM A FAN, BUT WHEN WE CROSS PATHS IN DEADPOOL ISSUE #19 I'M GONNA DUTCH OVEN YOU WITH YOUR OWN WEBS.

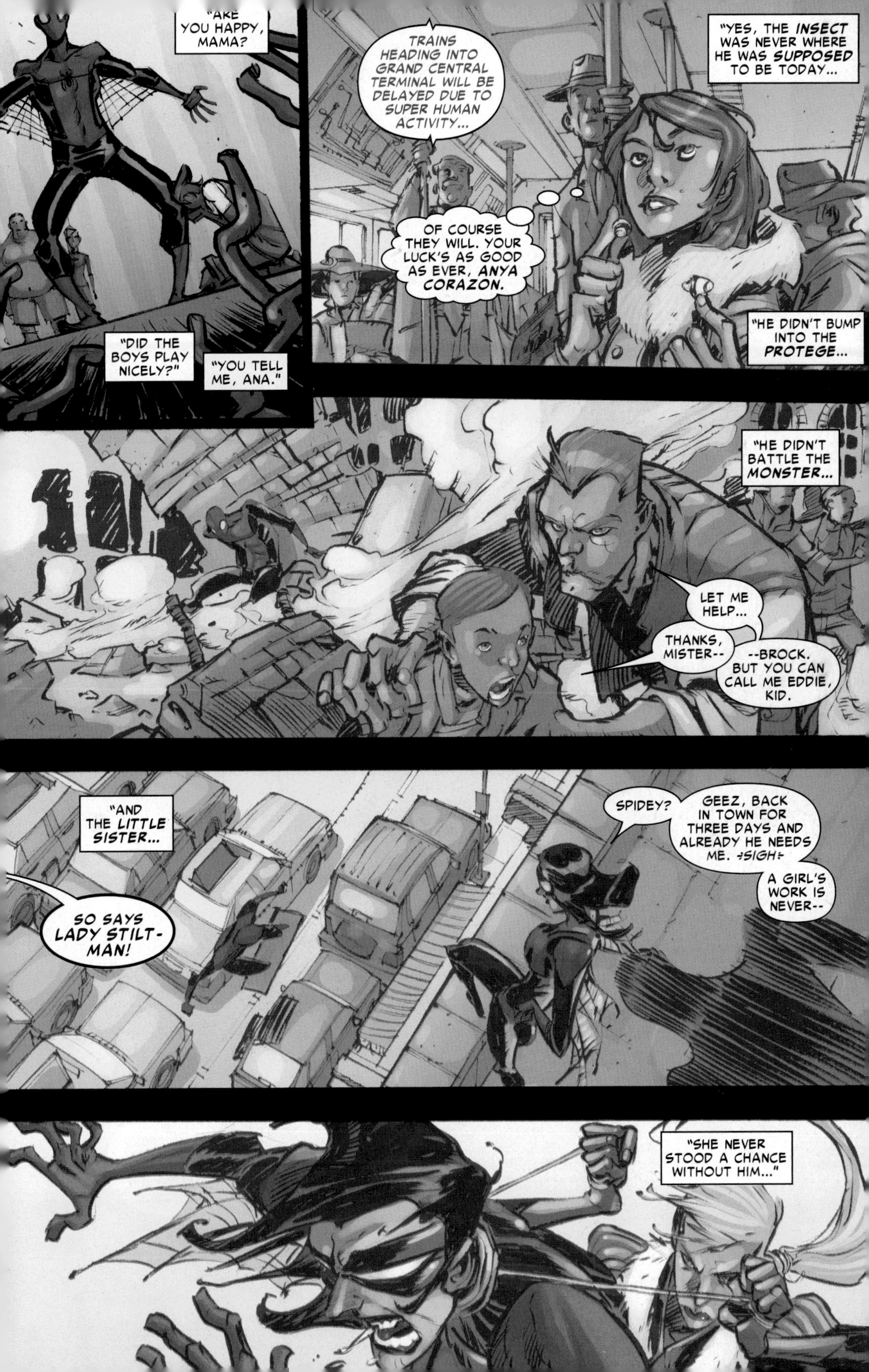
"ARE YOU HAPPY, MAMA?
"DID THE BOYS PLAY NICELY?"
"YOU TELL ME, ANA."
TRAINS HEADING INTO GRAND CENTRAL TERMINAL WILL BE DELAYED DUE TO SUPER HUMAN ACTIVITY...
OF COURSE THEY WILL. YOUR LUCK'S AS GOOD AS EVER, ANYA CORAZON.
"YES, THE INSECT WAS NEVER WHERE HE WAS SUPPOSED TO BE TODAY...
"HE DIDN'T BUMP INTO THE PROTEGE...
"HE DIDN'T BATTLE THE MONSTER...
LET ME HELP...
THANKS, MISTER--
--BROCK. BUT YOU CAN CALL ME EDDIE, KID.
"AND THE LITTLE SISTER...
SO SAYS LADY STILT-MAN!
SPIDEY?
GEEZ, BACK IN TOWN FOR THREE DAYS AND ALREADY HE NEEDS ME. ‹SIGH›
A GIRL'S WORK IS NEVER--
"SHE NEVER STOOD A CHANCE WITHOUT HIM..."

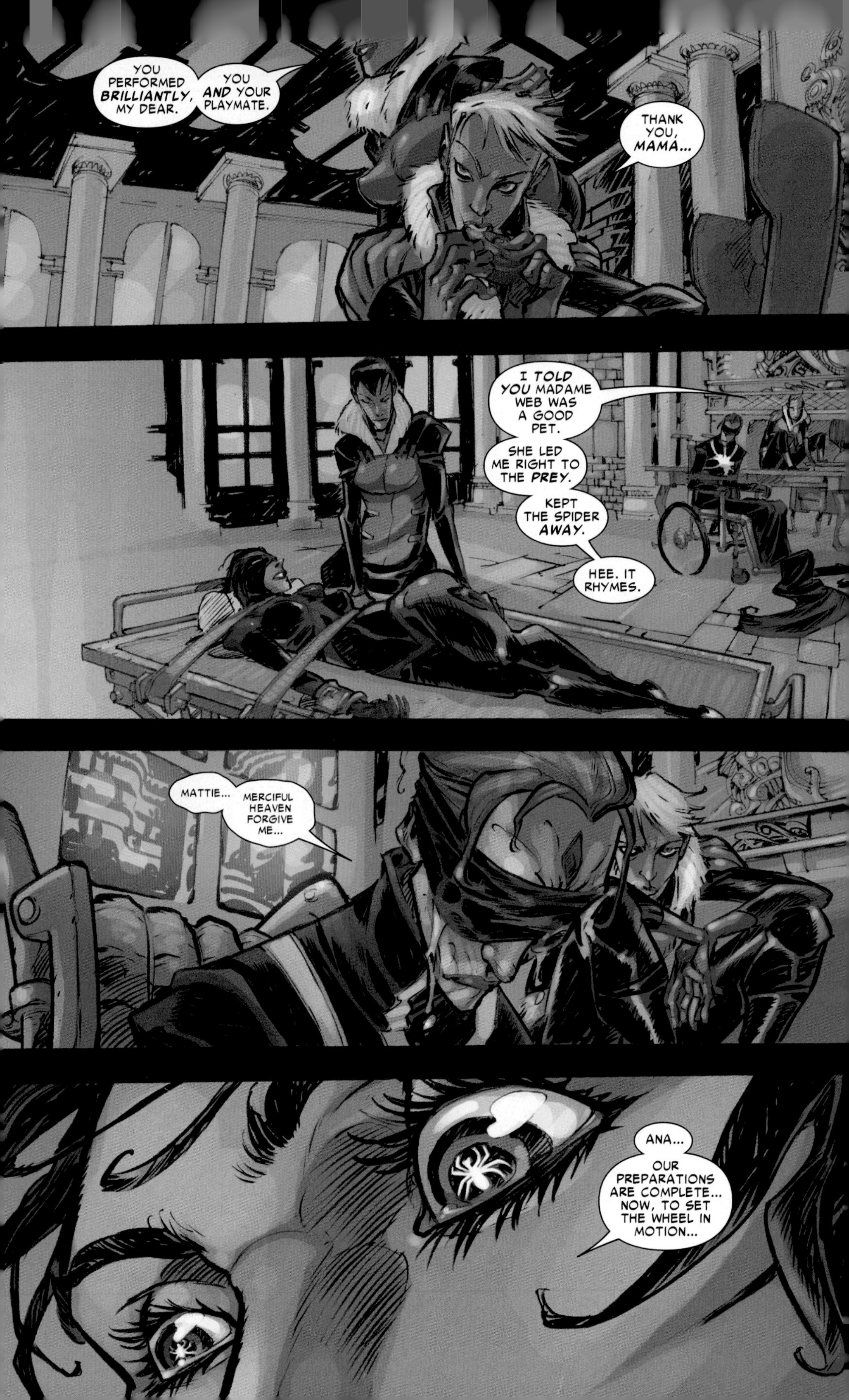
YOU PERFORMED BRILLIANTLY, MY DEAR.
YOU AND YOUR PLAYMATE.
THANK YOU, MAMA...
I TOLD YOU MADAME WEB WAS A GOOD PET.
SHE LED ME RIGHT TO THE PREY.
KEPT THE SPIDER AWAY.
HEE. IT RHYMES.
MATTIE...
MERCIFUL HEAVEN FORGIVE ME...
ANA...
OUR PREPARATIONS ARE COMPLETE... NOW, TO SET THE WHEEL IN MOTION...

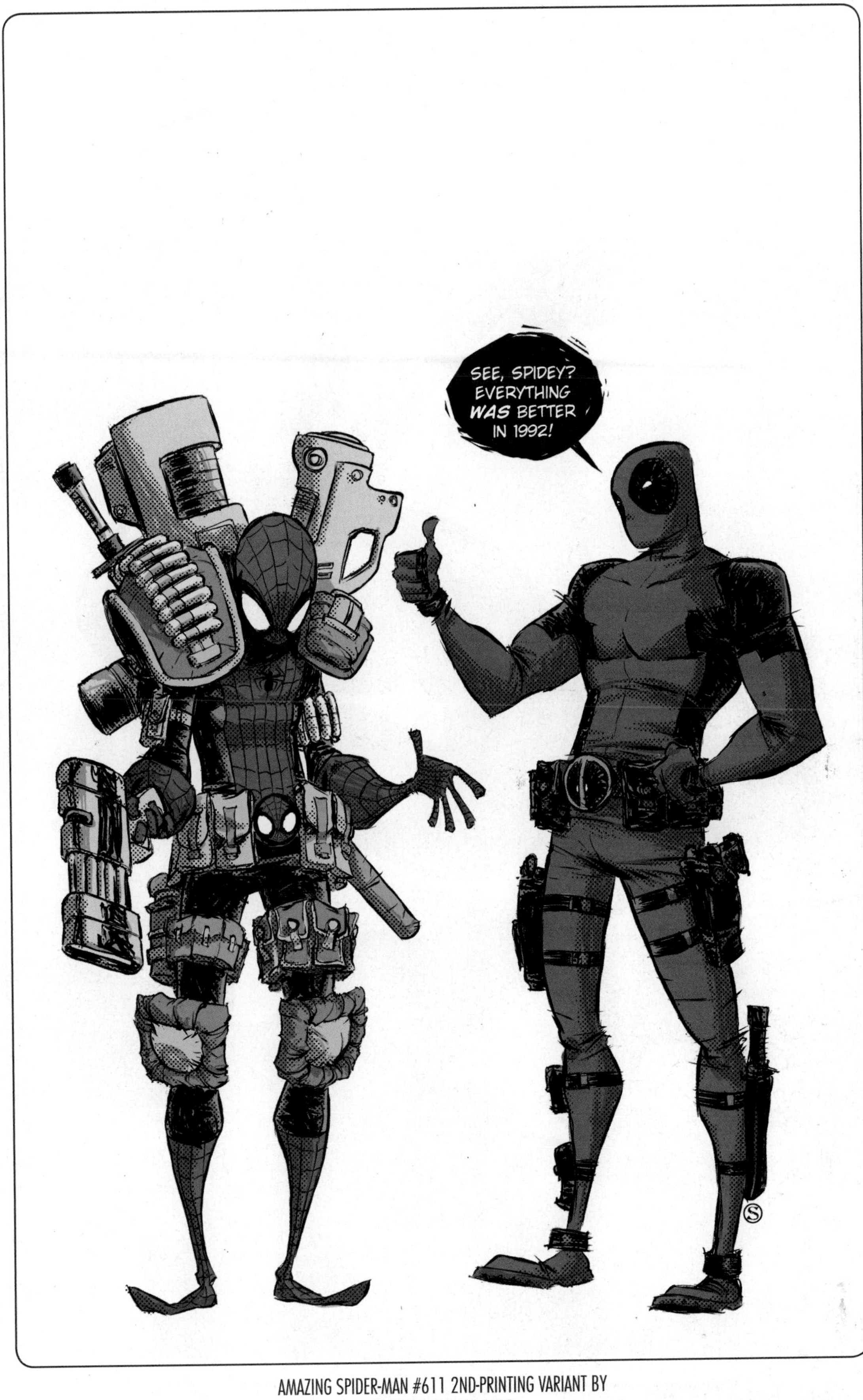
SEE, SPIDEY? EVERYTHING WAS BETTER IN 1992!

AMAZING SPIDER-MAN #611 2ND-PRINTING VARIANT BY
SKOTTIE YOUNG

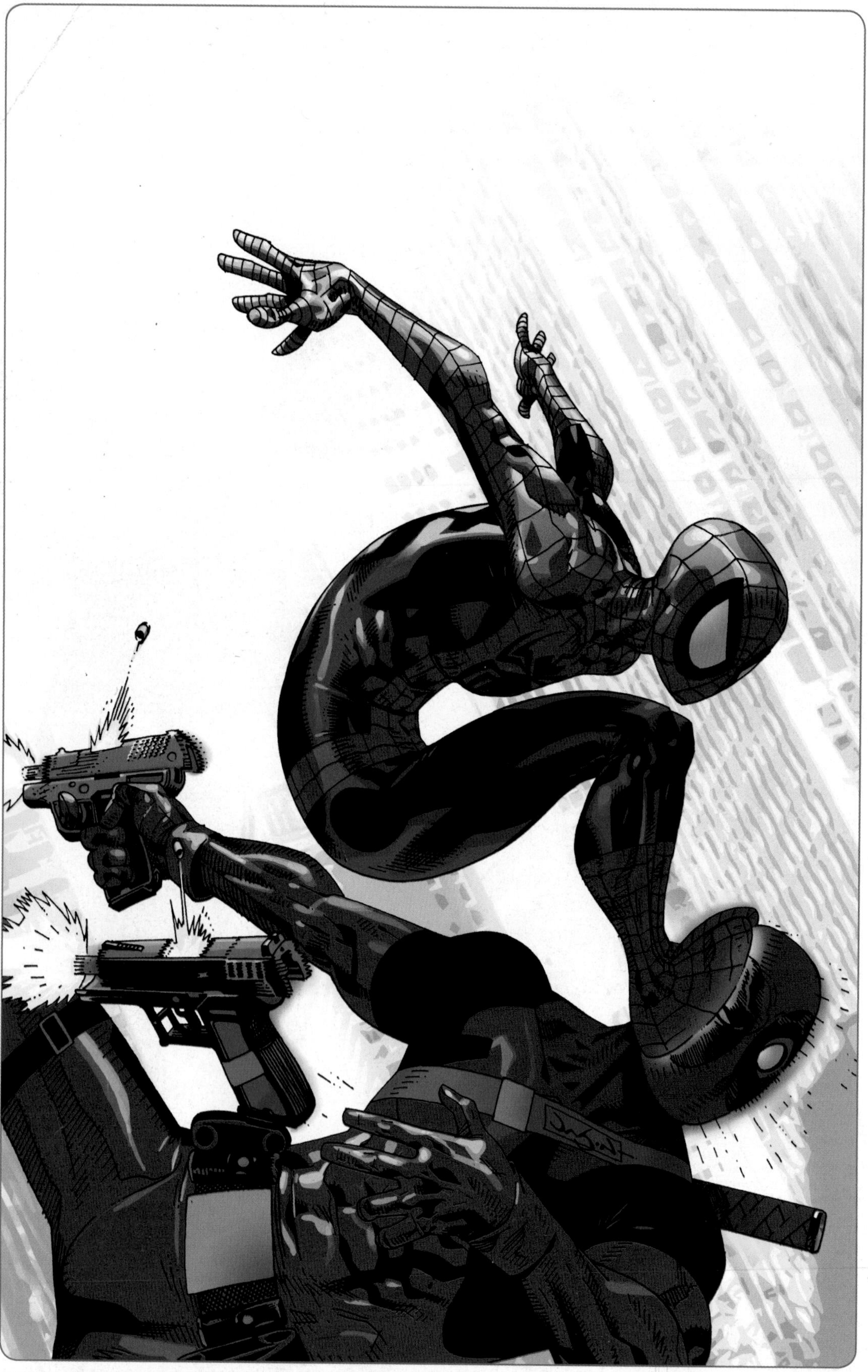

DEADPOOL (2008) #19

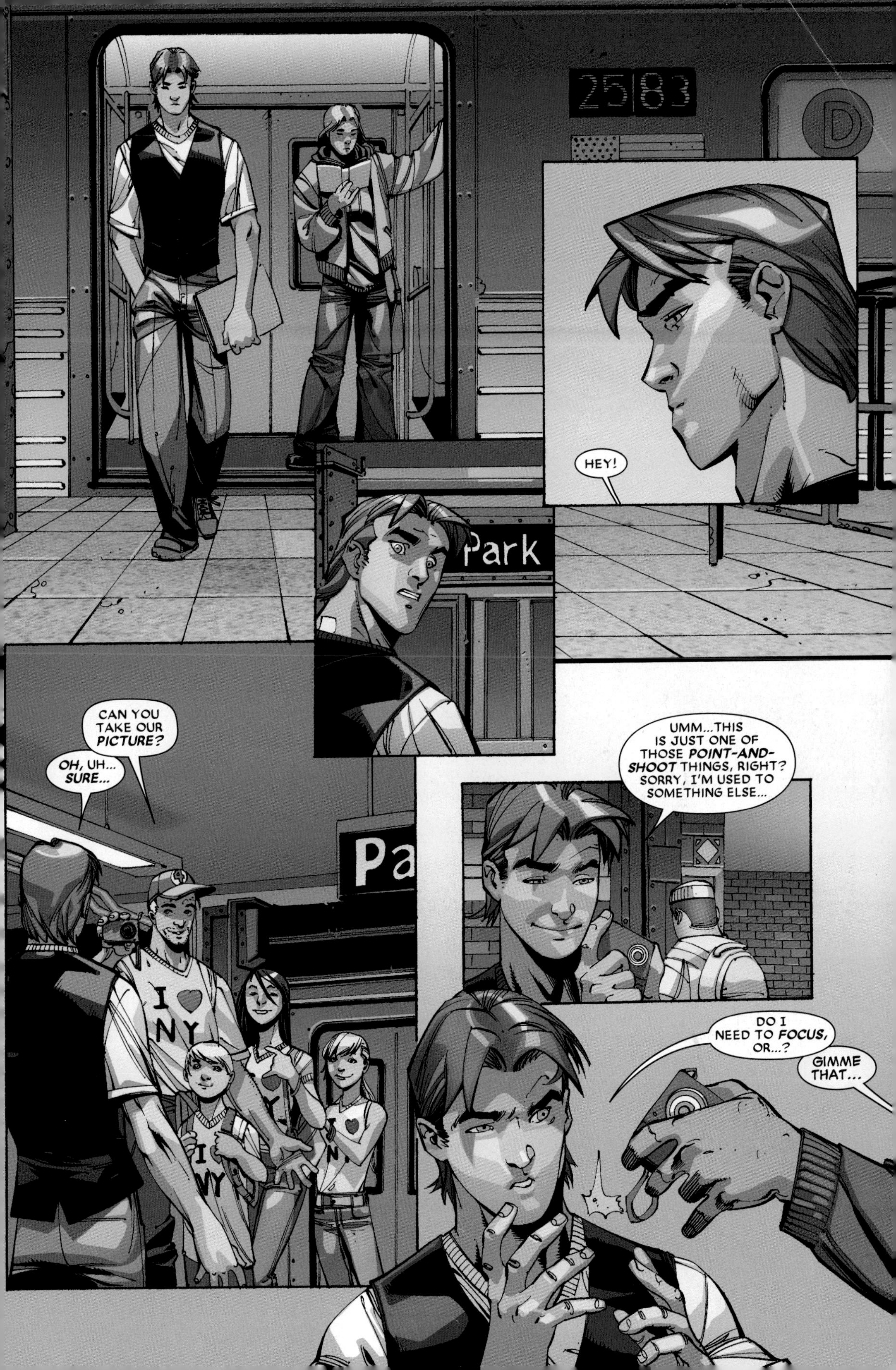
2583
D
HEY!
Park
CAN YOU TAKE OUR *PICTURE?*
OH, UH... *SURE...*
Pa
UMM...THIS IS JUST ONE OF THOSE *POINT-AND-SHOOT* THINGS, RIGHT? SORRY, I'M USED TO SOMETHING ELSE...
DO I NEED TO *FOCUS,* OR...?
GIMME THAT...

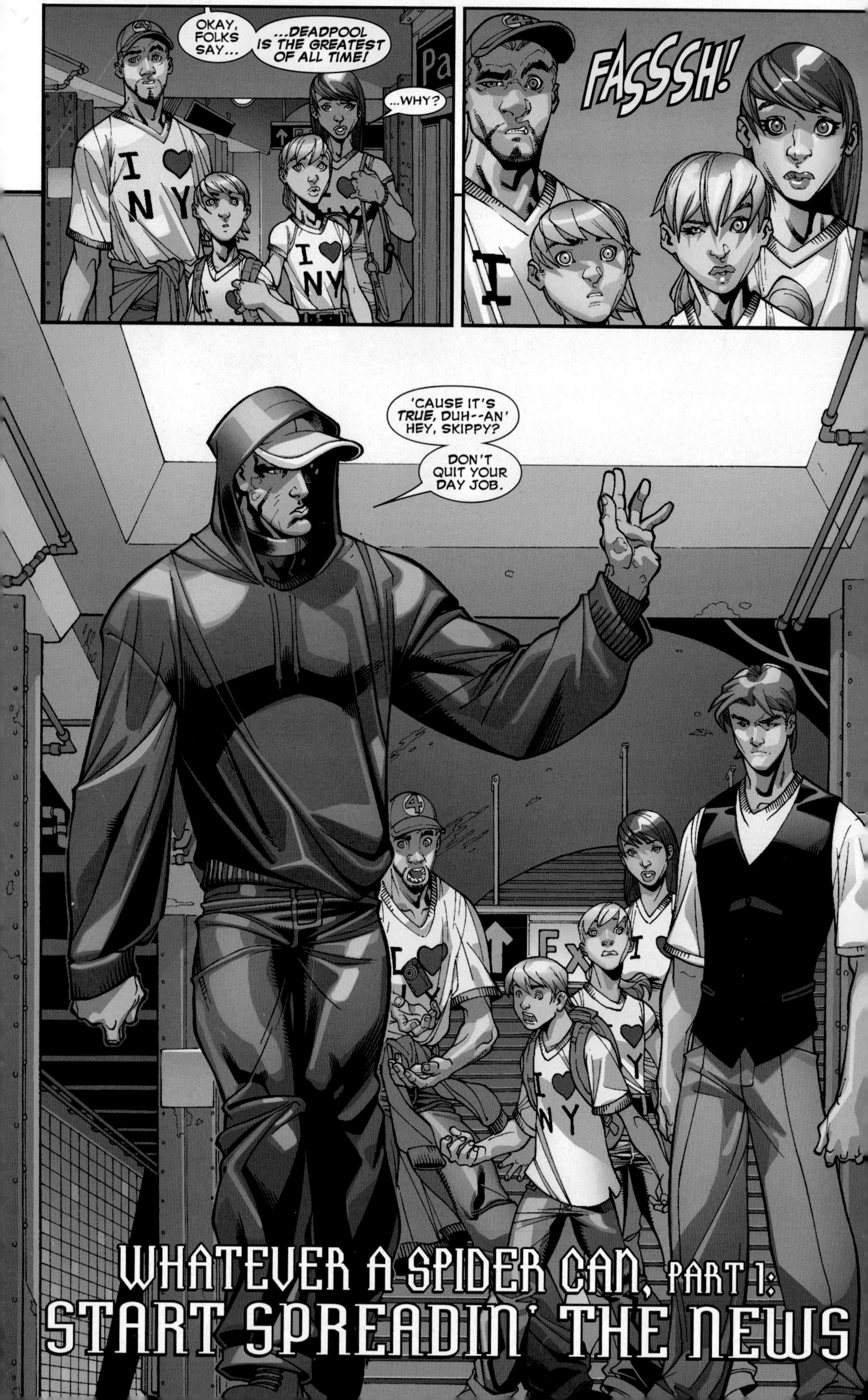
OKAY, FOLKS SAY...
...DEADPOOL IS THE GREATEST OF ALL TIME!
...WHY?
FASSSH!
'CAUSE IT'S *TRUE*, DUH--AN' HEY, SKIPPY?
DON'T QUIT YOUR DAY JOB.
WHATEVER A SPIDER CAN, PART 1:
START SPREADIN' THE NEWS

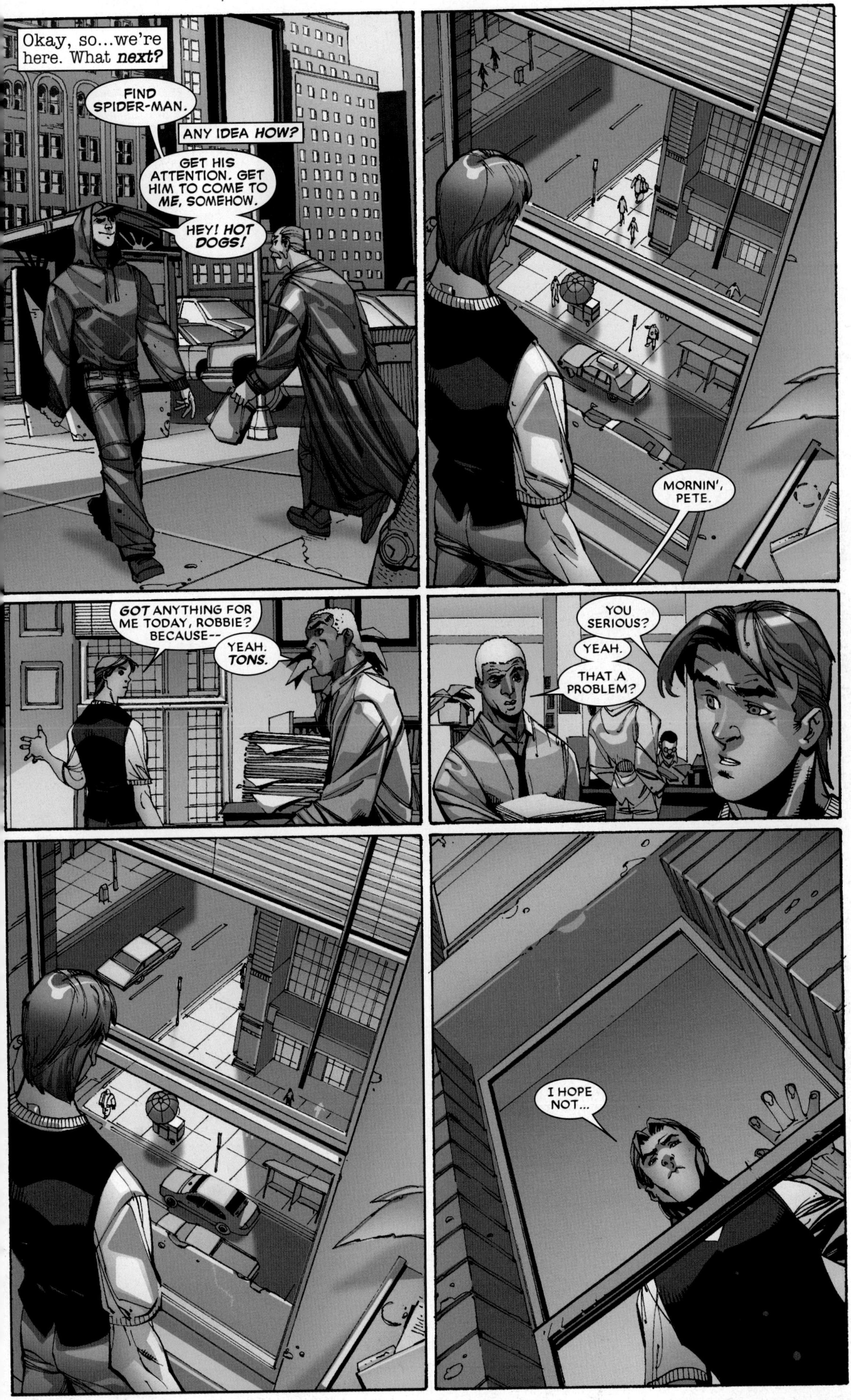
Okay, so...we're here. What *next?*
FIND SPIDER-MAN.
ANY IDEA *HOW?*
GET HIS ATTENTION. GET HIM TO COME TO *ME*, SOMEHOW.
HEY! *HOT DOGS!*
MORNIN', PETE.
GOT ANYTHING FOR ME TODAY, ROBBIE? BECAUSE--
YEAH. *TONS.*
YOU SERIOUS?
YEAH.
THAT A PROBLEM?
I HOPE NOT...

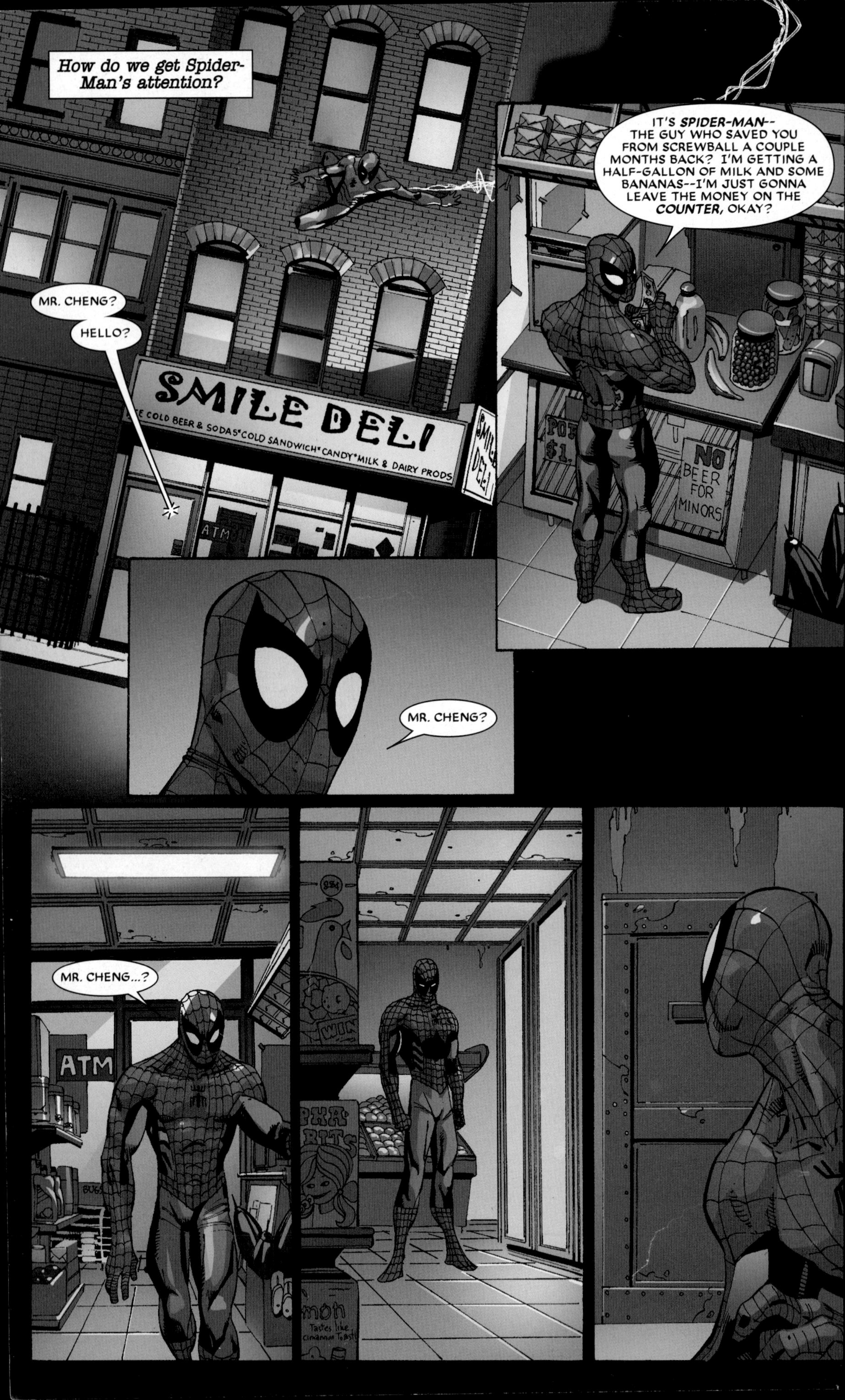
How do we get Spider-Man's attention?
MR. CHENG?
HELLO?
SMILE DELI
ICE COLD BEER & SODAS*COLD SANDWICH*CANDY*MILK & DAIRY PRODS
SMILE DELI
IT'S SPIDER-MAN--THE GUY WHO SAVED YOU FROM SCREWBALL A COUPLE MONTHS BACK? I'M GETTING A HALF-GALLON OF MILK AND SOME BANANAS--I'M JUST GONNA LEAVE THE MONEY ON THE COUNTER, OKAY?
NO BEER FOR MINORS
MR. CHENG?
MR. CHENG...?
ATM
Tastes like cinnamon Toast!

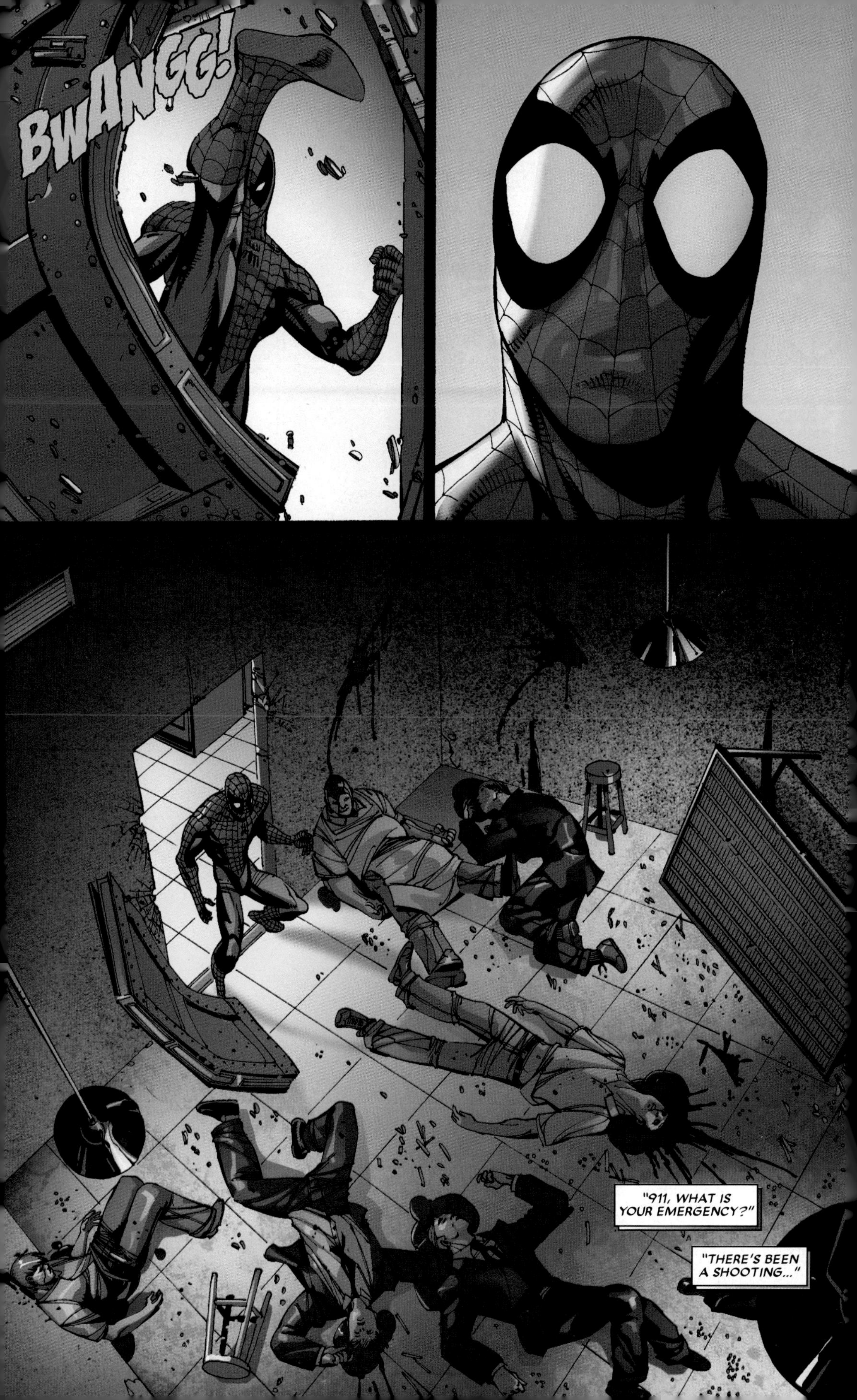
BWANGG!
"911, WHAT IS YOUR EMERGENCY?"
"THERE'S BEEN A SHOOTING..."

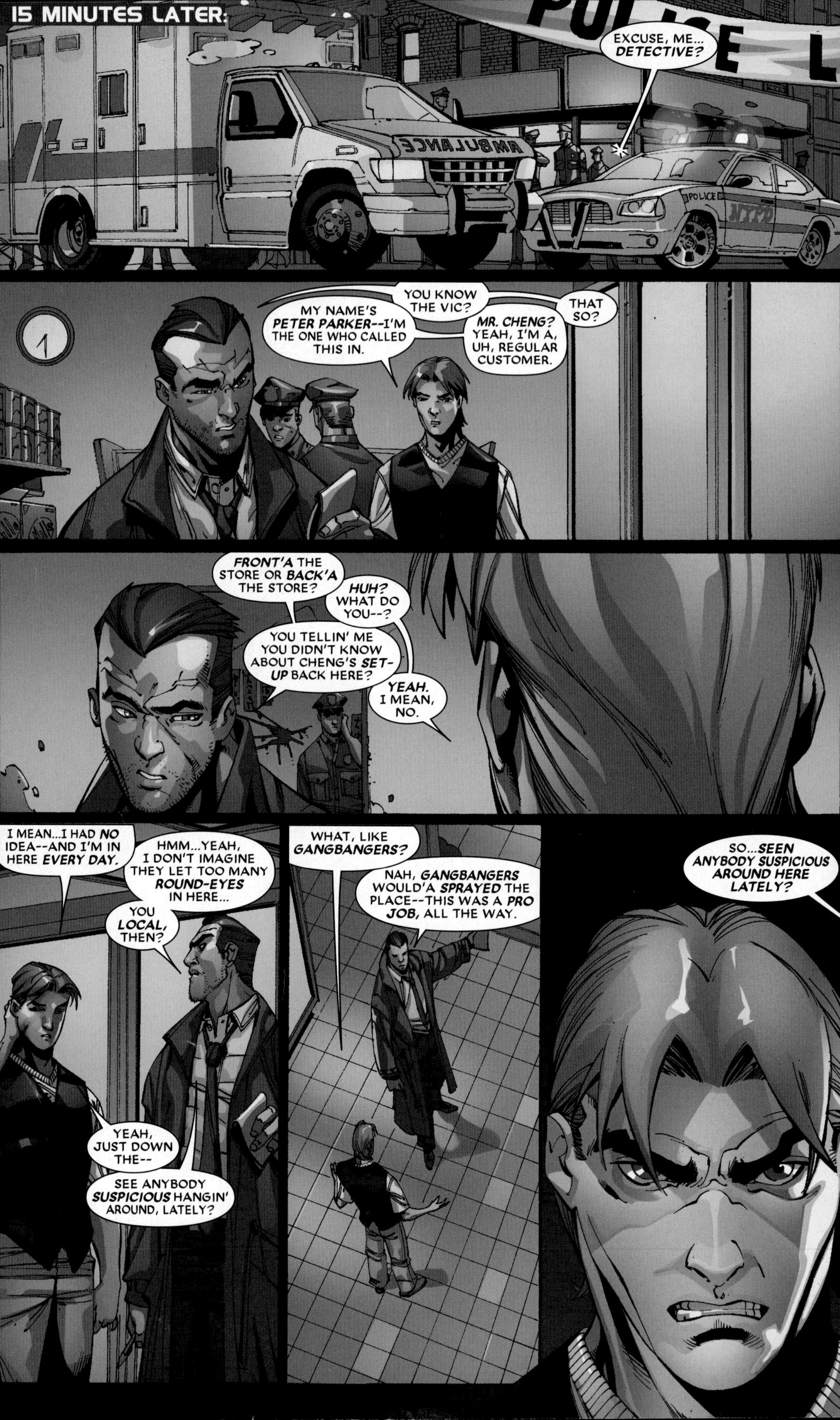
15 MINUTES LATER:
EXCUSE, ME... DETECTIVE?
AMBULANCE
POLICE
MY NAME'S PETER PARKER--I'M THE ONE WHO CALLED THIS IN.
YOU KNOW THE VIC?
MR. CHENG? YEAH, I'M A, UH, REGULAR CUSTOMER.
THAT SO?
FRONT'A THE STORE OR BACK'A THE STORE?
HUH? WHAT DO YOU--?
YOU TELLIN' ME YOU DIDN'T KNOW ABOUT CHENG'S SET-UP BACK HERE?
YEAH. I MEAN, NO.
I MEAN...I HAD NO IDEA--AND I'M IN HERE EVERY DAY.
HMM...YEAH, I DON'T IMAGINE THEY LET TOO MANY ROUND-EYES IN HERE...
YOU LOCAL, THEN?
YEAH, JUST DOWN THE--
SEE ANYBODY SUSPICIOUS HANGIN' AROUND, LATELY?
WHAT, LIKE GANGBANGERS?
NAH, GANGBANGERS WOULD'A SPRAYED THE PLACE--THIS WAS A PRO JOB, ALL THE WAY.
SO...SEEN ANYBODY SUSPICIOUS AROUND HERE LATELY?

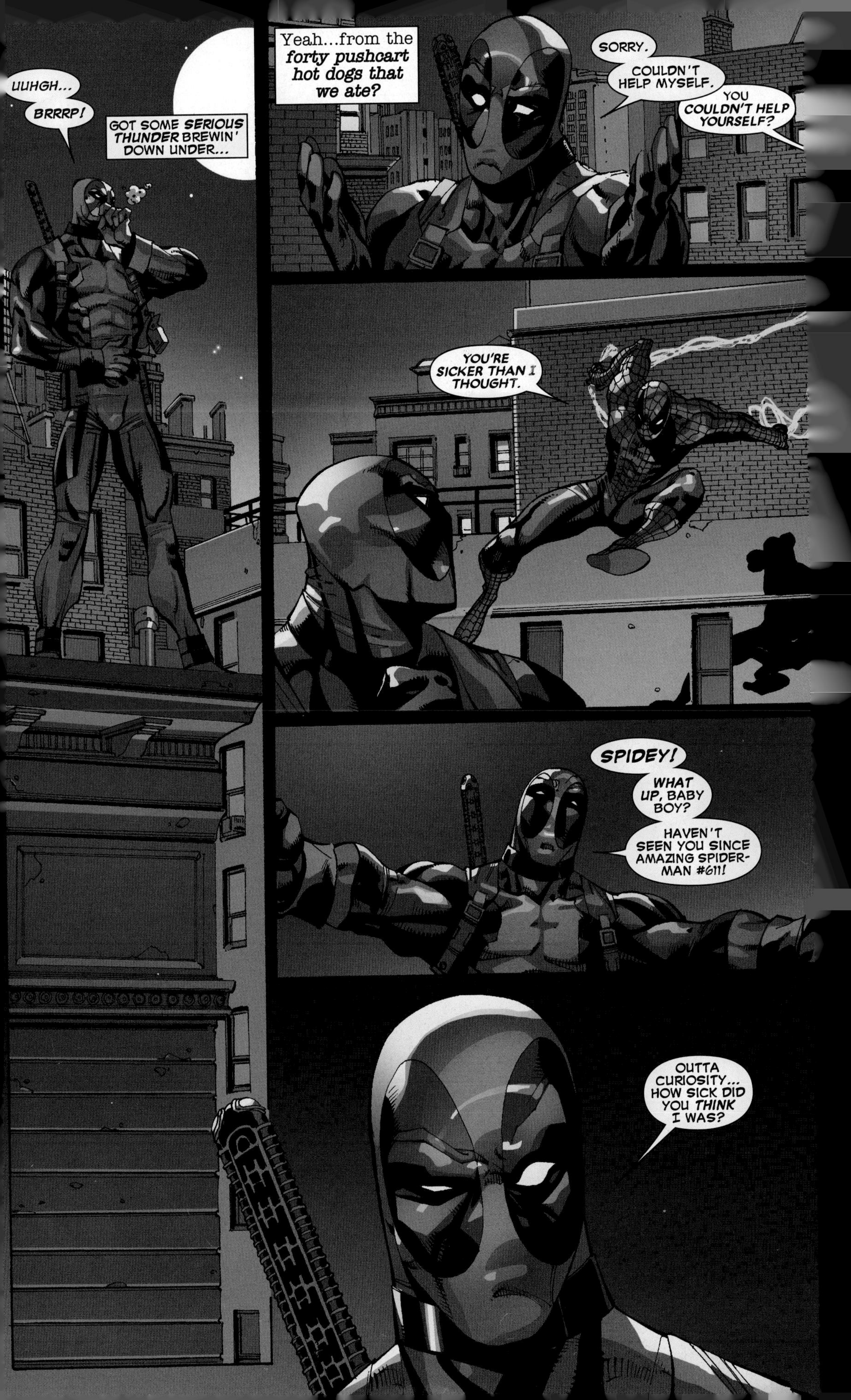
UUHGH...
BRRRP!
GOT SOME SERIOUS THUNDER BREWIN' DOWN UNDER...
Yeah...from the forty pushcart hot dogs that we ate?
SORRY.
COULDN'T HELP MYSELF.
YOU COULDN'T HELP YOURSELF?
YOU'RE SICKER THAN I THOUGHT.
SPIDEY!
WHAT UP, BABY BOY?
HAVEN'T SEEN YOU SINCE AMAZING SPIDER-MAN #611!
OUTTA CURIOSITY... HOW SICK DID YOU THINK I WAS?

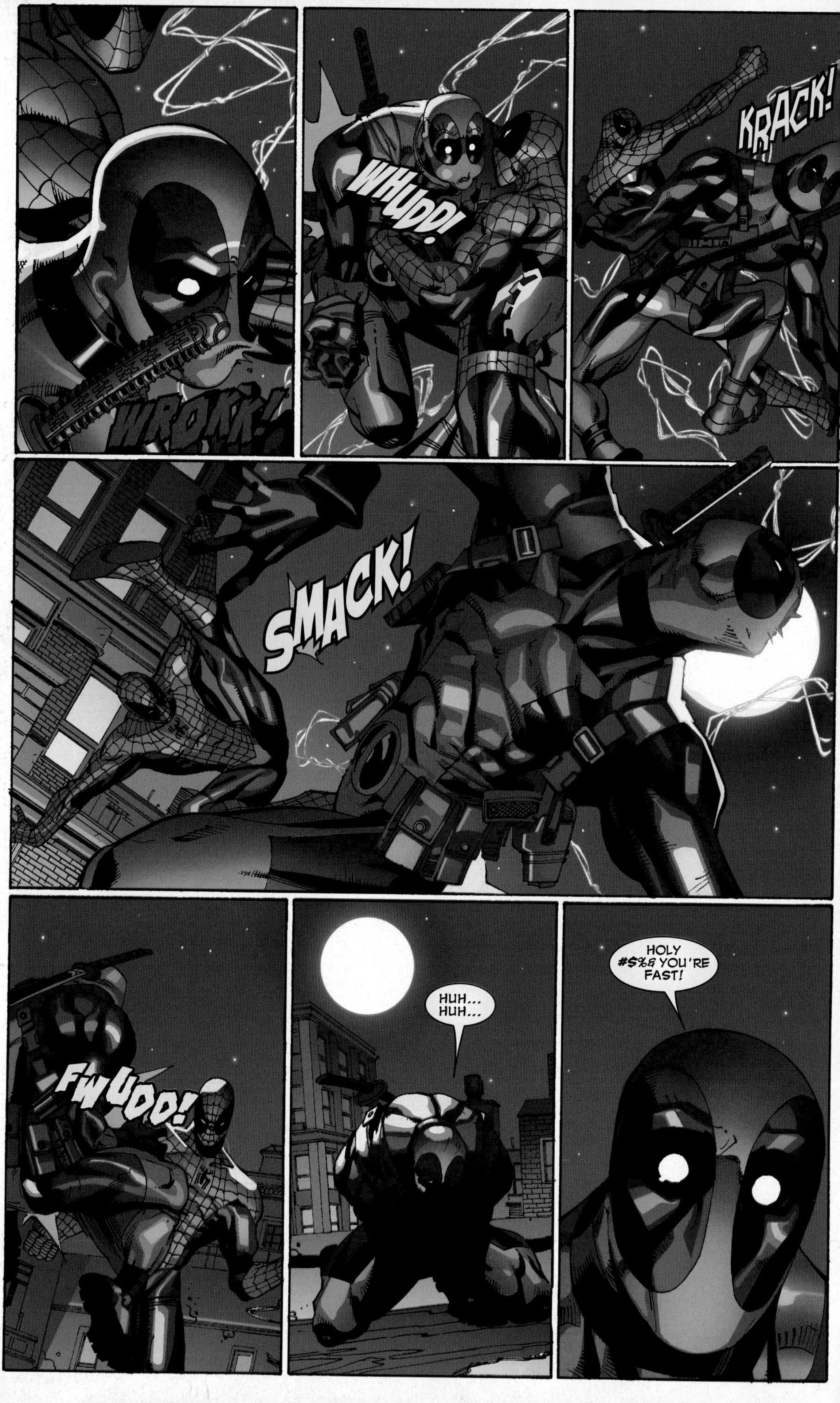
WROKK!
WHUDD!
KRACK!
SMACK!
FWUDD!
HUH... HUH...
HOLY #$%& YOU'RE FAST!

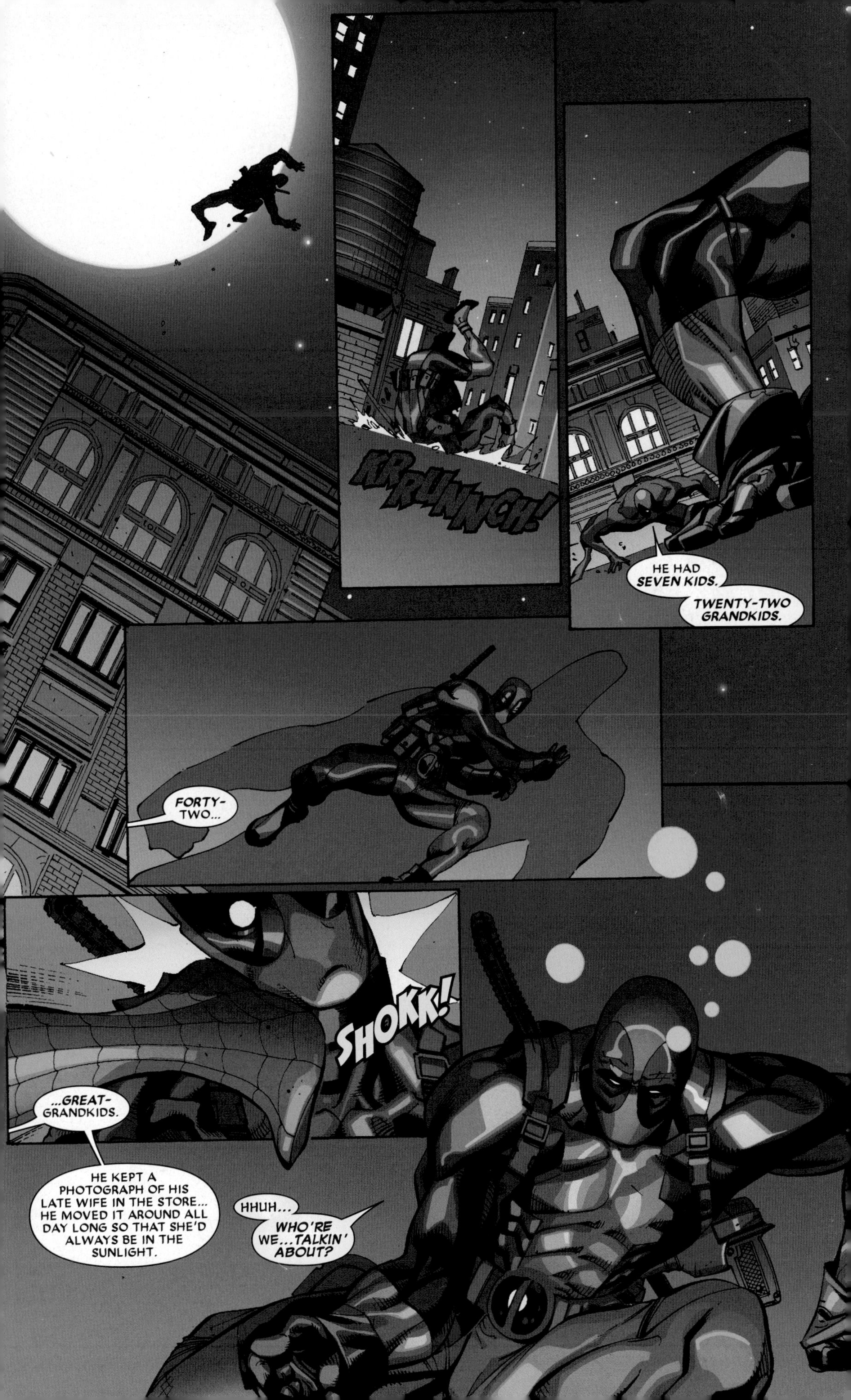
KRRUNNCH!
HE HAD SEVEN KIDS.
TWENTY-TWO GRANDKIDS.
FORTY-TWO...
SHOKK!
...GREAT-GRANDKIDS.
HE KEPT A PHOTOGRAPH OF HIS LATE WIFE IN THE STORE... HE MOVED IT AROUND ALL DAY LONG SO THAT SHE'D ALWAYS BE IN THE SUNLIGHT.
HHUH...
WHO'RE WE...TALKIN' ABOUT?

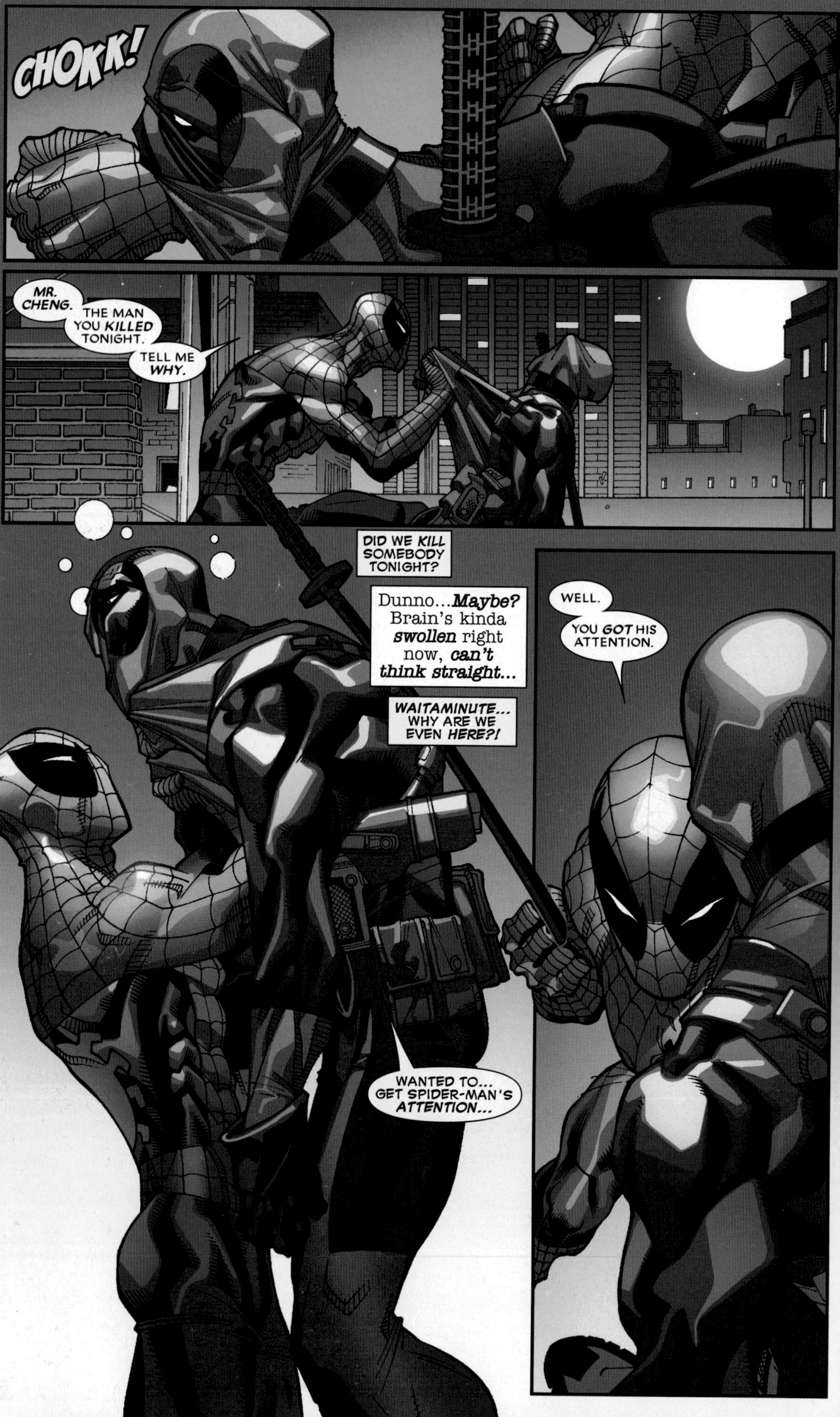
CHOKK!
MR. CHENG.
THE MAN YOU KILLED TONIGHT.
TELL ME WHY.
DID WE KILL SOMEBODY TONIGHT?
Dunno...Maybe? Brain's kinda swollen right now, can't think straight...
WAITAMINUTE... WHY ARE WE EVEN HERE?!
WANTED TO... GET SPIDER-MAN'S ATTENTION...
WELL.
YOU GOT HIS ATTENTION.

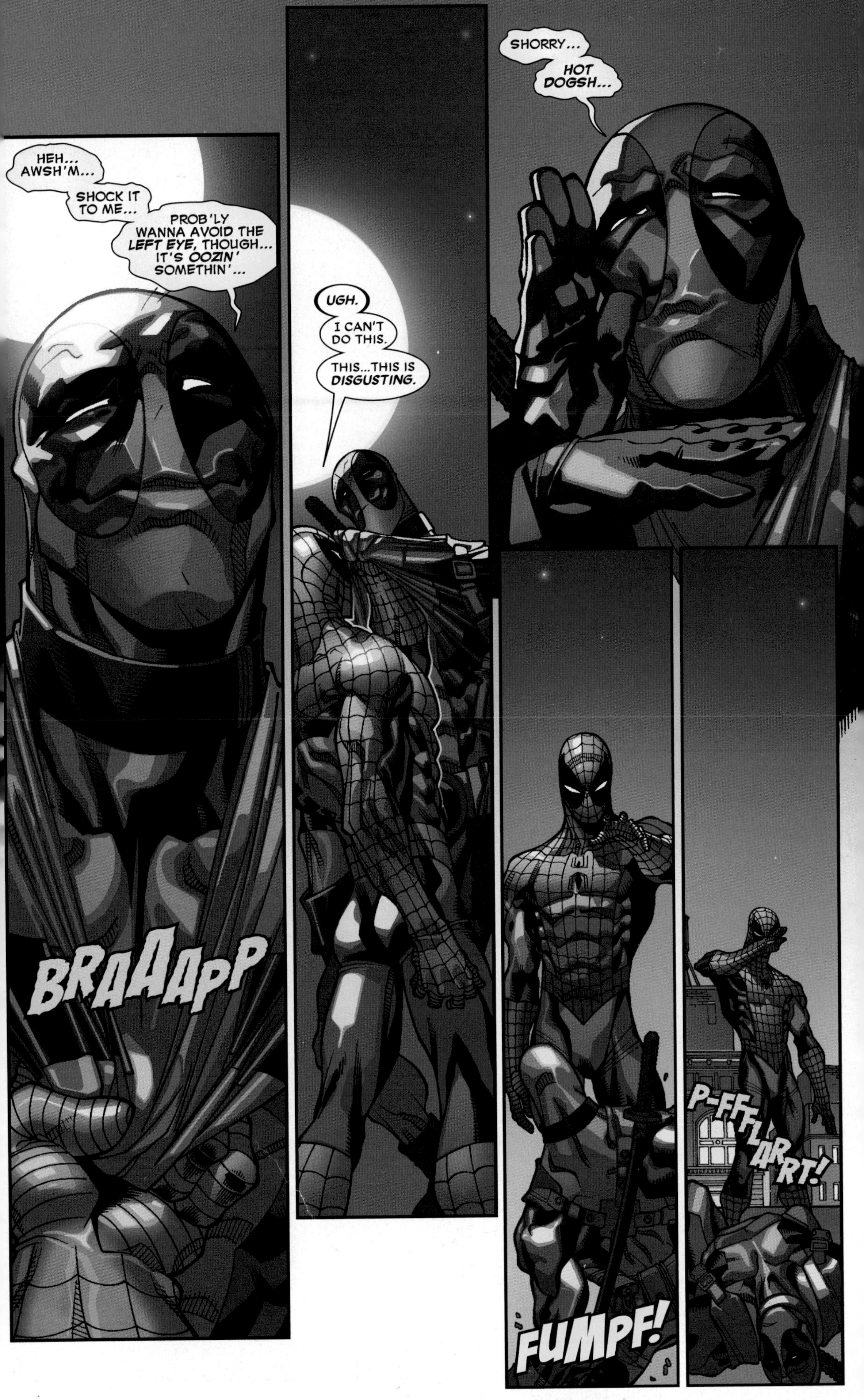
HEH... AWSH'M...
SHOCK IT TO ME...
PROB'LY WANNA AVOID THE LEFT EYE, THOUGH... IT'S OOZIN' SOMETHIN'...
BRAAAPP
UGH.
I CAN'T DO THIS.
THIS...THIS IS DISGUSTING.
SHORRY...
HOT DOGSH...
FUMPF!
P-FFFLARRT!

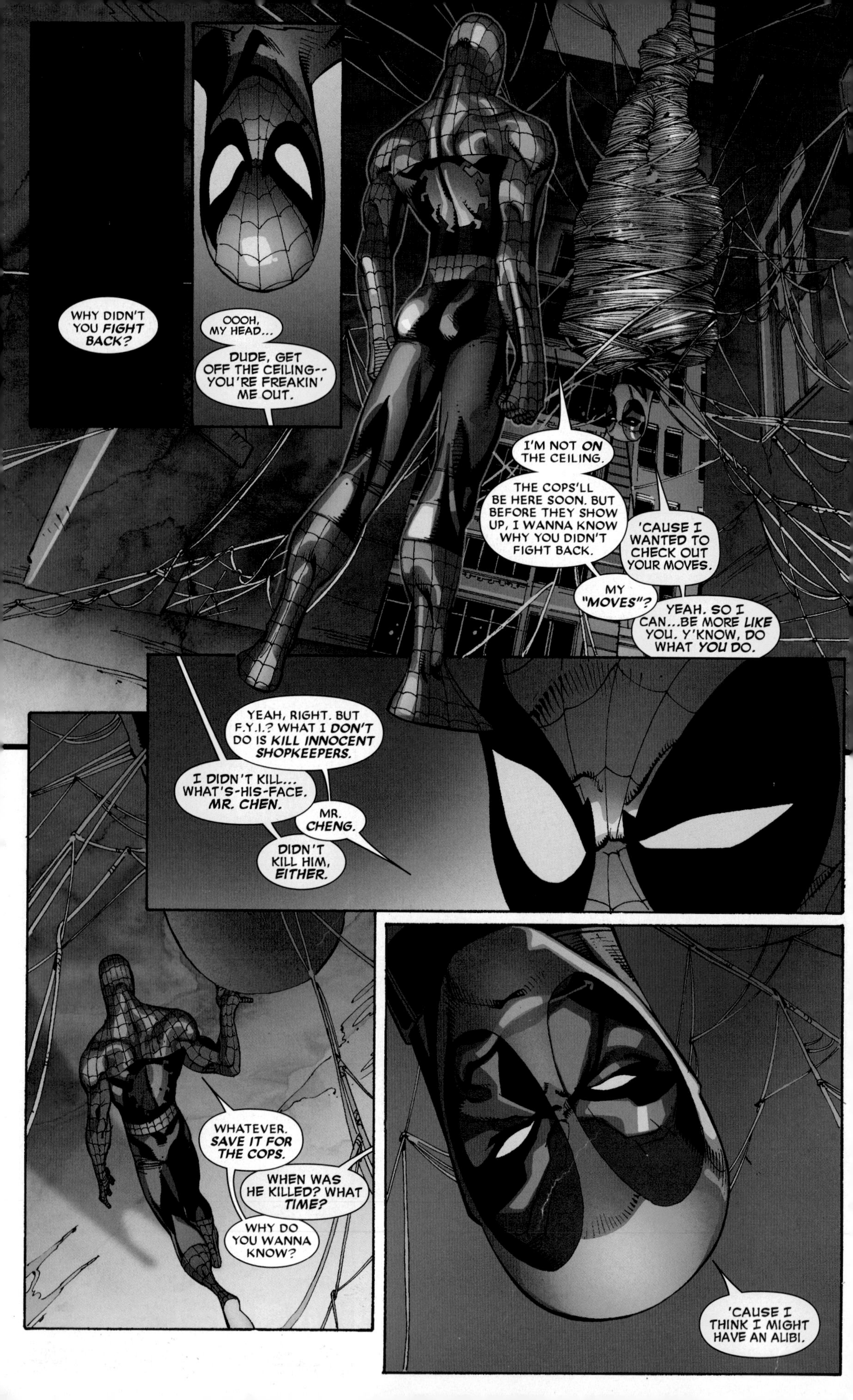
WHY DIDN'T YOU *FIGHT* BACK?
OOOH, MY HEAD...
DUDE, GET OFF THE CEILING--YOU'RE FREAKIN' ME OUT.
I'M NOT *ON* THE CEILING.
THE COPS'LL BE HERE SOON. BUT BEFORE THEY SHOW UP, I WANNA KNOW WHY YOU DIDN'T FIGHT BACK.
'CAUSE I WANTED TO CHECK OUT YOUR MOVES.
MY *"MOVES"*?
YEAH. SO I CAN...BE MORE *LIKE* YOU. Y'KNOW, DO WHAT *YOU* DO.
YEAH, RIGHT. BUT F.Y.I.? WHAT I *DON'T* DO IS *KILL INNOCENT SHOPKEEPERS.*
I DIDN'T KILL... WHAT'S-HIS-FACE. *MR. CHEN.*
MR. *CHENG.*
DIDN'T KILL HIM, *EITHER.*
WHATEVER. *SAVE IT FOR THE COPS.*
WHEN WAS HE KILLED? WHAT *TIME?*
WHY DO YOU WANNA KNOW?
'CAUSE I THINK I MIGHT HAVE AN ALIBI.

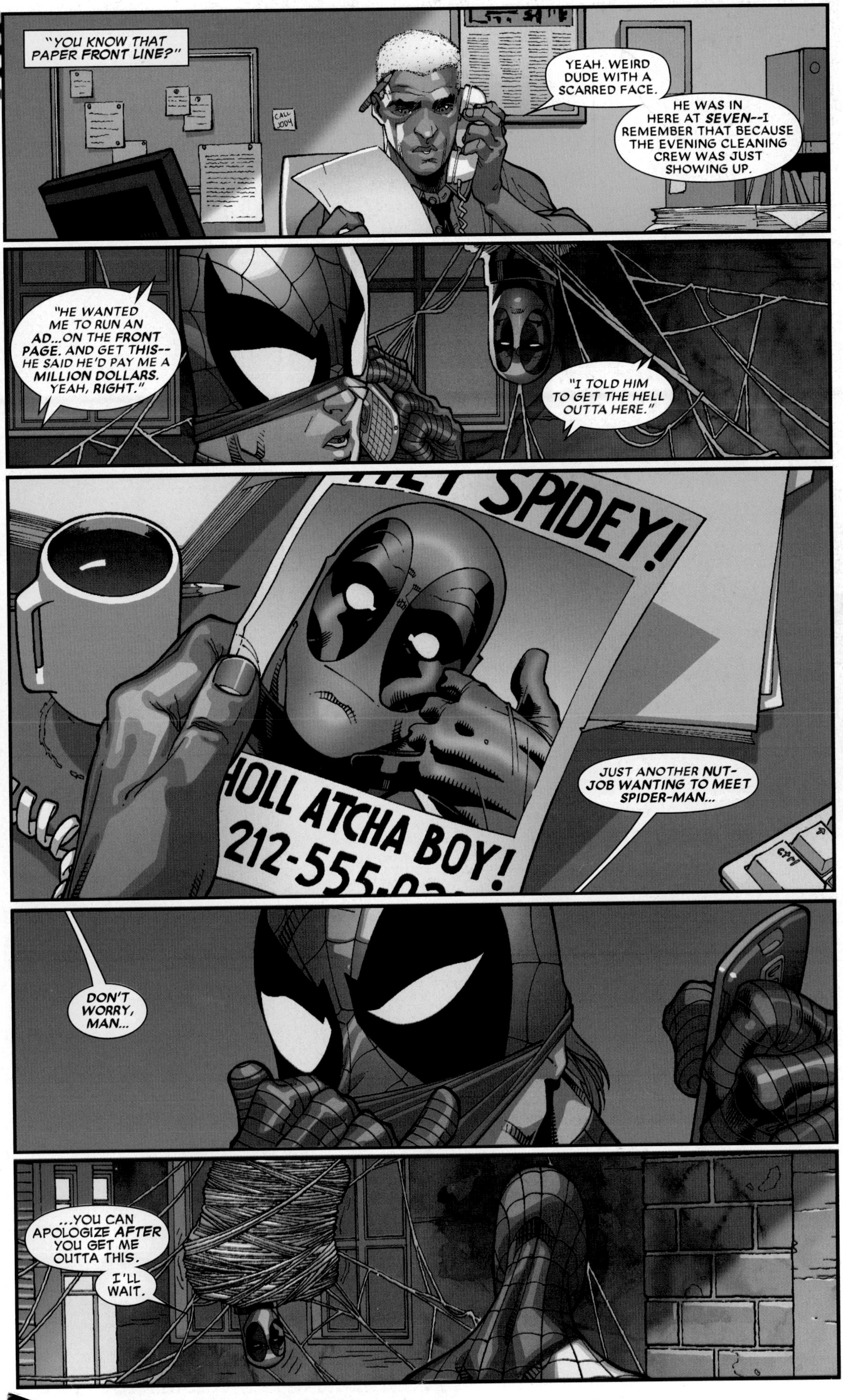
"YOU KNOW THAT PAPER FRONT LINE?"
YEAH. WEIRD DUDE WITH A SCARRED FACE.
HE WAS IN HERE AT SEVEN--I REMEMBER THAT BECAUSE THE EVENING CLEANING CREW WAS JUST SHOWING UP.
CALL JODY
"HE WANTED ME TO RUN AN AD...ON THE FRONT PAGE. AND GET THIS--HE SAID HE'D PAY ME A MILLION DOLLARS. YEAH, RIGHT."
"I TOLD HIM TO GET THE HELL OUTTA HERE."
SPIDEY!
HOLL ATCHA BOY!
212-555-
JUST ANOTHER NUT-JOB WANTING TO MEET SPIDER-MAN...
ctrl
DON'T WORRY, MAN...
...YOU CAN APOLOGIZE AFTER YOU GET ME OUTTA THIS.
I'LL WAIT.

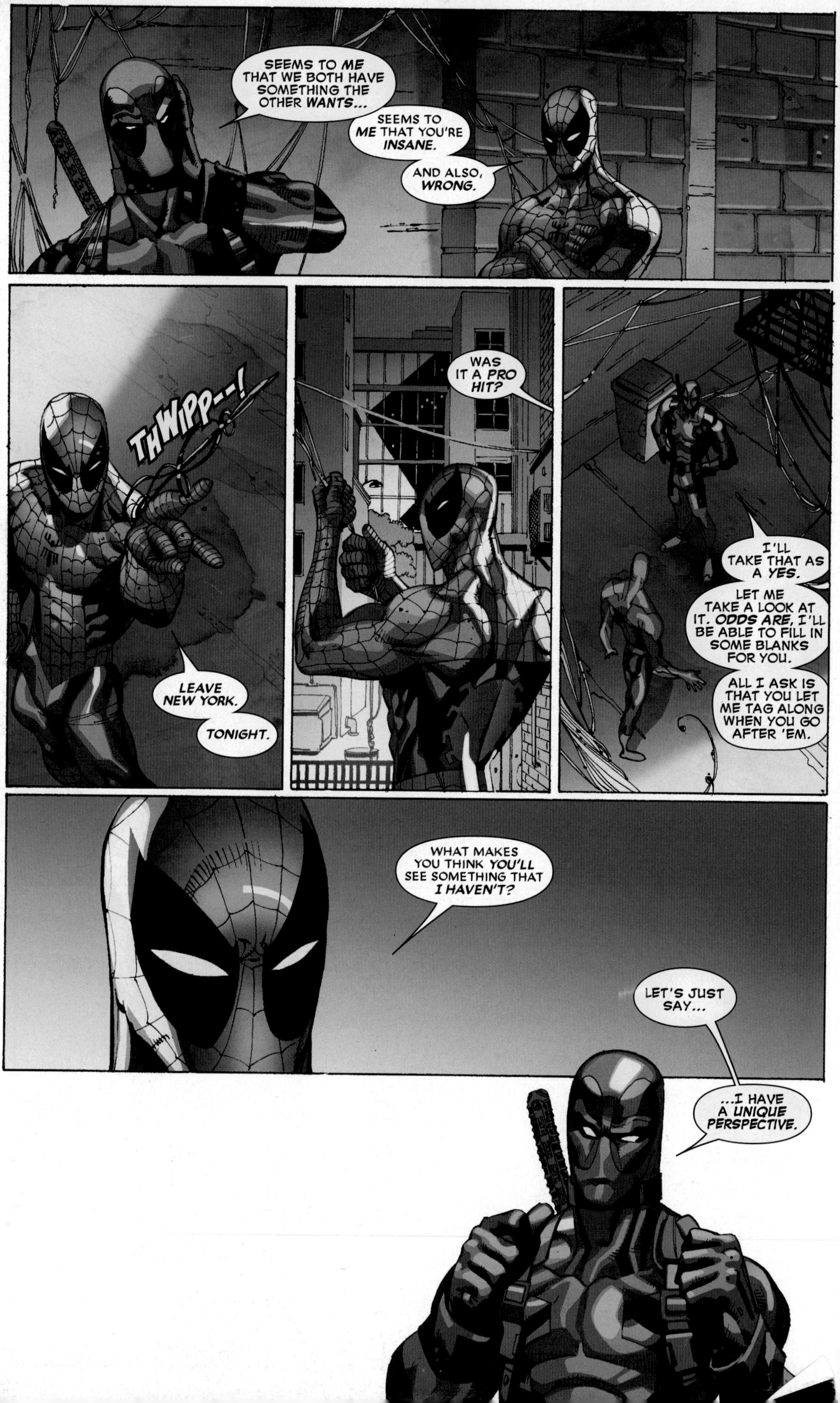
SEEMS TO ME THAT WE BOTH HAVE SOMETHING THE OTHER WANTS...
SEEMS TO ME THAT YOU'RE INSANE.
AND ALSO, WRONG.
THWIPP--!
LEAVE NEW YORK.
TONIGHT.
WAS IT A PRO HIT?
I'LL TAKE THAT AS A YES.
LET ME TAKE A LOOK AT IT. ODDS ARE, I'LL BE ABLE TO FILL IN SOME BLANKS FOR YOU.
ALL I ASK IS THAT YOU LET ME TAG ALONG WHEN YOU GO AFTER 'EM.
WHAT MAKES YOU THINK YOU'LL SEE SOMETHING THAT I HAVEN'T?
LET'S JUST SAY...
...I HAVE A UNIQUE PERSPECTIVE.

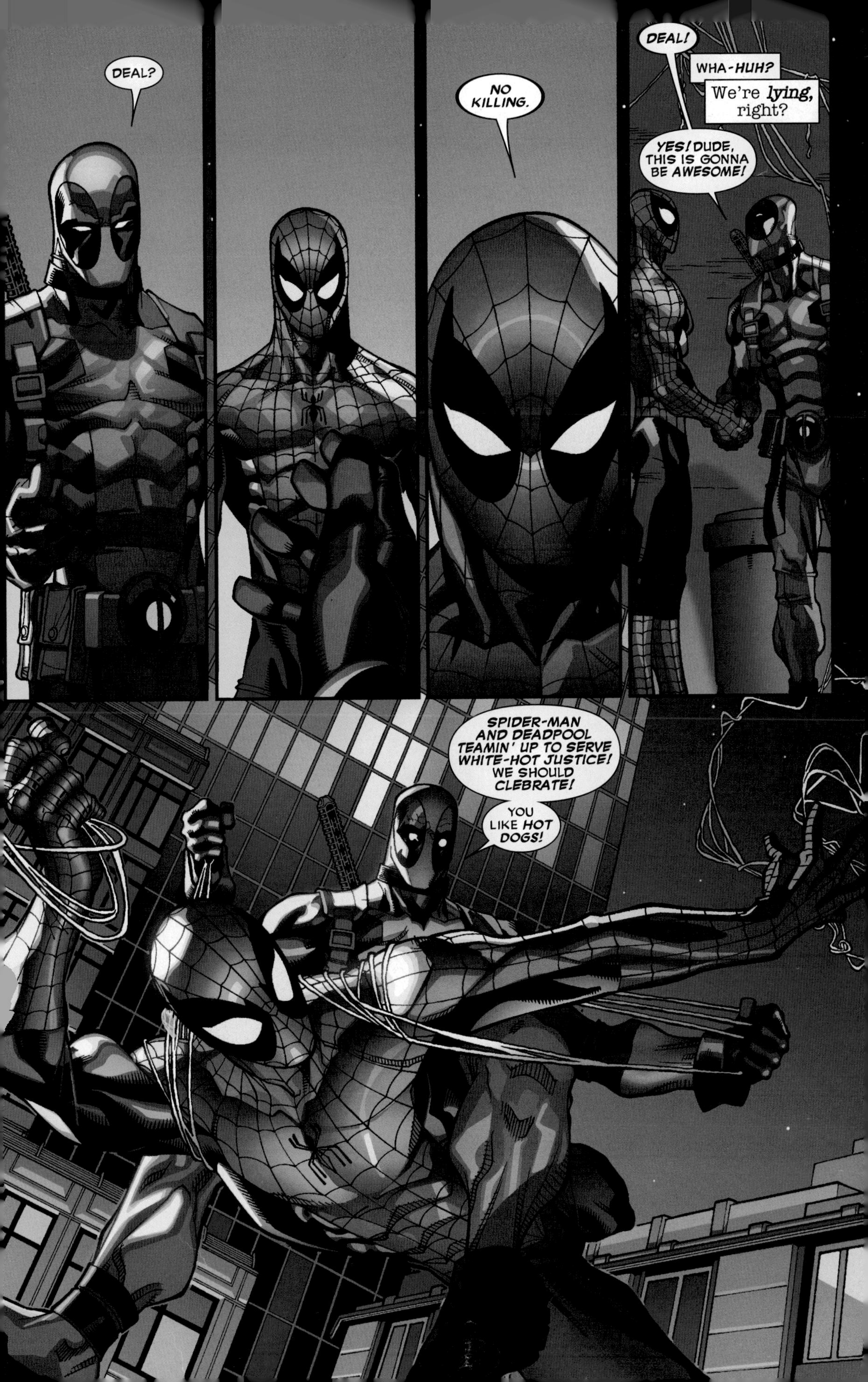
DEAL?
NO KILLING.
DEAL!
WHA-HUH?
We're lying, right?
YES! DUDE, THIS IS GONNA BE AWESOME!
SPIDER-MAN AND DEADPOOL TEAMIN' UP TO SERVE WHITE-HOT JUSTICE! WE SHOULD CLEBRATE!
YOU LIKE HOT DOGS!

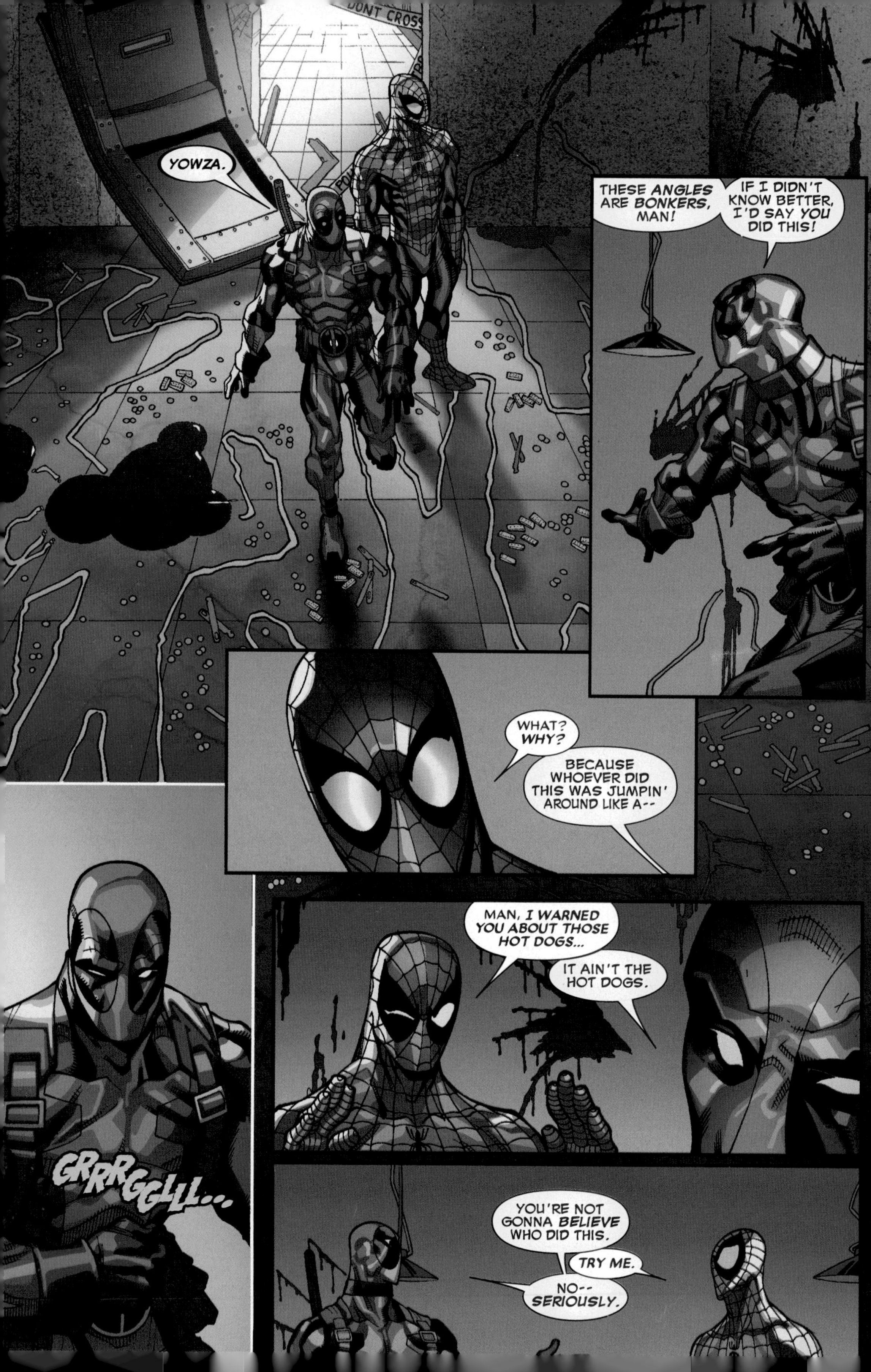
DONT CROSS
YOWZA.
THESE ANGLES ARE BONKERS, MAN!
IF I DIDN'T KNOW BETTER, I'D SAY YOU DID THIS!
WHAT? WHY?
BECAUSE WHOEVER DID THIS WAS JUMPIN' AROUND LIKE A--
GRRRGGLLL...
MAN, I WARNED YOU ABOUT THOSE HOT DOGS...
IT AIN'T THE HOT DOGS.
YOU'RE NOT GONNA BELIEVE WHO DID THIS.
TRY ME.
NO-- SERIOUSLY.

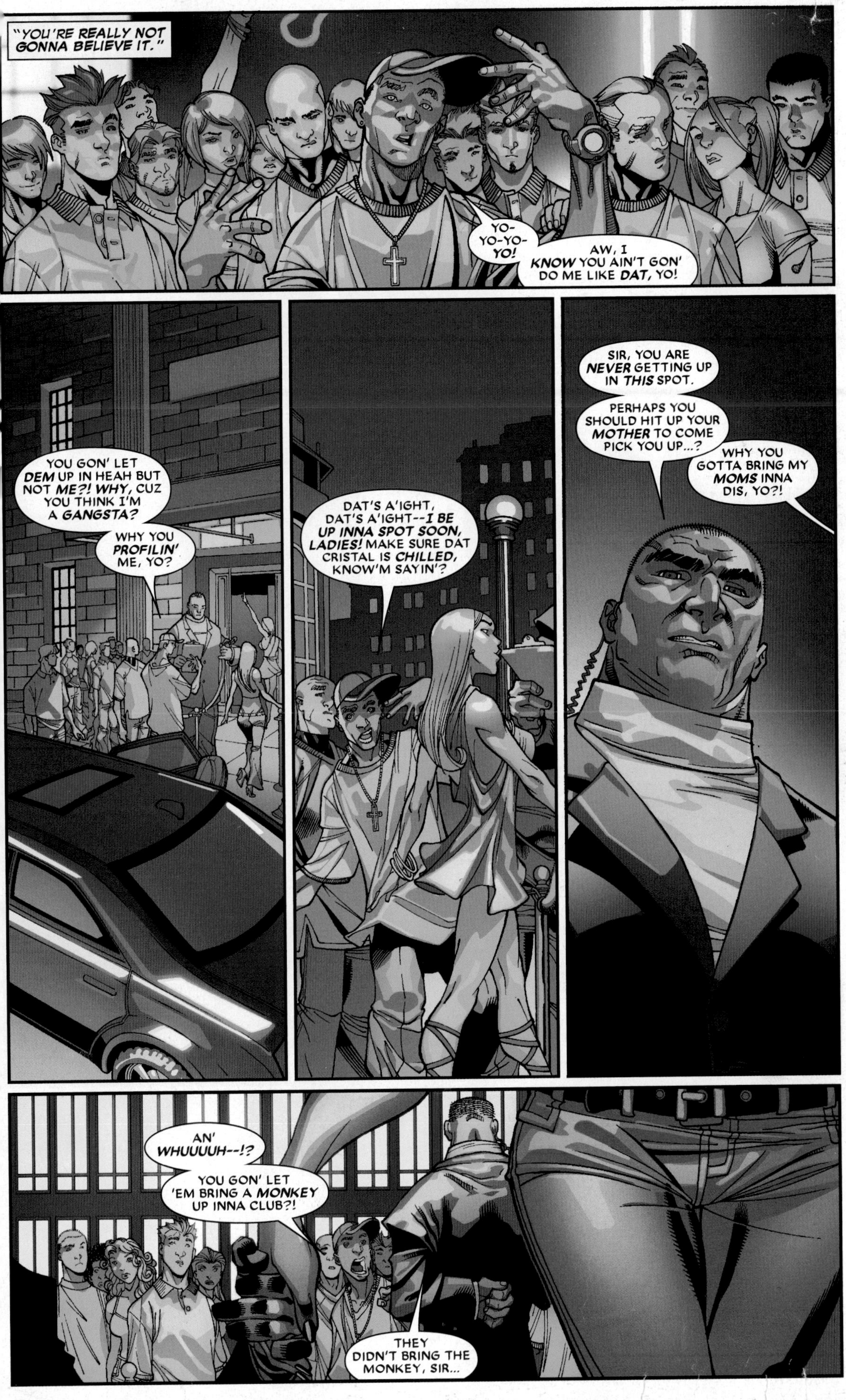
"YOU'RE REALLY NOT GONNA BELIEVE IT."
YO-YO-YO-YO!
AW, I KNOW YOU AIN'T GON' DO ME LIKE DAT, YO!
YOU GON' LET DEM UP IN HEAH BUT NOT ME?! WHY, CUZ YOU THINK I'M A GANGSTA?
WHY YOU PROFILIN' ME, YO?
DAT'S A'IGHT, DAT'S A'IGHT--I BE UP INNA SPOT SOON, LADIES! MAKE SURE DAT CRISTAL IS CHILLED, KNOW'M SAYIN'?
SIR, YOU ARE NEVER GETTING UP IN THIS SPOT.
PERHAPS YOU SHOULD HIT UP YOUR MOTHER TO COME PICK YOU UP...?
WHY YOU GOTTA BRING MY MOMS INNA DIS, YO?!
AN' WHUUUUH--!?
YOU GON' LET 'EM BRING A MONKEY UP INNA CLUB?!
THEY DIDN'T BRING THE MONKEY, SIR...

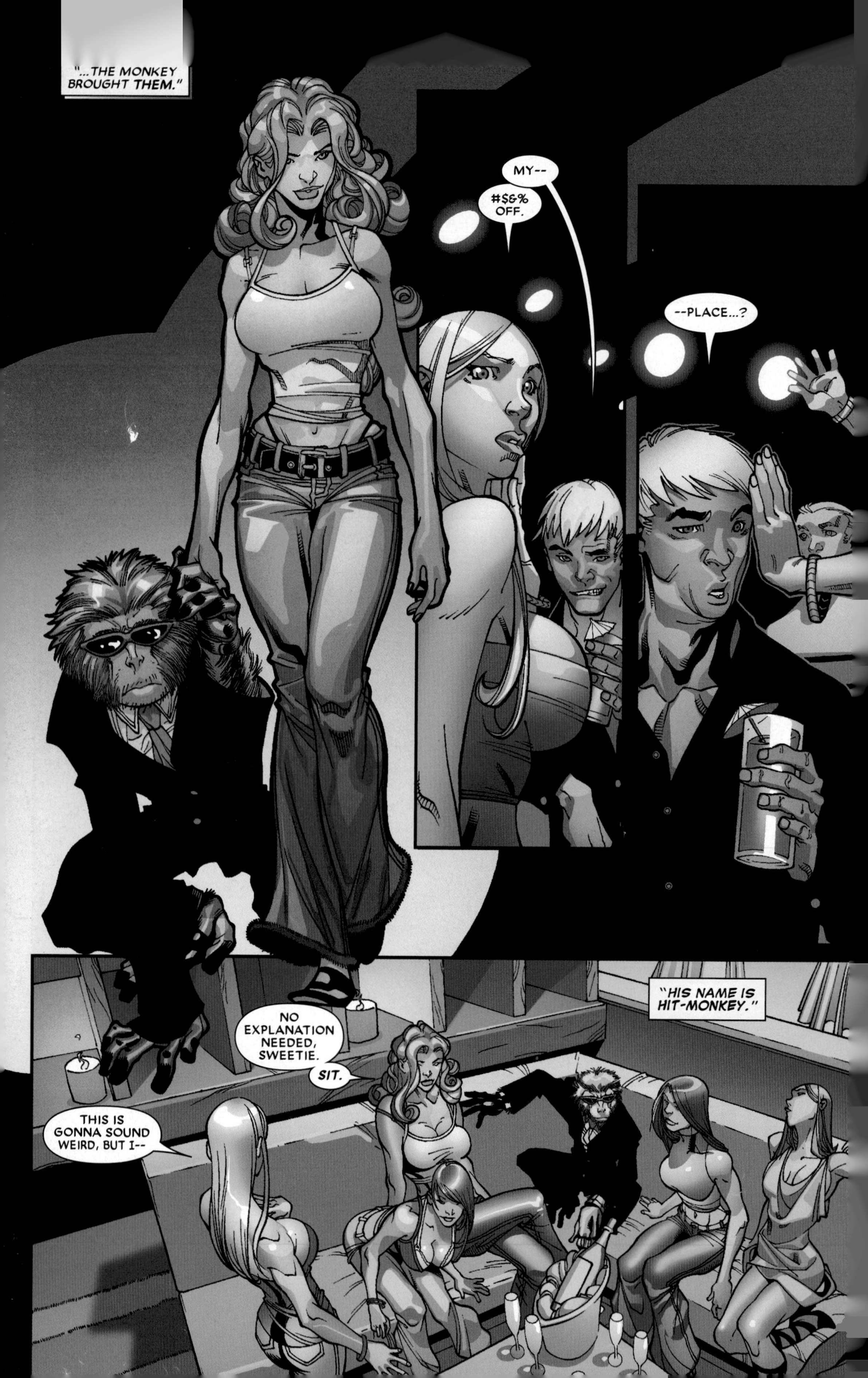
"...THE MONKEY BROUGHT THEM."
MY--
#$&% OFF.
--PLACE...?
"HIS NAME IS HIT-MONKEY."
NO EXPLANATION NEEDED, SWEETIE.
SIT.
THIS IS GONNA SOUND WEIRD, BUT I--

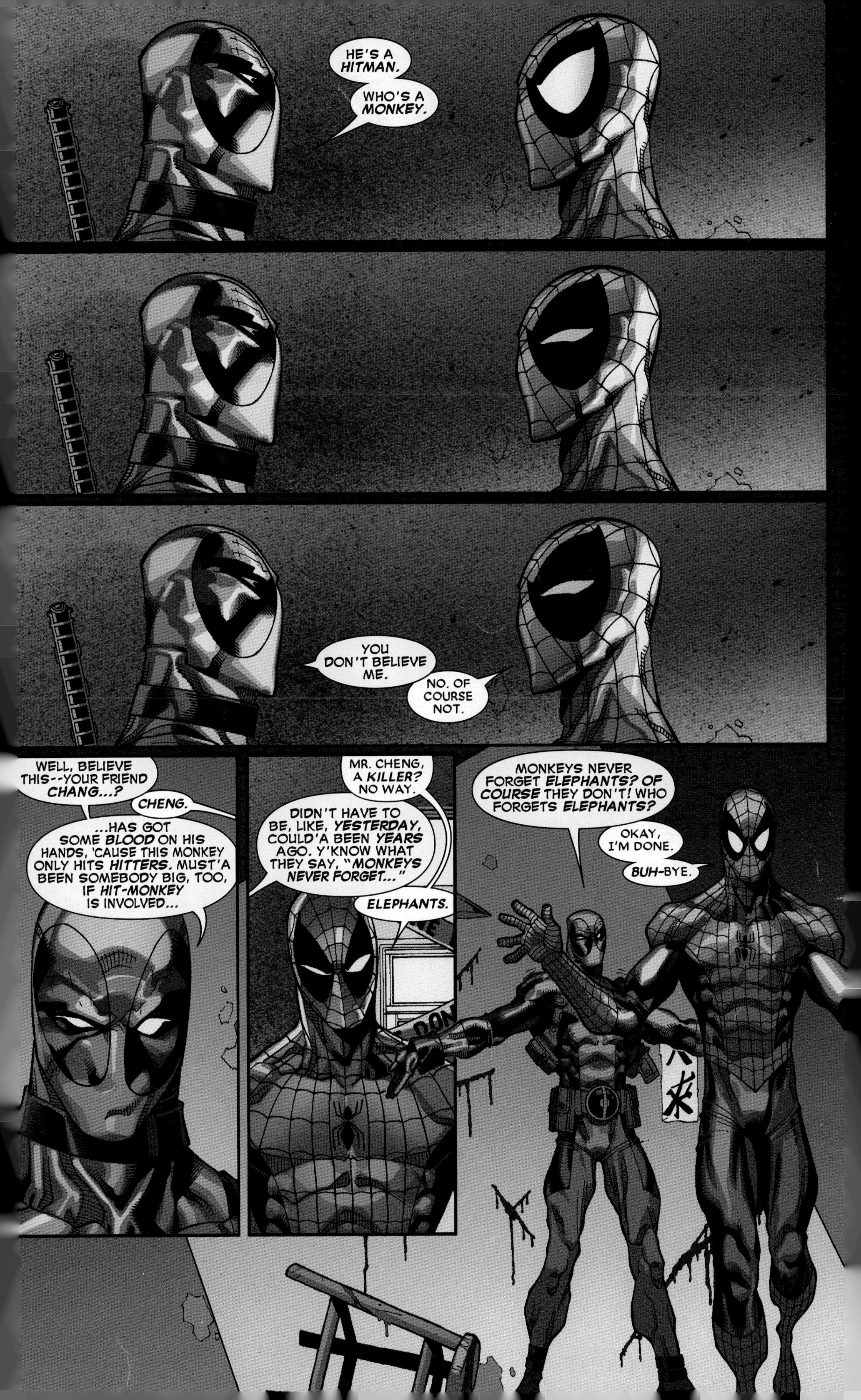
HE'S A HITMAN.
WHO'S A MONKEY.
YOU DON'T BELIEVE ME.
NO. OF COURSE NOT.
WELL, BELIEVE THIS--YOUR FRIEND CHANG...?
CHENG.
...HAS GOT SOME BLOOD ON HIS HANDS, 'CAUSE THIS MONKEY ONLY HITS HITTERS. MUST'A BEEN SOMEBODY BIG, TOO, IF HIT-MONKEY IS INVOLVED...
MR. CHENG, A KILLER? NO WAY.
DIDN'T HAVE TO BE, LIKE, YESTERDAY, COULD'A BEEN YEARS AGO. Y'KNOW WHAT THEY SAY, "MONKEYS NEVER FORGET..."
ELEPHANTS.
MONKEYS NEVER FORGET ELEPHANTS? OF COURSE THEY DON'T! WHO FORGETS ELEPHANTS?
OKAY, I'M DONE.
BUH-BYE.

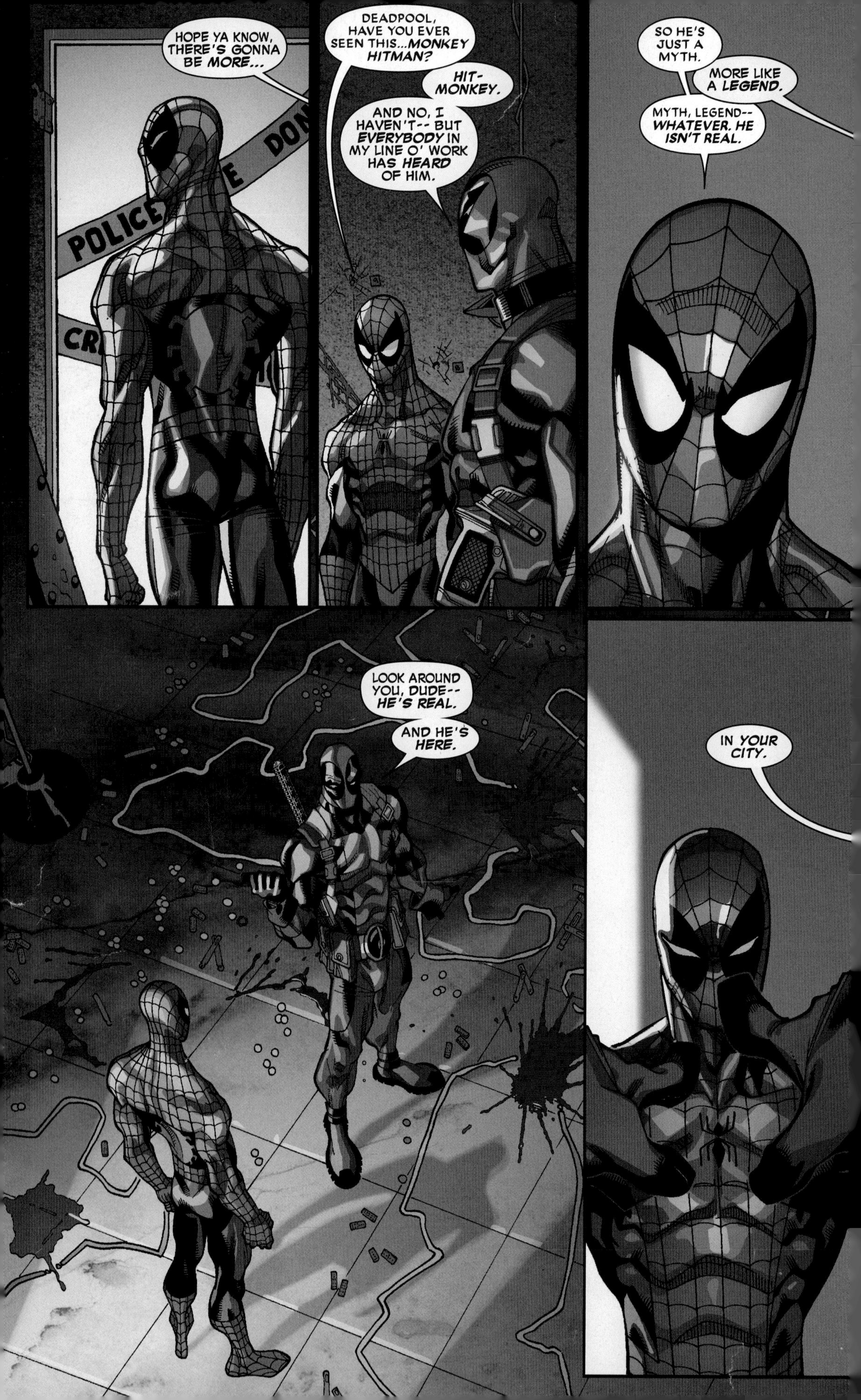
HOPE YA KNOW, THERE'S GONNA BE MORE...
POLICE
CR
DEADPOOL, HAVE YOU EVER SEEN THIS...MONKEY HITMAN?
HIT-MONKEY.
AND NO, I HAVEN'T-- BUT EVERYBODY IN MY LINE O' WORK HAS HEARD OF HIM.
SO HE'S JUST A MYTH.
MORE LIKE A LEGEND.
MYTH, LEGEND-- WHATEVER. HE ISN'T REAL.
LOOK AROUND YOU, DUDE-- HE'S REAL.
AND HE'S HERE.
IN YOUR CITY.

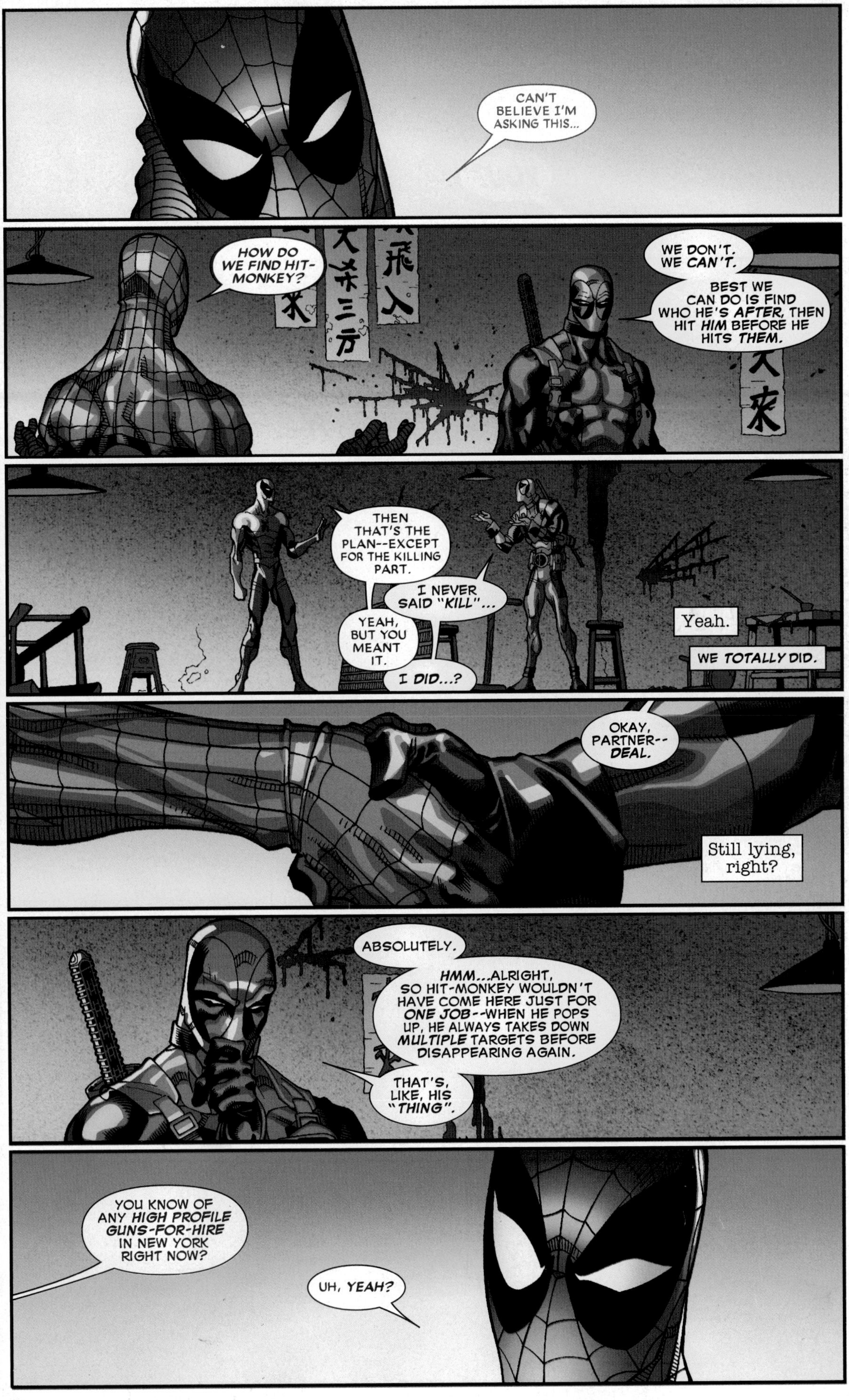
CAN'T BELIEVE I'M ASKING THIS...
HOW DO WE FIND HIT-MONKEY?
WE DON'T. WE CAN'T.
BEST WE CAN DO IS FIND WHO HE'S AFTER, THEN HIT HIM BEFORE HE HITS THEM.
THEN THAT'S THE PLAN--EXCEPT FOR THE KILLING PART.
I NEVER SAID "KILL"...
YEAH, BUT YOU MEANT IT.
I DID...?
Yeah.
WE TOTALLY DID.
OKAY, PARTNER--DEAL.
Still lying, right?
ABSOLUTELY.
HMM...ALRIGHT, SO HIT-MONKEY WOULDN'T HAVE COME HERE JUST FOR ONE JOB--WHEN HE POPS UP, HE ALWAYS TAKES DOWN MULTIPLE TARGETS BEFORE DISAPPEARING AGAIN.
THAT'S, LIKE, HIS "THING".
YOU KNOW OF ANY HIGH PROFILE GUNS-FOR-HIRE IN NEW YORK RIGHT NOW?
UH, YEAH?

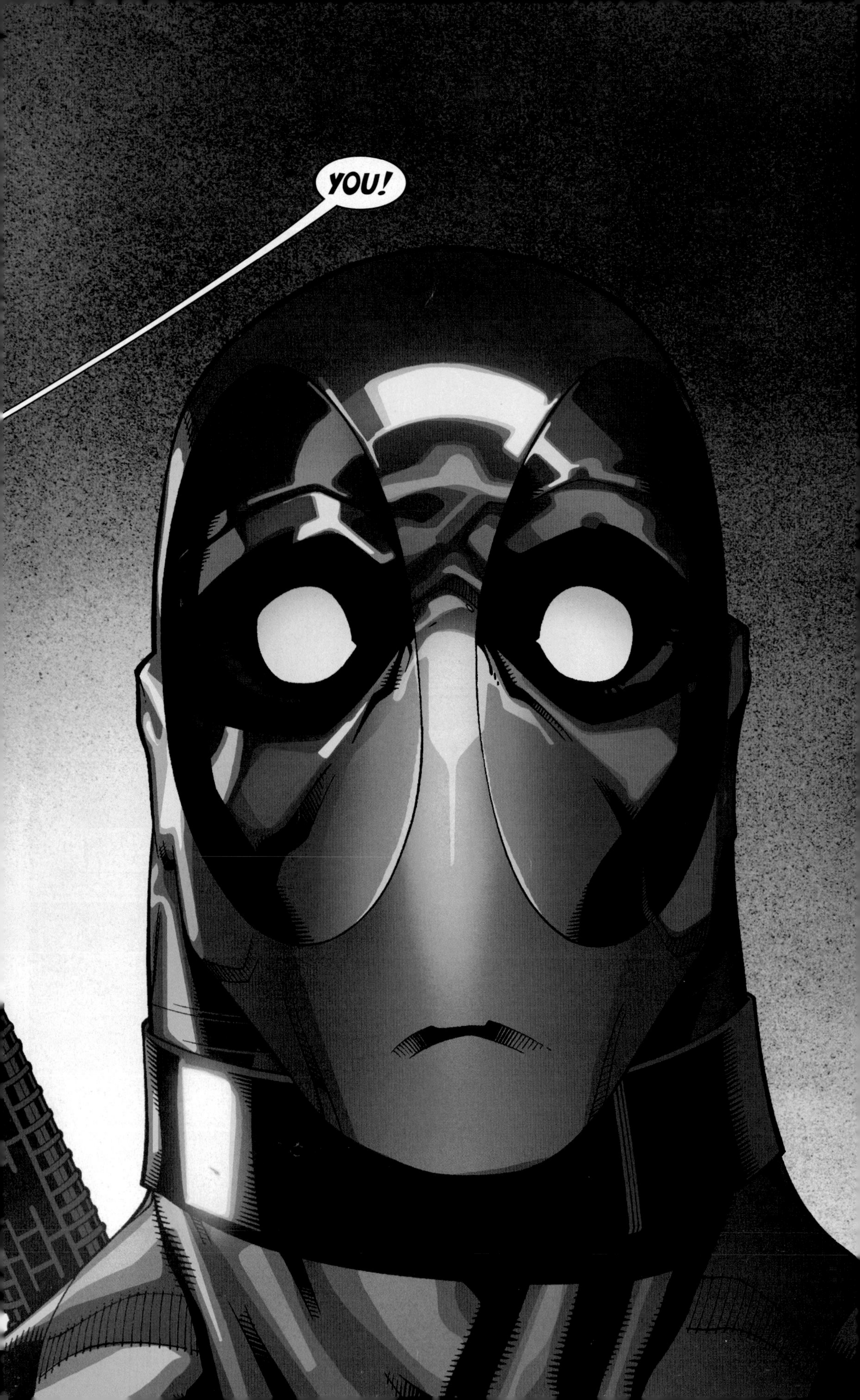
YOU!

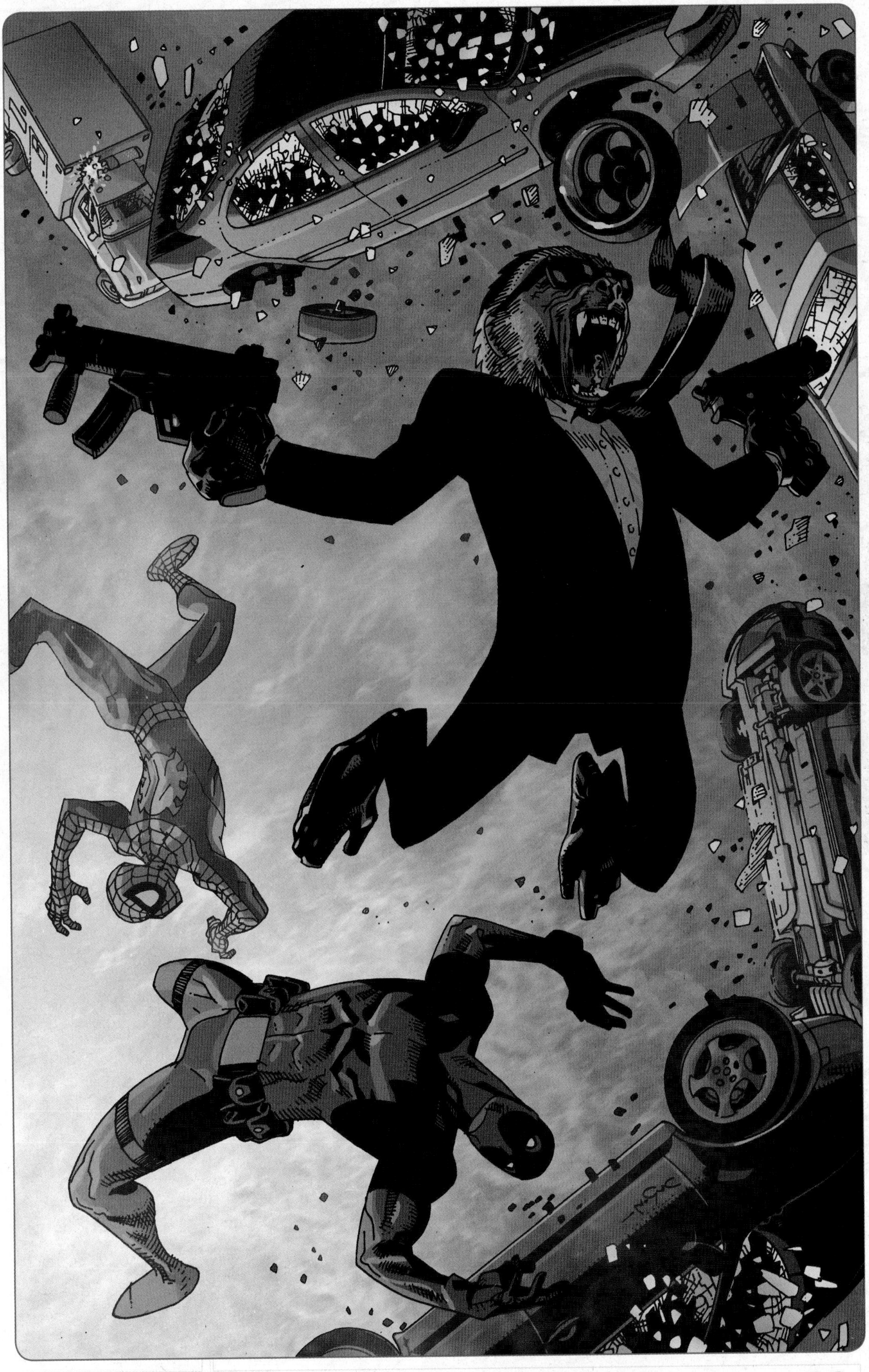

DEADPOOL (2008) #20

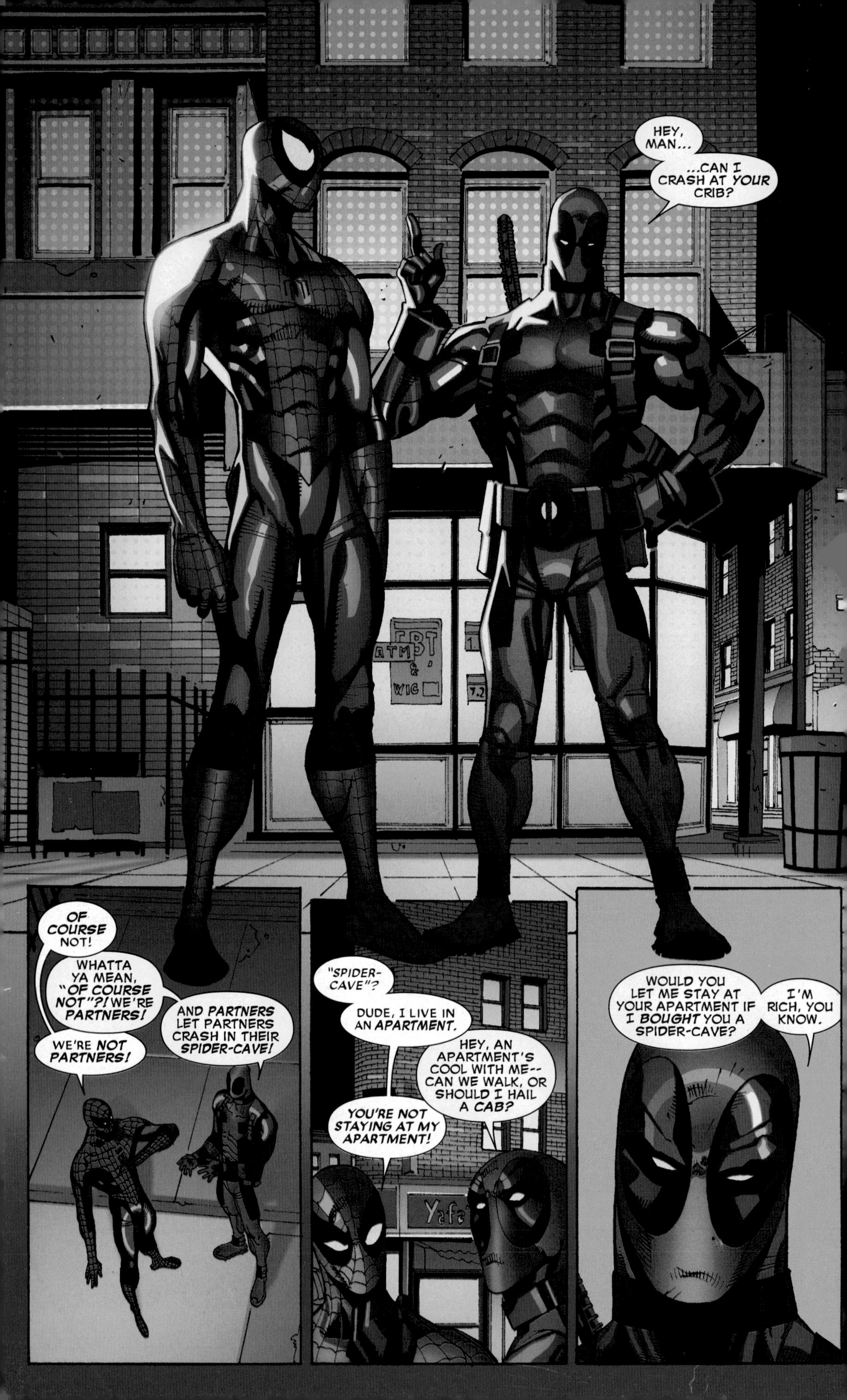

HEY, MAN...
...CAN I CRASH AT YOUR CRIB?
OF COURSE NOT!
WHATTA YA MEAN, "OF COURSE NOT"?! WE'RE PARTNERS!
AND PARTNERS LET PARTNERS CRASH IN THEIR SPIDER-CAVE!
WE'RE NOT PARTNERS!
"SPIDER-CAVE"?
DUDE, I LIVE IN AN APARTMENT.
HEY, AN APARTMENT'S COOL WITH ME-- CAN WE WALK, OR SHOULD I HAIL A CAB?
YOU'RE NOT STAYING AT MY APARTMENT!
WOULD YOU LET ME STAY AT YOUR APARTMENT IF I BOUGHT YOU A SPIDER-CAVE?
I'M RICH, YOU KNOW.

WAIT A MINUTE... YOU'RE *SCARED*, AREN'T YOU?

WHAT? NO...

Yes.

TERRIFIED.

YOU REALLY THINK A *"HIT-MONKEY"* IS OUT TO *GET* YOU?

NO, I'M REALLY *"CONVINCED"* THAT *"HIT-MONKEY"* IS GONNA *"BLOW MY FREAKIN' BRAINS OUT"*!

I KNOW HE'S *HERE*, AND I KNOW WHAT HE *DOES*--HE KILLS GUYS LIKE ME.

ASSASSINS.

I'M NOT AN ASSASSIN!

PEOPLE PAY YOU MONEY TO SHOOT *OTHER* PEOPLE.

THAT MAKES YOU AN ASSASSIN.

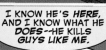

FORMER ASSASSIN.

I HAVEN'T PULLED A TRIGGER FOR *MONEY* IN... LEMME THINK...

WHEN DID I DO THAT PIZZA DELIVERY GUY?

Issue #10.

YEAH! AND THAT WAS, LIKE, *TEN* ISSUES AG--

HELLO?

WHATEVER A SPIDER CAN
PART 2 OF 3

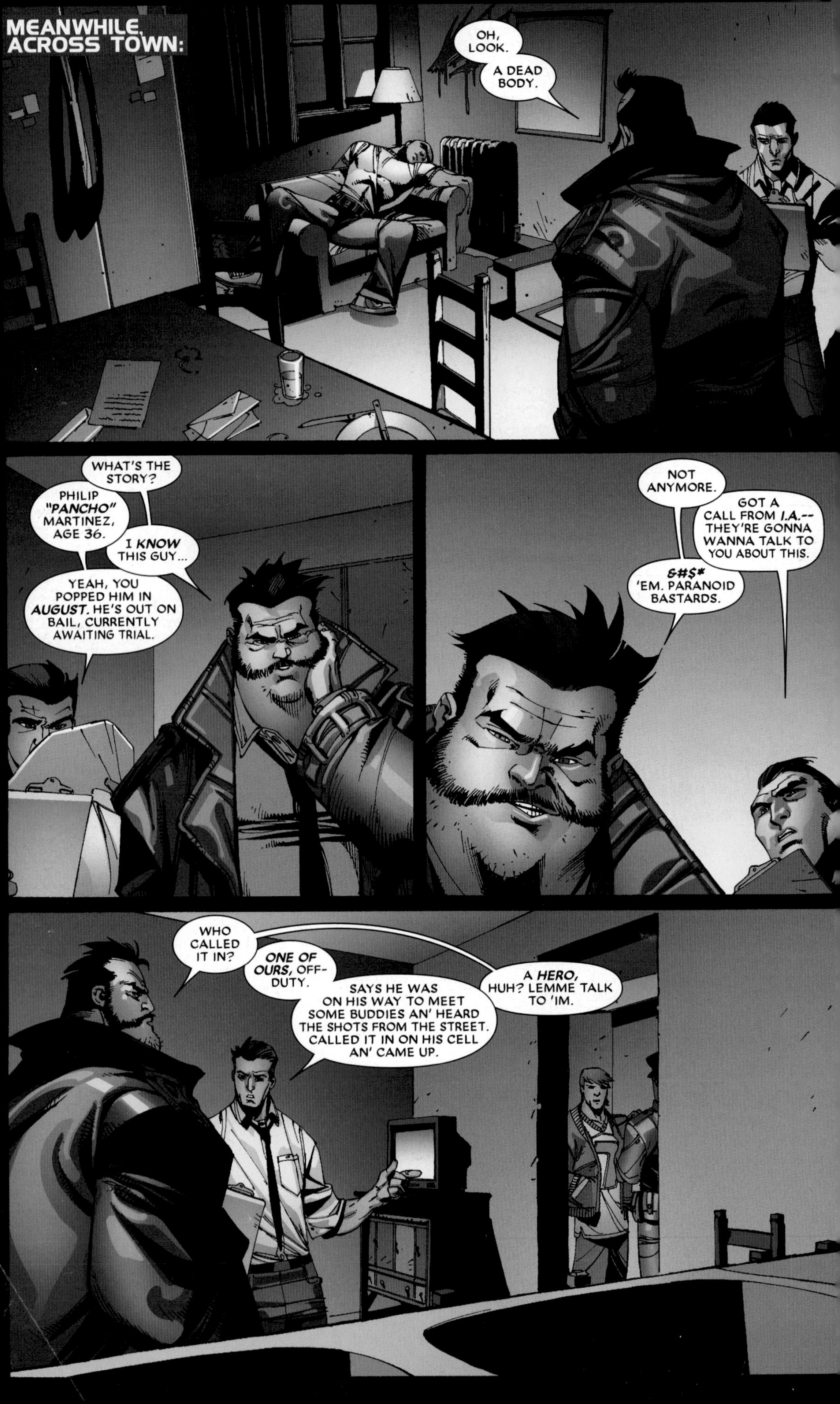
MEANWHILE, ACROSS TOWN:
OH, LOOK.
A DEAD BODY.
WHAT'S THE STORY?
PHILIP "PANCHO" MARTINEZ, AGE 36.
I KNOW THIS GUY...
YEAH, YOU POPPED HIM IN AUGUST. HE'S OUT ON BAIL, CURRENTLY AWAITING TRIAL.
NOT ANYMORE.
GOT A CALL FROM I.A.-- THEY'RE GONNA WANNA TALK TO YOU ABOUT THIS.
&#$* 'EM. PARANOID BASTARDS.
WHO CALLED IT IN?
ONE OF OURS, OFF-DUTY.
SAYS HE WAS ON HIS WAY TO MEET SOME BUDDIES AN' HEARD THE SHOTS FROM THE STREET. CALLED IT IN ON HIS CELL AN' CAME UP.
A HERO, HUH? LEMME TALK TO 'IM.

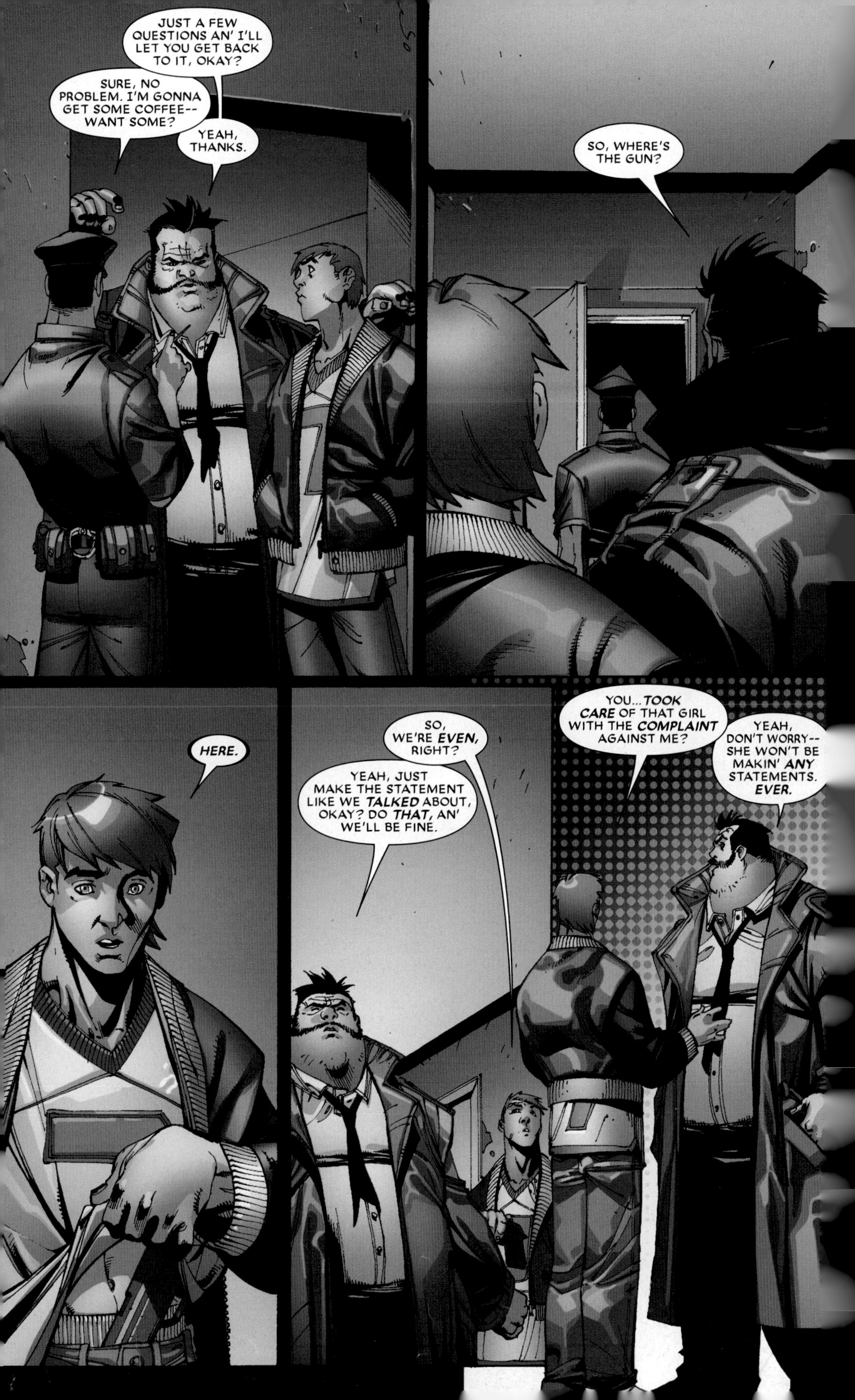

JUST A FEW QUESTIONS AN' I'LL LET YOU GET BACK TO IT, OKAY?
SURE, NO PROBLEM. I'M GONNA GET SOME COFFEE-- WANT SOME?
YEAH, THANKS.
SO, WHERE'S THE GUN?
HERE.
SO, WE'RE EVEN, RIGHT?
YEAH, JUST MAKE THE STATEMENT LIKE WE TALKED ABOUT, OKAY? DO THAT, AN' WE'LL BE FINE.
YOU...TOOK CARE OF THAT GIRL WITH THE COMPLAINT AGAINST ME?
YEAH, DON'T WORRY-- SHE WON'T BE MAKIN' ANY STATEMENTS. EVER.

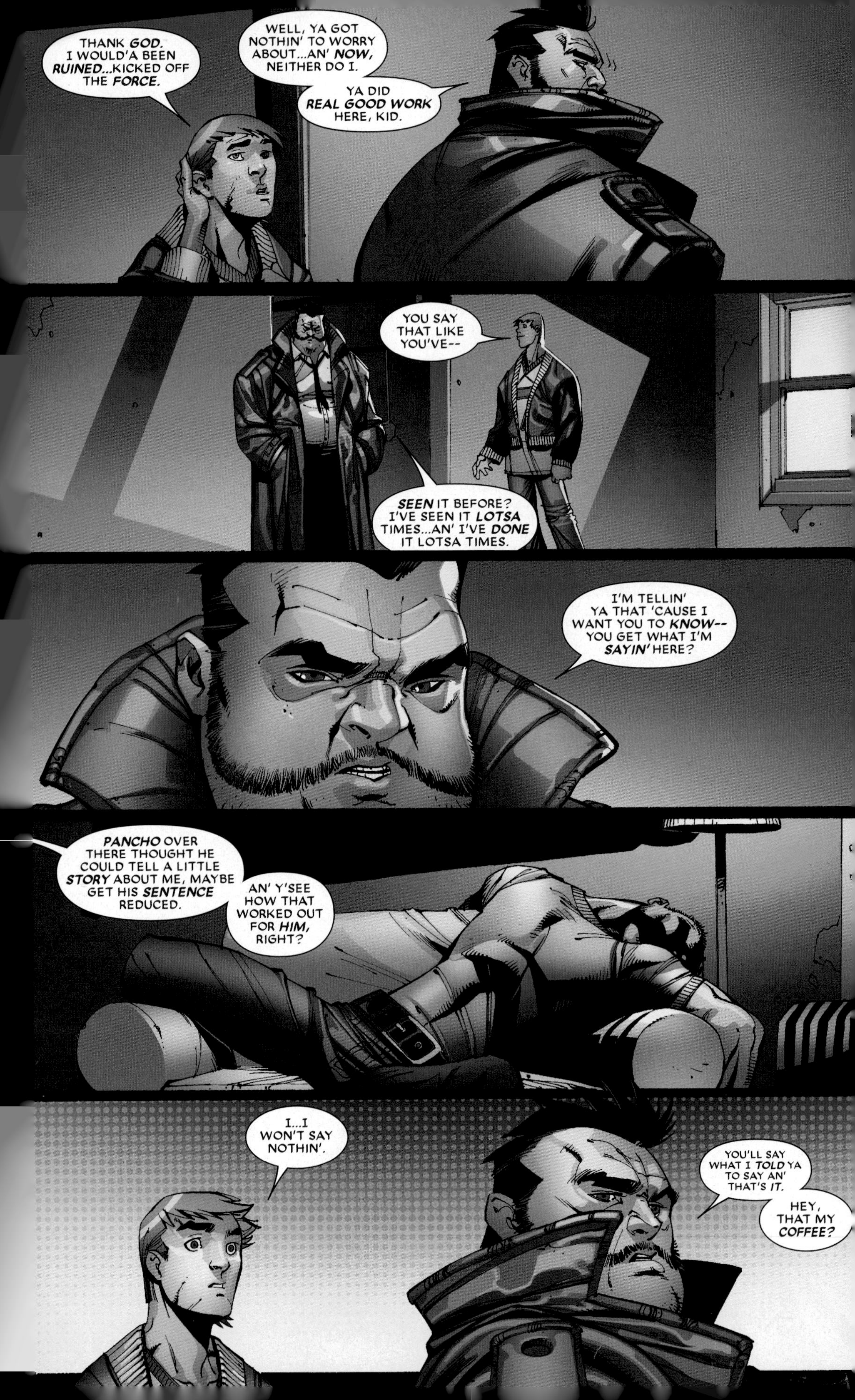

THANK GOD. I WOULD'A BEEN RUINED...KICKED OFF THE FORCE.
WELL, YA GOT NOTHIN' TO WORRY ABOUT...AN' NOW, NEITHER DO I.
YA DID REAL GOOD WORK HERE, KID.
YOU SAY THAT LIKE YOU'VE--
SEEN IT BEFORE? I'VE SEEN IT LOTSA TIMES...AN' I'VE DONE IT LOTSA TIMES.
I'M TELLIN' YA THAT 'CAUSE I WANT YOU TO KNOW-- YOU GET WHAT I'M SAYIN' HERE?
PANCHO OVER THERE THOUGHT HE COULD TELL A LITTLE STORY ABOUT ME, MAYBE GET HIS SENTENCE REDUCED.
AN' Y'SEE HOW THAT WORKED OUT FOR HIM, RIGHT?
I...I WON'T SAY NOTHIN'.
YOU'LL SAY WHAT I TOLD YA TO SAY AN' THAT'S IT.
HEY, THAT MY COFFEE?

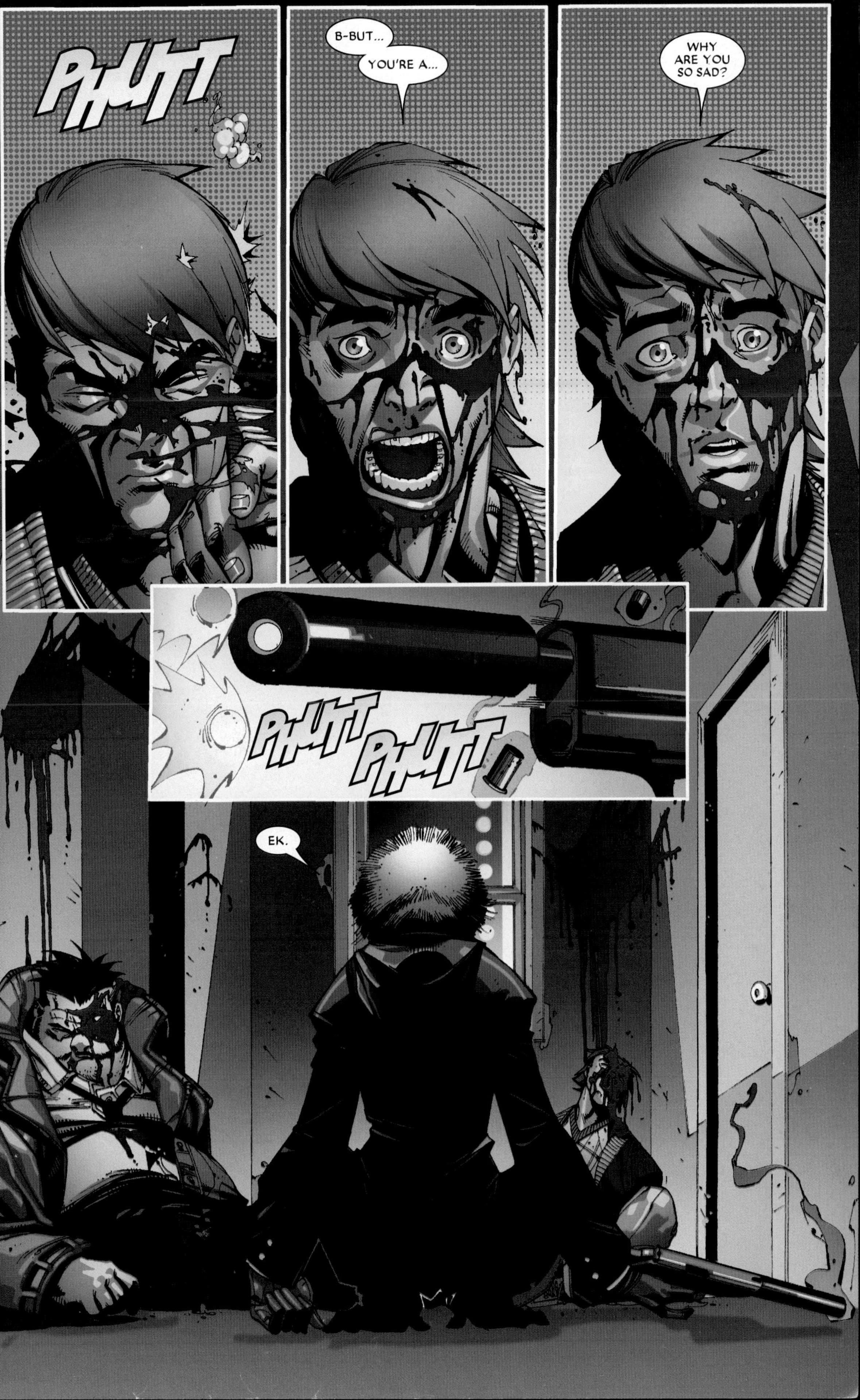
PHUTT
B-BUT...
YOU'RE A...
WHY ARE YOU SO SAD?
PHUTT PHUTT
EK.

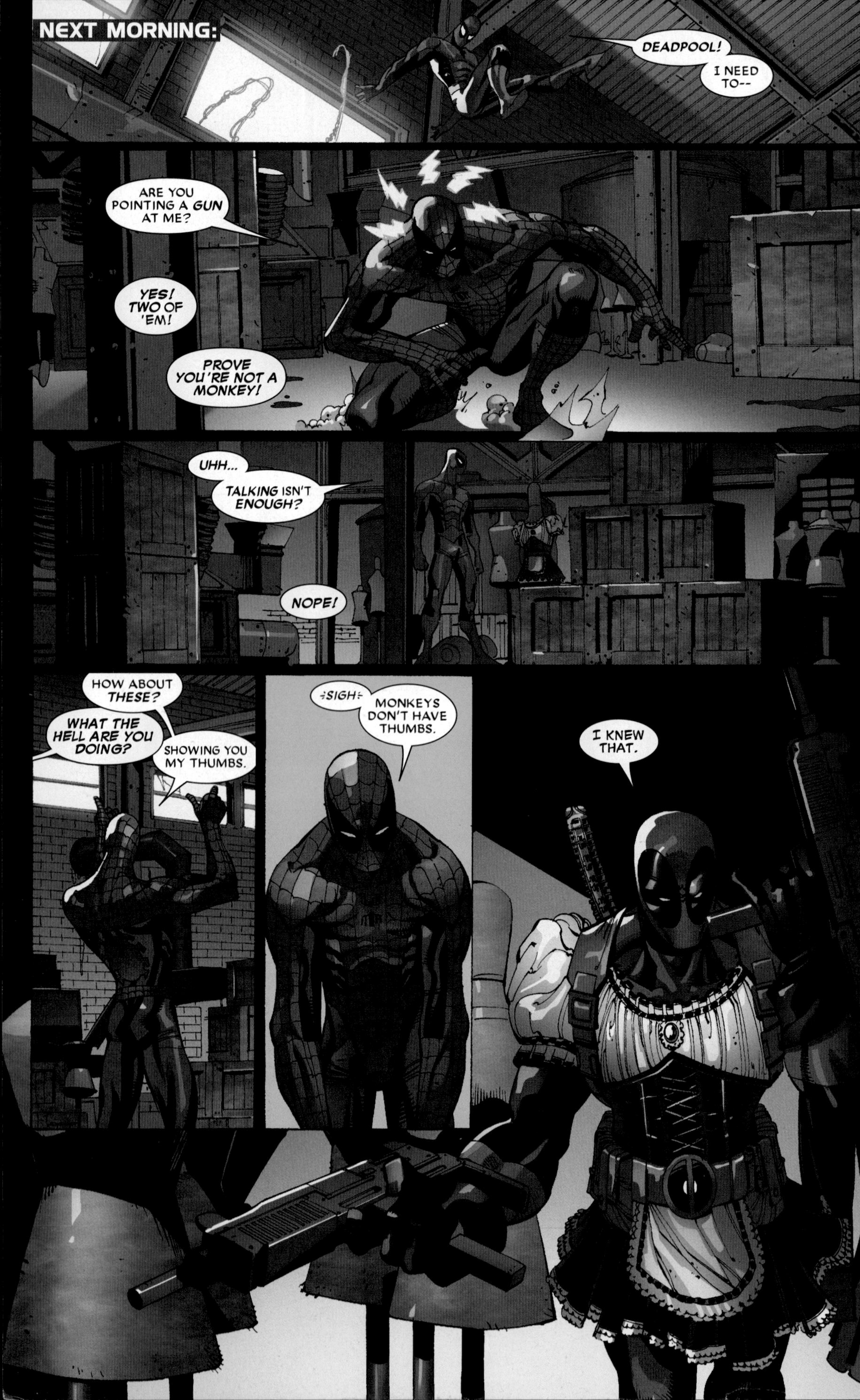
NEXT MORNING:
DEADPOOL!
I NEED TO--
ARE YOU POINTING A GUN AT ME?
YES! TWO OF 'EM!
PROVE YOU'RE NOT A MONKEY!
UHH...
TALKING ISN'T ENOUGH?
NOPE!
HOW ABOUT THESE?
WHAT THE HELL ARE YOU DOING?
SHOWING YOU MY THUMBS.
=SIGH=
MONKEYS DON'T HAVE THUMBS.
I KNEW THAT.

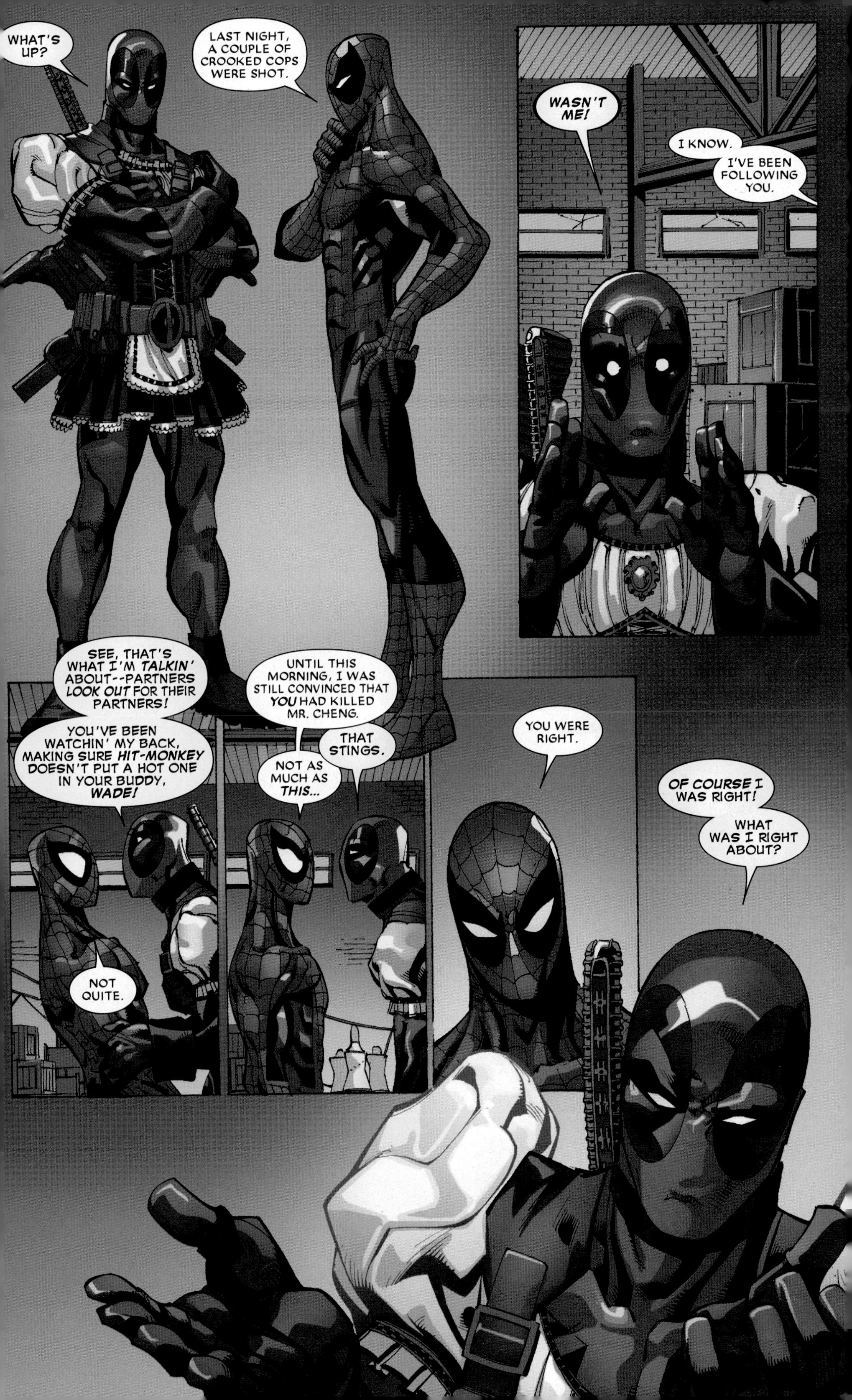
WHAT'S UP?
LAST NIGHT, A COUPLE OF CROOKED COPS WERE SHOT.
WASN'T ME!
I KNOW. I'VE BEEN FOLLOWING YOU.
SEE, THAT'S WHAT I'M TALKIN' ABOUT--PARTNERS LOOK OUT FOR THEIR PARTNERS!
YOU'VE BEEN WATCHIN' MY BACK, MAKING SURE HIT-MONKEY DOESN'T PUT A HOT ONE IN YOUR BUDDY, WADE!
NOT QUITE.
UNTIL THIS MORNING, I WAS STILL CONVINCED THAT YOU HAD KILLED MR. CHENG.
THAT STINGS.
NOT AS MUCH AS THIS...
YOU WERE RIGHT.
OF COURSE I WAS RIGHT!
WHAT WAS I RIGHT ABOUT?

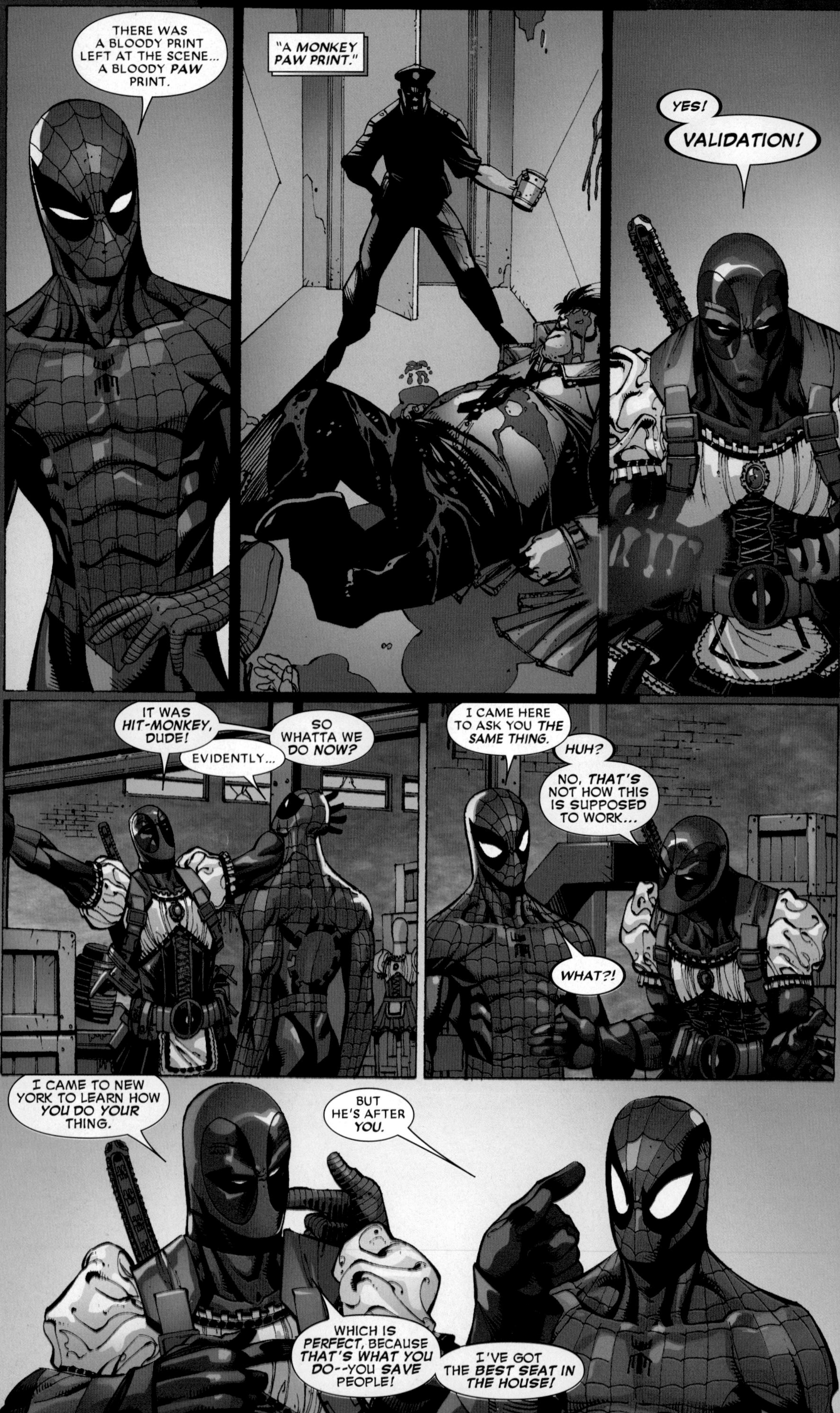

THERE WAS A BLOODY PRINT LEFT AT THE SCENE... A BLOODY PAW PRINT.
"A MONKEY PAW PRINT."
YES!
VALIDATION!
IT WAS HIT-MONKEY, DUDE!
EVIDENTLY...
SO WHATTA WE DO NOW?
I CAME HERE TO ASK YOU THE SAME THING.
HUH?
NO, THAT'S NOT HOW THIS IS SUPPOSED TO WORK...
WHAT?!
I CAME TO NEW YORK TO LEARN HOW YOU DO YOUR THING.
BUT HE'S AFTER YOU.
WHICH IS PERFECT, BECAUSE THAT'S WHAT YOU DO--YOU SAVE PEOPLE!
I'VE GOT THE BEST SEAT IN THE HOUSE!

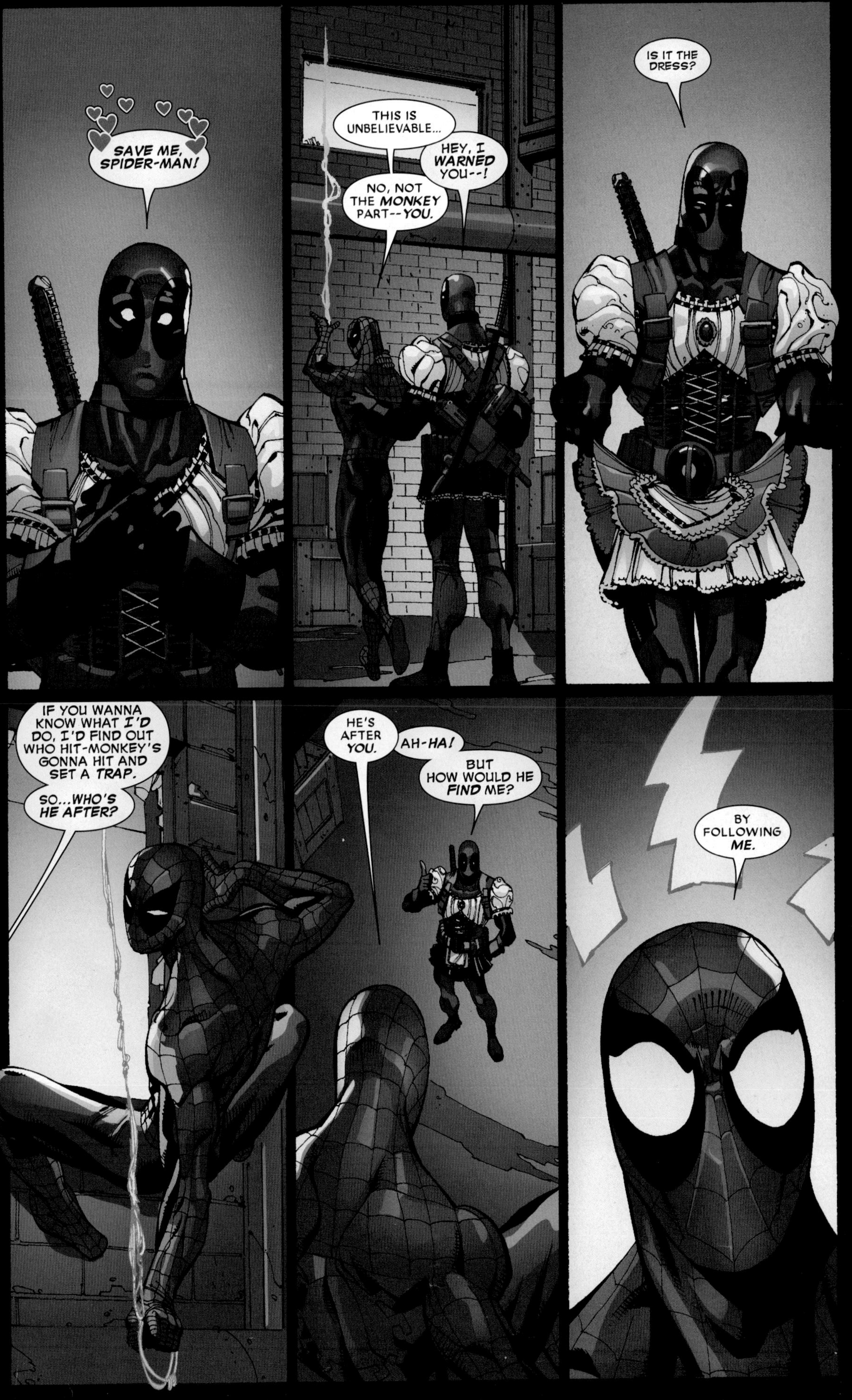

SAVE ME, SPIDER-MAN!
THIS IS UNBELIEVABLE...
HEY, I WARNED YOU--!
NO, NOT THE MONKEY PART--YOU.
IS IT THE DRESS?
IF YOU WANNA KNOW WHAT I'D DO, I'D FIND OUT WHO HIT-MONKEY'S GONNA HIT AND SET A TRAP.
SO...WHO'S HE AFTER?
HE'S AFTER YOU.
AH-HA!
BUT HOW WOULD HE FIND ME?
BY FOLLOWING ME.

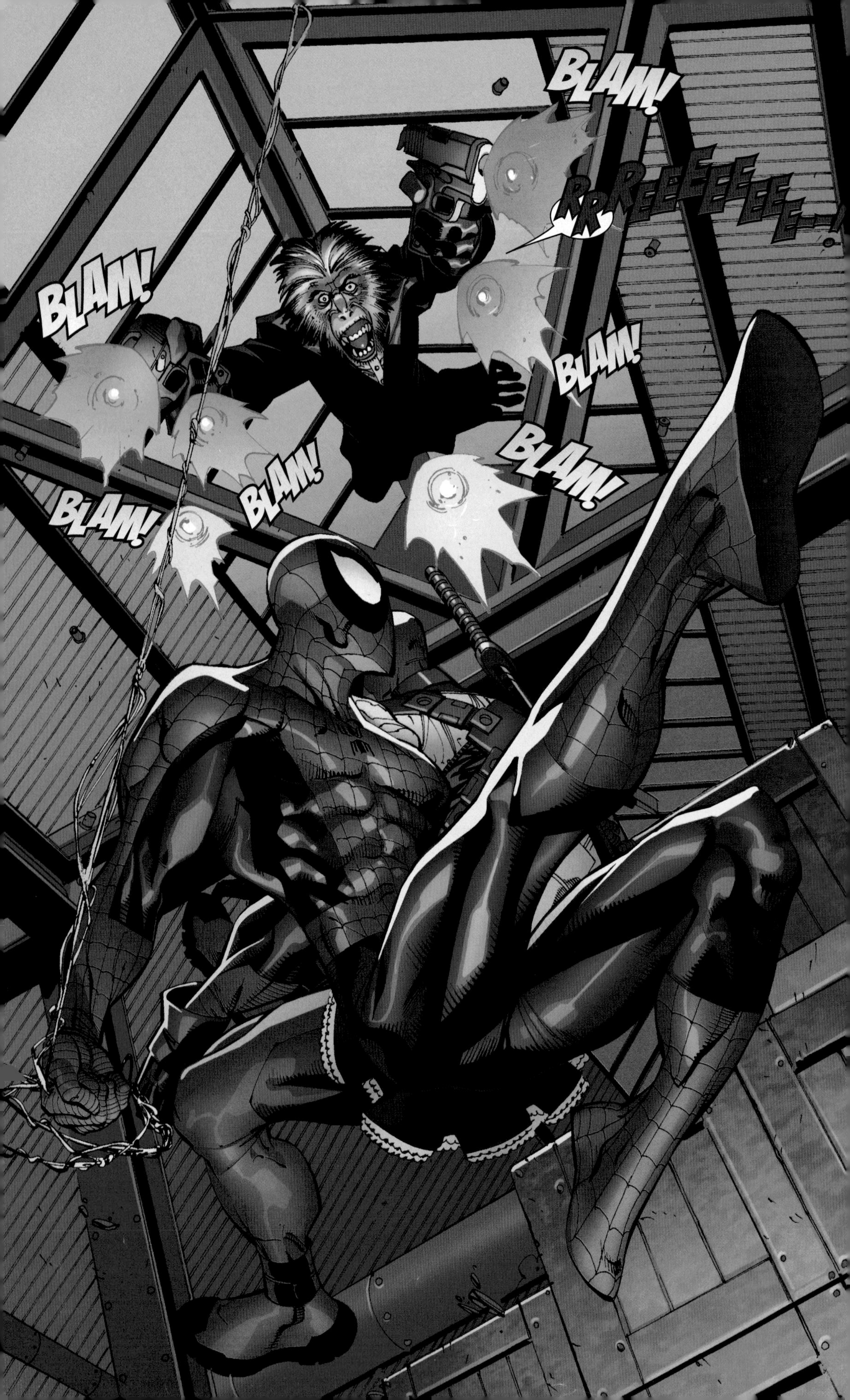
BLAM!
RRREEEEEEEEEE--!
BLAM!
BLAM!
BLAM!
BLAM!
BLAM!
BLAM!

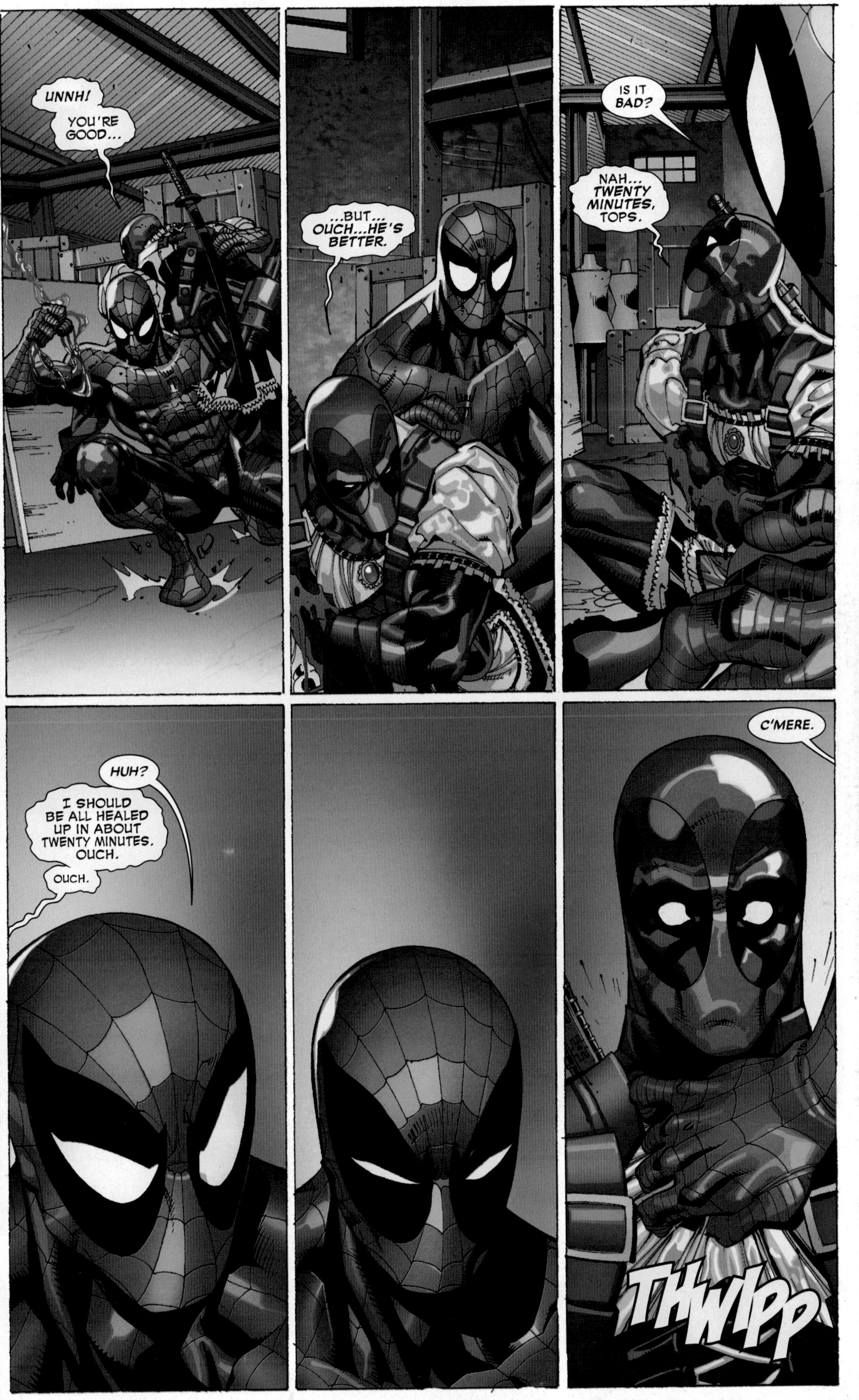
UNNH!
YOU'RE GOOD...
...BUT... OUCH...HE'S BETTER.
IS IT BAD?
NAH... TWENTY MINUTES, TOPS.
HUH?
I SHOULD BE ALL HEALED UP IN ABOUT TWENTY MINUTES. OUCH.
OUCH.
C'MERE.
THWIPP

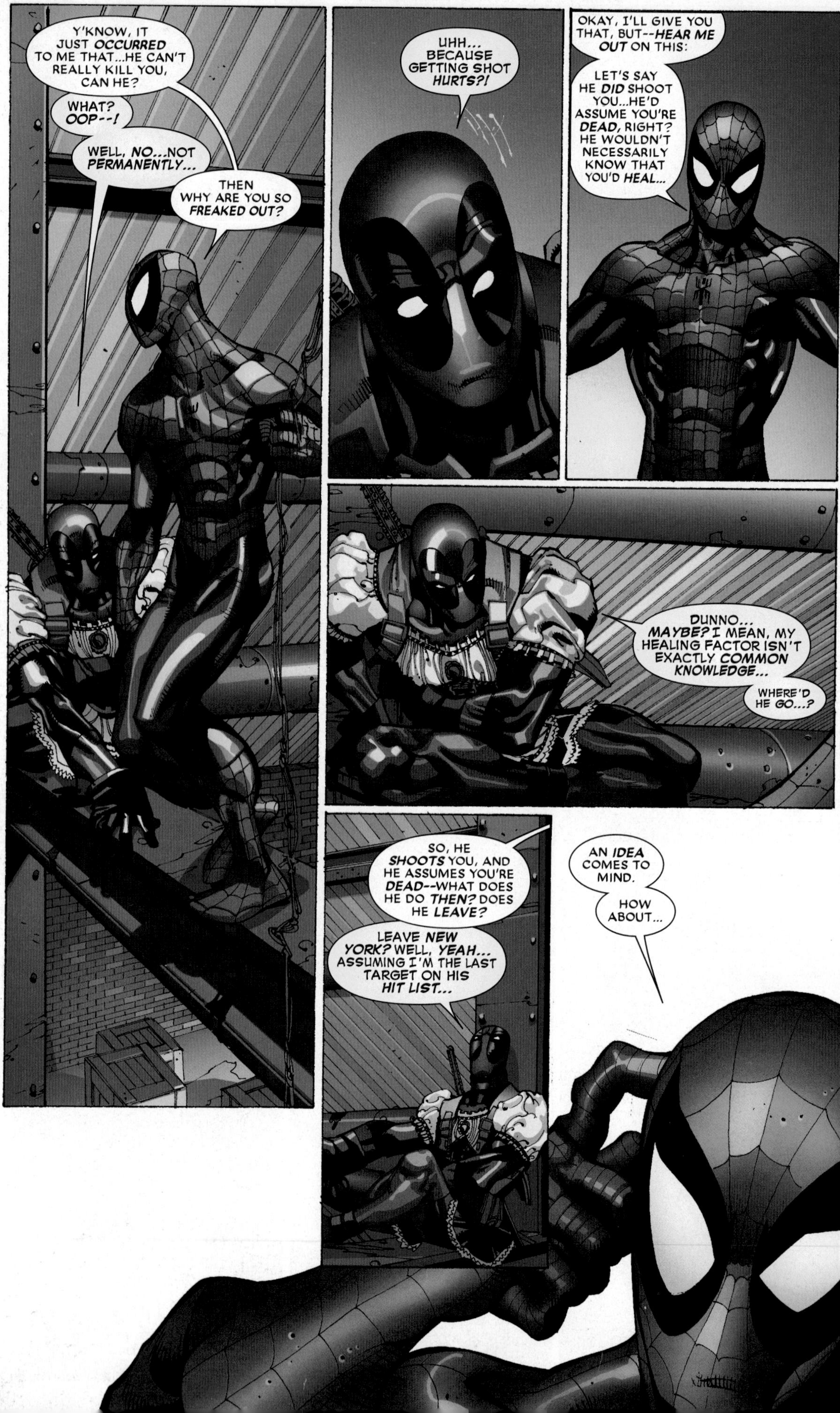
Y'KNOW, IT JUST OCCURRED TO ME THAT...HE CAN'T REALLY KILL YOU, CAN HE?
WHAT? OOP--!
WELL, NO...NOT PERMANENTLY...
THEN WHY ARE YOU SO FREAKED OUT?
UHH... BECAUSE GETTING SHOT HURTS?!
OKAY, I'LL GIVE YOU THAT, BUT--HEAR ME OUT ON THIS:
LET'S SAY HE DID SHOOT YOU...HE'D ASSUME YOU'RE DEAD, RIGHT? HE WOULDN'T NECESSARILY KNOW THAT YOU'D HEAL...
DUNNO... MAYBE? I MEAN, MY HEALING FACTOR ISN'T EXACTLY COMMON KNOWLEDGE...
WHERE'D HE GO...?
SO, HE SHOOTS YOU, AND HE ASSUMES YOU'RE DEAD--WHAT DOES HE DO THEN? DOES HE LEAVE?
LEAVE NEW YORK? WELL, YEAH... ASSUMING I'M THE LAST TARGET ON HIS HIT LIST...
AN IDEA COMES TO MIND.
HOW ABOUT...

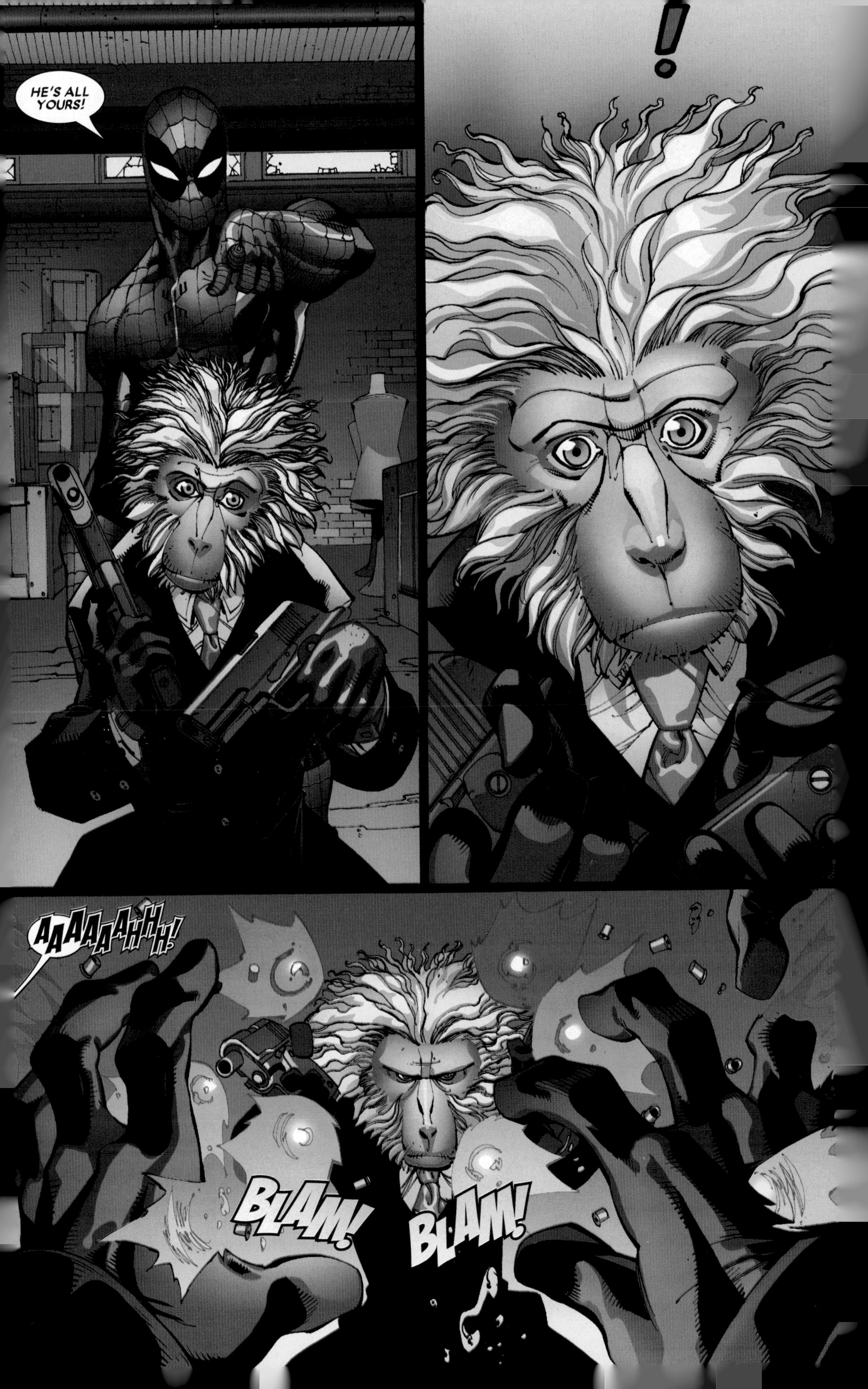
HE'S ALL YOURS!
!
AAAAAAHHH!
BLAM!
BLAM!

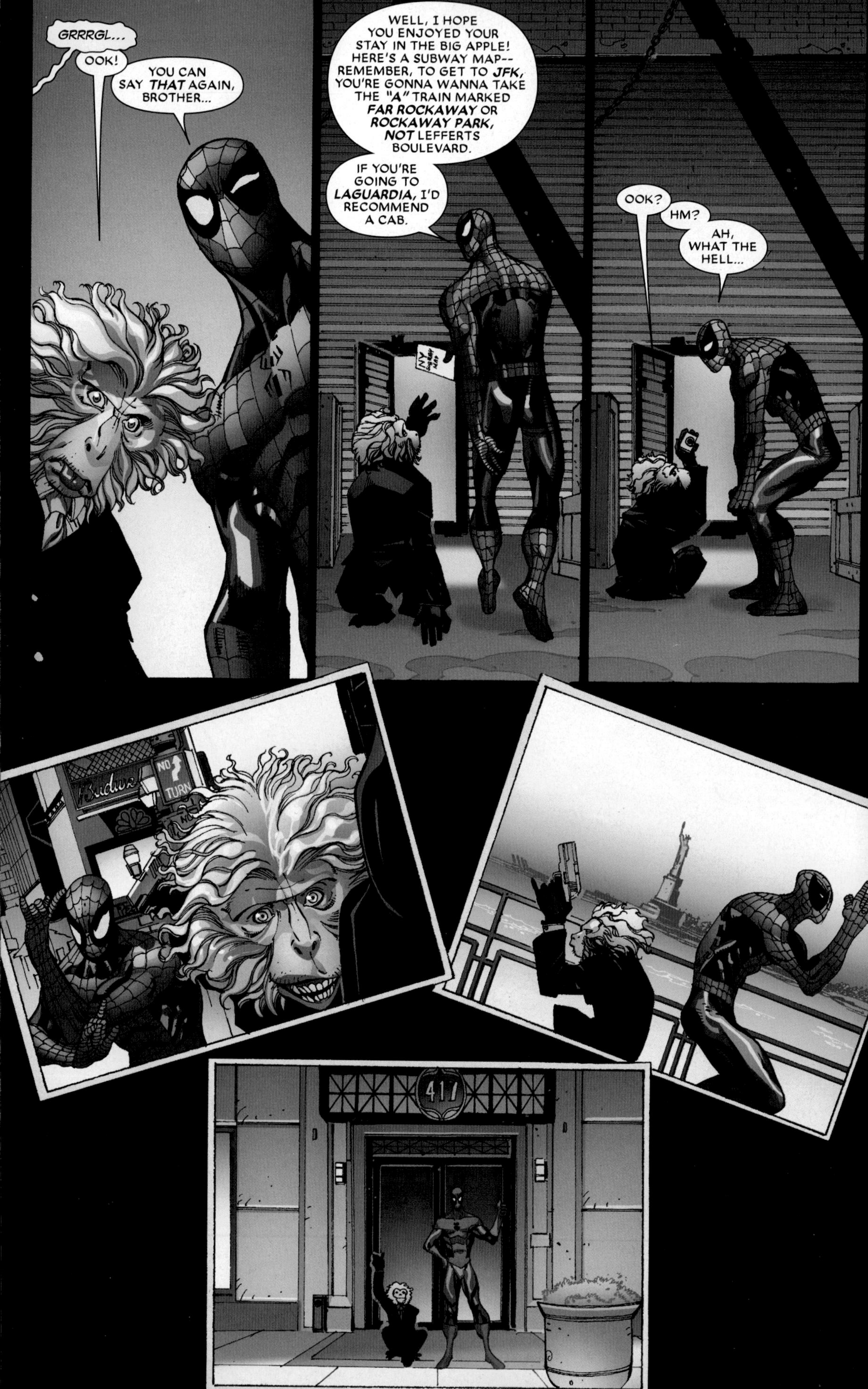
GRRRGL...
OOK!
YOU CAN SAY THAT AGAIN, BROTHER...
WELL, I HOPE YOU ENJOYED YOUR STAY IN THE BIG APPLE! HERE'S A SUBWAY MAP-- REMEMBER, TO GET TO JFK, YOU'RE GONNA WANNA TAKE THE "A" TRAIN MARKED FAR ROCKAWAY OR ROCKAWAY PARK, NOT LEFFERTS BOULEVARD.
IF YOU'RE GOING TO LAGUARDIA, I'D RECOMMEND A CAB.
OOK?
HM?
AH, WHAT THE HELL...
NO TURN
417

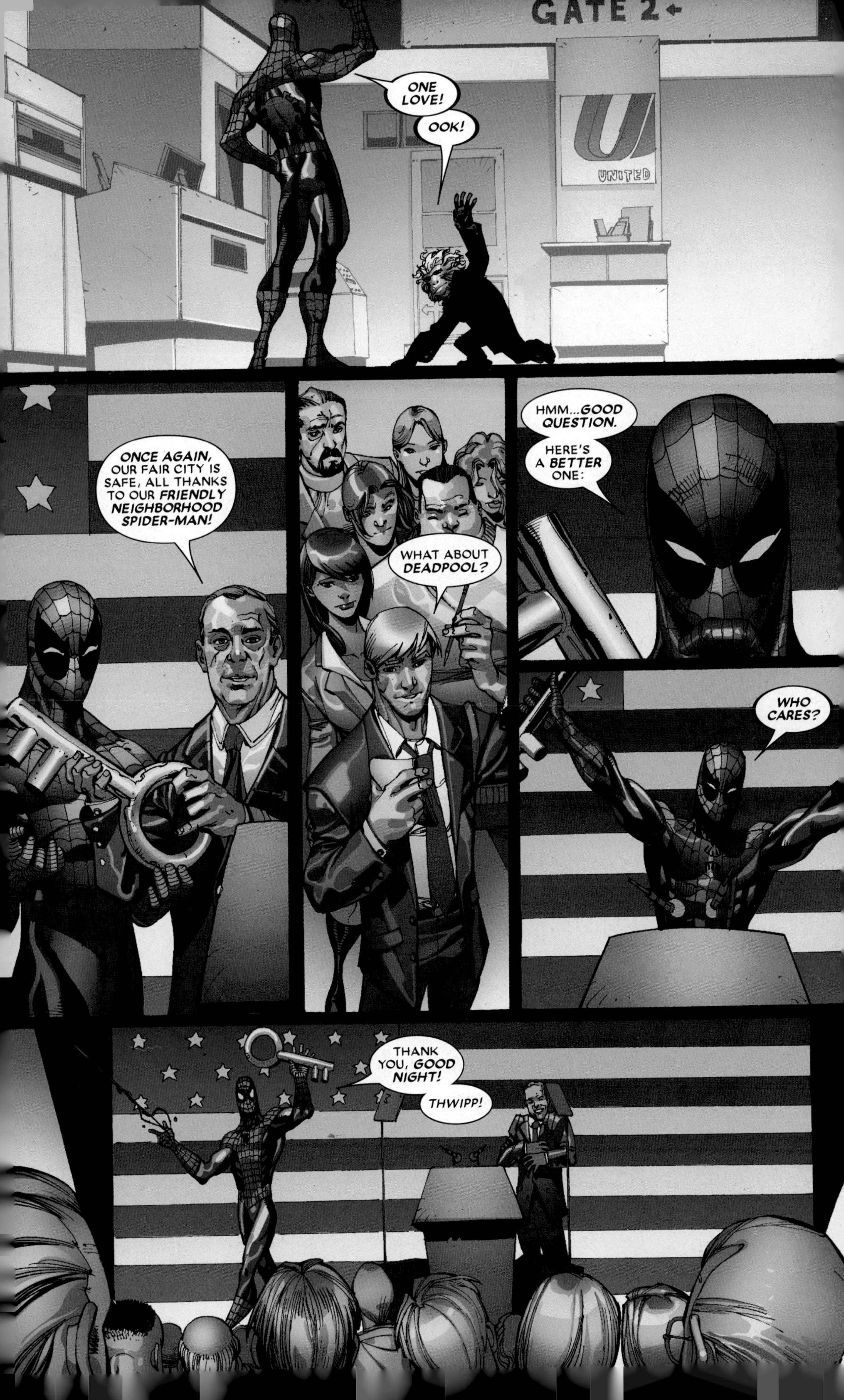
GATE 2
UNITED
ONE LOVE!
OOK!
ONCE AGAIN, OUR FAIR CITY IS SAFE, ALL THANKS TO OUR FRIENDLY NEIGHBORHOOD SPIDER-MAN!
WHAT ABOUT DEADPOOL?
HMM...GOOD QUESTION.
HERE'S A BETTER ONE:
WHO CARES?
THANK YOU, GOOD NIGHT!
THWIPP!

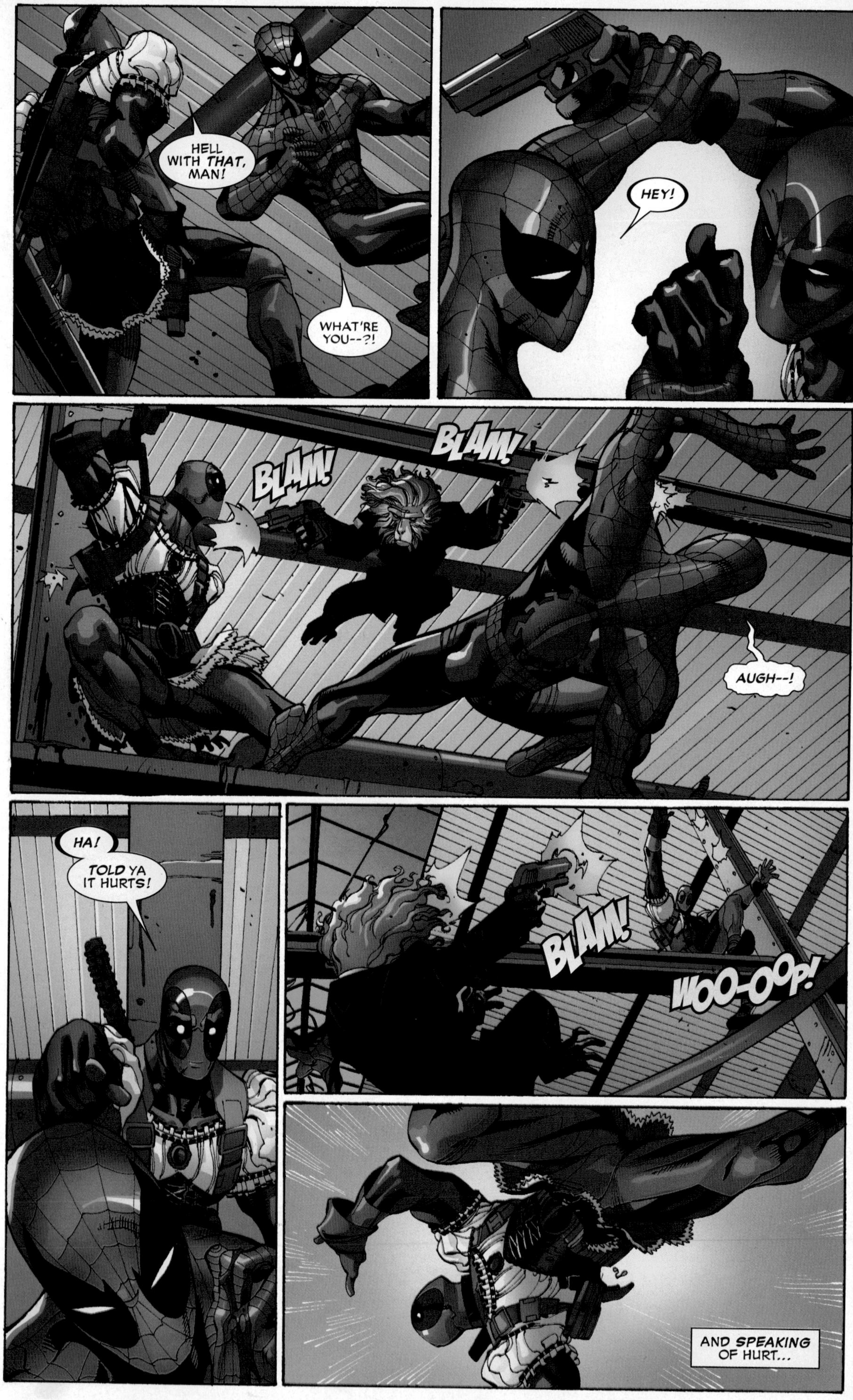

HELL WITH *THAT*, MAN!
WHAT'RE YOU--?!
HEY!
BLAM!
BLAM!
AUGH--!
HA!
TOLD YA IT HURTS!
BLAM!
WOO-OOP!
AND *SPEAKING* OF HURT...

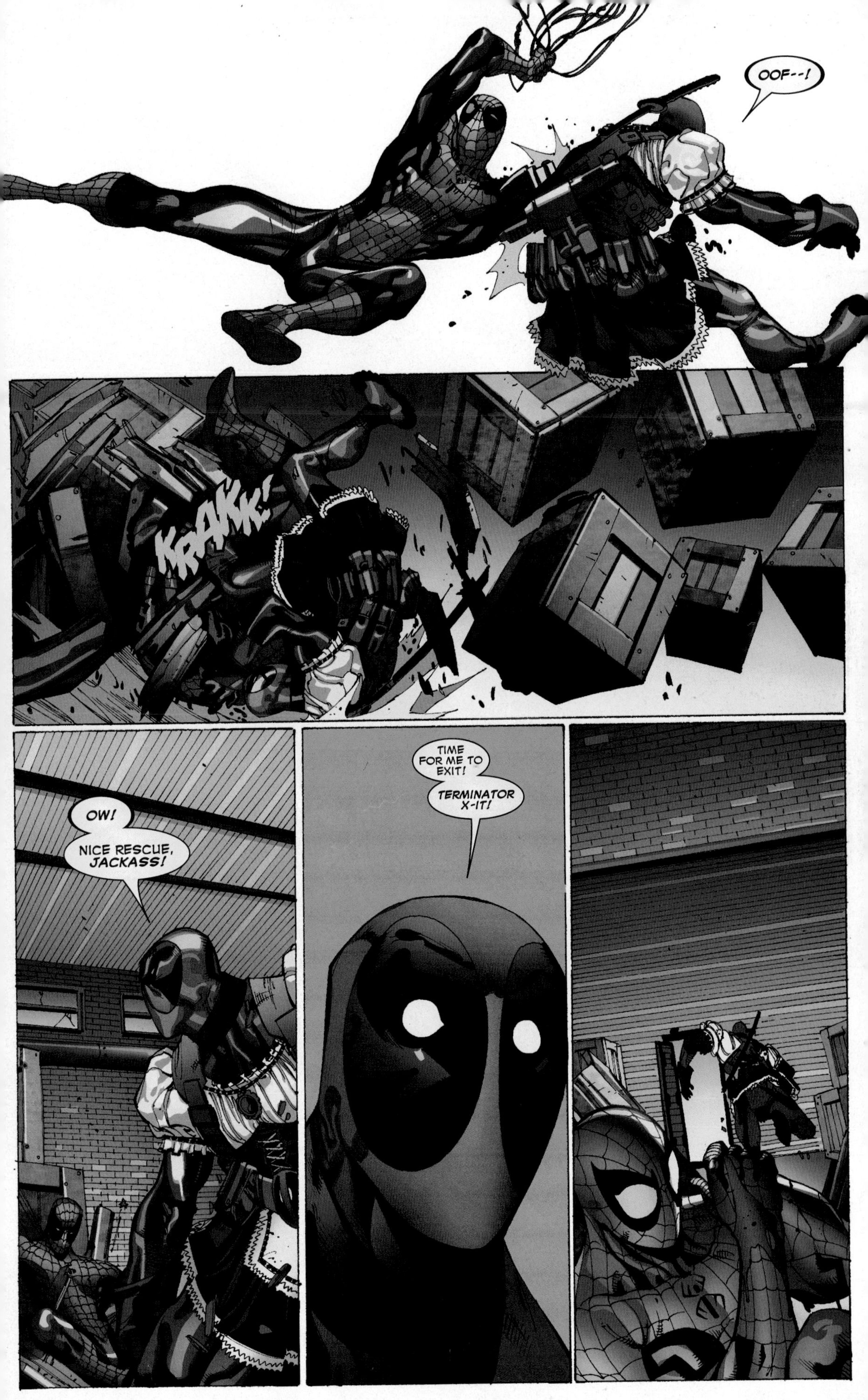
OOF--!
KRAKK!
OW!
NICE RESCUE, JACKASS!
TIME FOR ME TO EXIT!
TERMINATOR X-IT!

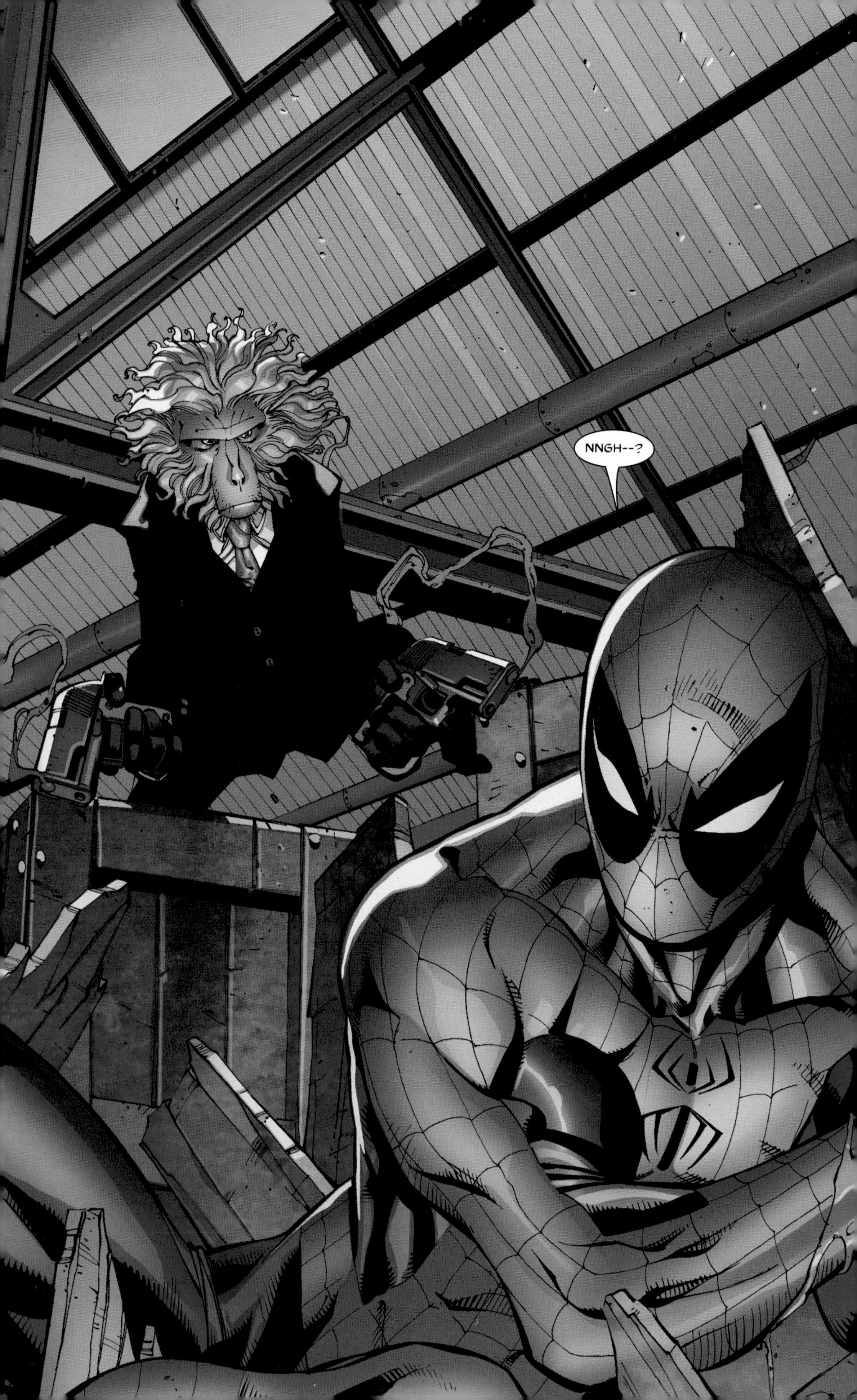
NNGH--?

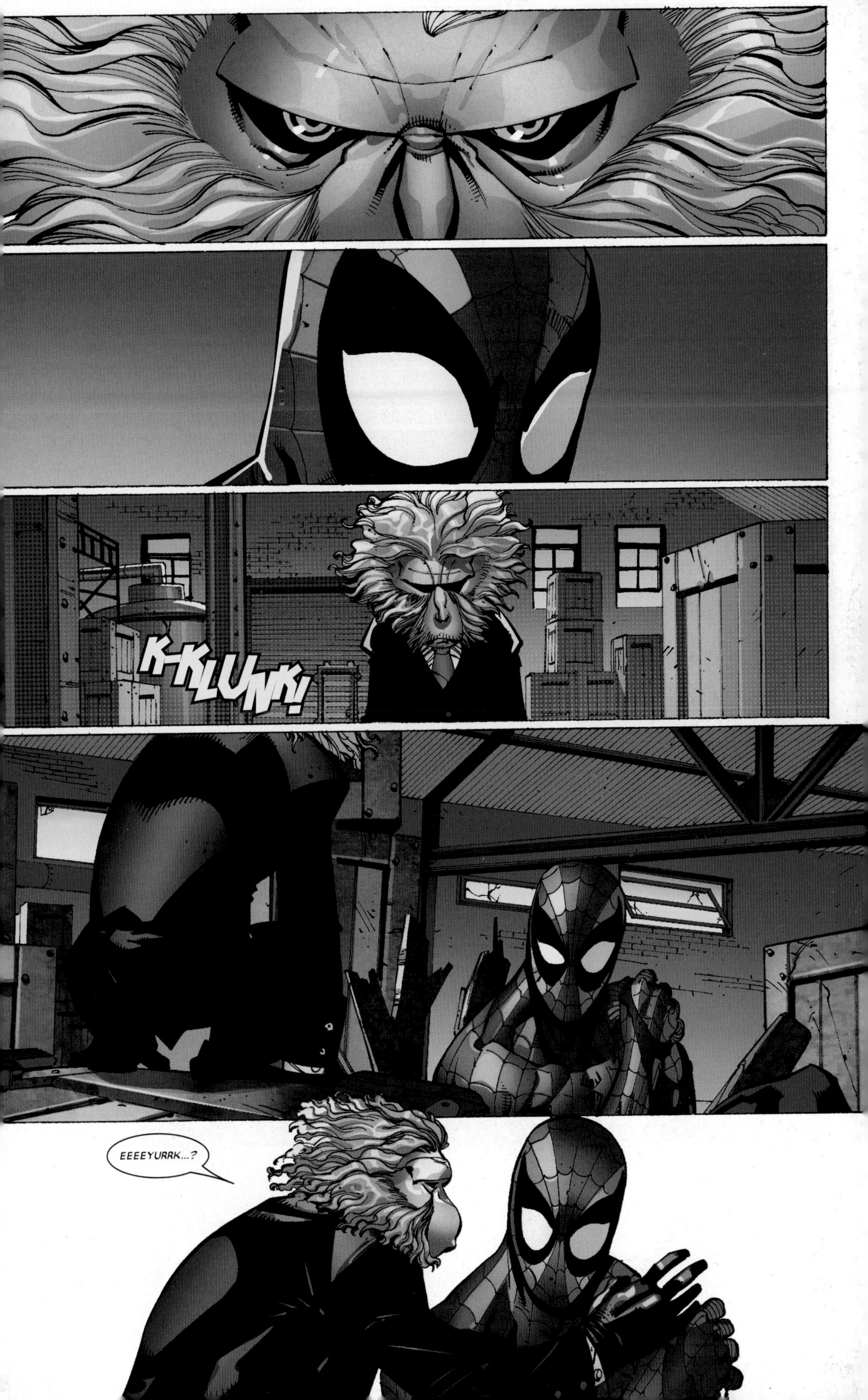
K-KLUNK!
EEEEYURRK...?

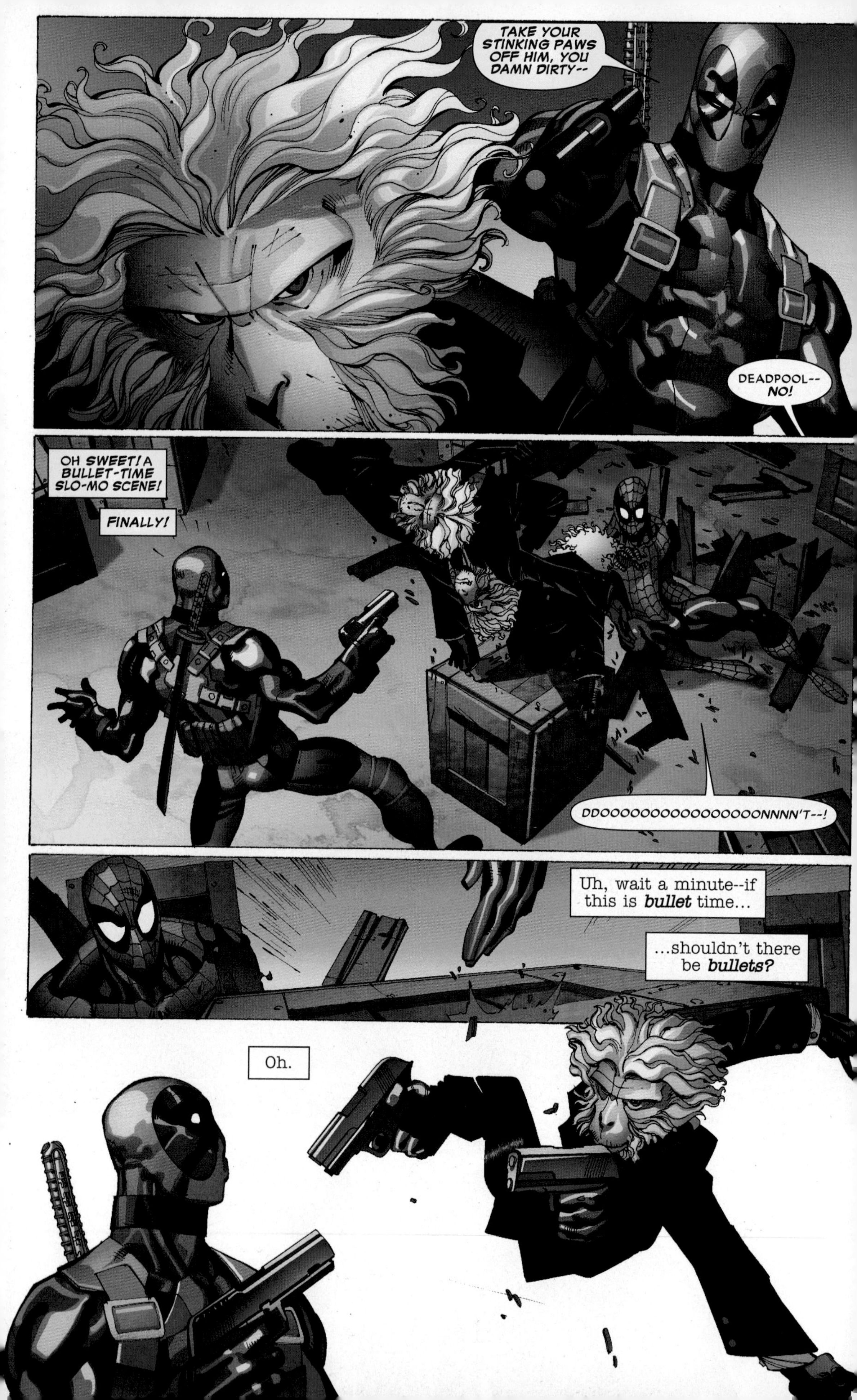
TAKE YOUR STINKING PAWS OFF HIM, YOU DAMN DIRTY--
DEADPOOL-- NO!
OH SWEET! A BULLET-TIME SLO-MO SCENE!
FINALLY!
DDOOOOOOOOOOOOOOOONNNN'T--!
Uh, wait a minute--if this is bullet time...
...shouldn't there be bullets?
Oh.

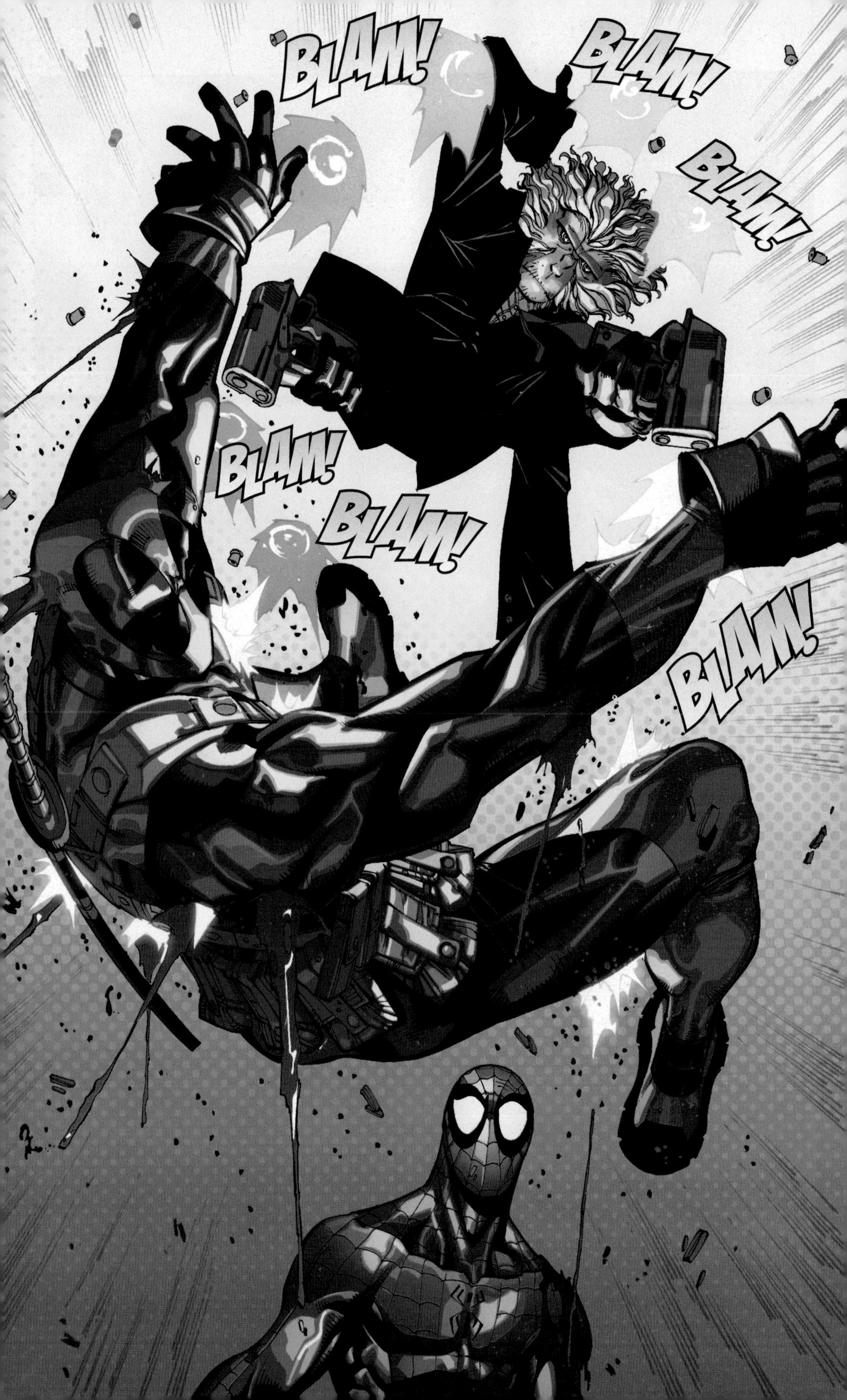
BLAM!
BLAM!
BLAM!
BLAM!
BLAM!
BLAM!

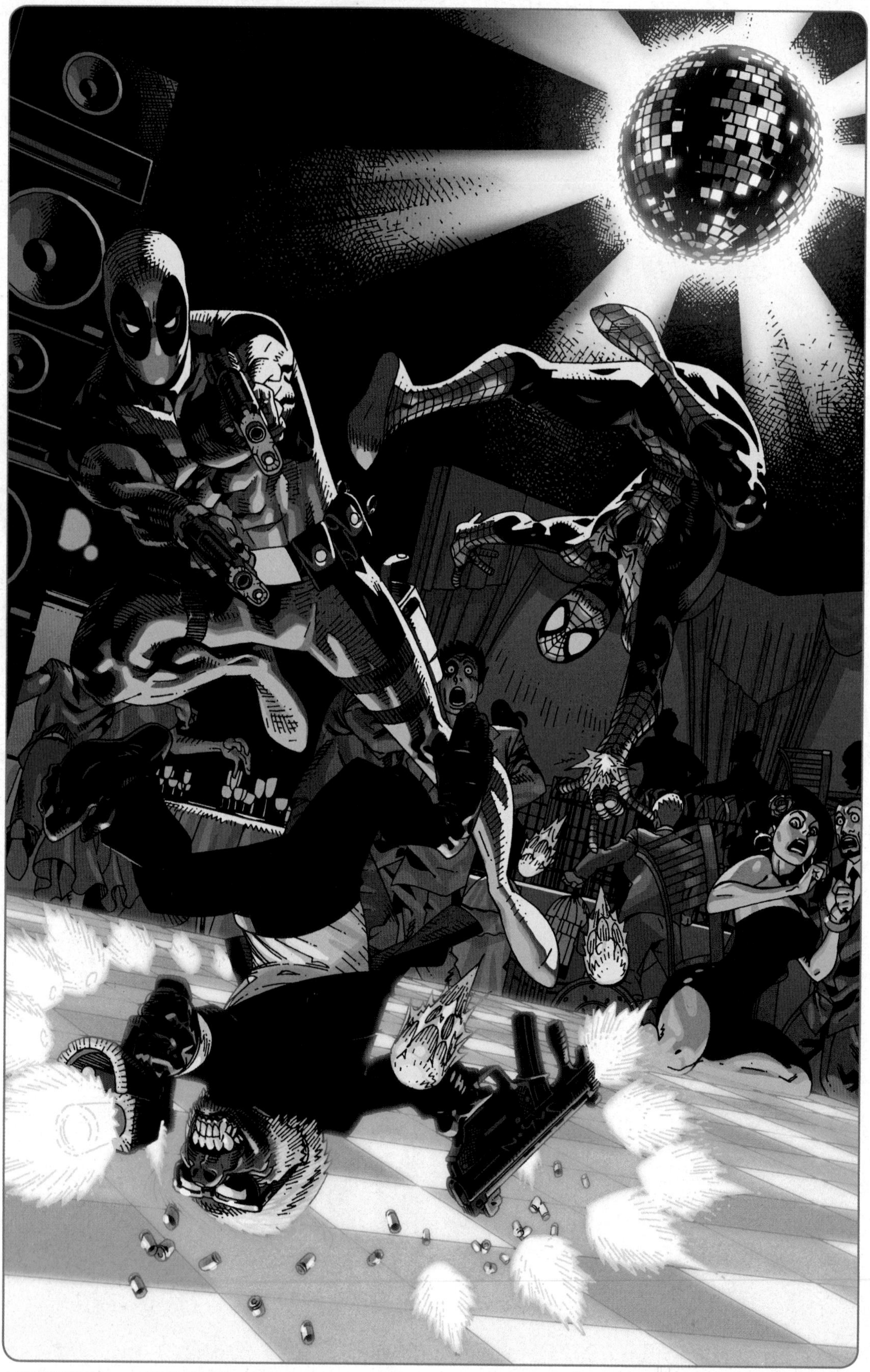

DEADPOOL (2008) #21

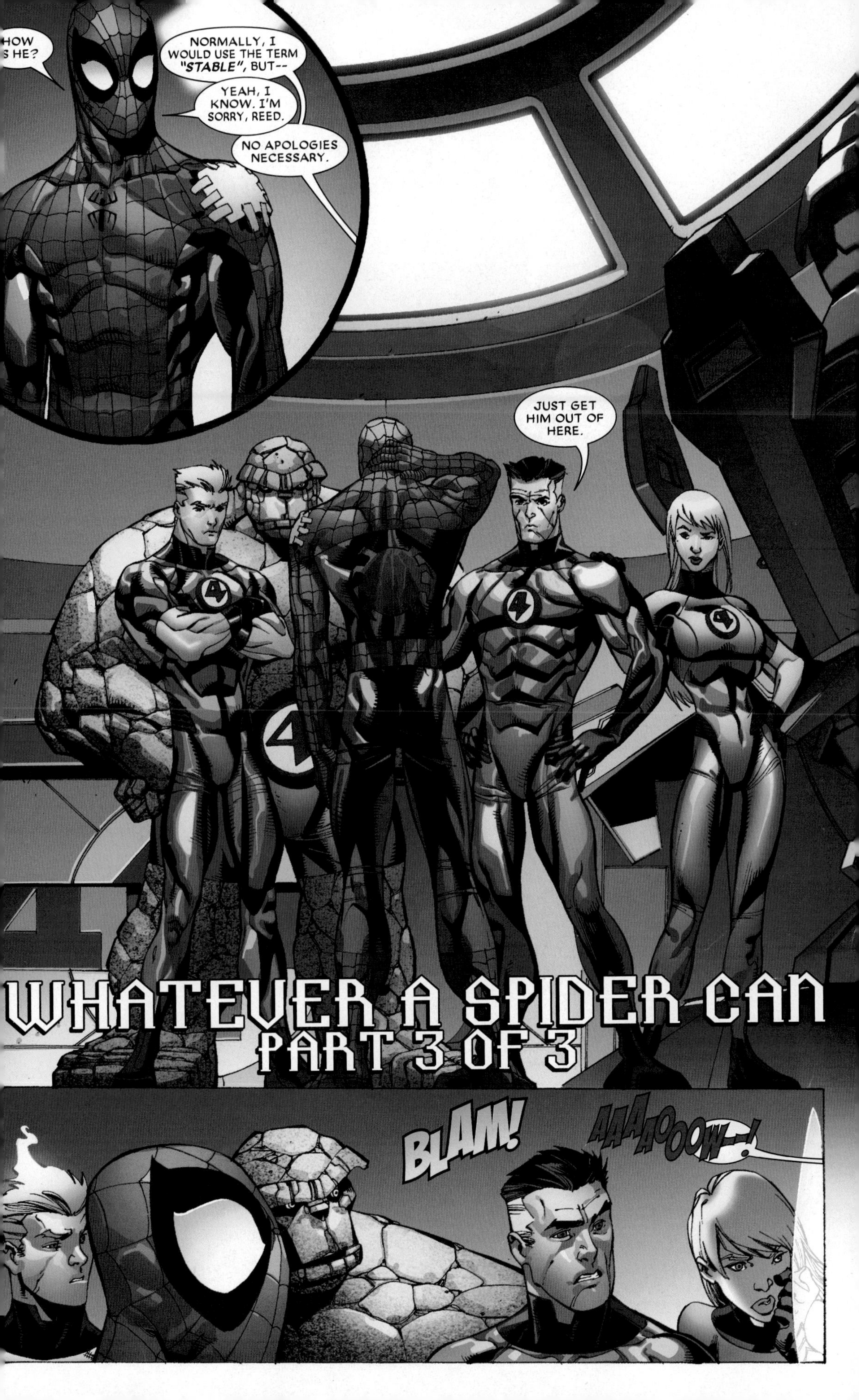
HOW IS HE?
NORMALLY, I WOULD USE THE TERM "STABLE", BUT--
YEAH, I KNOW. I'M SORRY, REED.
NO APOLOGIES NECESSARY.
JUST GET HIM OUT OF HERE.
WHATEVER A SPIDER CAN
PART 3 OF 3
BLAM!
AAAAOOOW--!

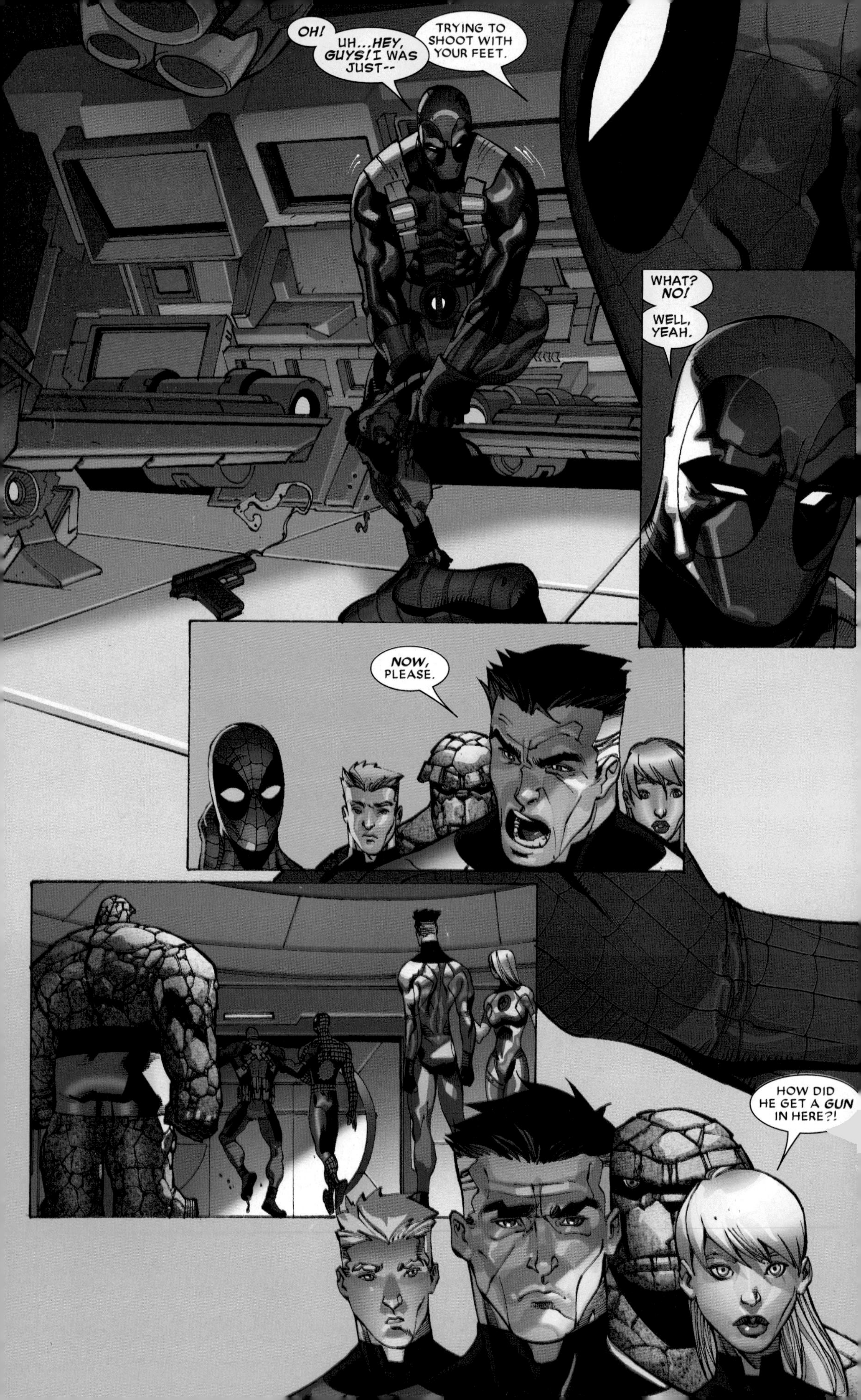
OH!
UH...HEY, GUYS! I WAS JUST--
TRYING TO SHOOT WITH YOUR FEET.
WHAT? NO!
WELL, YEAH.
NOW, PLEASE.
HOW DID HE GET A GUN IN HERE?!

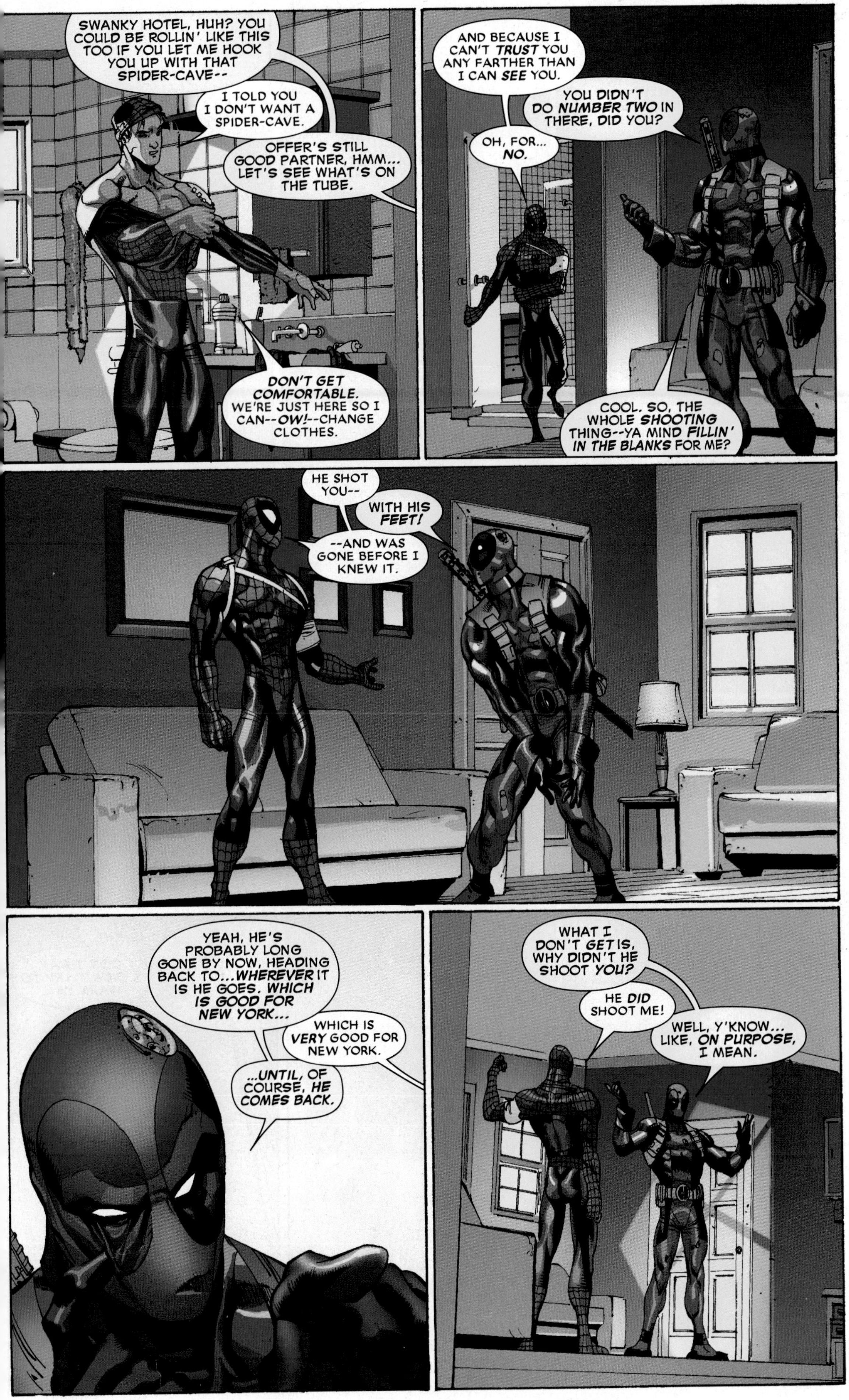
SWANKY HOTEL, HUH? YOU COULD BE ROLLIN' LIKE THIS TOO IF YOU LET ME HOOK YOU UP WITH THAT SPIDER-CAVE--
I TOLD YOU I DON'T WANT A SPIDER-CAVE.
OFFER'S STILL GOOD PARTNER, HMM... LET'S SEE WHAT'S ON THE TUBE.
DON'T GET COMFORTABLE. WE'RE JUST HERE SO I CAN--OW!--CHANGE CLOTHES.
AND BECAUSE I CAN'T TRUST YOU ANY FARTHER THAN I CAN SEE YOU.
YOU DIDN'T DO NUMBER TWO IN THERE, DID YOU?
OH, FOR... NO.
COOL. SO, THE WHOLE SHOOTING THING--YA MIND FILLIN' IN THE BLANKS FOR ME?
HE SHOT YOU--
WITH HIS FEET!
--AND WAS GONE BEFORE I KNEW IT.
YEAH, HE'S PROBABLY LONG GONE BY NOW, HEADING BACK TO...WHEREVER IT IS HE GOES. WHICH IS GOOD FOR NEW YORK...
WHICH IS VERY GOOD FOR NEW YORK.
...UNTIL, OF COURSE, HE COMES BACK.
WHAT I DON'T GET IS, WHY DIDN'T HE SHOOT YOU?
HE DID SHOOT ME!
WELL, Y'KNOW... LIKE, ON PURPOSE, I MEAN.

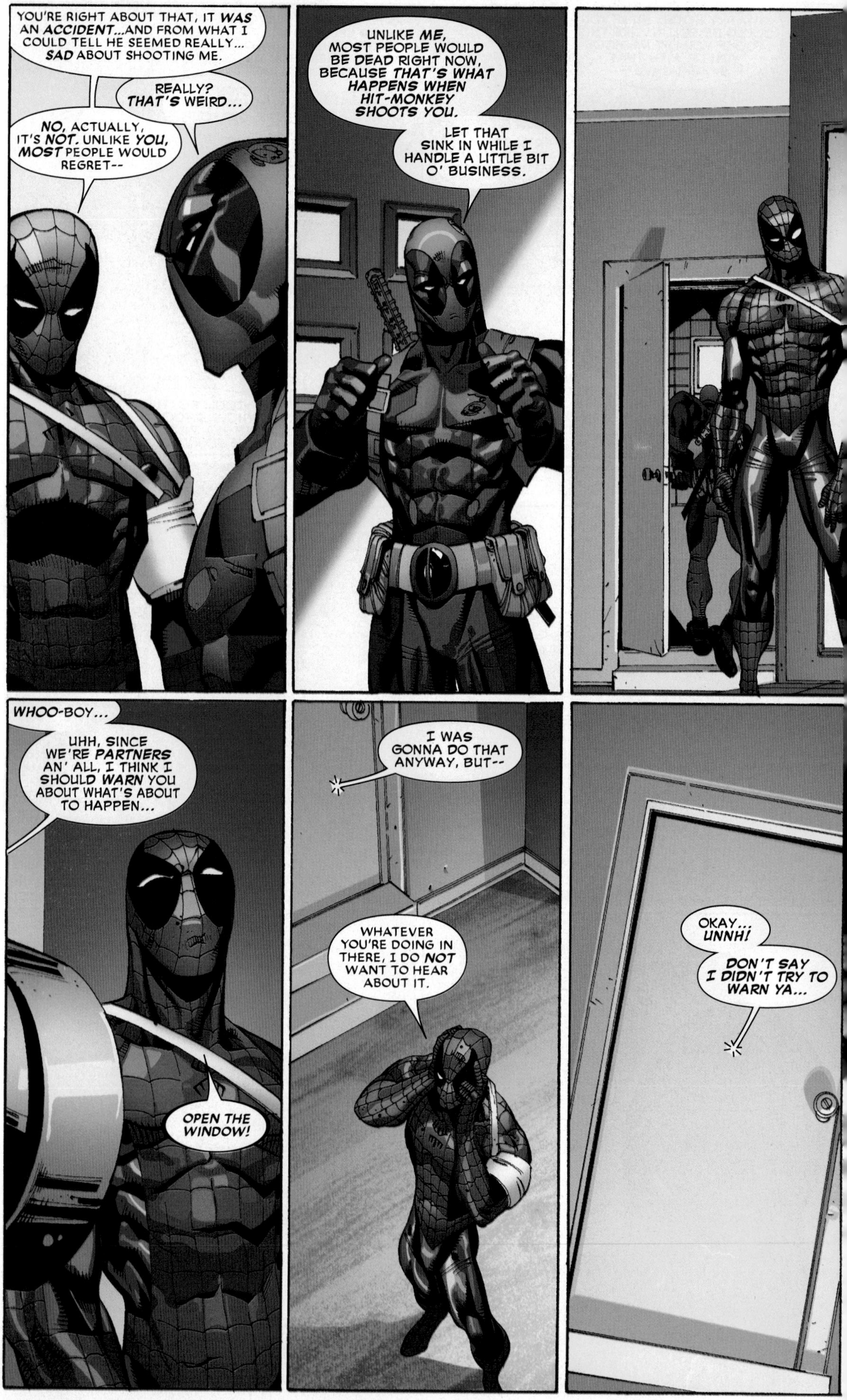
YOU'RE RIGHT ABOUT THAT, IT WAS AN ACCIDENT...AND FROM WHAT I COULD TELL HE SEEMED REALLY... SAD ABOUT SHOOTING ME.
REALLY? THAT'S WEIRD...
NO, ACTUALLY, IT'S NOT. UNLIKE YOU, MOST PEOPLE WOULD REGRET--
UNLIKE ME, MOST PEOPLE WOULD BE DEAD RIGHT NOW, BECAUSE THAT'S WHAT HAPPENS WHEN HIT-MONKEY SHOOTS YOU.
LET THAT SINK IN WHILE I HANDLE A LITTLE BIT O' BUSINESS.
WHOO-BOY...
UHH, SINCE WE'RE PARTNERS AN' ALL, I THINK I SHOULD WARN YOU ABOUT WHAT'S ABOUT TO HAPPEN...
OPEN THE WINDOW!
I WAS GONNA DO THAT ANYWAY, BUT--
WHATEVER YOU'RE DOING IN THERE, I DO NOT WANT TO HEAR ABOUT IT.
OKAY... UNNH!
DON'T SAY I DIDN'T TRY TO WARN YA...

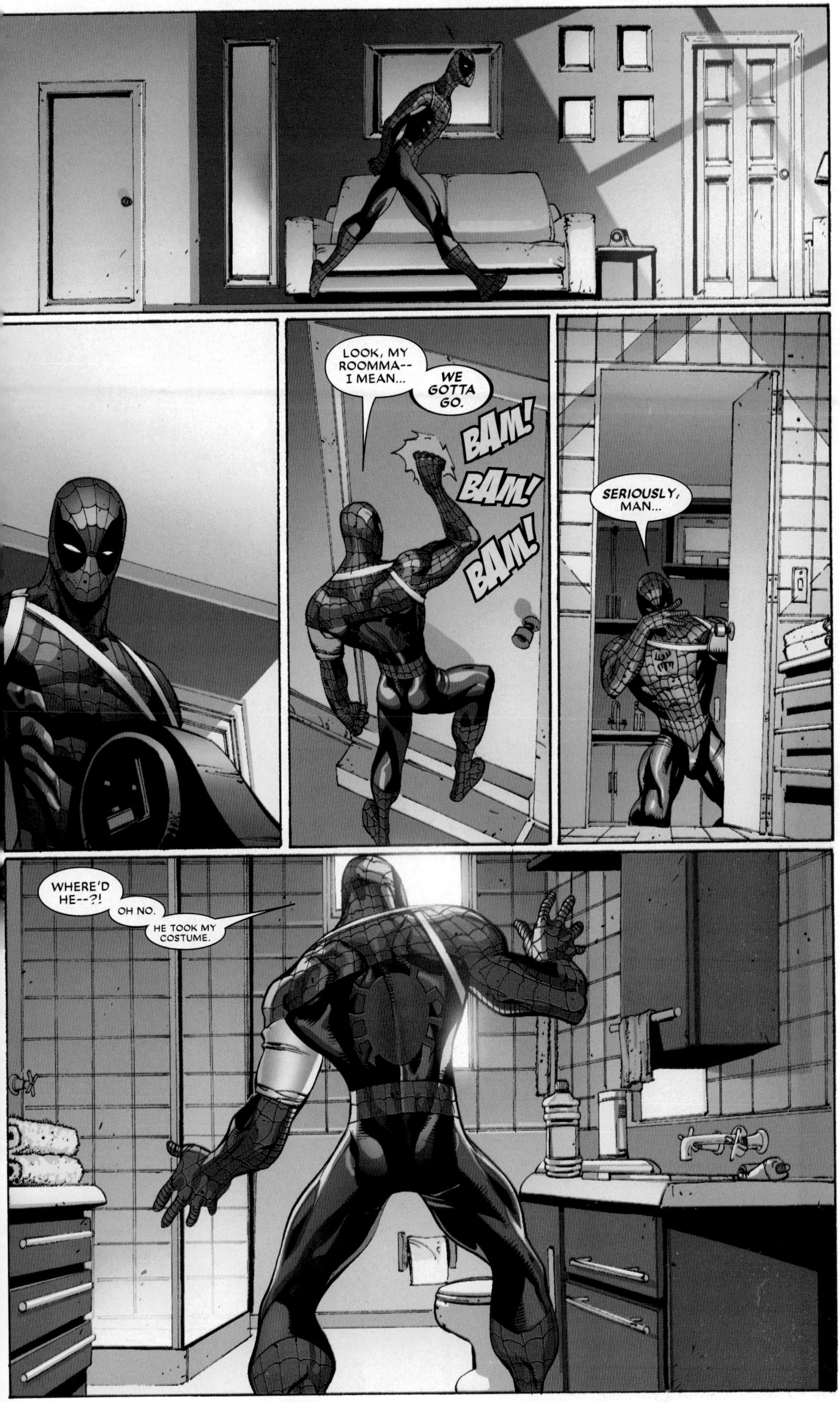
LOOK, MY ROOMMA-- I MEAN...
WE GOTTA GO.
BAM!
BAM!
BAM!
SERIOUSLY, MAN...
WHERE'D HE--?!
OH NO.
HE TOOK MY COSTUME.

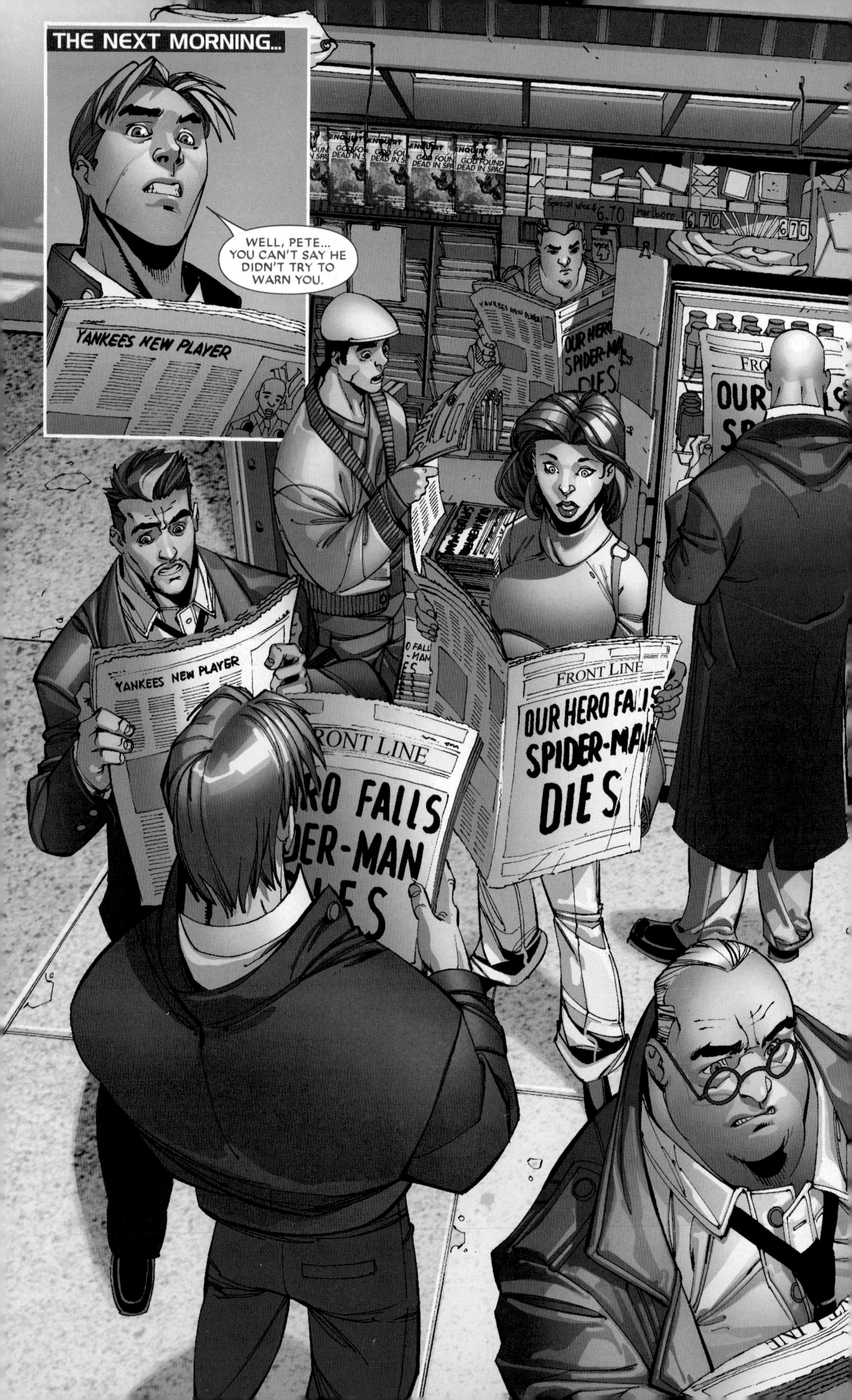
THE NEXT MORNING...
WELL, PETE... YOU CAN'T SAY HE DIDN'T TRY TO WARN YOU.
YANKEES NEW PLAYER
GOD FOUND DEAD IN SPACE
OUR HERO SPIDER-MAN DIES
YANKEES NEW PLAYER
FRONT LINE
OUR HERO FALLS SPIDER-MA DIES
FRONT LINE
RO FALLS DER-MAN

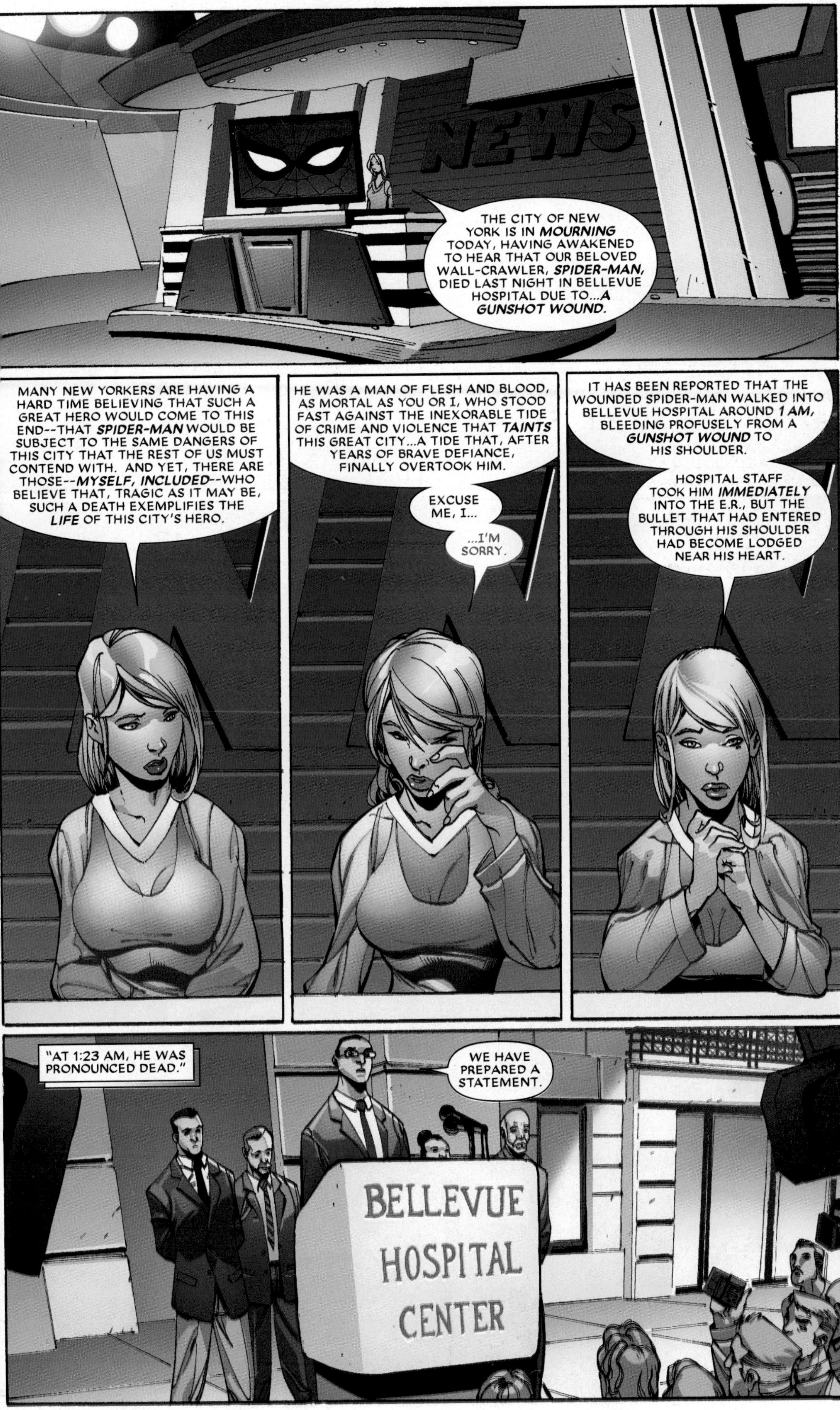
NEWS
THE CITY OF NEW YORK IS IN MOURNING TODAY, HAVING AWAKENED TO HEAR THAT OUR BELOVED WALL-CRAWLER, SPIDER-MAN, DIED LAST NIGHT IN BELLEVUE HOSPITAL DUE TO...A GUNSHOT WOUND.
MANY NEW YORKERS ARE HAVING A HARD TIME BELIEVING THAT SUCH A GREAT HERO WOULD COME TO THIS END--THAT SPIDER-MAN WOULD BE SUBJECT TO THE SAME DANGERS OF THIS CITY THAT THE REST OF US MUST CONTEND WITH. AND YET, THERE ARE THOSE--MYSELF, INCLUDED--WHO BELIEVE THAT, TRAGIC AS IT MAY BE, SUCH A DEATH EXEMPLIFIES THE LIFE OF THIS CITY'S HERO.
HE WAS A MAN OF FLESH AND BLOOD, AS MORTAL AS YOU OR I, WHO STOOD FAST AGAINST THE INEXORABLE TIDE OF CRIME AND VIOLENCE THAT TAINTS THIS GREAT CITY...A TIDE THAT, AFTER YEARS OF BRAVE DEFIANCE, FINALLY OVERTOOK HIM.
EXCUSE ME, I...
...I'M SORRY.
IT HAS BEEN REPORTED THAT THE WOUNDED SPIDER-MAN WALKED INTO BELLEVUE HOSPITAL AROUND 1 AM, BLEEDING PROFUSELY FROM A GUNSHOT WOUND TO HIS SHOULDER.
HOSPITAL STAFF TOOK HIM IMMEDIATELY INTO THE E.R., BUT THE BULLET THAT HAD ENTERED THROUGH HIS SHOULDER HAD BECOME LODGED NEAR HIS HEART.
"AT 1:23 AM, HE WAS PRONOUNCED DEAD."
WE HAVE PREPARED A STATEMENT.
BELLEVUE HOSPITAL CENTER

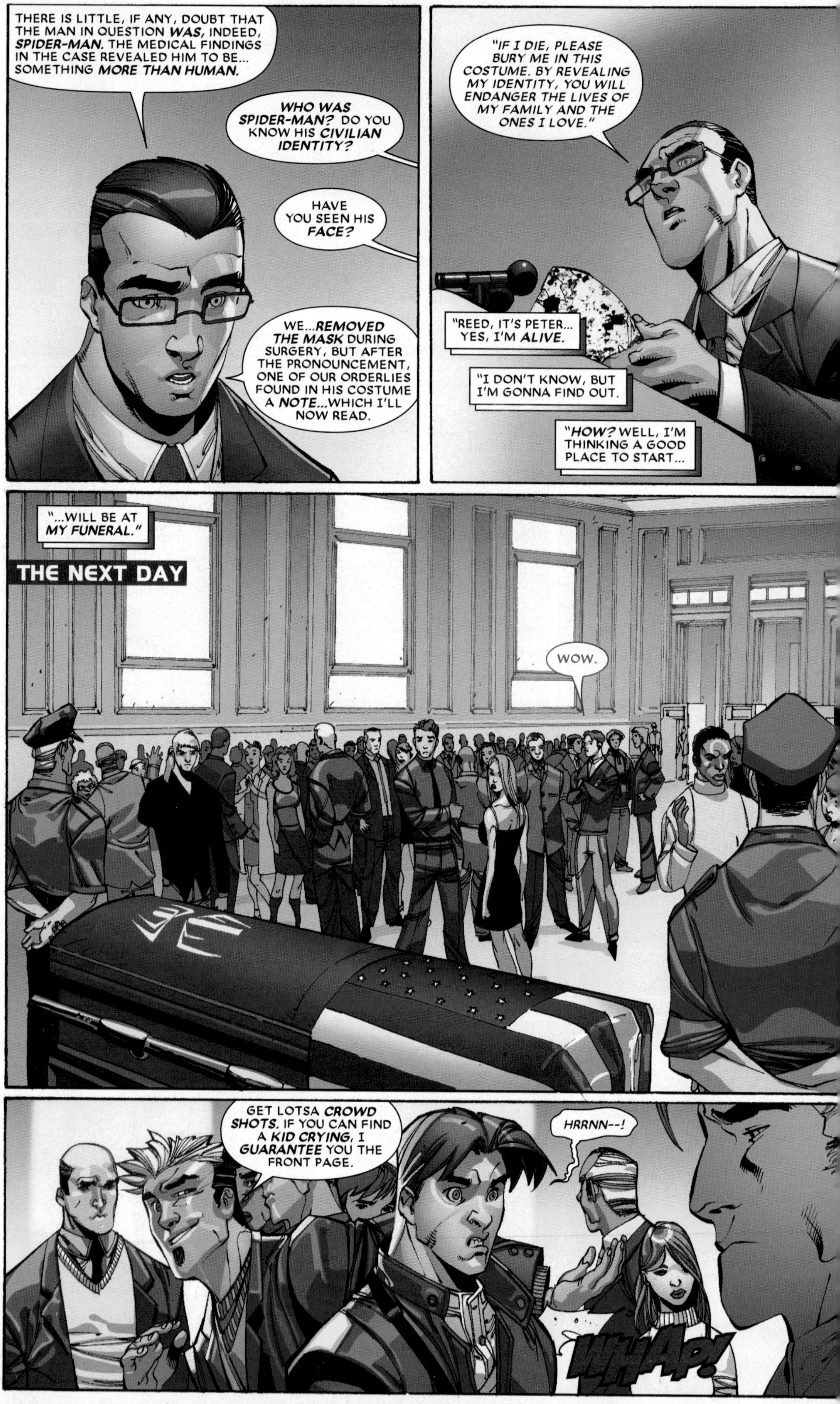
THERE IS LITTLE, IF ANY, DOUBT THAT THE MAN IN QUESTION WAS, INDEED, SPIDER-MAN. THE MEDICAL FINDINGS IN THE CASE REVEALED HIM TO BE... SOMETHING MORE THAN HUMAN.
WHO WAS SPIDER-MAN? DO YOU KNOW HIS CIVILIAN IDENTITY?
HAVE YOU SEEN HIS FACE?
WE...REMOVED THE MASK DURING SURGERY, BUT AFTER THE PRONOUNCEMENT, ONE OF OUR ORDERLIES FOUND IN HIS COSTUME A NOTE...WHICH I'LL NOW READ.
"IF I DIE, PLEASE BURY ME IN THIS COSTUME. BY REVEALING MY IDENTITY, YOU WILL ENDANGER THE LIVES OF MY FAMILY AND THE ONES I LOVE."
"REED, IT'S PETER... YES, I'M ALIVE.
"I DON'T KNOW, BUT I'M GONNA FIND OUT.
"HOW? WELL, I'M THINKING A GOOD PLACE TO START...
"...WILL BE AT MY FUNERAL."
THE NEXT DAY
WOW.
GET LOTSA CROWD SHOTS. IF YOU CAN FIND A KID CRYING, I GUARANTEE YOU THE FRONT PAGE.
HRRNN--!
WHAP!

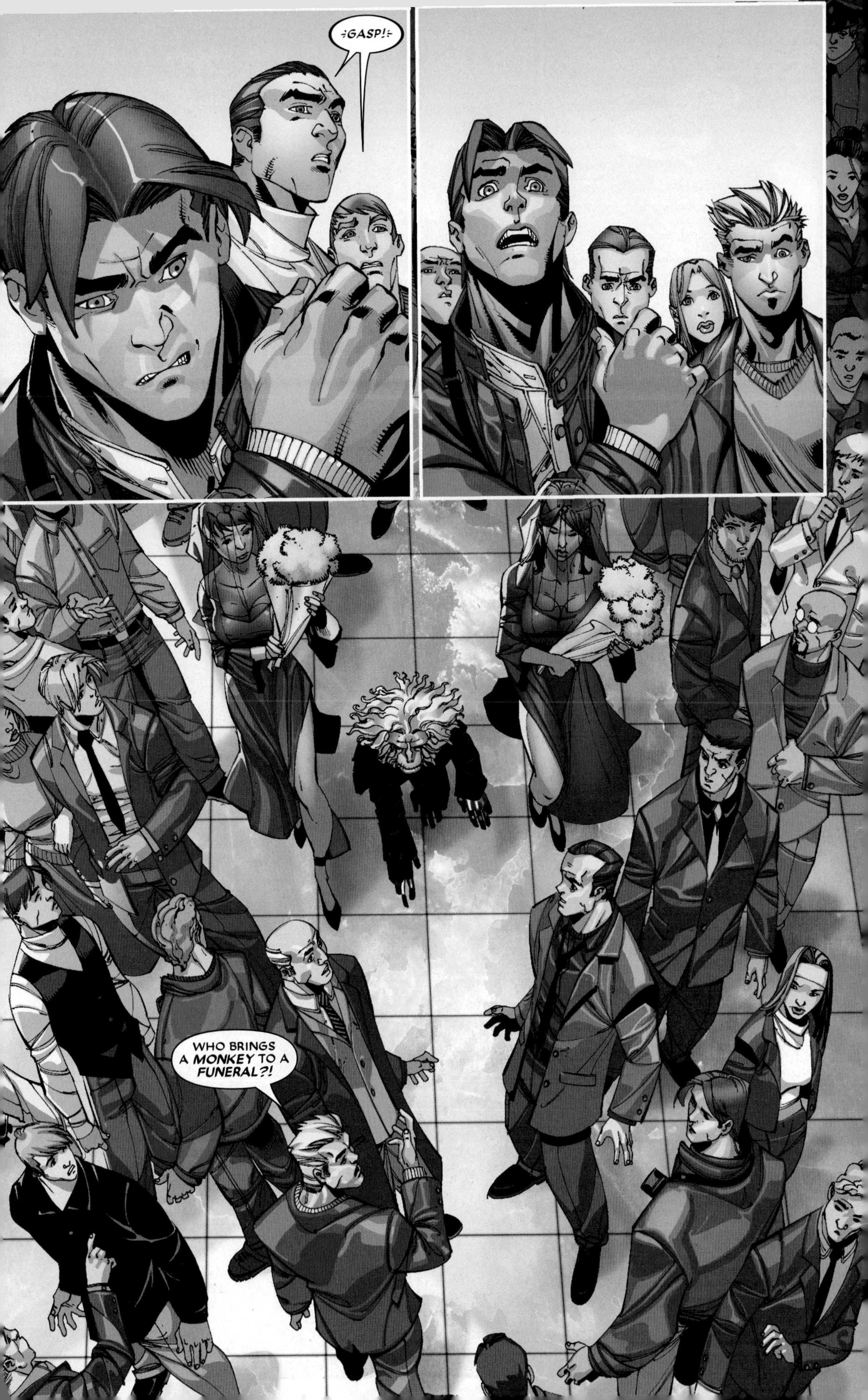
GASP!
WHO BRINGS A MONKEY TO A FUNERAL?!

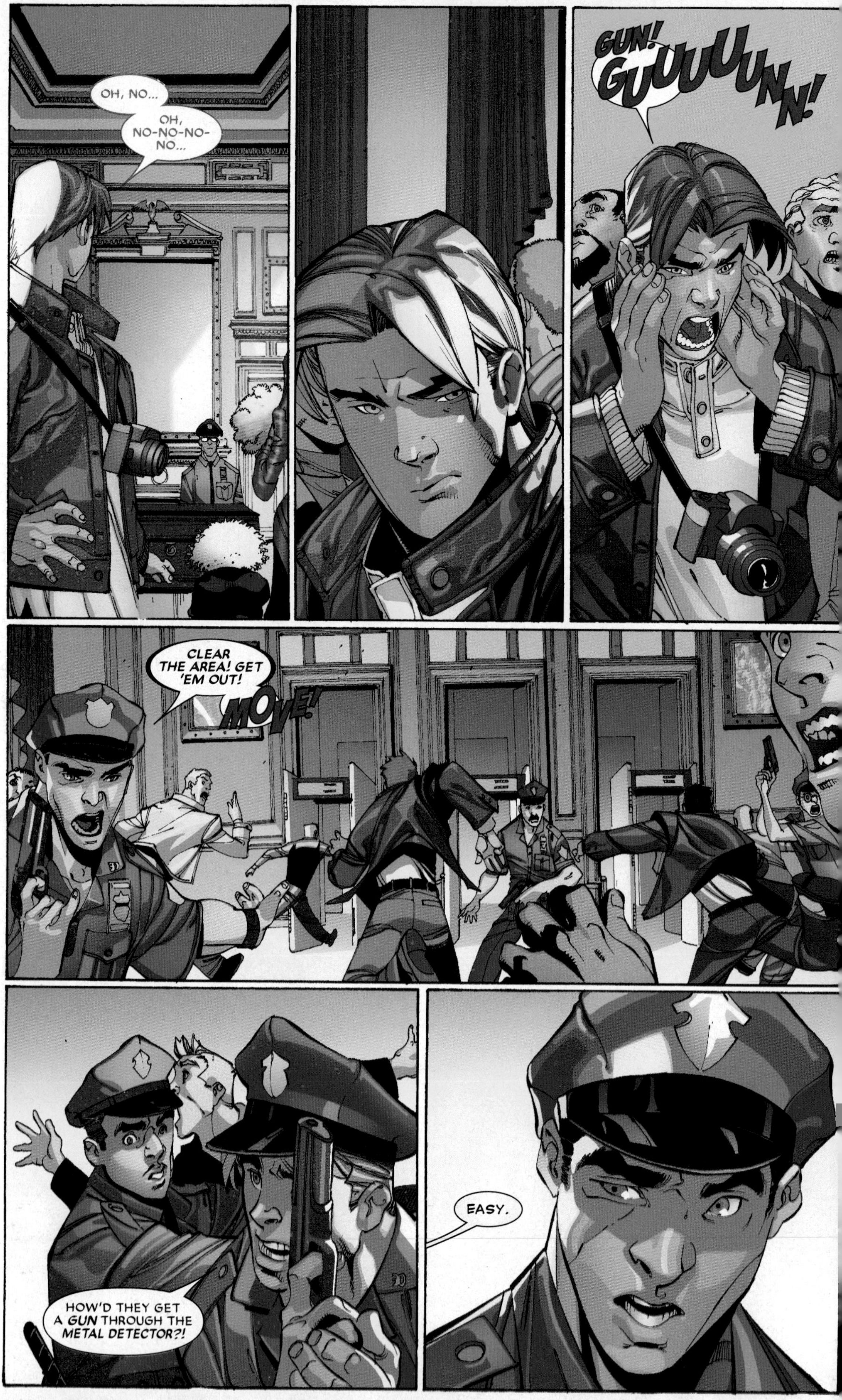
OH, NO...
OH, NO-NO-NO-NO...
GUN! GUUUUUNN!
CLEAR THE AREA! GET 'EM OUT!
MOVE!
HOW'D THEY GET A GUN THROUGH THE METAL DETECTOR?!
EASY.

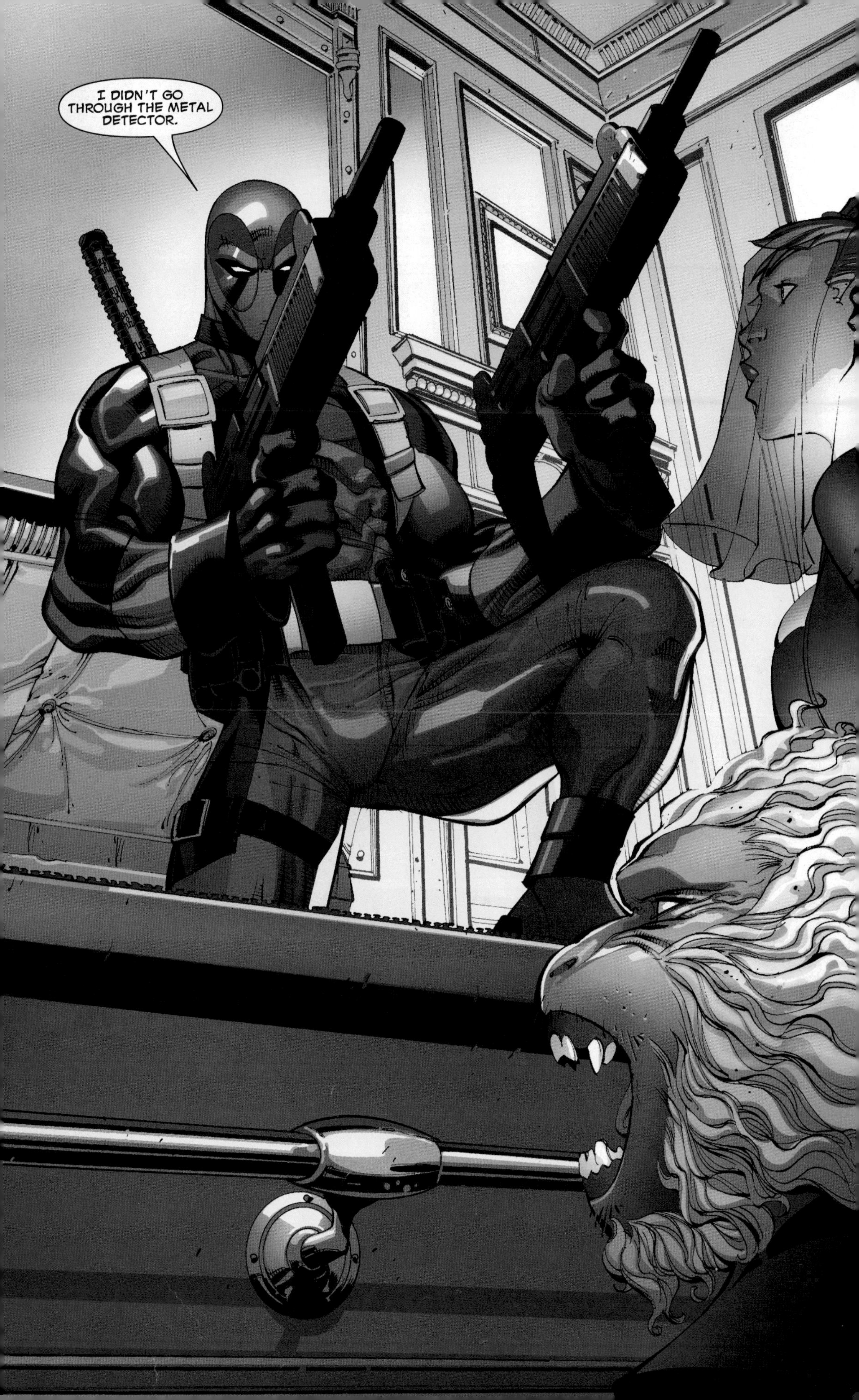
I DIDN'T GO THROUGH THE METAL DETECTOR.

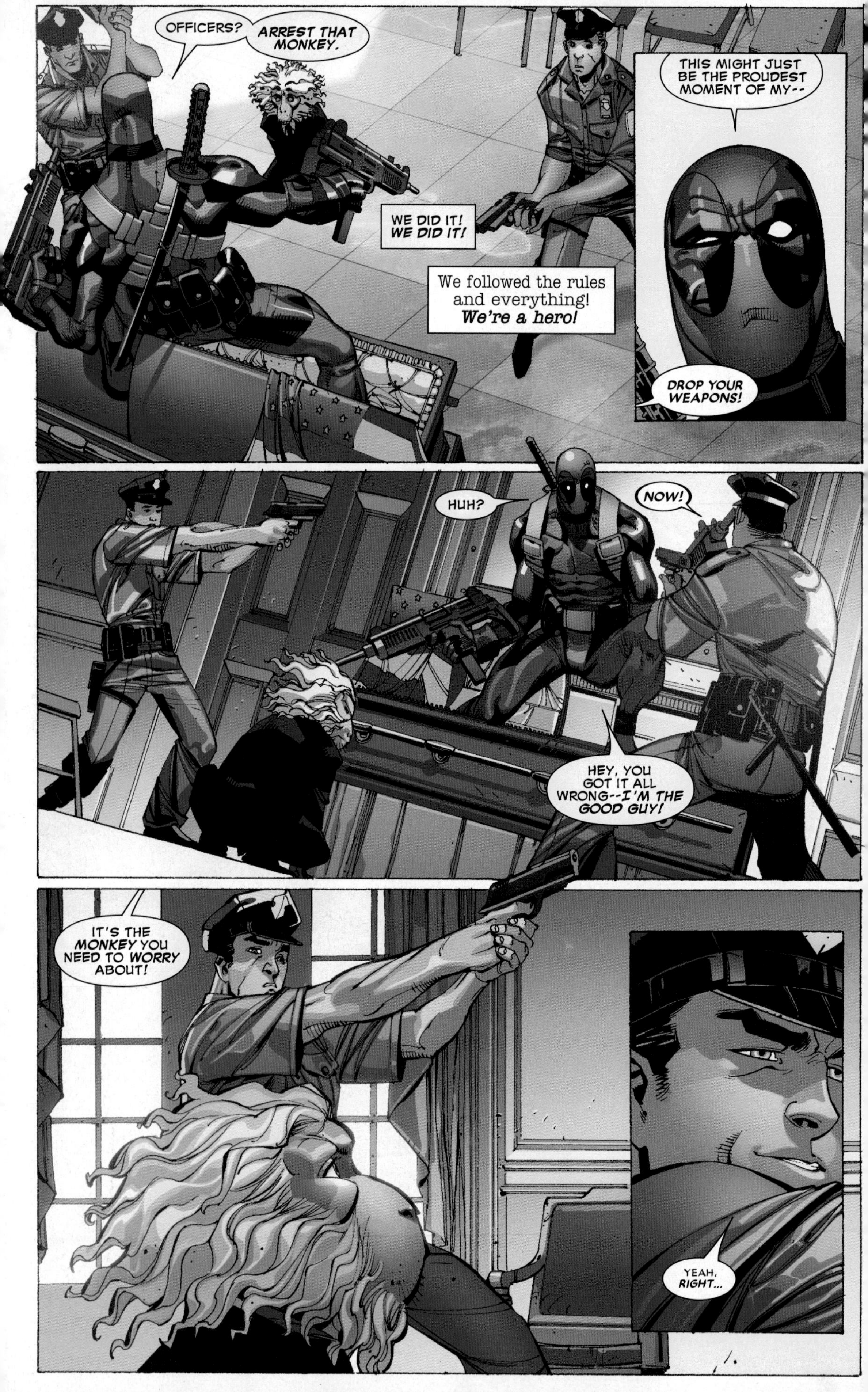

OFFICERS?
ARREST THAT MONKEY.
THIS MIGHT JUST BE THE PROUDEST MOMENT OF MY--
WE DID IT! WE DID IT!
We followed the rules and everything! We're a hero!
DROP YOUR WEAPONS!
HUH?
NOW!
HEY, YOU GOT IT ALL WRONG--I'M THE GOOD GUY!
IT'S THE MONKEY YOU NEED TO WORRY ABOUT!
YEAH, RIGHT...

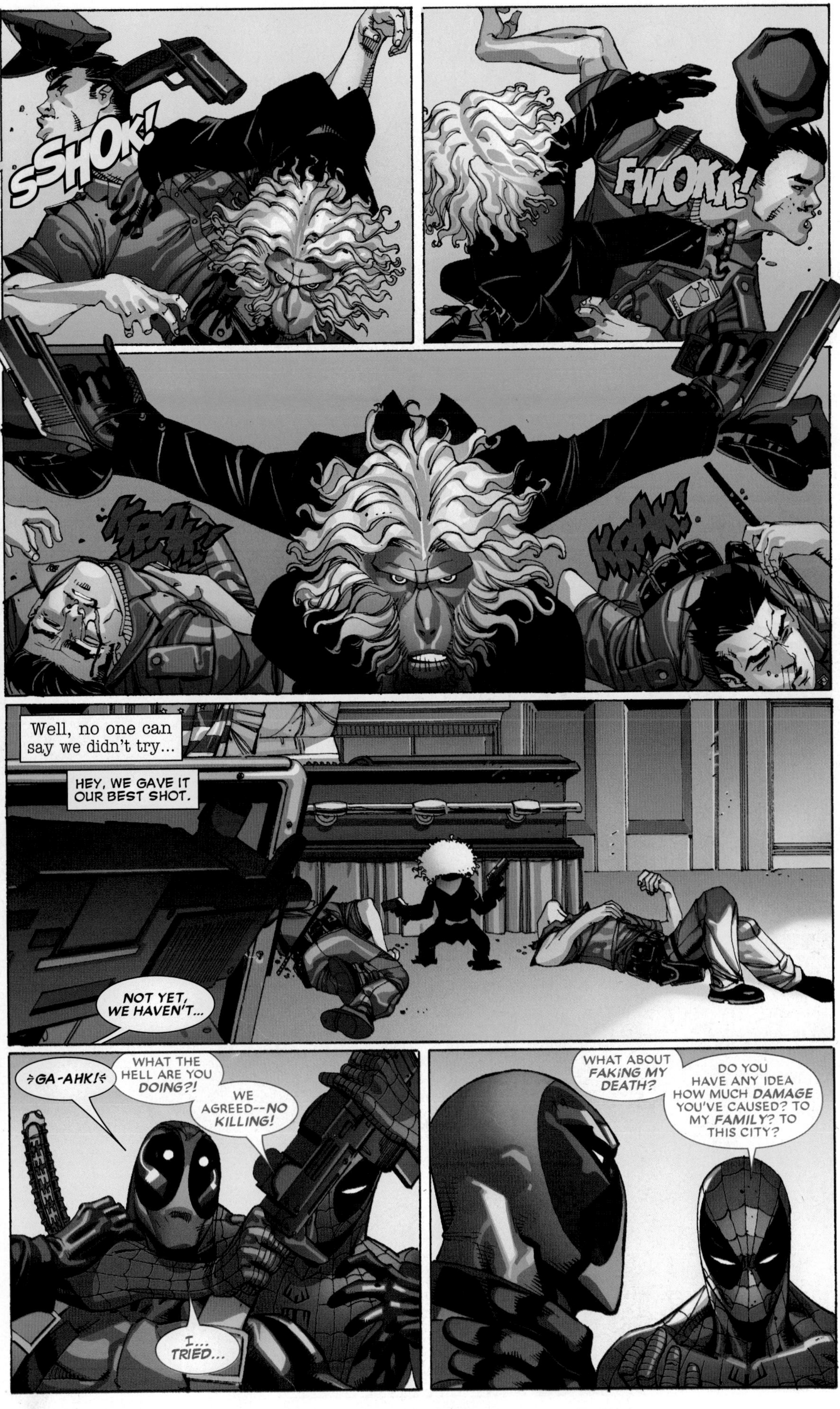

S-SHOK!
FWOKK!
KRAK!
KRAK!
Well, no one can say we didn't try...
HEY, WE GAVE IT OUR BEST SHOT.
NOT YET, WE HAVEN'T...
GA-AHK!
WHAT THE HELL ARE YOU DOING?!
WE AGREED--NO KILLING!
I... TRIED...
WHAT ABOUT FAKING MY DEATH?
DO YOU HAVE ANY IDEA HOW MUCH DAMAGE YOU'VE CAUSED? TO MY FAMILY? TO THIS CITY?

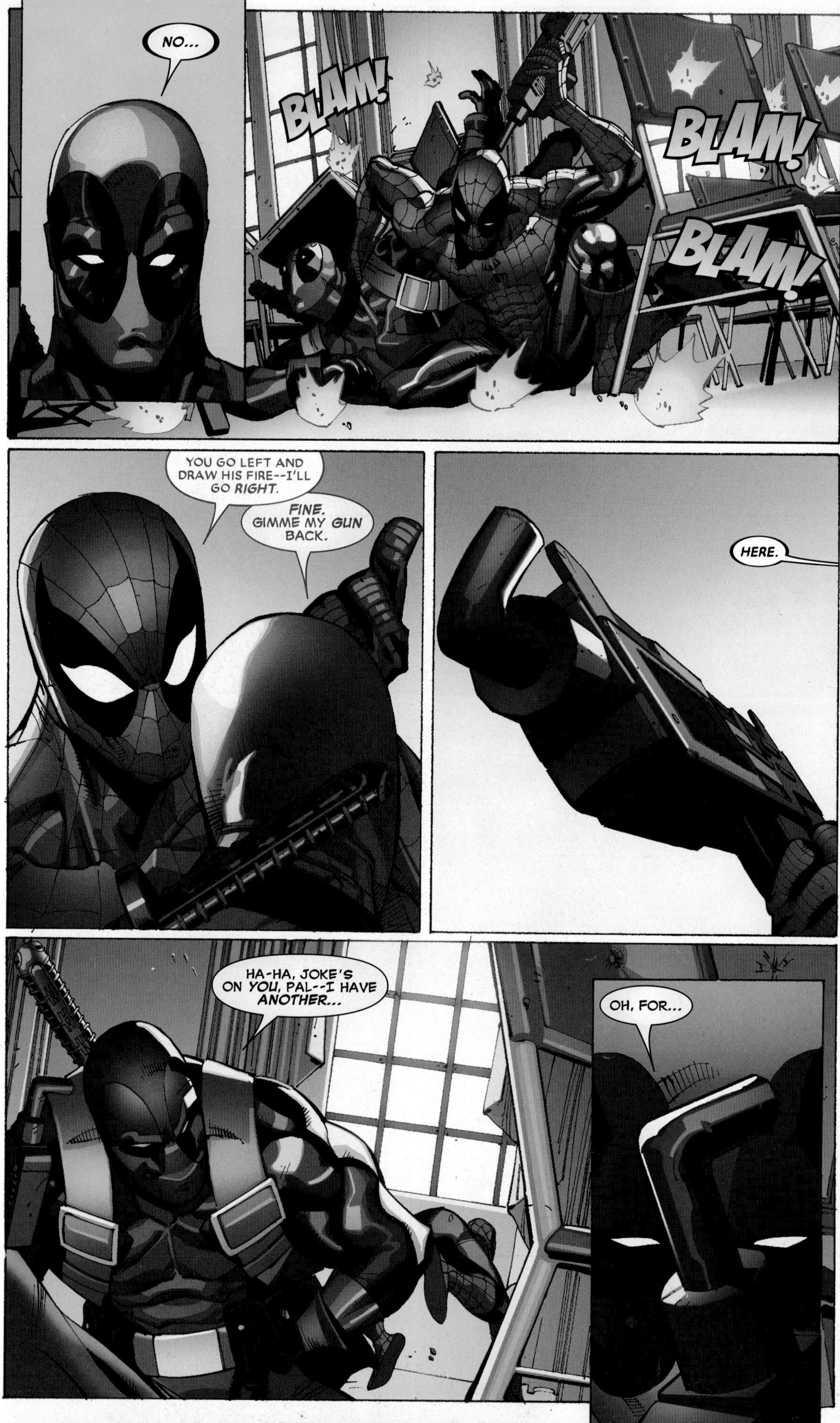
NO...
BLAM!
BLAM!
BLAM!
YOU GO LEFT AND DRAW HIS FIRE--I'LL GO RIGHT.
FINE. GIMME MY GUN BACK.
HERE.
HA-HA, JOKE'S ON YOU, PAL--I HAVE ANOTHER...
OH, FOR...

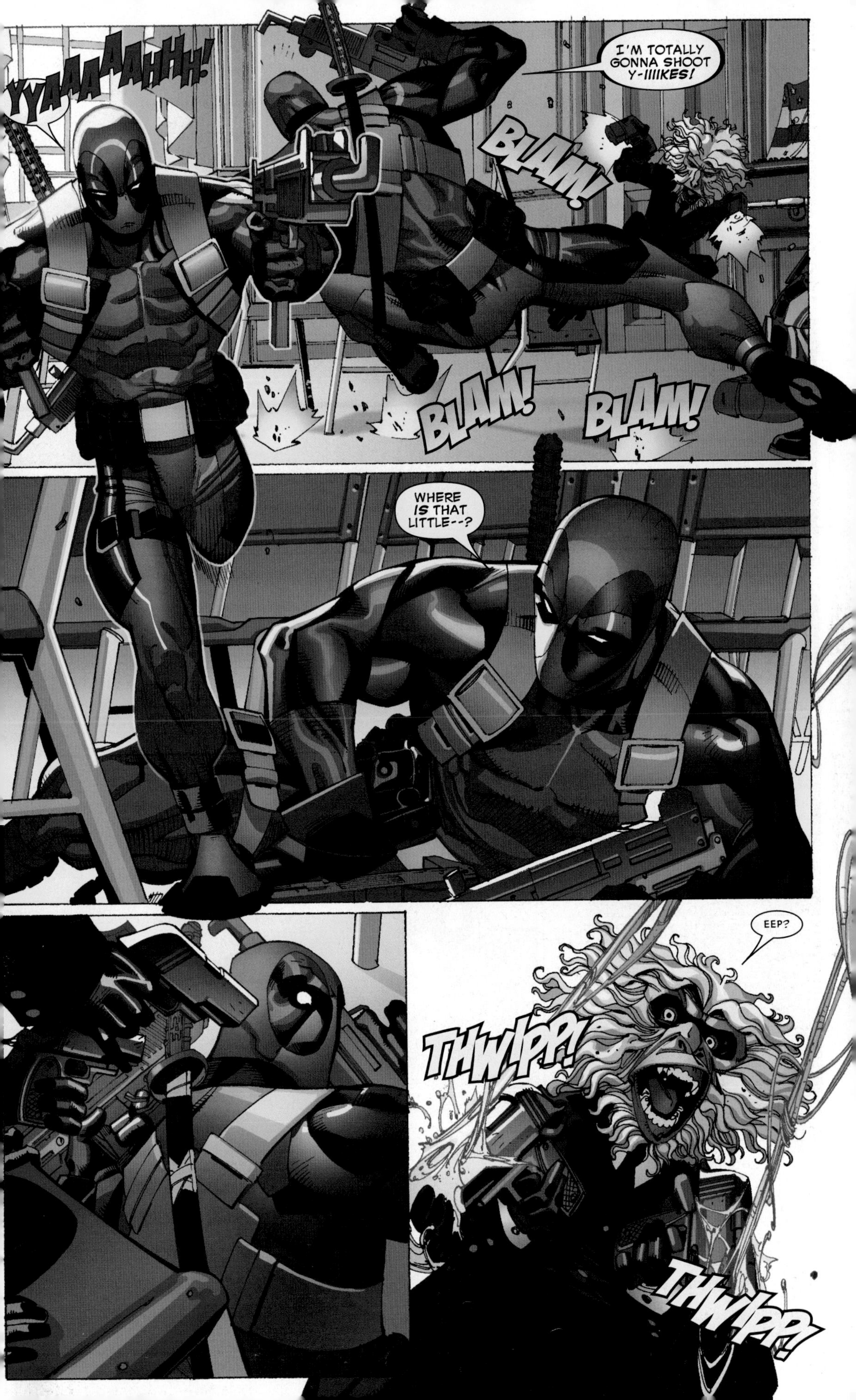
YYAAAAAHHH!
I'M TOTALLY GONNA SHOOT Y-IIIIKES!
BLAM!
BLAM!
BLAM!
WHERE IS THAT LITTLE--?
EEP?
THWIPP!
THWIPP!

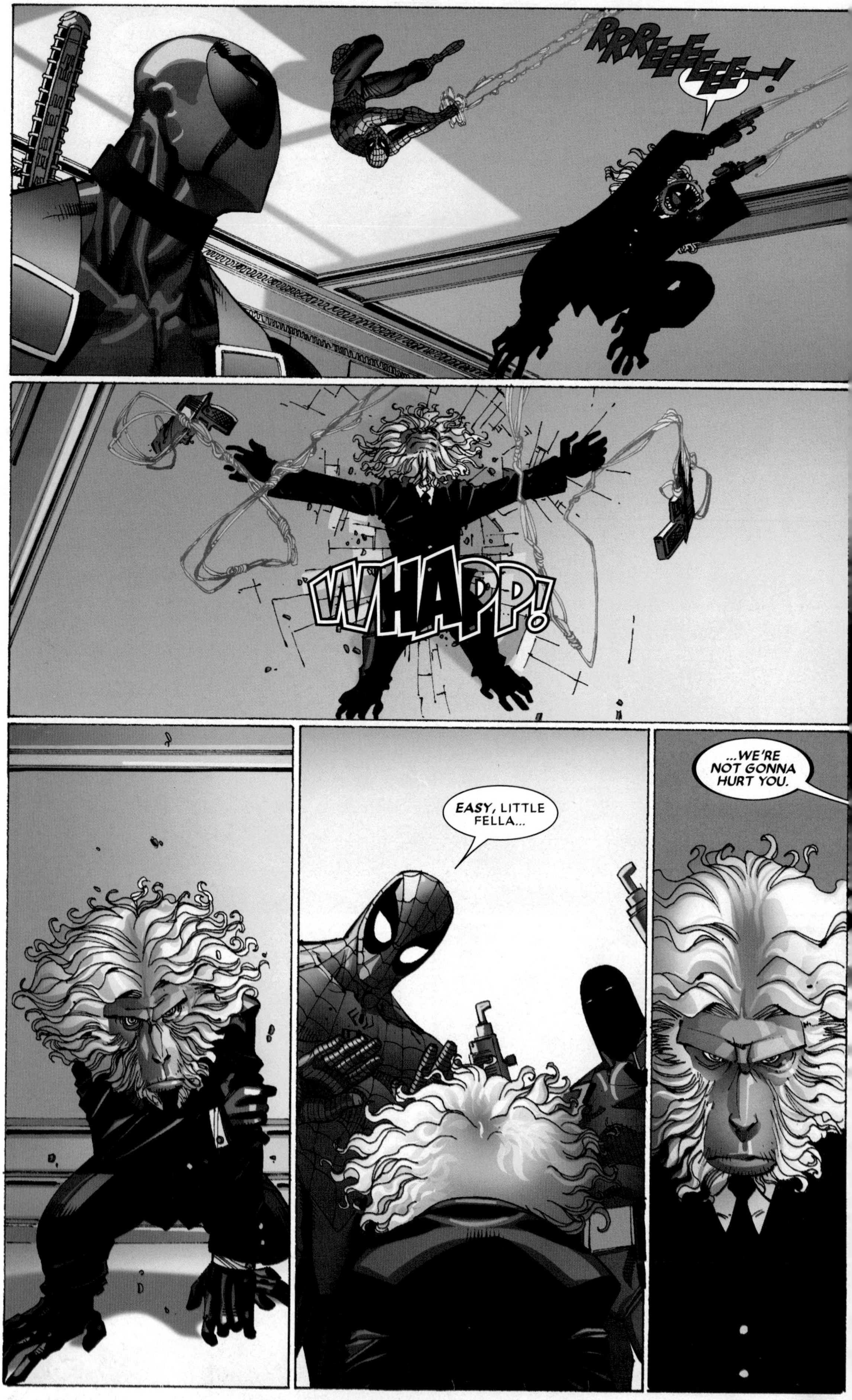
RRREEEEEEE--!
WHAPP!
EASY, LITTLE FELLA...
...WE'RE NOT GONNA HURT YOU.

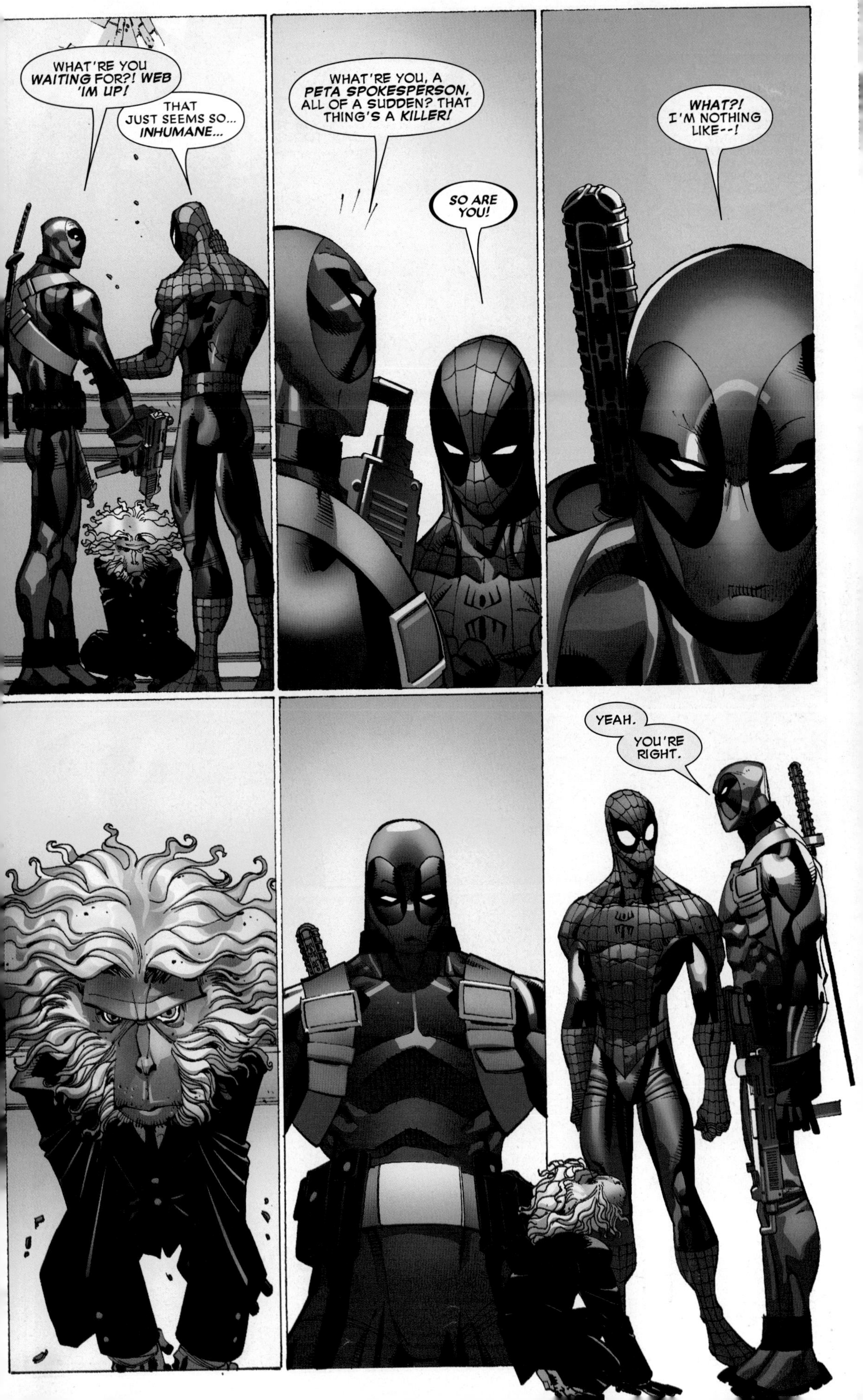
WHAT'RE YOU WAITING FOR?! WEB 'IM UP!
THAT JUST SEEMS SO... INHUMANE...
WHAT'RE YOU, A PETA SPOKESPERSON, ALL OF A SUDDEN? THAT THING'S A KILLER!
SO ARE YOU!
WHAT?! I'M NOTHING LIKE--!
YEAH.
YOU'RE RIGHT.

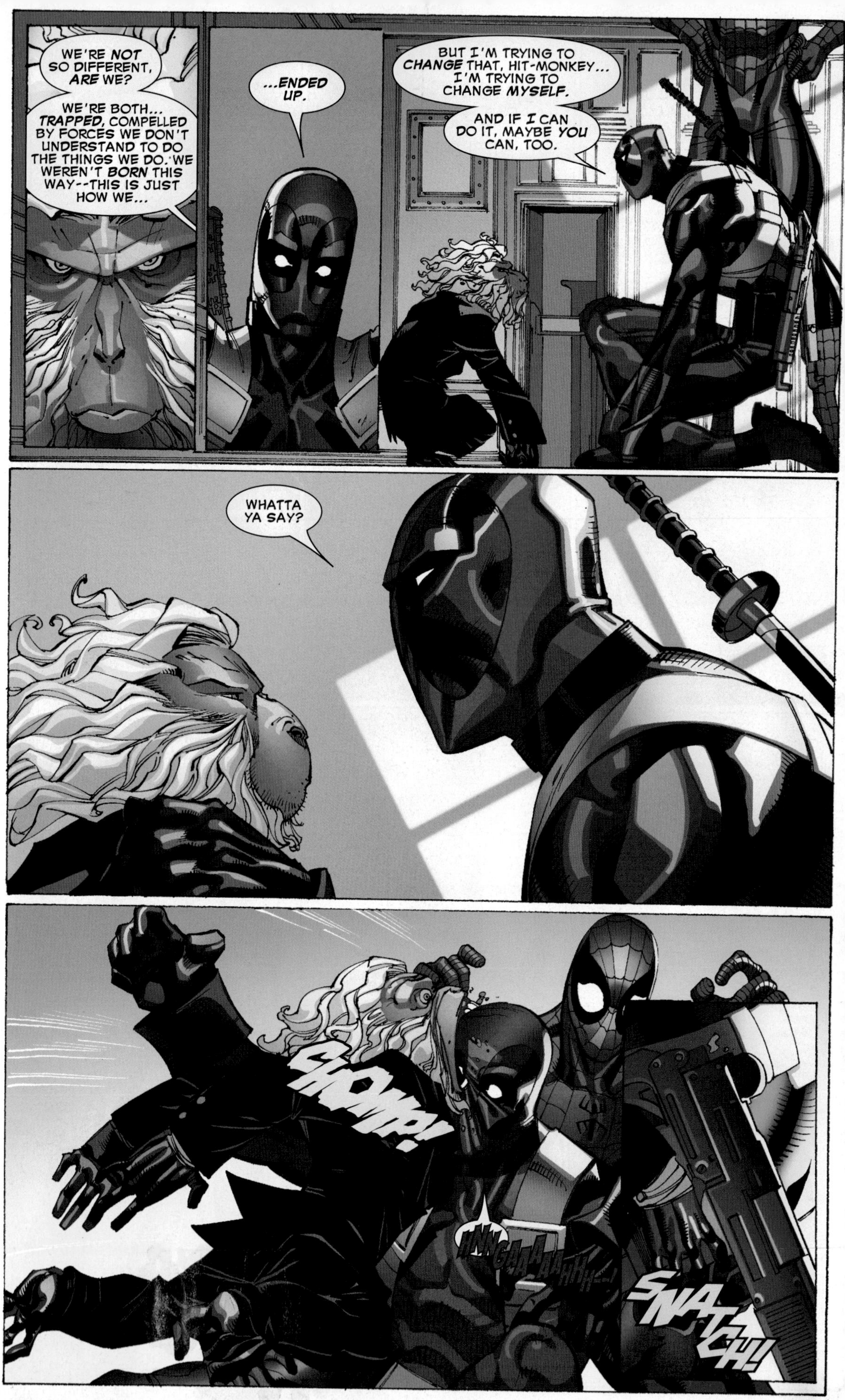
WE'RE NOT SO DIFFERENT, ARE WE?
WE'RE BOTH... TRAPPED, COMPELLED BY FORCES WE DON'T UNDERSTAND TO DO THE THINGS WE DO. WE WEREN'T BORN THIS WAY--THIS IS JUST HOW WE...
...ENDED UP.
BUT I'M TRYING TO CHANGE THAT, HIT-MONKEY... I'M TRYING TO CHANGE MYSELF.
AND IF I CAN DO IT, MAYBE YOU CAN, TOO.
WHATTA YA SAY?
CHOMP!
HNNGAAAAAHHH--!
SNATCH!

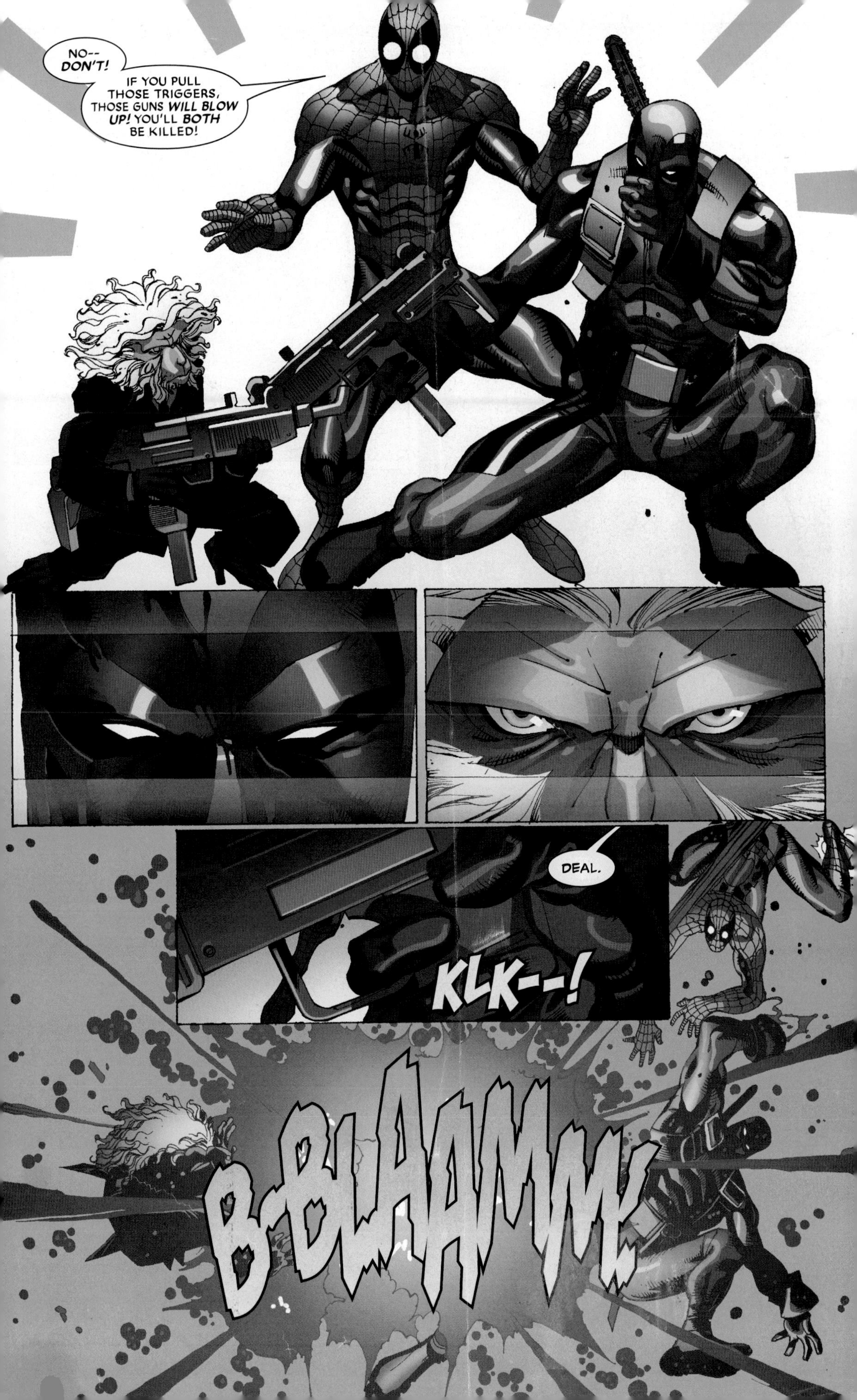
NO-- DON'T!
IF YOU PULL THOSE TRIGGERS, THOSE GUNS WILL BLOW UP! YOU'LL BOTH BE KILLED!
DEAL.
KLK--!
B-BLAAMM!

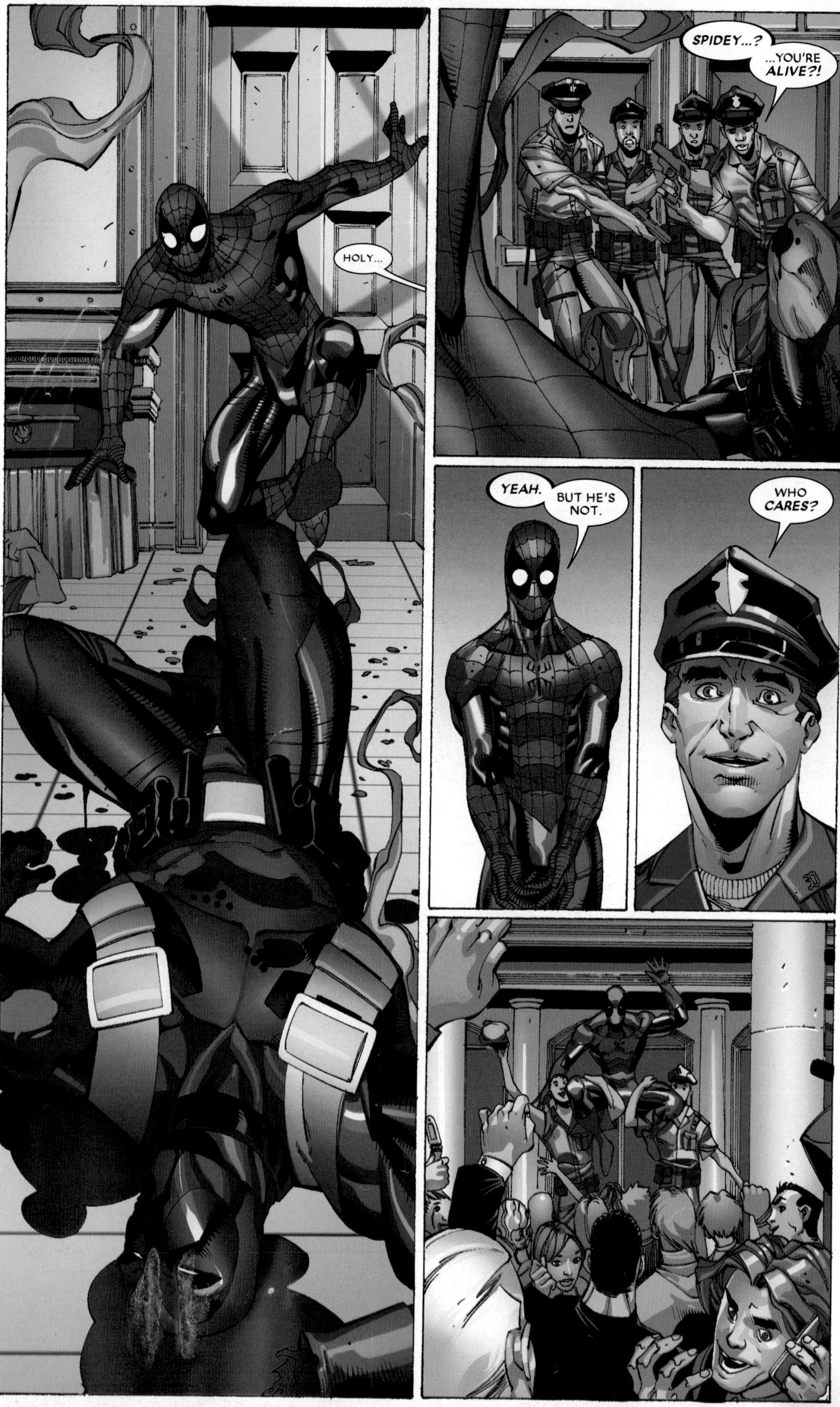
HOLY...
SPIDEY...?
...YOU'RE ALIVE?!
YEAH.
BUT HE'S NOT.
WHO CARES?

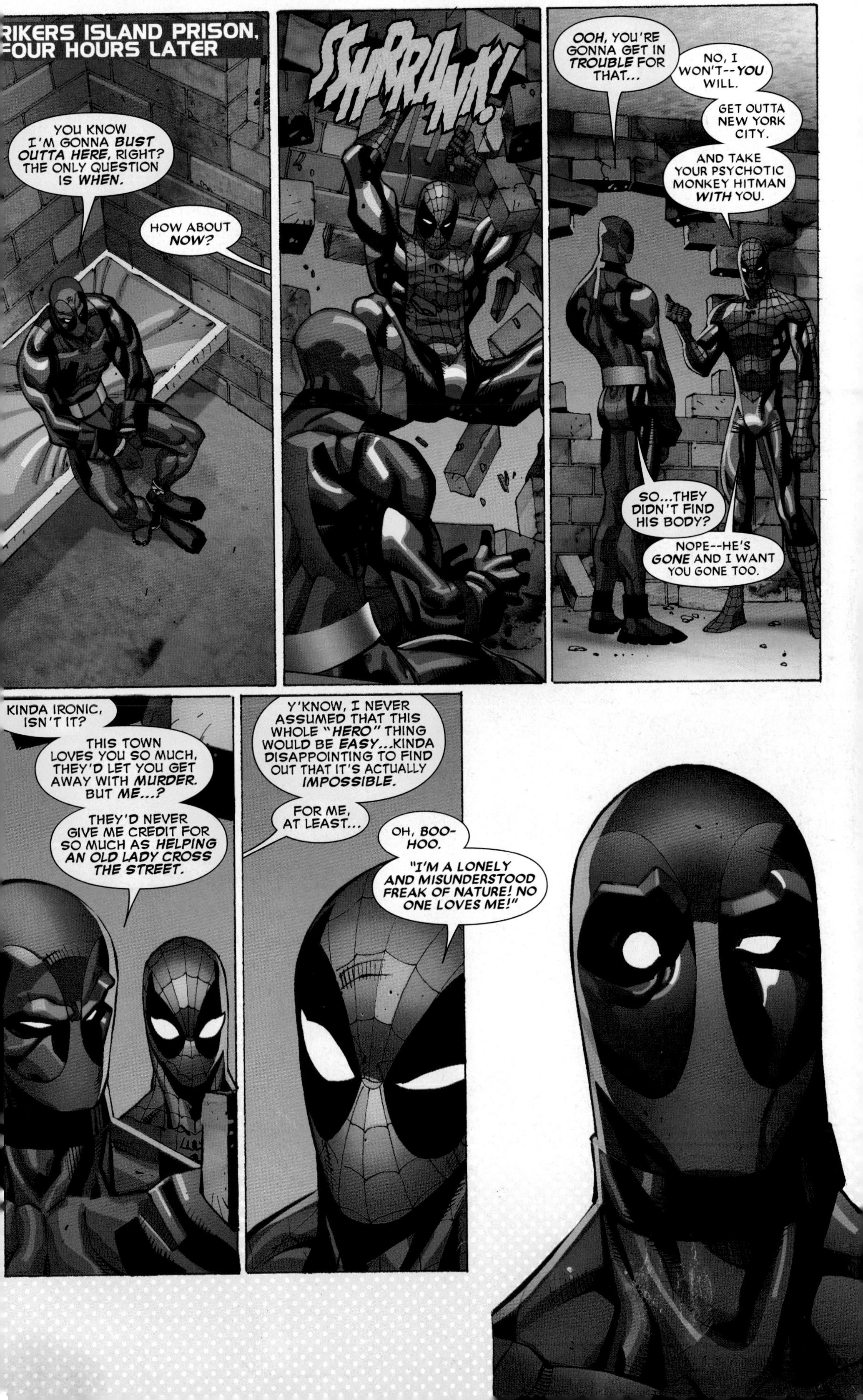
RIKERS ISLAND PRISON, FOUR HOURS LATER
YOU KNOW I'M GONNA BUST OUTTA HERE, RIGHT? THE ONLY QUESTION IS WHEN.
HOW ABOUT NOW?
SSHRRANK!
OOH, YOU'RE GONNA GET IN TROUBLE FOR THAT...
NO, I WON'T--YOU WILL.
GET OUTTA NEW YORK CITY.
AND TAKE YOUR PSYCHOTIC MONKEY HITMAN WITH YOU.
SO...THEY DIDN'T FIND HIS BODY?
NOPE--HE'S GONE AND I WANT YOU GONE TOO.
KINDA IRONIC, ISN'T IT?
THIS TOWN LOVES YOU SO MUCH, THEY'D LET YOU GET AWAY WITH MURDER. BUT ME...?
THEY'D NEVER GIVE ME CREDIT FOR SO MUCH AS HELPING AN OLD LADY CROSS THE STREET.
Y'KNOW, I NEVER ASSUMED THAT THIS WHOLE "HERO" THING WOULD BE EASY...KINDA DISAPPOINTING TO FIND OUT THAT IT'S ACTUALLY IMPOSSIBLE.
FOR ME, AT LEAST...
OH, BOO-HOO.
"I'M A LONELY AND MISUNDERSTOOD FREAK OF NATURE! NO ONE LOVES ME!"

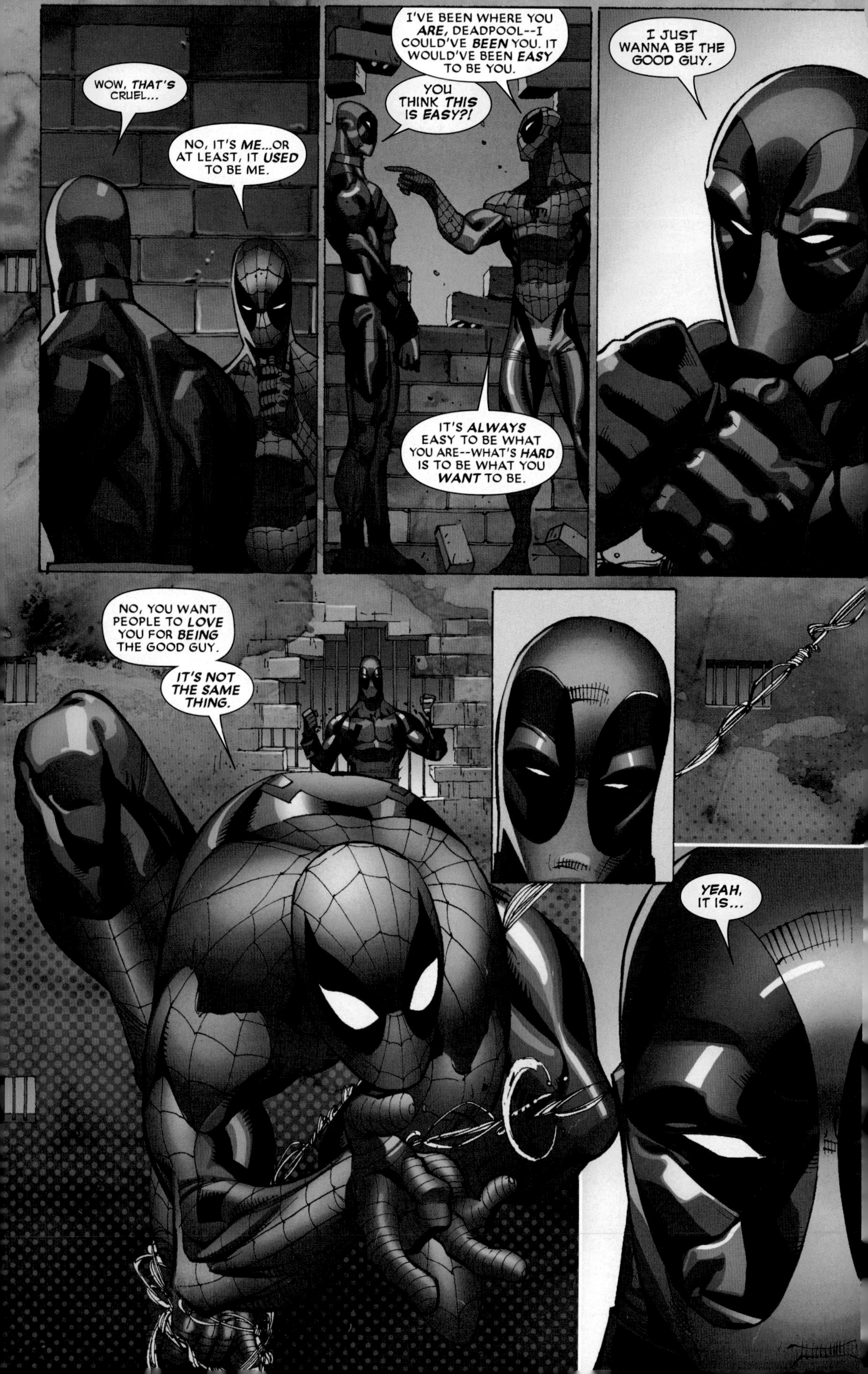
WOW, THAT'S CRUEL...
NO, IT'S ME...OR AT LEAST, IT USED TO BE ME.
I'VE BEEN WHERE YOU ARE, DEADPOOL--I COULD'VE BEEN YOU. IT WOULD'VE BEEN EASY TO BE YOU.
YOU THINK THIS IS EASY?!
IT'S ALWAYS EASY TO BE WHAT YOU ARE--WHAT'S HARD IS TO BE WHAT YOU WANT TO BE.
I JUST WANNA BE THE GOOD GUY.
NO, YOU WANT PEOPLE TO LOVE YOU FOR BEING THE GOOD GUY.
IT'S NOT THE SAME THING.
YEAH, IT IS...

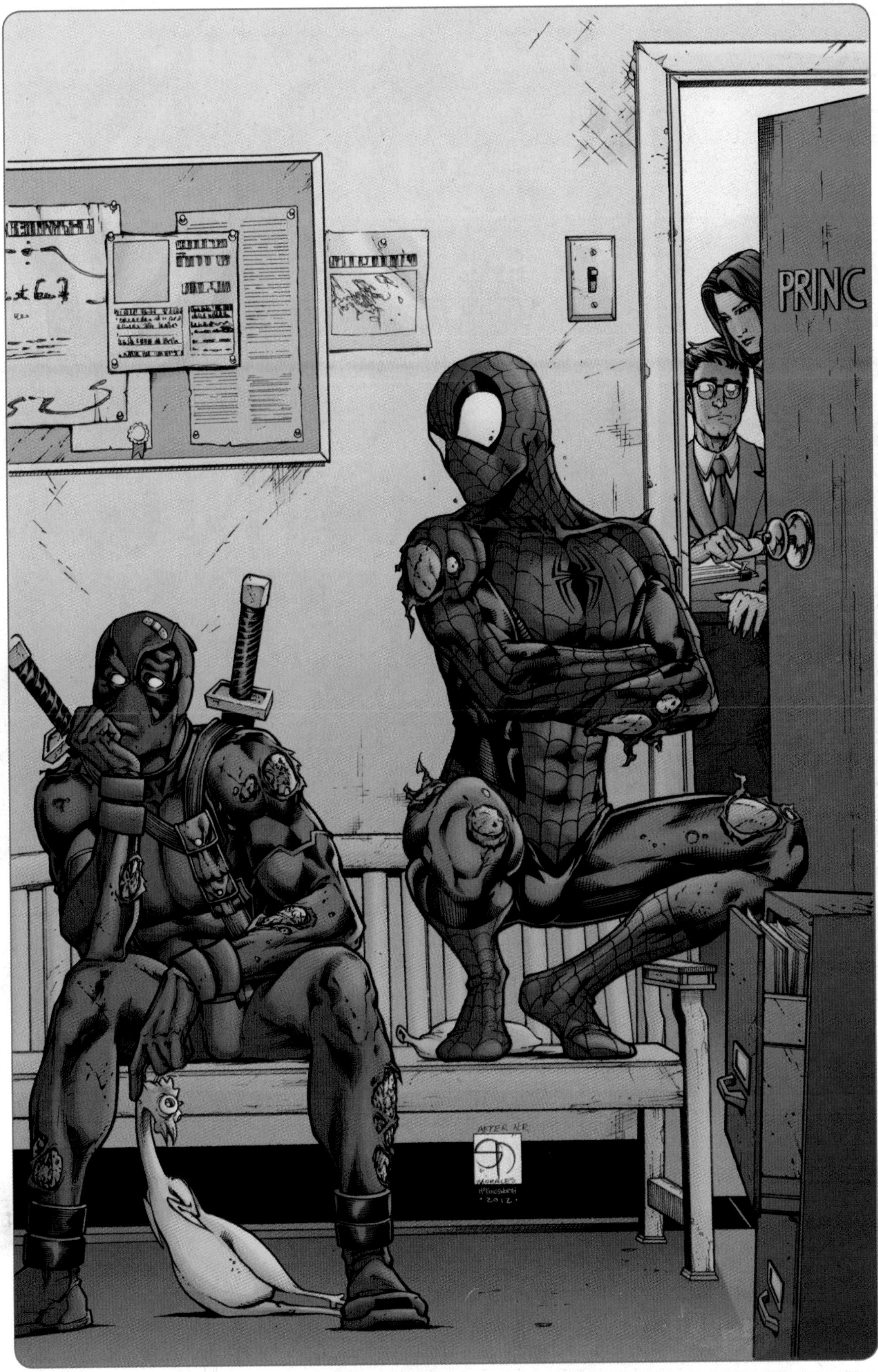
PRINC

AVENGING SPIDER-MAN #12

While attending a demonstration in radiology, high school student Peter Parker was bitten by a spider which had accidentally been exposed to radioactive rays. Through a miracle of science Peter soon found that he had gained the spider's powers…and had, in effect, become a human spider! Later he joined the Avengers. And now he is the...

AVENGING SPIDER-MAN

After being diagnosed with cancer, the deadly mercenary Wade Wilson volunteered for the Weapon X program, hoping that they would be able to give him a cure. Their solution was to give him a healing factor similar Wolverine's. Now, he's the Merc with a Mouth, the Regeneratin' Degenerate. He's…

DEADPOOL

AVENGING SPIDER-MAN

PREVIOUSLY...

Spider-Man celebrated the 50th anniversary of his debut

Before that, Spider-Man teamed up with Captain Marvel on a failed flight to Bosto... the tim... because this story probably takes place before both...

> WHY DO THEY NEED TO KNOW WHAT HAPPENED PREVIOUSLY? I WASN'T HERE, IT COULDN'T HAVE BEEN THAT IMPORTANT.

> Well, sometimes, Deadpool, readers are new, either to comics or reading this book, and they need to know things upfront so that they can jump right in and feel included.

> LIKE THE FACT THAT I TALK TO MYSELF IN CAPTIONS?

> Yes, and sometimes there are things even long-standing readers need to know.

> LIKE THE FACT THAT THIS STORY TAKES PLACE BEFORE DEADPOOL #50?

> Exactly!

> CAN I START SHOOTING PEOPLE YET?

> Probably not, it is a Spider-Man book.

WRITER: **KEVIN SHINICK** ART: **AARON KUDER**

COLOR ART: **MATT HOLLINGSWORTH** LETTERER: **VC's JOE CARAMAGNA**

COVER: **DAVIS, MORALES AND HOLLINGSWORTH**

ASSISTANT EDITOR: **ELLIE PYLE** ASSOCIATE EDITOR: **SANA AMANAT** EDITOR: **STEPHEN WACKER**

> OMG! THIS DUDE'S LAST NAME IS "WACKER"!

EXECUTIVE EDITOR: **TOM BREVOORT** EDITOR IN CHIEF: **AXEL ALONSO**

CHIEF CREATIVE OFFICER: **JOE QUESADA** PUBLISHER: **DAN BUCKLEY** EXECUTIVE PRODUCER: **ALAN FINE**

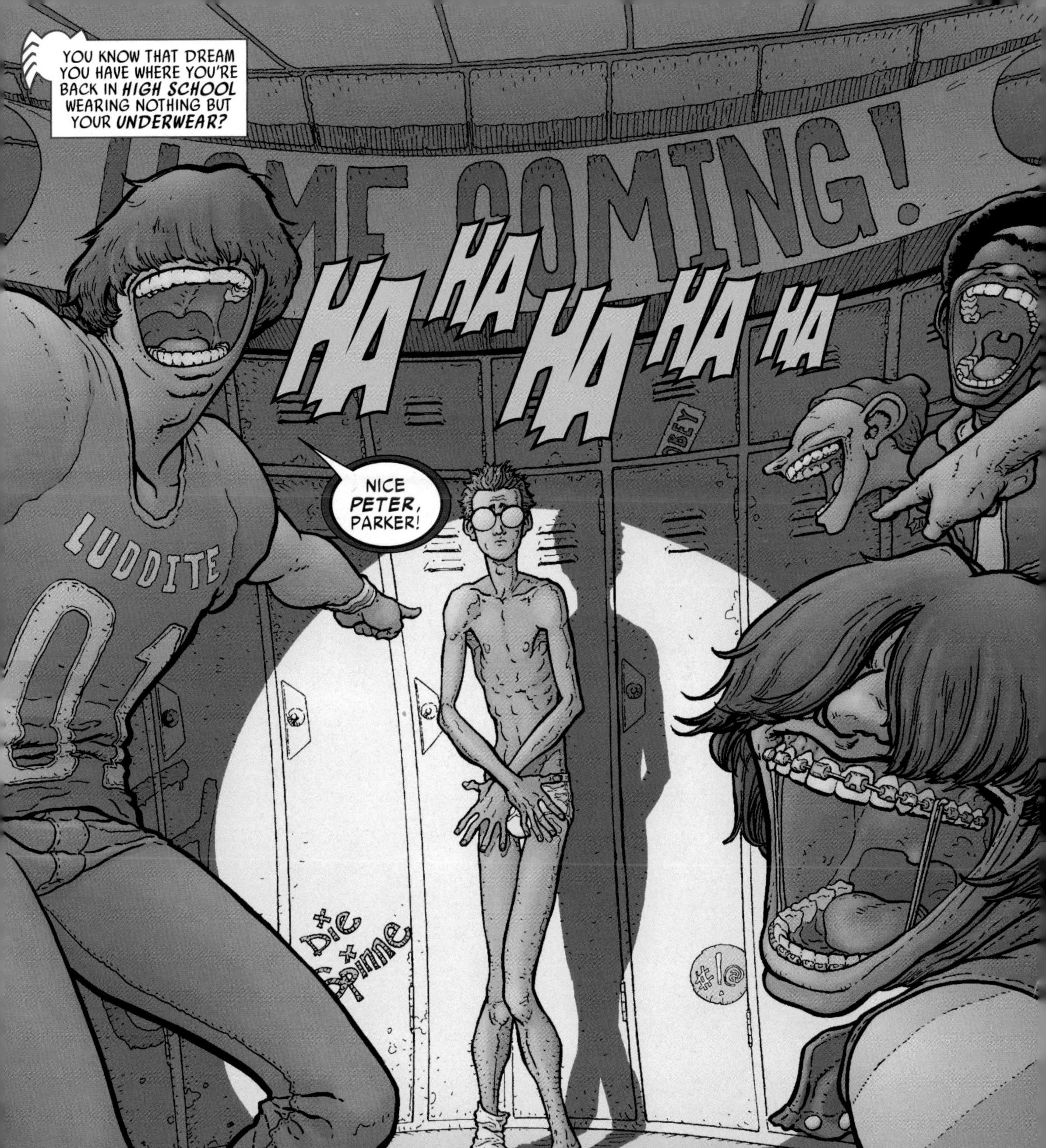
YOU KNOW THAT DREAM YOU HAVE WHERE YOU'RE BACK IN HIGH SCHOOL WEARING NOTHING BUT YOUR UNDERWEAR?
HOME COMING!
HA HA HA HA HA HA
NICE PETER, PARKER!
LUDDITE
Die Spinne

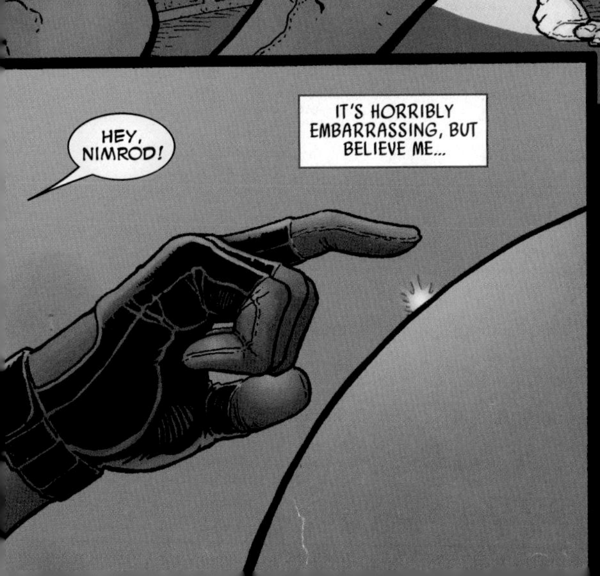
HEY, NIMROD!
IT'S HORRIBLY EMBARRASSING, BUT BELIEVE ME...

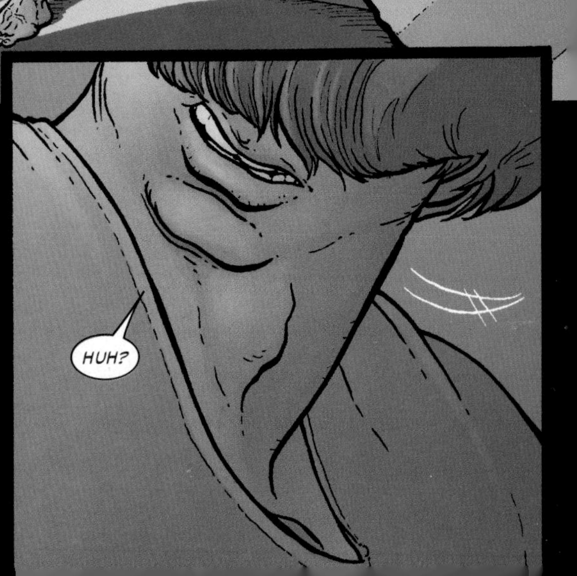
HUH?

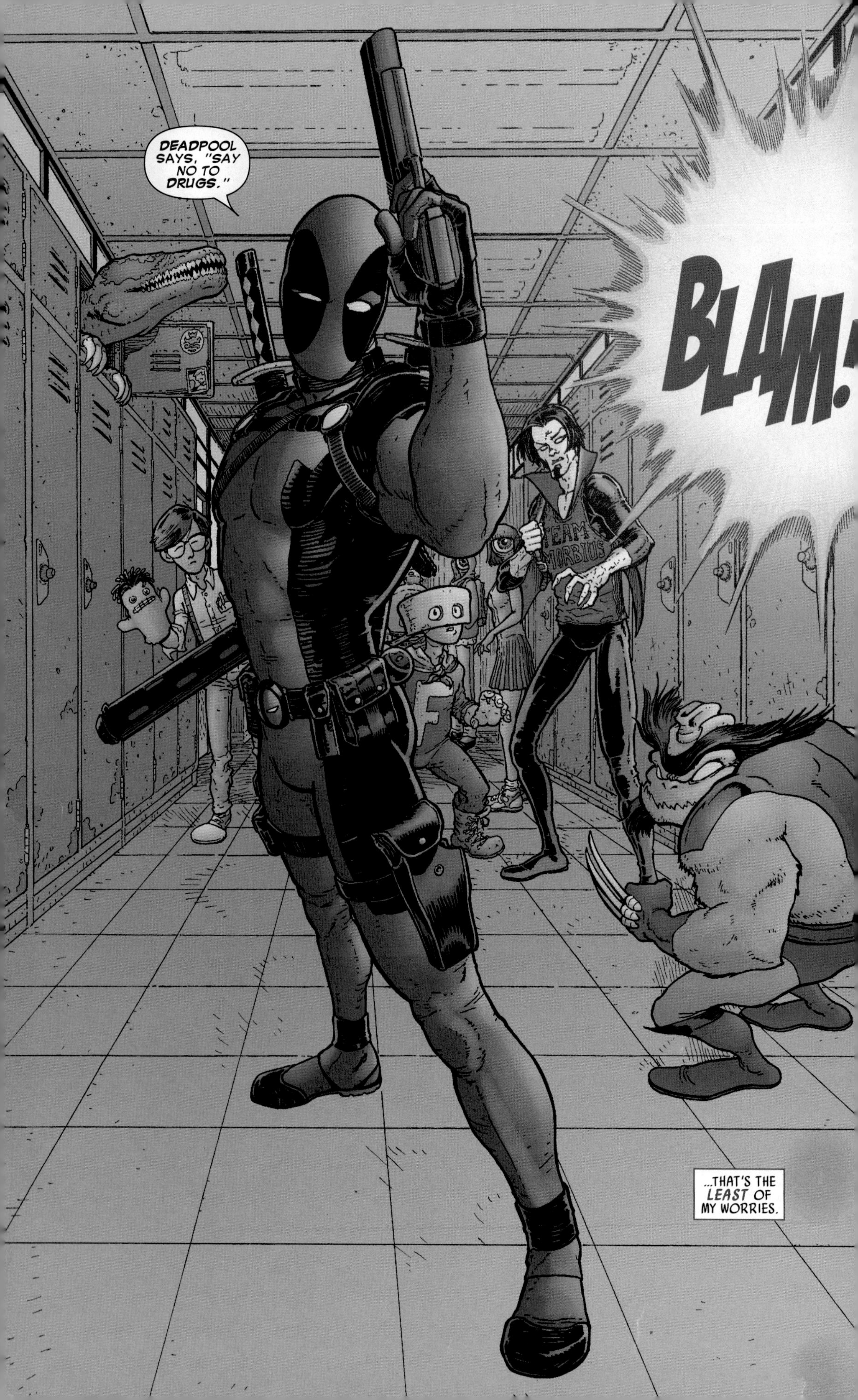
DEADPOOL SAYS, "SAY NO TO DRUGS."
BLAM!
TEAM MORBIUS
...THAT'S THE LEAST OF MY WORRIES.

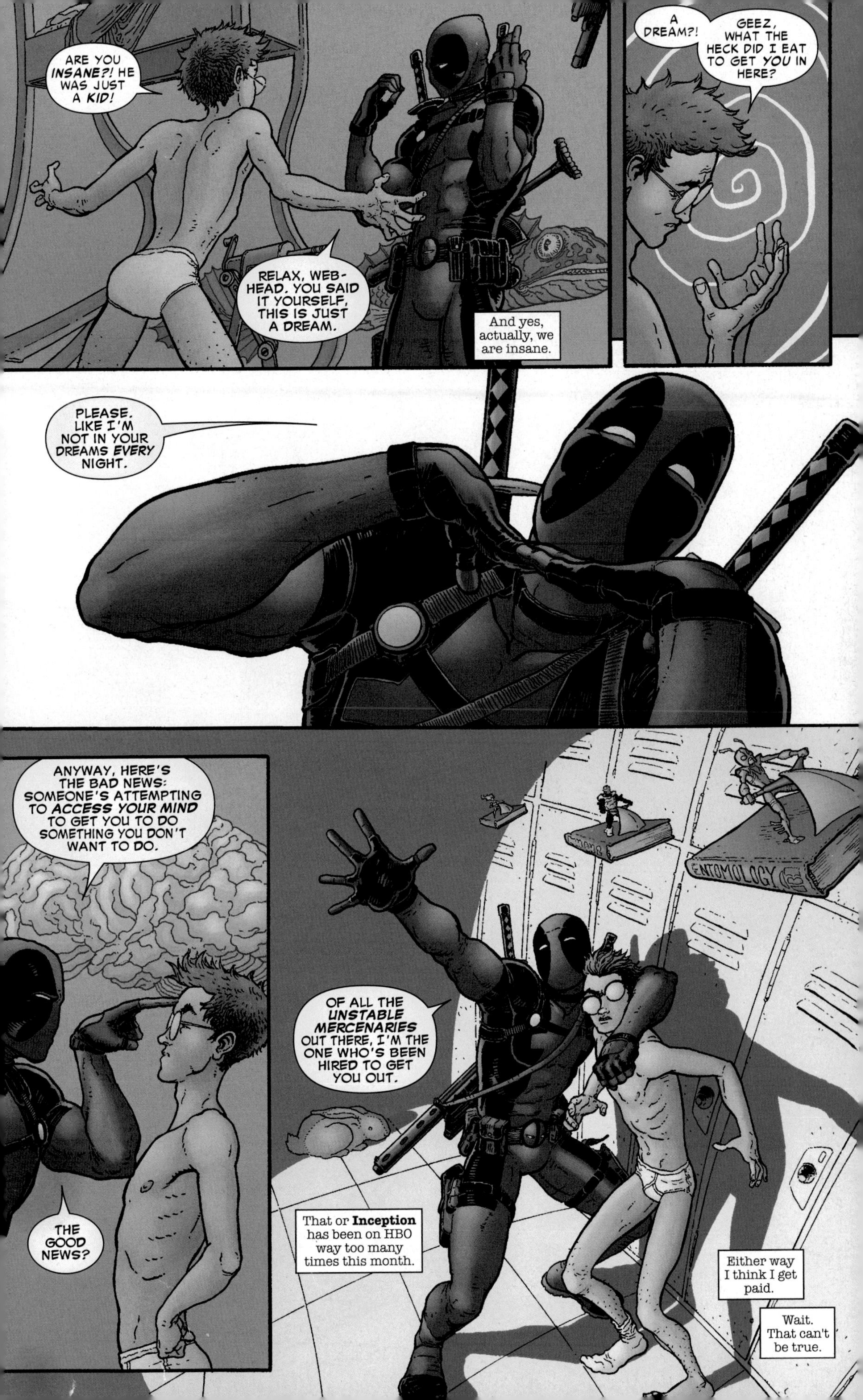

ARE YOU *INSANE?!* HE WAS JUST A *KID!*
RELAX, WEB-HEAD. YOU SAID IT YOURSELF, THIS IS JUST A DREAM.
And yes, actually, we are insane.
A DREAM?!
GEEZ, WHAT THE HECK DID I EAT TO GET *YOU* IN HERE?
PLEASE. LIKE I'M NOT IN YOUR DREAMS *EVERY* NIGHT.
ANYWAY, HERE'S THE BAD NEWS: SOMEONE'S ATTEMPTING TO *ACCESS YOUR MIND* TO GET YOU TO DO SOMETHING YOU DON'T WANT TO DO.
THE GOOD NEWS?
ENTOMOLOGY
OF ALL THE *UNSTABLE MERCENARIES* OUT THERE, I'M THE ONE WHO'S BEEN HIRED TO GET YOU OUT.
That or **Inception** has been on HBO way too many times this month.
Either way I think I get paid.
Wait. That can't be true.

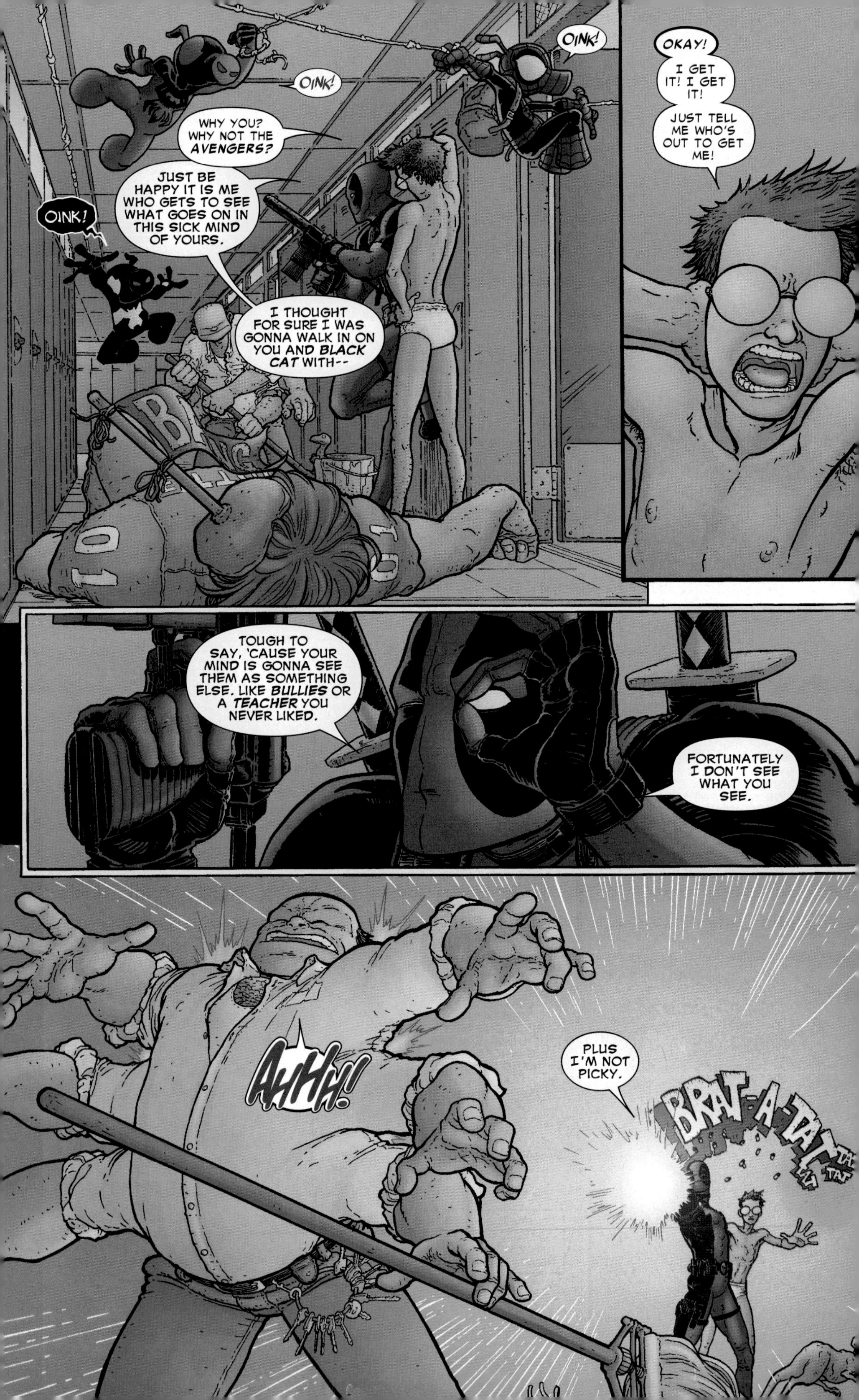
OINK!
OINK!
WHY YOU? WHY NOT THE AVENGERS?
JUST BE HAPPY IT IS ME WHO GETS TO SEE WHAT GOES ON IN THIS SICK MIND OF YOURS.
OINK!
I THOUGHT FOR SURE I WAS GONNA WALK IN ON YOU AND BLACK CAT WITH--
OKAY!
I GET IT! I GET IT!
JUST TELL ME WHO'S OUT TO GET ME!
TOUGH TO SAY, 'CAUSE YOUR MIND IS GONNA SEE THEM AS SOMETHING ELSE. LIKE BULLIES OR A TEACHER YOU NEVER LIKED.
FORTUNATELY I DON'T SEE WHAT YOU SEE.
AHHH!
PLUS I'M NOT PICKY.
BRAT-A-TAT

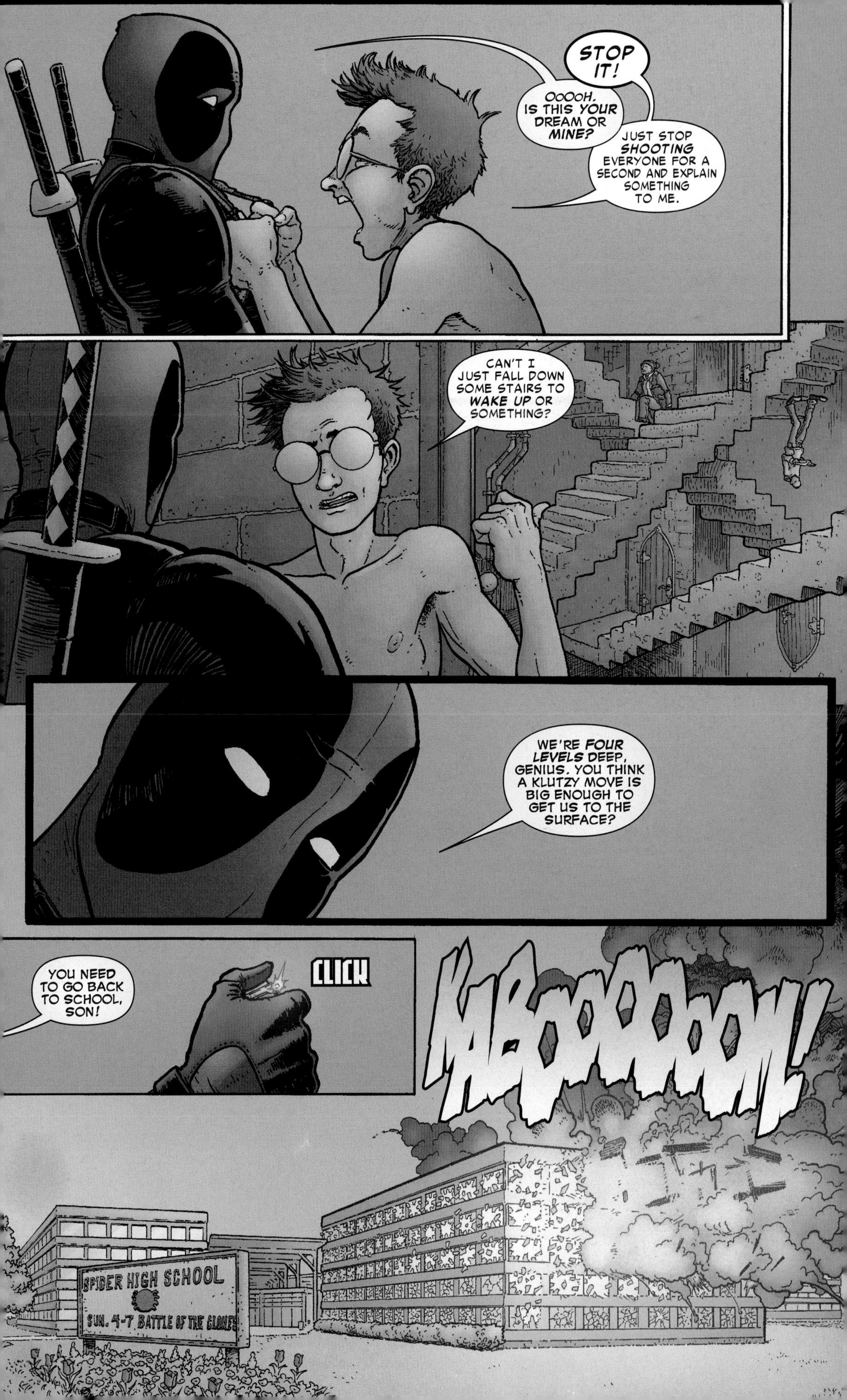
STOP IT!
OOOOH. IS THIS YOUR DREAM OR MINE?
JUST STOP SHOOTING EVERYONE FOR A SECOND AND EXPLAIN SOMETHING TO ME.
CAN'T I JUST FALL DOWN SOME STAIRS TO WAKE UP OR SOMETHING?
WE'RE FOUR LEVELS DEEP, GENIUS. YOU THINK A KLUTZY MOVE IS BIG ENOUGH TO GET US TO THE SURFACE?
YOU NEED TO GO BACK TO SCHOOL, SON!
CLICK
KABOOOOOOM!
SPIDER HIGH SCHOOL
SUN. 4-7 BATTLE OF THE CLONES

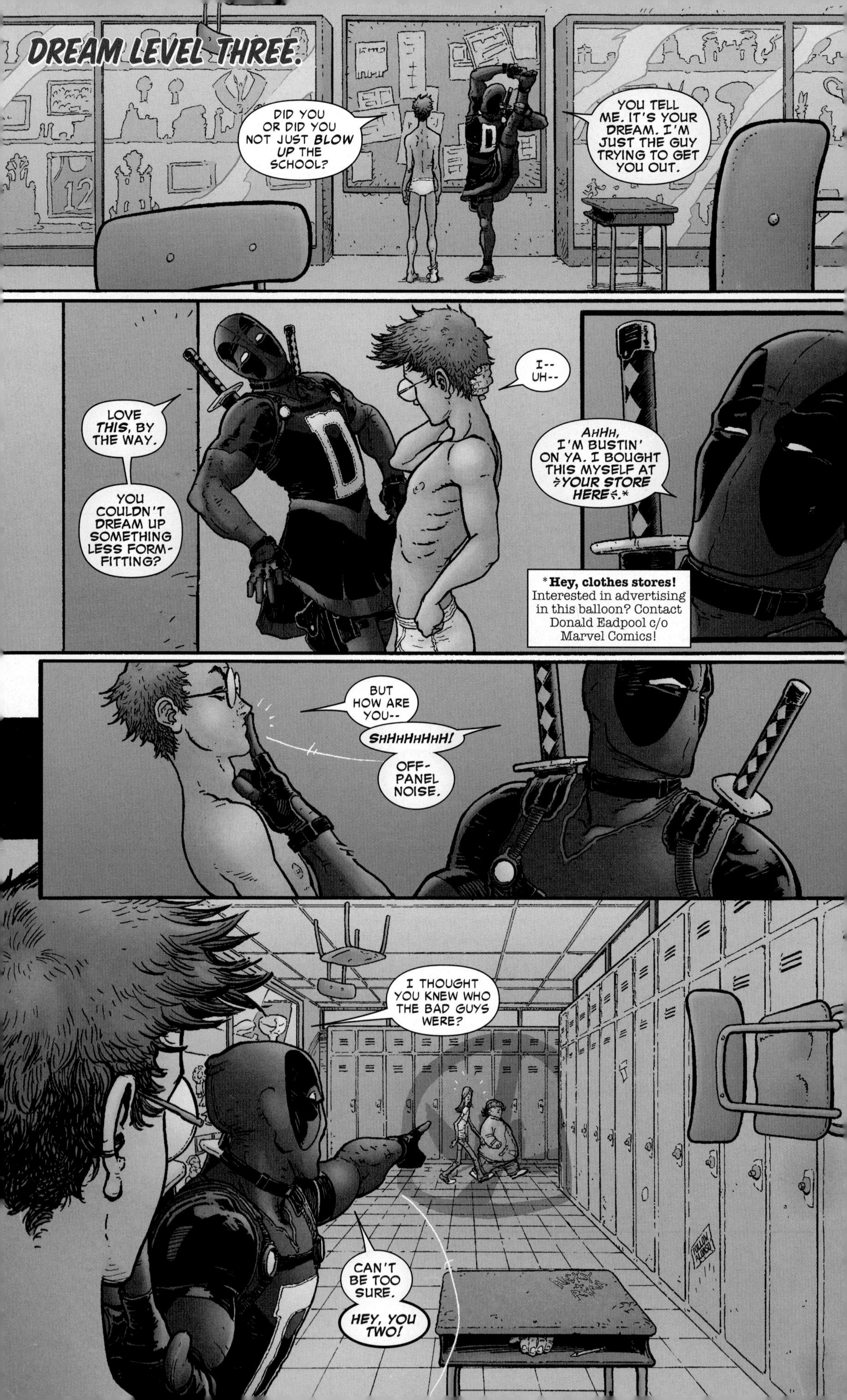
DREAM LEVEL THREE.
DID YOU OR DID YOU NOT JUST BLOW UP THE SCHOOL?
YOU TELL ME. IT'S YOUR DREAM. I'M JUST THE GUY TRYING TO GET YOU OUT.
LOVE THIS, BY THE WAY.
YOU COULDN'T DREAM UP SOMETHING LESS FORM-FITTING?
I-- UH--
AHHH, I'M BUSTIN' ON YA. I BOUGHT THIS MYSELF AT ≥YOUR STORE HERE≤.*
*Hey, clothes stores! Interested in advertising in this balloon? Contact Donald Eadpool c/o Marvel Comics!
BUT HOW ARE YOU--
SHHHHHHH!
OFF-PANEL NOISE.
I THOUGHT YOU KNEW WHO THE BAD GUYS WERE?
CAN'T BE TOO SURE.
HEY, YOU TWO!

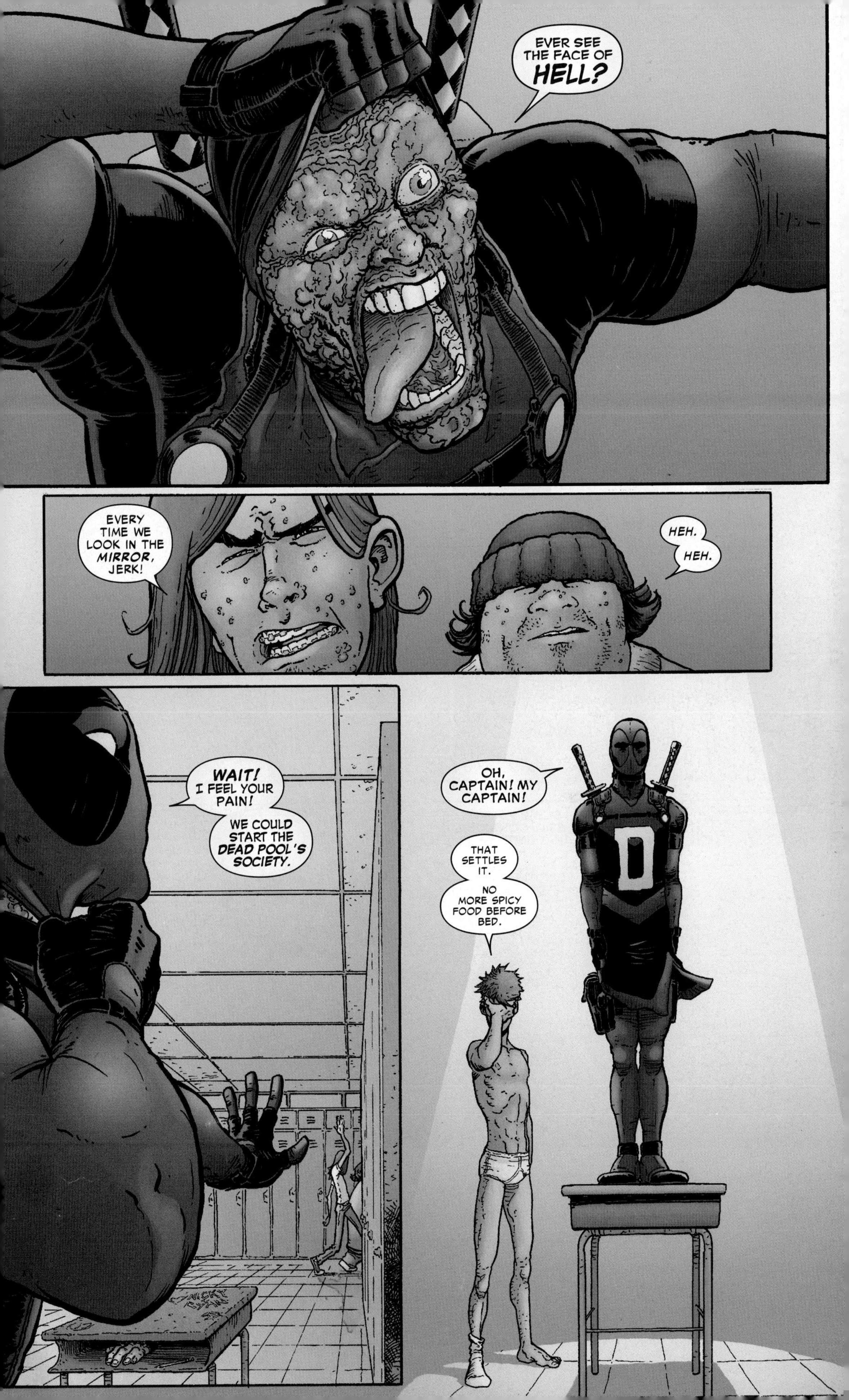
EVER SEE THE FACE OF HELL?
EVERY TIME WE LOOK IN THE MIRROR, JERK!
HEH. HEH.
WAIT! I FEEL YOUR PAIN!
WE COULD START THE DEAD POOL'S SOCIETY.
OH, CAPTAIN! MY CAPTAIN!
THAT SETTLES IT.
NO MORE SPICY FOOD BEFORE BED.

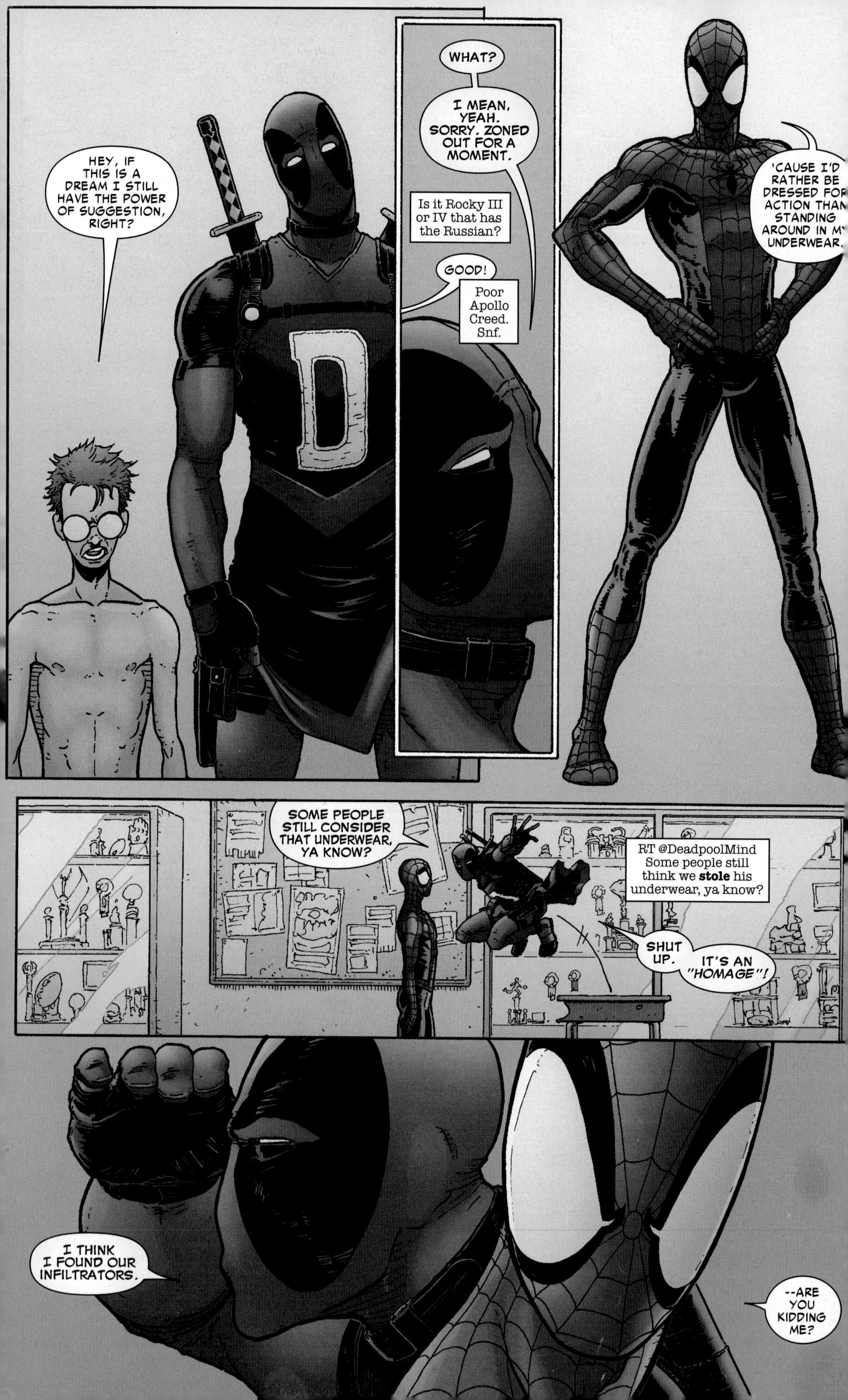
HEY, IF THIS IS A DREAM I STILL HAVE THE POWER OF SUGGESTION, RIGHT?
WHAT?
I MEAN, YEAH. SORRY. ZONED OUT FOR A MOMENT.
Is it Rocky III or IV that has the Russian?
GOOD!
Poor Apollo Creed. Snf.
'CAUSE I'D RATHER BE DRESSED FOR ACTION THAN STANDING AROUND IN MY UNDERWEAR.
SOME PEOPLE STILL CONSIDER THAT UNDERWEAR, YA KNOW?
RT @DeadpoolMind Some people still think we **stole** his underwear, ya know?
SHUT UP.
IT'S AN "HOMAGE"!
I THINK I FOUND OUR INFILTRATORS.
--ARE YOU KIDDING ME?

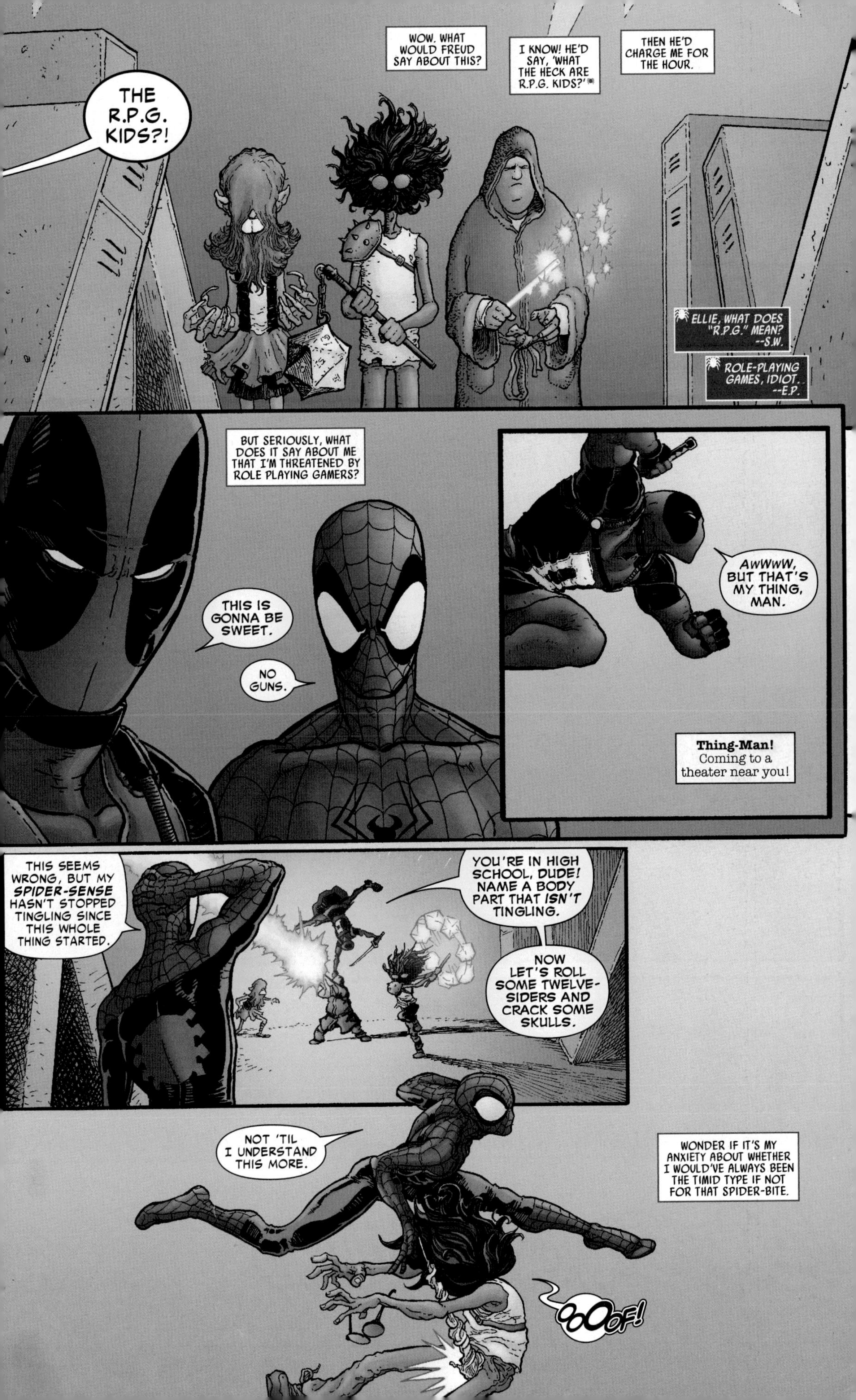
THE R.P.G. KIDS?!
WOW. WHAT WOULD FREUD SAY ABOUT THIS?
I KNOW! HE'D SAY, 'WHAT THE HECK ARE R.P.G. KIDS?'
THEN HE'D CHARGE ME FOR THE HOUR.
ELLIE, WHAT DOES "R.P.G." MEAN? --S.W.
ROLE-PLAYING GAMES, IDIOT. --E.P.
BUT SERIOUSLY, WHAT DOES IT SAY ABOUT ME THAT I'M THREATENED BY ROLE PLAYING GAMERS?
THIS IS GONNA BE SWEET.
NO GUNS.
AWWWW, BUT THAT'S MY THING, MAN.
Thing-Man! Coming to a theater near you!
THIS SEEMS WRONG, BUT MY SPIDER-SENSE HASN'T STOPPED TINGLING SINCE THIS WHOLE THING STARTED.
YOU'RE IN HIGH SCHOOL, DUDE! NAME A BODY PART THAT ISN'T TINGLING.
NOW LET'S ROLL SOME TWELVE-SIDERS AND CRACK SOME SKULLS.
NOT 'TIL I UNDERSTAND THIS MORE.
WONDER IF IT'S MY ANXIETY ABOUT WHETHER I WOULD'VE ALWAYS BEEN THE TIMID TYPE IF NOT FOR THAT SPIDER-BITE.
OOOOF!

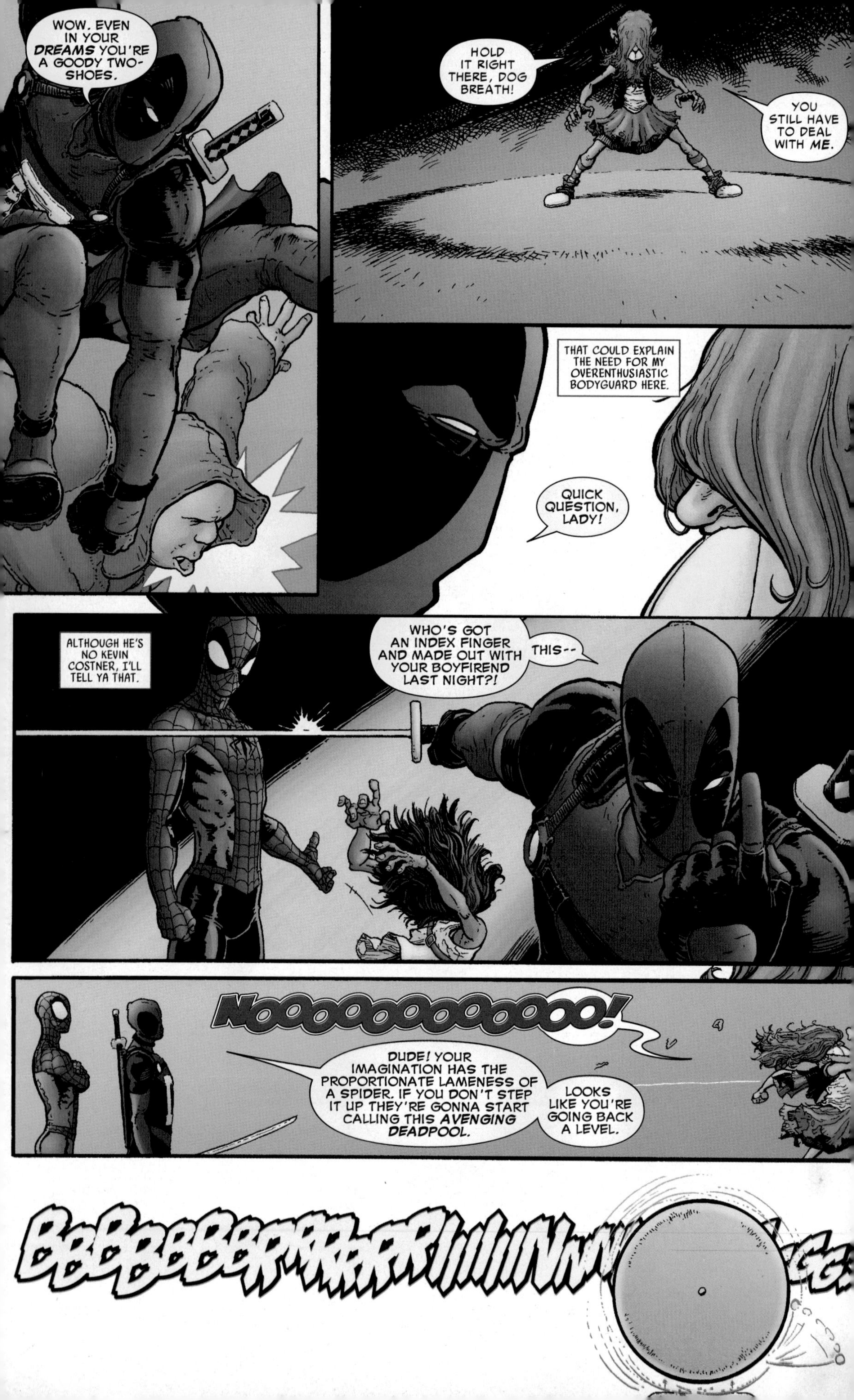
WOW. EVEN IN YOUR DREAMS YOU'RE A GOODY TWO-SHOES.
HOLD IT RIGHT THERE, DOG BREATH!
YOU STILL HAVE TO DEAL WITH ME.
THAT COULD EXPLAIN THE NEED FOR MY OVERENTHUSIASTIC BODYGUARD HERE.
QUICK QUESTION, LADY!
ALTHOUGH HE'S NO KEVIN COSTNER, I'LL TELL YA THAT.
WHO'S GOT AN INDEX FINGER AND MADE OUT WITH YOUR BOYFIREND LAST NIGHT?!
THIS--
NOOOOOOOOOOOOO!
DUDE! YOUR IMAGINATION HAS THE PROPORTIONATE LAMENESS OF A SPIDER. IF YOU DON'T STEP IT UP THEY'RE GONNA START CALLING THIS AVENGING DEADPOOL.
LOOKS LIKE YOU'RE GOING BACK A LEVEL.

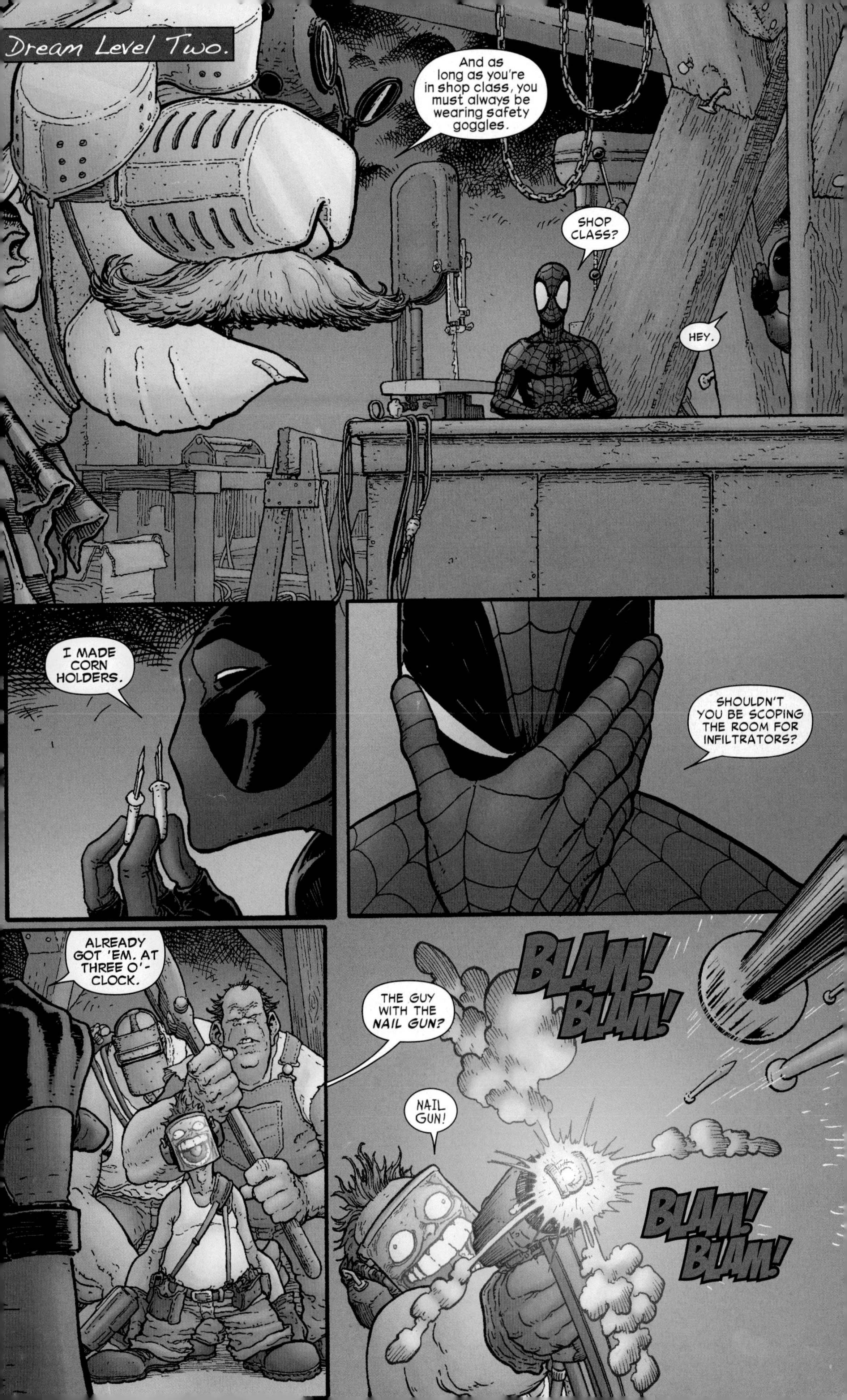
Dream Level Two.
And as long as you're in shop class, you must always be wearing safety goggles.
SHOP CLASS?
HEY.
I MADE CORN HOLDERS.
SHOULDN'T YOU BE SCOPING THE ROOM FOR INFILTRATORS?
ALREADY GOT 'EM. AT THREE O'-CLOCK.
THE GUY WITH THE *NAIL GUN?*
BLAM! BLAM!
NAIL GUN!
BLAM! BLAM!

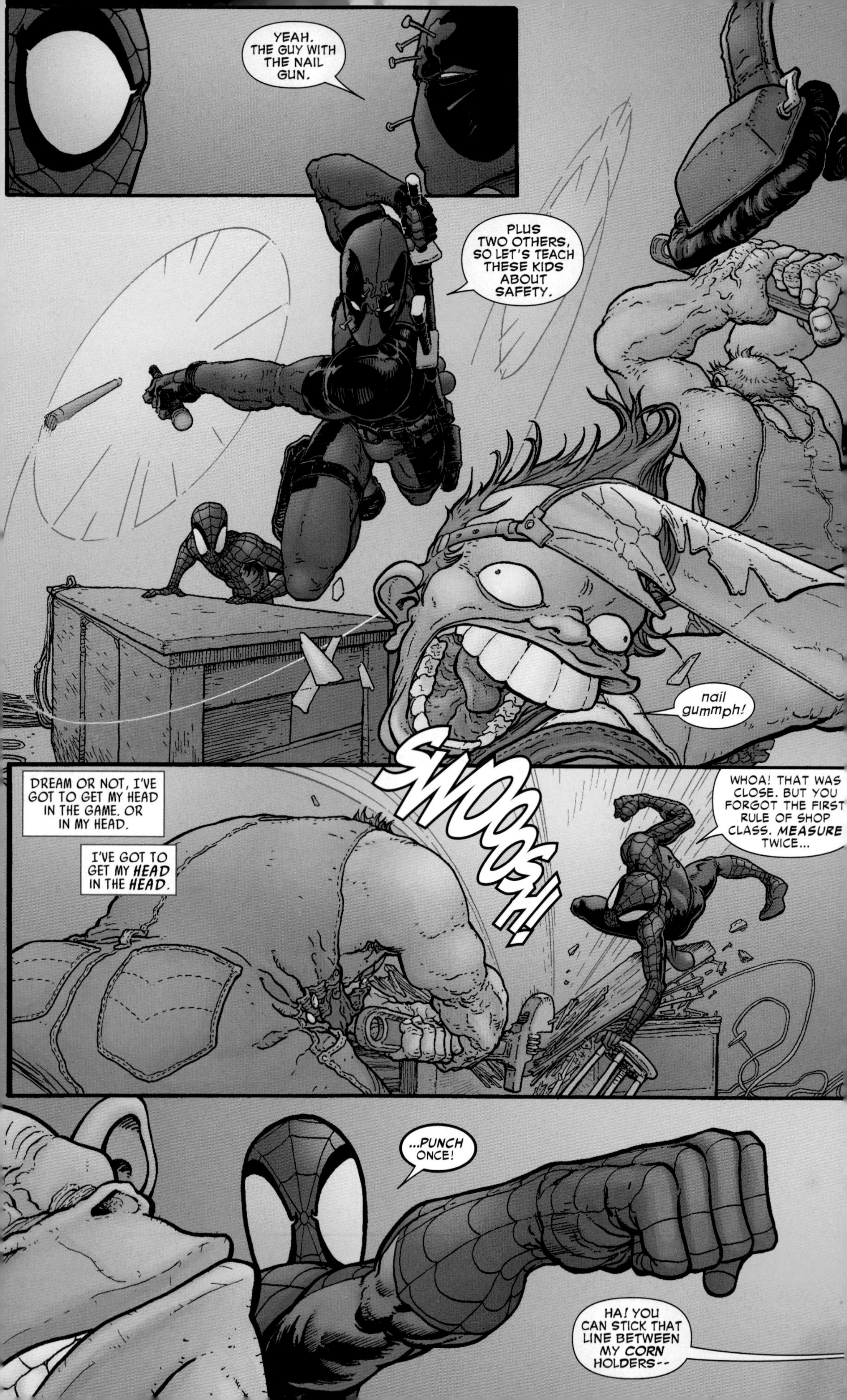
YEAH. THE GUY WITH THE NAIL GUN.
PLUS TWO OTHERS, SO LET'S TEACH THESE KIDS ABOUT SAFETY.
nail gummph!
SWOOOSH!
DREAM OR NOT, I'VE GOT TO GET MY HEAD IN THE GAME. OR IN MY HEAD.
I'VE GOT TO GET MY HEAD IN THE HEAD.
WHOA! THAT WAS CLOSE. BUT YOU FORGOT THE FIRST RULE OF SHOP CLASS. MEASURE TWICE...
...PUNCH ONCE!
HA! YOU CAN STICK THAT LINE BETWEEN MY CORN HOLDERS--

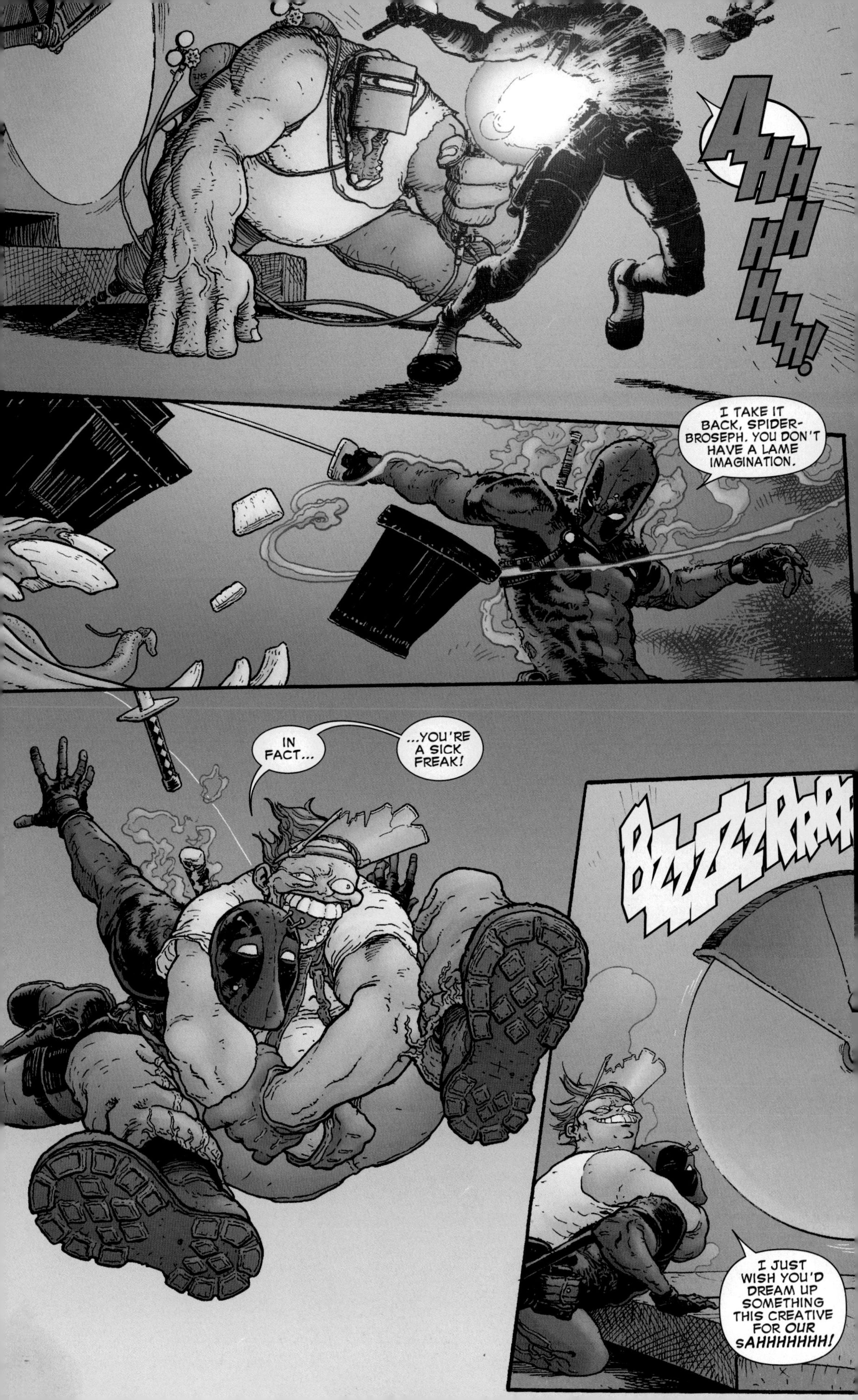
AHHHHHHHHH!
I TAKE IT BACK, SPIDER-BROSEPH. YOU DON'T HAVE A LAME IMAGINATION.
IN FACT...
...YOU'RE A SICK FREAK!
BZZZRRRR
I JUST WISH YOU'D DREAM UP SOMETHING THIS CREATIVE FOR OUR SAHHHHHHH!

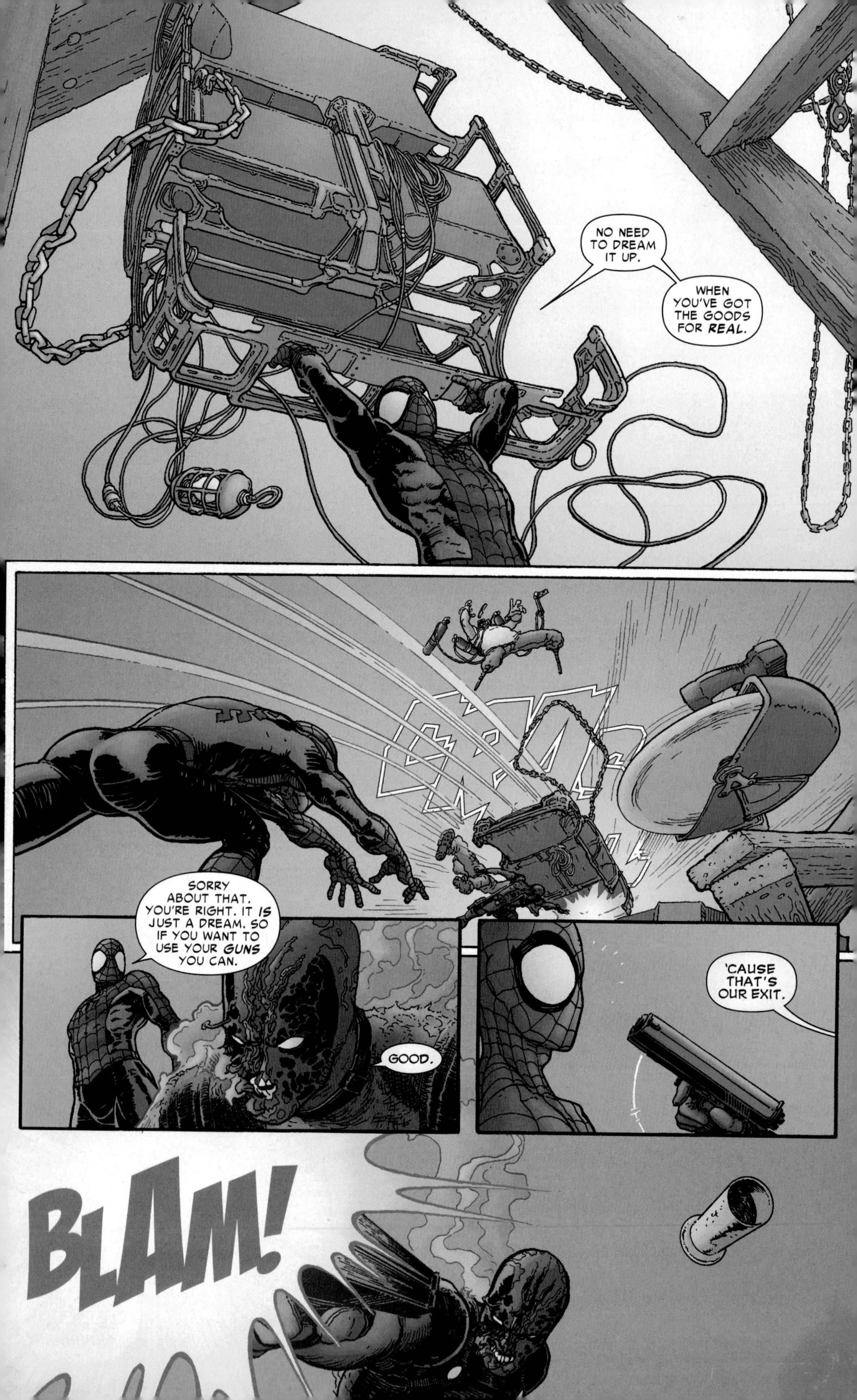
NO NEED TO DREAM IT UP.
WHEN YOU'VE GOT THE GOODS FOR REAL.
SORRY ABOUT THAT. YOU'RE RIGHT. IT IS JUST A DREAM. SO IF YOU WANT TO USE YOUR GUNS YOU CAN.
GOOD.
'CAUSE THAT'S OUR EXIT.
BLAM!

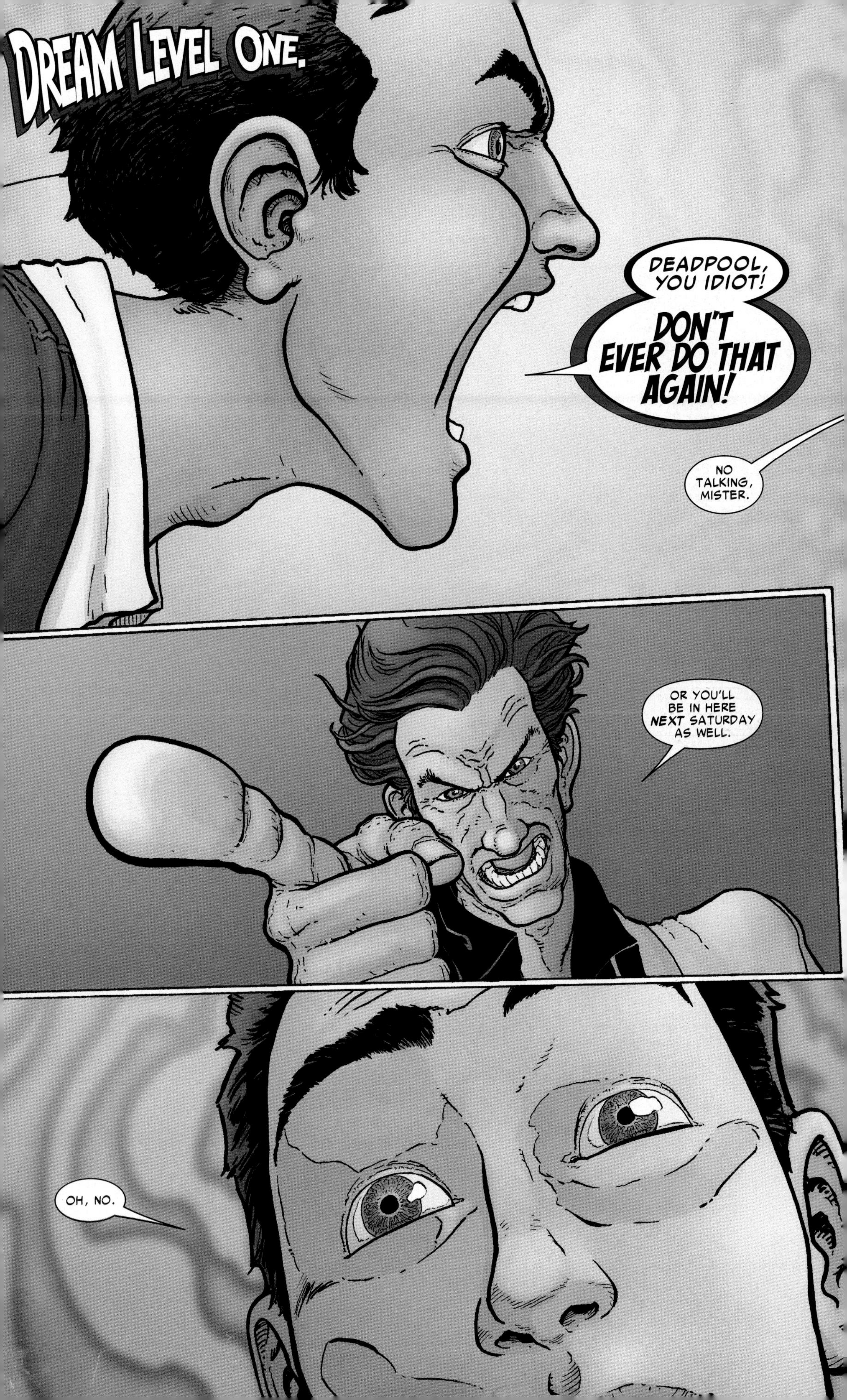
DREAM LEVEL ONE.
DEADPOOL, YOU IDIOT!
DON'T EVER DO THAT AGAIN!
NO TALKING, MISTER.
OR YOU'LL BE IN HERE NEXT SATURDAY AS WELL.
OH, NO.

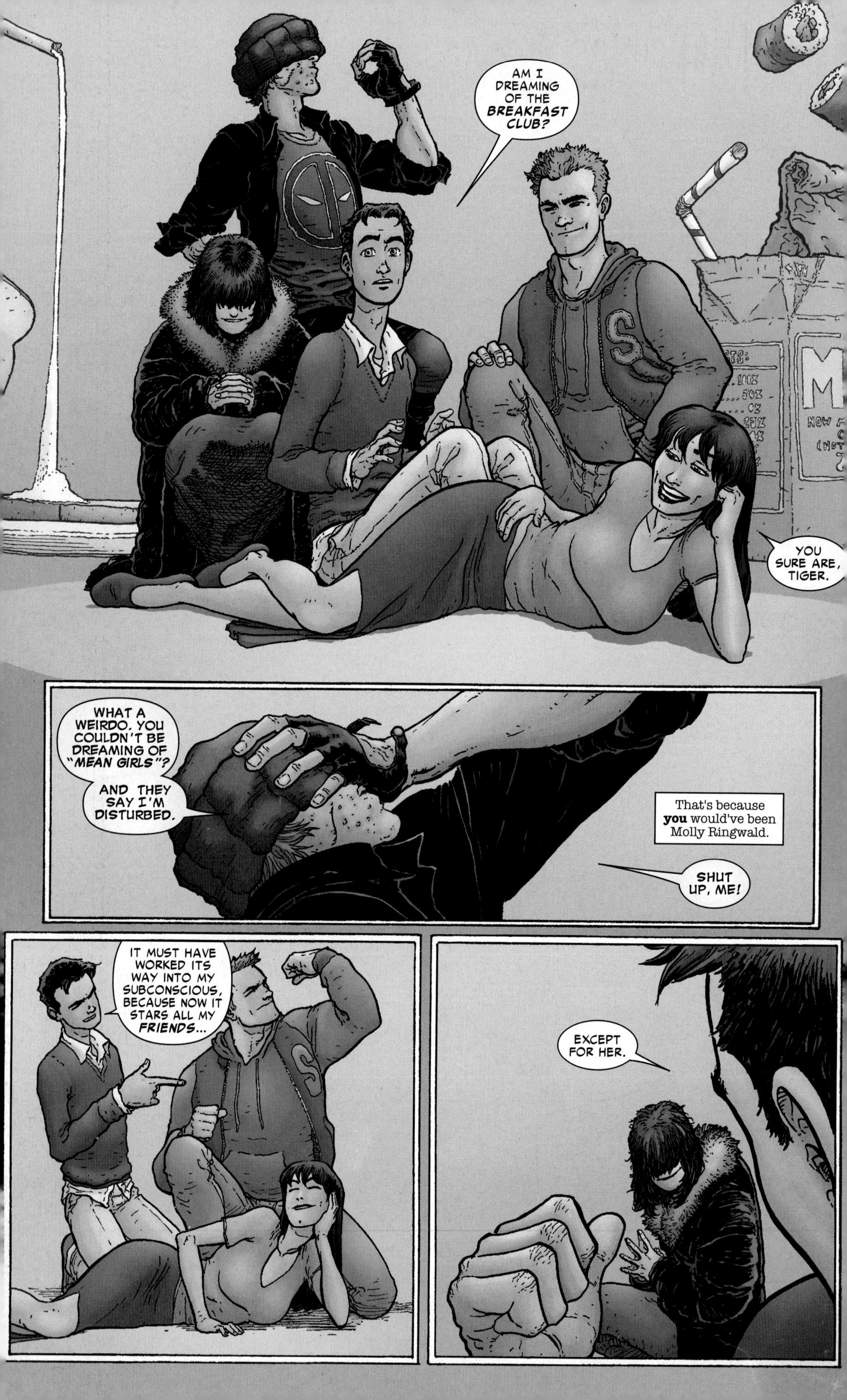
AM I DREAMING OF THE BREAKFAST CLUB?
YOU SURE ARE, TIGER.
WHAT A WEIRDO. YOU COULDN'T BE DREAMING OF "MEAN GIRLS"?
AND THEY SAY I'M DISTURBED.
That's because you would've been Molly Ringwald.
SHUT UP, ME!
IT MUST HAVE WORKED ITS WAY INTO MY SUBCONSCIOUS, BECAUSE NOW IT STARS ALL MY FRIENDS...
EXCEPT FOR HER.

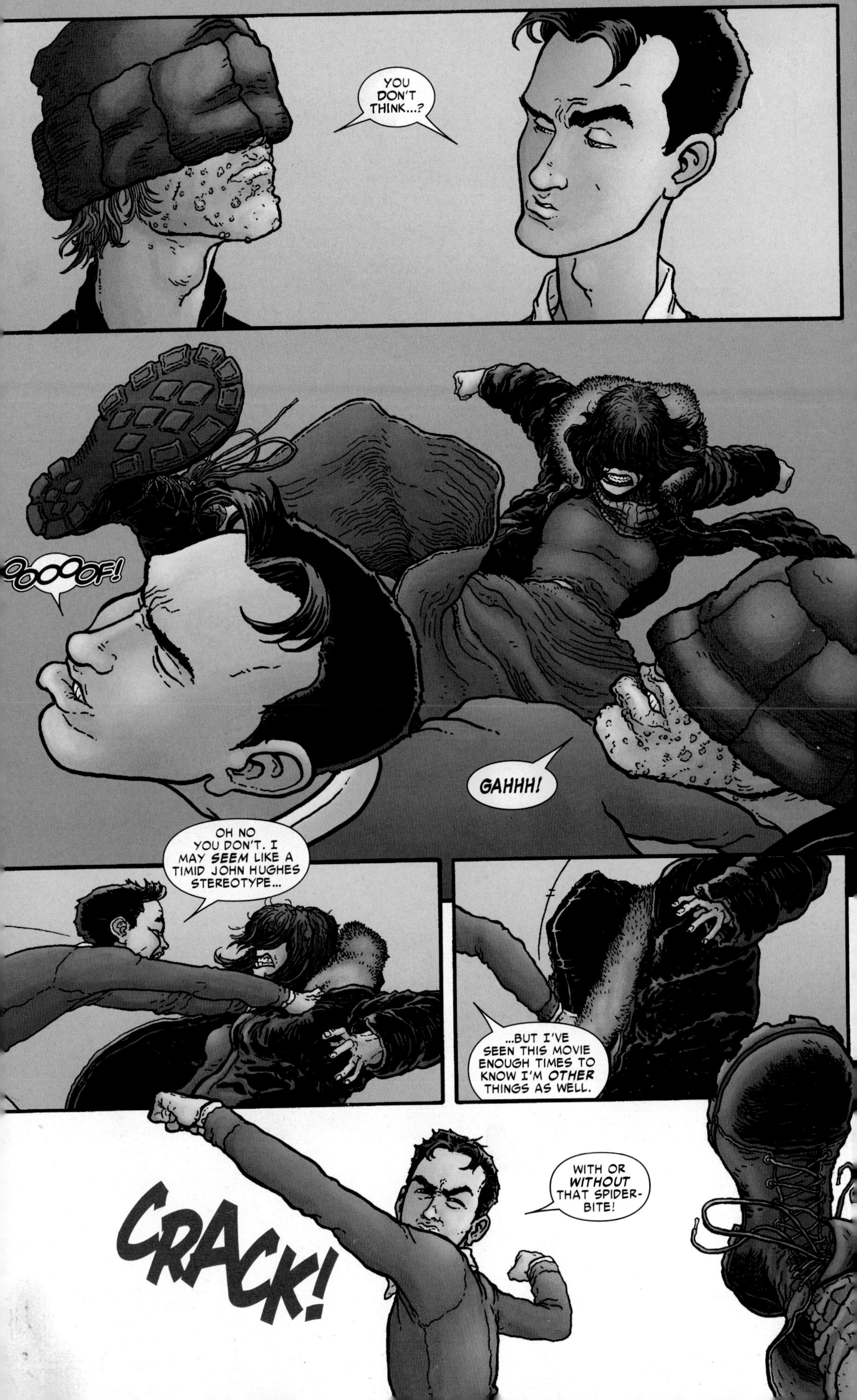
YOU DON'T THINK...?
OOOOOF!
GAHHH!
OH NO YOU DON'T. I MAY SEEM LIKE A TIMID JOHN HUGHES STEREOTYPE...
...BUT I'VE SEEN THIS MOVIE ENOUGH TIMES TO KNOW I'M OTHER THINGS AS WELL.
CRACK!
WITH OR WITHOUT THAT SPIDER-BITE!

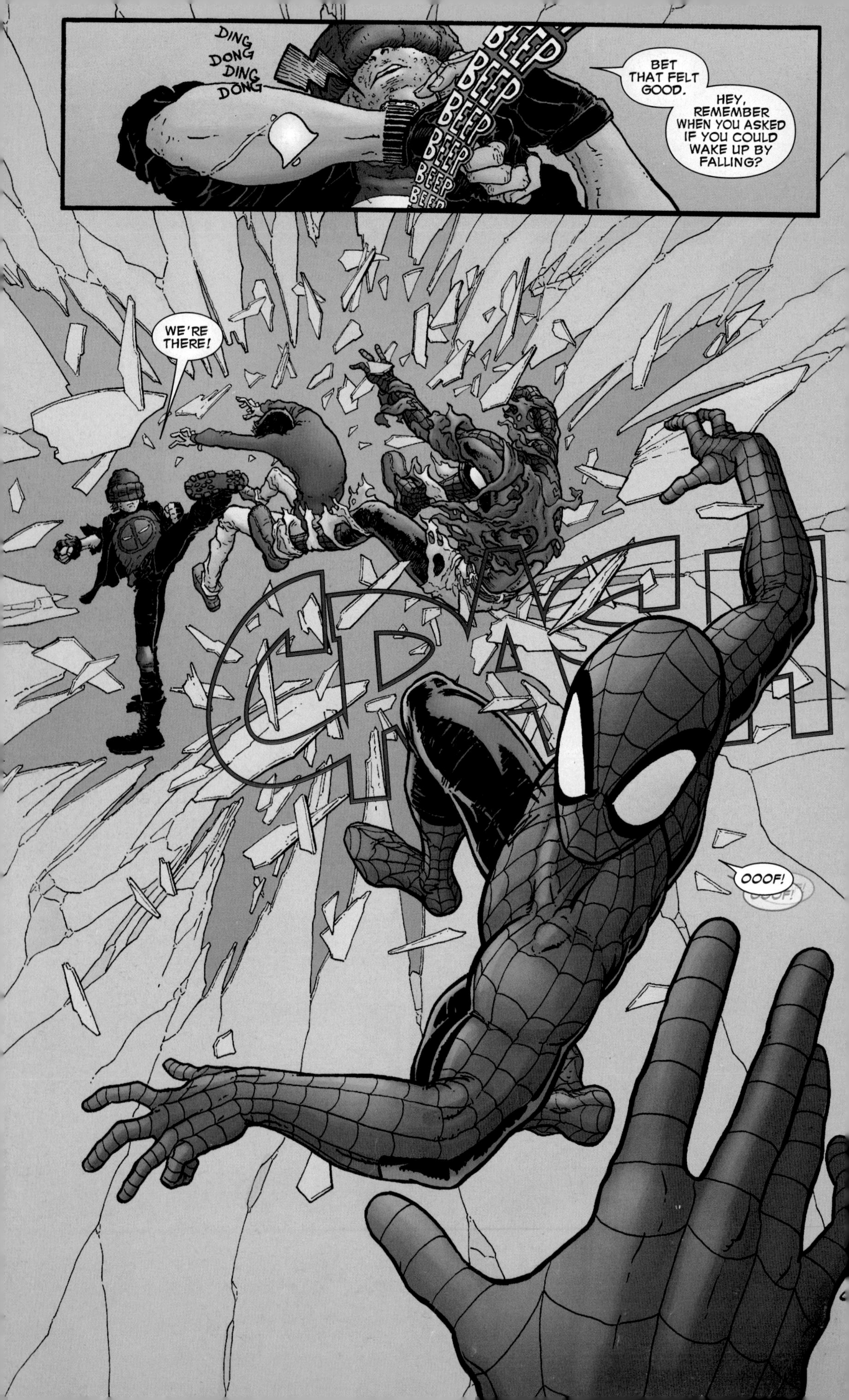
DING
DONG
DING
DONG
BEEP
BEEP
BEEP
BEEP
BEEP
BEEP
BET THAT FELT GOOD.
HEY, REMEMBER WHEN YOU ASKED IF YOU COULD WAKE UP BY FALLING?
WE'RE THERE!
CRASH
OOOF!

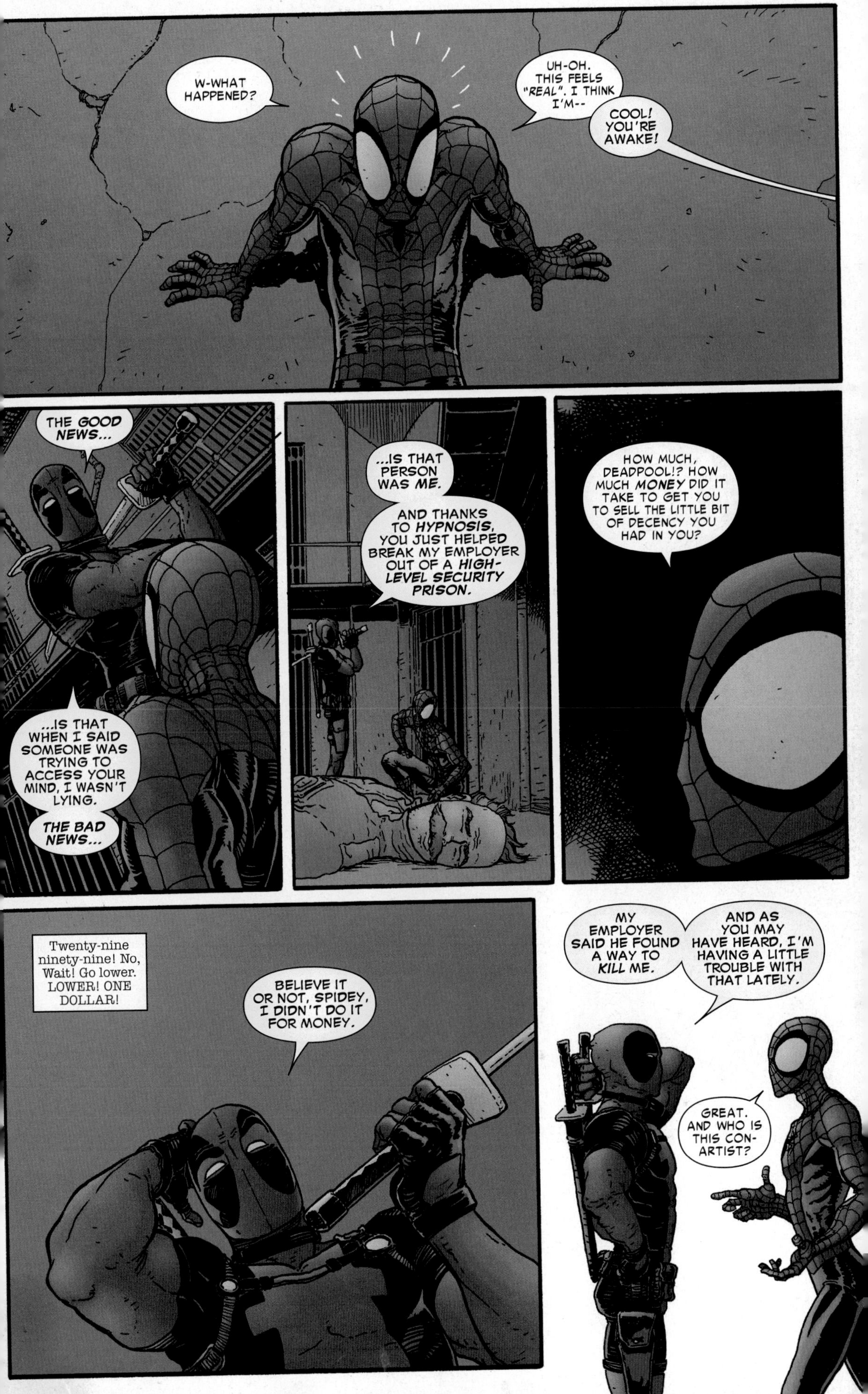
W-WHAT HAPPENED?
UH-OH. THIS FEELS "REAL". I THINK I'M--
COOL! YOU'RE AWAKE!
THE GOOD NEWS...
...IS THAT WHEN I SAID SOMEONE WAS TRYING TO ACCESS YOUR MIND, I WASN'T LYING.
THE BAD NEWS...
...IS THAT PERSON WAS ME.
AND THANKS TO HYPNOSIS, YOU JUST HELPED BREAK MY EMPLOYER OUT OF A HIGH-LEVEL SECURITY PRISON.
HOW MUCH, DEADPOOL!? HOW MUCH MONEY DID IT TAKE TO GET YOU TO SELL THE LITTLE BIT OF DECENCY YOU HAD IN YOU?
Twenty-nine ninety-nine! No, Wait! Go lower. LOWER! ONE DOLLAR!
BELIEVE IT OR NOT, SPIDEY, I DIDN'T DO IT FOR MONEY.
MY EMPLOYER SAID HE FOUND A WAY TO KILL ME.
AND AS YOU MAY HAVE HEARD, I'M HAVING A LITTLE TROUBLE WITH THAT LATELY.
GREAT. AND WHO IS THIS CON-ARTIST?

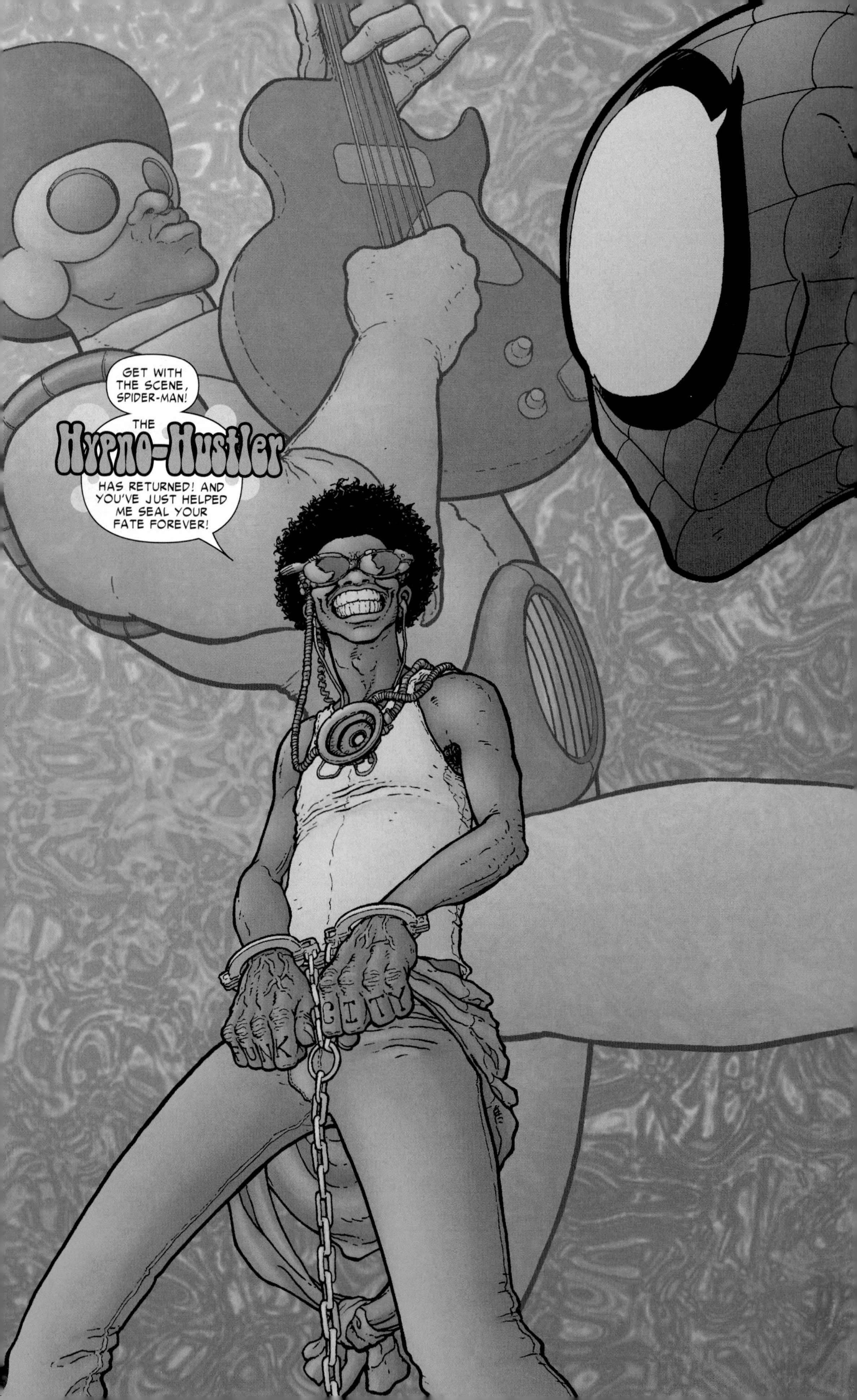

GET WITH THE SCENE, SPIDER-MAN!
THE Hypno-Hustler HAS RETURNED! AND YOU'VE JUST HELPED ME SEAL YOUR FATE FOREVER!
FUNK
CITY

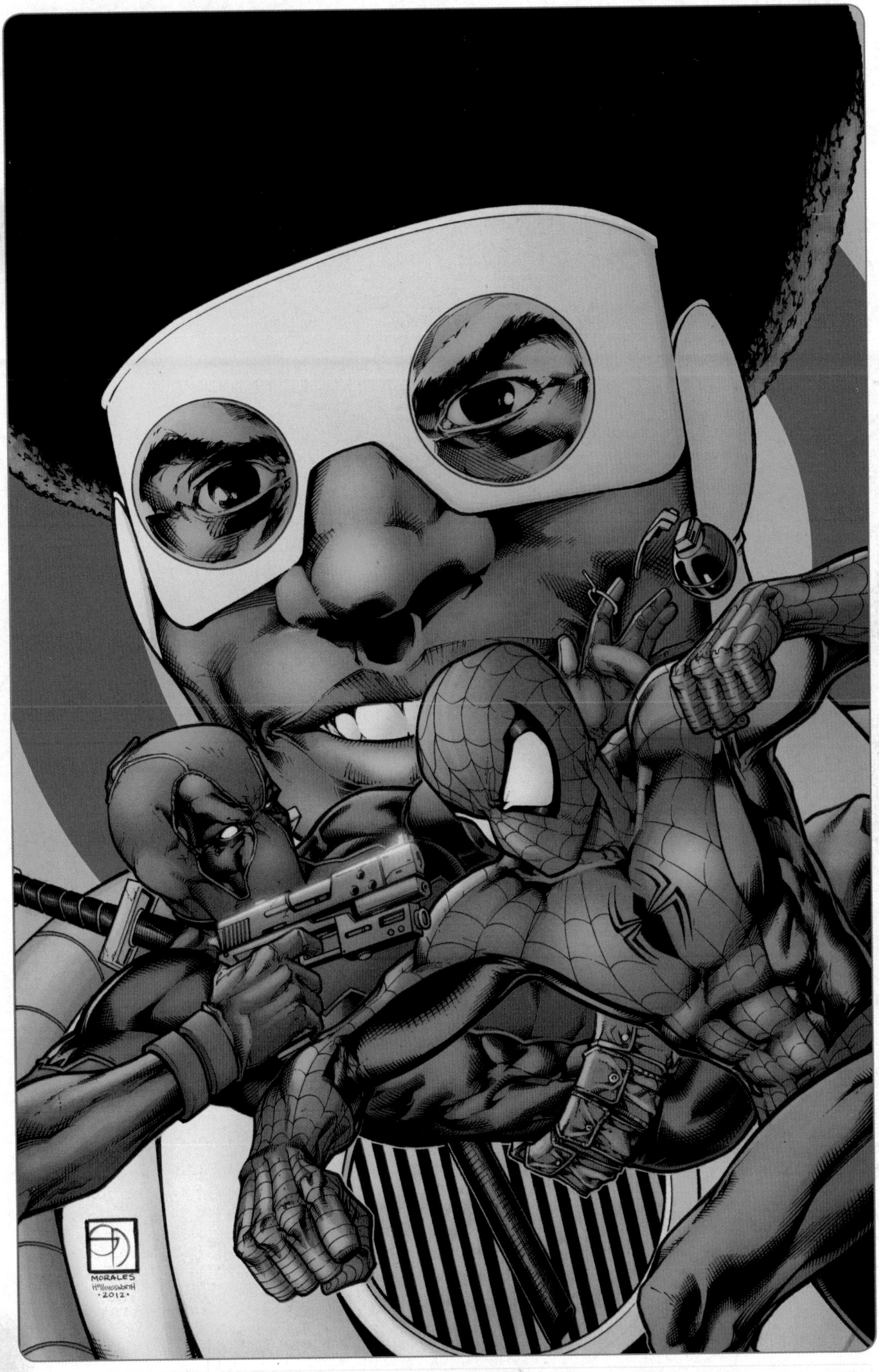
MORALES
HOLLINGSWORTH
2012

AVENGING SPIDER-MAN #13

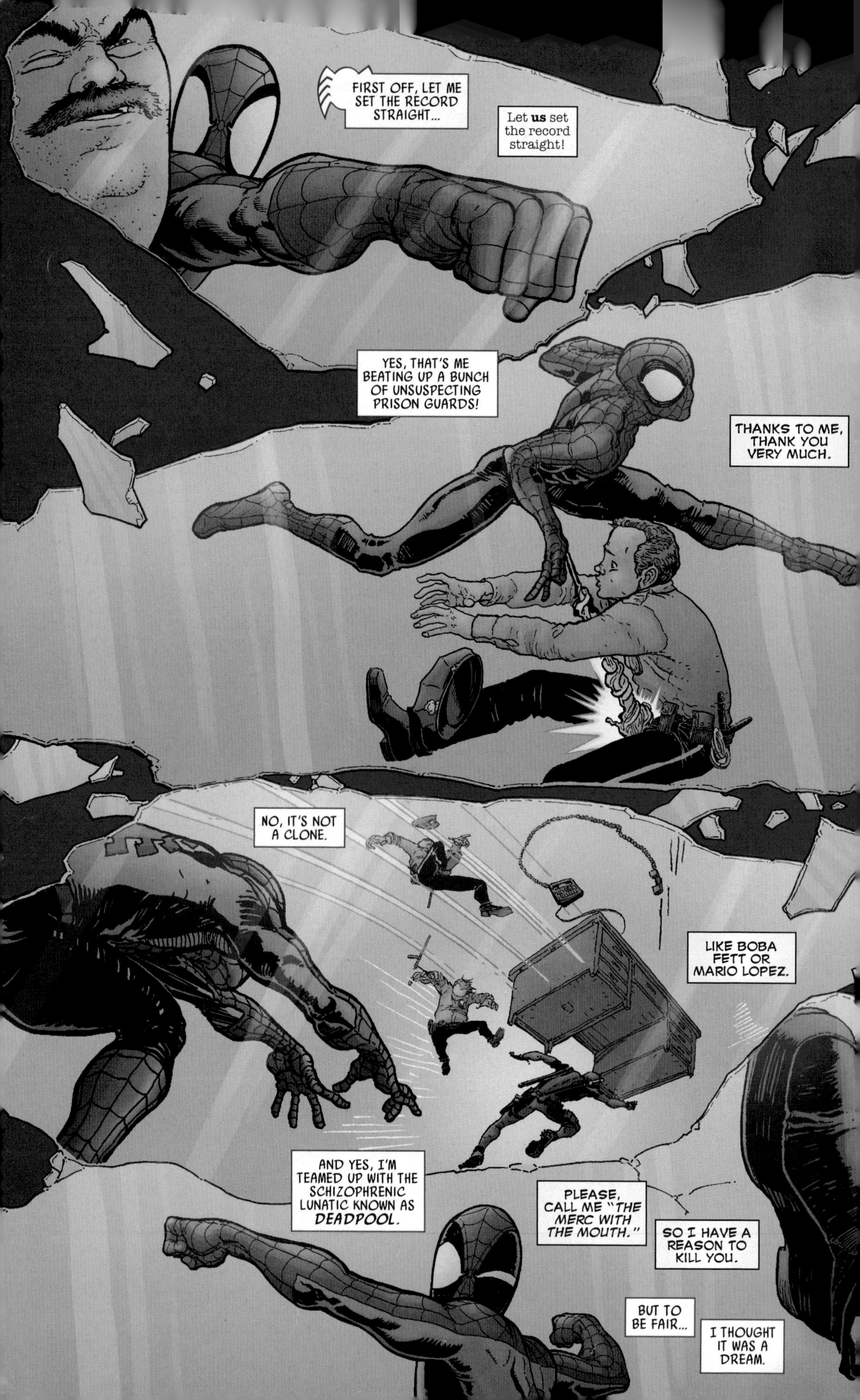
FIRST OFF, LET ME SET THE RECORD STRAIGHT...
Let **us** set the record straight!
YES, THAT'S ME BEATING UP A BUNCH OF UNSUSPECTING PRISON GUARDS!
THANKS TO ME, THANK YOU VERY MUCH.
NO, IT'S NOT A CLONE.
LIKE BOBA FETT OR MARIO LOPEZ.
AND YES, I'M TEAMED UP WITH THE SCHIZOPHRENIC LUNATIC KNOWN AS *DEADPOOL*.
PLEASE, CALL ME "*THE MERC WITH THE MOUTH.*"
SO I HAVE A REASON TO KILL YOU.
BUT TO BE FAIR...
I THOUGHT IT WAS A DREAM.

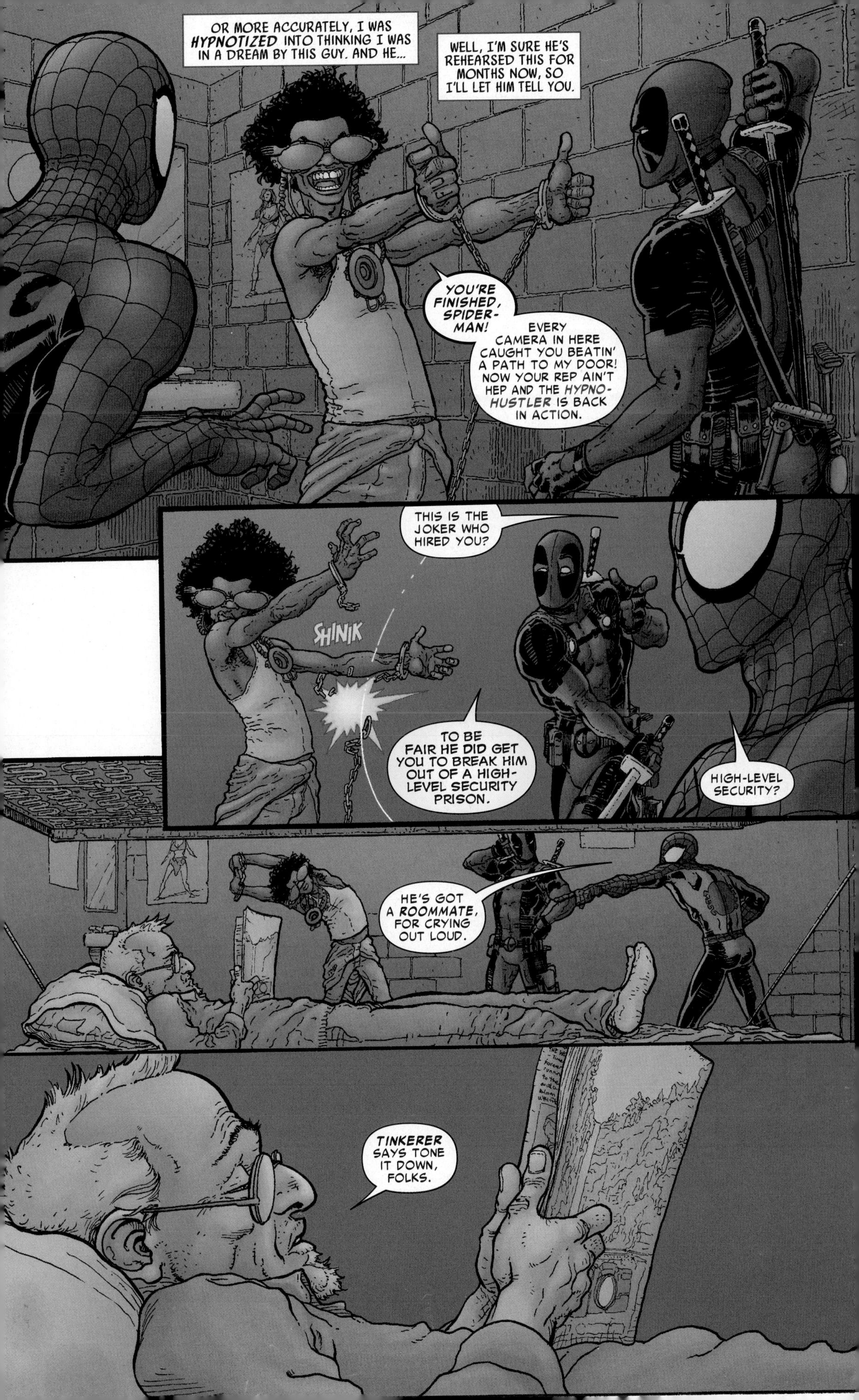

OR MORE ACCURATELY, I WAS HYPNOTIZED INTO THINKING I WAS IN A DREAM BY THIS GUY. AND HE...
WELL, I'M SURE HE'S REHEARSED THIS FOR MONTHS NOW, SO I'LL LET HIM TELL YOU.
YOU'RE FINISHED, SPIDER-MAN!
EVERY CAMERA IN HERE CAUGHT YOU BEATIN' A PATH TO MY DOOR! NOW YOUR REP AIN'T HEP AND THE HYPNO-HUSTLER IS BACK IN ACTION.
THIS IS THE JOKER WHO HIRED YOU?
SHINIK
TO BE FAIR HE DID GET YOU TO BREAK HIM OUT OF A HIGH-LEVEL SECURITY PRISON.
HIGH-LEVEL SECURITY?
HE'S GOT A ROOMMATE, FOR CRYING OUT LOUD.
TINKERER SAYS TONE IT DOWN, FOLKS.

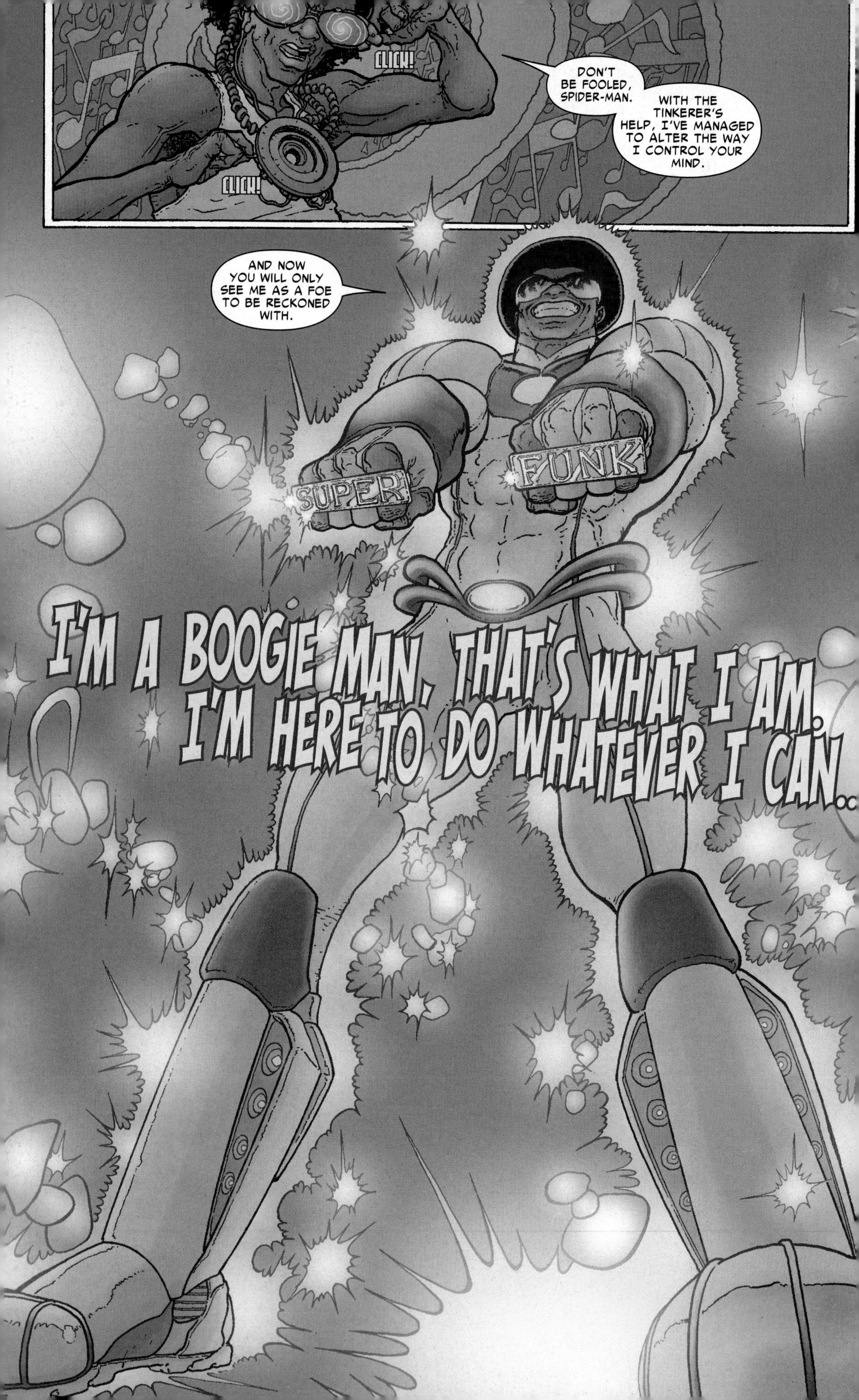
CLICK!
CLICK!
DON'T BE FOOLED, SPIDER-MAN.
WITH THE TINKERER'S HELP, I'VE MANAGED TO ALTER THE WAY I CONTROL YOUR MIND.
AND NOW YOU WILL ONLY SEE ME AS A FOE TO BE RECKONED WITH.
SUPER
FUNK
I'M A BOOGIE MAN, THAT'S WHAT I AM.
I'M HERE TO DO WHATEVER I CAN...

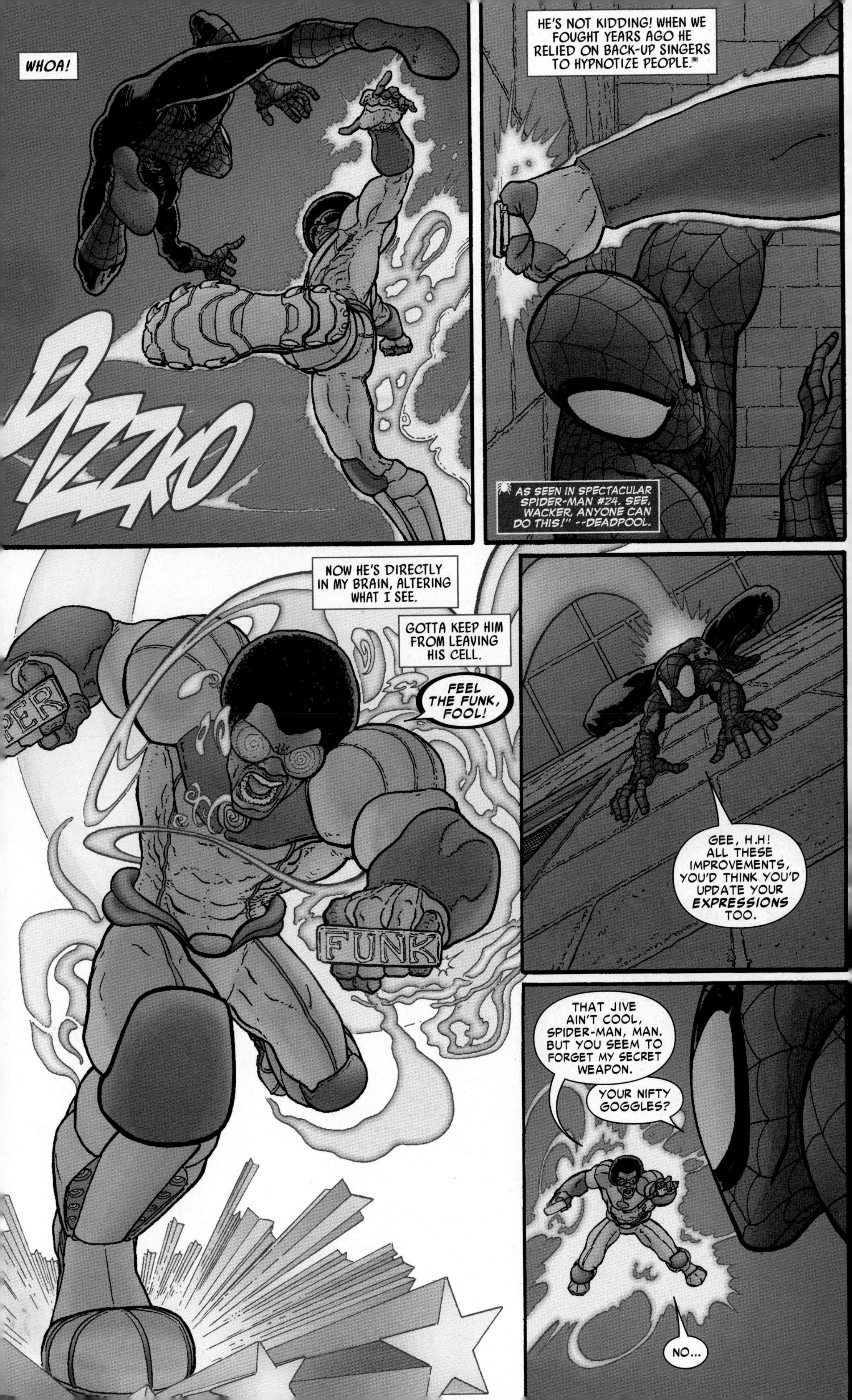

WHOA!
DZZZKO
HE'S NOT KIDDING! WHEN WE FOUGHT YEARS AGO HE RELIED ON BACK-UP SINGERS TO HYPNOTIZE PEOPLE.*
*AS SEEN IN SPECTACULAR SPIDER-MAN #24. SEE, WACKER, ANYONE CAN DO THIS!" --DEADPOOL.
NOW HE'S DIRECTLY IN MY BRAIN, ALTERING WHAT I SEE.
GOTTA KEEP HIM FROM LEAVING HIS CELL.
FEEL THE FUNK, FOOL!
PER
FUNK
GEE, H.H! ALL THESE IMPROVEMENTS, YOU'D THINK YOU'D UPDATE YOUR EXPRESSIONS TOO.
THAT JIVE AIN'T COOL, SPIDER-MAN, MAN. BUT YOU SEEM TO FORGET MY SECRET WEAPON.
YOUR NIFTY GOGGLES?
NO...

RATATATATATAT!

DEADPOOL!

NERTZ! HE'S RIGHT. I FORGOT THAT JERK SOLD ME OUT.

TOK TOK TOK TOK TOK TOK TOK

YOU CAN OUTRUN DEADPOOL, BUGMAN! BUT YOU CAN'T OUTRUN YOUR *FEARS*.

CLICK

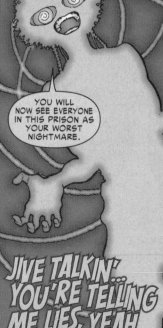

YOU WILL NOW SEE EVERYONE IN THIS PRISON AS YOUR WORST NIGHTMARE.

JIVE TALKIN'... YOU'RE TELLING ME LIES, YEAH...

YA KNOW, THAT *MUSIC* ISN'T EXACTLY HELPING YOUR THREATS.

Nor is that cologne. What is that, English Leather?

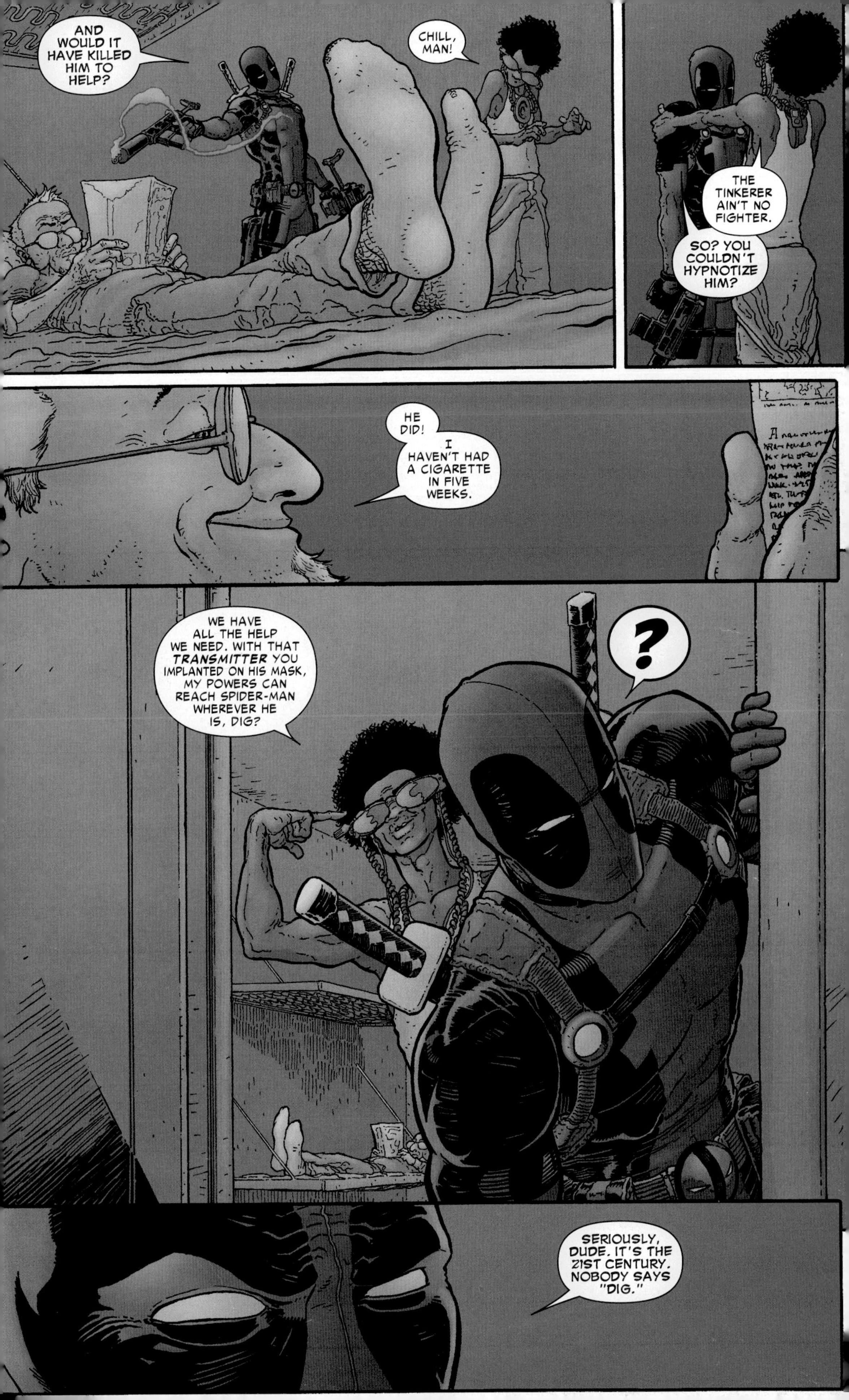

AND WOULD IT HAVE KILLED HIM TO HELP?
CHILL, MAN!
THE TINKERER AIN'T NO FIGHTER.
SO? YOU COULDN'T HYPNOTIZE HIM?
HE DID!
I HAVEN'T HAD A CIGARETTE IN FIVE WEEKS.
WE HAVE ALL THE HELP WE NEED. WITH THAT *TRANSMITTER* YOU IMPLANTED ON HIS MASK, MY POWERS CAN REACH SPIDER-MAN WHEREVER HE IS, DIG?
?
SERIOUSLY, DUDE. IT'S THE 21ST CENTURY. NOBODY SAYS "DIG."

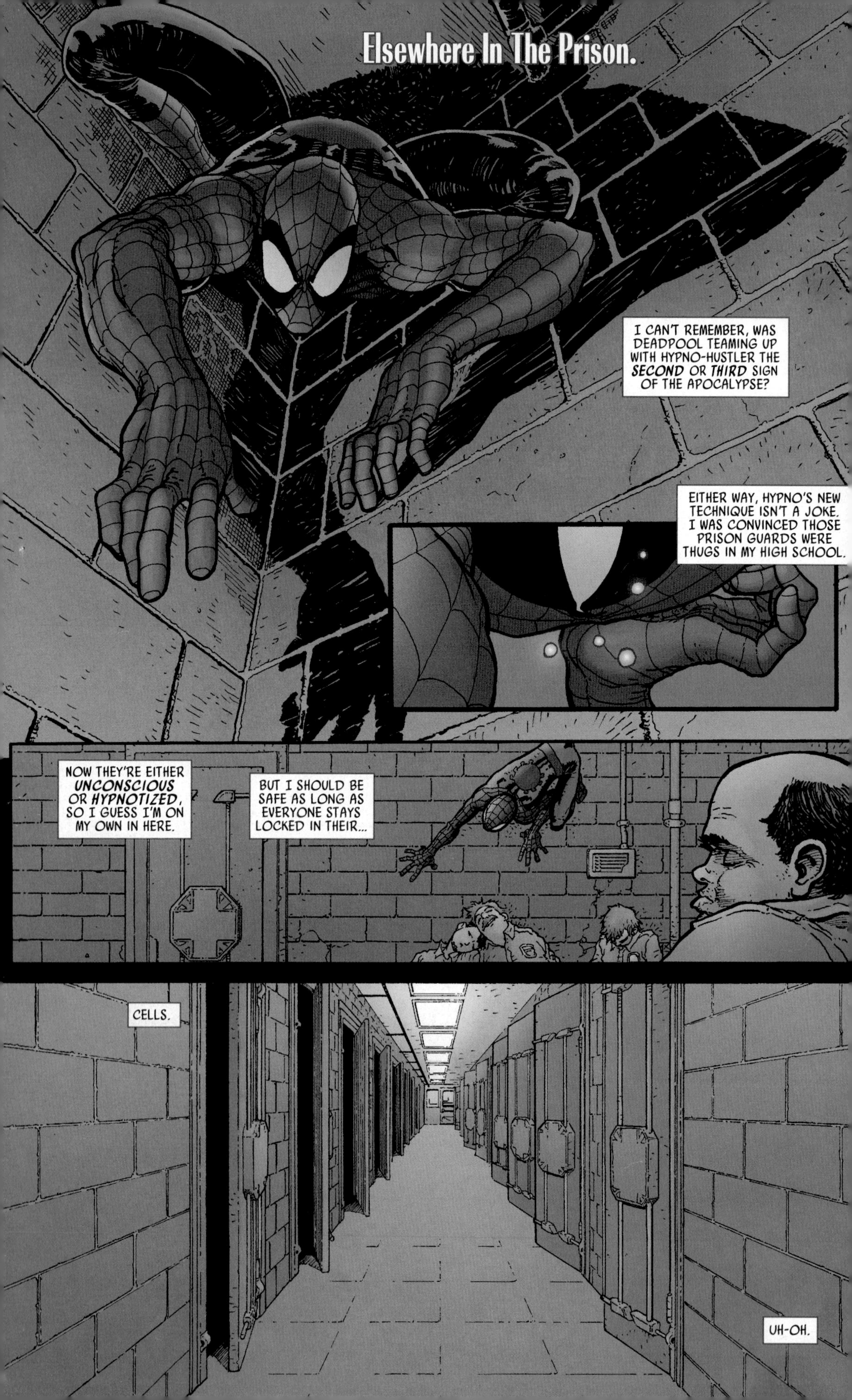
Elsewhere In The Prison.
I CAN'T REMEMBER, WAS DEADPOOL TEAMING UP WITH HYPNO-HUSTLER THE SECOND OR THIRD SIGN OF THE APOCALYPSE?
EITHER WAY, HYPNO'S NEW TECHNIQUE ISN'T A JOKE. I WAS CONVINCED THOSE PRISON GUARDS WERE THUGS IN MY HIGH SCHOOL.
NOW THEY'RE EITHER UNCONSCIOUS OR HYPNOTIZED, SO I GUESS I'M ON MY OWN IN HERE.
BUT I SHOULD BE SAFE AS LONG AS EVERYONE STAYS LOCKED IN THEIR...
CELLS.
UH-OH.

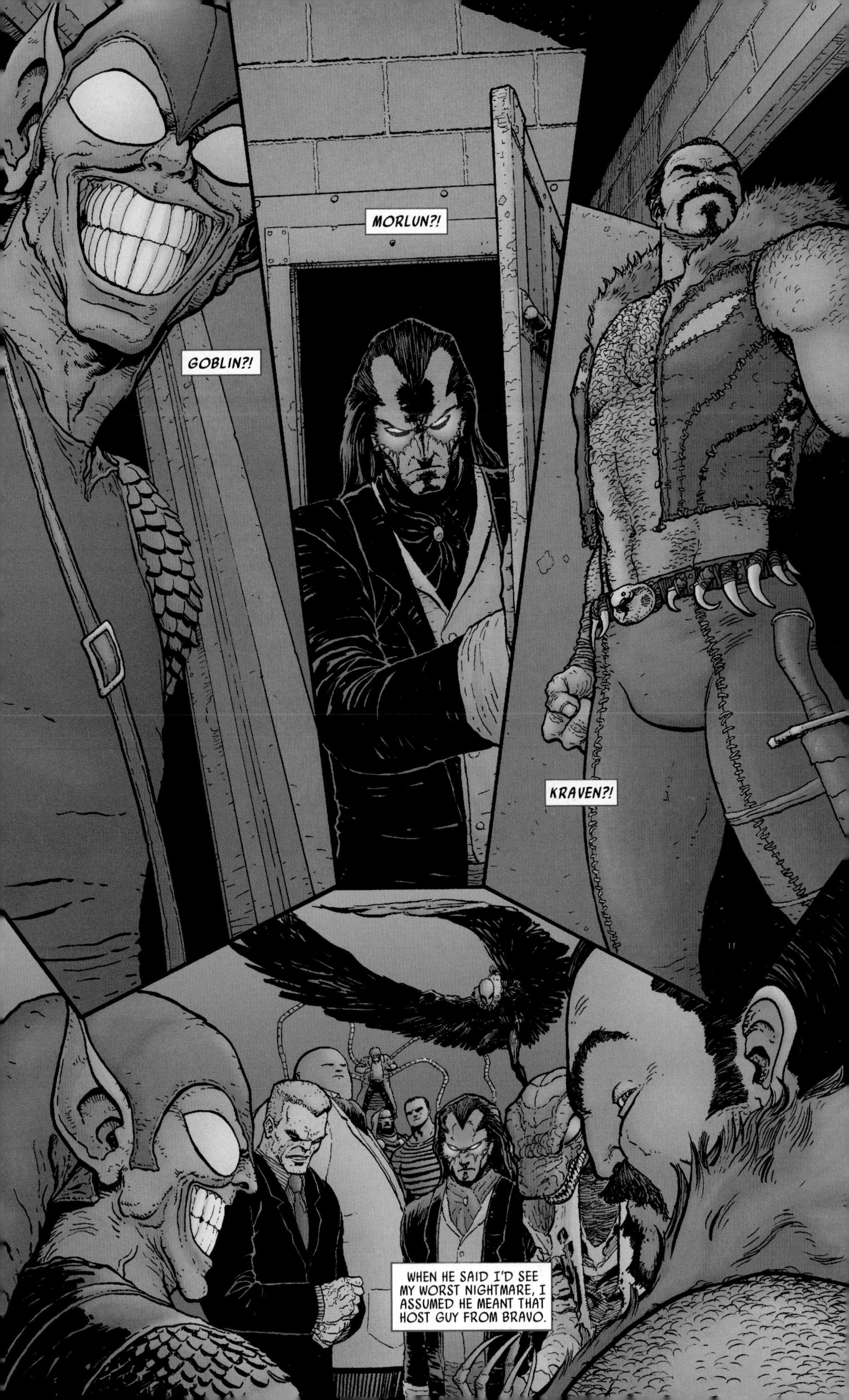
MORLUN?!
GOBLIN?!
KRAVEN?!
WHEN HE SAID I'D SEE MY WORST NIGHTMARE, I ASSUMED HE MEANT THAT HOST GUY FROM BRAVO.

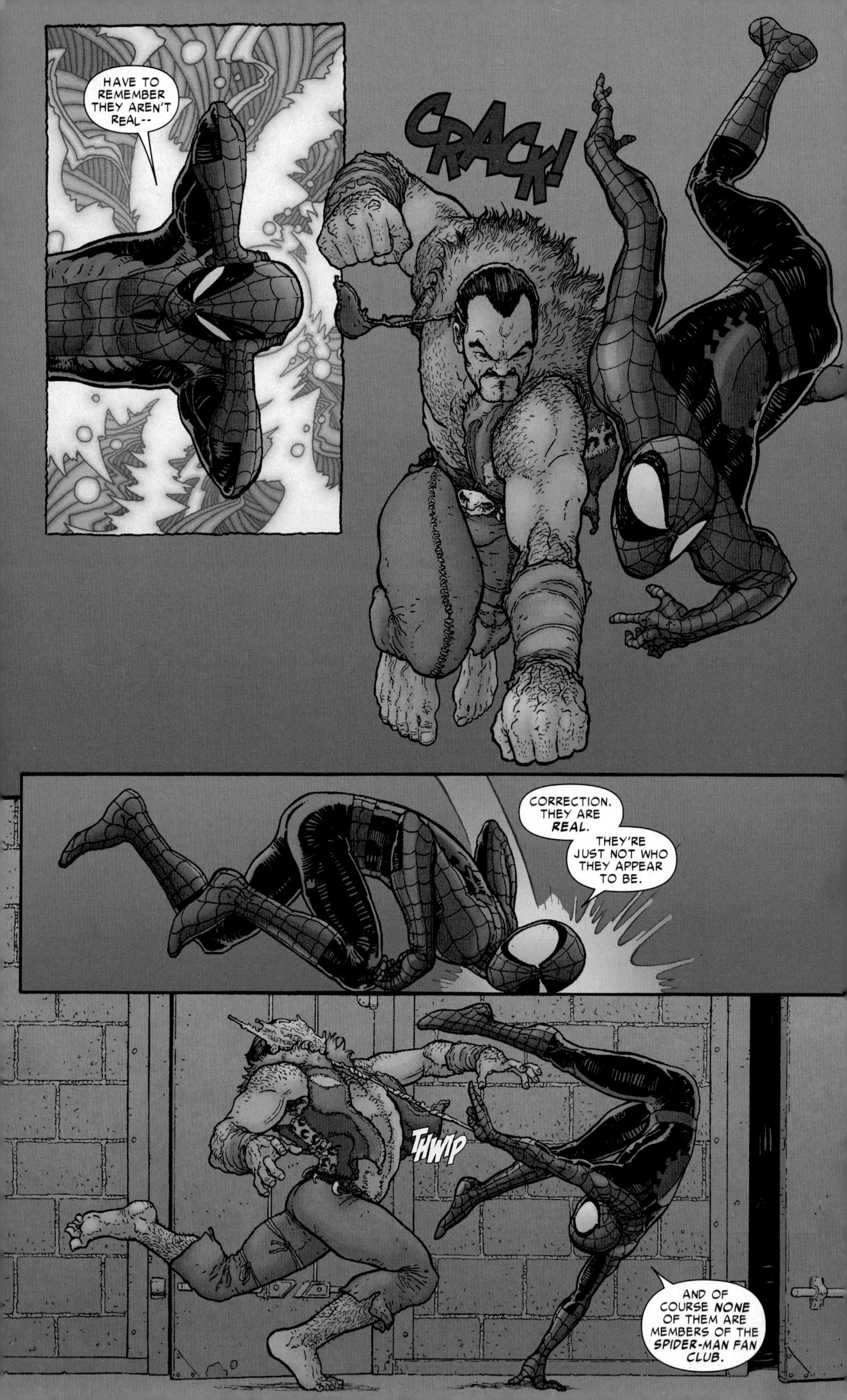
HAVE TO REMEMBER THEY AREN'T REAL--
CRACK!
CORRECTION. THEY ARE REAL.
THEY'RE JUST NOT WHO THEY APPEAR TO BE.
THWIP
AND OF COURSE NONE OF THEM ARE MEMBERS OF THE SPIDER-MAN FAN CLUB.

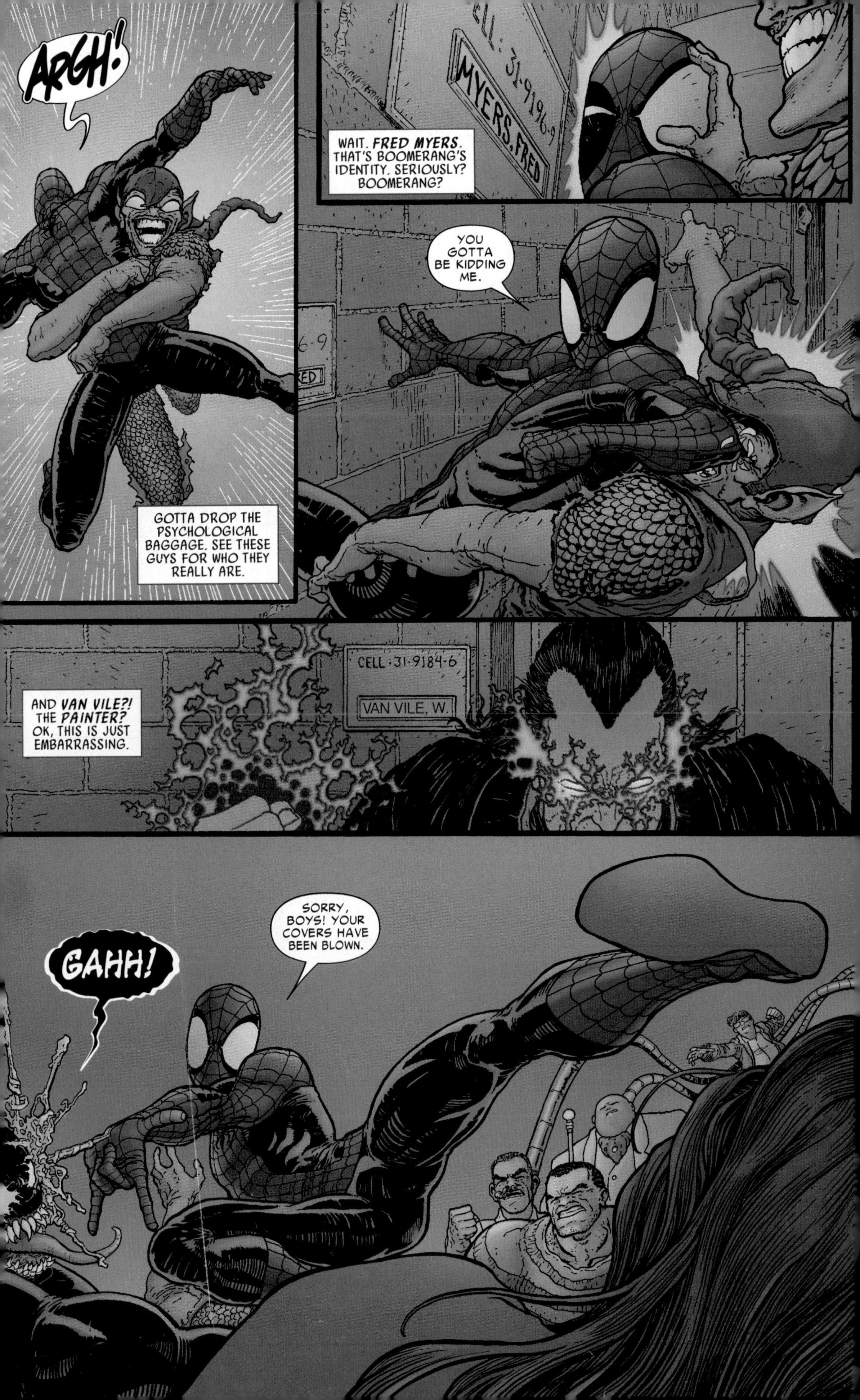
ARGH!
GOTTA DROP THE PSYCHOLOGICAL BAGGAGE. SEE THESE GUYS FOR WHO THEY REALLY ARE.
WAIT. FRED MYERS. THAT'S BOOMERANG'S IDENTITY. SERIOUSLY? BOOMERANG?
MYERS, FRED
YOU GOTTA BE KIDDING ME.
AND VAN VILE?! THE PAINTER? OK, THIS IS JUST EMBARRASSING.
CELL: 31-9184-6
VAN VILE, W.
GAHH!
SORRY, BOYS! YOUR COVERS HAVE BEEN BLOWN.

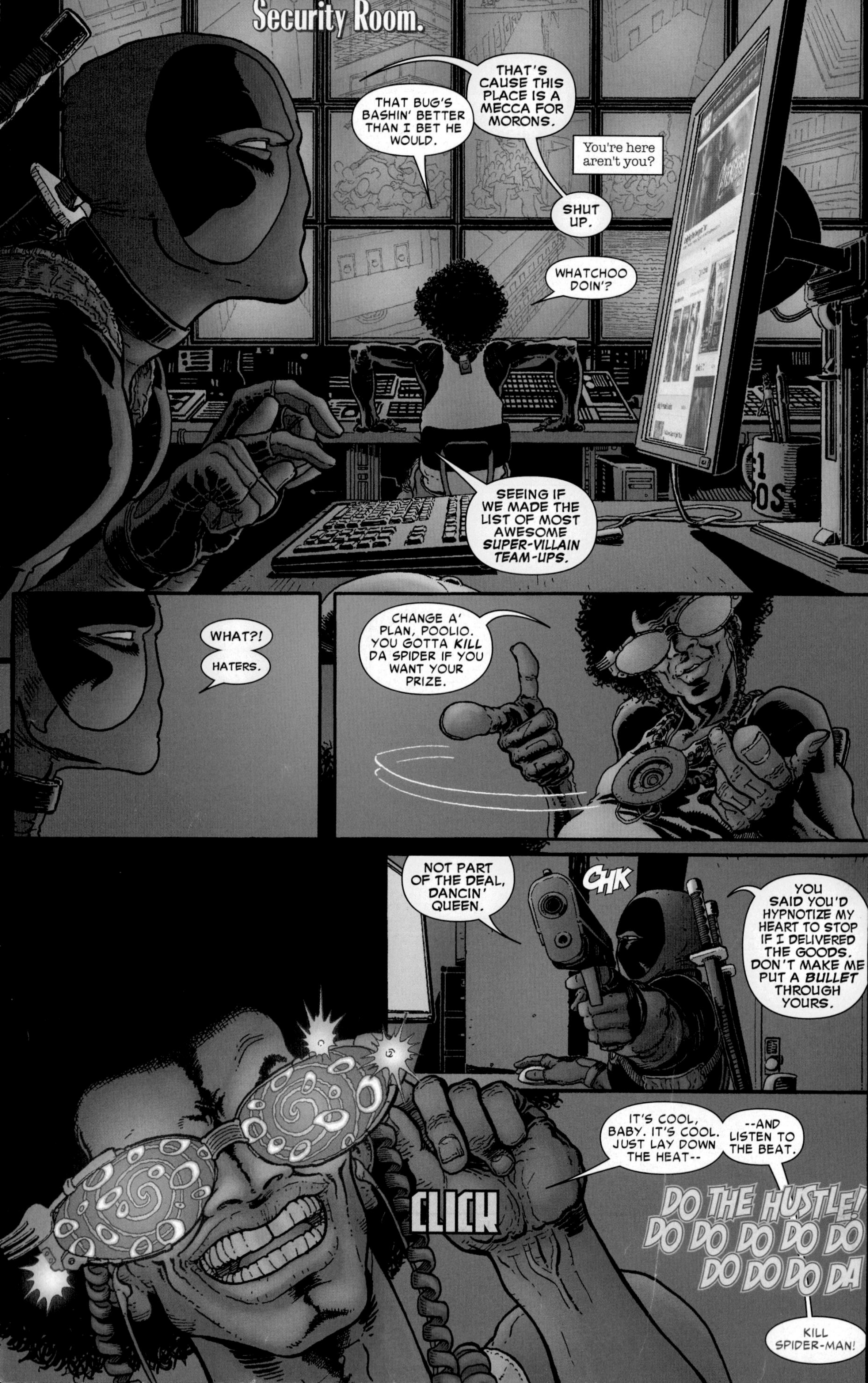
Security Room.
THAT BUG'S BASHIN' BETTER THAN I BET HE WOULD.
THAT'S CAUSE THIS PLACE IS A MECCA FOR MORONS.
You're here aren't you?
SHUT UP.
WHATCHOO DOIN'?
SEEING IF WE MADE THE LIST OF MOST AWESOME SUPER-VILLAIN TEAM-UPS.
WHAT?!
HATERS.
CHANGE A' PLAN, POOLIO. YOU GOTTA KILL DA SPIDER IF YOU WANT YOUR PRIZE.
NOT PART OF THE DEAL, DANCIN' QUEEN.
CHK
YOU SAID YOU'D HYPNOTIZE MY HEART TO STOP IF I DELIVERED THE GOODS. DON'T MAKE ME PUT A BULLET THROUGH YOURS.
IT'S COOL, BABY. IT'S COOL. JUST LAY DOWN THE HEAT--
--AND LISTEN TO THE BEAT.
CLICK
DO THE HUSTLE! DO DO DO DO DO DO DO DO DA
KILL SPIDER-MAN!

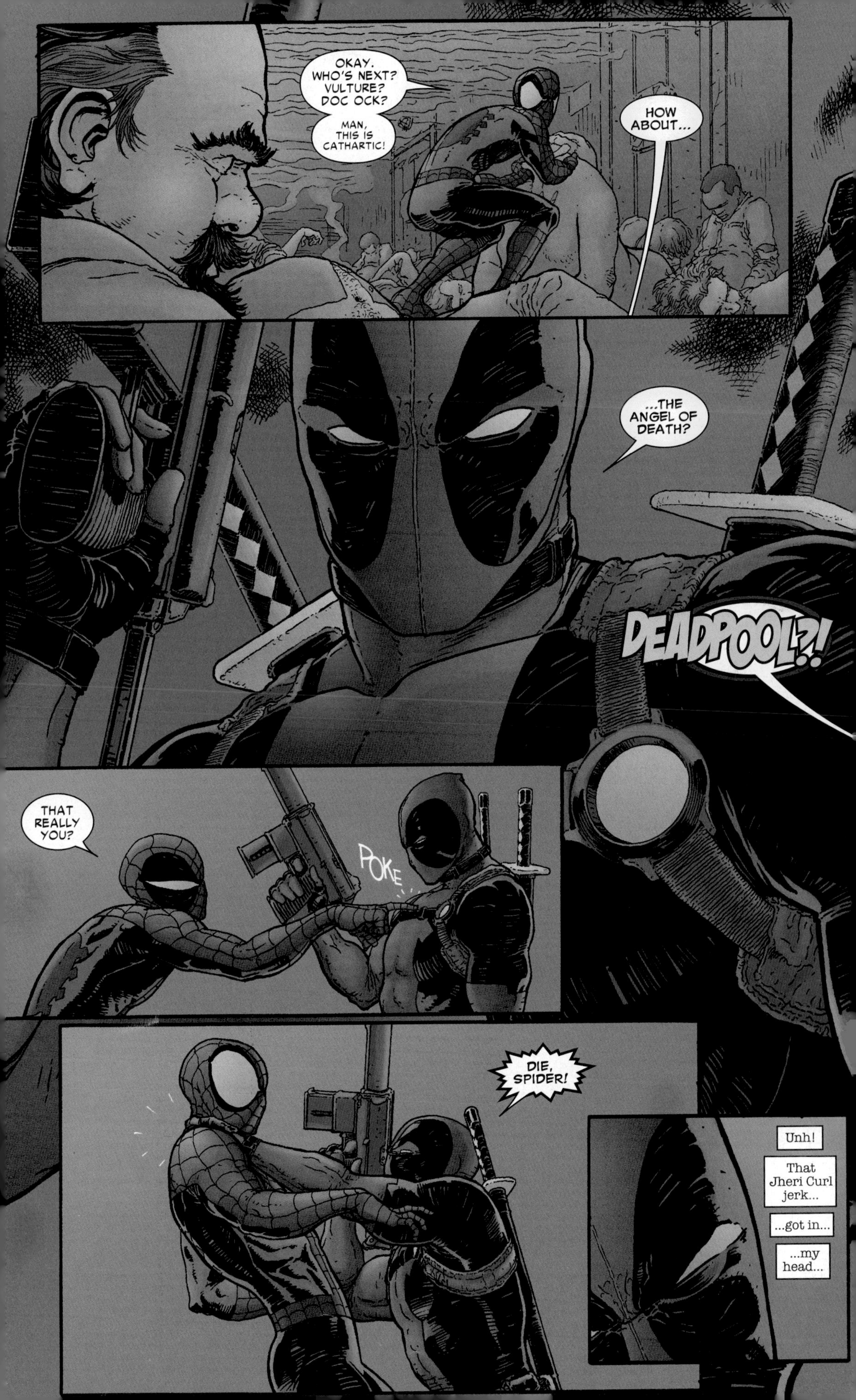
OKAY. WHO'S NEXT? VULTURE? DOC OCK?
MAN, THIS IS CATHARTIC!
HOW ABOUT...
...THE ANGEL OF DEATH?
DEADPOOL?!
THAT REALLY YOU?
POKE
DIE, SPIDER!
Unh!
That Jheri Curl jerk...
...got in...
...my head...

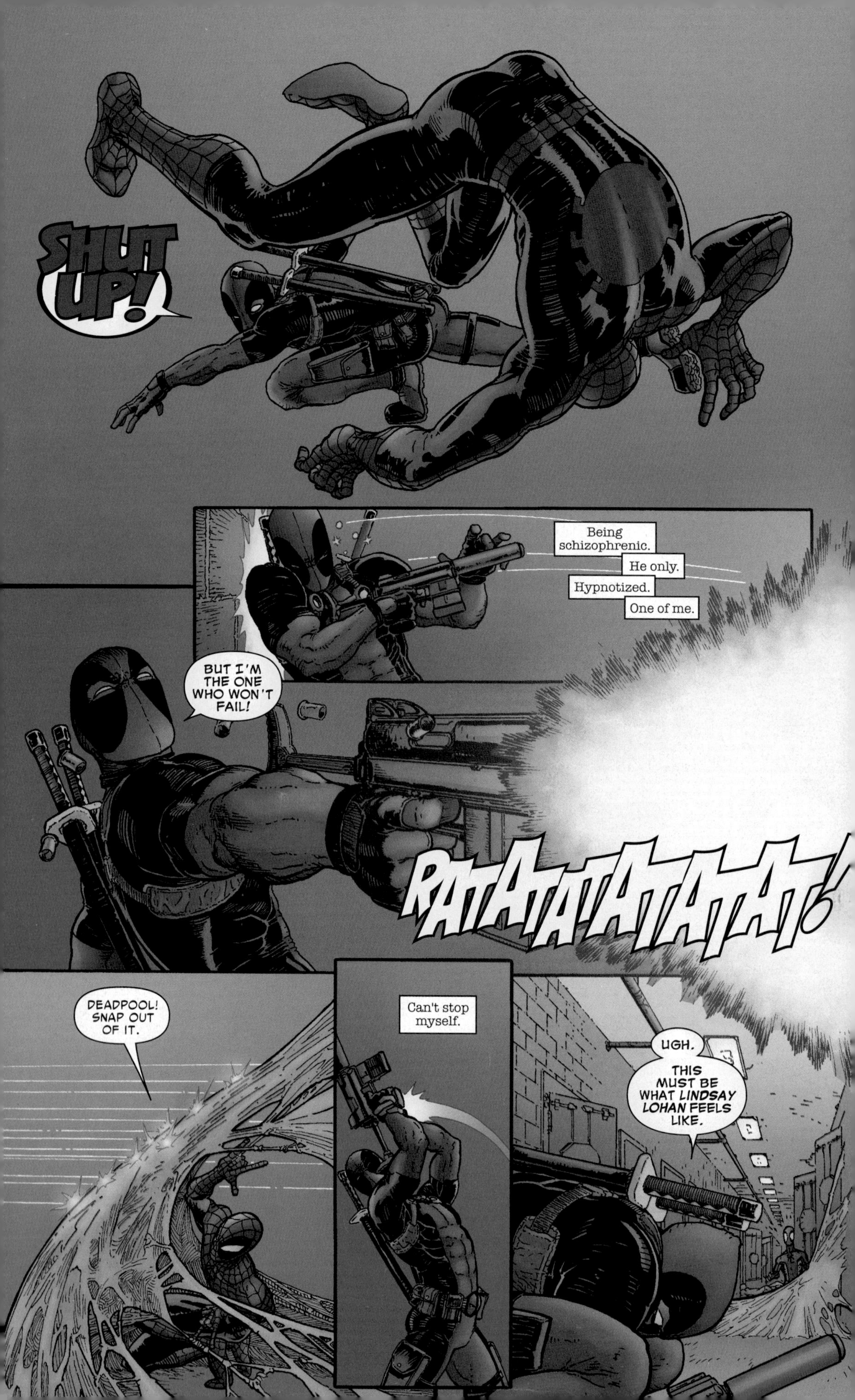

SHUT UP!
Being schizophrenic.
He only.
Hypnotized.
One of me.
BUT I'M THE ONE WHO WON'T FAIL!
RATATATATATATAT!
DEADPOOL! SNAP OUT OF IT.
Can't stop myself.
UGH.
THIS MUST BE WHAT LINDSAY LOHAN FEELS LIKE.

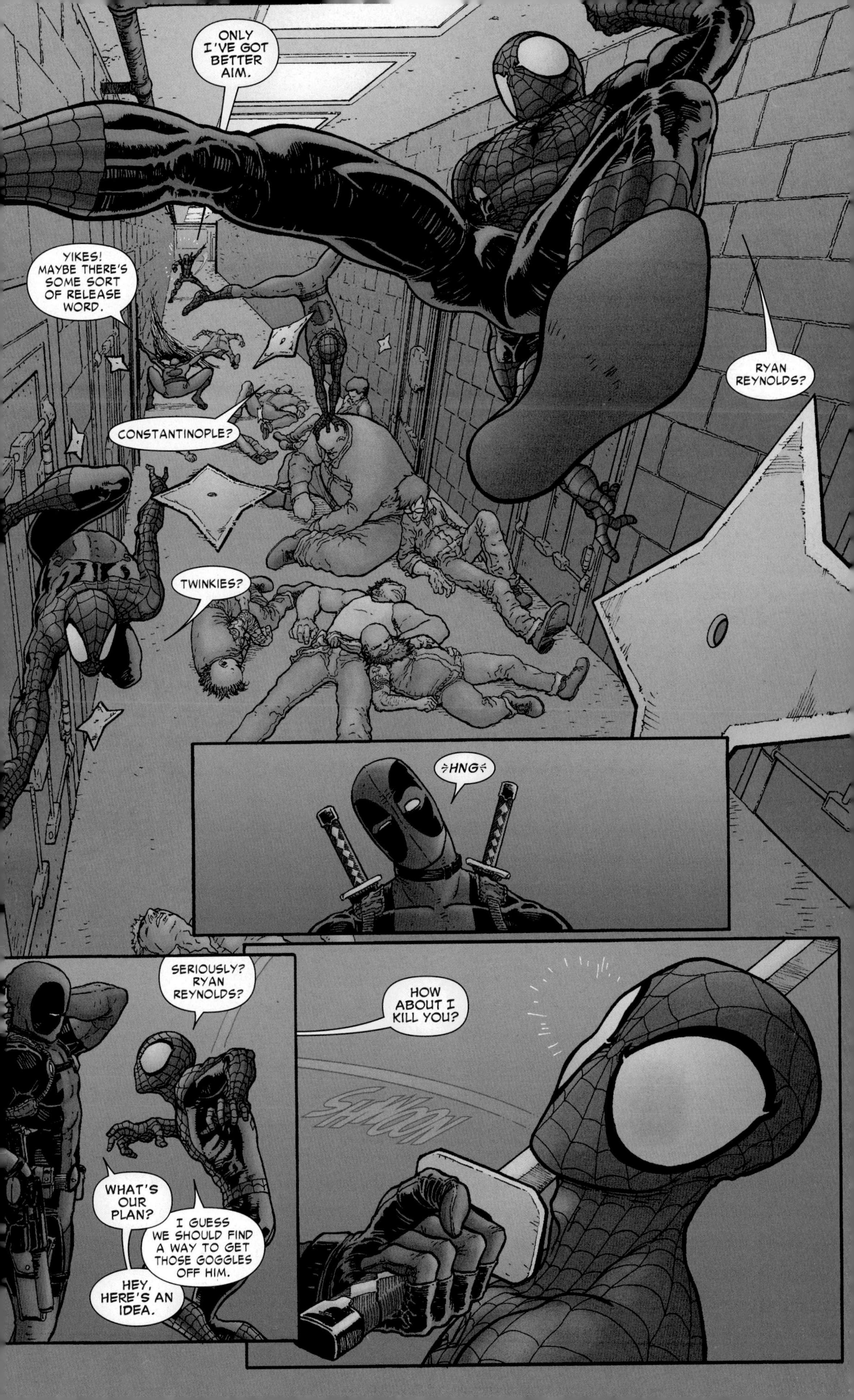
ONLY I'VE GOT BETTER AIM.
YIKES! MAYBE THERE'S SOME SORT OF RELEASE WORD.
CONSTANTINOPLE?
TWINKIES?
RYAN REYNOLDS?
HNG
SERIOUSLY? RYAN REYNOLDS?
HOW ABOUT I KILL YOU?
WHAT'S OUR PLAN?
I GUESS WE SHOULD FIND A WAY TO GET THOSE GOGGLES OFF HIM.
HEY, HERE'S AN IDEA.

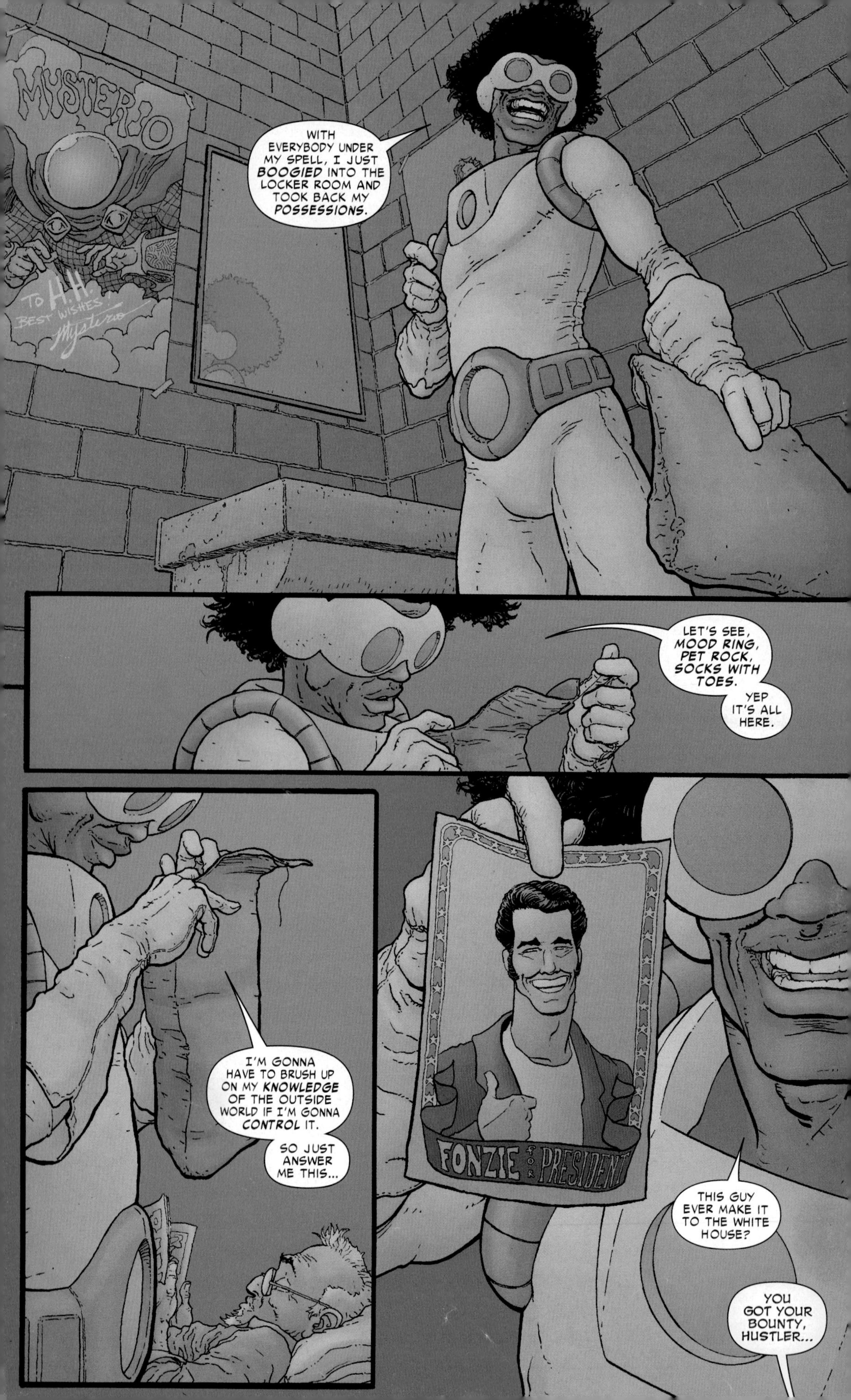
MYSTERIO
TO H.H. BEST WISHES! Mysterio
WITH EVERYBODY UNDER MY SPELL, I JUST BOOGIED INTO THE LOCKER ROOM AND TOOK BACK MY POSSESSIONS.
LET'S SEE, MOOD RING, PET ROCK, SOCKS WITH TOES.
YEP IT'S ALL HERE.
I'M GONNA HAVE TO BRUSH UP ON MY KNOWLEDGE OF THE OUTSIDE WORLD IF I'M GONNA CONTROL IT.
SO JUST ANSWER ME THIS...
FONZIE FOR PRESIDENT
THIS GUY EVER MAKE IT TO THE WHITE HOUSE?
YOU GOT YOUR BOUNTY, HUSTLER...

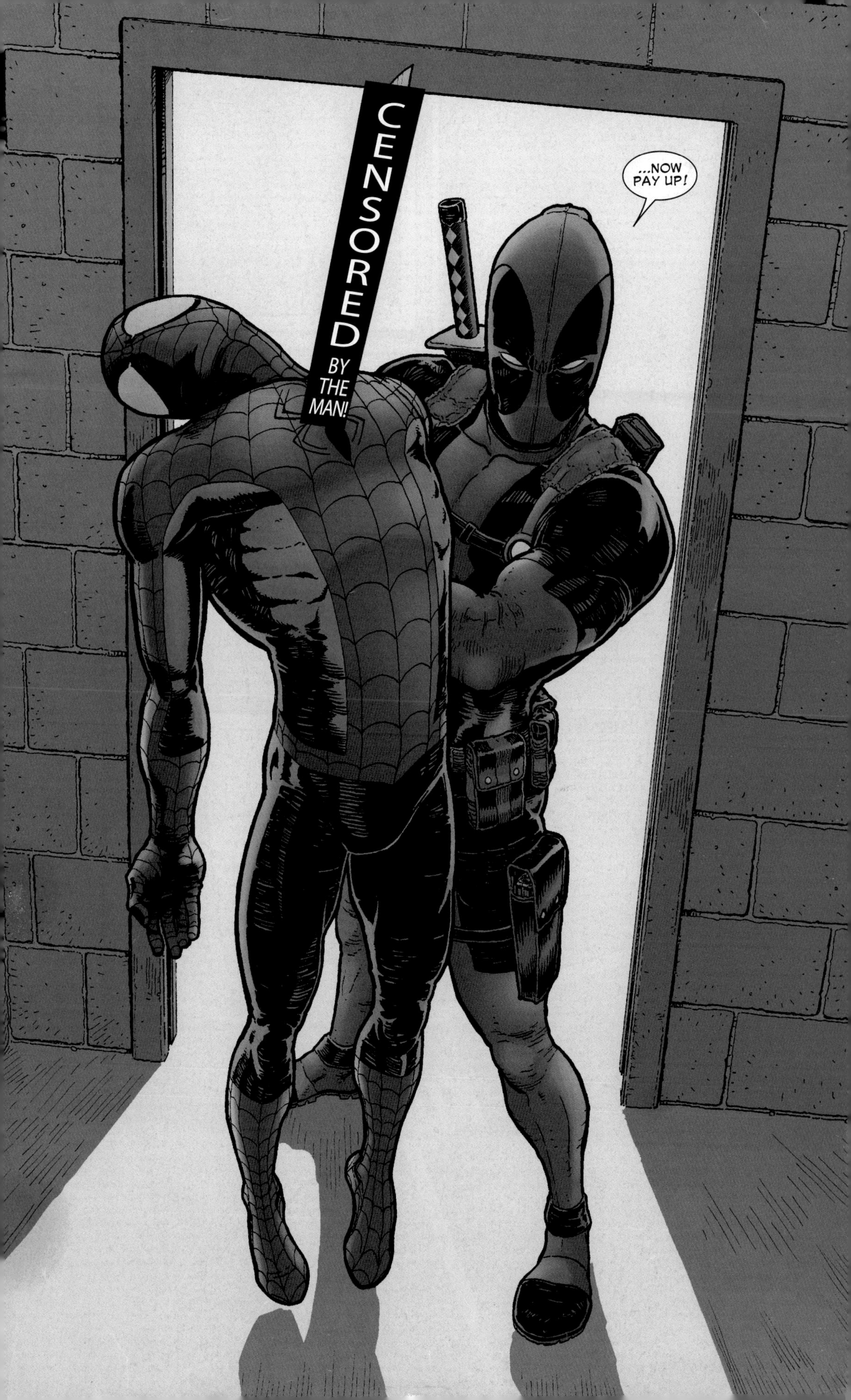
CENSORED BY THE MAN!
...NOW PAY UP!

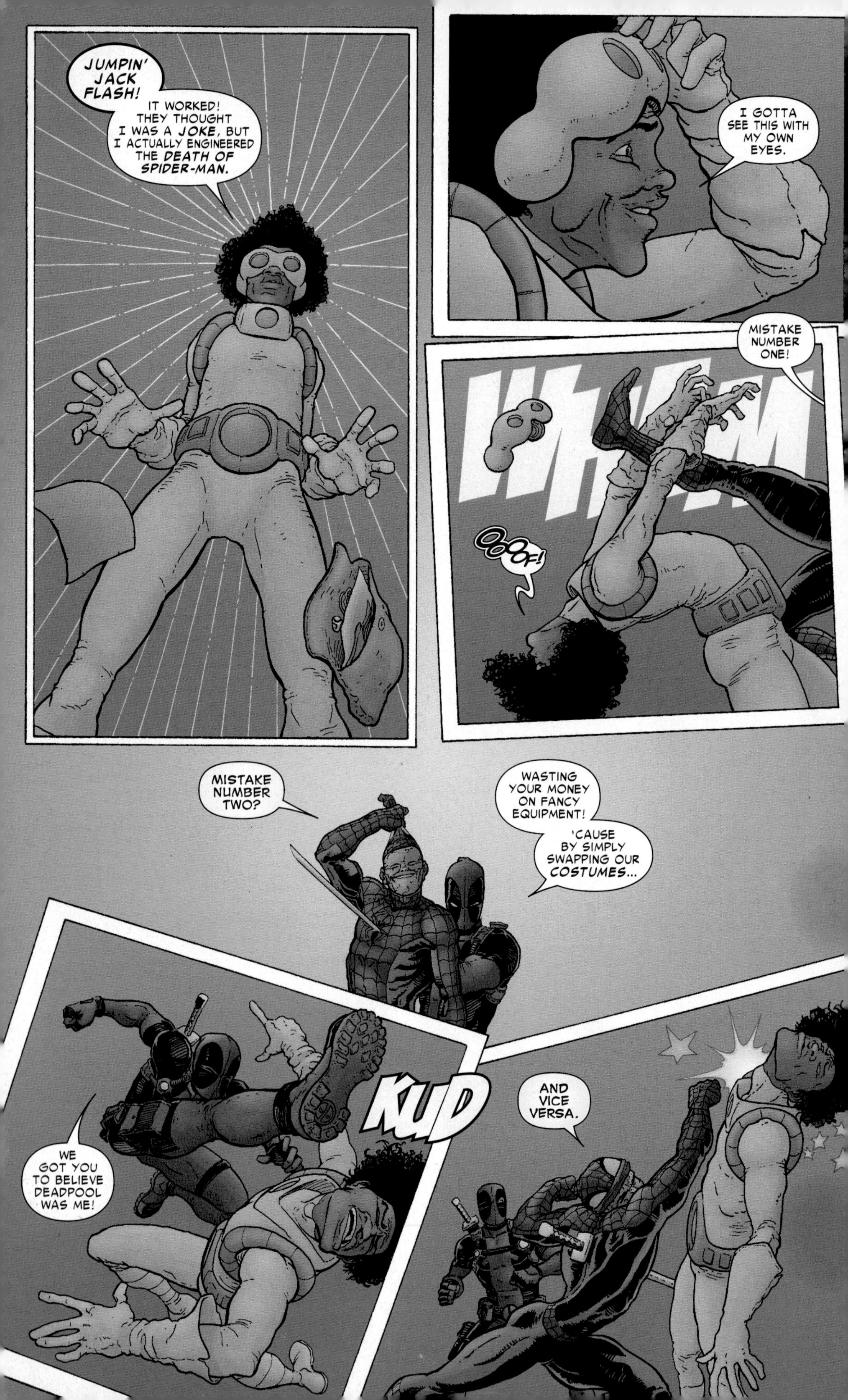
JUMPIN' JACK FLASH!
IT WORKED! THEY THOUGHT I WAS A JOKE, BUT I ACTUALLY ENGINEERED THE DEATH OF SPIDER-MAN.
I GOTTA SEE THIS WITH MY OWN EYES.
MISTAKE NUMBER ONE!
OOOF!
MISTAKE NUMBER TWO?
WASTING YOUR MONEY ON FANCY EQUIPMENT!
'CAUSE BY SIMPLY SWAPPING OUR COSTUMES...
WE GOT YOU TO BELIEVE DEADPOOL WAS ME!
KUD
AND VICE VERSA.

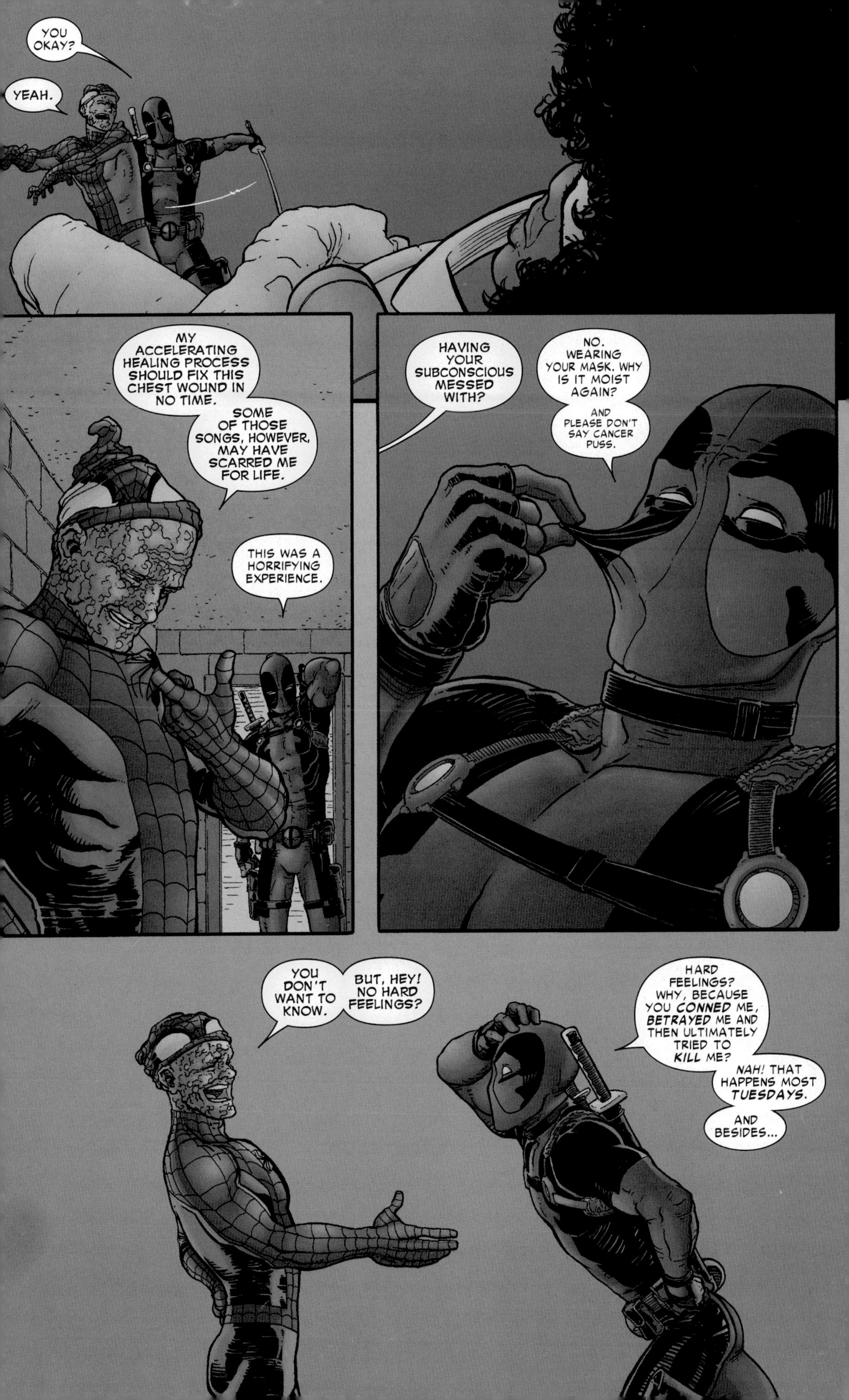

YOU OKAY?
YEAH.
MY ACCELERATING HEALING PROCESS SHOULD FIX THIS CHEST WOUND IN NO TIME.
SOME OF THOSE SONGS, HOWEVER, MAY HAVE SCARRED ME FOR LIFE.
THIS WAS A HORRIFYING EXPERIENCE.
HAVING YOUR SUBCONSCIOUS MESSED WITH?
NO. WEARING YOUR MASK. WHY IS IT MOIST AGAIN?
AND PLEASE DON'T SAY CANCER PUSS.
YOU DON'T WANT TO KNOW.
BUT, HEY! NO HARD FEELINGS?
HARD FEELINGS? WHY, BECAUSE YOU CONNED ME, BETRAYED ME AND THEN ULTIMATELY TRIED TO KILL ME?
NAH! THAT HAPPENS MOST TUESDAYS.
AND BESIDES...

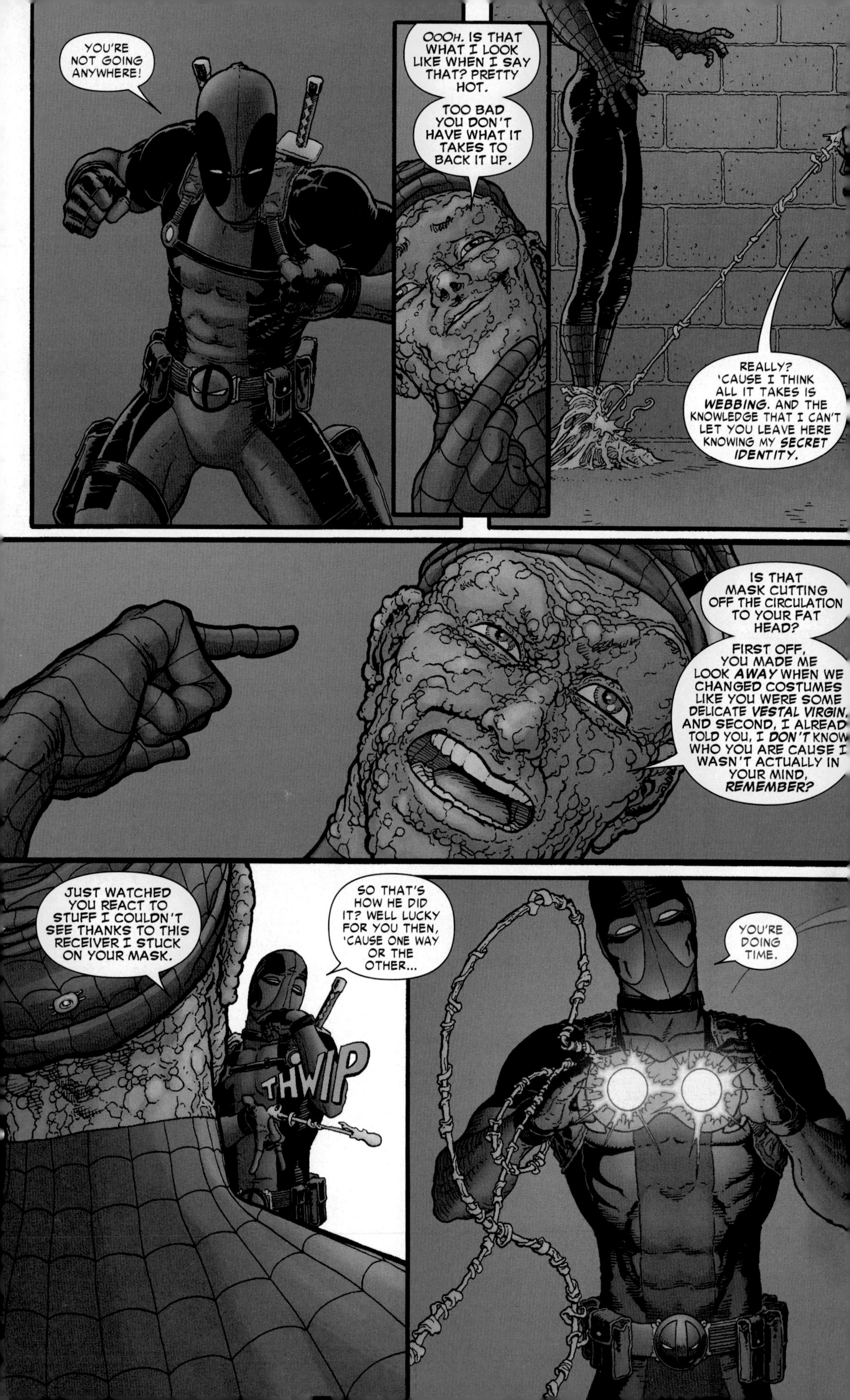
YOU'RE NOT GOING ANYWHERE!
OOOH. IS THAT WHAT I LOOK LIKE WHEN I SAY THAT? PRETTY HOT.
TOO BAD YOU DON'T HAVE WHAT IT TAKES TO BACK IT UP.
REALLY? 'CAUSE I THINK ALL IT TAKES IS WEBBING. AND THE KNOWLEDGE THAT I CAN'T LET YOU LEAVE HERE KNOWING MY SECRET IDENTITY.
IS THAT MASK CUTTING OFF THE CIRCULATION TO YOUR FAT HEAD?
FIRST OFF, YOU MADE ME LOOK AWAY WHEN WE CHANGED COSTUMES LIKE YOU WERE SOME DELICATE VESTAL VIRGIN. AND SECOND, I ALREAD TOLD YOU, I DON'T KNOW WHO YOU ARE CAUSE I WASN'T ACTUALLY IN YOUR MIND, REMEMBER?
JUST WATCHED YOU REACT TO STUFF I COULDN'T SEE THANKS TO THIS RECEIVER I STUCK ON YOUR MASK.
SO THAT'S HOW HE DID IT? WELL LUCKY FOR YOU THEN, 'CAUSE ONE WAY OR THE OTHER...
THWIP
YOU'RE DOING TIME.

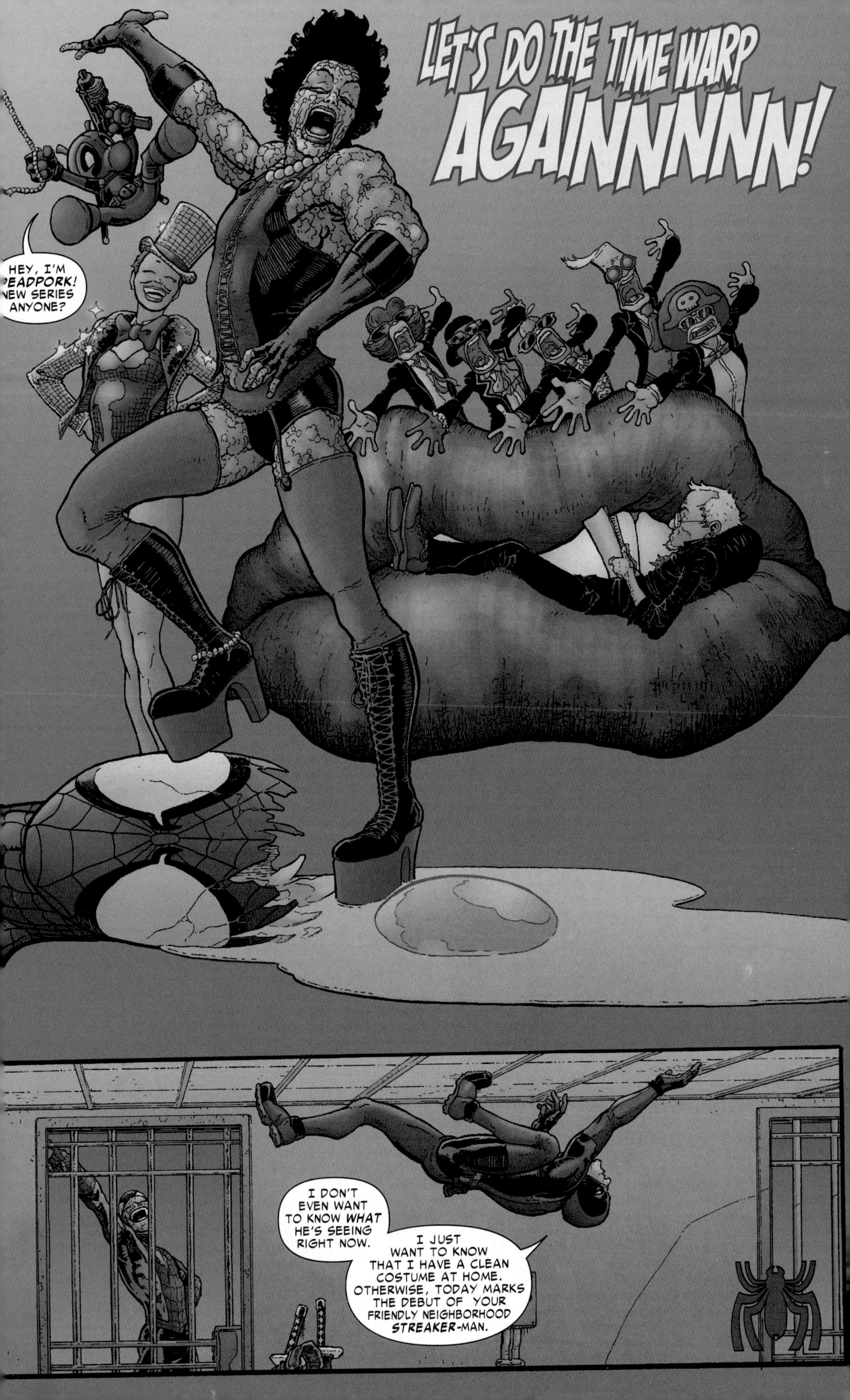

LET'S DO THE TIME WARP AGAINNNNN!
HEY, I'M DEADPORK! NEW SERIES ANYONE?
I DON'T EVEN WANT TO KNOW *WHAT* HE'S SEEING RIGHT NOW.
I JUST WANT TO KNOW THAT I HAVE A CLEAN COSTUME AT HOME. OTHERWISE, TODAY MARKS THE DEBUT OF YOUR FRIENDLY NEIGHBORHOOD *STREAKER*-MAN.

Recently, a dying Doctor Octopus transferred his brainwaves into Spider-Man's body, displacing Peter Parker's mind. Now, Doc Ock has used his engineering genius and ruthless temperament to become a superior Spider-Man! Deadpool doesn't know this. Shh, don't tell Deadpool…

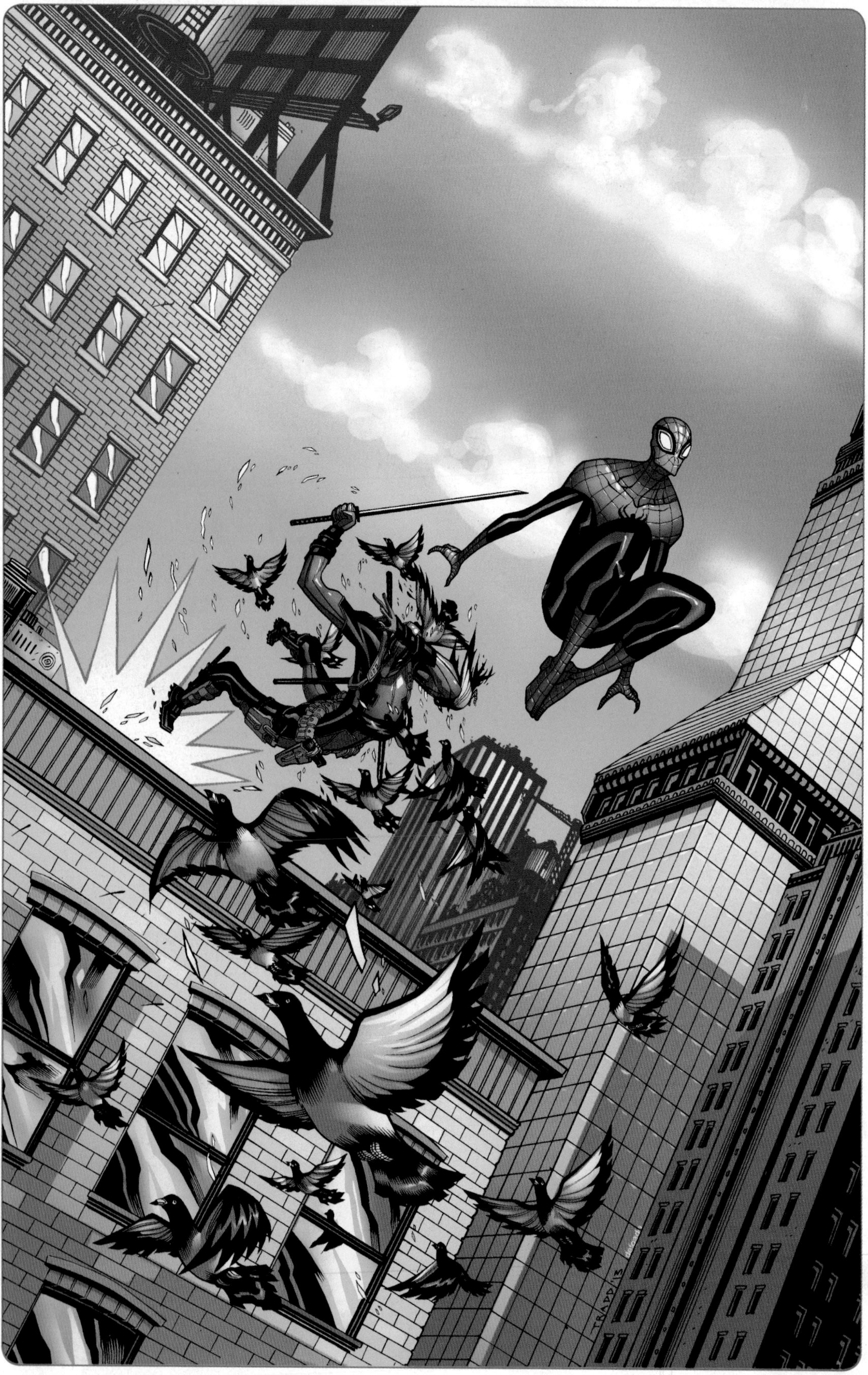

DEADPOOL (2012) **#10**

Possibly the world's most skilled mercenary, definitely the world's most annoying, Wade Wilson was chosen for a top-secret government program that gave him a healing factor allowing him to heal from any wound. Now, Wade makes his way as a gun for hire, shooting his prey's faces off while talking his friends' ears off. Call him the Merc with the Mouth...call him the Regeneratin' Degenerate...call him...

DEADPOOL

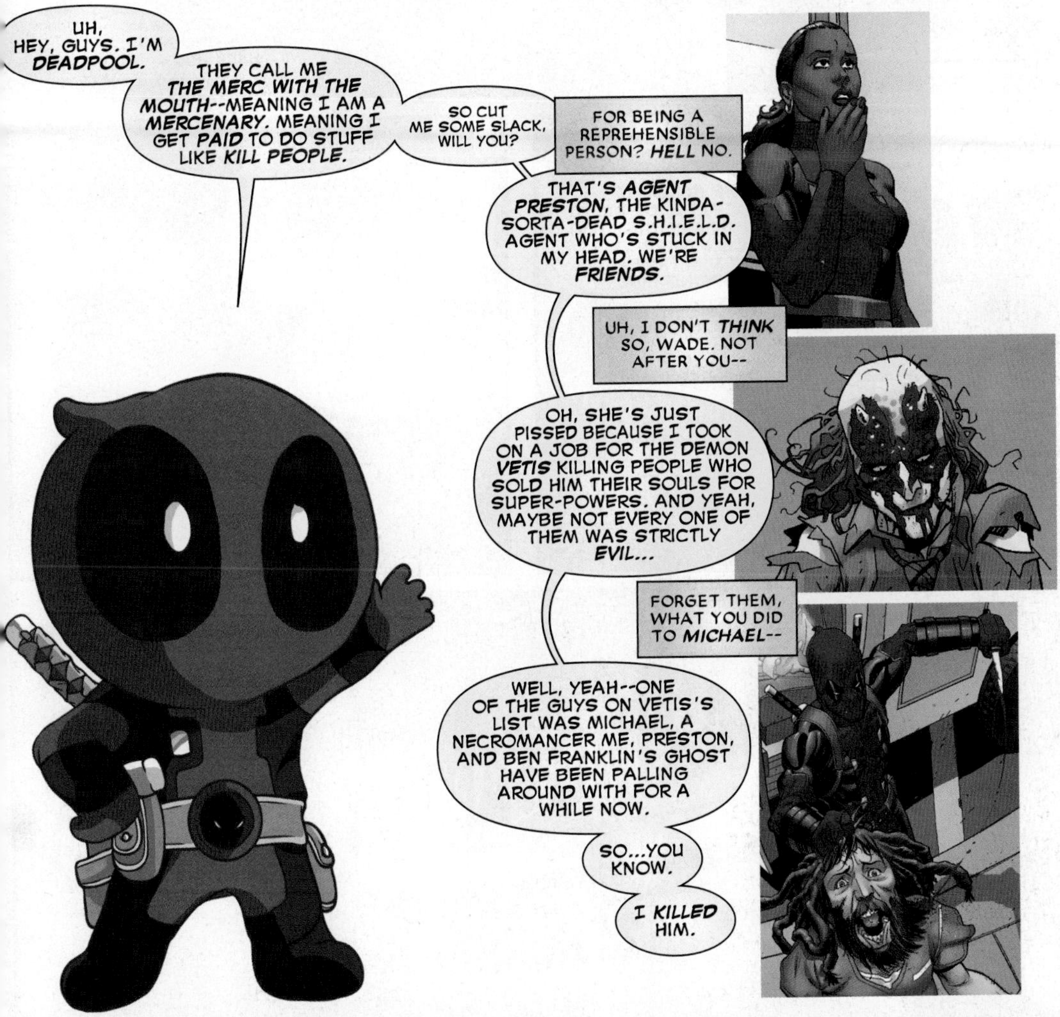

UH, HEY, GUYS. I'M DEADPOOL.

THEY CALL ME THE MERC WITH THE MOUTH--MEANING I AM A MERCENARY. MEANING I GET PAID TO DO STUFF LIKE KILL PEOPLE.

SO CUT ME SOME SLACK, WILL YOU?

FOR BEING A REPREHENSIBLE PERSON? HELL NO.

THAT'S AGENT PRESTON, THE KINDA-SORTA-DEAD S.H.I.E.L.D. AGENT WHO'S STUCK IN MY HEAD. WE'RE FRIENDS.

UH, I DON'T THINK SO, WADE. NOT AFTER YOU--

OH, SHE'S JUST PISSED BECAUSE I TOOK ON A JOB FOR THE DEMON VETIS KILLING PEOPLE WHO SOLD HIM THEIR SOULS FOR SUPER-POWERS. AND YEAH, MAYBE NOT EVERY ONE OF THEM WAS STRICTLY EVIL...

FORGET THEM, WHAT YOU DID TO MICHAEL--

WELL, YEAH--ONE OF THE GUYS ON VETIS'S LIST WAS MICHAEL, A NECROMANCER ME, PRESTON, AND BEN FRANKLIN'S GHOST HAVE BEEN PALLING AROUND WITH FOR A WHILE NOW.

SO...YOU KNOW.

I KILLED HIM.

EIGHT LEGS TO KICK YOU

Brian Posehn & Gerry Duggan
writers

Mike Hawthorne
artist

Val Staples
colorist

VC's Joe Sabino
letterer

Tradd Moore & Edgar Delgado
cover artists

Jordan D. White
editor

Axel Alonso
editor in chief

Joe Quesada
chief creative officer

Dan Buckley
publisher

Alan Fine
executive producer

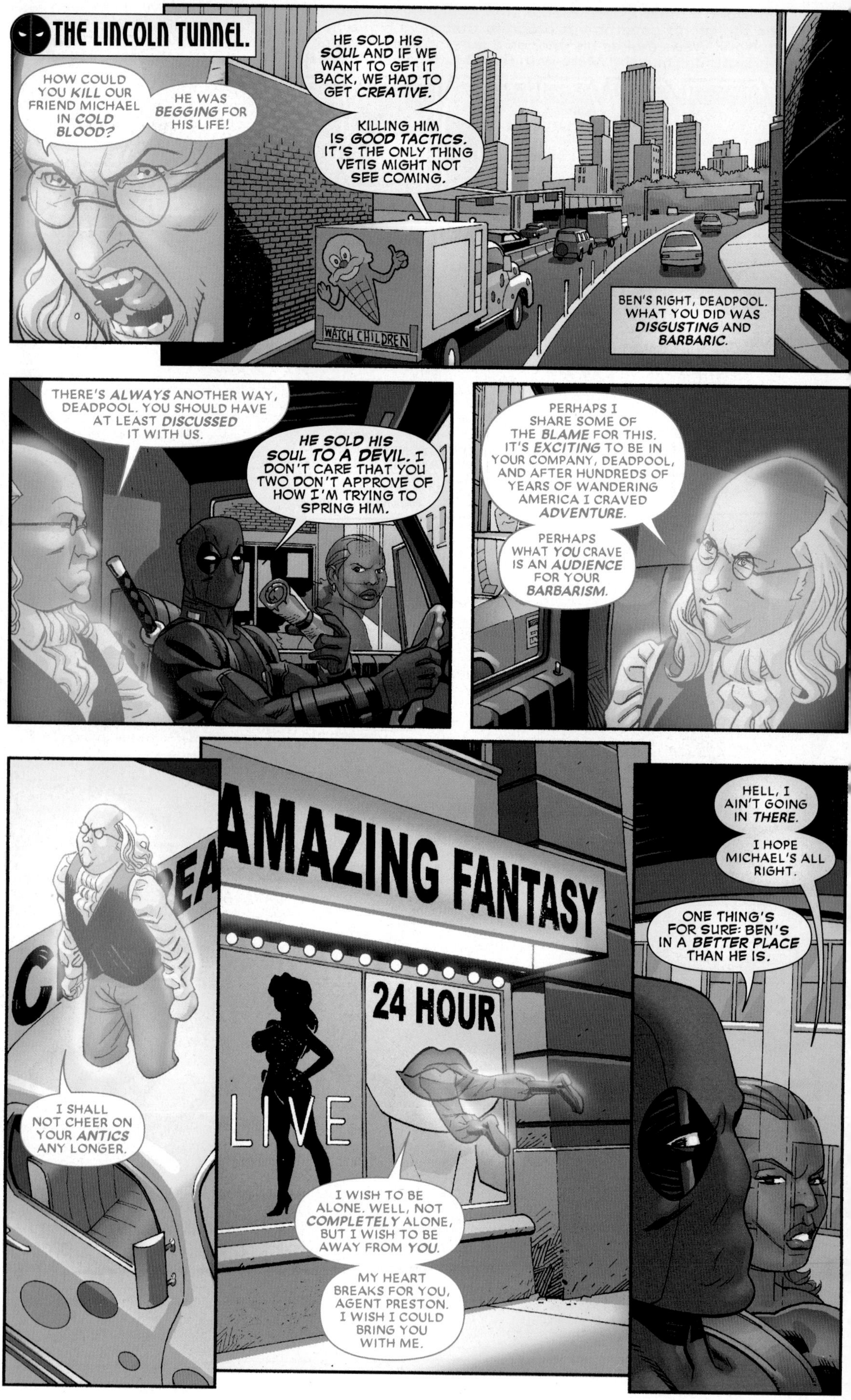
THE LINCOLN TUNNEL.
HOW COULD YOU KILL OUR FRIEND MICHAEL IN COLD BLOOD?
HE WAS BEGGING FOR HIS LIFE!
HE SOLD HIS SOUL AND IF WE WANT TO GET IT BACK, WE HAD TO GET CREATIVE.
KILLING HIM IS GOOD TACTICS. IT'S THE ONLY THING VETIS MIGHT NOT SEE COMING.
WATCH CHILDREN
BEN'S RIGHT, DEADPOOL. WHAT YOU DID WAS DISGUSTING AND BARBARIC.
THERE'S ALWAYS ANOTHER WAY, DEADPOOL. YOU SHOULD HAVE AT LEAST DISCUSSED IT WITH US.
HE SOLD HIS SOUL TO A DEVIL. I DON'T CARE THAT YOU TWO DON'T APPROVE OF HOW I'M TRYING TO SPRING HIM.
PERHAPS I SHARE SOME OF THE BLAME FOR THIS. IT'S EXCITING TO BE IN YOUR COMPANY, DEADPOOL, AND AFTER HUNDREDS OF YEARS OF WANDERING AMERICA I CRAVED ADVENTURE.
PERHAPS WHAT YOU CRAVE IS AN AUDIENCE FOR YOUR BARBARISM.
AMAZING FANTASY
24 HOUR
LIVE
I SHALL NOT CHEER ON YOUR ANTICS ANY LONGER.
I WISH TO BE ALONE. WELL, NOT COMPLETELY ALONE, BUT I WISH TO BE AWAY FROM YOU.
MY HEART BREAKS FOR YOU, AGENT PRESTON. I WISH I COULD BRING YOU WITH ME.
HELL, I AIN'T GOING IN THERE.
I HOPE MICHAEL'S ALL RIGHT.
ONE THING'S FOR SURE: BEN'S IN A BETTER PLACE THAN HE IS.

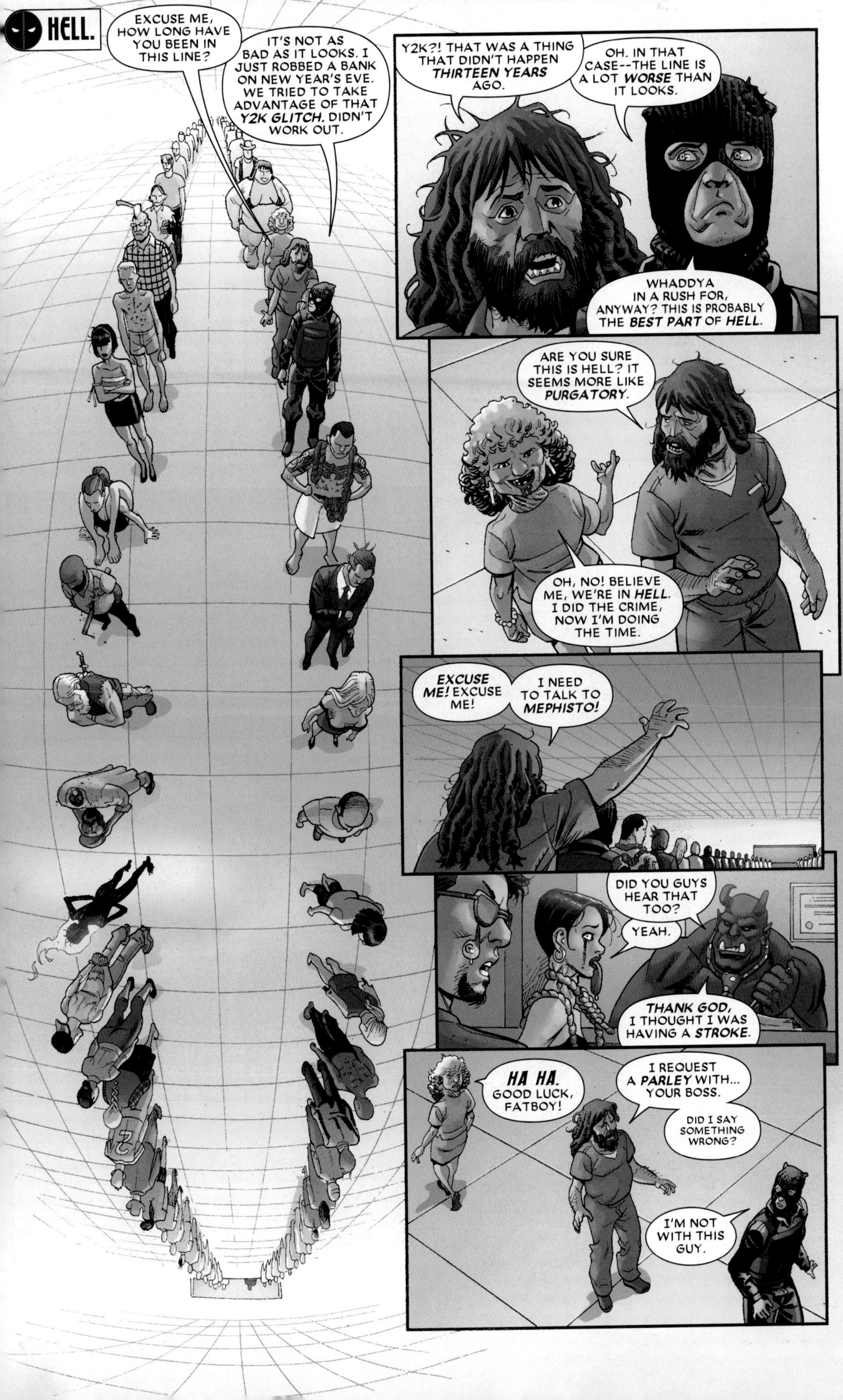
HELL.
EXCUSE ME, HOW LONG HAVE YOU BEEN IN THIS LINE?
IT'S NOT AS BAD AS IT LOOKS. I JUST ROBBED A BANK ON NEW YEAR'S EVE. WE TRIED TO TAKE ADVANTAGE OF THAT Y2K GLITCH. DIDN'T WORK OUT.
Y2K?! THAT WAS A THING THAT DIDN'T HAPPEN THIRTEEN YEARS AGO.
OH. IN THAT CASE--THE LINE IS A LOT WORSE THAN IT LOOKS.
WHADDYA IN A RUSH FOR, ANYWAY? THIS IS PROBABLY THE BEST PART OF HELL.
ARE YOU SURE THIS IS HELL? IT SEEMS MORE LIKE PURGATORY.
OH, NO! BELIEVE ME, WE'RE IN HELL. I DID THE CRIME, NOW I'M DOING THE TIME.
EXCUSE ME! EXCUSE ME!
I NEED TO TALK TO MEPHISTO!
DID YOU GUYS HEAR THAT TOO?
YEAH.
THANK GOD, I THOUGHT I WAS HAVING A STROKE.
HA HA. GOOD LUCK, FATBOY!
I REQUEST A PARLEY WITH... YOUR BOSS.
DID I SAY SOMETHING WRONG?
I'M NOT WITH THIS GUY.

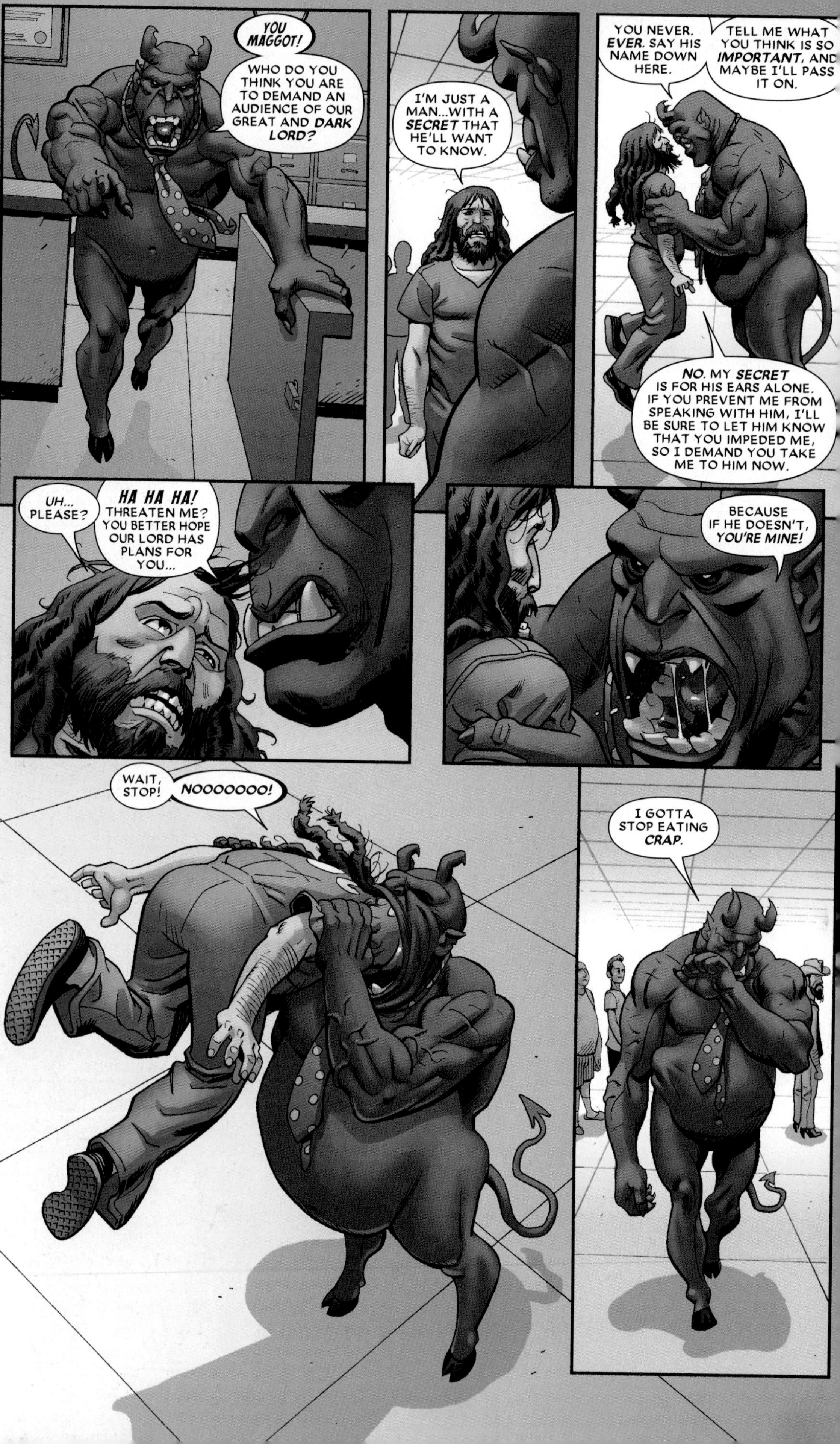
YOU MAGGOT!
WHO DO YOU THINK YOU ARE TO DEMAND AN AUDIENCE OF OUR GREAT AND DARK LORD?
I'M JUST A MAN...WITH A SECRET THAT HE'LL WANT TO KNOW.
YOU NEVER. EVER. SAY HIS NAME DOWN HERE.
TELL ME WHAT YOU THINK IS SO IMPORTANT, AND MAYBE I'LL PASS IT ON.
NO. MY SECRET IS FOR HIS EARS ALONE. IF YOU PREVENT ME FROM SPEAKING WITH HIM, I'LL BE SURE TO LET HIM KNOW THAT YOU IMPEDED ME, SO I DEMAND YOU TAKE ME TO HIM NOW.
UH... PLEASE?
HA HA HA! THREATEN ME? YOU BETTER HOPE OUR LORD HAS PLANS FOR YOU...
BECAUSE IF HE DOESN'T, YOU'RE MINE!
WAIT, STOP!
NOOOOOOO!
I GOTTA STOP EATING CRAP.

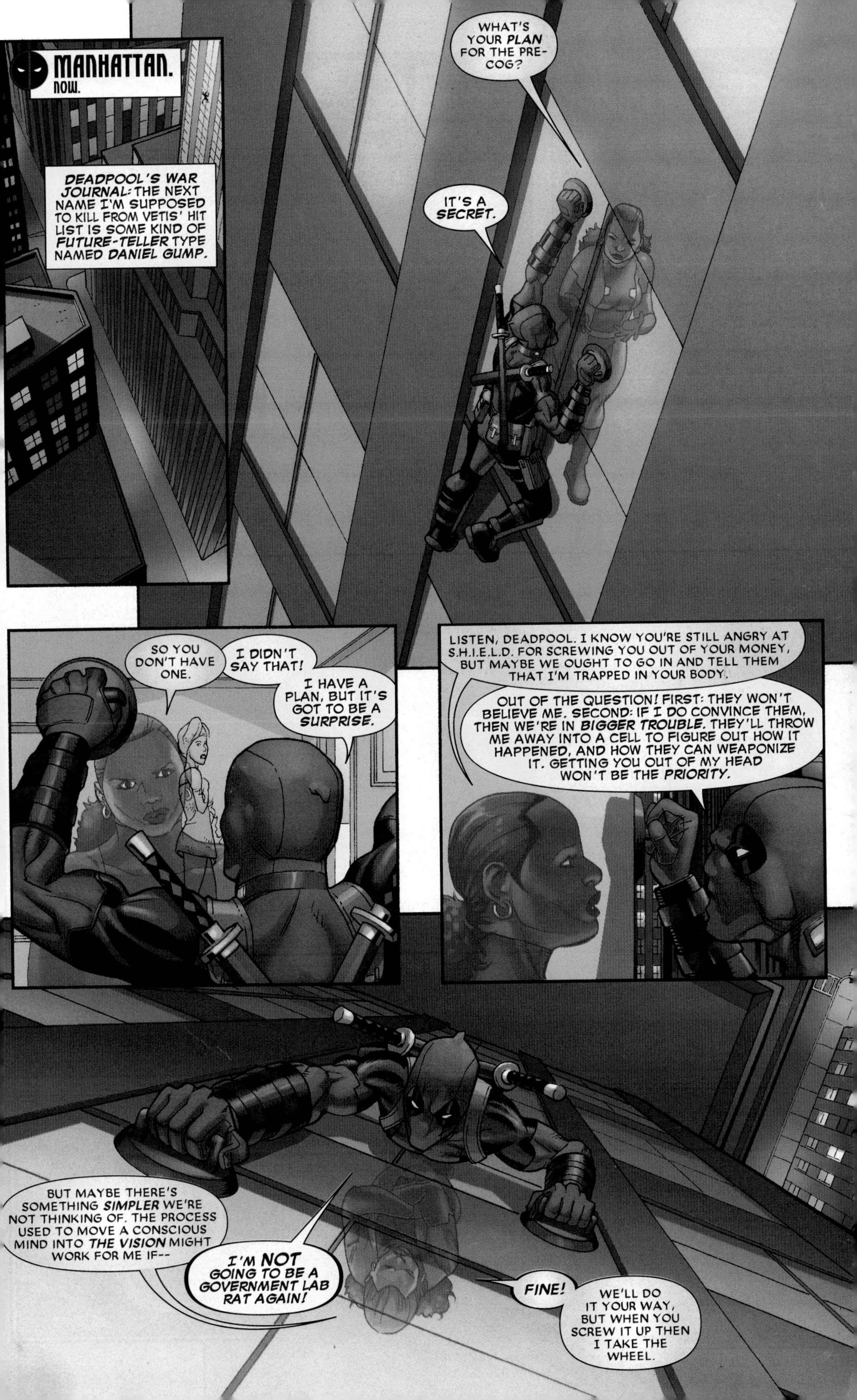

MANHATTAN.
now.
DEADPOOL'S WAR JOURNAL: THE NEXT NAME I'M SUPPOSED TO KILL FROM VETIS' HIT LIST IS SOME KIND OF FUTURE-TELLER TYPE NAMED DANIEL GUMP.
WHAT'S YOUR PLAN FOR THE PRE-COG?
IT'S A SECRET.
SO YOU DON'T HAVE ONE.
I DIDN'T SAY THAT!
I HAVE A PLAN, BUT IT'S GOT TO BE A SURPRISE.
LISTEN, DEADPOOL. I KNOW YOU'RE STILL ANGRY AT S.H.I.E.L.D. FOR SCREWING YOU OUT OF YOUR MONEY, BUT MAYBE WE OUGHT TO GO IN AND TELL THEM THAT I'M TRAPPED IN YOUR BODY.
OUT OF THE QUESTION! FIRST: THEY WON'T BELIEVE ME. SECOND: IF I DO CONVINCE THEM, THEN WE'RE IN BIGGER TROUBLE. THEY'LL THROW ME AWAY INTO A CELL TO FIGURE OUT HOW IT HAPPENED, AND HOW THEY CAN WEAPONIZE IT. GETTING YOU OUT OF MY HEAD WON'T BE THE PRIORITY.
BUT MAYBE THERE'S SOMETHING SIMPLER WE'RE NOT THINKING OF. THE PROCESS USED TO MOVE A CONSCIOUS MIND INTO THE VISION MIGHT WORK FOR ME IF--
I'M NOT GOING TO BE A GOVERNMENT LAB RAT AGAIN!
FINE!
WE'LL DO IT YOUR WAY, BUT WHEN YOU SCREW IT UP THEN I TAKE THE WHEEL.

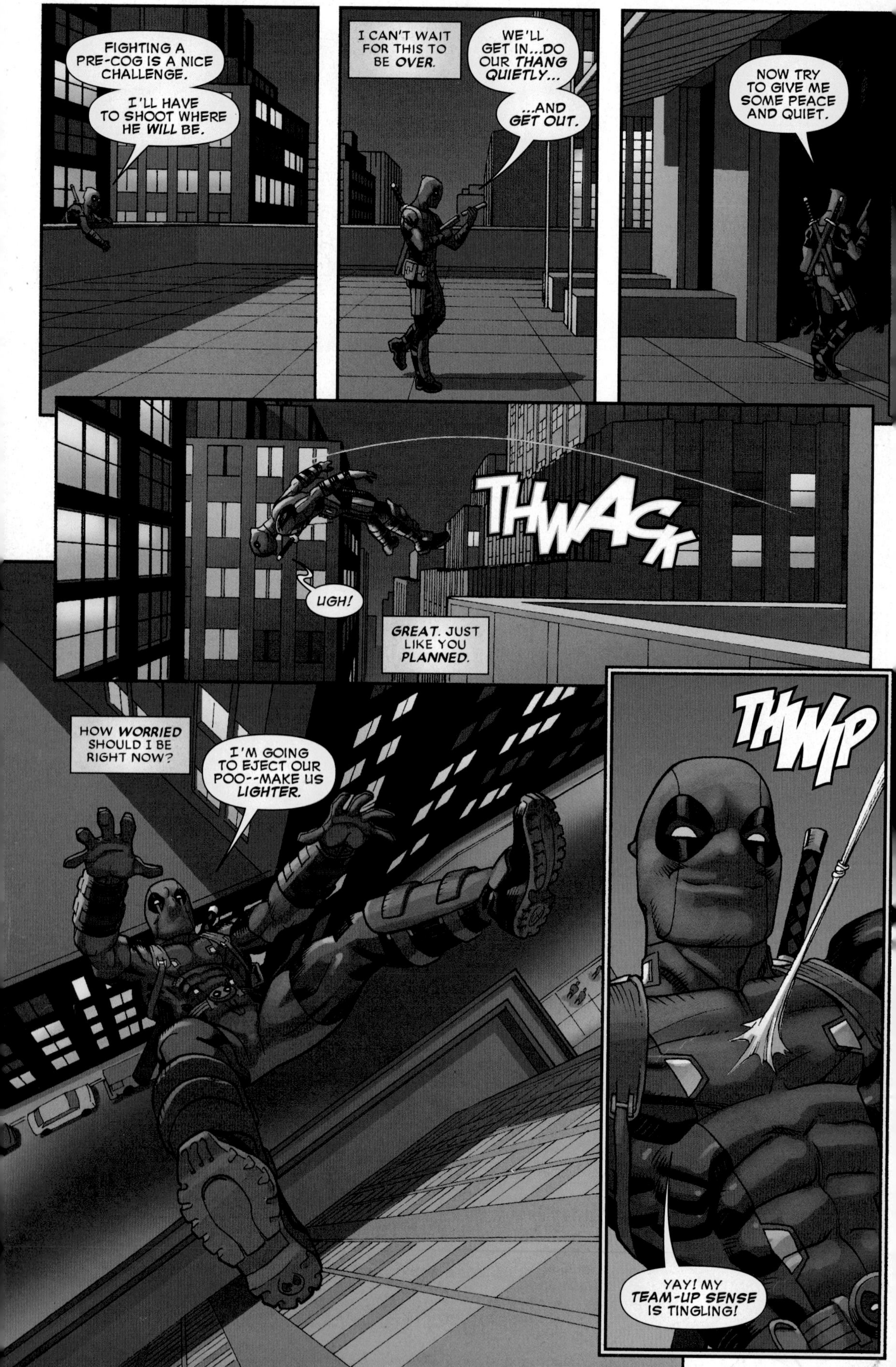
FIGHTING A PRE-COG IS A NICE CHALLENGE.
I'LL HAVE TO SHOOT WHERE HE WILL BE.
I CAN'T WAIT FOR THIS TO BE OVER.
WE'LL GET IN...DO OUR THANG QUIETLY...
...AND GET OUT.
NOW TRY TO GIVE ME SOME PEACE AND QUIET.
THWACK
UGH!
GREAT. JUST LIKE YOU PLANNED.
HOW WORRIED SHOULD I BE RIGHT NOW?
I'M GOING TO EJECT OUR POO--MAKE US LIGHTER.
THWIP
YAY! MY TEAM-UP SENSE IS TINGLING!

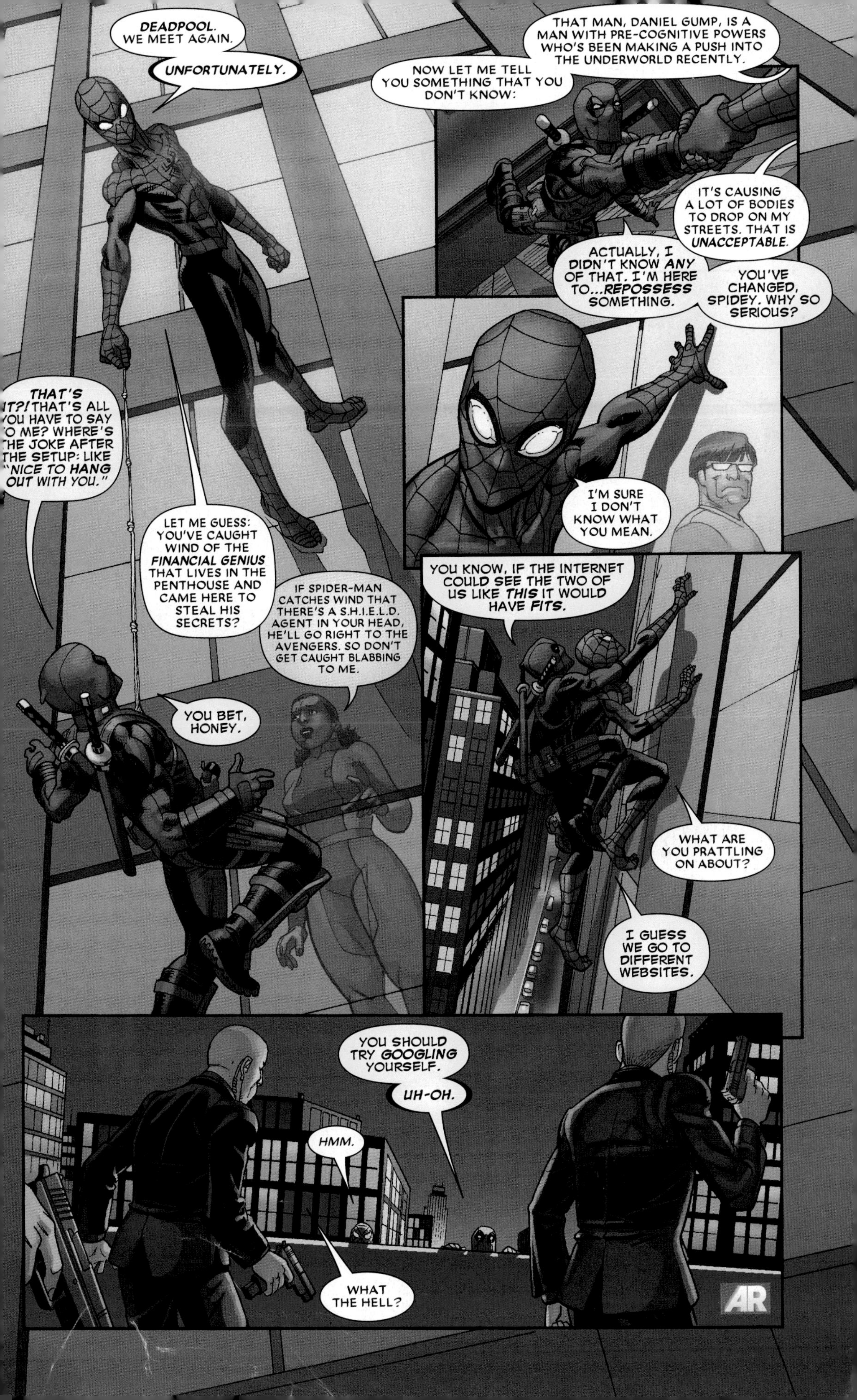

DEADPOOL. WE MEET AGAIN.
UNFORTUNATELY.
NOW LET ME TELL YOU SOMETHING THAT YOU DON'T KNOW:
THAT MAN, DANIEL GUMP, IS A MAN WITH PRE-COGNITIVE POWERS WHO'S BEEN MAKING A PUSH INTO THE UNDERWORLD RECENTLY.
IT'S CAUSING A LOT OF BODIES TO DROP ON MY STREETS. THAT IS UNACCEPTABLE.
ACTUALLY, I DIDN'T KNOW ANY OF THAT. I'M HERE TO...REPOSSESS SOMETHING.
YOU'VE CHANGED, SPIDEY. WHY SO SERIOUS?
I'M SURE I DON'T KNOW WHAT YOU MEAN.
THAT'S IT?! THAT'S ALL YOU HAVE TO SAY TO ME? WHERE'S THE JOKE AFTER THE SETUP: LIKE "NICE TO HANG OUT WITH YOU."
LET ME GUESS: YOU'VE CAUGHT WIND OF THE FINANCIAL GENIUS THAT LIVES IN THE PENTHOUSE AND CAME HERE TO STEAL HIS SECRETS?
IF SPIDER-MAN CATCHES WIND THAT THERE'S A S.H.I.E.L.D. AGENT IN YOUR HEAD, HE'LL GO RIGHT TO THE AVENGERS. SO DON'T GET CAUGHT BLABBING TO ME.
YOU BET, HONEY.
YOU KNOW, IF THE INTERNET COULD SEE THE TWO OF US LIKE THIS IT WOULD HAVE FITS.
WHAT ARE YOU PRATTLING ON ABOUT?
I GUESS WE GO TO DIFFERENT WEBSITES.
YOU SHOULD TRY GOOGLING YOURSELF.
UH-OH.
HMM.
WHAT THE HELL?
AR

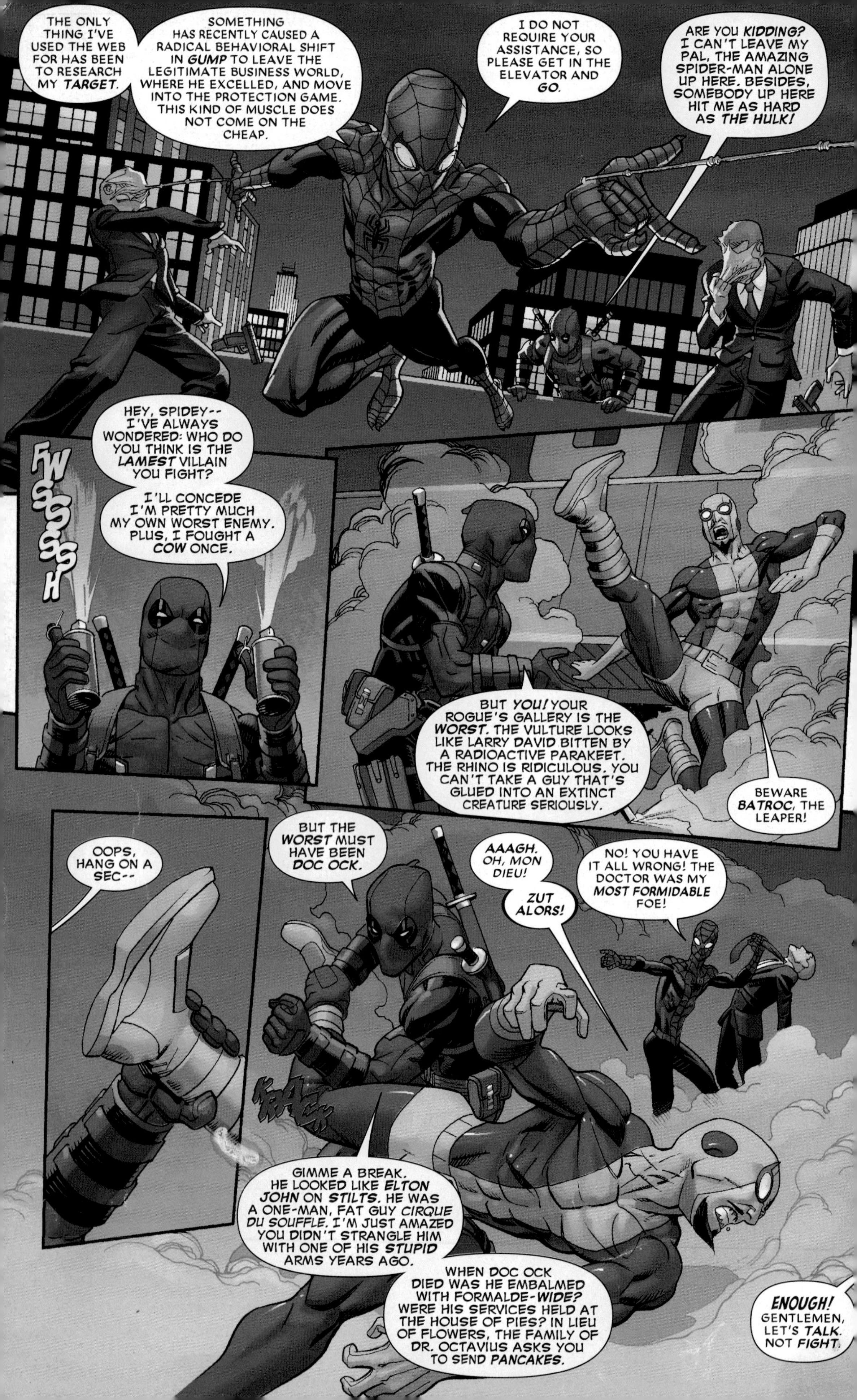
THE ONLY THING I'VE USED THE WEB FOR HAS BEEN TO RESEARCH MY TARGET.
SOMETHING HAS RECENTLY CAUSED A RADICAL BEHAVIORAL SHIFT IN GUMP TO LEAVE THE LEGITIMATE BUSINESS WORLD, WHERE HE EXCELLED, AND MOVE INTO THE PROTECTION GAME. THIS KIND OF MUSCLE DOES NOT COME ON THE CHEAP.
I DO NOT REQUIRE YOUR ASSISTANCE, SO PLEASE GET IN THE ELEVATOR AND GO.
ARE YOU KIDDING? I CAN'T LEAVE MY PAL, THE AMAZING SPIDER-MAN ALONE UP HERE. BESIDES, SOMEBODY UP HERE HIT ME AS HARD AS THE HULK!
FWSSSSH
HEY, SPIDEY-- I'VE ALWAYS WONDERED: WHO DO YOU THINK IS THE LAMEST VILLAIN YOU FIGHT?
I'LL CONCEDE I'M PRETTY MUCH MY OWN WORST ENEMY. PLUS, I FOUGHT A COW ONCE.
BUT YOU! YOUR ROGUE'S GALLERY IS THE WORST. THE VULTURE LOOKS LIKE LARRY DAVID BITTEN BY A RADIOACTIVE PARAKEET. THE RHINO IS RIDICULOUS. YOU CAN'T TAKE A GUY THAT'S GLUED INTO AN EXTINCT CREATURE SERIOUSLY.
BEWARE BATROC, THE LEAPER!
OOPS, HANG ON A SEC--
BUT THE WORST MUST HAVE BEEN DOC OCK.
AAAGH. OH, MON DIEU!
ZUT ALORS!
NO! YOU HAVE IT ALL WRONG! THE DOCTOR WAS MY MOST FORMIDABLE FOE!
KRAACK
GIMME A BREAK. HE LOOKED LIKE ELTON JOHN ON STILTS. HE WAS A ONE-MAN, FAT GUY CIRQUE DU SOUFFLE. I'M JUST AMAZED YOU DIDN'T STRANGLE HIM WITH ONE OF HIS STUPID ARMS YEARS AGO.
WHEN DOC OCK DIED WAS HE EMBALMED WITH FORMALDE-WIDE? WERE HIS SERVICES HELD AT THE HOUSE OF PIES? IN LIEU OF FLOWERS, THE FAMILY OF DR. OCTAVIUS ASKS YOU TO SEND PANCAKES.
ENOUGH! GENTLEMEN, LET'S TALK. NOT FIGHT.

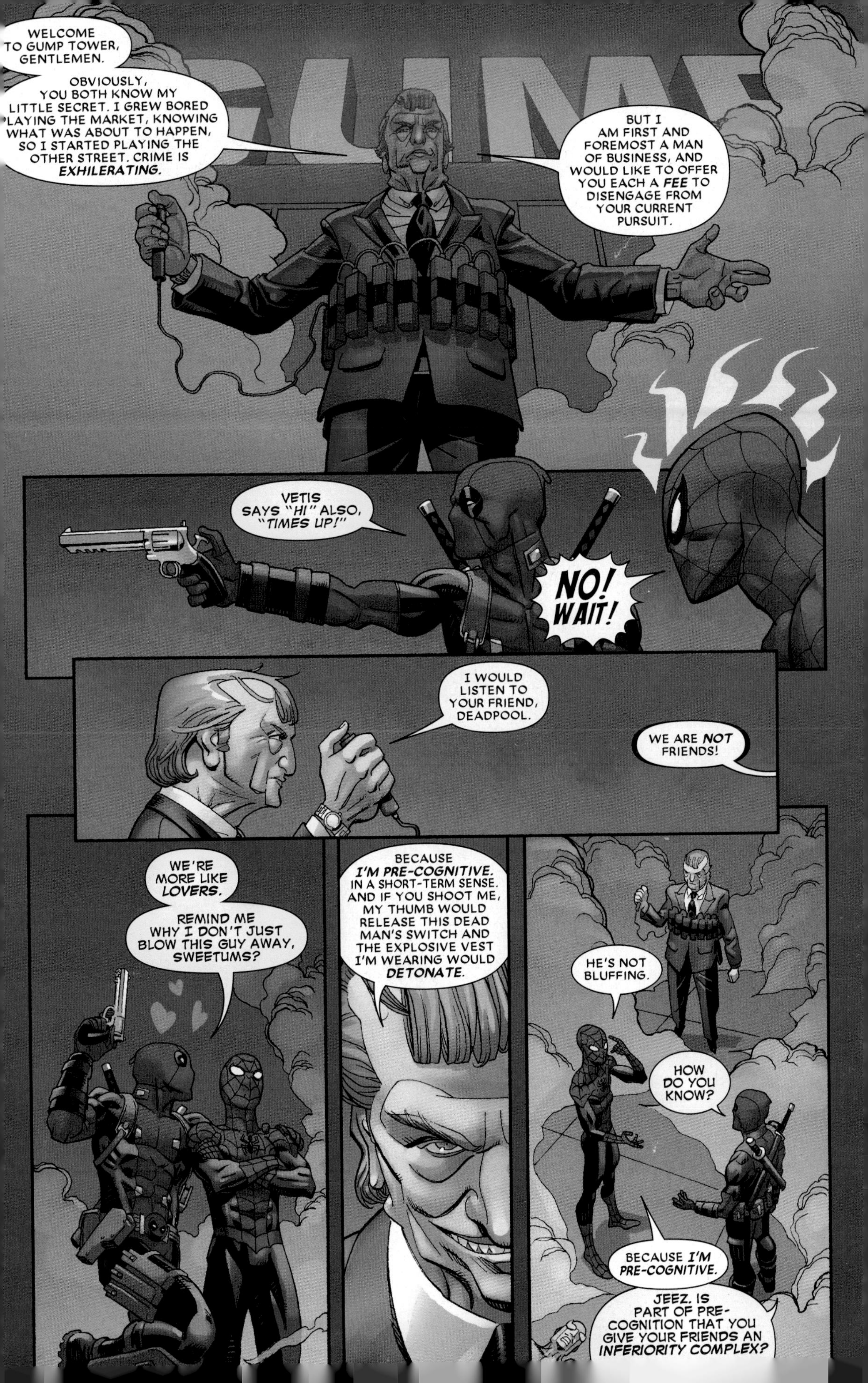
WELCOME TO GUMP TOWER, GENTLEMEN.
OBVIOUSLY, YOU BOTH KNOW MY LITTLE SECRET. I GREW BORED PLAYING THE MARKET, KNOWING WHAT WAS ABOUT TO HAPPEN, SO I STARTED PLAYING THE OTHER STREET. CRIME IS *EXHILERATING.*
BUT I AM FIRST AND FOREMOST A MAN OF BUSINESS, AND WOULD LIKE TO OFFER YOU EACH A *FEE* TO DISENGAGE FROM YOUR CURRENT PURSUIT.
VETIS SAYS "*HI*" ALSO, "*TIMES UP!*"
NO! WAIT!
I WOULD LISTEN TO YOUR FRIEND, DEADPOOL.
WE ARE *NOT* FRIENDS!
WE'RE MORE LIKE *LOVERS.*
REMIND ME WHY I DON'T JUST BLOW THIS GUY AWAY, SWEETUMS?
BECAUSE *I'M PRE-COGNITIVE.* IN A SHORT-TERM SENSE. AND IF YOU SHOOT ME, MY THUMB WOULD RELEASE THIS DEAD MAN'S SWITCH AND THE EXPLOSIVE VEST I'M WEARING WOULD *DETONATE.*
HE'S NOT BLUFFING.
HOW DO YOU KNOW?
BECAUSE *I'M* PRE-COGNITIVE.
JEEZ. IS PART OF PRE-COGNITION THAT YOU GIVE YOUR FRIENDS AN *INFERIORITY COMPLEX?*

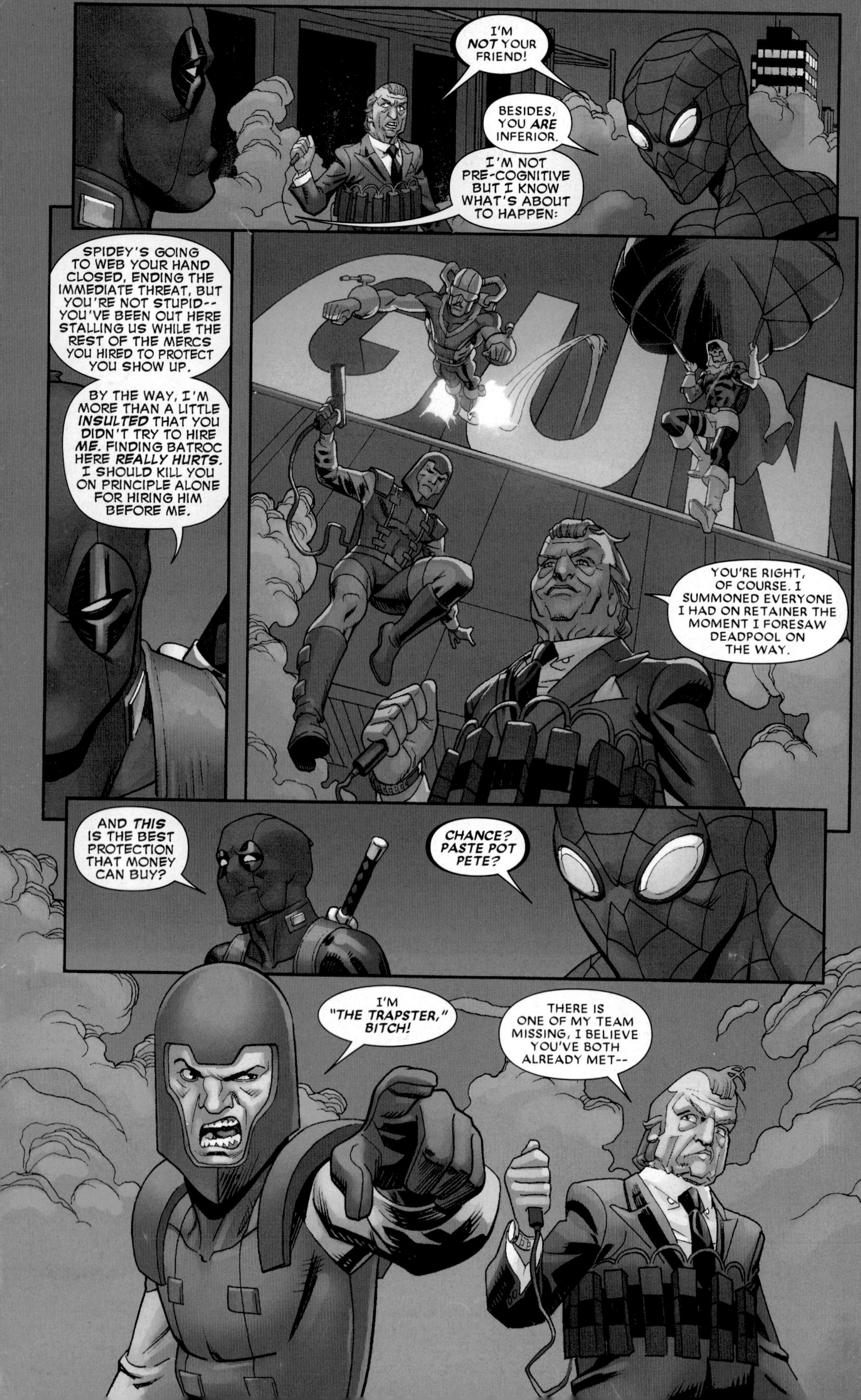
I'M NOT YOUR FRIEND!
BESIDES, YOU ARE INFERIOR.
I'M NOT PRE-COGNITIVE BUT I KNOW WHAT'S ABOUT TO HAPPEN:
SPIDEY'S GOING TO WEB YOUR HAND CLOSED, ENDING THE IMMEDIATE THREAT, BUT YOU'RE NOT STUPID-- YOU'VE BEEN OUT HERE STALLING US WHILE THE REST OF THE MERCS YOU HIRED TO PROTECT YOU SHOW UP.
BY THE WAY, I'M MORE THAN A LITTLE INSULTED THAT YOU DIDN'T TRY TO HIRE ME. FINDING BATROC HERE REALLY HURTS. I SHOULD KILL YOU ON PRINCIPLE ALONE FOR HIRING HIM BEFORE ME.
YOU'RE RIGHT, OF COURSE. I SUMMONED EVERYONE I HAD ON RETAINER THE MOMENT I FORESAW DEADPOOL ON THE WAY.
AND THIS IS THE BEST PROTECTION THAT MONEY CAN BUY?
CHANCE? PASTE POT PETE?
I'M "THE TRAPSTER," BITCH!
THERE IS ONE OF MY TEAM MISSING, I BELIEVE YOU'VE BOTH ALREADY MET--

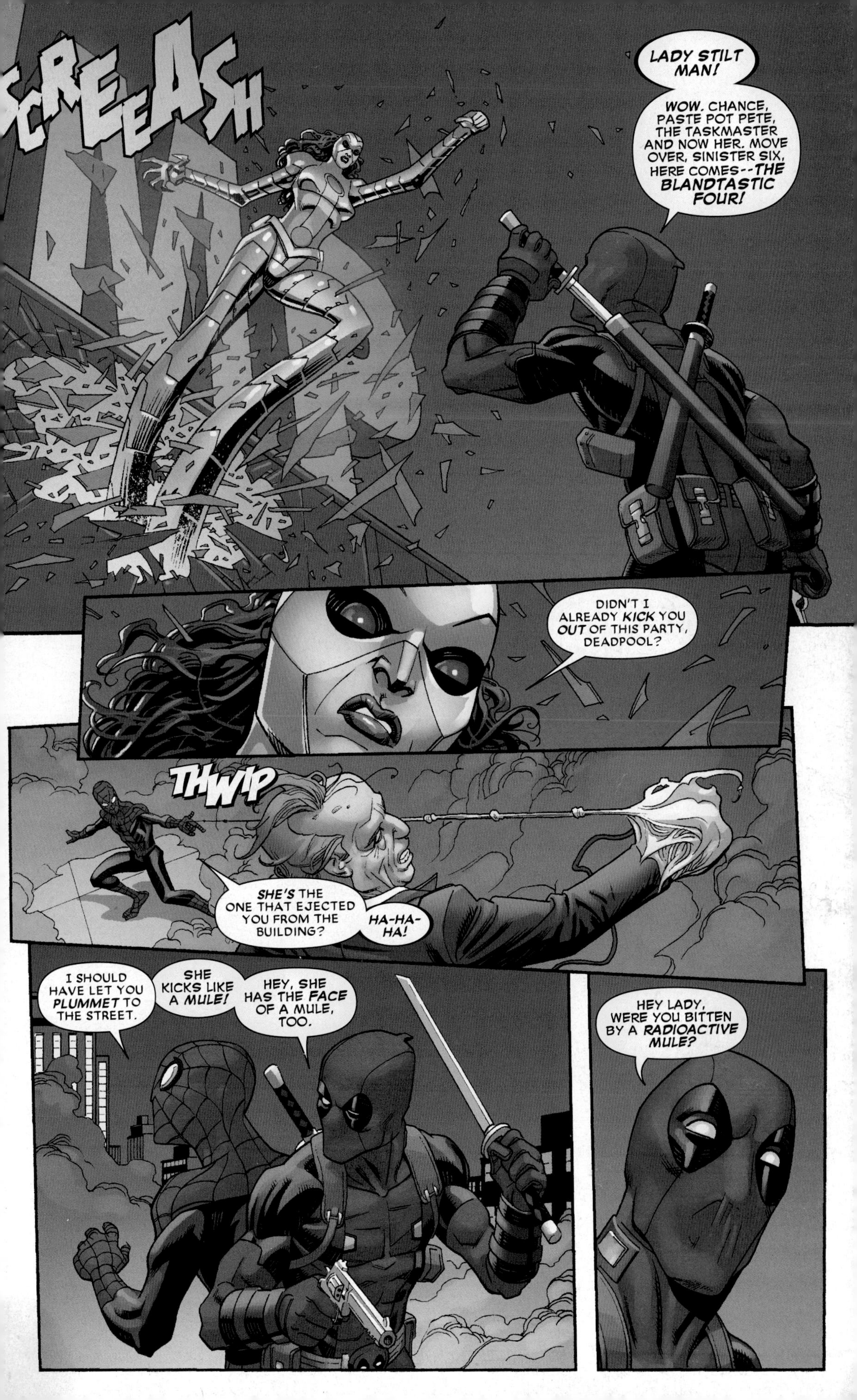
SCREEASH
LADY STILT MAN!
WOW. CHANCE, PASTE POT PETE, THE TASKMASTER AND NOW HER. MOVE OVER, SINISTER SIX, HERE COMES--THE BLANDTASTIC FOUR!
DIDN'T I ALREADY KICK YOU OUT OF THIS PARTY, DEADPOOL?
THWIP
SHE'S THE ONE THAT EJECTED YOU FROM THE BUILDING?
HA-HA-HA!
I SHOULD HAVE LET YOU PLUMMET TO THE STREET.
SHE KICKS LIKE A MULE!
HEY, SHE HAS THE FACE OF A MULE, TOO.
HEY LADY, WERE YOU BITTEN BY A RADIOACTIVE MULE?

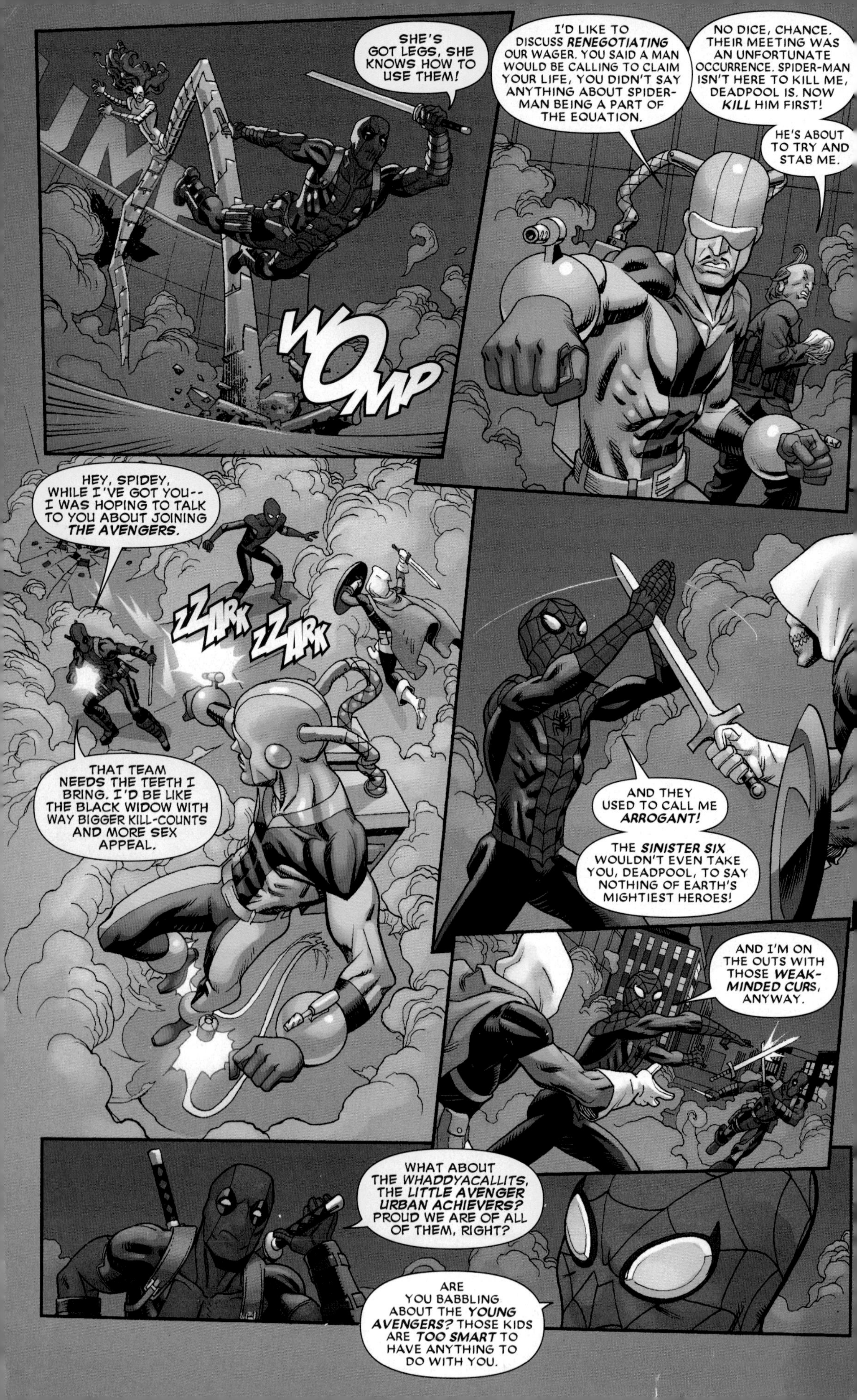
SHE'S GOT LEGS, SHE KNOWS HOW TO USE THEM!
WOMP
I'D LIKE TO DISCUSS RENEGOTIATING OUR WAGER. YOU SAID A MAN WOULD BE CALLING TO CLAIM YOUR LIFE, YOU DIDN'T SAY ANYTHING ABOUT SPIDER-MAN BEING A PART OF THE EQUATION.
NO DICE, CHANCE. THEIR MEETING WAS AN UNFORTUNATE OCCURRENCE. SPIDER-MAN ISN'T HERE TO KILL ME, DEADPOOL IS. NOW KILL HIM FIRST!
HE'S ABOUT TO TRY AND STAB ME.
HEY, SPIDEY, WHILE I'VE GOT YOU-- I WAS HOPING TO TALK TO YOU ABOUT JOINING THE AVENGERS.
ZZARK ZZARK
THAT TEAM NEEDS THE TEETH I BRING. I'D BE LIKE THE BLACK WIDOW WITH WAY BIGGER KILL-COUNTS AND MORE SEX APPEAL.
AND THEY USED TO CALL ME ARROGANT!
THE SINISTER SIX WOULDN'T EVEN TAKE YOU, DEADPOOL, TO SAY NOTHING OF EARTH'S MIGHTIEST HEROES!
AND I'M ON THE OUTS WITH THOSE WEAK-MINDED CURS, ANYWAY.
WHAT ABOUT THE WHADDYACALLITS, THE LITTLE AVENGER URBAN ACHIEVERS? PROUD WE ARE OF ALL OF THEM, RIGHT?
ARE YOU BABBLING ABOUT THE YOUNG AVENGERS? THOSE KIDS ARE TOO SMART TO HAVE ANYTHING TO DO WITH YOU.

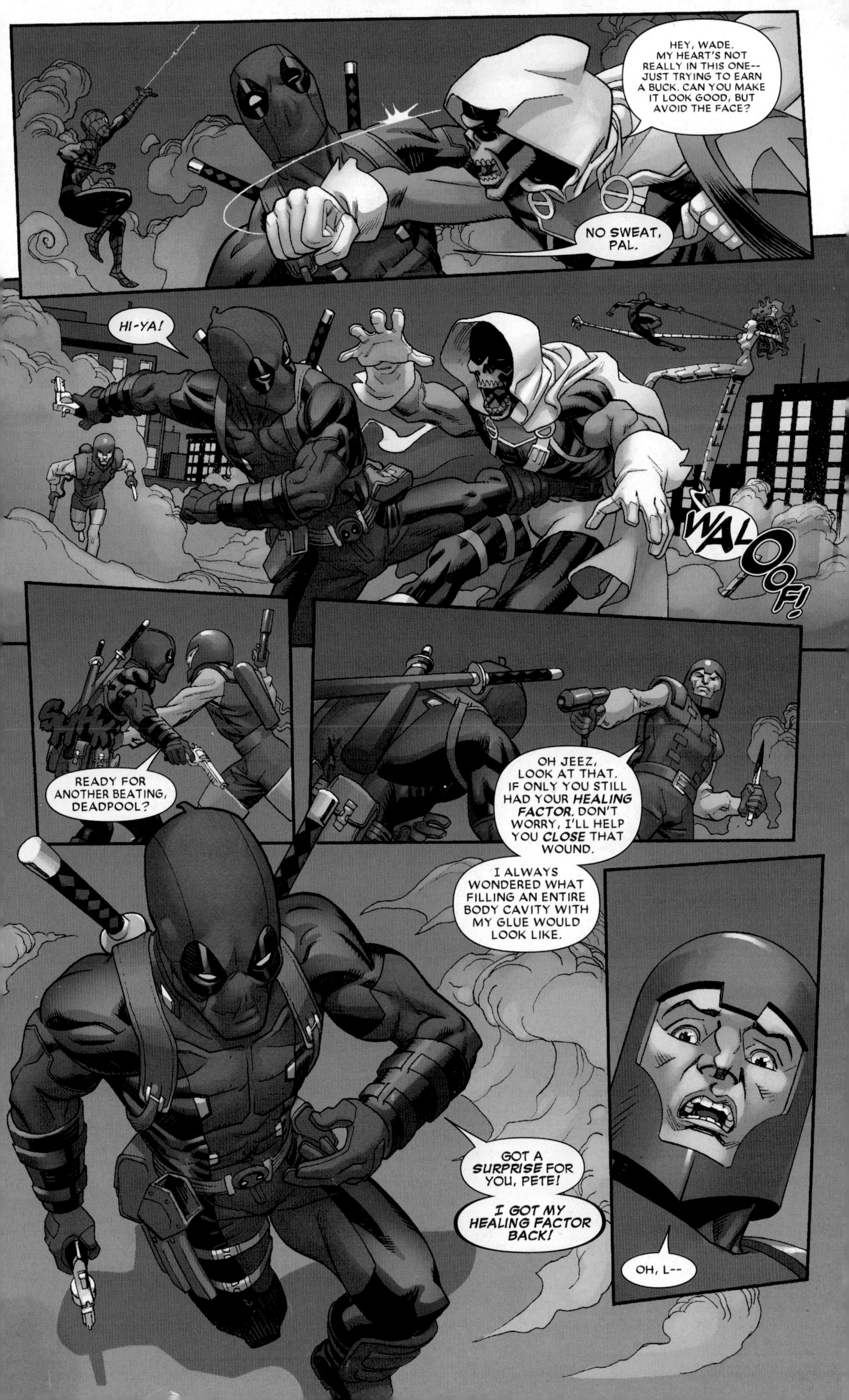

HEY, WADE. MY HEART'S NOT REALLY IN THIS ONE--JUST TRYING TO EARN A BUCK. CAN YOU MAKE IT LOOK GOOD, BUT AVOID THE FACE?
NO SWEAT, PAL.
HI-YA!
WALOOOF!
READY FOR ANOTHER BEATING, DEADPOOL?
OH JEEZ, LOOK AT THAT. IF ONLY YOU STILL HAD YOUR HEALING FACTOR. DON'T WORRY, I'LL HELP YOU CLOSE THAT WOUND.
I ALWAYS WONDERED WHAT FILLING AN ENTIRE BODY CAVITY WITH MY GLUE WOULD LOOK LIKE.
GOT A SURPRISE FOR YOU, PETE!
I GOT MY HEALING FACTOR BACK!
OH, L--

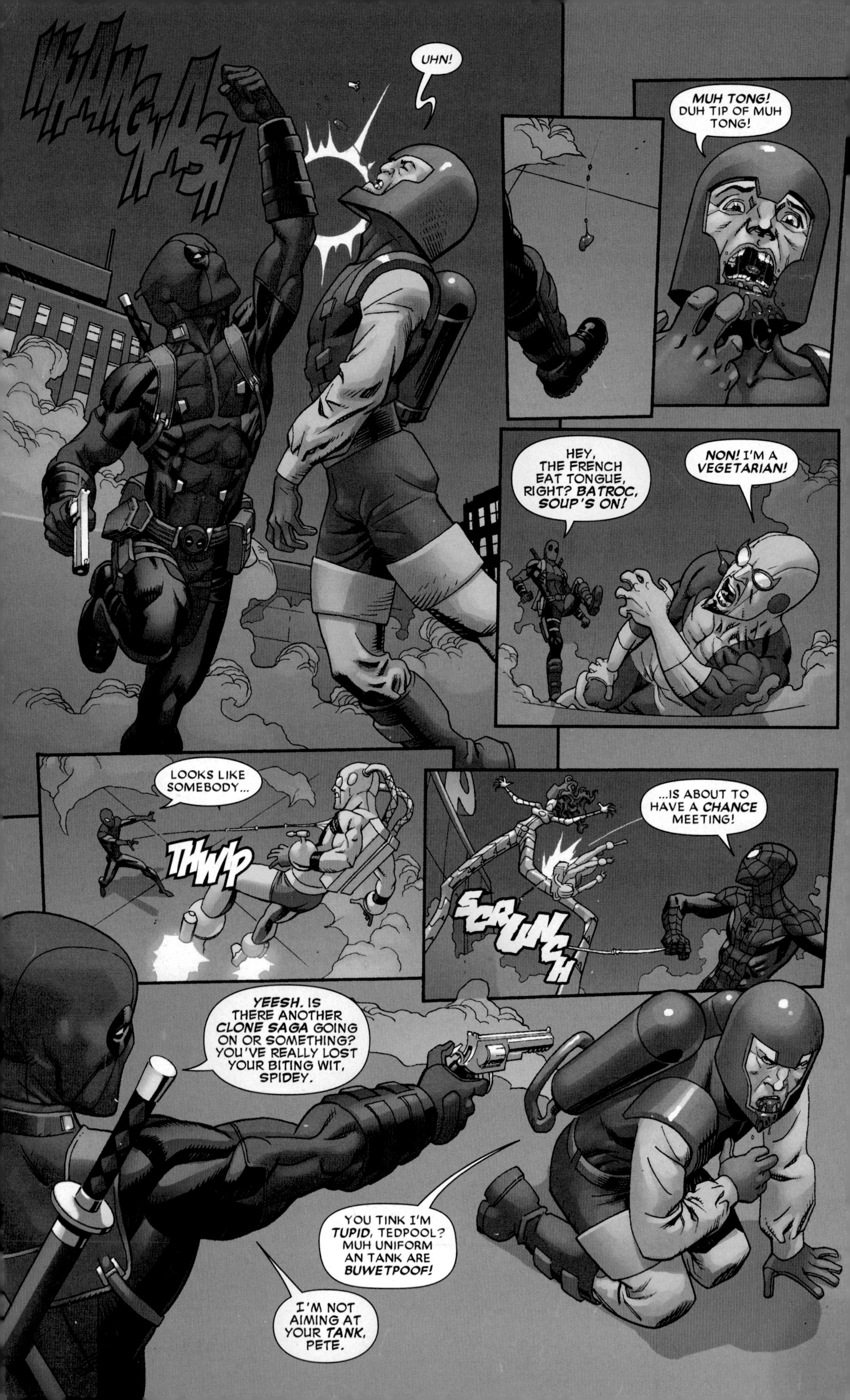
WHAKKAAA-TCH
UHN!
MUH TONG! DUH TIP OF MUH TONG!
HEY, THE FRENCH EAT TONGUE, RIGHT? BATROC, SOUP'S ON!
NON! I'M A VEGETARIAN!
LOOKS LIKE SOMEBODY...
THWIP
...IS ABOUT TO HAVE A CHANCE MEETING!
SCRUNCH
YEESH. IS THERE ANOTHER CLONE SAGA GOING ON OR SOMETHING? YOU'VE REALLY LOST YOUR BITING WIT, SPIDEY.
YOU TINK I'M TUPID, TEDPOOL? MUH UNIFORM AN TANK ARE BUWETPOOF!
I'M NOT AIMING AT YOUR TANK, PETE.

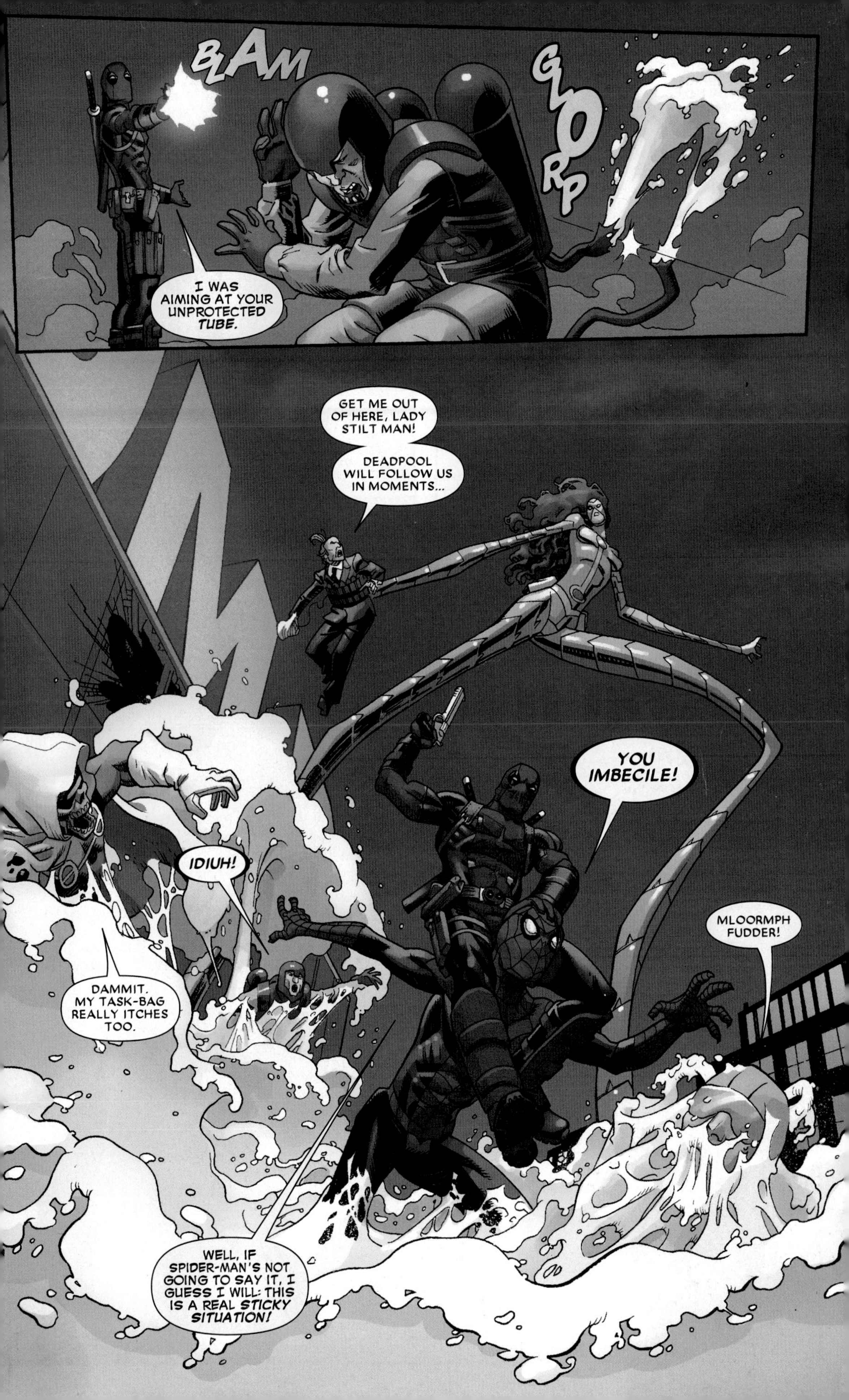
BLAM
GLORP
I WAS AIMING AT YOUR UNPROTECTED TUBE.
GET ME OUT OF HERE, LADY STILT MAN!
DEADPOOL WILL FOLLOW US IN MOMENTS...
YOU IMBECILE!
IDIUH!
MLOORMPH FUDDER!
DAMMIT. MY TASK-BAG REALLY ITCHES TOO.
WELL, IF SPIDER-MAN'S NOT GOING TO SAY IT, I GUESS I WILL: THIS IS A REAL STICKY SITUATION!

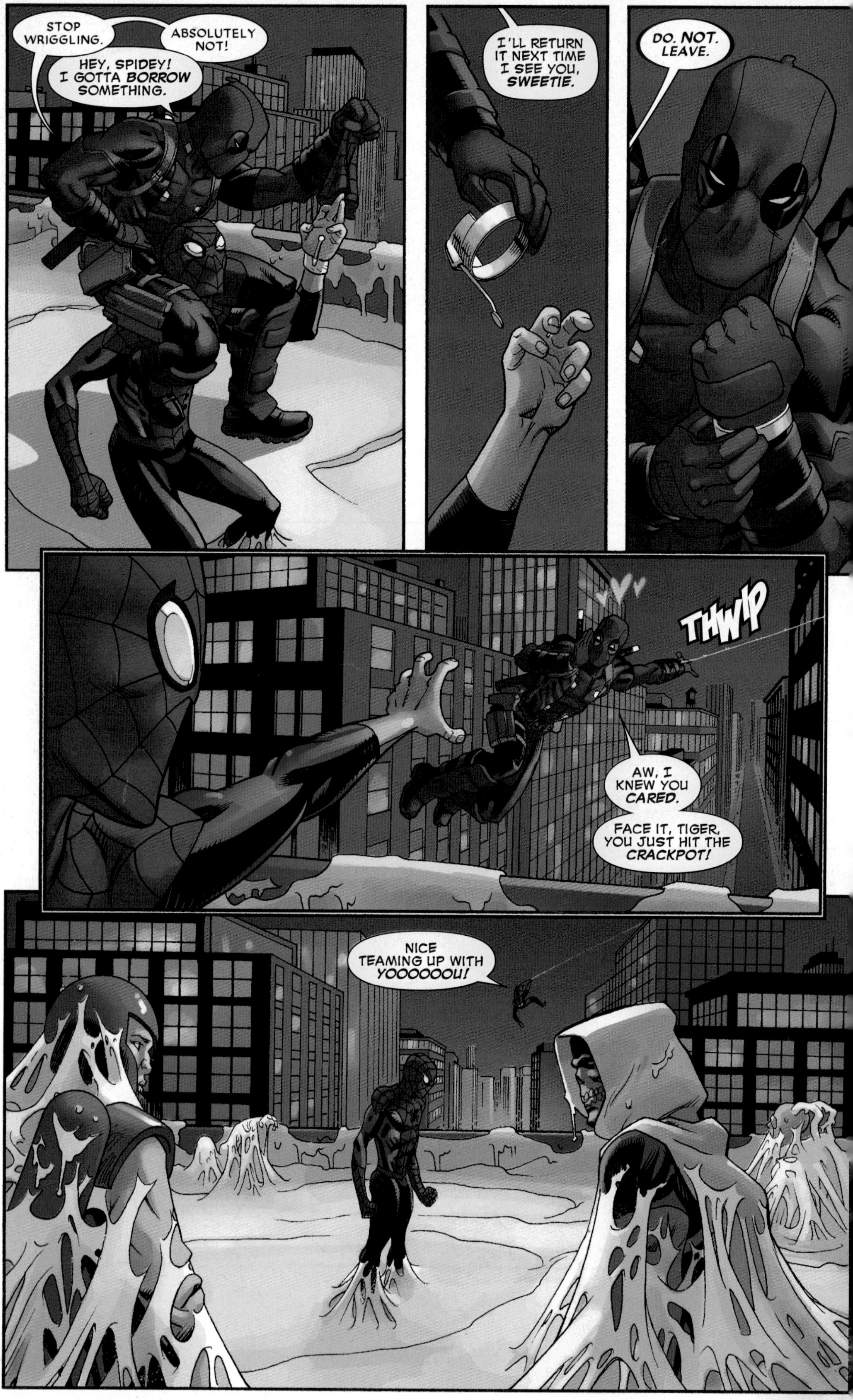

HEY, SPIDEY! I GOTTA BORROW SOMETHING.
STOP WRIGGLING.
ABSOLUTELY NOT!
I'LL RETURN IT NEXT TIME I SEE YOU, SWEETIE.
DO. NOT. LEAVE.
THWIP
AW, I KNEW YOU CARED.
FACE IT, TIGER, YOU JUST HIT THE CRACKPOT!
NICE TEAMING UP WITH YOOOOOOU!

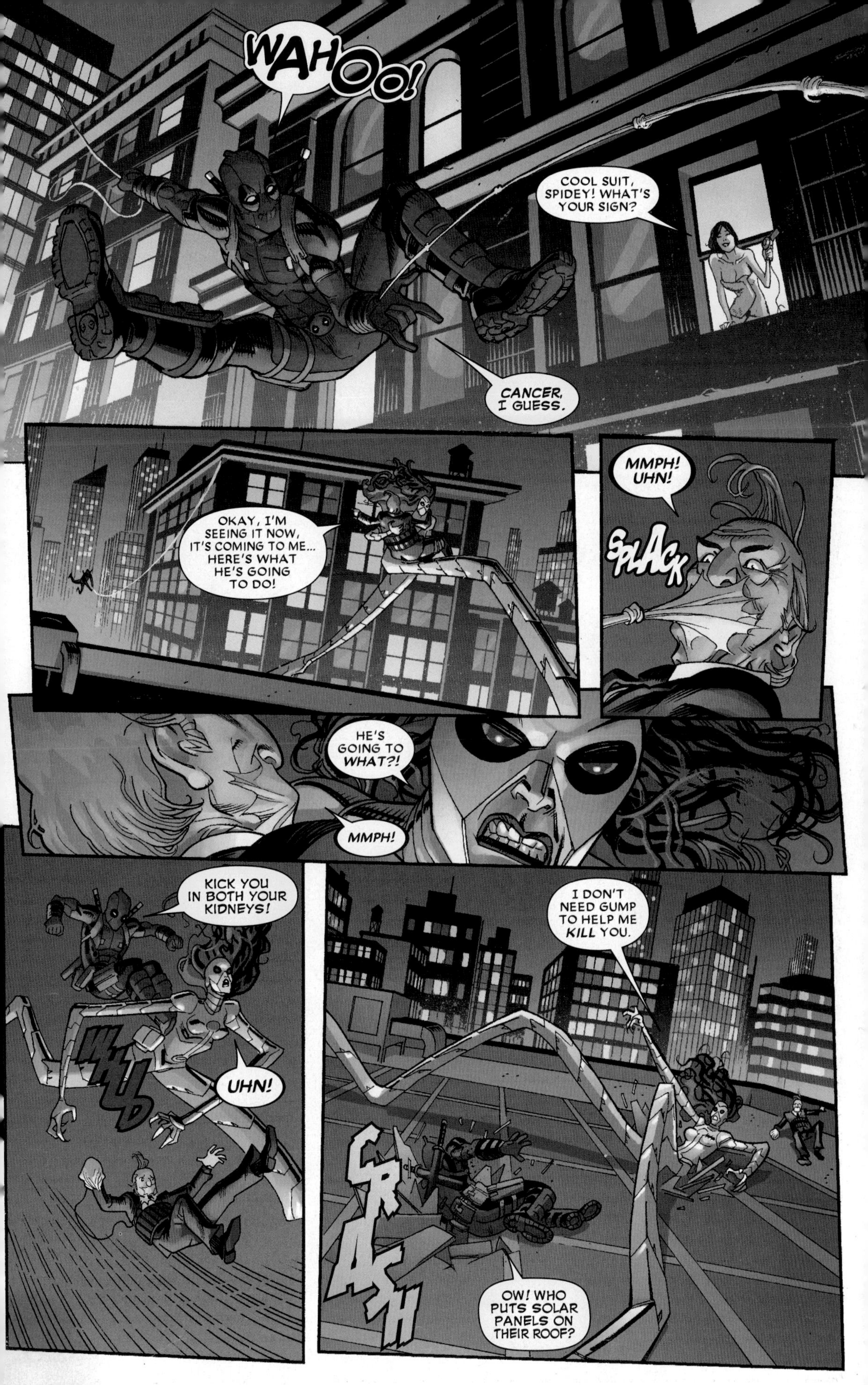
WAHOO!
COOL SUIT, SPIDEY! WHAT'S YOUR SIGN?
CANCER, I GUESS.
OKAY, I'M SEEING IT NOW, IT'S COMING TO ME... HERE'S WHAT HE'S GOING TO DO!
MMPH! UHN!
SPLACK
HE'S GOING TO WHAT?!
MMPH!
KICK YOU IN BOTH YOUR KIDNEYS!
UHN!
I DON'T NEED GUMP TO HELP ME KILL YOU.
CRASH
OW! WHO PUTS SOLAR PANELS ON THEIR ROOF?

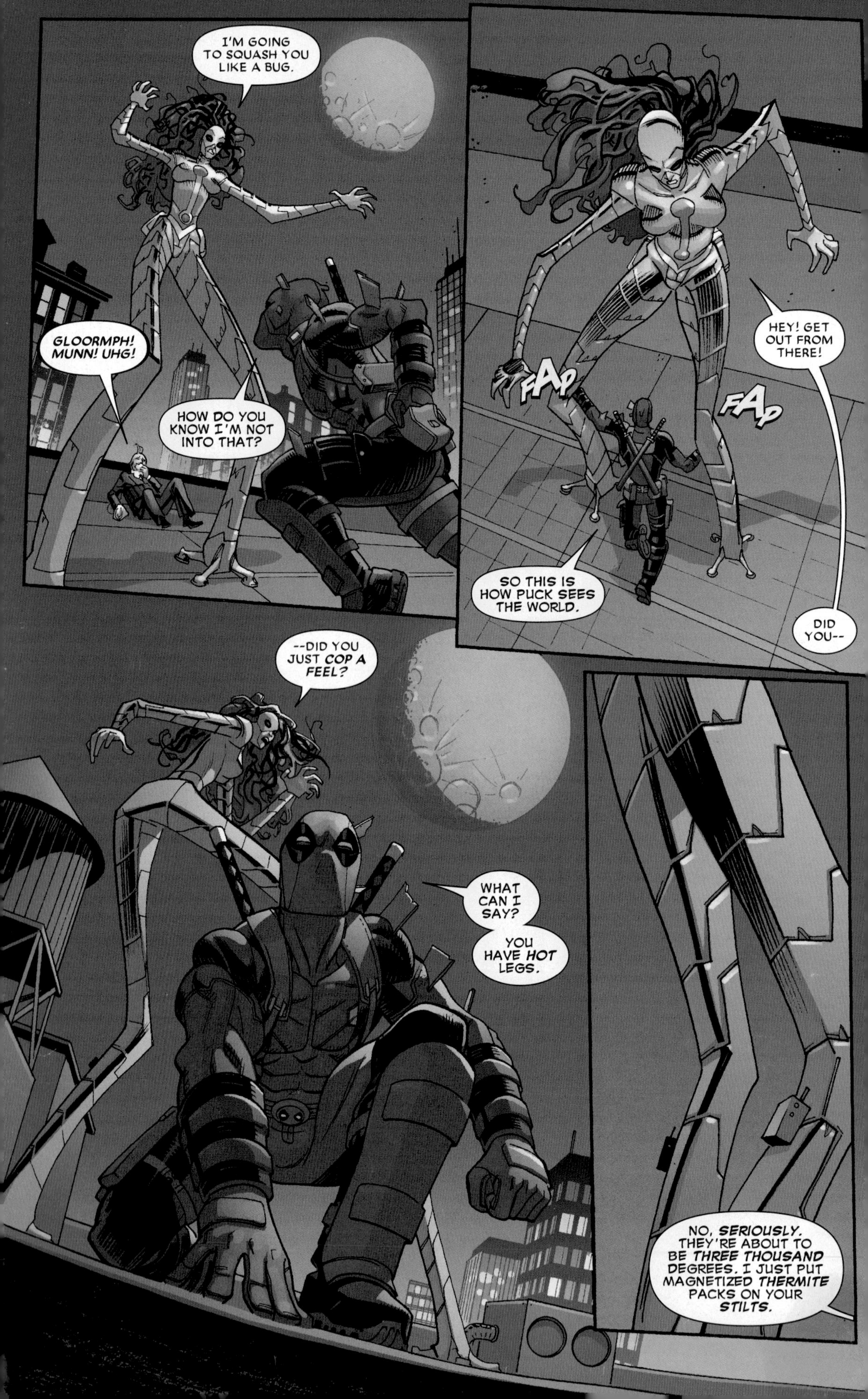
I'M GOING TO SQUASH YOU LIKE A BUG.
GLOORMPH! MUNN! UHG!
HOW DO YOU KNOW I'M NOT INTO THAT?
FAP
FAP
SO THIS IS HOW PUCK SEES THE WORLD.
HEY! GET OUT FROM THERE!
DID YOU--
--DID YOU JUST COP A FEEL?
WHAT CAN I SAY?
YOU HAVE HOT LEGS.
NO, SERIOUSLY. THEY'RE ABOUT TO BE THREE THOUSAND DEGREES. I JUST PUT MAGNETIZED THERMITE PACKS ON YOUR STILTS.

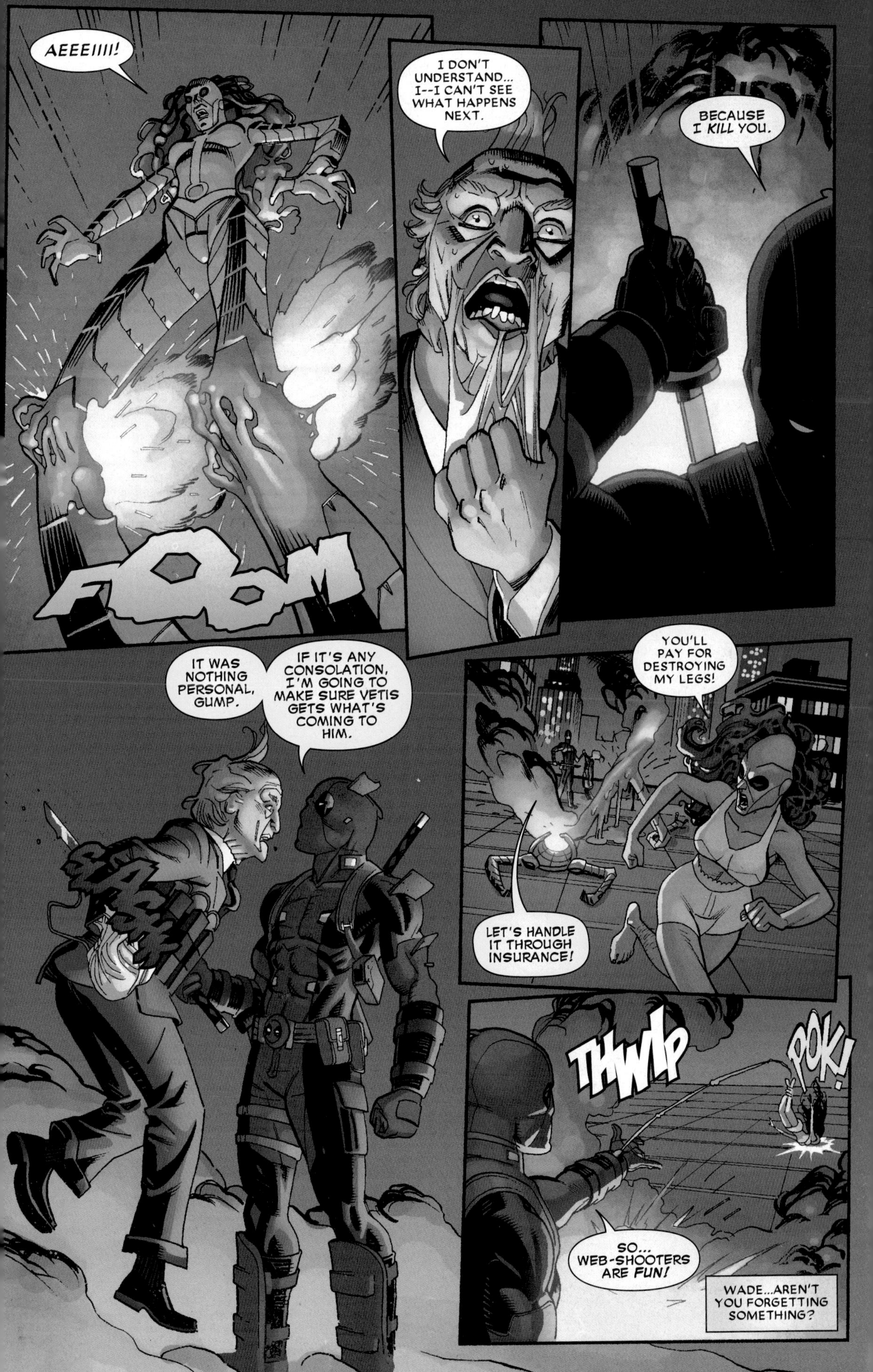
AEEEIIII!
FOOM
I DON'T UNDERSTAND... I--I CAN'T SEE WHAT HAPPENS NEXT.
BECAUSE I KILL YOU.
IT WAS NOTHING PERSONAL, GUMP.
IF IT'S ANY CONSOLATION, I'M GOING TO MAKE SURE VETIS GETS WHAT'S COMING TO HIM.
YOU'LL PAY FOR DESTROYING MY LEGS!
LET'S HANDLE IT THROUGH INSURANCE!
THWIP
POK!
SO... WEB-SHOOTERS ARE FUN!
WADE...AREN'T YOU FORGETTING SOMETHING?

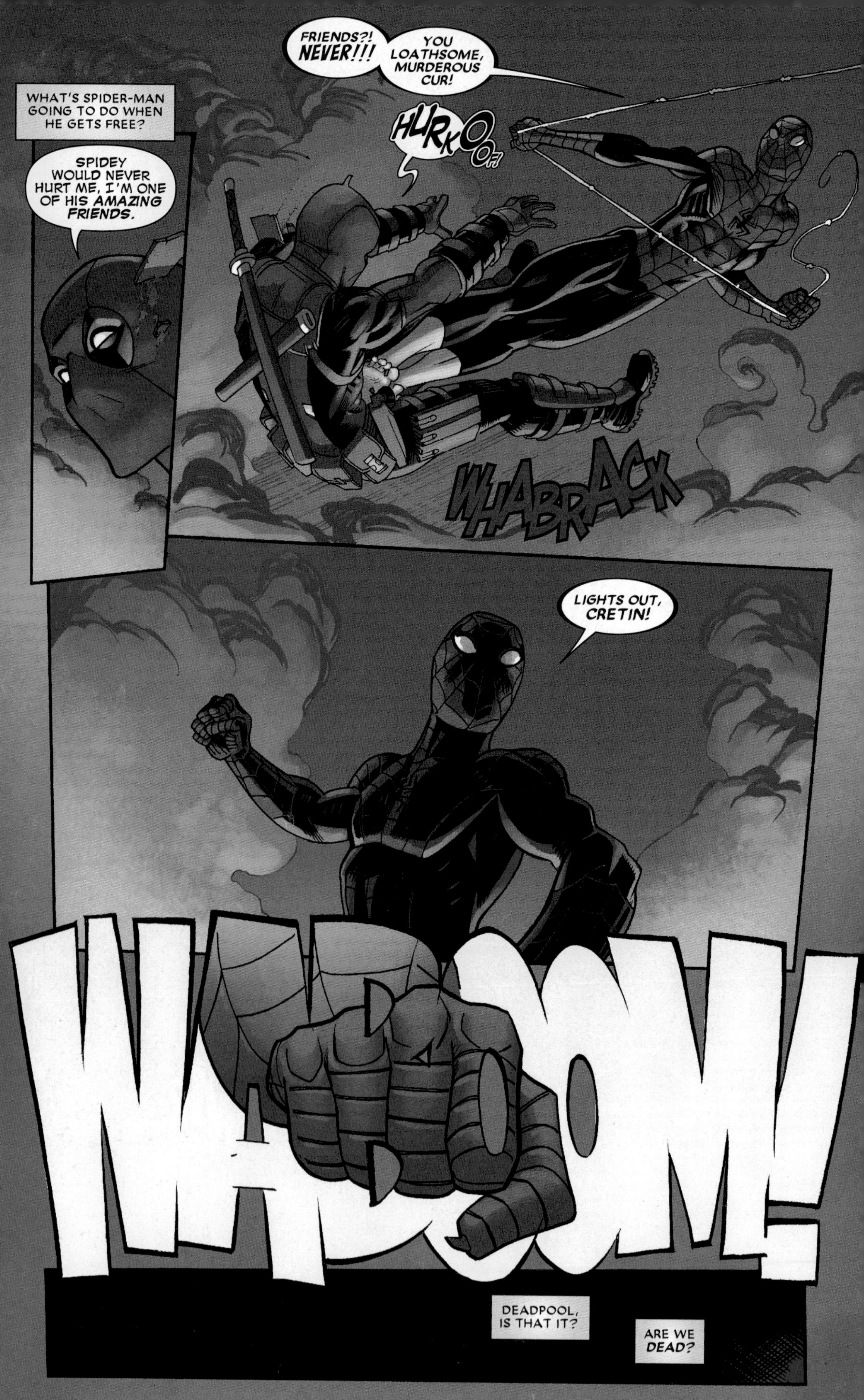

FRIENDS?! NEVER!!!
YOU LOATHSOME, MURDEROUS CUR!
WHAT'S SPIDER-MAN GOING TO DO WHEN HE GETS FREE?
SPIDEY WOULD NEVER HURT ME, I'M ONE OF HIS AMAZING FRIENDS.
HURK
OOF!
WHABRACK
LIGHTS OUT, CRETIN!
DEADPOOL, IS THAT IT?
ARE WE DEAD?

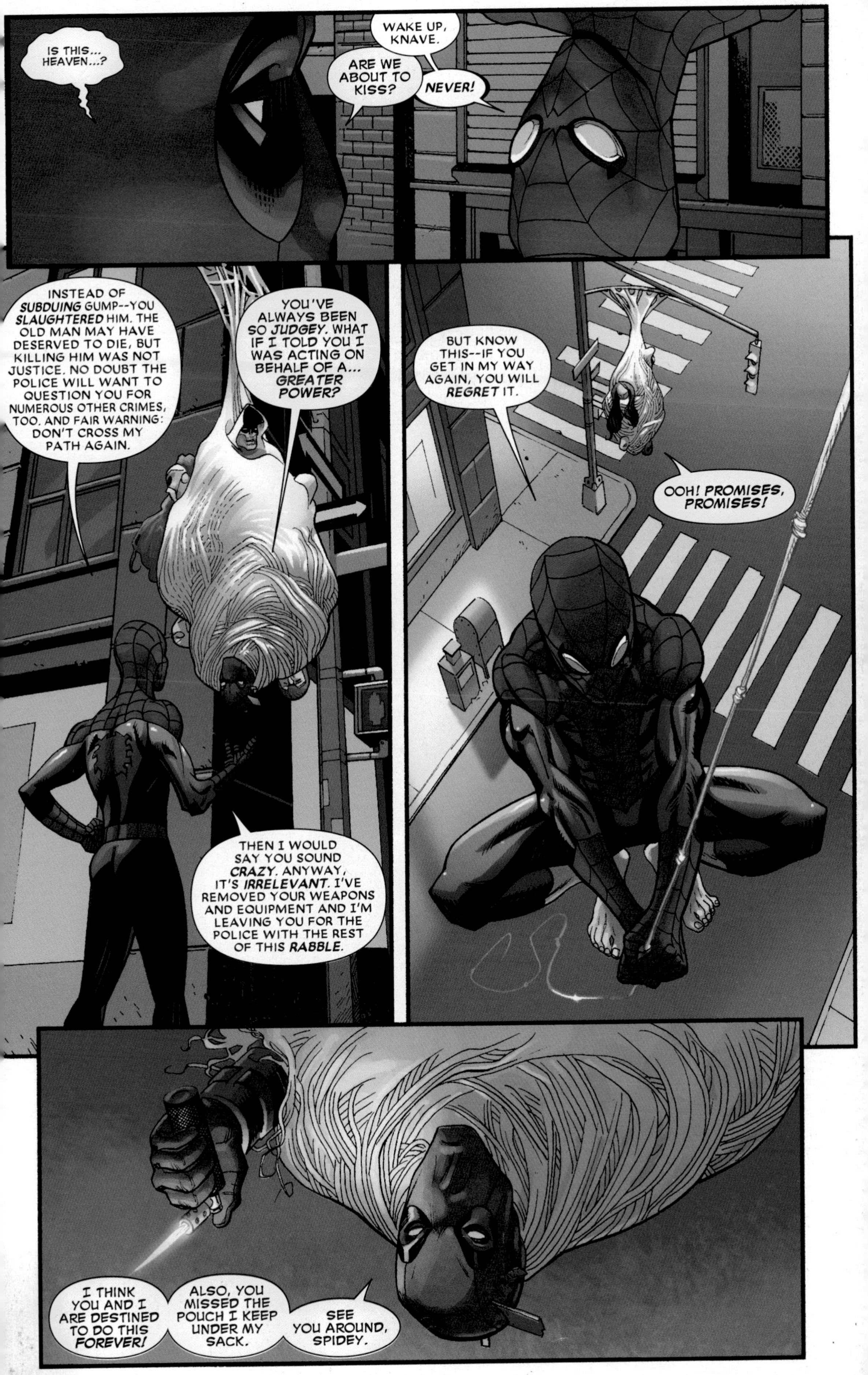
IS THIS... HEAVEN...?
WAKE UP, KNAVE.
ARE WE ABOUT TO KISS?
NEVER!
INSTEAD OF SUBDUING GUMP--YOU SLAUGHTERED HIM. THE OLD MAN MAY HAVE DESERVED TO DIE, BUT KILLING HIM WAS NOT JUSTICE. NO DOUBT THE POLICE WILL WANT TO QUESTION YOU FOR NUMEROUS OTHER CRIMES, TOO. AND FAIR WARNING: DON'T CROSS MY PATH AGAIN.
YOU'VE ALWAYS BEEN SO JUDGEY. WHAT IF I TOLD YOU I WAS ACTING ON BEHALF OF A... GREATER POWER?
THEN I WOULD SAY YOU SOUND CRAZY. ANYWAY, IT'S IRRELEVANT. I'VE REMOVED YOUR WEAPONS AND EQUIPMENT AND I'M LEAVING YOU FOR THE POLICE WITH THE REST OF THIS RABBLE.
BUT KNOW THIS--IF YOU GET IN MY WAY AGAIN, YOU WILL REGRET IT.
OOH! PROMISES, PROMISES!
I THINK YOU AND I ARE DESTINED TO DO THIS FOREVER!
ALSO, YOU MISSED THE POUCH I KEEP UNDER MY SACK.
SEE YOU AROUND, SPIDEY.

And now Peter Parker's back in charge of his brain! The magic of comics, everyone!

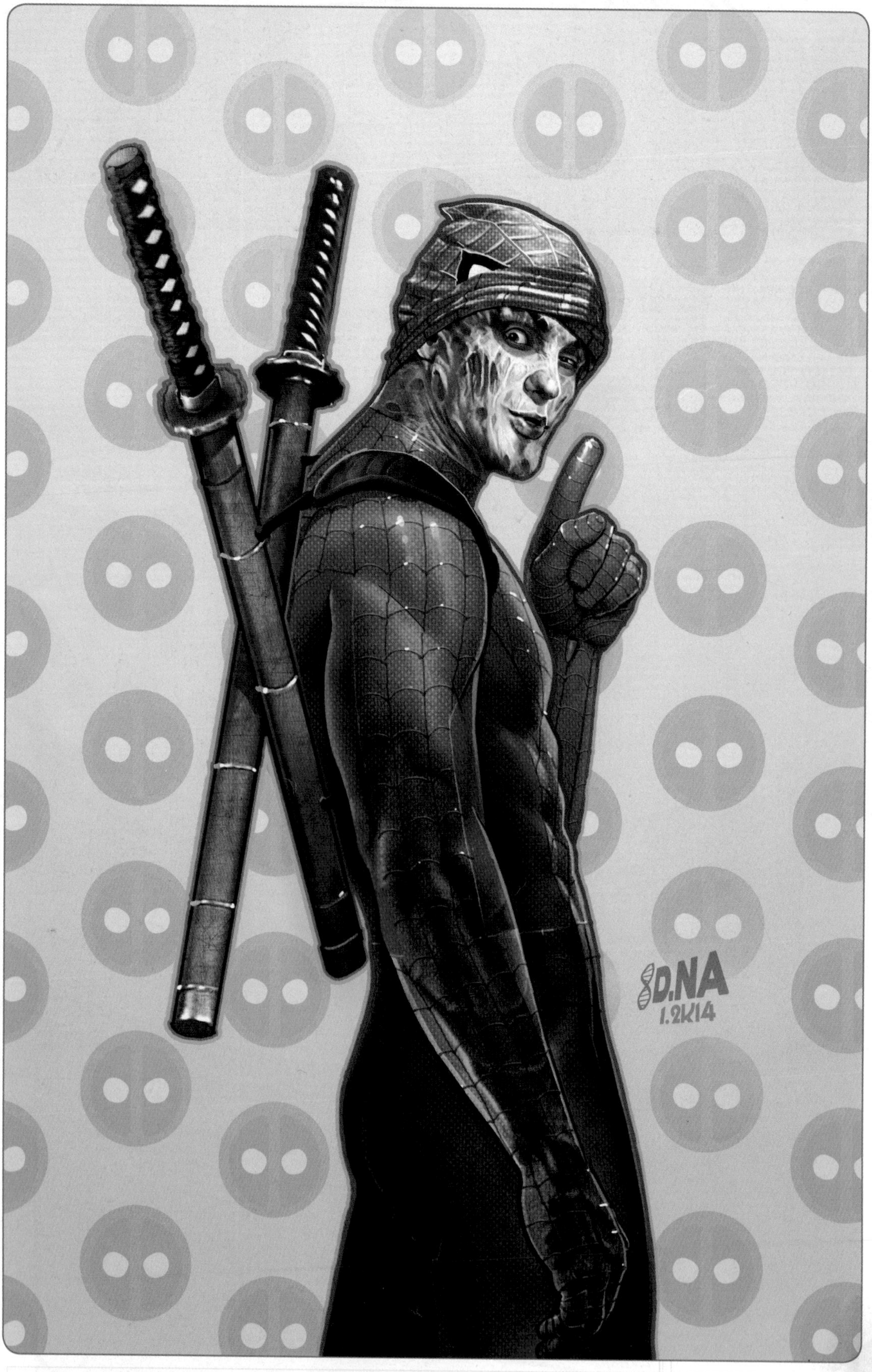
D.NA
1.2K14

DEADPOOL ANNUAL #2

Possibly the world's most skilled mercenary, definitely the world's most annoying, Wade Wilson was chosen for a top-secret government program that gave him a healing factor allowing him to heal from any wound. Now, Wade makes his way as a gun for hire, shooting his prey's faces off while talking his friends' ears off. Call him the Merc with the Mouth...call him the Regeneratin' Degenerate...call him...

DEADPOOL

HEY THERE, FRIENDS! MY NAME IS *DEADPOOL*--THE *MERC* WITH THE *MOUTH!*

I AM, LIKE...A *MERCENARY.* I ALSO HAVE A *MOUTH.* BUT LIKE... DON'T MOST MERCENARIES? I LIKE TO USE MINE TO SPOUT A CONSTANT STREAM OF *JOKES.* AND EAT *CHIMICHANGAS.* ALSO, I HAVE A *HEALING FACTOR*--WHICH I *ALSO* USE TO EAT *CHIMICHANGAS.*

YOU MAY KNOW ME FROM ME BEING YOUR FAVORITE CHARACTER IN *ULTIMATE ALLIANCE.*

THE GOOD NEWS IS THAT'S ALL YOU NEED TO KNOW TO ENJOY THIS ISSUE-- THAT I *EXIST!*

OH, EXCEPT... THERE IS THIS OTHER OBSCURE CHARACTER, *"SPIDER-MAN,"* THAT I SHOULD PROBABLY TELL YOU ABOUT. HE GOT BIT BY A *RADIOACTIVE SPIDER* A WHILE BACK, AND IT GAVE HIM THE PROPORTIONAL *SPEED* AND *STRENGTH* OF A SPIDER, AS WELL AS AN AMAZING *SPIDER-SENSE* TO WARN HIM OF DANGER!

PLUS, HE'S PRETTY SMART, AND HE MADE THESE MECHANICAL *"WEB-SHOOTERS"* THAT LET HIM SWING AROUND THE CITY!

AND FOR SOME REASON, PEOPLE DON'T LIKE HIM.

WELL, EXCEPT *ME.* I LIKE HIM JUST *FINE.*

LI'L DEADPOOL ART BY
IRENE Y. LEE

SPIDEYPOOL

Christopher Hastings
writer

Jacopo Camagni
artist

Matt Milla
colorist

VC's Joe Sabino
letterer

David Nakayama
cover artists

Frankie Johnson
assistant editor

Jordan D. White
editor

Mike Marts
X-Men group editor

Axel Alonso
editor in chief

Joe Quesada
chief creative officer

Dan Buckley
publisher

Alan Fine
executive producer

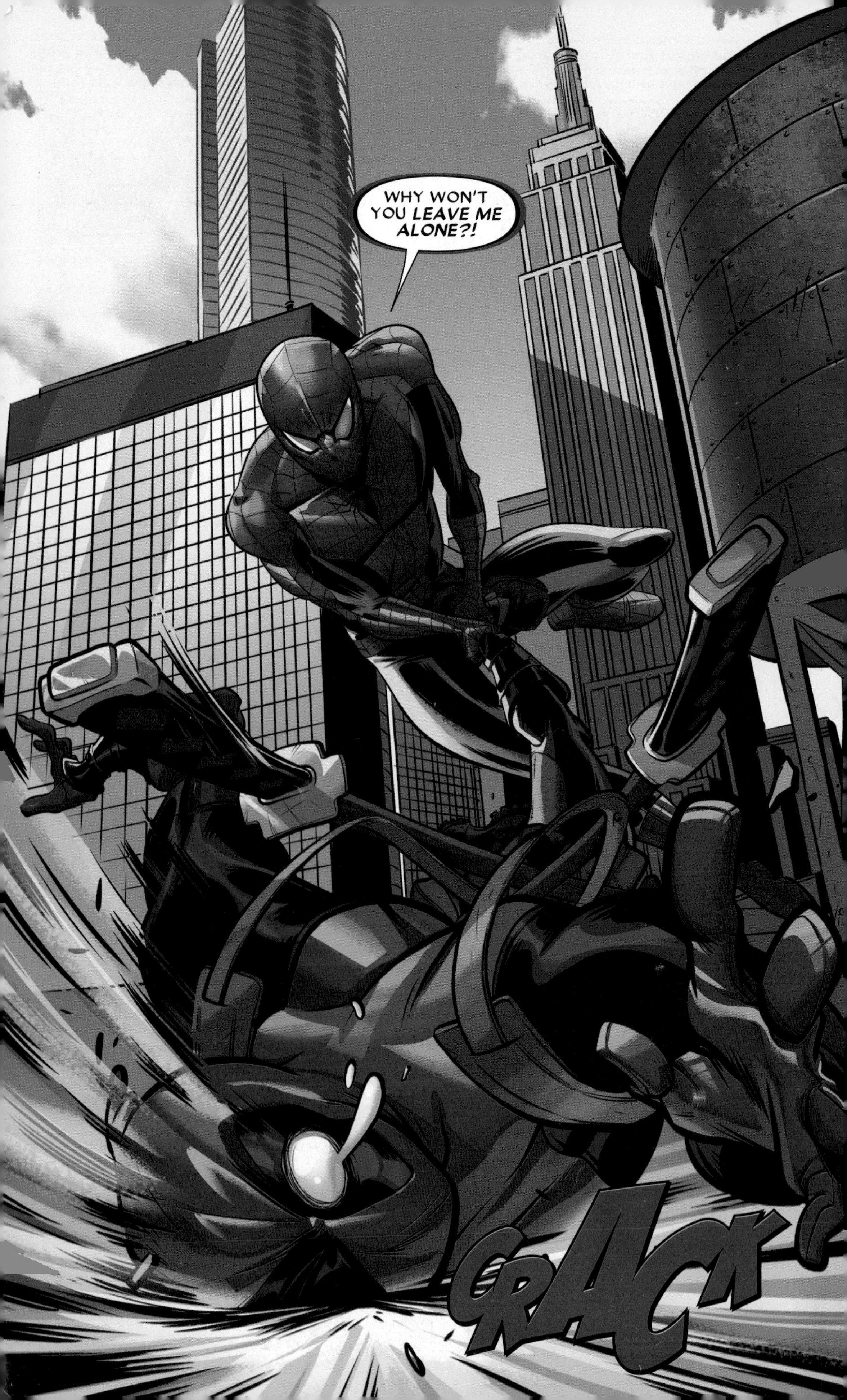
WHY WON'T YOU *LEAVE ME ALONE?!*
CRACK

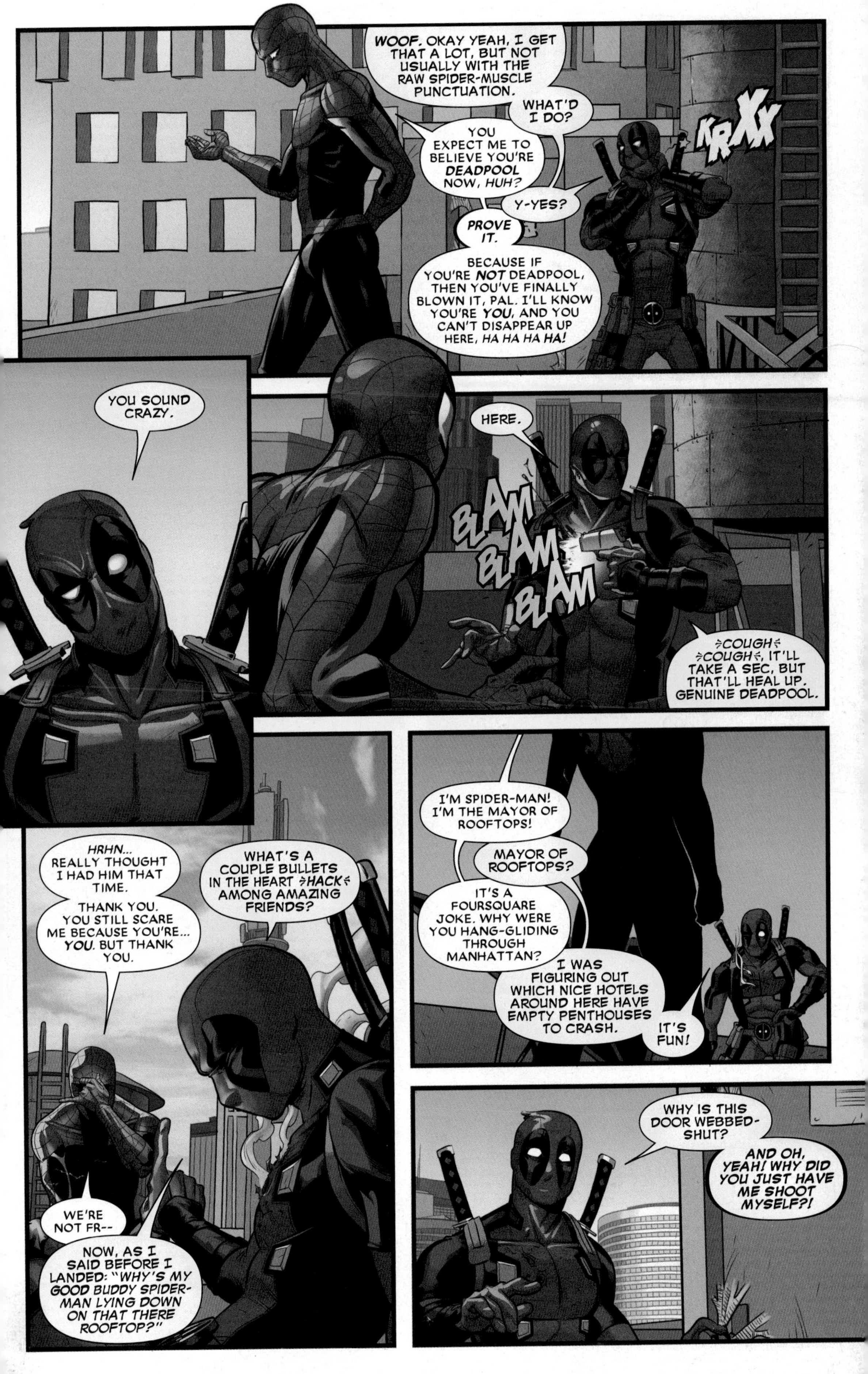
WOOF. OKAY YEAH, I GET THAT A LOT, BUT NOT USUALLY WITH THE RAW SPIDER-MUSCLE PUNCTUATION.
KRXX
WHAT'D I DO?
YOU EXPECT ME TO BELIEVE YOU'RE DEADPOOL NOW, HUH?
Y-YES?
PROVE IT.
BECAUSE IF YOU'RE NOT DEADPOOL, THEN YOU'VE FINALLY BLOWN IT, PAL. I'LL KNOW YOU'RE YOU, AND YOU CAN'T DISAPPEAR UP HERE, HA HA HA HA!
YOU SOUND CRAZY.
HERE.
BLAM BLAM BLAM
COUGH *COUGH*, IT'LL TAKE A SEC, BUT THAT'LL HEAL UP. GENUINE DEADPOOL.
HRHN... REALLY THOUGHT I HAD HIM THAT TIME.
THANK YOU. YOU STILL SCARE ME BECAUSE YOU'RE... YOU. BUT THANK YOU.
WHAT'S A COUPLE BULLETS IN THE HEART *HACK* AMONG AMAZING FRIENDS?
WE'RE NOT FR--
NOW, AS I SAID BEFORE I LANDED: "WHY'S MY GOOD BUDDY SPIDER-MAN LYING DOWN ON THAT THERE ROOFTOP?"
I'M SPIDER-MAN! I'M THE MAYOR OF ROOFTOPS!
MAYOR OF ROOFTOPS?
IT'S A FOURSQUARE JOKE. WHY WERE YOU HANG-GLIDING THROUGH MANHATTAN?
I WAS FIGURING OUT WHICH NICE HOTELS AROUND HERE HAVE EMPTY PENTHOUSES TO CRASH.
IT'S FUN!
WHY IS THIS DOOR WEBBED-SHUT?
AND OH, YEAH! WHY DID YOU JUST HAVE ME SHOOT MYSELF?!

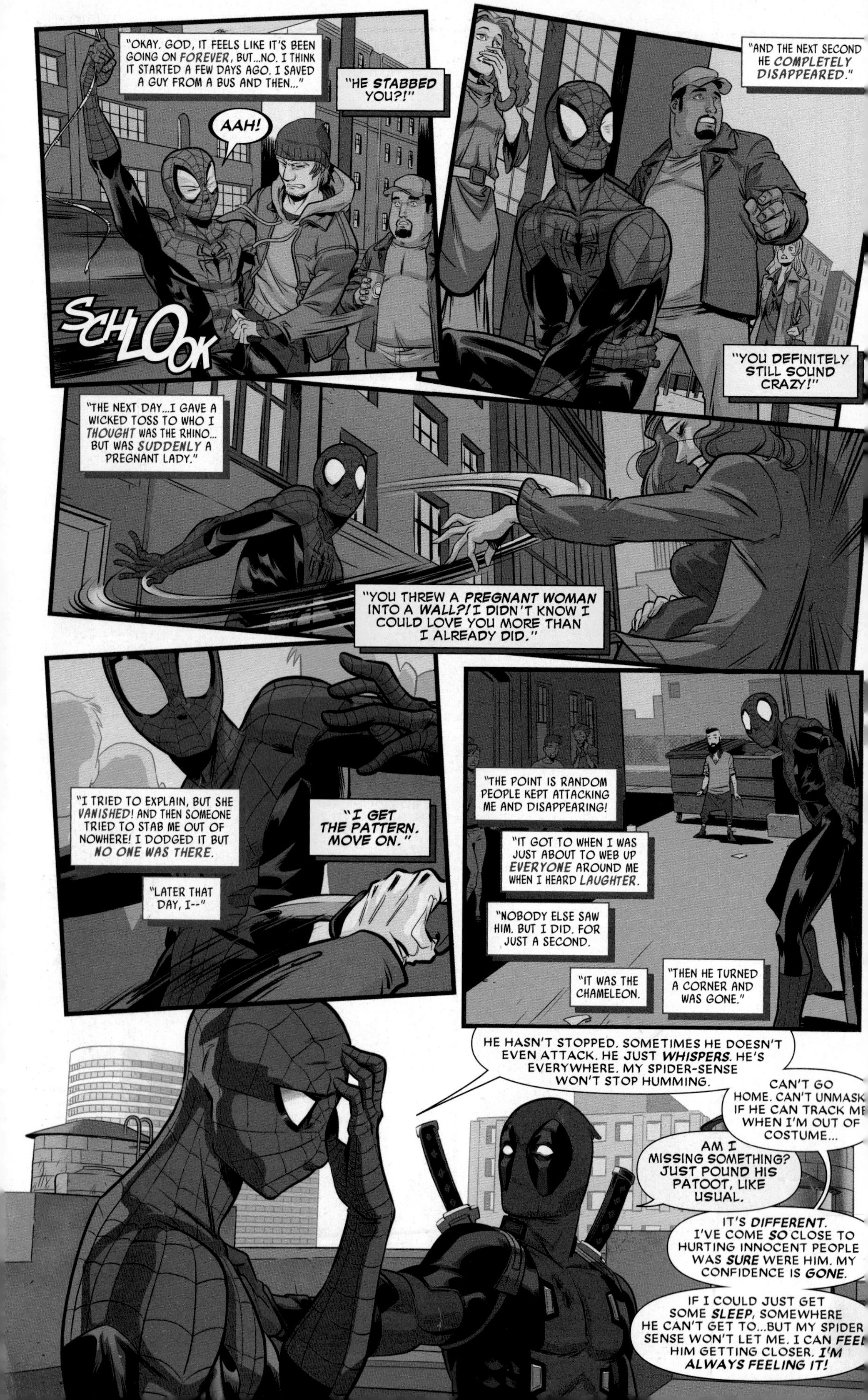
"OKAY. GOD, IT FEELS LIKE IT'S BEEN GOING ON FOREVER, BUT...NO. I THINK IT STARTED A FEW DAYS AGO. I SAVED A GUY FROM A BUS AND THEN..."
"HE STABBED YOU?!"
AAH!
SCHLOOK
"AND THE NEXT SECOND HE COMPLETELY DISAPPEARED."
"YOU DEFINITELY STILL SOUND CRAZY!"
"THE NEXT DAY...I GAVE A WICKED TOSS TO WHO I THOUGHT WAS THE RHINO... BUT WAS SUDDENLY A PREGNANT LADY."
"YOU THREW A PREGNANT WOMAN INTO A WALL?! I DIDN'T KNOW I COULD LOVE YOU MORE THAN I ALREADY DID."
"I TRIED TO EXPLAIN, BUT SHE VANISHED! AND THEN SOMEONE TRIED TO STAB ME OUT OF NOWHERE! I DODGED IT BUT NO ONE WAS THERE.
"LATER THAT DAY, I--"
"I GET THE PATTERN. MOVE ON."
"THE POINT IS RANDOM PEOPLE KEPT ATTACKING ME AND DISAPPEARING!
"IT GOT TO WHEN I WAS JUST ABOUT TO WEB UP EVERYONE AROUND ME WHEN I HEARD LAUGHTER.
"NOBODY ELSE SAW HIM. BUT I DID. FOR JUST A SECOND.
"IT WAS THE CHAMELEON.
"THEN HE TURNED A CORNER AND WAS GONE."
HE HASN'T STOPPED. SOMETIMES HE DOESN'T EVEN ATTACK. HE JUST WHISPERS. HE'S EVERYWHERE. MY SPIDER-SENSE WON'T STOP HUMMING.
CAN'T GO HOME. CAN'T UNMASK IF HE CAN TRACK ME WHEN I'M OUT OF COSTUME...
AM I MISSING SOMETHING? JUST POUND HIS PATOOT, LIKE USUAL.
IT'S DIFFERENT. I'VE COME SO CLOSE TO HURTING INNOCENT PEOPLE I WAS SURE WERE HIM. MY CONFIDENCE IS GONE.
IF I COULD JUST GET SOME SLEEP, SOMEWHERE HE CAN'T GET TO...BUT MY SPIDER SENSE WON'T LET ME. I CAN FEEL HIM GETTING CLOSER. I'M ALWAYS FEELING IT!

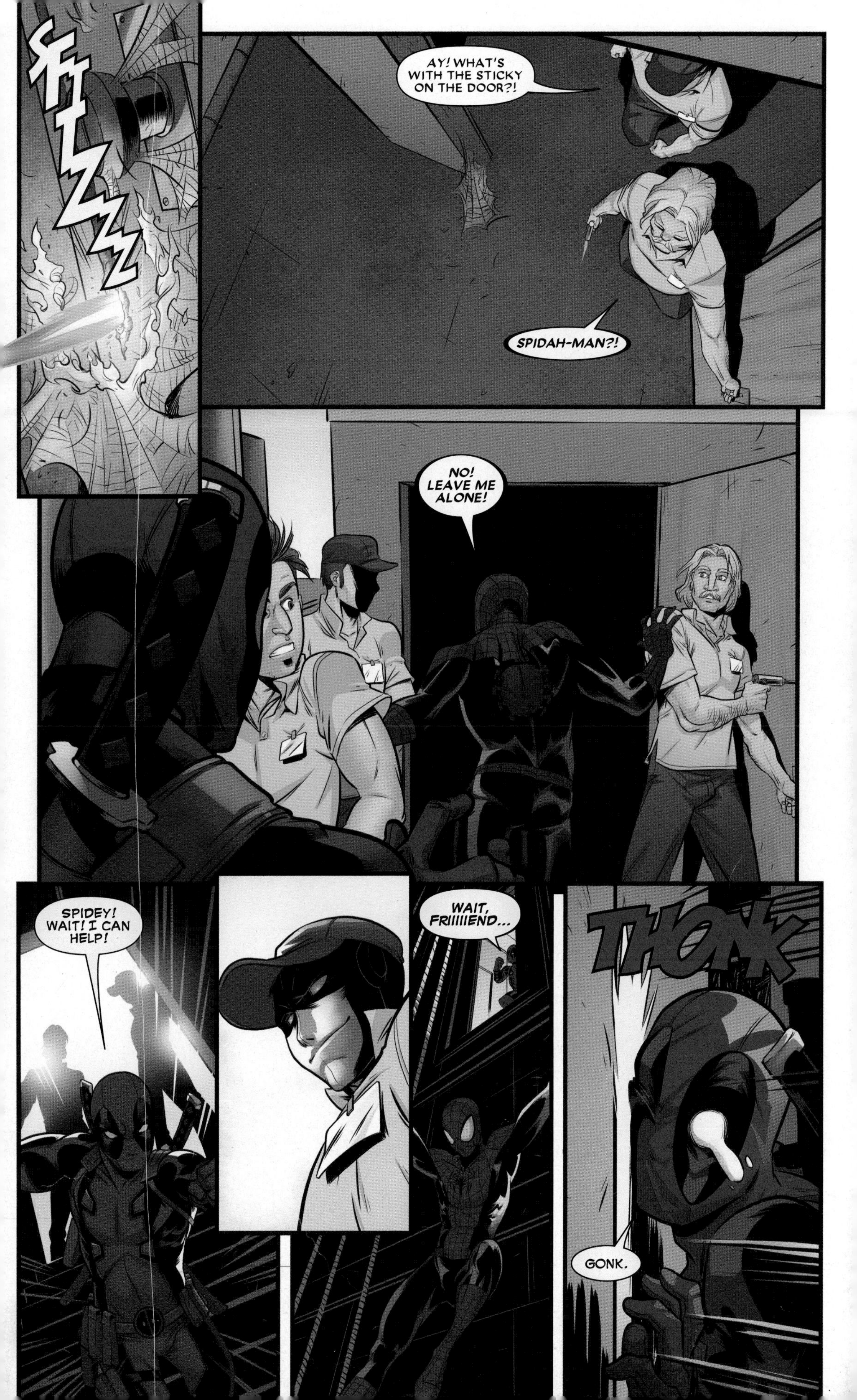
SFTTZZZZ
AY! WHAT'S WITH THE STICKY ON THE DOOR?!
SPIDAH-MAN?!
NO! LEAVE ME ALONE!
SPIDEY! WAIT! I CAN HELP!
WAIT, FRIIIIIEND...
THONK
GONK.

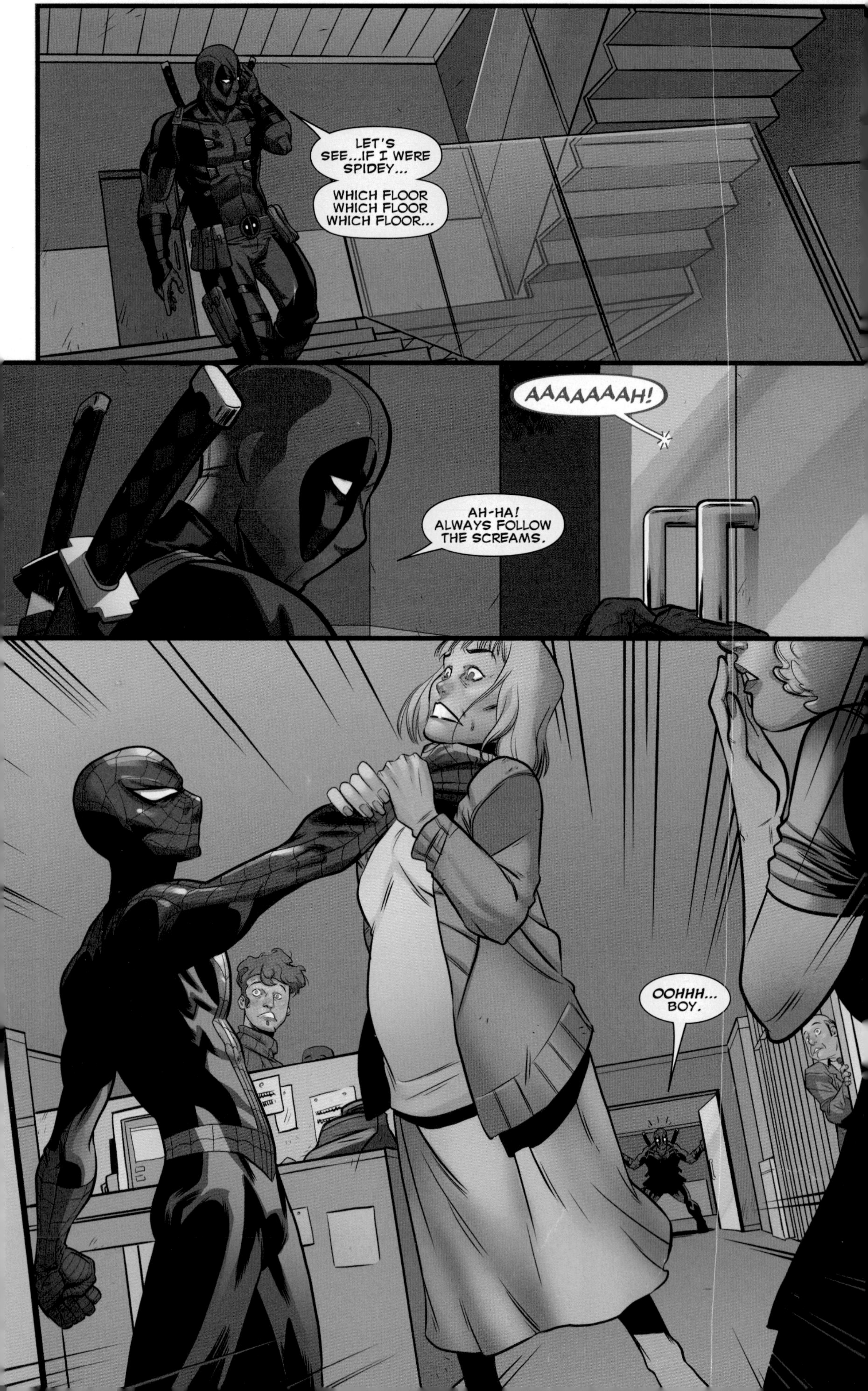
LET'S SEE...IF I WERE SPIDEY...
WHICH FLOOR WHICH FLOOR WHICH FLOOR...
AAAAAAAH!
AH-HA! ALWAYS FOLLOW THE SCREAMS.
OOHHH... BOY.

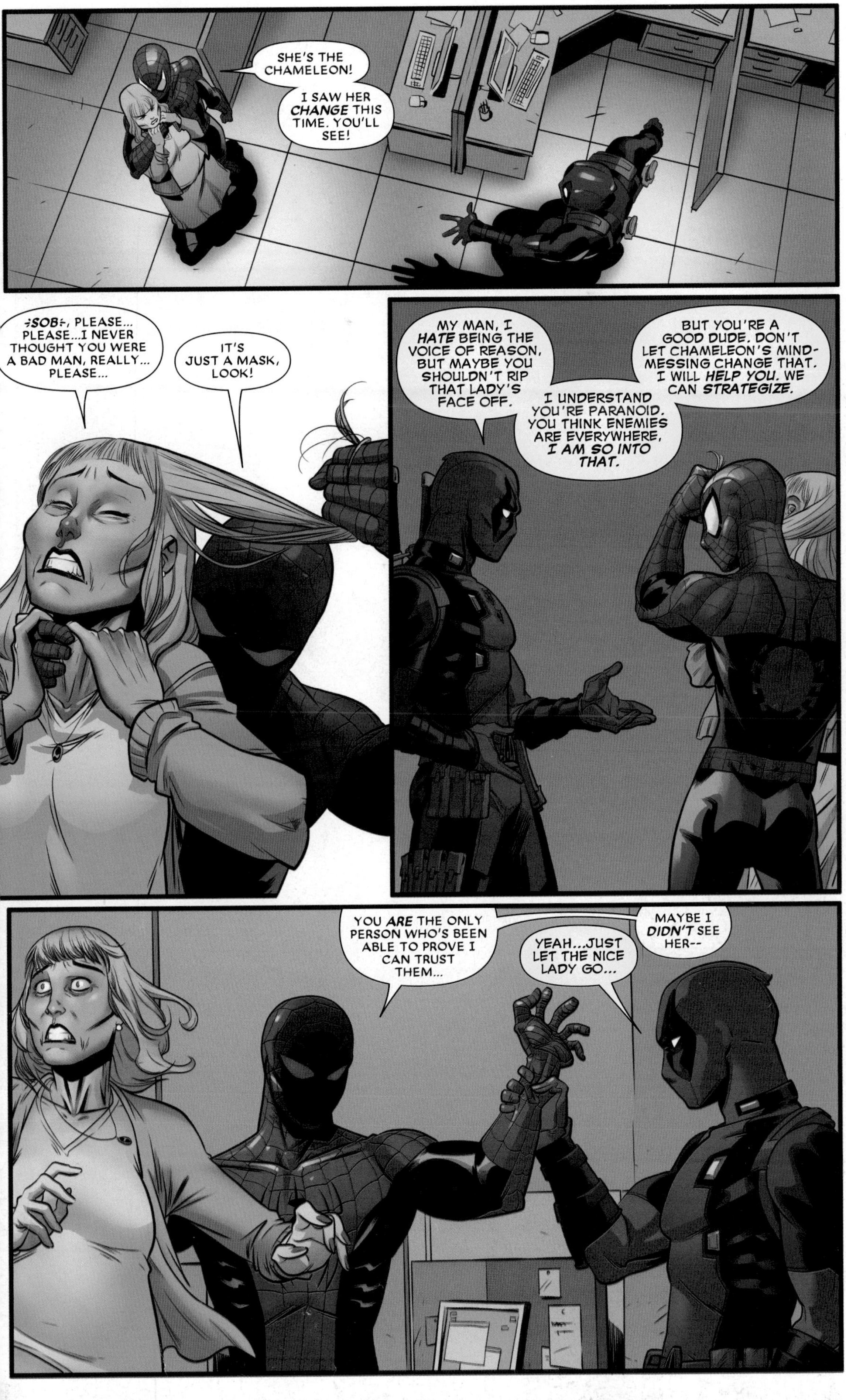
SHE'S THE CHAMELEON!
I SAW HER CHANGE THIS TIME. YOU'LL SEE!
-SOB-, PLEASE... PLEASE...I NEVER THOUGHT YOU WERE A BAD MAN, REALLY... PLEASE...
IT'S JUST A MASK, LOOK!
MY MAN, I HATE BEING THE VOICE OF REASON, BUT MAYBE YOU SHOULDN'T RIP THAT LADY'S FACE OFF.
I UNDERSTAND YOU'RE PARANOID. YOU THINK ENEMIES ARE EVERYWHERE, I AM SO INTO THAT.
BUT YOU'RE A GOOD DUDE. DON'T LET CHAMELEON'S MIND-MESSING CHANGE THAT. I WILL HELP YOU. WE CAN STRATEGIZE.
YOU ARE THE ONLY PERSON WHO'S BEEN ABLE TO PROVE I CAN TRUST THEM...
MAYBE I DIDN'T SEE HER--
YEAH...JUST LET THE NICE LADY GO...

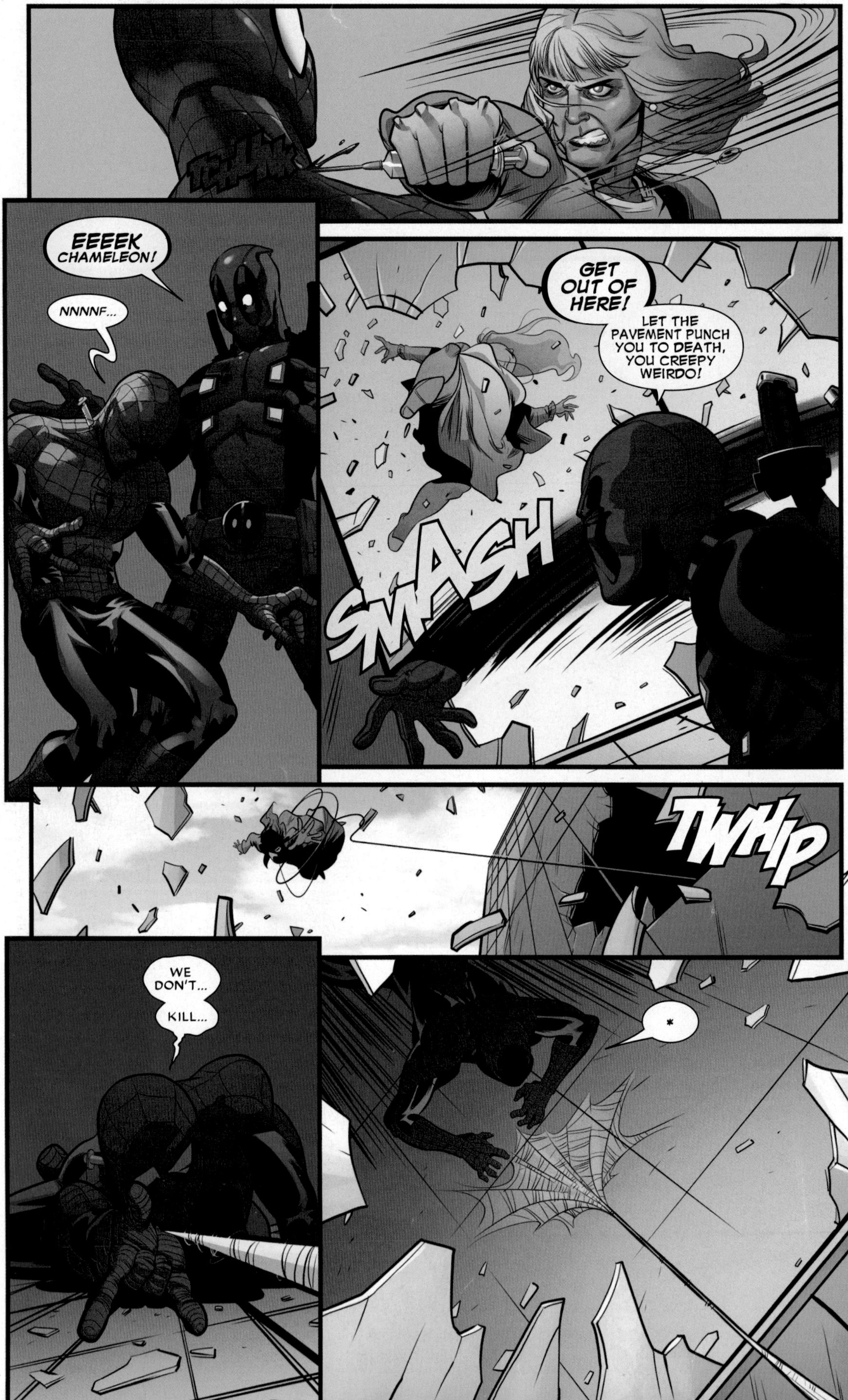
EEEEK CHAMELEON!
NNNNF...
GET OUT OF HERE!
LET THE PAVEMENT PUNCH YOU TO DEATH, YOU CREEPY WEIRDO!
SMASH
TWHIP
WE DON'T...
KILL...
*

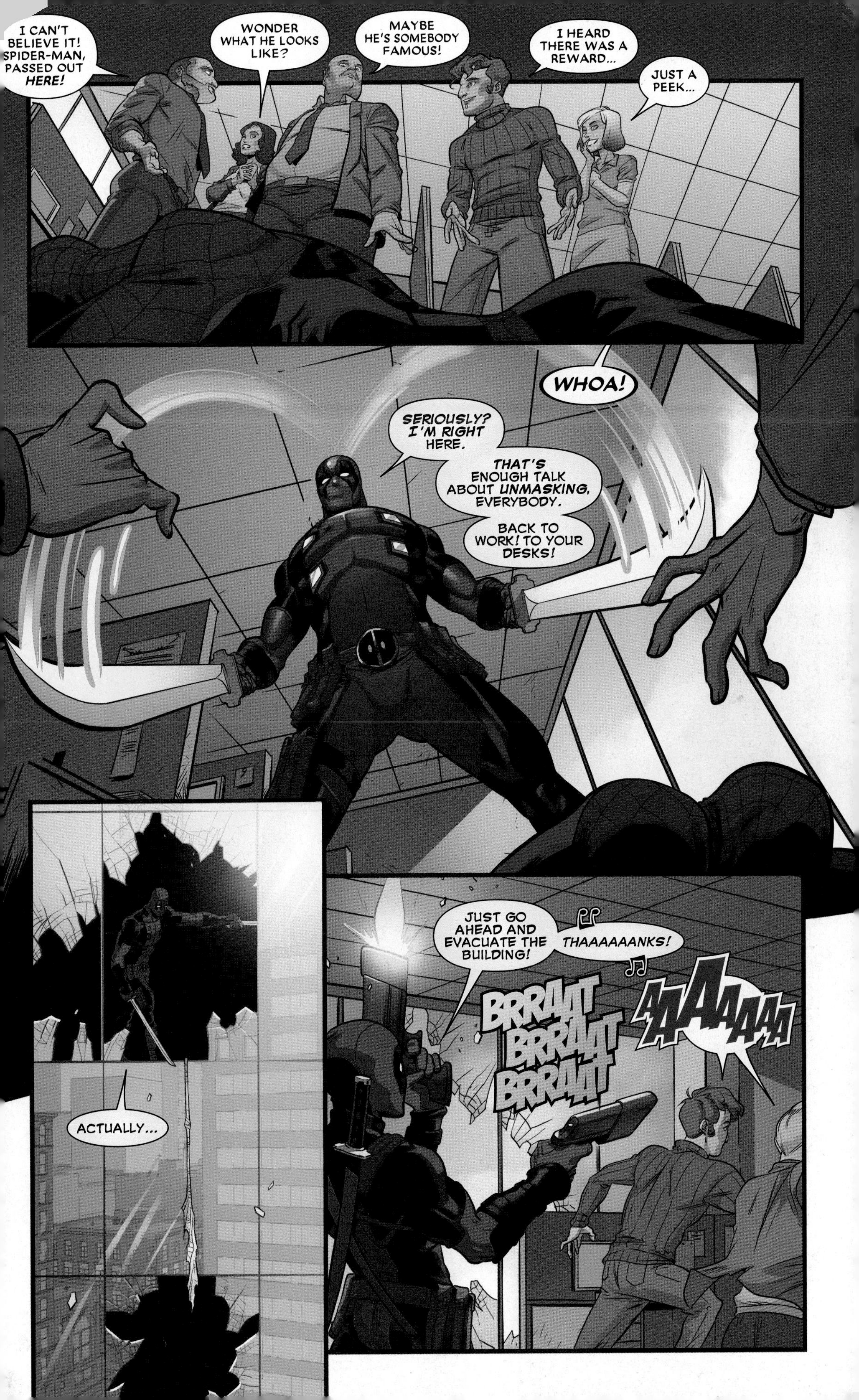
I CAN'T BELIEVE IT! SPIDER-MAN, PASSED OUT HERE!
WONDER WHAT HE LOOKS LIKE?
MAYBE HE'S SOMEBODY FAMOUS!
I HEARD THERE WAS A REWARD...
JUST A PEEK...
WHOA!
SERIOUSLY? I'M RIGHT HERE.
THAT'S ENOUGH TALK ABOUT UNMASKING, EVERYBODY.
BACK TO WORK! TO YOUR DESKS!
ACTUALLY...
JUST GO AHEAD AND EVACUATE THE BUILDING!
THAAAAAAANKS!
BRRAAT BRRAAT BRRAAT
AAAAAAA

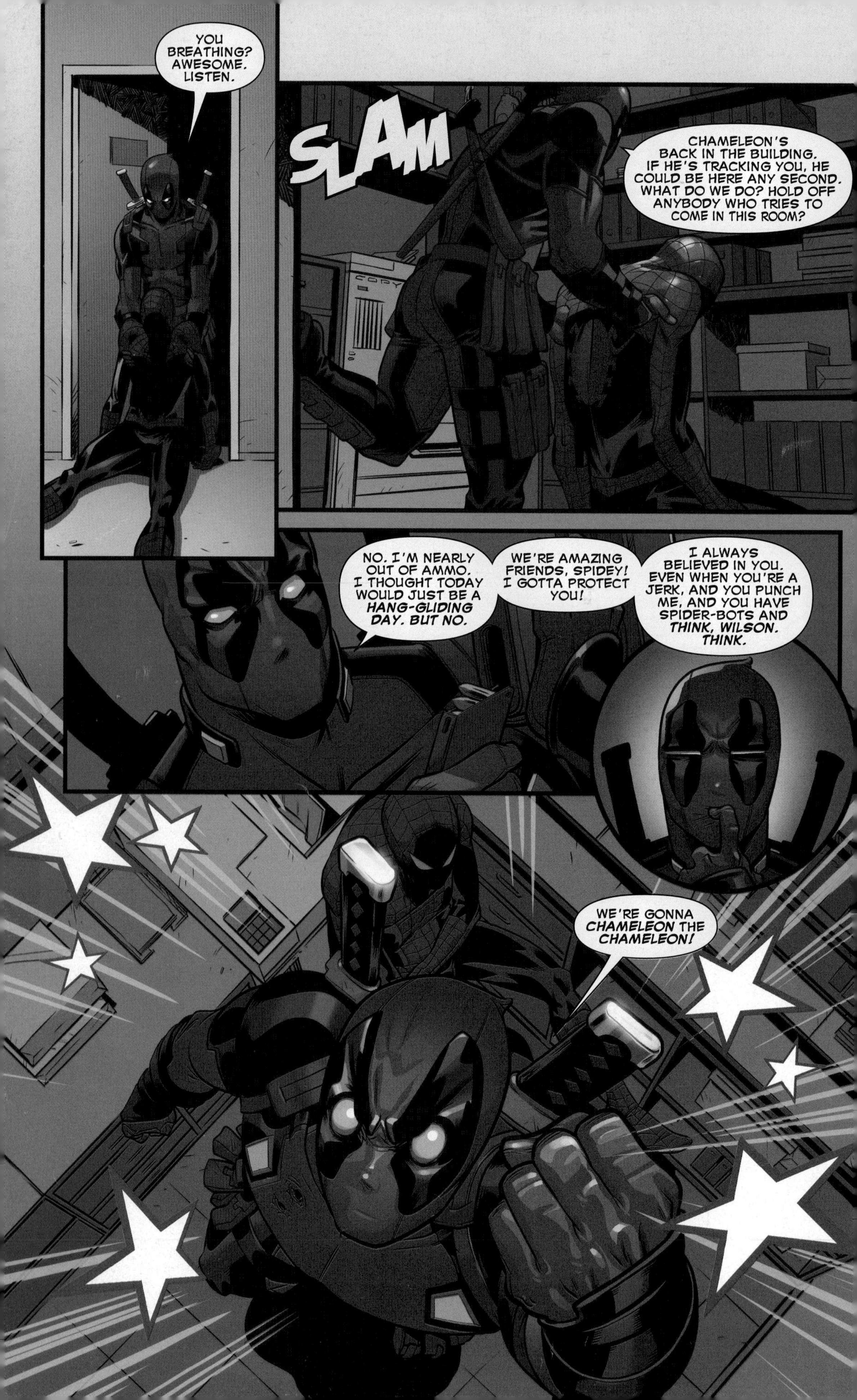
YOU BREATHING? AWESOME. LISTEN.
SLAM
CHAMELEON'S BACK IN THE BUILDING. IF HE'S TRACKING YOU, HE COULD BE HERE ANY SECOND. WHAT DO WE DO? HOLD OFF ANYBODY WHO TRIES TO COME IN THIS ROOM?
NO. I'M NEARLY OUT OF AMMO. I THOUGHT TODAY WOULD JUST BE A *HANG-GLIDING* DAY. BUT NO.
WE'RE AMAZING FRIENDS, SPIDEY! I GOTTA PROTECT YOU!
I ALWAYS BELIEVED IN YOU. EVEN WHEN YOU'RE A JERK, AND YOU PUNCH ME, AND YOU HAVE SPIDER-BOTS AND *THINK, WILSON. THINK.*
COPY
WE'RE GONNA *CHAMELEON* THE *CHAMELEON!*

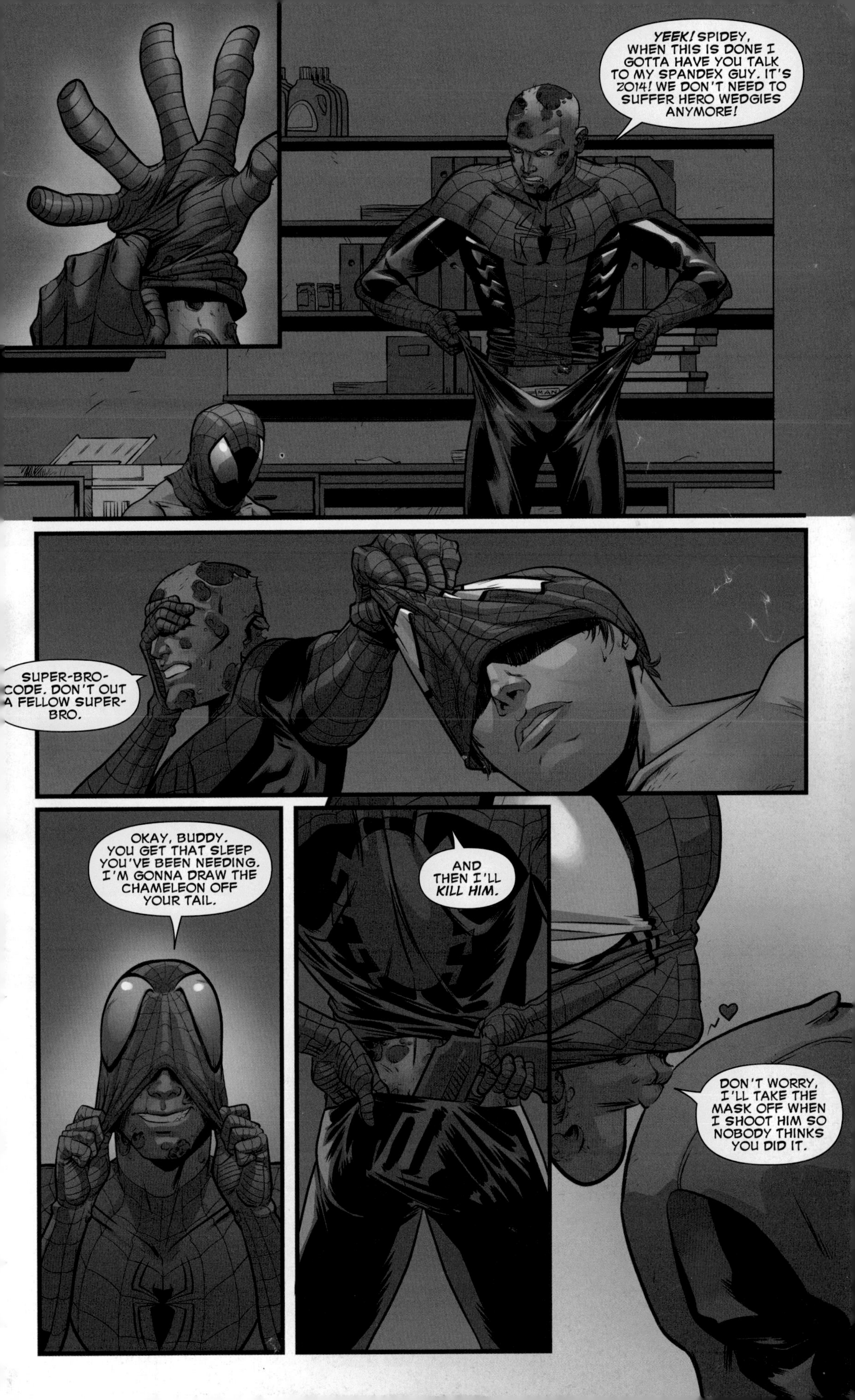

YEEK! SPIDEY, WHEN THIS IS DONE I GOTTA HAVE YOU TALK TO MY SPANDEX GUY. IT'S 2014! WE DON'T NEED TO SUFFER HERO WEDGIES ANYMORE!
MAN
SUPER-BRO-CODE. DON'T OUT A FELLOW SUPER-BRO.
OKAY, BUDDY. YOU GET THAT SLEEP YOU'VE BEEN NEEDING. I'M GONNA DRAW THE CHAMELEON OFF YOUR TAIL.
AND THEN I'LL KILL HIM.
DON'T WORRY, I'LL TAKE THE MASK OFF WHEN I SHOOT HIM SO NOBODY THINKS YOU DID IT.

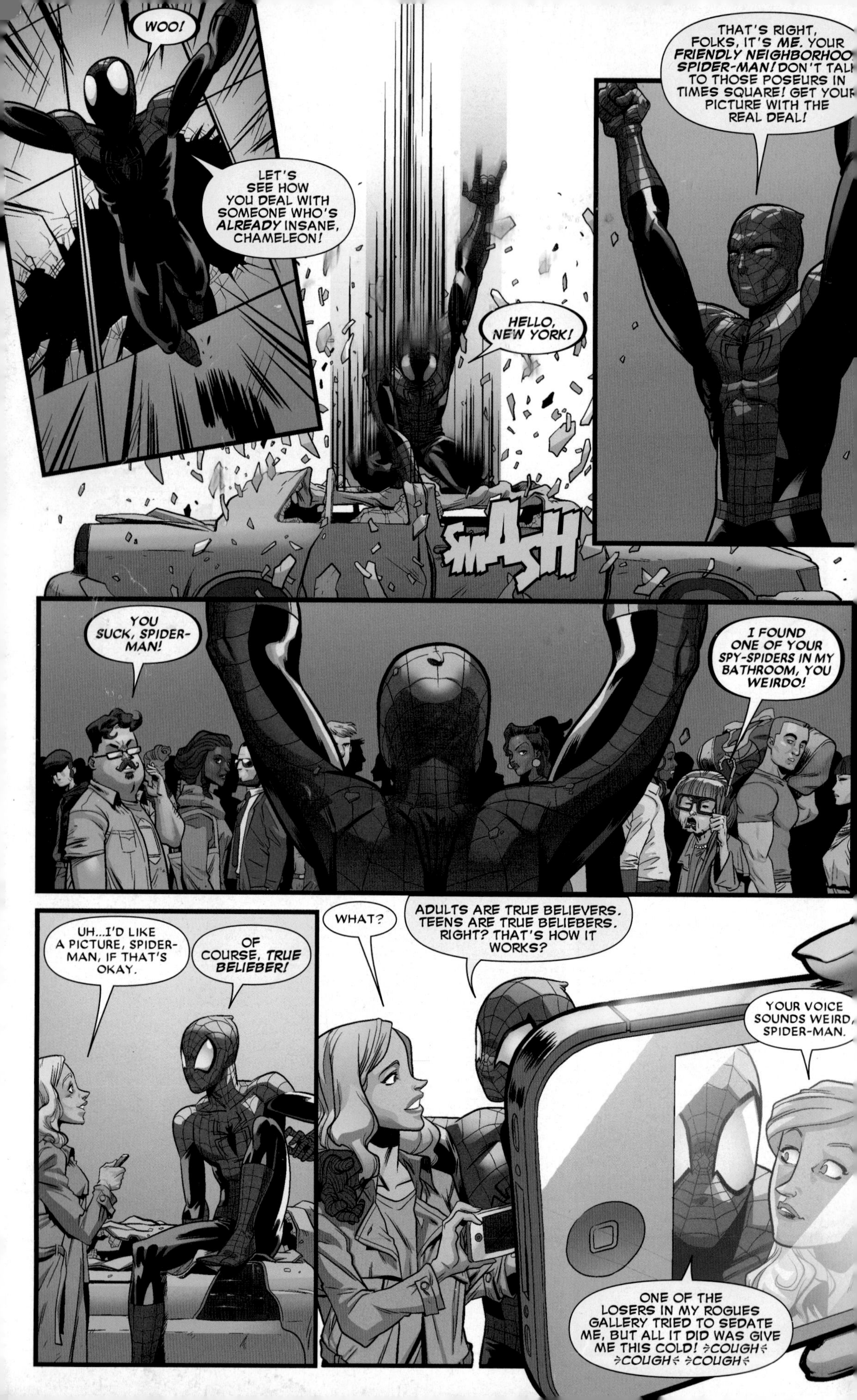
WOO!
LET'S SEE HOW YOU DEAL WITH SOMEONE WHO'S ALREADY INSANE, CHAMELEON!
HELLO, NEW YORK!
SMASH
THAT'S RIGHT, FOLKS, IT'S ME. YOUR FRIENDLY NEIGHBORHOO SPIDER-MAN! DON'T TAL TO THOSE POSEURS IN TIMES SQUARE! GET YOUR PICTURE WITH THE REAL DEAL!
YOU SUCK, SPIDER-MAN!
I FOUND ONE OF YOUR SPY-SPIDERS IN MY BATHROOM, YOU WEIRDO!
UH...I'D LIKE A PICTURE, SPIDER-MAN, IF THAT'S OKAY.
OF COURSE, TRUE BELIEBER!
WHAT?
ADULTS ARE TRUE BELIEVERS. TEENS ARE TRUE BELIEBERS. RIGHT? THAT'S HOW IT WORKS?
YOUR VOICE SOUNDS WEIRD, SPIDER-MAN.
ONE OF THE LOSERS IN MY ROGUES GALLERY TRIED TO SEDATE ME, BUT ALL IT DID WAS GIVE ME THIS COLD! *COUGH* *COUGH* *COUGH*

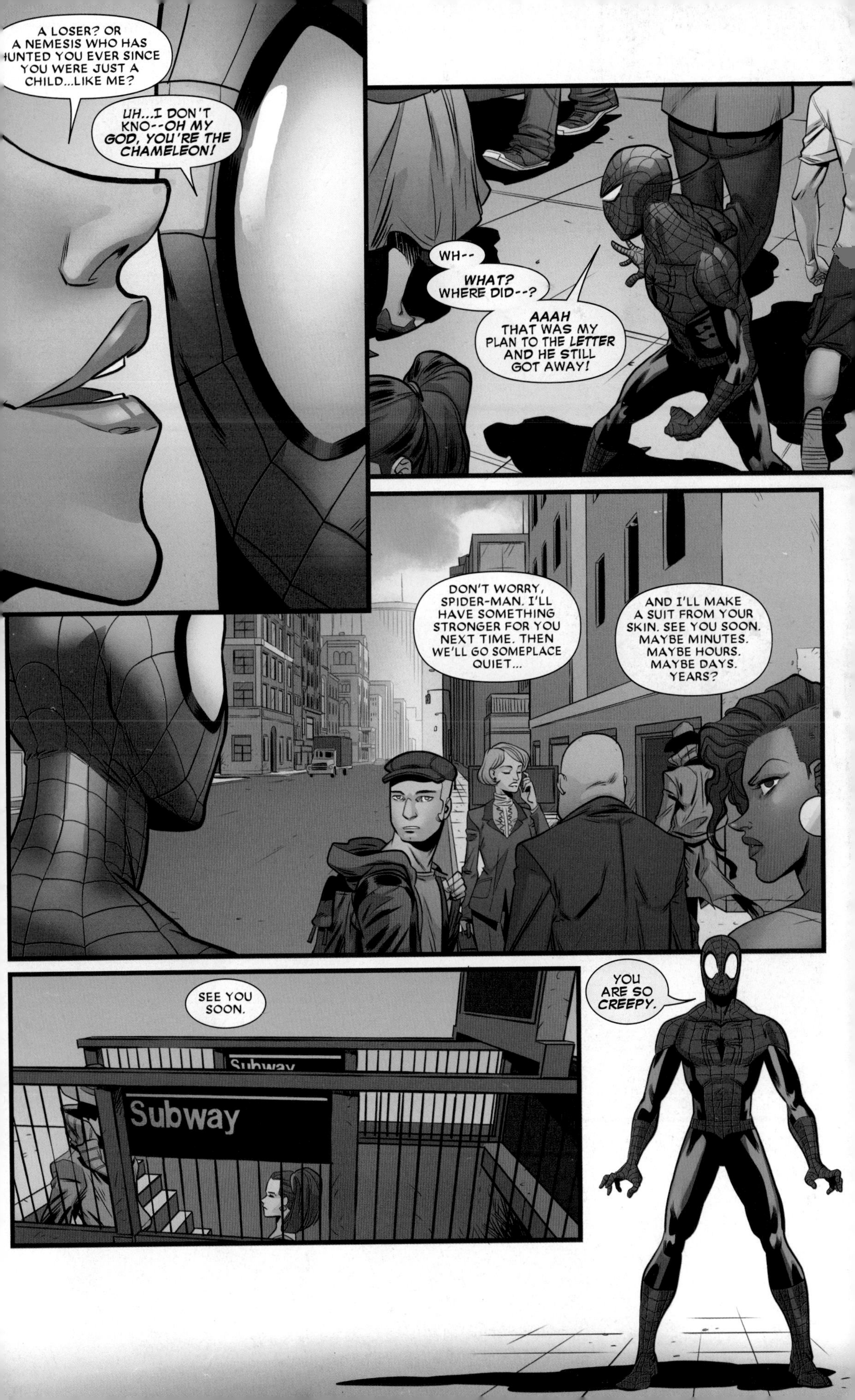
A LOSER? OR A NEMESIS WHO HAS HUNTED YOU EVER SINCE YOU WERE JUST A CHILD...LIKE ME?
UH...I DON'T KNO--OH MY GOD, YOU'RE THE CHAMELEON!
WH--
WHAT? WHERE DID--?
AAAH THAT WAS MY PLAN TO THE LETTER AND HE STILL GOT AWAY!
DON'T WORRY, SPIDER-MAN. I'LL HAVE SOMETHING STRONGER FOR YOU NEXT TIME. THEN WE'LL GO SOMEPLACE QUIET...
AND I'LL MAKE A SUIT FROM YOUR SKIN. SEE YOU SOON. MAYBE MINUTES. MAYBE HOURS. MAYBE DAYS. YEARS?
SEE YOU SOON.
Subway
Subway
YOU ARE SO CREEPY.

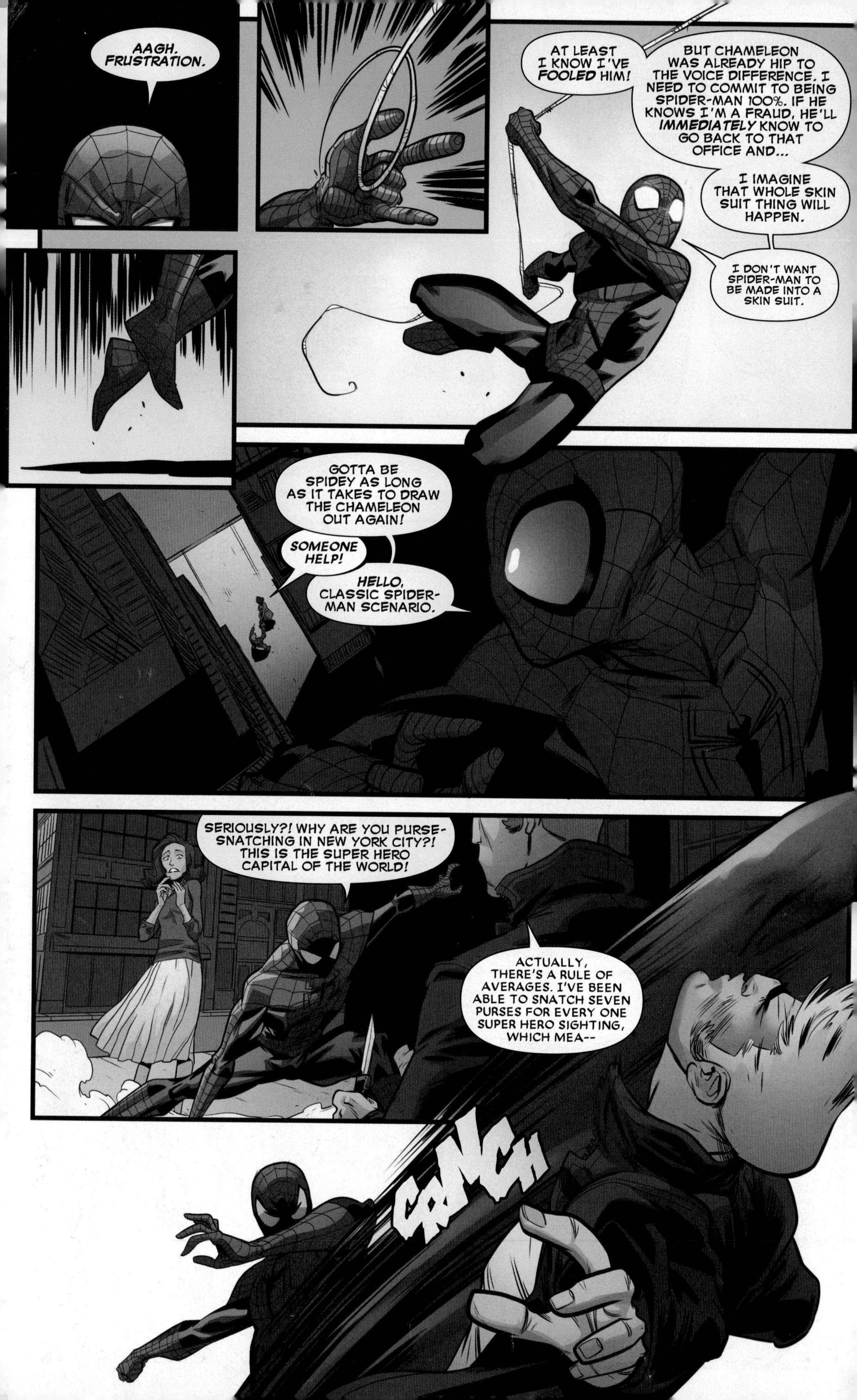
AAGH. FRUSTRATION.
AT LEAST I KNOW I'VE FOOLED HIM!
BUT CHAMELEON WAS ALREADY HIP TO THE VOICE DIFFERENCE. I NEED TO COMMIT TO BEING SPIDER-MAN 100%. IF HE KNOWS I'M A FRAUD, HE'LL IMMEDIATELY KNOW TO GO BACK TO THAT OFFICE AND...
I IMAGINE THAT WHOLE SKIN SUIT THING WILL HAPPEN.
I DON'T WANT SPIDER-MAN TO BE MADE INTO A SKIN SUIT.
GOTTA BE SPIDEY AS LONG AS IT TAKES TO DRAW THE CHAMELEON OUT AGAIN!
SOMEONE HELP!
HELLO, CLASSIC SPIDER-MAN SCENARIO.
SERIOUSLY?! WHY ARE YOU PURSE-SNATCHING IN NEW YORK CITY?! THIS IS THE SUPER HERO CAPITAL OF THE WORLD!
ACTUALLY, THERE'S A RULE OF AVERAGES. I'VE BEEN ABLE TO SNATCH SEVEN PURSES FOR EVERY ONE SUPER HERO SIGHTING, WHICH MEA--
CRNCH

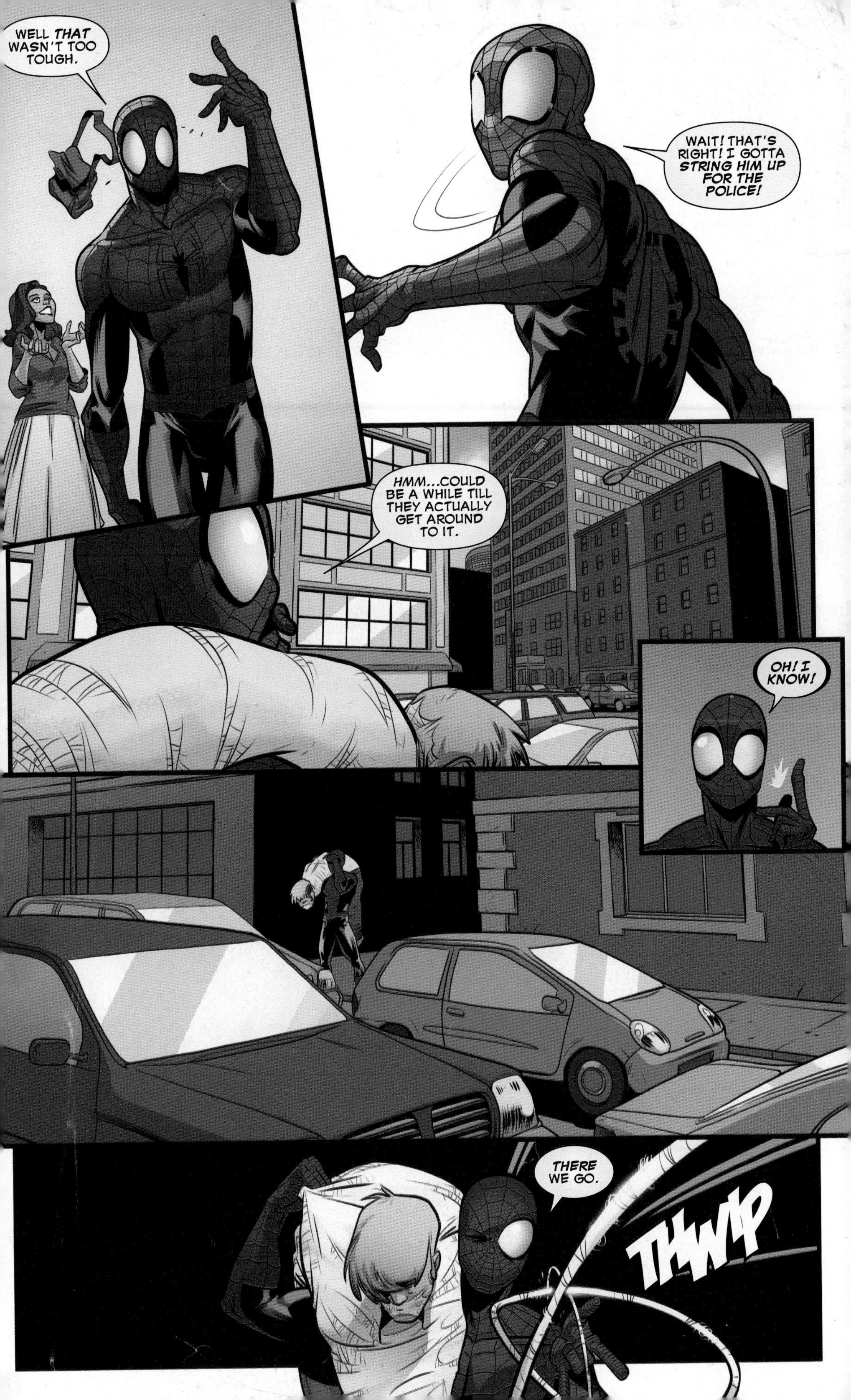
WELL THAT WASN'T TOO TOUGH.
WAIT! THAT'S RIGHT! I GOTTA STRING HIM UP FOR THE POLICE!
HMM...COULD BE A WHILE TILL THEY ACTUALLY GET AROUND TO IT.
OH! I KNOW!
THERE WE GO.
THWIP

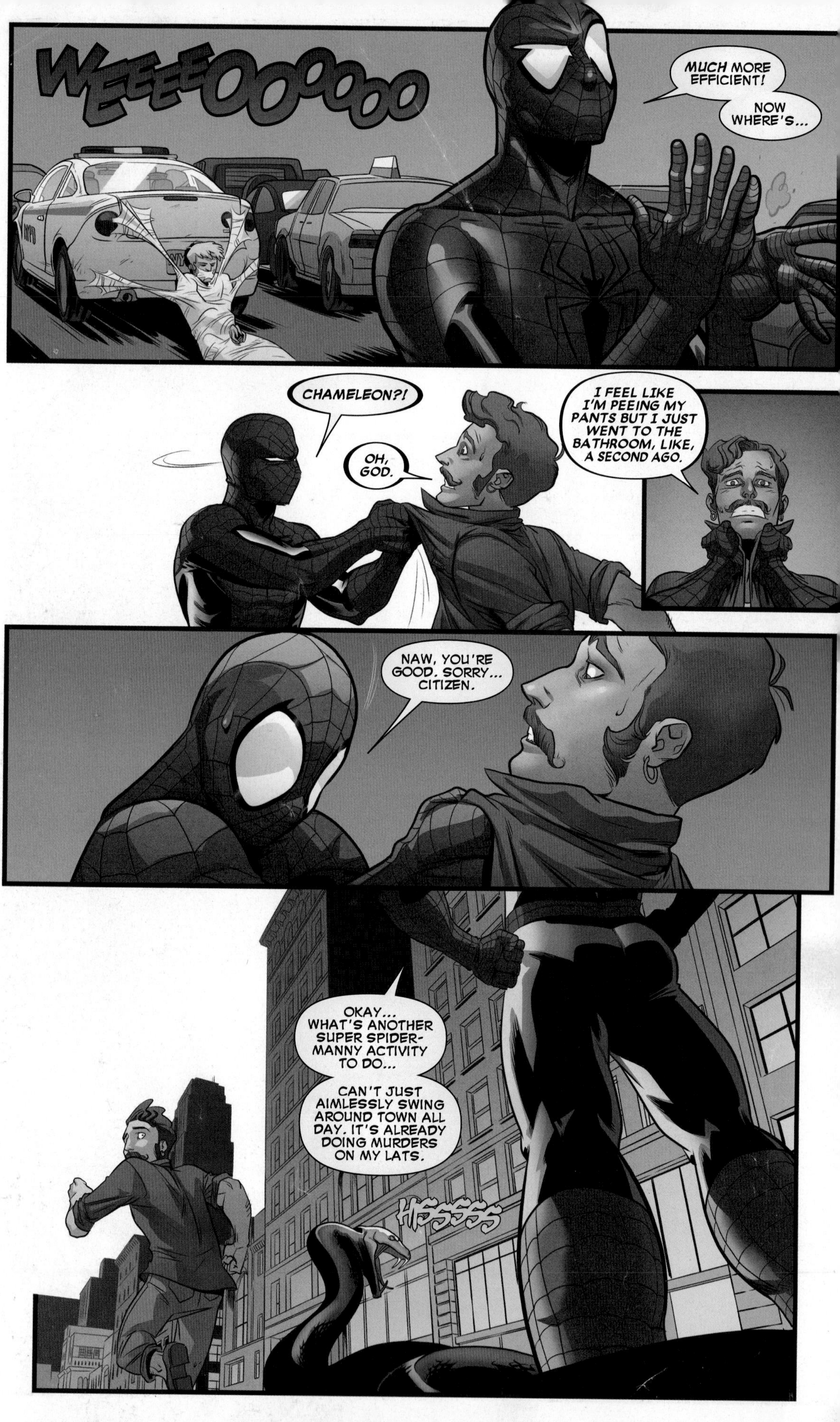
WEEEEOOOOOOO
MUCH MORE EFFICIENT!
NOW WHERE'S...
CHAMELEON?!
OH, GOD.
I FEEL LIKE I'M PEEING MY PANTS BUT I JUST WENT TO THE BATHROOM, LIKE, A SECOND AGO.
NAW, YOU'RE GOOD. SORRY... CITIZEN.
OKAY... WHAT'S ANOTHER SUPER SPIDER-MANNY ACTIVITY TO DO...
CAN'T JUST AIMLESSLY SWING AROUND TOWN ALL DAY. IT'S ALREADY DOING MURDERS ON MY LATS.
HSSSSS

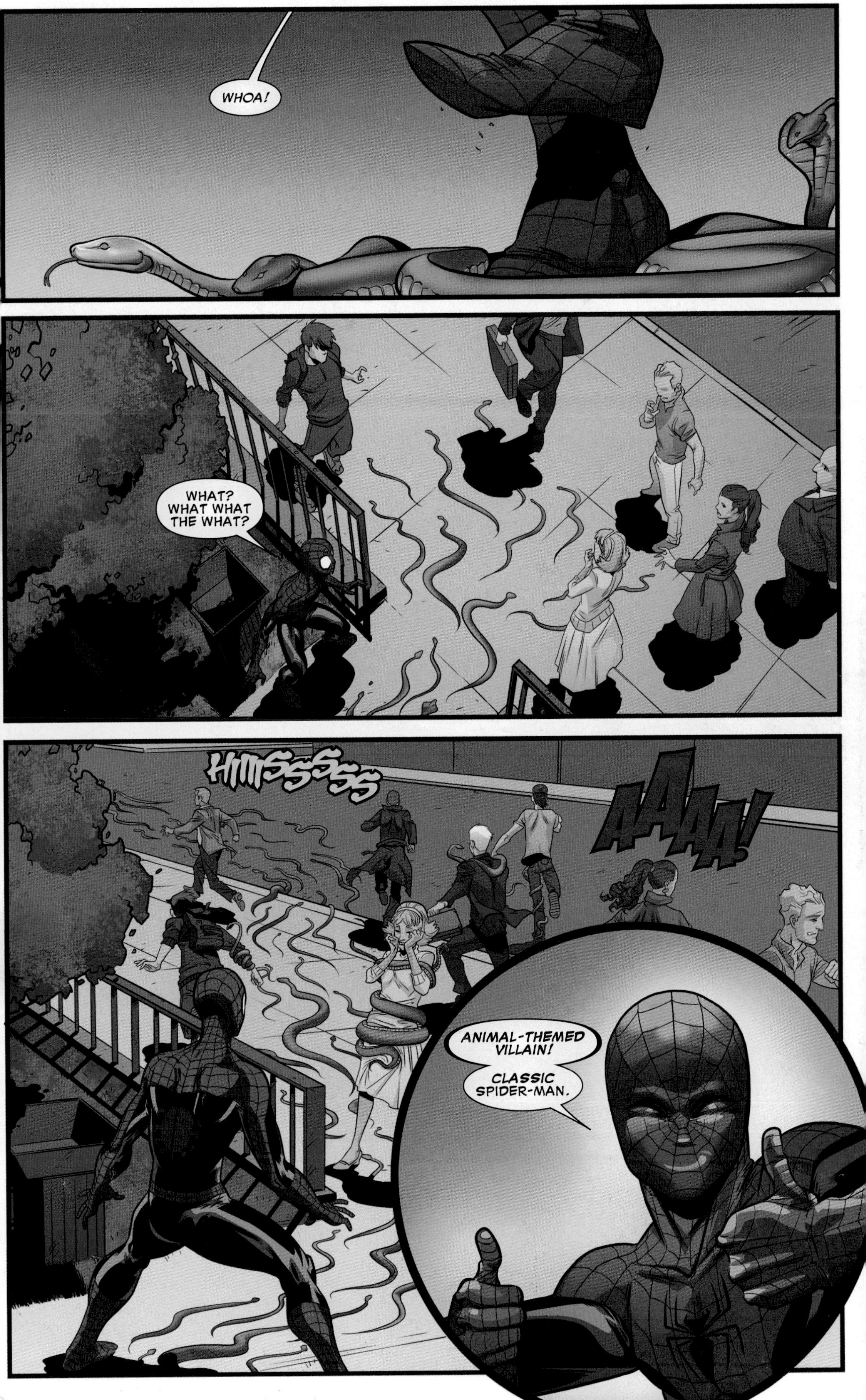
WHOA!
WHAT? WHAT WHAT THE WHAT?
HIIISSSSSS
AAAA!
ANIMAL-THEMED VILLAIN!
CLASSIC SPIDER-MAN.

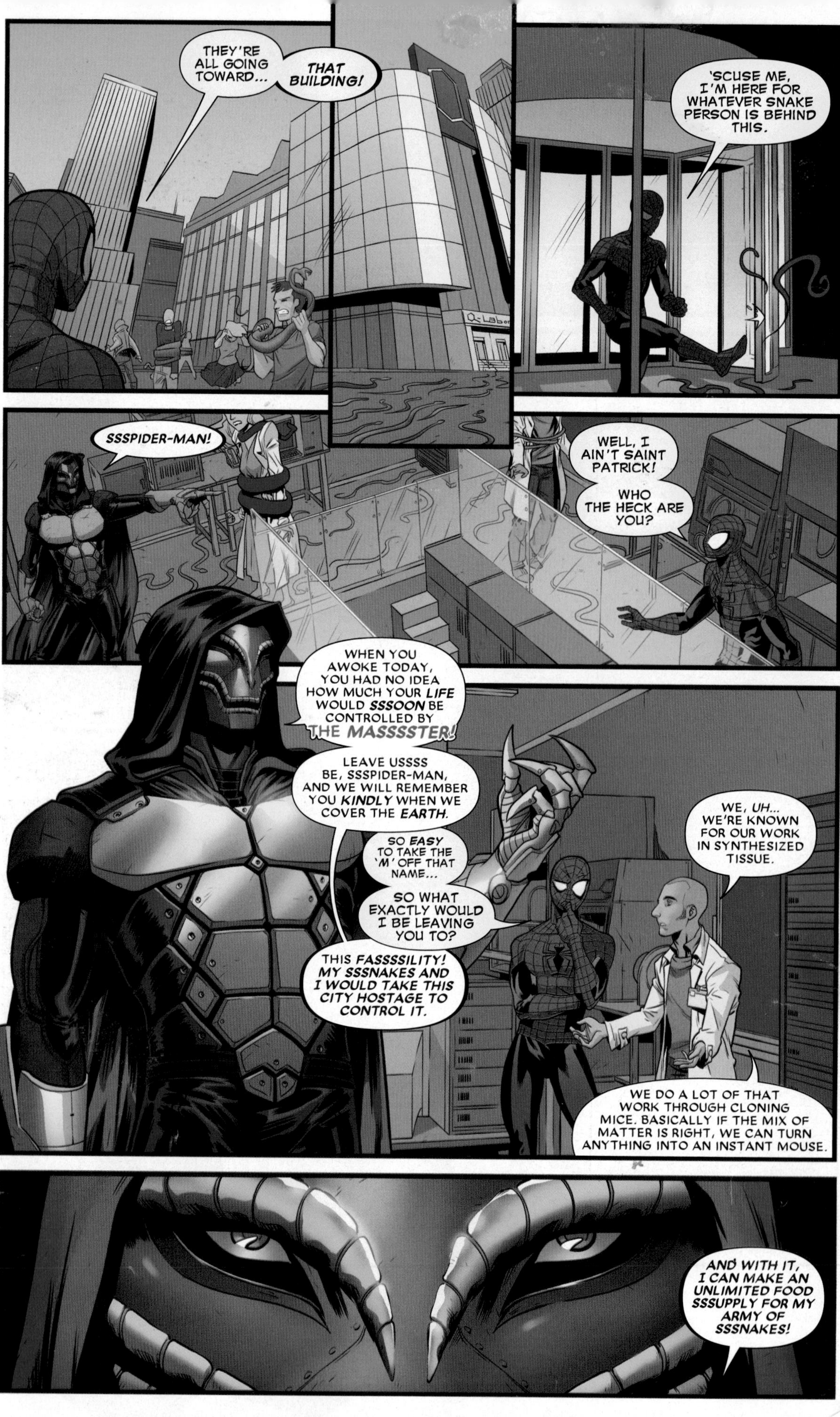
THEY'RE ALL GOING TOWARD...
THAT BUILDING!
'SCUSE ME, I'M HERE FOR WHATEVER SNAKE PERSON IS BEHIND THIS.
SSSPIDER-MAN!
WELL, I AIN'T SAINT PATRICK!
WHO THE HECK ARE YOU?
WHEN YOU AWOKE TODAY, YOU HAD NO IDEA HOW MUCH YOUR LIFE WOULD SSSOON BE CONTROLLED BY THE MASSSSTER!
LEAVE USSSS BE, SSSPIDER-MAN, AND WE WILL REMEMBER YOU KINDLY WHEN WE COVER THE EARTH.
SO EASY TO TAKE THE 'M' OFF THAT NAME...
SO WHAT EXACTLY WOULD I BE LEAVING YOU TO?
THIS FASSSSILITY! MY SSSNAKES AND I WOULD TAKE THIS CITY HOSTAGE TO CONTROL IT.
WE, UH... WE'RE KNOWN FOR OUR WORK IN SYNTHESIZED TISSUE.
WE DO A LOT OF THAT WORK THROUGH CLONING MICE. BASICALLY IF THE MIX OF MATTER IS RIGHT, WE CAN TURN ANYTHING INTO AN INSTANT MOUSE.
AND WITH IT, I CAN MAKE AN UNLIMITED FOOD SSSUPPLY FOR MY ARMY OF SSSNAKES!

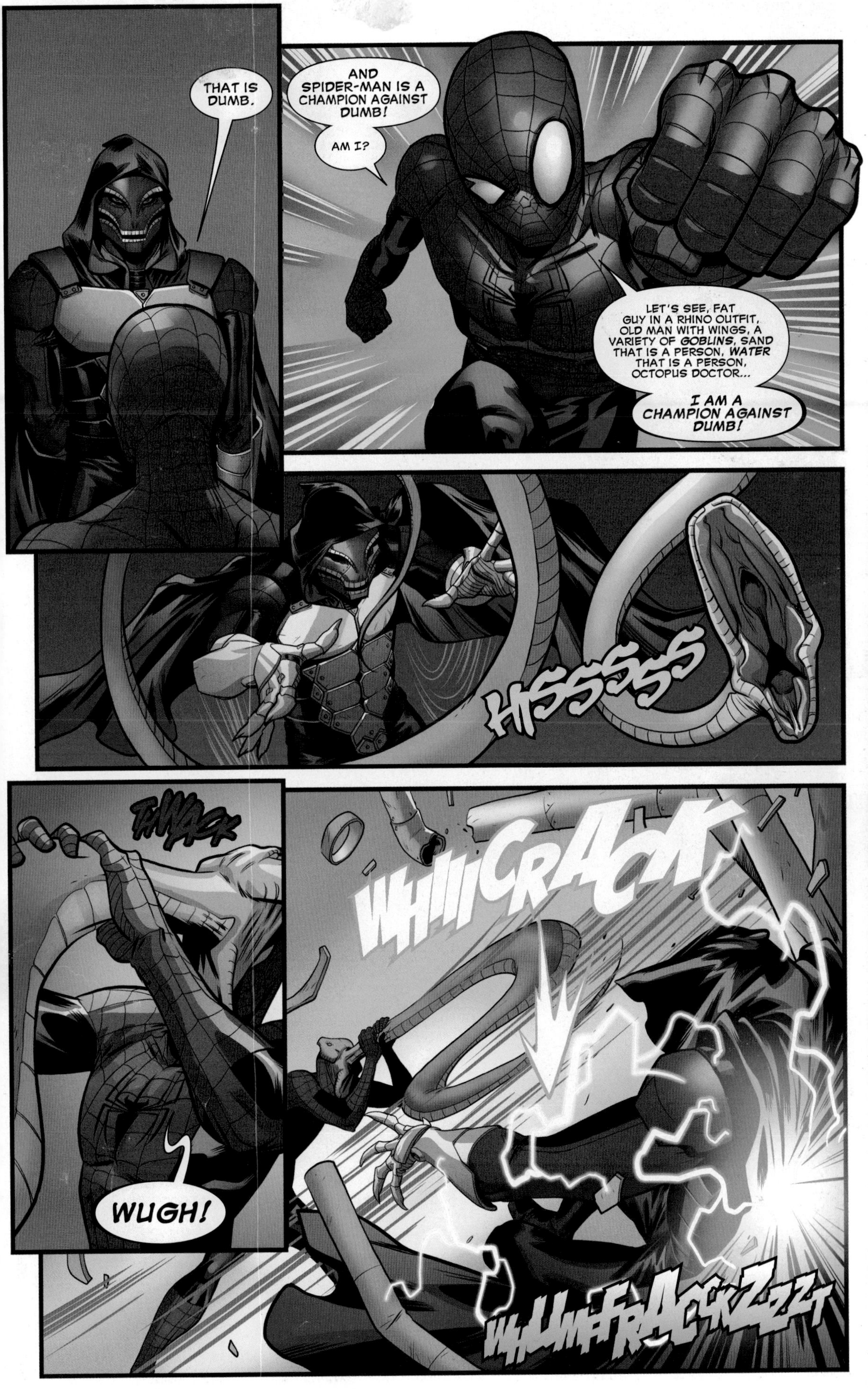
THAT IS DUMB.
AND SPIDER-MAN IS A CHAMPION AGAINST DUMB!
AM I?
LET'S SEE, FAT GUY IN A RHINO OUTFIT, OLD MAN WITH WINGS, A VARIETY OF GOBLINS, SAND THAT IS A PERSON, WATER THAT IS A PERSON, OCTOPUS DOCTOR...
I AM A CHAMPION AGAINST DUMB!
HISSSSS
THWACK
WUGH!
WHIIICRACK
WHUMFRACKZZZT

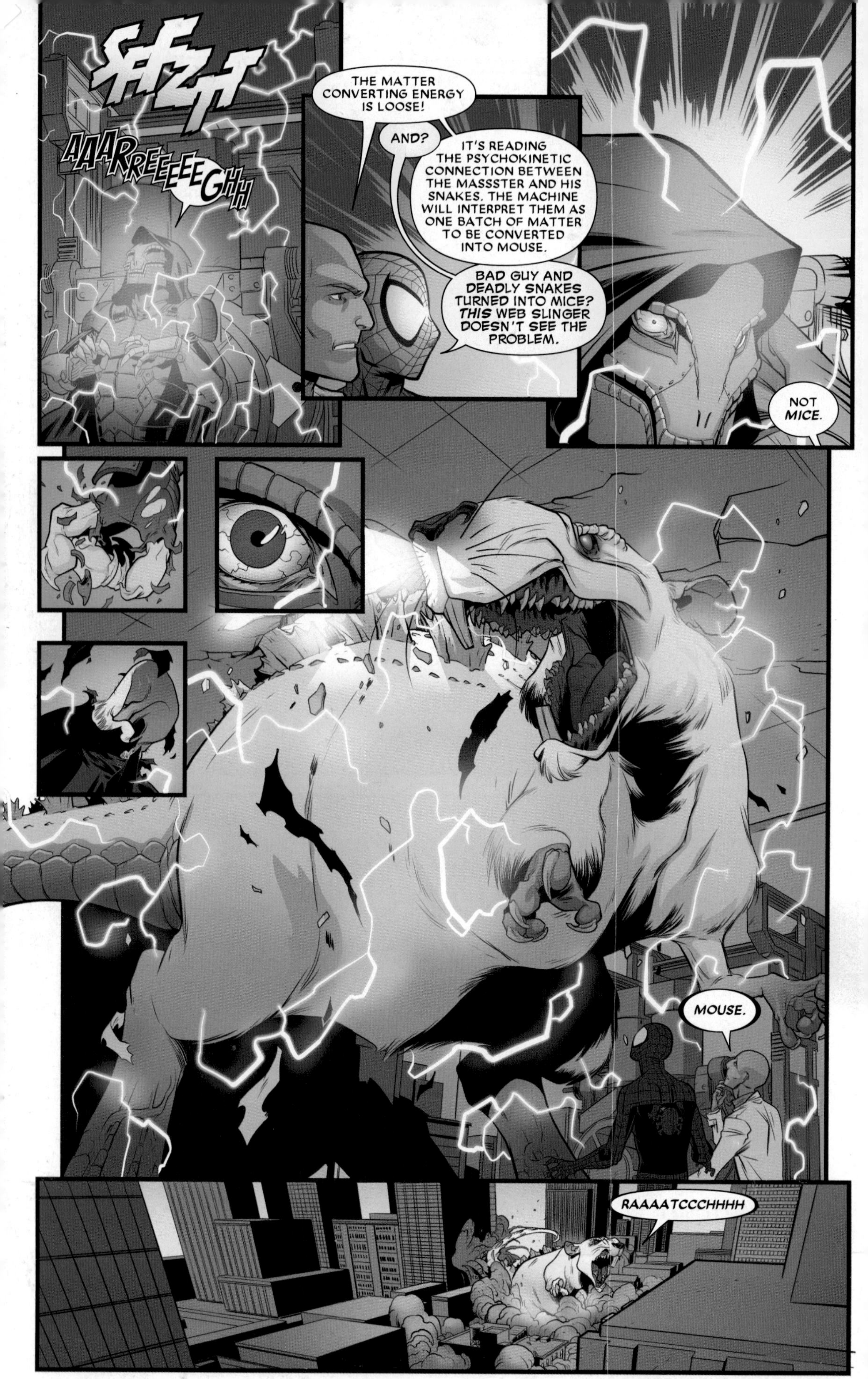
SFFZZTT
AAARREEEEEGHH
THE MATTER CONVERTING ENERGY IS LOOSE!
AND?
IT'S READING THE PSYCHOKINETIC CONNECTION BETWEEN THE MASSSTER AND HIS SNAKES. THE MACHINE WILL INTERPRET THEM AS ONE BATCH OF MATTER TO BE CONVERTED INTO MOUSE.
BAD GUY AND DEADLY SNAKES TURNED INTO MICE? THIS WEB SLINGER DOESN'T SEE THE PROBLEM.
NOT MICE.
MOUSE.
RAAAATCCCHHHH

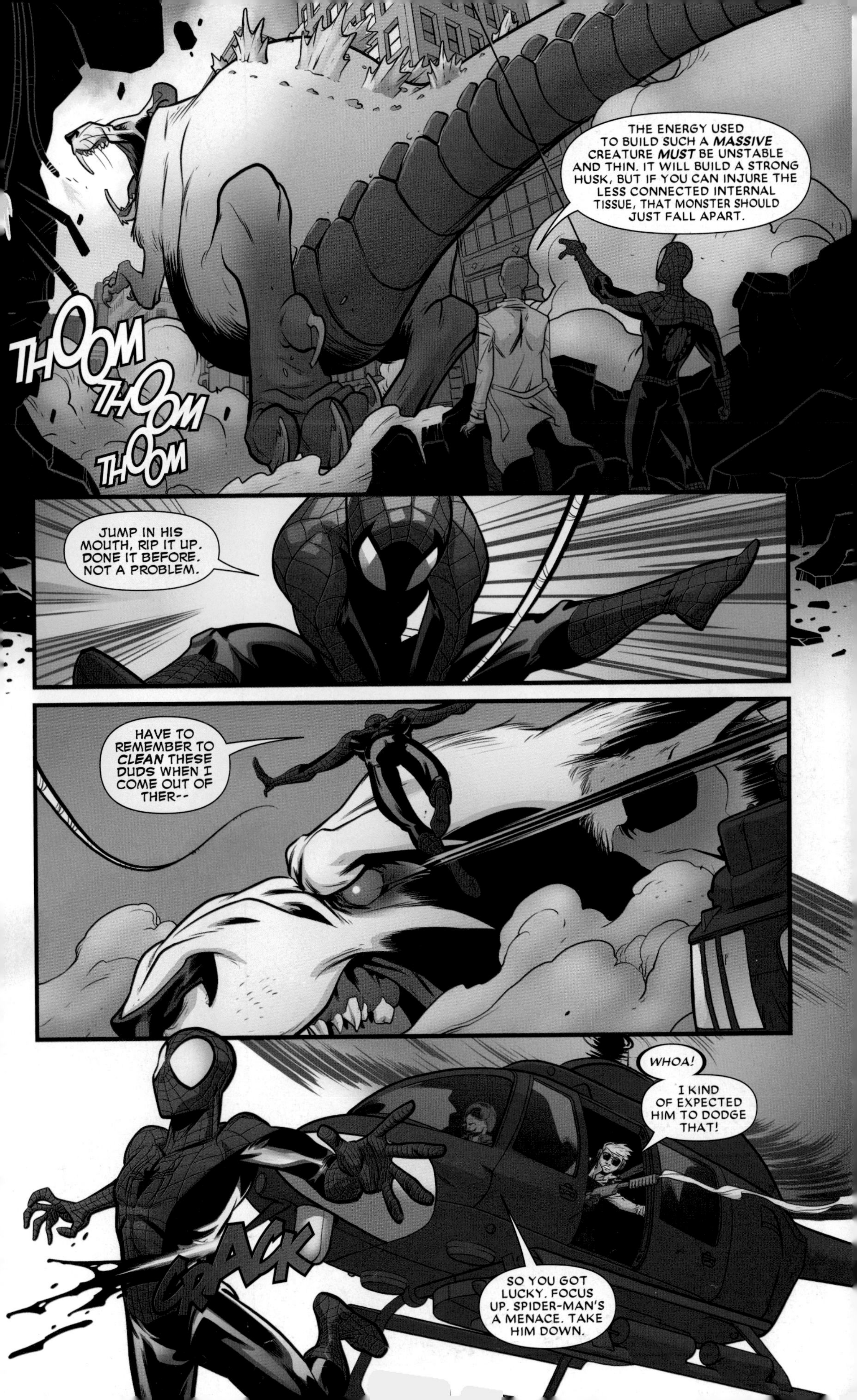
THE ENERGY USED TO BUILD SUCH A MASSIVE CREATURE MUST BE UNSTABLE AND THIN. IT WILL BUILD A STRONG HUSK, BUT IF YOU CAN INJURE THE LESS CONNECTED INTERNAL TISSUE, THAT MONSTER SHOULD JUST FALL APART.
THOOM THOOM THOOM
JUMP IN HIS MOUTH, RIP IT UP. DONE IT BEFORE. NOT A PROBLEM.
HAVE TO REMEMBER TO CLEAN THESE DUDS WHEN I COME OUT OF THER--
WHOA!
I KIND OF EXPECTED HIM TO DODGE THAT!
CRACK
SO YOU GOT LUCKY. FOCUS UP. SPIDER-MAN'S A MENACE. TAKE HIM DOWN.

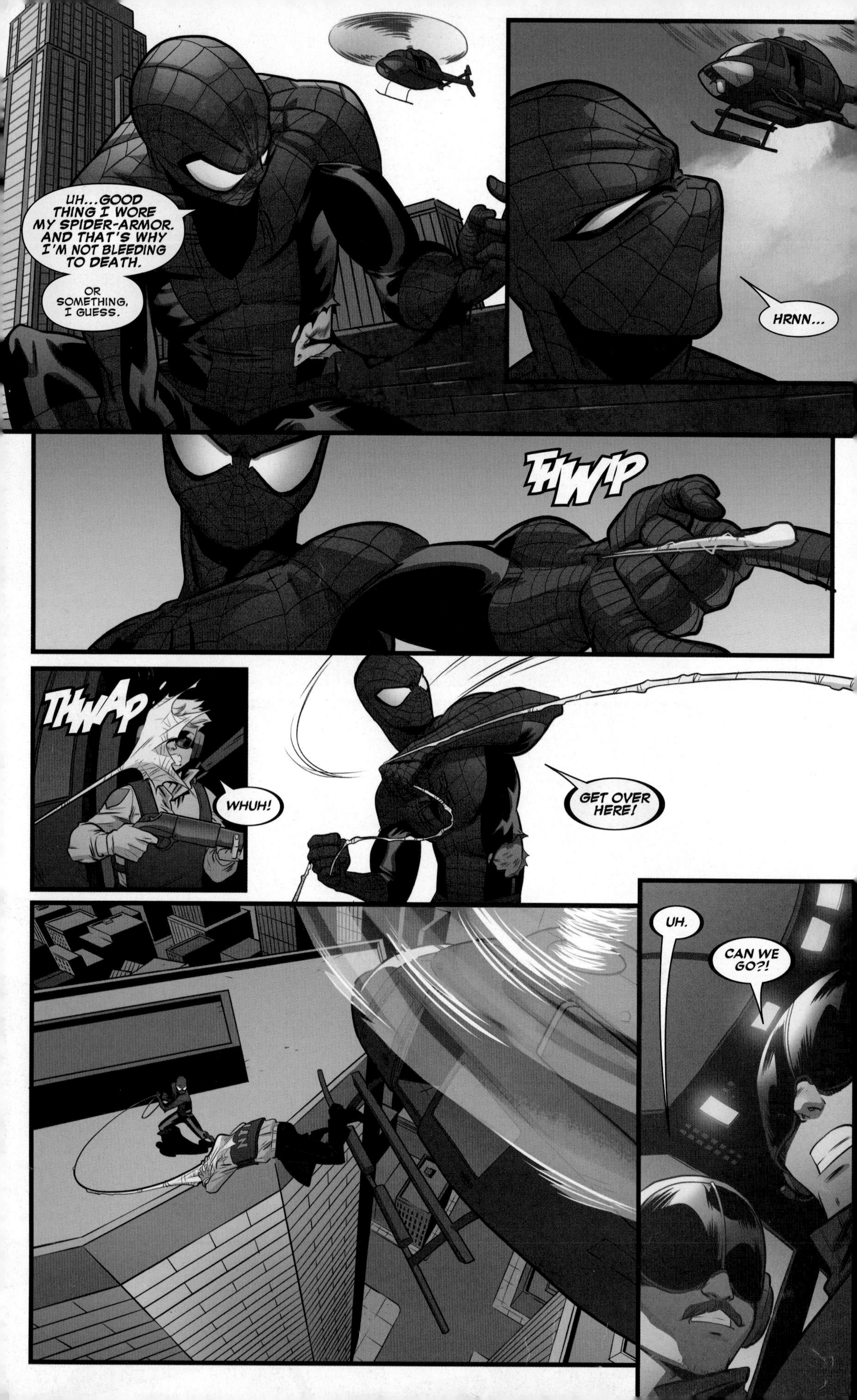
UH...GOOD THING I WORE MY SPIDER-ARMOR. AND THAT'S WHY I'M NOT BLEEDING TO DEATH.
OR SOMETHING, I GUESS.
HRNN...
THWIP
THWAP
WHUH!
GET OVER HERE!
UH.
CAN WE GO?!

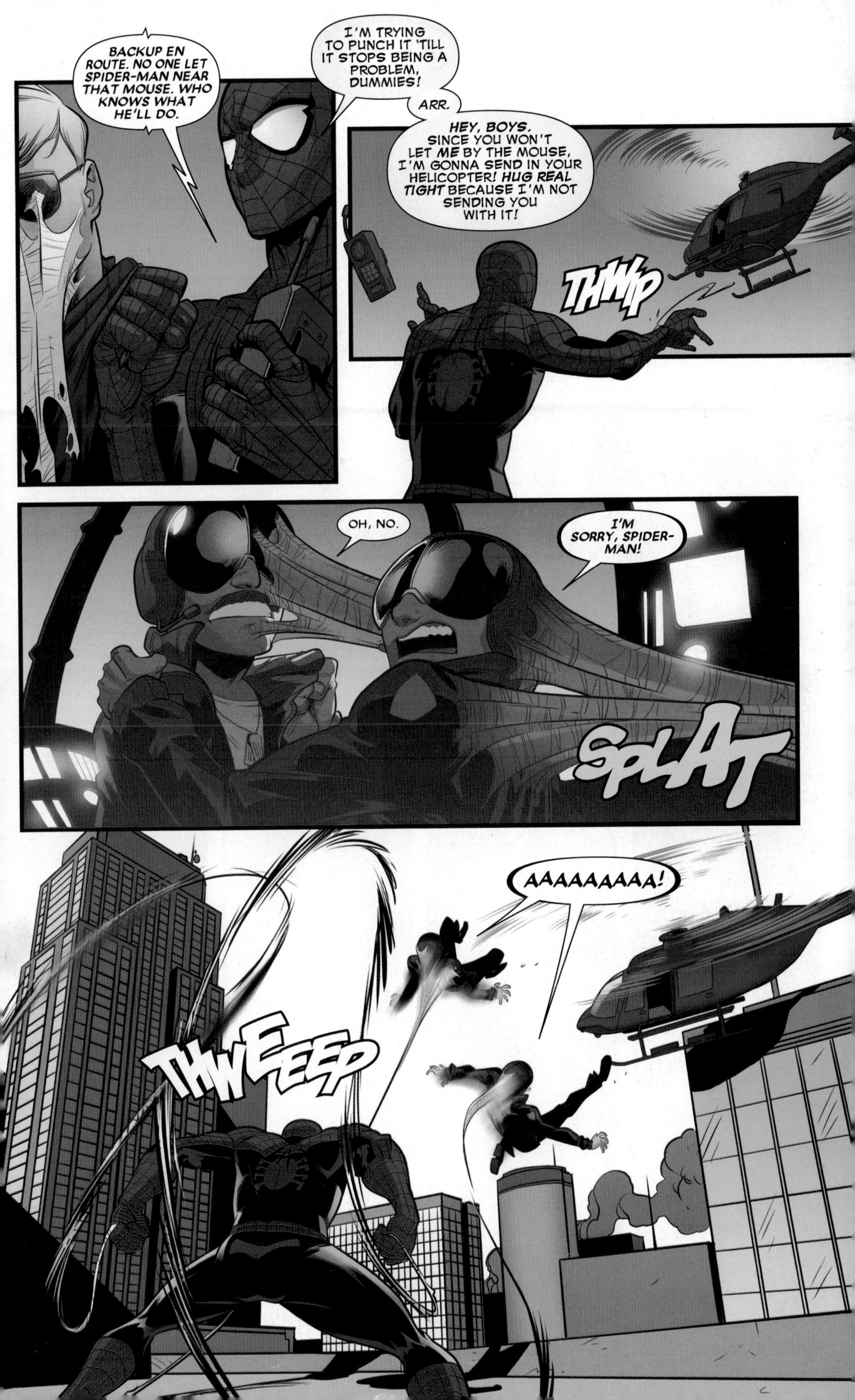
BACKUP EN ROUTE. NO ONE LET SPIDER-MAN NEAR THAT MOUSE. WHO KNOWS WHAT HE'LL DO.
I'M TRYING TO PUNCH IT 'TILL IT STOPS BEING A PROBLEM, DUMMIES!
ARR.
HEY, BOYS. SINCE YOU WON'T LET ME BY THE MOUSE, I'M GONNA SEND IN YOUR HELICOPTER! HUG REAL TIGHT BECAUSE I'M NOT SENDING YOU WITH IT!
THWIP
OH, NO.
I'M SORRY, SPIDER-MAN!
SPLAT
AAAAAAAAA!
THWEEEP

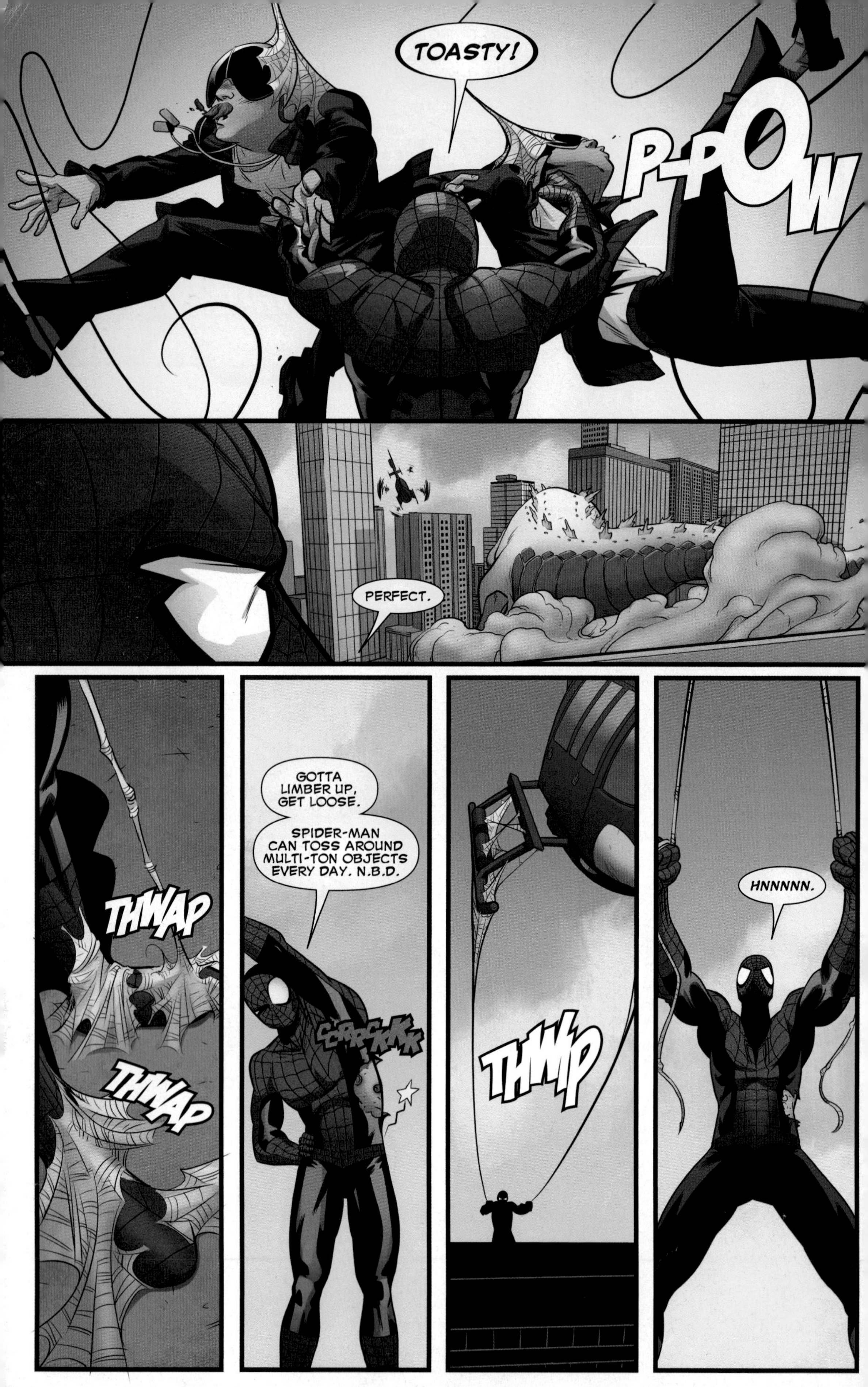
TOASTY!
P-POW
PERFECT.
THWAP
THWAP
GOTTA LIMBER UP, GET LOOSE.
SPIDER-MAN CAN TOSS AROUND MULTI-TON OBJECTS EVERY DAY. N.B.D.
CRRCKKK
THWIP
HNNNNN.

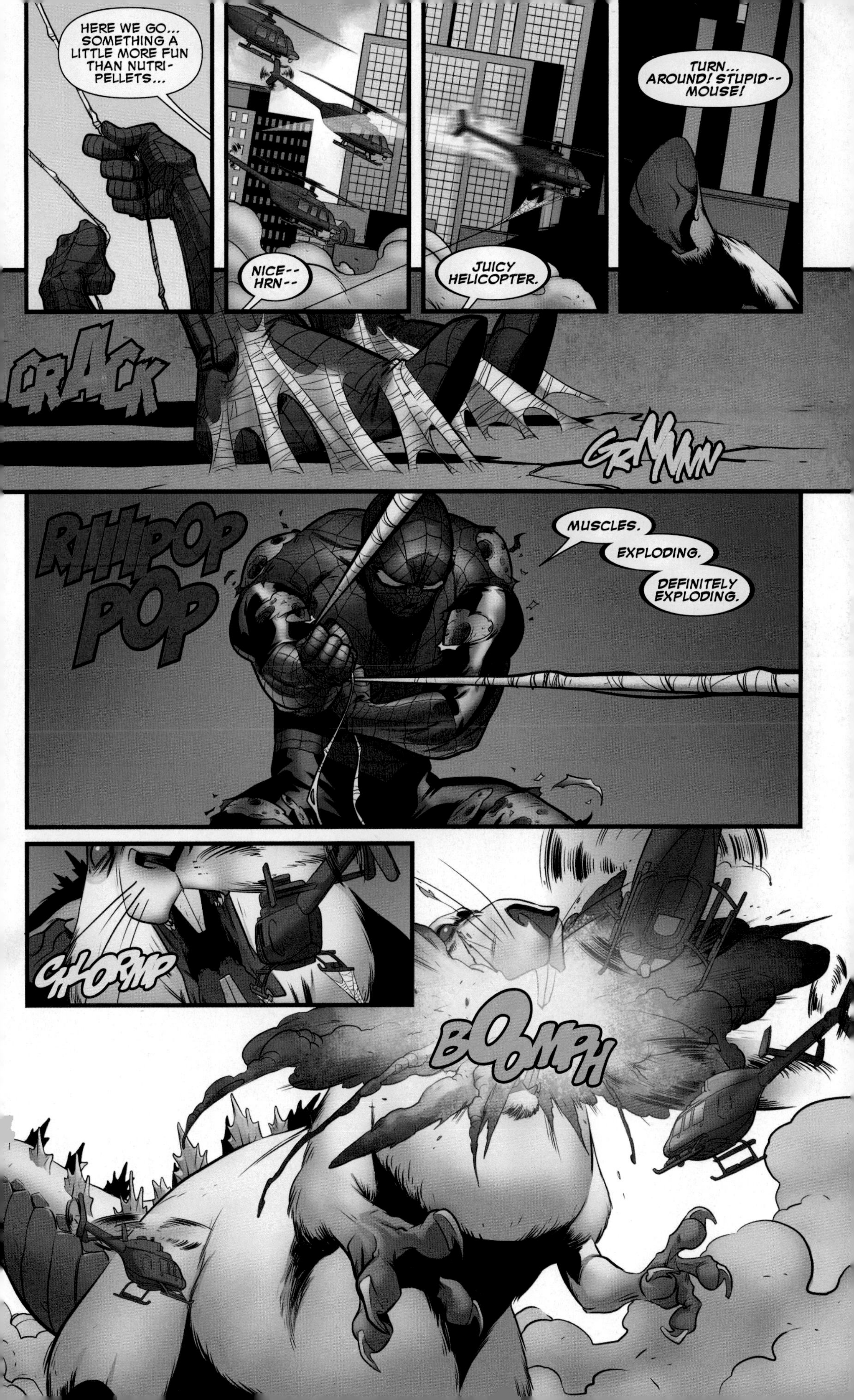
HERE WE GO... SOMETHING A LITTLE MORE FUN THAN NUTRI-PELLETS...
NICE-- HRN--
JUICY HELICOPTER.
TURN... AROUND! STUPID-- MOUSE!
CRACK
GRNNNN
RIIIPOP POP
MUSCLES.
EXPLODING.
DEFINITELY EXPLODING.
CHORMP
BOOMPH

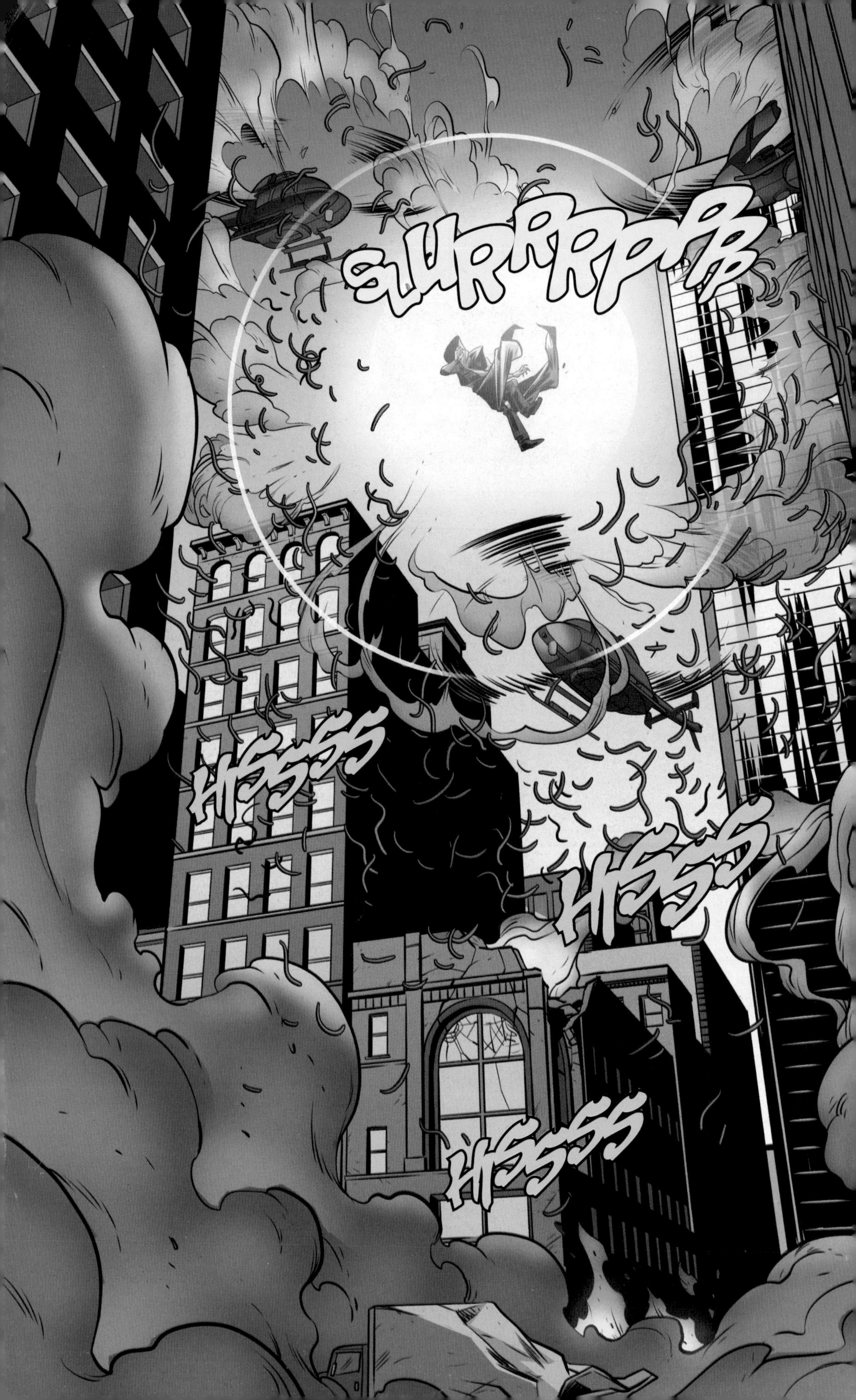
SLURRRPPP
HISSSS
HISSS
HISSSS

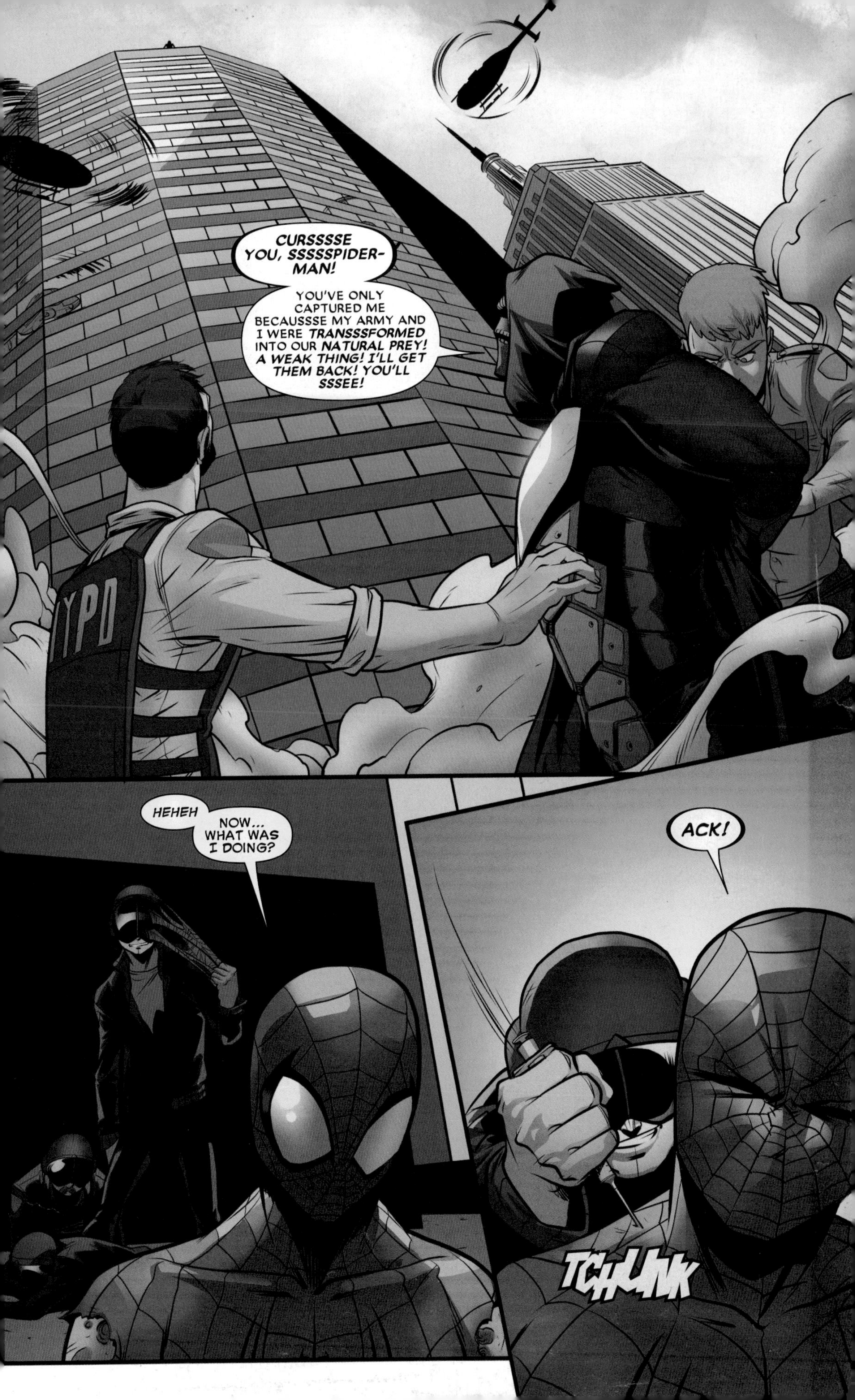
CURSSSSE YOU, SSSSSPIDER-MAN!
YOU'VE ONLY CAPTURED ME BECAUSSSE MY ARMY AND I WERE TRANSSSFORMED INTO OUR NATURAL PREY! A WEAK THING! I'LL GET THEM BACK! YOU'LL SSSEE!
NYPD
HEHEH
NOW... WHAT WAS I DOING?
ACK!
TCHUNK

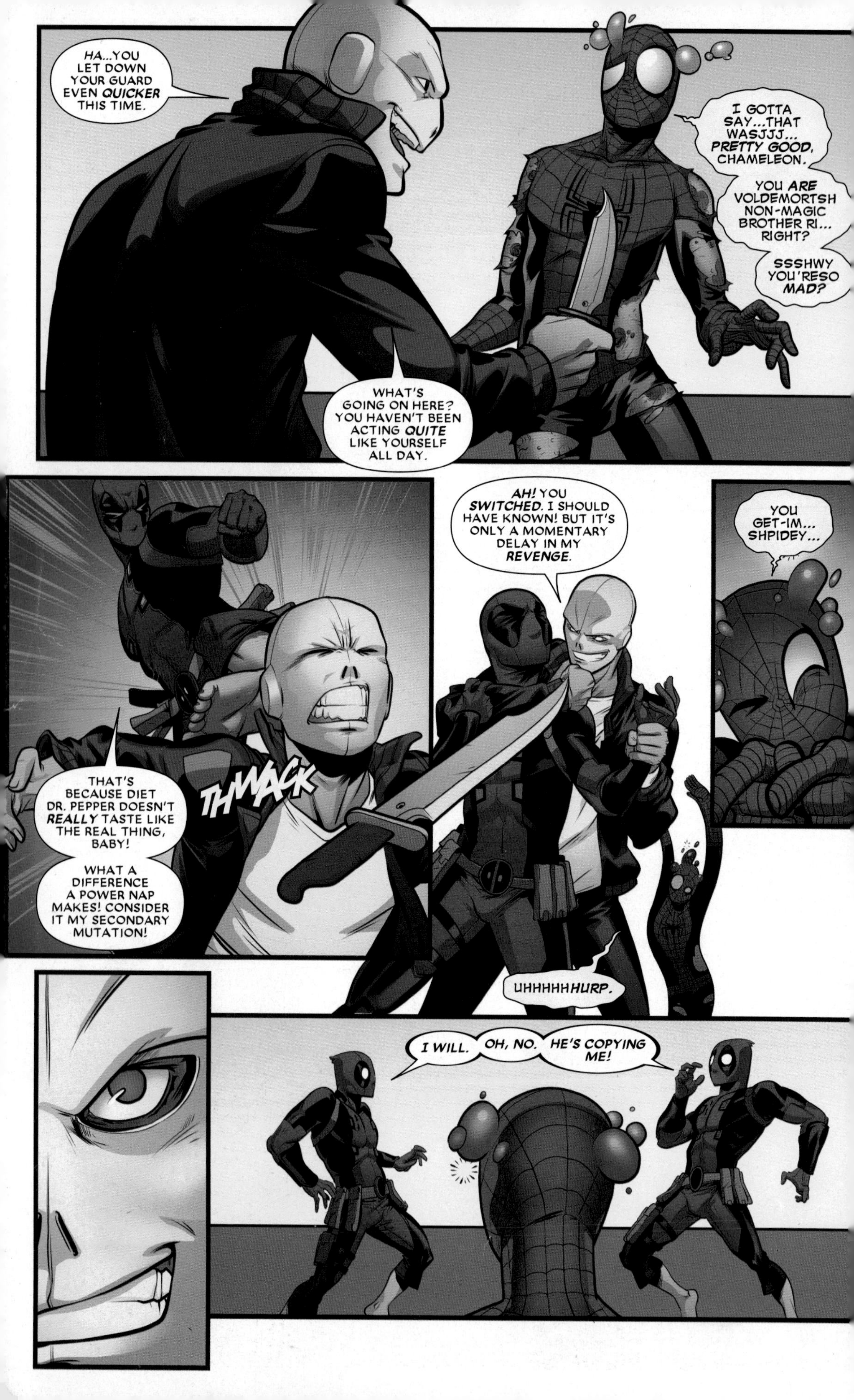
HA...YOU LET DOWN YOUR GUARD EVEN QUICKER THIS TIME.
I GOTTA SAY...THAT WASJJJ... PRETTY GOOD, CHAMELEON.
YOU ARE VOLDEMORTSH NON-MAGIC BROTHER RI... RIGHT?
SSSHWY YOU'RESO MAD?
WHAT'S GOING ON HERE? YOU HAVEN'T BEEN ACTING QUITE LIKE YOURSELF ALL DAY.
THAT'S BECAUSE DIET DR. PEPPER DOESN'T REALLY TASTE LIKE THE REAL THING, BABY!
WHAT A DIFFERENCE A POWER NAP MAKES! CONSIDER IT MY SECONDARY MUTATION!
THWACK
AH! YOU SWITCHED. I SHOULD HAVE KNOWN! BUT IT'S ONLY A MOMENTARY DELAY IN MY REVENGE.
YOU GET-IM... SHPIDEY...
UHHHHHHURP.
I WILL.
OH, NO.
HE'S COPYING ME!

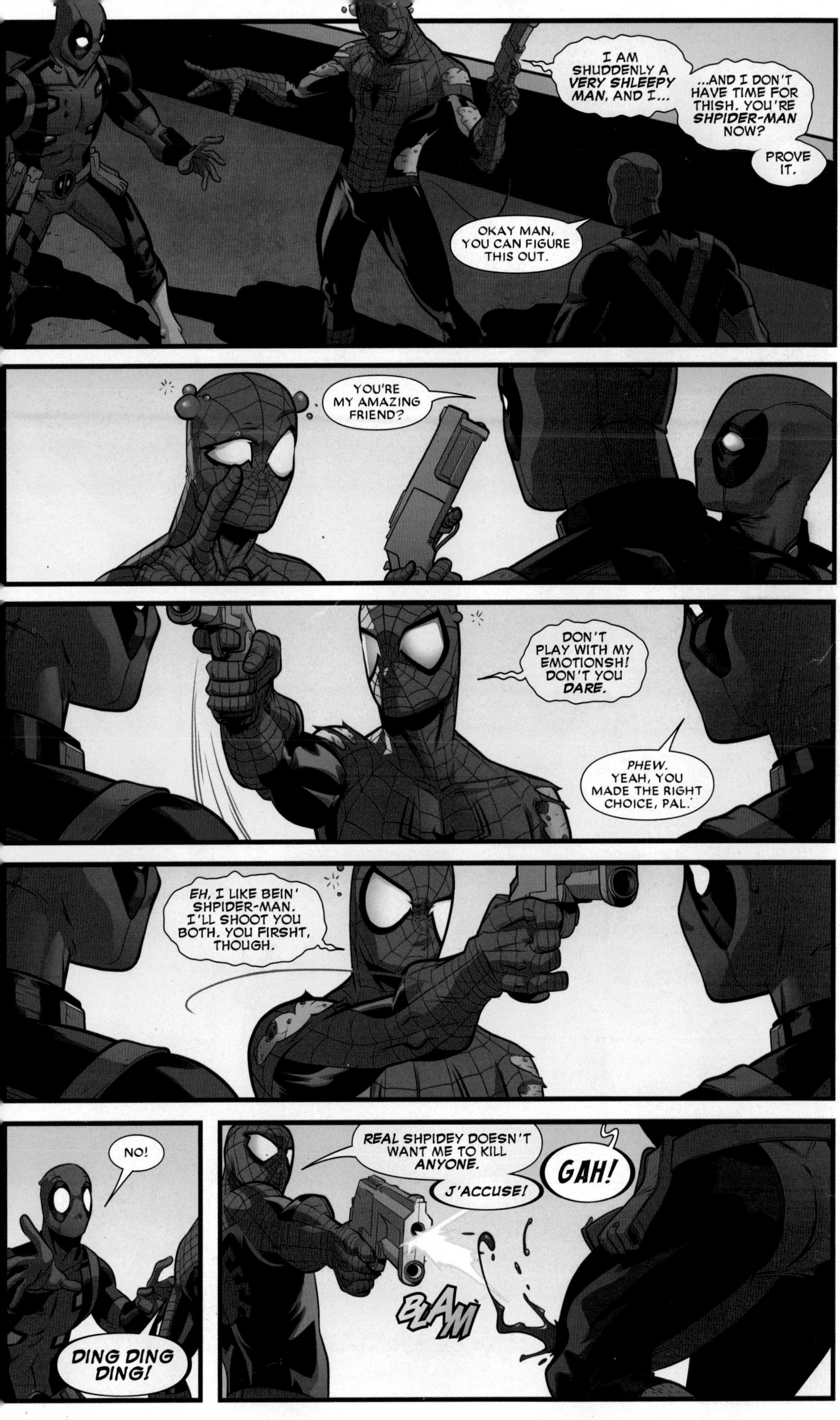

I AM SHUDDENLY A VERY SHLEEPY MAN, AND I...
...AND I DON'T HAVE TIME FOR THISH. YOU'RE SHPIDER-MAN NOW?
PROVE IT.
OKAY MAN, YOU CAN FIGURE THIS OUT.
YOU'RE MY AMAZING FRIEND?
DON'T PLAY WITH MY EMOTIONSH! DON'T YOU DARE.
PHEW. YEAH, YOU MADE THE RIGHT CHOICE, PAL.
EH, I LIKE BEIN' SHPIDER-MAN. I'LL SHOOT YOU BOTH. YOU FIRSHT, THOUGH.
NO!
DING DING DING!
REAL SHPIDEY DOESN'T WANT ME TO KILL ANYONE.
J'ACCUSE!
GAH!
BLAM

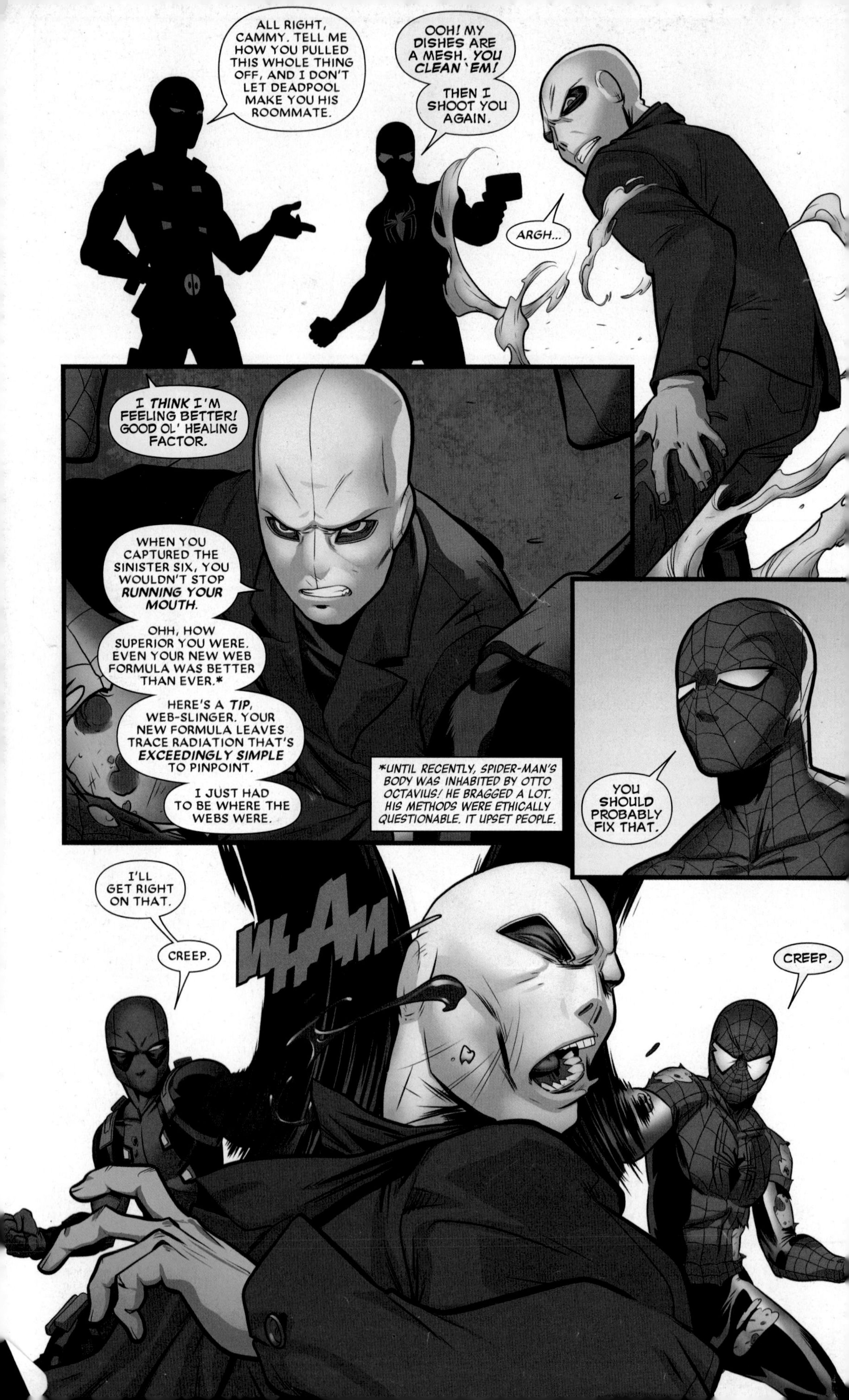
ALL RIGHT, CAMMY. TELL ME HOW YOU PULLED THIS WHOLE THING OFF, AND I DON'T LET DEADPOOL MAKE YOU HIS ROOMMATE.
OOH! MY DISHES ARE A MESH. *YOU CLEAN 'EM!*
THEN I SHOOT YOU AGAIN.
ARGH...
I *THINK* I'M FEELING BETTER! GOOD OL' HEALING FACTOR.
WHEN YOU CAPTURED THE SINISTER SIX, YOU WOULDN'T STOP **RUNNING YOUR MOUTH**.
OHH, HOW SUPERIOR YOU WERE. EVEN YOUR NEW WEB FORMULA WAS BETTER THAN EVER.*
HERE'S A *TIP*, WEB-SLINGER. YOUR NEW FORMULA LEAVES TRACE RADIATION THAT'S ***EXCEEDINGLY SIMPLE*** TO PINPOINT.
I JUST HAD TO BE WHERE THE WEBS WERE.
*UNTIL RECENTLY, SPIDER-MAN'S BODY WAS INHABITED BY OTTO OCTAVIUS! HE BRAGGED A LOT. HIS METHODS WERE ETHICALLY QUESTIONABLE. IT UPSET PEOPLE.
YOU SHOULD PROBABLY FIX THAT.
I'LL GET RIGHT ON THAT.
CREEP.
WHAM
CREEP.

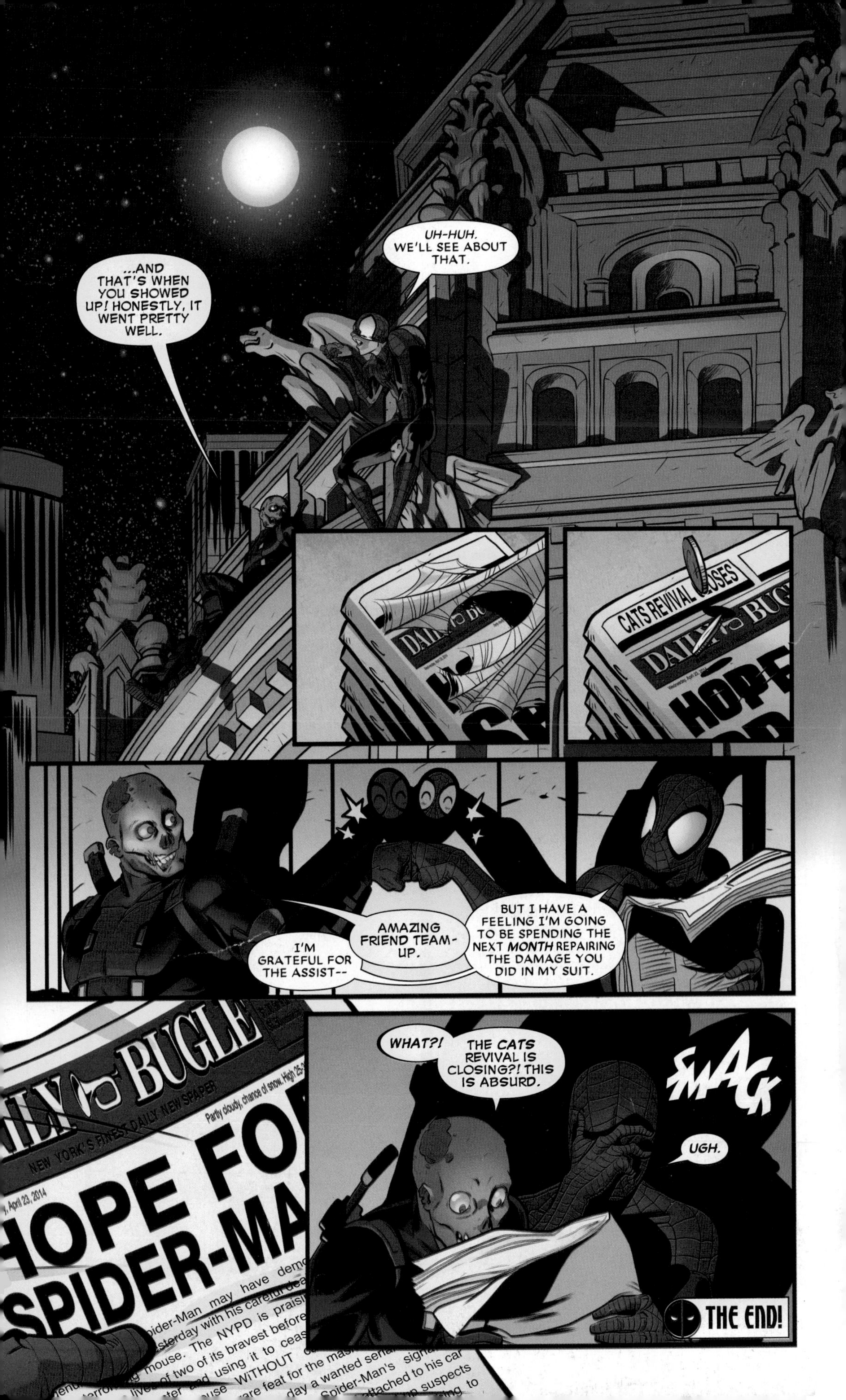
...AND THAT'S WHEN YOU SHOWED UP! HONESTLY, IT WENT PRETTY WELL.
UH-HUH. WE'LL SEE ABOUT THAT.
CATS REVIVAL CLOSES
I'M GRATEFUL FOR THE ASSIST--
AMAZING FRIEND TEAM-UP.
BUT I HAVE A FEELING I'M GOING TO BE SPENDING THE NEXT MONTH REPAIRING THE DAMAGE YOU DID IN MY SUIT.
BUGLE
Partly cloudy, chance of snow.
NEW YORK'S FINEST DAILY NEWSPAPER
WHAT?!
THE CATS REVIVAL IS CLOSING?! THIS IS ABSURD.
SMACK
UGH.
THE END!

MARVEL COMICS
ART PAPER FOR BLEED PAGES (BOOKSHELF FORMAT OR SADDLE STITCH)
PRINTS AT 67%
ILLUSTRATION QUALITY

BEHIND THE SCENES

60's vs 90's

Hola, kids! Welcome to another installment of "Behind the Scenes"! This month's topic: our upcoming, 64-page, 11th issue extravaganza! Since everyone and their brother has been clamoring for a Spidey/Deadpool story, we figured it was time to deliver. But if there's one thing you folks have no doubt learned by now, it's that when it comes to DEADPOOL, expect the unexpected (and thank you, New Universe)!

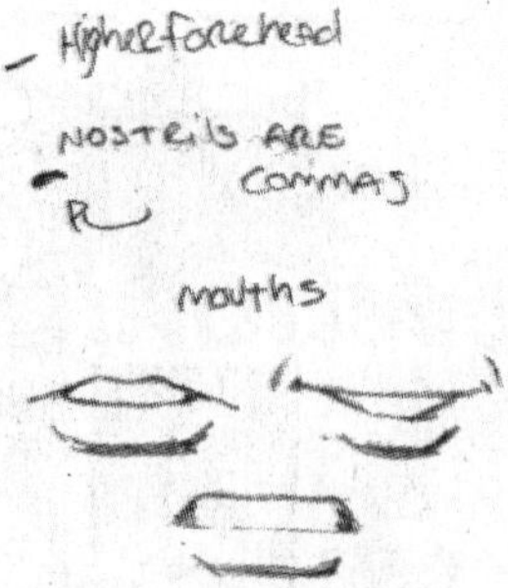

We're going to be trying something which, to the best of our knowledge, has never been attempted: Gumping! Deadpool will be taking a short jaunt back in time, where he'll hang out and interact with some of your favorite Spidey characters from the past! (We'll be taking a sneak-peek at how that's done next month.)

— Higher forehead
NOSTRILS ARE COMMAS
R
mouths

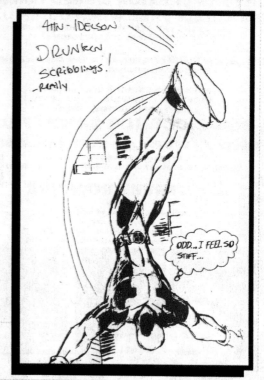

4th - IDELSON
DRUNKEN SCRIBBLINGS!
— really

ODD... I FEEL SO STIFF...

What you see here is some of the conceptual sketchwork being done by the man of the hour, Pete Woods. Pete, who will be handling the penciling chores for our 49-page tale, spent long hours at the drafting table trying to capture the essence of that which is John Romita, Sr.!

The sketches at the top of the page are Pete's early attempts at drawing a certain Mr. Parker. So far, so good! (Although the shot at the upper right of the next page is slightly un-Pete-like, wouldn't you say?)

INSTRUCTIONS FOR DOUBLE PAGE SPREAD: CUT AS SHOWN. ABUT PAGE EDGES. TAPE ON BACK. DO NOT OVERLAP

ART PAPER FOR BLEED PAGES (BOOKSHELF FORMAT OR SADDLE STITCH)   PRINTS   ILLUSTRATION QUALITY
ALL BLEED   TO SOLID LINE   AT 67%   KEEP AL
Book   Line Up   LETTERING INSI
Page #   BROKEN-LINE B

BEHIND THE SCENES

Notice anything special about these sketches? How 'bout the fact that Blind Al has been drawn with her hair in a bun! Plot point alert! Do you think Al will be making the trip? (So much for not messing with the timestream!)

Here's another giveaway. Pete captures the magic that is young Weasel! Indeed, this earlier form of our favorite sidekick will be playing a pivotal role in the events of this story, and at last gaining his moment in the sun. (Note to historians: Weasel is based loosely on Pete Woods' dad!)

The shot below shows our favorite nephew very much out of character, threatening a certain supporting player we all know and love. (And if this doesn't hint at a major plot point, nothing will!)

And so, that's our little hint at things-to-come for today! Thanks for joining us. See you next month when the term "Gump" will take on a whole new meaning!

INSTRUCTIONS FOR DOUBLE PAGE SPREAD: CUT AS SHOWN, ABUT PAGE EDGES, TAPE ON BACK DO NOT OVERLA

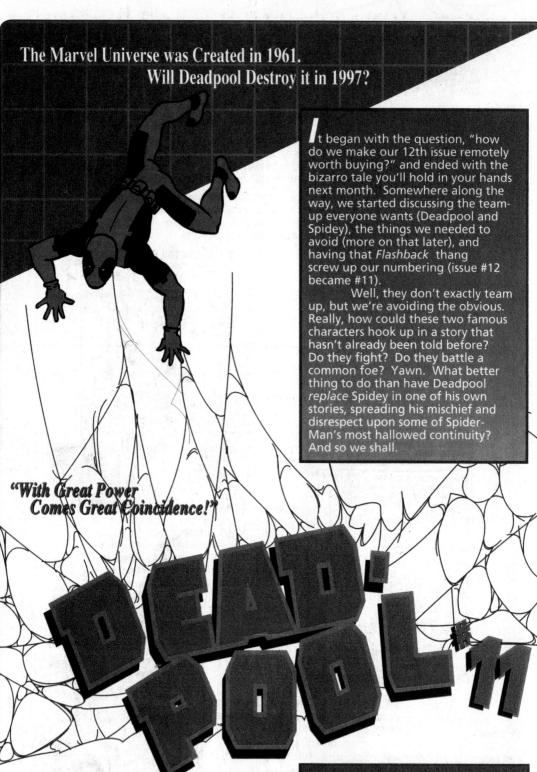

The Marvel Universe was Created in 1961.
Will Deadpool Destroy it in 1997?

*I*t began with the question, "how do we make our 12th issue remotely worth buying?" and ended with the bizarro tale you'll hold in your hands next month. Somewhere along the way, we started discussing the team-up everyone wants (Deadpool and Spidey), the things we needed to avoid (more on that later), and having that *Flashback* thang screw up our numbering (issue #12 became #11).

Well, they don't exactly team up, but we're avoiding the obvious. Really, how could these two famous characters hook up in a story that hasn't already been told before? Do they fight? Do they battle a common foe? Yawn. What better thing to do than have Deadpool *replace* Spidey in one of his own stories, spreading his mischief and disrespect upon some of Spider-Man's most hallowed continuity? And so we shall.

*"With Great Power
Comes Great Coincidence!"*

DEAD-POOL #11

A SPECIAL
BEHIND THE SCENES
PREVIEW

In the pages that follow, we'll take a quick look at how past and present meet in a most original way, and give you a few cheap laughs, courtesy of a sneak peek at our upcoming cover. So read on, true believer, and always face front!

BEHIND THE SCENES

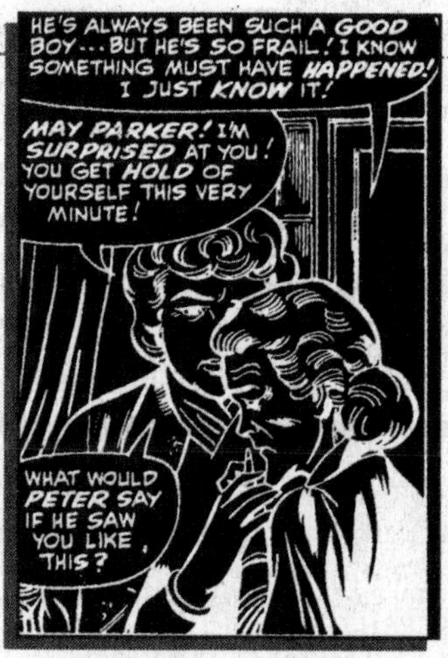
HE'S ALWAYS BEEN SUCH A GOOD BOY... BUT HE'S SO FRAIL! I KNOW SOMETHING MUST HAVE HAPPENED! I JUST KNOW IT!
MAY PARKER! I'M SURPRISED AT YOU! YOU GET HOLD OF YOURSELF THIS VERY MINUTE!
WHAT WOULD PETER SAY IF HE SAW YOU LIKE THIS?

Displayed on this page is our initial attempt at "Gumping"--Deadpool style--using a panel from AMAZING SPIDER-MAN #40, by Stan Lee and John Romita, Sr.

The first thing we had to do was obtain the black-and-white film which, like any film negative is in reverse. That's the film there to your left.

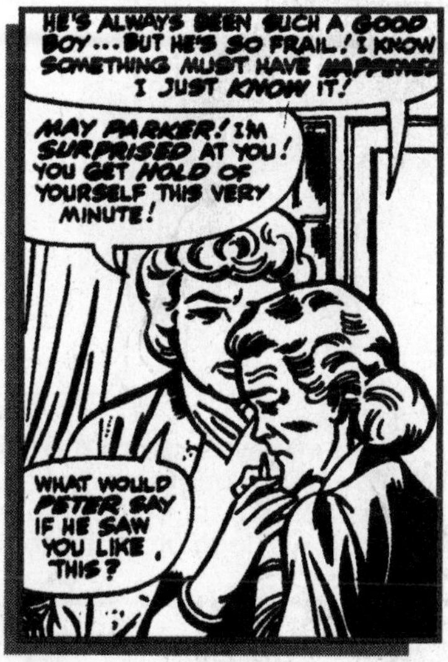
HE'S ALWAYS BEEN SUCH A GOOD BOY... BUT HE'S SO FRAIL! I KNOW SOMETHING MUST HAVE HAPPENE I JUST KNOW IT!
MAY PARKER! I'M SURPRISED AT YOU! YOU GET HOLD OF YOURSELF THIS VERY MINUTE!
WHAT WOULD PETER SAY IF HE SAW YOU LIKE THIS?

What we have here is a photostat of the film, reversing the negative film into a positive image.

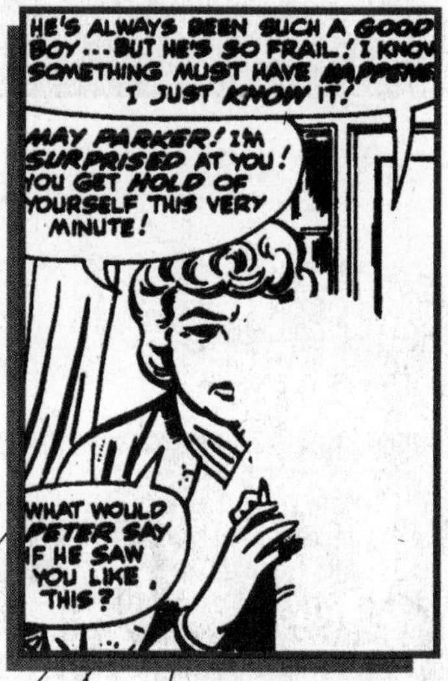
HE'S ALWAYS BEEN SUCH A GOOD BOY... BUT HE'S SO FRAIL! I KNOW SOMETHING MUST HAVE HAPPENE I JUST KNOW IT!
MAY PARKER! I'M SURPRISED AT YOU! YOU GET HOLD OF YOURSELF THIS VERY MINUTE!
WHAT WOULD PETER SAY IF HE SAW YOU LIKE THIS?

Now that you know what it *should* look like, let's get into some "Gumping!" We applied some black patch tape to the film, covering up Aunt May, so that when we made a photostat of the panel, she'd be removed from the image.

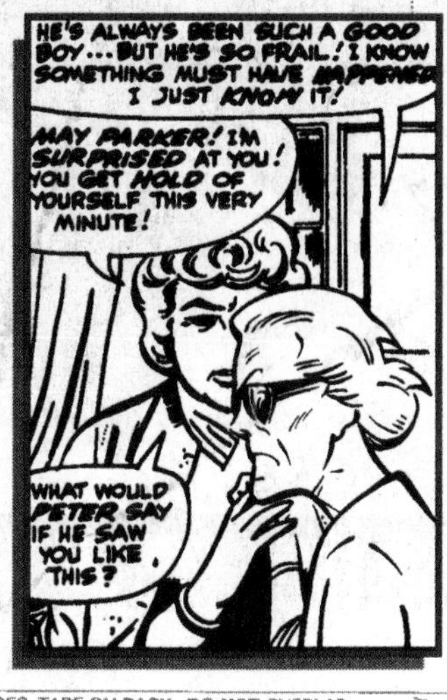
HE'S ALWAYS BEEN SUCH A GOOD BOY... BUT HE'S SO FRAIL! I KNOW SOMETHING MUST HAVE HAPPENED I JUST KNOW IT!
MAY PARKER! I'M SURPRISED AT YOU! YOU GET HOLD OF YOURSELF THIS VERY MINUTE!
WHAT WOULD PETER SAY IF HE SAW YOU LIKE THIS?

With that out of the way, we then proceeded to drop in a shot of our favorite cranky old lady, Blind Al. And there you have it: history rewritten!

As you can imagine, with each successive test, we got the final product to blend into the original art more seamlessly, but we thought we'd treat you folks to our very first attempt!

BEHIND THE SCENES

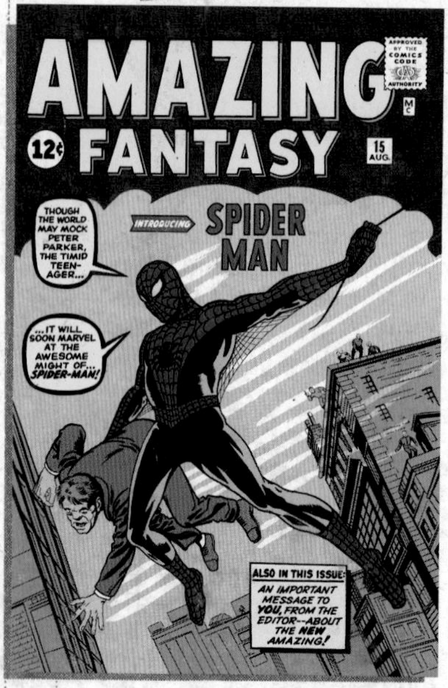

AMAZING FANTASY
12¢
15 AUG.
INTRODUCING SPIDER MAN
THOUGH THE WORLD MAY MOCK PETER PARKER, THE TIMID TEEN-AGER...
...IT WILL SOON MARVEL AT THE AWESOME MIGHT OF... SPIDER-MAN!
ALSO IN THIS ISSUE: AN IMPORTANT MESSAGE TO YOU, FROM THE EDITOR--ABOUT THE NEW AMAZING!

To our left is perhaps the most famous cover in comics history. The first appearance of Spider-Man! When going forward with our story, we decided to emulate a famous Spidey cover. The cover to the story we used didn't quite work right, so we decided to go for broke and pick the big one! It was then that we noticed a bizarre cosmic coincidence: Spidey has the same style word balloons as Deadpool!

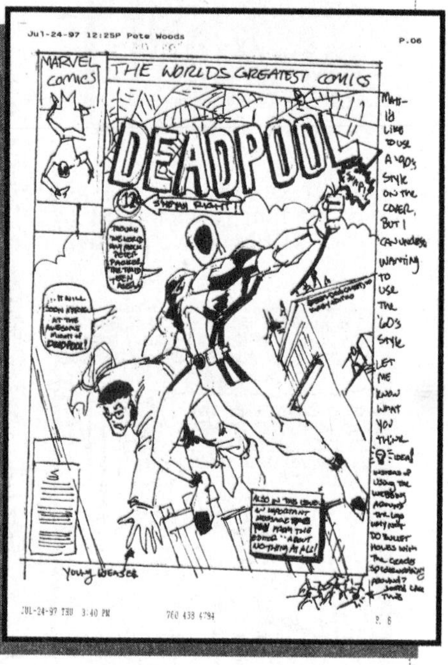

Jul-24-97 12:25P Pete Woods P.06
MARVEL comics
THE WORLDS GREATEST COMICS
DEADPOOL

Here we have a sketch by Pete Woods for our version of the cover. Notice the Spidey-esque logo up at the top?

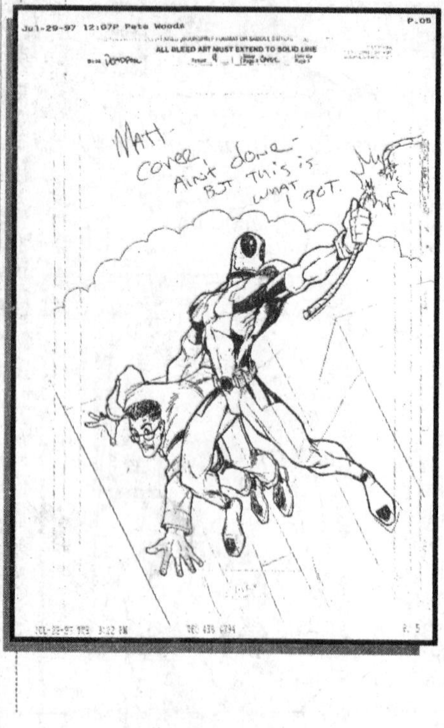

Jul-29-97 12:07P Pete Woods P.05
ALL BLEED ART MUST EXTEND TO SOLID LINE
Matt-
Cover ain't done-
but this is what I got.

Finally, we have the finished pencils—well, of the main figures, anyway. Can you guess who that is under Deadpool's arm? As you can see, we decided to vary slightly away from a straight emulation. The breaking rope is a result of that choice.

Well, that's all the sneak peeks you're going to get for now! See ya next month for 64 titanic pages of laughter, disrespect, and inappropriate behavior, as Deadpool and Blind Al engage in a true tale to admonish!

INSTRUCTIONS FOR DOUBLE PAGE SPREAD: CUT AS SHOWN, ABUT PAGE EDGES, TAPE ON BACK. DO NOT OVERLAP.